Essays in the History of Canadian Law, Volume V
Crime and Criminal Justice
Edited by Jim Phillips, Tina Loo, and Susan Lewthwaite

This fifth volume in the Osgoode Society's distinguished essay series on the history of Canadian law turns to the important issues of crime and criminal justice. In examining crime and criminal law specifically, the volume contributes to the long-standing concern of Canadian historians with law, order, and authority.

The volume covers criminal justice history at various times in British Columbia, Ontario, Quebec, and the Maritimes. It is a study which opens up greater vistas of understanding to all those interested in the interstices of law, crime, and punishment.

(The Osgoode Society for Canadian Legal History)

JIM PHILLIPS is Associate Professor and Associate Dean, Faculty of Law, University of Toronto.

TINA LOO is Associate Professor, Department of History, Simon Fraser University.

SUSAN LEWTHWAITE teaches in the Division of Social Science, York University.

P9-BJA-019

PATRONS OF THE OSGOODE SOCIETY

Aird Berlis
Blake, Cassels & Graydon
Davies Ward Beck
McCarthy Tétrault
Osler Hoskin & Harcourt
The Harweg Foundation
Tory Tory DesLauriers & Binnington
Weir Foulds

The Society also thanks The Law Foundation of Ontario
and the Law Society of Upper Canada for their continuing support.

Essays in the History of Canadian Law

VOLUME V

CRIME AND CRIMINAL JUSTICE

Edited by
JIM PHILLIPS, TINA LOO
and SUSAN LEWTHWAITE

Published for The Osgoode Society for Canadian Legal History by

University of Toronto Press

Toronto Buffalo London

© The Osgoode Society for Canadian Legal History 1994
Printed in Canada

ISBN 0-8020-0633-7 (cloth)
ISBN 0-8020-7587-8 (paper)

Printed on acid-free paper

Canadian Cataloguing in Publication Data

Main entry under title:

Essays in the history of Canadian law

Includes bibliographical references and index.
Partial contents: v. 5. Crime and criminal
justice / edited by Jim Phillips, Tina Loo and Susan Lewthwaite.
ISBN 0-8020-0633-7 (v. 5 : bound)
ISBN 0-8020-7587-8 (v. 5 : pbk.)

1. Law – Canada – History and criticism.
I. Flaherty, David H.   II. Osgoode Society for Canadian Legal History.

KE394.Z85E87 1981   349.71   C81-095131-2
KF345.E87   1981

Contents

AUGUSTANA UNIVERSITY COLLEGE
LIBRARY

Foreword

THE OSGOODE SOCIETY
FOR CANADIAN LEGAL HISTORY

The purpose of the Osgoode Society for Canadian Legal History is to encourage research and writing in the history of Canadian law. The Society, which was incorporated in 1979 and is registered as a charity, was founded at the initiative of the Honourable R. Roy McMurtry, former attorney general for Ontario, and officials of the Law Society of Upper Canada. Its efforts to stimulate the study of legal history in Canada include a research support programme, a graduate student research assistance programme, and work in the fields of oral history and legal archives. The Society publishes (at the rate of about one a year) volumes of interest to the Society's members that contribute to legal-historical scholarship in Canada, including studies of the courts, the judiciary, and the legal profession, biographies, collections of documents, studies in criminology and penology, accounts of great trials, and work in the social and economic history of the law.

Current directors of The Osgoode Society for Canadian Legal History are Jane Banfield, Marion Boyd, Brian Bucknall, Archie Campbell, J. Douglas Ewart, Martin Friedland, John Honsberger, Kenneth Jarvis, Paul Lamek, Allen Linden, Colin McKinnon, Roy McMurtry, Brendan O'Brien, Peter Oliver, James Spence, and Richard Tinsley. The annual report and information about membership may be obtained by writing to The Osgoode Society for Canadian Legal History, Osgoode Hall, 130 Queen Street West, Toronto, Ontario, Canada M5H 2N6. Members receive the annual volumes published by the Society.

Collections of essays, usually organized around a specific theme, have become a tradition at the Osgoode Society. As the fifth volume in the series, these essays on *Crime and Criminal Justice* maintain the high standards of previous collections and will appeal to a wide audience of legal practitioners, academics, and members of the general public. In recent years, as the volume editors point out, there has been a proliferation of literature on this topic, but not in Canada, and these essays add greatly to our understanding of criminal justice themes in Canadian historiography.

We wish to thank Susan Lewthwaite, Tina Loo, and Jim Phillips who undertook a heavy editorial burden and performed their task with good humour and great efficiency.

R. Roy McMurtry
President

Peter Oliver
Editor-in-Chief

Acknowledgments

As editors our greatest debt is to the contributors to this volume, who have throughout displayed equal measures of scholarship and patience with our many demands. One of those contributors, Professor Peter Oliver, deserves special thanks also for his role as editor-in-chief of the Osgoode Society. He has been an enthusiastic supporter of this volume from the outset, providing encouragement, practical support, and much useful criticism. Canadian legal history generally, and the Osgoode Society publications programme in particular, owe Professor Oliver a great debt, which we are very pleased to acknowledge. One of the great pleasures of publishing with the Osgoode Society is to work with Marilyn MacFarlane, whose efficiency and good humour are by now legendary. Finally, we thank the anonymous reviewers of the volume for their detailed and considered commentaries, the substance of which is reflected in its final manifestation.

Jim Phillips
Tina Loo
Susan Lewthwaite

Contributors

CONSTANCE BACKHOUSE is Professor of Law at the University of Western Ontario. She received her LLB in 1975 from Osgoode Hall Law School and her LLM in 1979 from Harvard Law School. She is the author of *Petticoats and Prejudice: Women and Law in Nineteenth-Century Canada* (1991), which was awarded the 1992 Willard Hurst Prize in American Legal History by the Law and Society Association.

RAINER BAEHRE is Associate Professor of History at Sir Wilfred Grenfell College, Memorial University of Newfoundland. A graduate of the University of Waterloo and York University, he has written several articles on nineteenth-century Canadian social history, and he is continuing his research on the state and nineteenth-century mechanisms of legal, social, and moral regulation in Canada.

JOSEPH GONDOR BERKOVITS is a PhD candidate in history at the University of Toronto. His research is on prison life in Ontario, c. 1870–1915.

HELEN BORITCH is an Associate Professor of Sociology at the University of Alberta. Her research interests focus on historical analyses of crime, criminal justice institutions, and female criminality.

JOHN DICKINSON is Professor of History, and Chair of the Department of History, at the University of Montreal. He has written extensively on the justice system, and on relations between native peoples and colonists in New France.

JEAN-MARIE FECTEAU is Professor of History, University of Quebec at Montreal. He is the author of many articles and of *Un nouvel ordre des choses: La pauvreté, le crime, l'État au Québec, de la fin du 18e siècle à 1840* (1989). He is continuing his researches into the socio-political history of Quebec in the nineteenth century, with a particular emphasis on the history of law and other systems of regulation.

HAMAR FOSTER is Professor of Law at the University of Victoria. His teaching and research interests include evidence, comparative criminal law, legal history, and the law of aboriginal title. He has published a number of articles in these fields and recently edited, with John McLaren and Chet Orloff, *Law for the Elephant, Law for the Beaver: Essays in the Legal History of the North American West.*

ANDRÉ LACHANCE is Professor of History at the University of Sherbrooke. He has written extensively on the history of crime and punishment in New France. In addition to many articles, he is the author of *La justice criminelle du roi au Canada au XVIII siècle* (1978), *Crimes et criminels en Nouvelle-France* (1984), *La vie urbaine en Nouvelle-France* (1987), and other books.

SUSAN LEWTHWAITE is a doctoral candidate at the University of Toronto. She is completing a thesis on justices of the peace in Upper Canada and teaching part-time at York University.

TINA LOO teaches social and legal history at Simon Fraser University. She is the author of *Making Law, Order, and Authority in British Columbia, 1821–1871* (1994).

PETER OLIVER is Professor of History at York University and Editor-in-Chief of the Osgoode Society. He has written extensively on Ontario's political and correctional history, and is currently engaged on a history of corrections in nineteenth-century Ontario.

JIM PHILLIPS is Associate Professor and Associate Dean in the Faculty of Law at the University of Toronto. He was co-editor (with Philip Girard) of *Essays in the History of Canadian Law: Volume Three – Nova Scotia* (1990). He has published in the fields of British imperial history, Canadian legal history, and trusts law, and is currently at work on a monograph on the history of crime and criminal justice in Nova Scotia.

PAUL ROMNEY is an independent scholar living in Baltimore. He is the author of *Mr Attorney: The Attorney General for Ontario in Court, Cabinet, and Legislature, 1791–1899* (1986) and of numerous papers on Canadian legal and constitutional history.

SYLVIE SAVOIE is a doctoral candidate at Laval University and lecturer in the history of New France at the University of Sherbrooke. She is investigating the problem of matrimonial alliances in New France.

CAROLYN STRANGE teaches legal history and criminal law at Carleton University. She has written on the history of gender, crime, and sexuality, and is currently working on a comparative project concerning capital punishment in Ontario and New South Wales, Australia. Her book *Toronto's Girl Problem: The Perils and Pleasures of the City, 1880–1930* is forthcoming.

Essays in the History of Canadian Law

1

Introduction

SUSAN LEWTHWAITE, TINA LOO,
AND JIM PHILLIPS

This is the fifth volume in the Osgoode Society's series of *Essays in the History of Canadian Law*. The previous volumes paid only a limited amount of attention to crime and criminal justice history,[1] perhaps unusually limited given the predominant place of criminal justice themes in the writing of legal history in Britain and the United States and the long-standing preoccupation of Canadian historians with law, order, and authority. This collection seems to us, in fact, to reflect the recent interest among historians in examining these latter issues through the law generally and the criminal law more specifically, and it is no accident that a majority of our contributors are relatively new to the field.[2]

The volume examines law and authority in a variety of times and regions from the seventeenth to the twentieth centuries. In doing so it broadens the inquiry about law and order beyond its traditional focus on elite ideology in Upper Canada.[3] We are particularly pleased to be able to include three essays on Quebec and thereby to introduce to an anglophone audience the extensive work of Jean-Marie Fecteau, which has previously appeared only in French and which is now summarized here.[4] These are joined by two essays on the Maritimes, two on British Columbia, and a number situated in Ontario. The essays are also topically and methodologically diverse. In dealing with native peoples, women, nineteenth-century prisons, and other criminal justice institutions and state authority, the contributors variously employ quantitative analysis, closely focused case studies, aspects of modern social theory, as well as more standard narrative forms. In the remainder of this introduction, we will sketch out in a little more detail the sections into which the volume is divided and the themes dealt with in each.

Like many of the histories of native peoples in Canada, the essays in the first section deal with the encounter between two cultures and the conflict and accommodation that resulted from their meeting, albeit in different ways. Sensitive to the diversity of interests of each group, John Dickinson examines the clash of two systems of law in New France – native and French. The former, he argues, was characterized by a concept of responsibility that was group-centred and was aimed at the restoration of amicable relations within or between the disputants' communities through the payment of reparations. French law, in contrast, focused on the individual and was aimed at punishing the offender. By simply pointing out these differences, Dickinson reminds us that we should define law not by its institutional form but rather by its social function as a means of ordering relations.[5] But the essay does more. Social ordering could be achieved in many ways, and these ways were not always comprehensible to cultural outsiders, as Dickinson shows. In New France, neither the many indigenous groups nor the French understood the other's system of law or considered it wholly legitimate. Misunderstandings were frequent in disputes between them and further conflict often the result. It is these 'international conflicts of law' that are the essay's chief focus.[6]

Looking at disputes between Indian and European nations over the seventeenth and eighteenth centuries, Dickinson sketches out the changes in French attitudes toward native law: missionaries had a much more accommodating view than the royal government did, though even the latter had to give in to native law eventually. He explains the actions of both the Indians and the French and the changes in French attitudes in terms of geopolitics; that is to say, in terms of the trade alliances that existed between various native nations and the French and the ability of the French to impose their will.[7]

Like Dickinson, Hamar Foster is concerned with international conflicts – in this case those involving native nations and the English west of the Rockies – and their subsequent impact on the legal regimes of both parties. Foster argues that the trial and execution in 1853 of Sque-is and Siam-a-sit, two Coast Salish men, for the execution of Hudson's Bay Company shepherd Peter Brown, represents a natural divide in the legal history of British Columbia. It was the first jury trial in the colony, and thus the first opportunity for Governor James Douglas to invoke the rhetoric and impose the reality of British justice. Prior to that time there had been no real attempt to apply English criminal law to the aboriginal peoples of British Columbia, even when the offence involved Europeans and natives;[8] rather, a hybrid of aboriginal and fur trader law coexisted. In dealing with this earlier period Foster asks who was adapting to whom, and how the fur traders in particular perceived the role and legitimacy of their laws.

After British Columbia became a colony aboriginal law played a less influential role in resolving disputes; however, the transition to English law brought difficulties of its own. One was that liberal legal ideology required formal equality before the law for native peoples in the criminal context in a society in which no such equality existed generally. Another was that European society at times used the full force of the criminal law for broader political purposes, to make 'examples' of aboriginal defendants as a means of bringing to heel a recalcitrant community in its midst. Finally, to complete a complex picture, Foster also suggests that native groups appear to have been able at times to manipulate the European legal system for their own advantage. Such manipulation was not just for the purpose of ordering relations between native peoples and European society, but was also employed in disputes internal to native communities. In turn, such a use of European law weakened aboriginal communities by exacerbating political and religious differences within them and by slowly destroying the traditional lack of distinction between what European law conceived of as the criminal and civil spheres. In all, we learn a great deal here about the enforcement of the criminal law in pre- and post-colonial British Columbia, and through that prism gain insights also into wider issues of cultural encounter and conflict.

Although 'The Road from Bute Inlet' takes us to the same destination as the other two pieces, it does so by journeying through different terrain. Like Dickinson, Tina Loo is concerned with the perceived 'incommensurability' of indigenous and European cultures and the conflict that resulted.[9] However, Loo's piece is somewhat different because it is concerned with how one group – the Europeans in mid-nineteenth-century British Columbia – dealt with the differences they encountered. This, then, is a piece about the encounter with encounter. Using the so-called Bute Inlet massacre – the killing of a number of European labourers allegedly by Chilcotin Indians in 1864 – as its focus, the essay explores how European British Columbians perceived the event and why they acted as they did in responding to it. Loo identifies a 'discourse of savagery' that both constructed the native killers as a barbaric 'Other' and in doing so also constructed a colonial identity centring on civility and the rule of law for the Europeans who articulated it.[10] In turn, this discourse of savagery and the colonial identity it forged structured how British Columbians responded to the Bute Inlet killings. The process of constructing the 'Self' through the 'Other' was, Loo argues, far from unproblematic. The distinctions between savagery and civility were not clear-cut and the relationship between 'Self' and 'Other' not straightforward; hence the actions they precipitated were both ambiguous and contradictory, reflecting, in large part, contradictions inherent in the rule of law.

The essays on native peoples all deal in some way with the exercise or attempted exercise of power by one group over another through law. What they also reveal, however, is that there were limitations to this use of law, limitations that were sometimes rooted in a particular context but which were also sometimes the result of the nature of law itself.[11] Both these themes are also dealt with in the essays concerned with women, crime, and criminal justice. This subject has excited much interest in the last decade or so among scholars involved with the social history of crime and those whose primary concern is women's history. For the former adding gender to the equation deepens an understanding of, among other things, discretionary prosecutorial, conviction, and sentencing practices, and punitive strategies; for the latter criminal justice records provide insight into the everyday lives of women and represent another site for the operation of gender controls.

The essay by André Lachance and Sylvie Savoie reveals much about gender relations in New France, and the role of law and community in shaping them. Using court records, Lachance and Savoie examine 'conflict, disorder, scandal, violence, and crime' – threats to the 'normal' functioning of the family. Women sought separation because of their husbands' alcoholism, mistreatment, or irresponsibility towards their families. As well, the authors discuss adultery, bigamy, and common law marriages, all of which undermined the traditional family. Though the law imposed sanctions against those who violated marital norms, community controls were often more immediate and more effective. In cases of domestic violence, for instance, neighbours often intervened to limit a husband's 'right of correction' when its use was perceived to be excessive. Because this was a society in which family honour was paramount, gossip was also a means by which the community could exercise indirect control over husbands and wives. In fact, formal law was only appealed to when these informal controls failed.

The other essays in this section have much to tell us about three interrelated topics: the formal operation of criminal justice institutions, the ways in which attitudes to women and women's roles influenced decision-making by them, and the experience of women, both within and outside of those institutions. Jim Phillips' essay deals with all three of these themes. Unlike other jurisdictions, Phillips argues, women in eighteenth-century Halifax were treated as harshly by the courts as were their male counterparts. He also argues that women in general were subject to high rates of violent victimization by men. Both of these phenomena are attributed to the authoritarian and militaristic nature of Halifax society. Phillips' study demonstrates the ways in which criminal court records shed light on both the internal workings of the criminal justice system as well as the experiences of women, particularly their collective experience of victimization.

Victimization and responses to it are also the subjects of Carolyn Strange's essay. Strange examines rape prosecutions, which have been of particular interest to women's historians,[12] by combining a statistical analysis of prevalence and outcomes with an assessment of results of prosecutions. Strange asks an unusual question in a history of rape – why were some men convicted? Most historians have been concerned to account for the failure of the legal system to protect the physical and sexual integrity of women, and while Strange does not deny that, she is primarily concerned with accounting for 'successes' within that general picture of failure. She argues that the class, status, and ethnicity of defendants played vital roles even though 'the outcome of individual cases was not predetermined.' She also contends that the character and actions of the alleged victims could be crucial, especially in an age of increasing concern over sexual 'purity' and the new freedoms being asserted by single women. In this regard we see rape prosecutions as a stage on which larger societal concerns about such matters as the corrosion of family life, the changing ethnic composition of late nineteenth-century Toronto, and changes wrought by the automobile were played out. Finally, she reminds us that as 'untidy' a process as a criminal trial was, some were simply decided on their facts, on the overwhelming preponderance, or marked inadequacy, of the evidence.

Constance Backhouse also uses criminal trials as the principal narrative vehicle of her essay on abortion, though unlike Strange she concentrates on just two high-profile cases. Abortion is another subject central to the history of women and crime, representing as it does the use of the criminal law to control women's reproductive choices, and

Backhouse adds to a considerable literature on the subject using a relatively unusual technique.[13] In telling the stories of two abortion prosecutions a half century apart she seeks to illustrate a variety of social and legal themes. We learn a great deal, for example, about the kinds of options available to women who sought abortions when they were completely illegal, about how a woman would have contacted someone willing to perform the procedure, about who the 'abortionists' were, and about availability, techniques, and costs. We can infer that the practice of abortion was relatively widespread, for the only kinds of cases that came consistently to the attention of the authorities were those where something went wrong. Backhouse also skilfully weaves legal and social considerations into her accounts of the trials themselves, showing us, for example, the importance of having the woman testify for the prosecution and the concomitant difficulty of obtaining convictions on accomplice evidence. Like Strange, she argues that extra-legal considerations, specifically the class status of women and abortionists, were crucial factors.

The links between formal legal institutions and their social and economic context are the subjects of the diverse collection of essays in the third section. Two of the essays concern Lower Canada and Upper Canada respectively, while the third looks at late nineteenth-century and early twentieth-century Ontario. In different ways each discusses the nature of state authority and its impact on the operation of the judicial system. Perhaps the most ambitious attempt to make such connections is Jean-Marie Fecteau's examination of the links between poverty and criminality in Lower Canada. Fecteau's subject – the changing ways in which social problems such as poverty and crime were dealt with in the late eighteenth and nineteenth centuries – is an international scholarly concern.[14] Whereas most studies emphasize the similarities which emerged during the period of transition to capitalism in the treatment of crime, mental illness, and poverty, Fecteau demonstrates that these problems were treated in distinct ways in Lower Canada. He describes the development of separate 'modes of regulation' aimed at poverty and crime, wherein the former came under the purview of private philanthropic organizations while the state came to dominate the repression of crime. Arguing that in their zeal to describe the 'new' historians often ignore aspects of continuity, Fecteau intriguingly links the emerging social control ideology of the nineteenth century and its faith in the power of institutions to the older feudal 'totalitarian ideal.' The individualization emphasized by capitalism and liberalism came to shape ideas about the treatment of crime; poverty, however, was viewed with greater equanimity by the state.

Whereas Fecteau is concerned with the growing state interest in acquiring a monopoly over criminal justice administration, Susan Lewthwaite demonstrates the difficulties confronted by the state in imposing such a monopolistic order in rural Upper Canada.[15] She suggests that there were limits to the ability of formal mechanisms of law enforcement to deal with criminal offences in the early nineteenth-century Ontario countryside. Building her argument around a series of disputes between inhabitants of Burford township between 1839 and 1841, Lewthwaite demonstrates that the authority of the officials representing formal state law and criminal justice was rendered quite powerless when faced with determined community hostility. Local inhabitants, on this occasion and on many others, were able at times to circumvent formal authority, at other times to exercise power or control over its agents. In turn those agents recognized the ambiguity of their position, of their dependence on the consent of the governed, and could themselves in response act in an 'extra-legal' fashion or encourage private settlement. Lewthwaite's argument, while principally concerned with the position of rural magistrates, has broader implications, for in showing that agents of the central government may not have been as influential in their localities as historians have generally assumed she also demonstrates the contingency of that central authority itself.

Just as Lewthwaite explores the difficulties in administering the law in rural Upper Canada, Paul Romney is concerned with a similar problem in Toronto in the 1830s due to the politicization of criminal justice administration. Romney examines one incident in William Lyon Mackenzie's career as mayor and magistrate to show how tory politicians interfered in the administration of criminal justice in an attempt to undermine the credibility of reformers. In late November 1834 Mackenzie sentenced two Irish Catholic prostitutes to terms in the city jail. Days later, the Toronto *Recorder* reported that the two women had been put to work at hard labour and denied heat on the authority of Mackenzie's warrant. Romney casts doubt on Mackenzie's responsibility for the harsh treatment of the prisoners and argues instead that the warrant was altered by persons unknown in an attempt to secure Mackenzie's defeat in the upcoming municipal election. The conspirators hoped that the publicity surrounding Mackenzie's alleged treatment of these two women would turn Irish Catholic voters against him. Though the conspiracy against Mackenzie failed, the incident reveals the deep political divisions that ran through Upper Canadian criminal justice from top to bottom as well as much about the operation of the municipal jail.

If administering the law in Upper Canada was difficult, Helen Boritch shows us that translating reform ideas of a different era into practice was an equally tricky task. Focusing on the population of the Middlesex County Jail Boritch asks if the patterns of the mid nineteenth century regarding the nature of crime, criminals, and punishment changed or remained the same in the late nineteenth and early twentieth centuries. The reform movement of the later period was characterized by rhetoric which focused on rehabilitation rather than punishment, and the development of specialized institutions to deal with various types of offenders. Boritch finds that despite the apparent demand for new directions little changed in practice in the overall patterns of crimes, criminals, or punishments. Great numbers of offenders continued to be sentenced to the county jail, and the underprivileged remained over-represented in the jail population (although the jail population only loosely fit contemporary ideas of a criminal class). Concern about public order was a major preoccupation of law enforcement and public order offences predominated in this period as they had done earlier.[16]

Nowhere in criminal justice history is the gap between theory and practice more marked than in nineteenth-century penal reform. Although this has been explored in the context of the Kingston and Halifax penitentiaries,[17] Rainer Baehre offers us a first look at the Saint John Penitentiary. A product of the enthusiasm for penal reform that swept the transatlantic world in the first half of the nineteenth century, the penitentiary represented New Brunswick's commitment to modernism in crime control – graduated, systematic, and reforming punishment. Baehre argues that the international movement for the reduction of capital and corporal punishment and their replacement by prison regimes of silence, religion, discipline, and labour provided the principal impetus for the construction of the penitentiary in the 1840s. He then charts a story familiar to prison historians – the story of failure. Administrative inefficiency and a punitive regime combined to dash the hopes of those who wanted a 'prison as factory,' although it did not destroy the enduring faith in labour as a reformative and cost-cutting device. As with the penitentiaries at Kingston and Halifax in the same period, inquiries, reports, and recommendations consistently reaffirmed the commitment to reform through labour while their very existence just as consistently demonstrated the unlikelihood that this would ever work.

The prison regime is likewise a central concern of Joseph Berkovits' essay on labour in Ontario's Central Prison in the late nineteenth century. Intended as an intermediate institution between local jails and the penitentiary, the Central Prison represented a reaffirmation of faith in the value of labour as a reforming tool and a new official optimism that incarceration could be made to pay. Berkovits' detailed analysis of the operation of prison labour demonstrates clearly that neither of these fond hopes was fulfilled. The labour process and the prison discipline needed to enforce it hardened rather than reformed most of the inmates, while they also maimed and killed some of them. At the same time, the prison not only failed to show a profit but it never came close to meeting its expenses. Berkovits' essay, which uncovers much new material about the organization, conditions, and effects of the prison work regime, attributes these failures to a variety of causes. Corruption, inefficient administration, the use of private contractors, and the poor health and inadequate skills of the inmates all played a role; nothing was more damaging to the high hopes of its founders, however, than the fact that the Central Prison was first and foremost an instrument for punishment, and labour served as much to augment this aspect of the prison as to give prisoners a sense of worth and a second chance in the world outside its walls. The Central Prison could not transcend its essential role as a prison.[18]

In contrast, Peter Oliver argues that it is necessary to see the Mercer Reformatory, a 'fascinating experiment in social engineering' involving the running of a women's prison on maternal feminist principles, as a more successful venture than historians have previously judged such late nineteenth-century separate facilities to have been. Taking issue with the work of American, British, and Canadian historians of women's prisons, all of whom have argued that these institutions failed because incarceration was contradictory to nurturing and because a class gulf separated inmates and reformers,[19] he suggests that its achievements were substantial. Mary Jane O'Reilly and her almost entirely female staff were able to establish and run a prison distinctly different from other contemporary institutions. It embodied a regime marked by what he terms 'essential kindness and humaneness,' and, as a result, by a complete lack of degrading discipline and punishments and their concomitant violent prisoner resistance. It was the ability of the Mercer to achieve this humane internal regime that Oliver uses to argue for the institution's success, and he does not contend that in other respects the Mercer 'worked,' that it actually improved the lives of its inmates after their release. But nor did the repressiveness of more traditional institutions, and that, in a sense, is Oliver's point – to compare the Mercer with other carceral institutions, and thereby to show it in a positive light, rather than to situate it within a debate about the nature and achievements of late nineteenth-century maternal feminism as others have done. His argument gains support from the other essays in this section, which reveal stark contrasts with the Mercer.

If there is an overriding theme in this volume, it is the complexity of the relationships among deviance, order, law, and authority. On the one hand, the state has ordered social relations repressively through the criminal law, or so one would conclude from the essays by, for example, Baehre, Berkovits, Phillips, and Boritch. On the other hand, according to Dickinson, Fecteau, Lewthwaite, Loo, and Strange, among others, the process of doing so was neither simple nor straightforward. This is not surprising, for the assertion of authority through the criminal law mirrored the ambiguities inherent in state formation, a process in which criminal law and criminal justice institutions played a significant role.

NOTES

1 Seven out of thirty essays dealt with criminal justice themes. See G. Parker 'The Origins of the Canadian Criminal Code' in D. Flaherty, ed. *Essays in the History of Canadian Law: Volume One* (Toronto: University of Toronto Press and Osgoode Society 1981); C. Backhouse 'Nineteenth-Century Canadian Rape Law 1800–92,' P. Craven 'Law and Ideology: The Toronto Police Court 1850–80,' and H. Foster 'The Kamloops Outlaws and Commissions of Assize in Nineteenth-Century British Columbia,' all in D.H. Flaherty, ed. *Essays in the History of Canadian Law: Volume Two* (Toronto: University of Toronto Press and Osgoode Society 1983); R. Baehre 'From Bridewell to Federal Penitentiary: Prisons and Punishment in Nova Scotia before 1880,' J. Phillips 'Poverty, Unemployment, and the Administration of the Criminal Law: Vagrancy Laws in Halifax, 1864–1890,' and B.J. Price '"Raised in Rockhead. Died in the Poor House": Female Petty Criminals in Halifax, 1864–1890,' all in P. Girard and J. Phillips, eds. *Essays in the History of Canadian Law: Volume Three – Nova Scotia* (Toronto: University of Toronto Press and Osgoode Society 1990).

2 For the recent increase in writing on criminal justice history themes see J. Phillips 'Crime and Punishment in the Dominion of the North: Canada from New France to the Present' in C. Emsley and L.A. Knafla, eds. *Crime History and Histories of Crime: Studies in the Historiography of Crime and Criminal Justice* (Westport, Conn.: Greenwood Press 1994).

3 There is a long-standing debate over this. Representative of some of its phases are G. Horowitz 'Conservatism, Liberalism and Socialism in Canada: An Interpretation' *Canadian Journal of Economics and Political Science* 32 (1966) 143–71; S.F. Wise 'Liberal Consensus or Ideological Battleground: Some Reflections on the Hartz Thesis' *Historical Papers* (1974) 1–14 and 'Upper Canada and the Conservative Tradition' in E.G. Firth, ed. *Profiles of a Province: Studies in the History of Ontario* (Toronto: Ontario Historical Society 1967); P. Romney 'Very Late Loyalist Fantasies: Nostalgic Tory "History" and the Rule of Law in Upper Canada' in W. Pue and J.B. Wright, eds. *Canadian Perspectives on Law and Society: Issues in Legal History* (Ottawa: Carleton University Press 1988) and 'From the Types Riot to the Rebellion: Elite Ideology, Anti-legal Sentiment, Political Violence, and the Rule of Law in Upper Canada' *Ontario History* 79 (1987) 113–44; G.B. Baker 'So Elegant a Web: Providential Order and the Rule of Law in Early Nineteenth Century Upper Canada' *University of Toronto Law Journal* 38 (1988) 184–205.

4 See principally J.-M. Fecteau *Un nouvel ordre des choses: La pauvreté, le crime, l'Etat au Québec, de la fin du XVIIIe siècle à 1840* (Montreal: VLB 1989), on which Professor Fecteau's contribution here is based. See also the same author's 'Régulation sociale et répression de la déviance au Bas-Canada au tournant du 19e siècle (1791–1815)' *Revue d'histoire de l'Amérique française* 38 (1985) 499–521.

5 In doing so, he follows much of the work on legal anthropology. For an introduction to this field, see Simon Roberts *Order and Dispute: An Introduction to Legal Anthropology* (Oxford: Robertson 1979). On native-European contact more generally, see O. Dickason *Canada's First Nations: A History of the Founding Peoples from Earliest Times* (Toronto: McClelland and Stewart 1992); R. Fisher *Contact and Conflict: Indian-European Relations in British Columbia 1774–1890* (Vancouver: University of British Columbia Press 1992); and J.R. Miller *Skyscrapers Hide the Heavens: A History of Indian-European Relations in Canada* (Toronto: University of Toronto Press 1991).

6 The only other work that deals with this theme is J.P. Reid 'Principles of Vengeance: Fur Trappers, Indians, and Retaliation for Homicide in the Transboundary North American West' *Western Historical Quarterly* 24 (1993) 21–43.

7 For these trading relationships and their effects on other aspects of native-European contact and conflict, see A.J. Ray and D. Freeman *'Give Us Good Measure': An Economic Analysis of Relations between the Indians and Hudson's Bay Company before 1763* (Toronto: University of Toronto Press 1978); R. White *The Middle Ground: Indians, Empires and Republics in the Great Lakes Region, 1650–1815* (Cambridge: Cambridge University Press 1991); B.G. Trigger *Natives and Newcomers: Canada's 'Heroic Age' Reconsidered* (Montreal and Kingston: McGill-Queen's University Press 1985).

8 For analyses of this see H. Foster 'Long Distance Justice: The Criminal Jurisdiction of Canadian Courts West of the Canadas, 1763–1859' *American Journal of Legal History* 34 (1990) 1–48, and 'Sins against the Great Spirit: The Law, the Hudson's Bay Company, and the Mackenzie's River Murders, 1835–1839' *Criminal Justice History* 10 (1989) 23–76.

9 For the notion of 'incommensurability' see generally A. Pagden *European Encounters with the New World from Renaissance to Romanticism* (New Haven: Yale University Press 1993).

10 The centrality of law to both defining European colonial identity and dispossessing the indigenous inhabitants of North America of their rights is explored in R. Williams *The American Indian in Western Legal Thought: The Discourses of Conquest* (New York: Knopf 1990) and F. Jennings *The Invasion of America: Indians, Colonialism and the Cant of Conquest* (Chapel Hill: University of North Carolina Press 1975).

11 The classic formulation of this notion, of course, is the conclusion to E.P. Thompson *Whigs and Hunters: The Origins of the Black Act* (London: Allen Lane 1975). For another application in the context of native-white relations in British Columbia see T. Loo 'Dan Cranmer's Potlatch: Law as Coercion, Symbol and Rhetoric in British Columbia, 1884–1951' *Canadian Historical Review* 73 (1992) 125–65.

12 Backhouse 'Nineteenth-Century Canadian Rape Law,' 'The Sayer Street Outrage: Gang Rape and Male Law in 19th Century Toronto' in W. Pue and D. Gibson, eds. *Glimpses of Canadian Legal History* (Winnipeg: Law Foundation of Manitoba 1991), and *Petticoats and Prejudice: Women and Law in Nineteenth-Century Canada* (Toronto: University of Toronto Press and Osgoode Society 1991) chap. 3; A. Clark *Women's Silence, Men's Violence: Sexual Assault in England, 1770–1845* (London: Pandora 1987); C. Conley 'Rape and Justice in Victorian England' *Victorian Studies* 29 (1986) 519–36

13 See A. and A.T. McLaren *The Bedroom and the State: The Changing Practices and Policies of Contraception and Abortion in Canada, 1880–1910* (Toronto: McClelland and Stewart 1986); C. Backhouse 'Involuntary Motherhood: Abortion, Birth

Control and the Law in Nineteenth Century Canada' *Windsor Yearbook of Access to Justice* 3 (1983) 61–130; S. Gavigan 'The Criminal Sanction as It Relates to Human Reproduction: The Genesis of the Statutory Prohibition of Abortion' *Journal of Legal History* 5 (1984) 20–43; D. Rhode *Justice and Gender: Sex Discrimination and the Law* (Cambridge, Mass.: Harvard University Press 1989).

14 See especially D. Rothman *The Discovery of the Asylum: Social Order and Disorder in the New Republic* (Boston: Little, Brown 1971); M. Ignatieff *A Just Measure of Pain: The Penitentiary in the Industrial Revolution, 1750–1850* (New York: Columbia University Press 1978), and 'State, Civil Society and Total Institutions: A Critique of Recent Social Histories of Punishment' in S. Cohen and A. Scull, eds. *Social Control and the State* (Oxford: Blackwell 1985); J. Innes 'Prisons for the Poor: English Bridewells 1550–1900' in D. Hay and F. Snyder, eds. *Labour, Law and Crime* (London: Routledge & Kegan Paul 1987).

15 For a similar investigation of such central-local tension see T. Loo 'A Delicate Game: The Meaning of Law on Grouse Creek' *BC Studies* 96 (1992) 41–65.

16 The early to mid nineteenth-century period has been much more thoroughly studied. See in particular M. Katz *The People of Hamilton, Canada West: Family and Class in a Mid-Nineteenth-Century City* (Cambridge, Mass.: Harvard University Press 1975) and Katz et al. *The Social Organisation of Early Industrial Capitalism* (Cambridge, Mass.: Harvard University Press 1982); J. Weaver 'Crime, Public Order and Repression: The Gore District in Upheaval' *Ontario History* 78 (1986) 175–207; J. Fingard *The Dark Side of Life in Victorian Halifax* (Porter's Lake, NS: Pottersfield Press 1989); S. Houston 'The Impetus to Reform: Urban Crime, Poverty and Ignorance in Ontario, 1850–1875' (PhD thesis, University of Toronto 1974).

17 The principal studies are J.M. Beattie *Attitudes towards Crime and Punishment in Upper Canada, 1830–1850: A Documentary Study* (Toronto: University of Toronto Centre of Criminology 1977); R. Baehre 'Origins of the Penitentiary System in Upper Canada' *Ontario History* 69 (1977) 185–207 and 'From Bridewell to Federal Penitentiary'; C.J. Taylor 'The Kingston, Ontario, Penitentiary and Moral Architecture' *Histoire sociale – Social History* 12 (1979) 385–408; W.A. Calder 'Convict Life in Canadian Federal Penitentiaries, 1867–1900' in L.A. Knafla, ed. *Crime and Criminal Justice in Europe and Canada* (Waterloo: Wilfrid Laurier University Press 1981); R.C. Smandych 'Beware of the "Evil American Monster": Upper Canadian Views on the Need for a Penitentiary' *Canadian Journal of Criminology* 33 (1991) 125–47, and 'Tory Paternalism and the Politics of Penal Reform in Upper Canada, 1830–1834: A

"Neo-Revisionist" Account of the Kingston Penitentiary' *Criminal Justice History* 12 (1991) 57–83.

18 For the repressiveness of the Central Prison see also P. Oliver '"A Terror to Evil-Doers": The Central Prison and the Criminal Class in Late Nineteenth-Century Ontario' in R. Hall et al., eds. *Patterns of the Past: Reinterpreting Ontario's History* (Toronto: Dundurn Press 1988).

19 N. Rafter 'Prisons for Women, 1790–1980' in M. Tonry and N. Morris, eds. *Crime and Justice: An Annual Review of Research* vol. 5 (Chicago: University of Chicago Press 1983); E.B. Freedman *Their Sisters' Keepers: Women's Prison Reform in America, 1830–1930* (Ann Arbor: University of Michigan Press 1981); C. Strange 'The Criminal and Fallen of Their Sex: The Establishment of Canada's First Women's Prison, 1874–1901' *Canadian Journal of Women and the Law* 1 (1985) 79–92 and 'The Velvet Glove: Maternalistic Reform at the Andrew Mercer Ontario Reformatory for Females, 1874–1927' (MA thesis, University of Ottawa 1983); L. Zedner *Women, Crime and Custody in Victorian England* (Oxford: Clarendon 1991)

2

Native Sovereignty and French Justice in Early Canada

JOHN A. DICKINSON

As native territorial claims and the issue of self-government become increasingly important on the Canadian political agenda, questions of native sovereignty in historical context take on new meaning. The United States recognizes Indian nations as sovereign entities to whom the federal government is legally bound to carry out its 'trust responsibility.'[1] Canada has not followed this lead, and although some recent decisions – notably the Sparrow (1987) and Sioui (1990) cases – have been more generous in recognizing native claims,[2] aboriginal rights are never taken for granted. In recent Quebec cases, for example, the Crown has tried to prove that the Mohawks are not a distinct native people, but merely provincial citizens with the same rights before the courts as any others.[3] This paper focuses on both native and French reactions to differing concepts of authority and sovereignty in the St Lawrence valley and the necessary accommodations that took place on both sides of the cultural divide before the fall of New France in 1760.

In Eastern Canada the situation is complex since France never made treaties with the populations on whose lands it established colonies. Historian William John Eccles has defined New France's relations with her native allies in peripheral regions as a form of sovereignty association and this term is equally applicable in the colony's core.[4] Unlike in other areas of North America where the initial period of 'non-directed cultural change'[5] did not long survive settlement, natives in the St Lawrence Valley and Upper State New York continued to control their destiny by playing off one imperial power against the other.

French imperial policy in the Americas did not recognize the existence of any native claims to the territory. By virtue of their cultural superiority, the French were masters of all lands they claimed through exploration. Natives were *Sauvages* who lived *sans foi et sans loi* – without any recognizable religious or civil institutions that would have made them the equals of Europeans.[6] Before they obtained any rights they had to be 'humanized' by accepting Catholicism, when they became reputed French subjects,[7] and this legal fiction was maintained throughout the French regime. Natives, however, considered themselves sovereign nations as the Seneca chief Cachouintioui made clear to Governor Roland-Michel Barrin de La Galissonière in 1748 when he stated that the Iroquois were happy to have the French and English settle among them to trade, but they had never ceded the lands that heaven had given them.[8] Two very different conceptions of authority and sovereignty were present in New France and came into conflict when deviance from accepted norms or problems of social control emerged.

NATIVE CONCEPTS OF SOVEREIGNTY AND AUTHORITY

Although native peoples did not have institutions that Europeans could easily recognize, they did possess effective mechanisms for social control within their communities and elaborate procedures for dealing with conflict with other groups. The historical record offers rich detail on the mechanisms for resolving conflict with other communities, and the basic underlying concept was understood: members of the offending group would offer reparation payments to the victim's family. If reparations were not made, the victim's family could seek revenge, inviting further retaliation. As regards internal controls, it is unlikely that French observers fully comprehended the intricacies involved. As Simon Roberts has noted, all acephalous societies manage to maintain relatively ordered social lives without structures of authority. The inevitable disputes that arise are settled through a variety of mechanisms, including physical violence, channelling conflict into ritual, shaming, supernatural agencies, migration, the withdrawal of cooperation or ostracism, and mediation.[9] The amount of disruptive behaviour that could be tolerated was variable, but most native societies in the Northeast encouraged subdued, self-effacing conduct and avoided confrontation within the community. In some specific circumstances, such as in cases of treason or witchcraft, however, it seems that Huron councils could execute offenders. Despite these exceptions, the aim of native mechanisms for dispute resolution was not punishment, but the restoration of amicable relations.[10]

The most informative source on Huron concepts of authority is the *Jesuit Relations*. In 1636 Jean de Brébeuf noted that the Huron punished 'murderers, thieves, traitors, and sorcerers.'[11] The most striking feature of Huron custom to these European observers was that the community rather than the individual was held responsible: 'for the relatives of the deceased pursue not only him who has committed the murder, but address themselves to the whole village, which must give satisfaction for it, and furnish as soon as possible, for this purpose as many as sixty presents, the least of which must be the value of a new beaver robe.'[12] Murder was the most serious crime and required thirty presents for an adult male, forty for a woman, and even more for a member of another nation.[13] Wounds were 'healed' by the presentation of wampum or hatchets. Thieves could be dispossessed of all their belongings (although the Jesuits did not understand Huron concepts of property and might have misinterpreted what they observed). Sorcerers who poisoned people could be put to death immediately.[14] There are two recorded cases of Huron sorcerers being executed, a woman in 1637 and a man in 1640, at a time when Huron society was severely disrupted by the appearance of new European diseases.[15] An isolated case suggests that internal controls involved a more rigorous concept of authority. In 1677, a Mohawk chief named Annontaguelté executed a member of his hunting party near Lachine for stabbing a drunk Iroquois woman in the back. Governor Louis de Buade de Frontenac and Montreal judge Charles D'Ailleboust initiated judicial procedures against Annontaguelté charging him with murder. The accused retorted 'that he was not sorry for the death of the said Savage being his master and having the right to punish him for his misdeed but he was sorry that blood had been spilt on [French territory].'[16] Executions of this sort might have been unusual, but this case stresses that natives considered that they alone were responsible for the resolution of internal conflicts.

The collective responsibility for deviance was a concept totally alien to the French. In French law the individual was responsible for his or her actions and had to bear the consequences. Punishment was personal and played out in elaborate public rituals aimed at impressing subjects with the power of the state and acting as a deterrent.[17] Native society also had an elaborate ritual to 'cover' or 'raise' the dead, but it did not seek to punish an individual. Rather it highlighted central features of native concepts of authority that relied on consensus and kin and community solidarity, rather than on coercive power.[18] The Jesuits had difficulty coming to terms with this concept of authority. Father Hierosme Lalemant wrote in 1646:

I do not believe that there is any people on earth freer than they, and less able to allow the subjection of their wills to any power whatever, – so much so that Fathers here have no control over their children, or Captains over their subjects, or the Laws of the country over any of them, except in so far as each is pleased to submit to them. There is no punishment which is inflicted on the guilty ... It is not because there are no Laws or punishments proportionate to the crimes, but it is not the guilty who suffer the penalty. It is the public that must make amends for the offenses of individuals ... the whole country assembles; and they come to an agreement respecting the number of presents to be given to the Tribe or relatives of him who has been killed, to stay the vengeance that they might take. The Captains urge their subjects to provide what is needed; no one is compelled to it, but those who are willing bring publicly what they wish to contribute; it seems as if they vied with one another according to the amount of their wealth, and as the desire for glory or appearing solicitous for the public welfare animate them on such occasions ... This form of justice ... is nevertheless a very mild proceeding, which leaves individuals in such a spirit of liberty that they never submit to any Laws and obey no other impulse than of their own will.[19]

The clash between different concepts of authority and individual as opposed to collective responsibility formed the basis of an ongoing struggle to find acceptable means of resolving interethnic conflict and violence in New France. Over time, both sides worked out a 'middle ground' that blended in the values and practices of the other culture to establish new conventions.[20]

THE EARLY YEARS

During the first quarter-century after the French established a trading post at Quebec in 1608, their inability to comprehend native customs[21] almost led to the sundering of the trade alliance. With never more than a few dozen traders wintering at Quebec,[22] the French were conscious of their vulnerability to native hostility. They were also completely dependent on native trading networks to supply them with furs, the sole economic incentive for colonization. Although Samuel de Champlain's participation in native warfare against the Iroquois and the desirability of access to trade goods put the alliance on a fairly sound footing, conflict between adventurous Frenchmen and independent natives was probably inevitable. The first incident occurred in 1616–17, when two Frenchmen were killed by Cherouny and another Montagnais in retaliation for a beating.[23] Although it is not known why the French beat the Montagnais, it is clear that, from the native viewpoint, reparations were called for to avoid revenge. The French insisted that the Montagnais hand over the culprits and explained that they were to be punished according to French law. The Montagnais withdrew to Three Rivers[24] and sent a delegation to offer reparations for the murders. Although the French traders were willing to accept native reparations because they were too few in number to resist an attack and feared disrupting the trading network, Recollet fathers Le Caron and Huet refused, arguing that a French life could not be sold for furs since this would be tantamount to licensing natives to kill Frenchmen at will.[25] It was finally decided to accept the presents and two hostages until Champlain arrived to settle the matter definitively. In no position to impose their concept of justice, the French refused to have further dealings with Cherouny until 1623, when he was granted an official pardon at Three Rivers. As a symbol of the pardon, Emery de Caen threw a sword in the St Lawrence to bury the crime. This was interpreted by the natives as a sign of weakness, and the Hurons spent the winter joking that it only cost a dozen beaver pelts to kill a Frenchman.[26]

The French learned little from this incident and persisted in wanting to impose their law on natives.[27] Another similar incident occurred in October 1627, when Mahican Alic Ouche got into an argument with Quebec's baker. The Montagnais sought revenge and killed two sleeping Frenchmen.[28] Champlain ordered his men to be armed at all times and to shoot any Montagnais that approached them without permission. He demanded that the murderer be handed over to the French, but had to settle for three hostages, and it was only in May 1628 that the suspect was brought to Quebec by Montagnais chief La Forière, who asked for his pardon. Champlain refused and had the suspect imprisoned. Although he should have been executed according to French law, the prisoner was held until the following spring, when he was freed without receiving an official pardon.

French weakness in this incident alienated the Montagnais, who helped David Kirke's expedition capture Quebec in July 1629. By refusing to accommodate to native customs, Champlain elicited only contempt since he did not have the necessary force to impose French justice. French failure to compromise was again evident in three separate incidents in 1633.

When the French retook possession of Quebec, they learned of Etienne Brûlé's murder by the Huron. Fearing a murder accusation, some Huron were uneasy about returning to the St Lawrence to trade but Louis Amantacha, a Huron who had spent two years in France, reassured them that Brûlé's death was unimportant since the French considered him a traitor for having dealt with the English during the Kirke interlude.[29] Such a reaction must have been disconcerting to the natives, whose conceptions of community would have incited them to seek revenge.[30] During the trading fair at Quebec in July 1633, a Petite Nation Algonquin killed a Frenchman washing his clothes near Quebec. The Montagnais informed the French of the murderer's identity, and he was seized and imprisoned. The Huron, Petite Nation, and Kichespirini demanded his release, saying they feared that Jesuits travelling West would be killed by the accused's relatives. French authorities tried to save face, with Father Le Jeune interceding for the prisoner. The execution was put off until orders came from the King. The fate of the prisoner is unknown but, if he survived the winter at Quebec, he was probably released.[31] Once again the French were unable to impose their law, and their actions alienated some of their allies and prevented the Jesuits from reaching the Huron country in 1633. The Huron, remarked Father Le Jeune, 'see that the French will not accept presents as compensation for the murder of one of their countrymen; they fear that their young men may do some reckless deed, for they would have to give up, alive or dead, any one who might have committed murder, or else break with the French. This makes them uneasy.'[32] The final incident involved a French drummer boy who wounded a Nippissing with his drumstick. The Nippissings' reaction conformed to their cultural values: 'Behold, one of thy people has wounded one of ours; thou knowest our custom well; give us presents for the wound.' The French refused to follow native custom and promised to punish the boy by whipping. This idea horrified the natives, who sought mercy, 'alleging that it was only a child, that he had no mind, that he did not know what he was doing.' One native threw his blanket over the boy, saying 'Strike me, if thou wilt, but thou shalt not strike him.' The boy escaped punishment.[33] The application of French conceptions of law was again thwarted by the natives.

Inability to recognize the cultural values of the dominant group forced the French to retreat with loss of prestige.[34] Although much better armed, the French were heavily outnumbered and could not risk the trade alliance by imposing their concept of law on their allies. Champlain and the Jesuits were probably satisfied that they had not given in to native custom, but their disregard for proper methods of resolving violence brought contempt and threatened to undermine the alliance. In the years immediately following the eventful summer of 1633, there seems to have been little violence directed against the French.[35] The onslaught of smallpox and measles that decimated the native peoples from the Atlantic to the Great Lakes eroded native confidence, however, and the French started to emerge as powerful sorcerers who were not affected by disease. Fortunately, as settlement around Quebec increased, the Montagnais withdrew to the north and there was less day-to-day contact that could cause friction.

THE MURDER OF JACQUES DOUART

As the French became better acquainted with native customs, they began to realize that more could be gained through compromise than through confrontation. It is significant, however, that the first explicit recognition of native custom occurred in the Huron country, isolated from the centre of French administration. There had been a precedent, although the main European actors were probably unaware of it at the time. In 1623, Father Joseph Le Caron was threatened by a Huron with a club. The Recollets complained to the village chief, who held a council and convinced the community to give the priests a few bags of corn in reparation.[36] By the 1640s, the Jesuits had abandoned the original policy of complete assimilation and were willing to allow some native customs, and by the time of the murder of Jesuit donné Jacques Douart in 1648,[37] they were prepared to accept native concepts of conflict resolution. Indeed, wrote Father Ragueneau, '[i]t would be attempting the impossible, and even make matters still worse, instead of improving them, to try and proceed with Savages according to the method in which justice is administered in France, where he who is convicted of murder is put to death.'[38] This event offers the most detailed description of a traditional reparation ceremony.[39]

On 28 April 1648 six chiefs from three villages, who had always been hostile to Christianity, incited two brothers to murder the first Frenchman they met. They fell upon Jacques Douart in the woods near the

Jesuit residence of Ste Marie and killed him with a hatchet blow to the head. This crime caused considerable turmoil among the Hurons since it threatened the French alliance at a time when the country was seriously threatened by Iroquois warfare. At the beginning of May, a general council decided that 'reparation should be made to [the Jesuits] in the name of the whole country.' The Huron presentation clearly demonstrated that the disruption of amicable relations rather than the murder of one individual by another was the main concern:

A bolt from the Heavens has fallen in the midst of our land, and has rent it open; shouldst thou cease to sustain us, we would fall into the abyss ... This country is now but a dried skeleton without flesh, without veins, without sinews, and without arteries, – like bones that hold together only by a very delicate thread. The blow that has fallen on the head of thy nephew, for whom we weep, has cut that bond ... the wretched murderer thought that he was aiming at the head of a young Frenchman; and with the same blow he struck his country, and inflicted on it a mortal wound. The earth opened up to receive the blood of an innocent, and has left an abyss that is to swallow us up, since we are the guilty ones.

... Thou alone can restore life to [the country]; it is for thee to collect all the scattered bones, for thee to close up the mouth of the abyss that seeks to swallow us.

Coached by Christian chiefs, the Jesuits presented the Huron with a small bundle of sticks to represent the presents they expected as atonement for this death.

When the presents had been collected from the different villages of the confederation, the reparation ceremony was held. The ceremony was divided into two distinct components: the *andaonhaan* designed 'to make peace, and to take away from their hearts all bitterness and desire for vengeance'; and the *andaerraehaan* that constituted the reparation.[40] The *andaonhaan* was made up of thirty-eight presents to calm the Jesuits, to erect a burial platform for the deceased, to reconstitute his body and to clothe him, to close the abyss that separated the Huron and the French, to appease the governor, and to make the Jesuits love the Huron and reopen their house to them. The *andaerraehaan* was composed of fifty presents.[41] Although Trigger states that this was the largest reparations payment ever recorded among the Huron,[42] it was not of unusual size. The *andaerraehaan* was standard for the murder of a stranger, but the *andaonhaan* was considerably larger than the nine presents enumerated by Brébeuf to settle internal disputes.[43] The size of the payment underlines the diplomatic importance of this ceremony, at which the Jesuits themselves reciprocated with a 3000-bead wampum[44] and other presents:

to all the eight nations individually, to strengthen our alliance with them, to the whole country in common, to exhort them to remain united together ... Another present of some value was given to complain of the calumnies that were circulated against the Faith, and against the Christians, as if all the misfortunes that happen in these countries – such as war, famine, and disease – were brought here by the Faith ... We also gave them some presents to console them for the loss they had recently suffered through the killing of some persons by the enemy. Finally we ended with a present which assured them the Monsieur the Governor and all the French ... would have nothing but love for them, and would forget the murder, since they had made reparation for it.

There is no mention of reciprocation by the victims in any of the early documents, but the Jesuits, counselled by the Christian chiefs, were probably following custom when different nations were involved. A few gifts could console the family and restore village harmony, but many were required to renew an alliance, avoid general warfare, and maintain trading relations. Reciprocity was required to acknowledge the resumption of normal relations. This incident demonstrates not only the Jesuits' remarkable ability to adapt, but also the fact that the French now understood native custom and its diplomatic underpinnings.

If native custom provided a means of accommodation in the Huron country, it was not so acceptable to authorities in the St Lawrence valley. By the 1640s, Mohawk raids along the St Lawrence were the major threat, and violence against the French was almost always attributed to this common foe. It is possible that some unaccounted disappearances were caused by allies rather than the Iroquois, but no action was taken to discover the true murderer.[45] During the truce of 1653–60, murders committed by Iroquois at French settlements were considered crimes, not acts of war. More often than not, the Iroquois made reparation for Frenchmen who were killed. In 1656, Father Léonard Gareau was fatally wounded when the Algonquin convoy carrying him was attacked by Mohawks. His aggressors brought him alive to Montreal and 'offered two wretched little presents according to their custom. One was to show their regret for the accident that had happened, and the other to dry our tears and assuage our grief.'[46] After the murder of three Montreal men in 1658, an Oneida delegation presented Montreal governor de Maisonneuve with seven reparation presents to cover the dead.[47] Despite atoning for the crimes following native custom, both de Maisonneuve and Governor Louis D'Ailleboust considered that murder had to be punished. In November 1657, five Mohawks were taken by 'subtlety' at Three Rivers and sent to Quebec, where they were placed in irons.[48] The following year, an Onondaga hunting near Montreal and on friendly terms with the French was imprisoned by de Maisonneuve, seven Mohawk and five Oneida were captured by 'stratagem' at Three Rivers, and three other Mohawks were taken when their canoe was wrecked near Quebec.[49] All but four of the prisoners had escaped or were released by the end of November, when a Mohawk delegation left Quebec carrying a wampum from the governor 'wiping away the blood at Three Rivers and Montreal.'[50] Although the French would have liked to punish the murderers, they had to bend to Iroquois custom and diplomacy to ensure the safety of French hostages in the Iroquois country.

REPRESSION OF VIOLENCE UNDER ROYAL GOVERNMENT

Iroquois warfare severely disrupted the trading networks of the French alliance after 1648. In the 1650s French *coureurs de bois* started ranging the West to collect furs and establish new networks less dependent on native middlemen. At the same time, the French population along the St Lawrence substantially increased, climbing from some 1250 in 1650 to about 7000 by 1670 and to over 15,000 by the turn of the century.[51] Although trade remained important, imperial politics gradually transformed New France into a 'military frontier' to impede British expansion. Native populations along the St Lawrence – especially in the Montreal area – were an essential link in French military strategy[52] and the importance of native warriors moulded official policy concerning mission communities.

The absolute monarchy of Louis XIV was more forceful in its desire to impose civilization on 'savagery.' After the Crown took control of the colony in 1663, French minister Jean-Baptiste Colbert instructed the intendant Jean Talon to induce the natives living near French settlements to abandon their customs and especially their language. Henceforth, official policy was clear: 'With one law and one master [French and natives] were to become a single nation with the same blood.'[53]

The Jesuit policy of accommodation was discredited and Talon blamed the priests for not having 'civilized' the natives. He assured the minister that the missionaries would insist on total acculturation in the future, starting with language.[54] Although the Jesuits, and later the Sulpicians, gave lip service to royal commands, they realized that assimilation was impracticable.[55] Towards the end of the French regime, Father Degonner, unable to learn Mohawk, was considered useless and had to leave Sault St Louis.[56]

The effort to impose French customs and language was accompanied by a more determined policy to force the growing native population[57] in the St Lawrence valley to accept French law.[58] Whereas few natives lived close to French settlements prior to 1650, the establishment of a Huron village near Quebec in the 1650s and of two missions in the neighbourhood of Montreal after 1667 brought settled natives and the French into close contact. As early as April 1664, the Sovereign Council was faced with a case of rape committed by Robet Hache. Local native chiefs protested that they were not aware that this was a capital offence, and the council remitted the punishment. However, after obtaining the consent of six chiefs, it issued an edict subjecting natives to 'the penalties prescribed by French law for murder and rape.'[59] Despite this policy, virtually all native offenders received different treatment from whites.[60]

The available documentation reveals few crimes committed by natives that normally entailed corporal or capital punishment. In 1669, four Sokokis – 8rambech, Chipai8angan, 8ichanigan, and an unidentified woman – broke into Pierre Dupas' cabin on the Richelieu River and threatened the occupants, Dupas' servants, Etienne Clemenceau and Pierre du Pineau. The last-named killed Chipai8angan and 8ichanigan in self-defence. In the fracas, the woman was also killed, apparently by one of her countrymen. Sokoki chiefs, represented by Maanitou 8amet, recognized that 8rambech was liable to be hanged by French law, but asked that, in consideration of their alliance, the French pardon 8rambech since two of the aggressors were already dead. In consideration of public welfare and peace, the council suspended procedures against 8rambech and freed him.[61]

In 1684 a Huron from Lorette named Nicolas Tonaktouan, who had spent the previous six years in the West, berated the Sulpician missionary Joseph Mariet and threatened him with an axe. The Sulpician tried to claim that the Indian was sober, but Tonaktouan repeatedly said that he was drunk and remembered nothing of the incident. The

Jesuit missionary from Sault St Louis interceded for Tonaktouan, 'for the good of the colony and to avoid the dangerous consequences a long trial and stern punishment might incur.' Threatening people in authority was considered a serious offence and deserved corporal punishment, yet Tonaktouan was merely banished from the Island of Montreal and fined 100 *livres*. While the fact that he was a stranger without close kin ties in Montreal explains why he was prosecuted, fear of alienating the Sault St Louis Iroquois probably explains the relative leniency of the sentence.[62]

Mariet was not the only Sulpician to be threatened by native people. René-Charles de Breslay was taken to task and shaken by the collar by two drunk Indians, a Nippissing named Pierre and an Iroquois named Tonnirata, in 1713. Despite the fact that de Breslay knew the aggressors, there was no prosecution.[63]

In the early eighteenth century, incidences of violence seem to have increased dramatically, natives killing both settlers and cattle,[64] but cases rarely came before the courts. In 1713, three Iroquois from Sault St Louis seriously injured Isaac Nafrechou, but after spending three weeks in prison, the case was dropped on the orders of Governor Philippe de Rigaud de Vaudreuil. Anxious to avoid conflict with the mission Indians, he accepted a reparation payment of thirty beaver skins.[65] In other known cases of assault causing bodily harm by mission Indians in the Montreal area, no legal procedures were initiated against the culprits and there is no record of reparations.[66] Indeed, when a man named Choret was severely beaten in Montreal in 1726, he was told by the local governor, de Longueuil, that his only recourse was against the Frenchman who had supplied the alcohol.[67]

Murder was equally difficult to deal with. There were four recorded cases of murder committed by natives against French settlers in the eighteenth century.[68] In 1719, two-year-old Pierre Gagnier of La Prairie was killed by H8atak8isoé, a resident of Sault St Louis, who managed to return to the mission before he could be apprehended. The native council refused to surrender the suspect and complained that Jacques Détailly, who sold brandy to the natives, was responsible. Given firm native opposition, the case was never brought to court.[69] The Sault council's attitude was different a year later when an Iroquois murdered a Chateauguay woman, probably Michelle Garnier: 'The murderer was surrendered by his nation, condemned to have his head broken open and executed in front of the natives who thanked us.'[70] When Honoré Dany was killed by five Iroquois from the Sault in 1721 and his son-in-law seriously wounded, the Montreal royal court initiated proceedings against them. The royal judge, François-Marie Bouat, had the matter taken out of his hands by Governor Vaudreuil, who pardoned the accused after meeting with a delegation from the Sault. The Iroquois vigorously protested French intervention, stating that they would never allow their people to be imprisoned and that armed intervention would be required to take them from the village. With the further threat of leaving the colony should the governor insist on trying the accused, they promised to pay reparations to the widow.[71] The final case occurred in 1735 and involved an Attikamek, Pierre 8aononasquesche or Le Chevreuil, who killed a soldier working on Montreal's fortifications. He was arrested on the spot and thrown in jail. Two days later, a court martial sentenced him to death and he was executed by firing-squad in the presence of a Sulpician missionary and an interpreter.[72]

Nocturnal theft was also a capital offence in New France. In the only known case, the offender, Sieur Douville's Montagnais maidservant Marie, was hanged at Montreal in 1756.[73] By leaving her nation and integrating into French society, she had forfeited the protection of kin groups and native councils.[74]

All these cases involved capital punishment, yet only three natives were executed. In the 1720 case, it was the local native council that surrendered the criminal, and they seem to have been glad to be rid of an habitual troublemaker. In the cases of the Attikamek and Montagnais, both were far from home with no relatives to come to their defence. Neither the Attikamek nor the Montagnais were important military allies in the eighteenth century and their population was centred far from French settlements. When Iroquois who had the support of their council were involved, the French proceeded with caution so as not to endanger the fragile alliance. Native warriors – there were between 350 and 400 of them during this period[75] – were essential to the Montreal region's security.

Alcohol was at the root of all the murder cases and continued to be a major social problem throughout the French regime. As early as 1664, the Sovereign Council had ordered all settlers to apprehend drunk natives in order to learn the names of their suppliers.[76] This ordinance was followed by the arrest of Ta8iskaron and Anaka8abemat on 10 May. They were released two days later when they accused a soldier, Rouvray, of supplying drink.[77] Despite the severe penalties imposed by successive ordinances,[78] natives remained immune from prosecution for drunkenness. Disorder was rife in the streets of Montreal and in neighbouring settlements and regularly resulted in natives wounding or killing other natives. Even when the identities of the belligerents were known, however, royal justice dropped the investigation of native violence and concentrated on prosecuting the French alcohol suppliers.[79] French settlers seemed to be convinced that they could obtain no redress from the regular courts for misdemeanours committed by drunk natives.[80] And this conviction seems justified, since the courts freed intoxicated natives arrested in town as soon as they had identified their supplier.[81]

The authorities' continuing ambiguity regarding the status of natives before the law was never resolved. Although theoretically French subjects, there was little consensus as to whether they should be subject to regular royal courts. Governors supported their use as witnesses but claimed that they should have jurisdiction over them since the defence of the colony was at stake. Intendants tried to preserve their hegemony over the judicial field and even questioned their use as witnesses.[82] The court agreed with the unreliability of native witnesses, but ordered that they be called to prosecute French suppliers of alcohol since there was no other alternative.[83] Such prosecutions were numerous and, for a time, quite rewarding for the natives, who received half the fine.[84]

The fur trade also brought the natives into conflict with French concepts of sovereignty and authority. The Iroquois living in the mission communities of the St Lawrence maintained close kin and commercial ties with their fellow-countrymen living in what Europeans considered British colonies to the south. This 'illegal' trade has been discussed extensively in the historical literature[85] and was the subject of numerous ordinances throughout the eighteenth century.[86] The law was clear: no furs were to be taken to Albany or other English posts and no English stroud was to be brought to New France. Natives, however, continued to take furs to the English with little regard for French law, and an exasperated Governor Beauharnois went as far as to state in a 1741 letter that the Mohawks of Sault St Louis 'have English hearts' because of the trade and that the mission 'has become a sort of Republic.'[87] Given the refusal of the Iroquois to obey French law, authorities sought compromise, and the court agreed that Vaudreuil should allow natives to trade the product of their hunt in Albany and bring back English goods for their personal use.[88] If goods were seized by overzealous soldiers, disputes were to be settled by the governor, the intendant, and another judicial official rather than by the regular courts to avoid cumbersome procedure that threatened to alienate the natives.[89] There were occasional seizures of goods being carried by native peoples, but one must presume that they were acting as agents for French merchants in most of these cases.[90] More significant is a well-documented case in 1716 involving goods brought to Sault St Louis by Ontachogo.[91] In this case, Governor Ramezay ordered the Sieur de Chauvignerie to convince Ontachogo to give up eight pieces of stroud that he was storing for Montreal merchants. The envoy was to promise the Mohawk a third of the goods as a reward but to return empty-handed in case of opposition. Ontachogo surrendered six pieces of cloth but kept two as an advance on his reward and asked the authorities to write the Albany merchants and tell them that the goods had been seized so that they would not accuse him of theft.

French authorities realized that the native alliance was indispensable for the security of New France and that they could not afford to alienate the Iroquois. As regards French justice, the natives felt that they were outside the law. Native councils, as we have seen in the murder cases of Gagnier and Dany, successfully defended their people, blaming murder on alcohol and not the Indians. According to the natives, imprisonment could not be imposed by the French unless accepted by native councils: '[The Iroquois] consider that they are not subject to the laws and jurisdictions of the kingdom. Indeed, they told [Governor] Ramezay that their consent was required to imprison their people found drunk or carrying liquor, saying that we had no authority to put them in jail.'[92] The Crown was forced to recognize this situation: 'As to the natives' claim that we cannot imprison them without their consent and that they are not subject to the law of the land, this is a very delicate matter and must be dealt with carefully ... We can hope to accustom them to military justice and then, little by little, they will get used to the same justice as the French settlers.'[93] This policy was never fulfilled. Any attempt at coercion was met with the threat that the mission communities would leave the country and join the English. Even towards the end of the French regime, action depended on concerting with native councils so as not to offend these valuable allies.[94] French authorities had to compromise with native tradition; accepting the concept that alcohol was responsible for crimes, and substituting reparation payments from the community for the corporal punishment of individuals, were major elements of this accommodation.

CONCLUSION

Although the state would have liked to treat the native population of Canada in the same way as its French subjects, it was never able to obtain this objective. Native alliances were vital for the protection of the colony and authorities could not risk alienating allies whose military prowess was indispensable for the defence of the settlements along the St Lawrence. These political considerations gave natives a relative immunity before the law since the French accepted that the maintenance of amicable relations was more important than the punishment of an individual.

This accommodation gave precedence to native mechanisms for conflict resolution involving different nations that were based on collective reparation payments to a victim's family. These mechanisms existed before the arrival of Europeans and continued to condition native responses to violence until the end of the French regime. Victims of violence had their wounds 'healed' or their corpses 'covered' with presents to ensure the resumption of amicable relations between communities. The French took almost half a century before they recognized the efficacy of native customs, but following the resolution of the Douart murder in 1648, reparations became an accepted means of meting out justice when natives were involved.

Missions were perceived as native territories controlled by the local population. They were havens where natives could find strong support from their communities, as was dramatically illustrated by the case of H8atak8isoé in 1719. Native councils refused state intervention in their internal affairs or interference with their people's freedom, as is illustrated by the claim that arrests could only be made with their consent. Regular courts could interrogate drunk natives and use their testimony to prosecute French liquor traders, but the natives were invariably set free as soon as they had identified their suppliers, regardless of the havoc they caused. Despite their reluctance to recognize native sovereignty, authorities were obliged to do so even if this was contrary to government policy. The instructions given to the Sieur de la Chauvignerie by Governor Ramezay not to use force to obtain contraband goods being stored at Sault St Louis is a good example. Unfortunately, documentation generated by the French administration tells little of how natives resolved conflict among themselves. There is clear evidence that natives were killed and injured by other natives during drunken brawls. Local councils probably had recourse to traditional mechanisms to maintain harmony within their communities, but violence, encouraged by alcohol abuse, was undoubtedly greater than in pre-contact times. The native councils' ready cooperation with colonial authorities to try and curb the sale of liquor is a reflection of the problems alcohol created and the degree to which they were willing to accommodate some external interference in their affairs. That native communities were able to overcome the disruptive effects of drunkenness is a tribute to the ongoing importance of native methods of mediation.

The Iroquois, Algonquin, and Abenaki mission communities were sorts of 'republics' that functioned independently of French authority. Their inhabitants were not subjects but allies who remained closely tied to the French through commercial and military bonds. A highly institutionalized legal system regulated French colonists, whereas a more informal concept of authority maintained ordered relations among natives. When interethnic conflict arose, native customs provided the most satisfactory means of restoring the alliance by recognizing the sovereignty of both parties.

NOTES

1 Christopher Vecsey 'The Issues Underlying Iroquois Land Claims' in Christopher Vecsey and William A. Starna, eds. *Iroquois Land Claims* (Syracuse: Syracuse University Press 1988) 3

2 Olive Patricia Dickason *Canada's First Nations: A History of Founding Peoples from Earliest Times* (Toronto: McClelland & Stewart 1992) 353–4

3 Marcel Trudel 'Rapport historique sur les Mohawks,' document submitted for the prosecution in *Quebec Ministry of Revenue v. Madeleine Meloche*

4 William John Eccles 'Sovereignty Association' in *Essays on New France* (New York: Oxford University Press 1988)

5 Robin Fisher sees natives as central forces in the historical process who adapted selectively to new forces and moulded them to serve their own ends in the initial period before being overwhelmed by major cultural change introduced by settlement: *Contact and Conflict: Indian-European Relations in British Columbia, 1774–1890* (Vancouver: University of British Columbia Press 1977) xi–xiv.

6 George F.G. Stanley 'The Policy of "Francisation" as Applied to the Indians during the Ancien Régime' *Revue d'histoire de l'Amérique française* 3 (1949) 334; Olive Patricia Dickason *The Myth of the Savage and the Beginnings of French Colonialism in the Americas* (Edmonton: University of Alberta Press 1984) 30 and Dickason *Canada's First Nations* 100, 108

7 Article 17 of the Charter of the Company of One Hundred Associates in 1627 recognized Indians who accepted Christianity as French subjects: Canada *Edits, ordonnances royaux, déclarations et arrêts du Conseil d'Etat du Roi concernant le*

Canada (Quebec: E.-R. Fréchette 1854) 1: 10. The same provisions can be found in article 34 of the Charter of the Compagnie des Indes occidentales in 1664: ibid. 1: 46.

8 Acte authentique des Six nations iroquoises sur leur indépendance (2 novembre 1748) *Rapport de l'Archiviste de la Province de Québec* (1921–2) facing p. 108

9 Simon Roberts *Order and Dispute: An Introduction to Legal Anthropology* (Harmondsworth: Penguin 1979) 12–13, 57–69

10 These mechanisms were analysed by Bruce G. Trigger 'Order and Freedom in Huron Society' *Anthropologica* 5 (1963) 151–69. Further research has validated their applicability to other Iroquoian and Algonquian societies in the Northeast and the Midwest: Richard White *The Middle Ground: Indians, Empires, and Republics in the Great Lakes Region, 1650–1815* (New York: Cambridge University Press 1991) 76. These mechanisms resemble those that Thomas Stone has characterized as 'forward-looking' whereby miners separated disputants or mediated between them to restore amicable relations: 'Atomistic Order and Frontier Violence: Miners and Whalemen in the Nineteeenth Century Yukon' *Ethnology* 22 (1983) 327–39.

11 Reuben Gold Thwaites *The Jesuit Relations and Allied Documents* (New York: Pageant Book Company 1959) 10: 215 (hereafter *JR*). This statement is mostly confirmed by François-Joseph Le Mercier, who wrote, in 1637, that those who 'kill, rob, bewitch someone' were punished. Only traitors were not mentioned: *JR* 13: 210.

12 *JR* 10: 215. Ragueneau remarked in 1648: 'their justice is no doubt very efficacious for repressing evil, though in France it would be looked upon as injustice; for it is the public who make reparation for the offences of individuals, whether the criminal be known or remain hidden. In a word, it is the crime that is punished': *JR* 33: 233–5.

13 *JR* 33: 243

14 *JR* 10: 223–5

15 *JR* 14: 37–9; 19: 85–7

16 Archives nationales du Québec à Montréal (hereafter ANQM), *Pièces judiciaires*, 06 MT 1-1, box 42, 9 Aug. 1677. My thanks to Jan Grabowski for bringing this document to my attention.

17 Michel Foucault *Surveiller et punir: Naissance de la prison* (Paris: Gallimard 1975) passim

18 Recent studies stress that small-scale societies dependent on interdependence and strong interrelationships are reluctant to label offenders since labelling breaks social and economic bonds. Rather actions are labelled and, only after a gradual process involving evaluation of the disruptive effects of

the action so that consensus can be achieved, is action taken. Once consensus is reached, however, punishment can be severe, including assassination. Douglas Raybeck 'Deviance, Labelling Theory, and the Concept of Scale' *Anthropologica* 33 (1991) 17–38.

19 *JR* 28: 49–51. A large part of this passage was rewritten almost verbatim in the 1648 *Relation* (33: 239–41). The translation of the second-last sentence is more felicitous and has been used here. On the absence of coercion see also *JR* 10: 233–5.

20 White *The Middle Ground* 52

21 Champlain, for example, was convinced that the natives had no legal code, and no form of punishment except revenge: Georges-Emile Giguère, ed. *Oeuvres de Champlain* (Montreal: Les Editions du Jour 1973) 2: 574.

22 Marcel Trudel *Histoire de la Nouvelle-France* vol. 2: *Le comptoir, 1604–1627* (Montreal: Fides 1966) 486–500

23 Sources for this event are Giguère *Oeuvres de Champlain* 2: 610–14 and Gabriel Sagard *Histoire du Canada et voyage que les frères mineurs récollets y ont faicts pour la conversion des infidèles depuis l'an 1615* (Paris: Tross 1866) 1: 54–7. Although Sagard states that this murder occurred in April 1617, it is unlikely that several nations would have been gathered at Three Rivers at that time. Champlain indicates that it was towards the end of the summer of 1616, but necessarily after his departure on 20 July when the Huron and Algonquin would have already been heading home. The summer of 1617 is also a possibility since the bodies seem to have been discovered only in the spring of 1618. This incident is also discussed by Bruce G. Trigger 'Champlain Judged by His Indian Policy: A Different View of Early Canadian History' *Anthropologica* 13 (1971) 95–8.

24 According to Sagard's account, 800 natives threatened to cut all the Frenchmen's throats to prevent the French from avenging the deaths: *Histoire du Canada* 1: 54.

25 Ibid. 1: 56

26 Giguère *Oeuvres de Champlain* 3: 1047–9; Sagard *Histoire du Canada* 1: 226

27 Unhappy at the Huron reaction, Sagard remarked that when the French were stronger than the natives they would impose their will on them: *Histoire du Canada* 1: 227.

28 Sources are Giguère *Oeuvres de Champlain* 3: 1133–8, 1145–9, 1204–5; Sagard *Histoire du Canada* 3: 813–21. Trigger discusses this case in 'Champlain Judged by His Indian Policy' 98–100.

29 *JR* 5: 239–41

30 John Phillip Reid has emphasized the role of kin in retaliation in the far West: 'Principles of Vengeance: Fur Trappers, Indians, and Retaliation for

Homicide in the Transboundary North American West' *Western Historical Quarterly* 24 (1993) 27. The Huron undoubtedly expected that Brûlé's kin would feel duty-bound to retaliate by killing the first Huron encountered.

31 *JR* 6: 7–17

32 *JR* 6: 19–21

33 *JR* 6: 219–21

34 Repeated violence directed against the French suggests that Reid is correct in concluding that failure to retaliate led to further aggression: 'Principles of Vengeance.'

35 That this violence was not more widespread is due to the importance of the trade alliance for the natives.

35 The Jesuits in the Huron country were threatened because they were seen as witches responsible for the calamities befalling the nation, but the Huron could not afford to break the trade alliance: Bruce G. Trigger *The Children of Aataentsic: A History of the Huron People to 1660* (Montreal and London: McGill-Queen's University Press 1976) 2: 526–46.

36 Gabriel Sagard *Le grand voyage du pays des Hurons* ed. Marcel Trudel (Montreal: Hurtubise HMH 1976) 154–6

37 Accounts and different interpretations of this case can be found in Trigger *The Children of Aataentsic* 2: 744–50 and Lucien Campeau *La mission des jésuites chez les Hurons, 1634–1650* (Montreal: Bellarmin 1987) 272–8.

38 *JR* 33: 233–5

39 The account of these events is found in chapter 17 of the 1648 *Relation*: *JR* 33: 229–47.

40 Brébeuf, who undoubtedly witnessed a similar ceremony, describes the different parts: *JR* 10: 215–21.

41 As noted above, standard reparations seem to have been thirty presents for a man, forty for a woman, and fifty for a stranger, but the total could be as much as sixty. It is not clear, however, whether these figures refer only to the *andaerraehaan* or include the *andoanhaan*.

42 Trigger *The Children of Aataentsic* 2: 748

43 *JR* 10: 217

44 This was a very considerable amount, equal to three normal reparation presents.

45 John A. Dickinson 'La guerre iroquoise et la mortalité en Nouvelle-France, 1608–1666' *Revue d'histoire de l'Amérique française* 35 (1982) 34–5

46 *JR* 42: 237

47 *JR* 44: 193–5

48 *JR* 43: 169

49 *JR* 44: 95–7, 107, 111, 119

50 JR 44: 129

51 John A. Dickinson 'Les Amérindiens et les débuts de la Nouvelle-France' in Giovanni Dotoli and Luca Codignola, eds. *Canada ieri e oggi* (Bari: Schena editore 1986) 87–108

52 William John Eccles *The Canadian Frontier* (New York: Holt, Rinehart and Winston 1969) passim

53 Colbert to Talon, 5 Apr. 1667, *Rapport de l'Archiviste de la Province de Québec* (1930–1) 72

54 Talon to Colbert, 27 Oct. 1667, ibid. 84

55 Louise Tremblay 'La politique missionnaire des sulpiciens au XVIIe et au début du XVIIIe siècle' (MA thesis, Département d'histoire, Université de Montréal 1981) 11–14, 61–70

56 JR 68: 225

57 John A. Dickinson and Jan Grabowski 'Les populations amrindiennes de la vallée laurentienne, 1608–1760' *Annales de démographie historique* (1993) 51–65

58 Similar problems were encountered in the West, where violence against Frenchmen was frequent. In the single year 1684, thirty-nine Frenchmen were killed by allied Indians. Occasionally the French made a show of force and executed murderers, but more generally they pardoned them or accepted reparation payments: White *The Middle Ground* 75–93. Other examples of interracial violence are found on pages 107–8, 203–5, 229–32, 246–7. The situation deteriorated at the end of the French regime and Governor la Jonquière was forced to grant a general amnesty to all natives who had killed Frenchmen in the West to maintain the crumbling alliance: ibid. 209. Given its peculiar geopolitical situation, crimes in the West will not be dealt with here.

59 Canada *Edits, ordonances royaux, déclarations et arrêts* 2: 16–17. In 1674, drunkenness was to be punished by imprisonment and a fine of one moose hide: Pierre-Georges Roy *Ordonnances, commissions, etc., etc. des gouverneurs et intendants de la Nouvelle-France, 1639–1706* (Beauceville: L'Eclaireur 1924) 1: 163. Article XXX of the general police regulations of 11 May 1676 widened the scope to all crimes. Article XXIX stipulated that natives would be subject to corporal punishment for drunkenness: ibid. 2: 70. Later ordinances only prescribed imprisonment for drunkenness: ibid. 2: 38–40; Quebec *Jugements et délibérations du Conseil Souverain* (Quebec: A. Côté 1885) 4: 256–7. As Cornelius J. Jaenen has remarked, it is significant that natives were treated as a distinct group as well as being subject to general ordinances: 'The Meeting of French and Amerindians in the Seventeenth Century' *Revue de l'Université d'Ottawa* 43 (1973) 136.

60 There are only three known cases of natives being condemned for drunken-

ness in the Montreal district and all occurred in a twenty-one-month period between January 1688 and October 1689. A Mohawk named Anonchotte was probably sentenced to be flogged (there is no evidence that the sentence was carried out) and two others were fined ten *livres*: ANQM, Pièces judiciaires, passim.

61 Quebec *Jugements et délibérations du Conseil Souverain* 1: 570-2

62 Archives du Séminaire de Saint-Sulpice à Montréal (hereafter ASSSM), *Fonds Faillon*, FF 68-73. Tonaktouan did not obey the terms of the sentence since he was involved in a brawl four years later.

63 Ibid. FF 117

64 Archives nationales, Colonies, C11A, 43, 220-3, *Mémoire* from de Ramezay to Council, 1 Oct. 1721. With the signing of the Treaty of Montreal in 1701, the Iroquois threat was over, and this might have influenced French authorities in their efforts to deal with alcohol-related violence. However, the threat of English aggression against the colony was still present, making native military resources essential for security.

65 Ibid. 34, 23-6, Vaudreuil and Bégon to the minister 13 Nov. 1713

66 Jan Grabowski 'Searching for the Common Ground: Natives & French in Montreal, 1700-1730' (paper read at the French Colonial Historical Society Meeting, Montreal, 1992) 7

67 Jan Grabowski 'Crime & Punishment: Sault-Saint-Louis, Lac des Deux-Montagnes and French Justice, 1713-1735' (paper read at a conference on Native Peoples and New France: Re-examining the Relationships, 1663-1763, McGill University, Montreal, 1992) 14

68 Slaves, either Indian or Black, cannot be considered on the same footing as mission Indians since their legal status was different and, without family and kin connections within the colony, they had no one to defend them. Madame de Francheville's Black slave, Marie-Joseph-Angélique, was sentenced to death in 1734 for arson: Pierre-Georges Roy *Inventaire des jugements et délibérations du Conseil Supérieur de 1716 à 1760* (Beauceville: L'Eclaireur 1932) 2: 147. Two Pawnee slaves were convicted by regular French courts in the 1750s. M. de Saint-Blin's slave, Constant, was put in the pillory and then banished for theft in 1757: ibid. 2: 203. Marie was hanged after stabbing her mistress in Three Rivers in 1759. The lower court sentence prescribed whipping, branding, and banishment, but, with the British occupying Quebec, the Superior Council sentenced her to death: ibid. 2: 213.

69 Grabowski 'Crime and Punishment' 10

70 ASSSM, L 581

71 ASSSM, HH 122

72 ANQM, Pièces judiciaires, box 132, 13 July 1735

73 Roy *Inventaire* 2: 202–3
74 By crossing the cultural divide separating Indians from Europeans, natives became outcasts in their own communities and could no longer count on the protection of their councils. Louis-Antoine de Bougainville mentions a Nippissing who was scorned by both native and Canadian society because he wore breeches and other French clothes, ate and slept like a Frenchman, and never went hunting or to war: Amédée Gosselin 'Le journal de M. de Bougainville' *Rapport de l'Archiviste de la Province de Québec* (1923–4) 271.
75 Dickinson and Grabowski 'Les populations amérindiennes' 57. During the 1720s there were only about 850 officers and men of the Troupes de la Marine for the whole colony. See, for example, Archives nationales, Colonies, C11A, 44: 26, Etat des troupes dans la colonie, 1721.
76 Quebec *Jugements et délibérations du Conseil Souverain* 1: 186, Ordinance of 25 Apr. 1664
77 Ibid. 1: 188–9
78 See note 59.
79 Grabowski 'Crime and Punishment' 6
80 In 1721, Marguerite Chorel declared that she was convinced that justice had nothing to do with natives but had she known the courts would act she would have complained to the judge: Grabowski 'Common Ground' 4–5.
81 Archives nationales, Colonies, C11A, 43: 220–3, *Mémoire* from de Ramezay to the Council, 1 Oct. 1721. In one case at least, the judge had to free a prisoner on the governor's orders before the interrogation: Grabowski 'Common Ground' 7.
82 The most dramatic example of this conflict is found in the joint letter of Governor Vaudreuil and Intendant Bégon to the minister, 5 Nov. 1713, Archives nationales, Colonies, C11A, 34: 23–6.
83 Ibid. C11B, 36: 28–9, *Mémoire* from the King to Vaudreuil and Bégon, 19 Mar. 1714
84 Grabowski 'Common Ground' 9–10. See also Roy *Inventaires* 2: 151, 165, 167, 170, 173, 202.
85 Jean Lunn 'The Illegal Fur Trade out of New France, 1713–1760' Canadian Historical Association *Annual Report* (1939) 61–76; Alice Jean Elizabeth Lunn *Développement économique de la Nouvelle-France, 1713–1760* (Montreal: Les Presses de l'Université de Montréal 1986); Thomas Wien 'Selling Beaver Skins in North America and Europe, 1720–1760: The Uses of Fur-Trade Imperialism' *Journal of the Canadian Historical Association* n.s. 1 (1990) 293–317; Denys Delâge 'Les Iroquoiens chrétiens des "réductions," 1667–1760' *Recherches amérindiennes au Québec* 21 (1991) 65
86 See, for example, Edict of 6 July 1709, *Arrêt* of 11 July 1718, *Arrêt* of 4 June

1719, *Déclaration* of 22 May 1718, Order of 14 May 1726: Canada *Edits, ordonnances royaux, déclarations et arrêts* 1: 320, 398, 401–2, 489, 505–6.

87 Edmund B. O'Callaghan, ed. *Documents Relative to the Colonial History of New York State* (Albany: Weed, Parsons 1856–87) 9: 1071

88 Archives nationales, Colonies, C11A, 43: 254–5, Vaudreuil and Bégon to the minister, 8 Oct. 1721

89 Ibid. 36: 411–12, *Arrêt* from the Conseil de Marine, 28 Apr. 1716

90 Only nine seizures of goods from natives were validated by the intendant: see Pierre-Georges Roy *Inventaire de ordonnances des intendants de la Nouvelle-France* (Beauceville: L'Eclaireur 1919) 1: 181, 229, 249, 267, 275; 2: 68, 75, 99, 130. In one of these cases some of the goods were returned to the native: ANQM, Pièces judiciaires, box 108, 28 Sept. 1724. Since natives had the right to transport personal effects, restitution followed. In 1740, for example, Governor Beauharnois informed the minister that three of the eleven pieces of stroud seized in 1738 had been given back to the natives because they had been purchased with the product of their hunt: Archives nationales, Colonies, C11A, 74: 4, Beauharnois to the minister, 28 Sept. 1740.

91 ASSSM, FF 194–200

92 Archives nationales, Colonies, C11A, 34: 23–6, Vaudreuil and Bégon to the minister, 5 Nov. 1713

93 Archives nationales, Colonies, C11B, 36: 28–9, *Mémoire* from the King to Vaudreuil and Bégon, 19 Mar. 1714

94 See, for example, the instructions given to the Marquis de la Jonquière in 1746: ibid. 83: 143, *Mémoire* from the King to La Jonquière, 1 Apr. 1746.

3

'The Queen's Law Is Better Than Yours': International Homicide in Early British Columbia

HAMAR FOSTER

In September 1884 the chiefs and people of Kit-au-max, a Gitksan village at the Forks of the Skeena River, wrote to the provincial government hundreds of miles to the south to explain their law of homicide. There was some urgency involved, because the police had recently arrested one of their number and taken him to Victoria to be tried for murdering a white man. The head chief, Geddum-Cal-Doe, said that he and his people wanted peace between the whites and the Indians, and asked that the prisoner be shown clemency.[1] A number of white miners also wrote to the government about the case, but they were of a different view. They blamed much of the growing discontent and danger in the region upon the 'wretched and disloyal teachings' of the missionaries, and dropped hints about taking the law into their own hands. But they decided to wait until the government acted 'on the side of civilization in its warfare against barbarism and fanaticism,' adding that it would be a good idea to set an example by hanging the murderer locally, at the Forks of the Skeena, instead of in far-off Victoria.[2]

Only a few facts about the case are contained in the record compiled for the provincial legislature. The deceased, one Amos Card Youmans, had been in charge of a canoe brigade on the river, and a young Kit-au-max man named Billy Owen had drowned. When Haatq (or Ha-at), Billy's father, learned of his son's death, he sought out Youmans and killed him. It seems that the drowning was an accident, so in his letter to Provincial Secretary John Robson Geddum-cal-doe explained Gitksan law regarding accidental deaths 'that occur in company with others.'

It is expected that the survivors shall immediately, or as soon as possible, make known to the friends of the ... deceased, what has taken place. If this is not done, it is taken as evidence that there has been foul play ...

The general custom ... is that if anyone calls another to hunt with him, to go canoeing, &c., and death occurs, the survivor always makes a present corresponding with his ability, to show his sympathy and good will to the friends of the deceased, and to show that there was no ill-feeling in the matter.[3]

According to Geddum-cal-doe, Youmans had not done this. When he arrived at Kit-au-max he stayed two days and three nights without mentioning the incident. Asked if those with him were all well, he said they were, except for one with sore feet. Because Youmans had neither spoken of the matter nor given a present, he came under suspicion. Geddum-cal-doe added that his people did not know that Haatq – a 'quiet, inoffensive man' – was going to kill Youmans, and said that they had offered no opposition to his arrest because they believed that the government would take all these circumstances into consideration.[4]

There was, of course, more to the story than this. Transporting heavy loads up and down the Skeena was a dangerous business, and relations between the Gitksan and the local miners and traders were uneven. Moreover, both Haatq and Youmans had experienced death and compensation before. The different sources are not entirely consistent, but it appears that a few years earlier Haatq had lost a nephew in a similar incident, but on that occasion the trader involved had not only immediately informed Haatq but had also paid for the search for the body, the burial, and the dead young man's wages up to the time that the canoes reached the Forks without him. There is also some evidence – albeit inadmissible at Haatq's trial – that Youmans had himself paid compensation for a man killed in his employ, and there is no doubt that he was familiar with this aspect of Gitksan law. He was in fact married to a Gitksan woman, and would have known that this 'would make the Indians ... more readily think that he was subject to their law, and notwithstanding in case of his death his children would have to be taken over by the tribe as their own under a well known tribal law, he would not be spared if he did not act rightly in the matter.'[5]

When word of Youmans' death reached the provincial authorities, they did what they and their colonial and fur trade predecessors often did in such circumstances: they sought Aboriginal assistance. The services of a young Nisga'a guide were secured to help the police locate and take Haatq into custody. (The Nisga'a, like the Gitksan, are a Tsimshian people, and the young guide was the son of a chief.) He led a party of officers to Haatq's house at Kit-au-max, where they made the arrest early in the morning and departed by canoe before anyone realized what had happened. According to missionary William Henry Collison, a hue and cry was raised, but not in time to have any effect.[6]

When Haatq was tried in Victoria in December, the evidence tended to confirm what Geddum-Cal-doe had told Robson. Billy Owen had drowned, and Youmans had left the canoe and gone on ahead to the Forks, arriving at least two days before the canoe. Yet he had said nothing to Haatq, who lived directly across the river from Youmans. He was probably afraid, and possibly unduly concerned about how much compensation would be demanded. In any event he seriously underestimated the effect of his silence: only two hours after he learned of his son's death, Haatq went to Youmans' store and, without a word, fatally stabbed him. As defence counsel put it in his speech to the jury, both the prisoner and the deceased were well acquainted with tribal law, and Haatq's reaction was that of a shocked and grieving parent: 'Consider the feelings of the prisoner. No information brought or given to him except by an Indian from another tribe and just before the killing. Suppose your own case. Suppose your own son was killed in the employment of another and he kept the news of his death from you for two or three days. What would you think?' He then suggested to the jury that they would not only have suspected foul play but, had they been Gitksan, they would have felt not only justified but positively obligated to 'follow the tribal laws' and exact blood.[7] Notwithstanding this, the jury convicted Haatq of murder.

Such a verdict was what the Queen's law seemed to require, and conformed to the description of that law contained in Robson's reply to Geddum-Cal-doe before the trial. It is, in effect, an emphatic statement of the changes wrought by the establishment of British Columbia as a colony in 1858, and its confederation with the Dominion of Canada in 1871.[8] Robson agreed that it would perhaps have been better if Youmans had acted in conformity with 'Indian custom,' but he told the Kit-au-max that they had to understand that their law was not binding. 'It is by the Queen's law that all people, Indians and whites, alike, are now governed,' Robson wrote, 'and those who disobey that law must be punished, no matter what they may have been accustomed to before.' 'Besides,' he added: 'the Queen's law is better than yours, as you will see: A man might kill an Indian and say that it was an accident as soon as he came to the dead man's relations, and make them the accustomed present, thereby satisfying the Indian law. But, under the Queen's law, the man would be taken in charge and a thorough investigation made ... and he would have a fair trial. If proved guilty of murder, he would be hanged. If ... the man was not to blame, he would be set free.'[9]

Of course, centuries before Youmans' death English law had also prescribed wergeld, or blood money, rather than execution for most homicides, but 'buying off the spear' was not an option in the British Columbia of 1884. Robson therefore does not explain why hanging is so clearly a better remedy than compensation, nor does he indicate why he thought that the Kit-au-max, unlike the Queen, were somehow bound to accept every protestation of innocence at face value. He also does not consider that the concepts of guilt, innocence, murder, and blame might function differently in Gitksan law, especially when the deceased and the suspected killer were from different nations, and he ignores the question of how Haatq should have sought redress if Youmans had refused to pay compensation. There is no suggestion that any coroner's inquest into Billy Owen's death would have been held, and although there was liability for accidental death in Gitksan law, there is none at common law. Even if there was, a civil suit in the Supreme Court of British Columbia was, in Haatq's case, hardly a realistic possibility. In this connection it is worth noting that the judge who presided at Haatq's trial took a more sympathetic view of Gitksan law, even though he too regarded it as 'external to the case.' Certainly he had no doubts about the Gitksan ability to conduct a thorough investigation. Even if a man immediately proclaims the accident and offers substantial compensation, wrote Justice Crease to the secretary of state in Ottawa, an inquiry is made: '[H]is every word and movement is watched and if the relatives are satisfied it is an accident, all goes on well. But if a simple word say at a Potlatch escapes him to show it was anything but an accident, his life is invariably forfeited.' Crease then gives a recent example of such a case.[10]

Instead of addressing such questions, Robson assured the Kit-au-max that the virtue of the Queen's law was that it applied equally to all.

'Had Youmans killed an Indian, instead of having been killed by one, he would have been subjected to the same treatment and trial as Haatq.' Perhaps to prepare the Kit-au-max for what he anticipated would happen to Haatq, Robson added that, a few months earlier, a white man had been executed at Victoria for killing an Indian. He provides no details.[11]

However, notwithstanding the jury's verdict and the seemingly implacable requirements of the Queen's law, Justice Crease recommended clemency and Ottawa commuted the sentence to ten years of penal servitude. The considerations that were 'external to the case' in so far as Haatq's guilt was concerned were deemed relevant when it came to his punishment. Unfortunately, ten year's imprisonment was a terrible sentence for Haatq, and it seems that he died in jail.[12]

John W. Mountain, the Nisga'a who helped the authorities locate Haatq, received a silver watch and a written testimonial, signed by Robson, acknowledging Mountain's contribution to 'the cause of law and order as opposed to barbarism and crime.' The young man, who ultimately became chief in his father's place, framed it and placed it on a wall in his house. 'But the best part,' recorded one of the missionaries, was that a 'surviving son of the murderer afterwards became a Christian, and having proved himself a clever student became our Native teacher in the Mission ... He proved faithful in that office ... until his death, and thus did much to remove the stain which his father's act had wrought.'[13] John W. Mountain was also a Christian, which may explain his willingness to assist in the capture of the pagan Haatq. But when the question of Indian title to the Naas valley arose, John Wesley – to use the good Methodist name bestowed upon Mountain by the missionaries – quickly learned that the white man's gratitude did not extend very much beyond watches and words.[14]

In January 1885 Robson told the Christian Indians of Metlakatla, a Tsimshian community founded in 1862 by lay missionary William Duncan, what he had told the Gitksan a few months earlier. A complaint filed by the Council of Metlakatla, he said,

speaks of 'Tsimpsean law' and 'our own law,' in contradistinction to 'the Queen's law,' in such a way as would lead one to suppose that the petitioners imagined themselves to be still under 'Tsimpsean law,' and that they are not under or amendable to the Queen's law, whenever it conflicts with their 'own law.'

Now, it is my duty to tell you that 'Tsimpsean law' is not known to nor recognized by either the Dominion or Provincial Government, and that the

Indians of Metlakatlah, in common with all the other Indians and whites, are under and bound to obey the Queen's laws.[15]

Robson told them that their council had no legal status, that it had no right to make and enforce laws, and that the implication that it could accept or reject aspects of British law as it saw fit was 'utterly inconsistent with the genius of our institutions.' He concluded by stating that it was his duty 'to tell you plainly that the sooner you dismiss from your minds all idea of setting up what you are pleased to term your "own law," and submit yourselves fully and loyally to the Queen's law the better it will be for you and all concerned; and, further, I would warn you that those who teach you to set yourselves above and against the Queen's law are not acting the part of good teachers or your true friends.'[16]

This was of course a reference to the missionaries, especially Duncan and Robert Tomlinson of the Church Missionary Society. By 1885 trouble had been brewing at Metlakatla for some time, and in 1886, two years after Robson's blunt warning, prolonged disputes with both church and government over land title led Duncan and the Metlakatlans to decide to move to Alaska.[17] In 1887, a delegation from many of the Tsimshian who had remained in British Columbia went to Victoria to complain about the government's land policy, and a commission was appointed to inquire into the developing unrest.[18] Then, a year later, troops were sent aboard HMS *Caroline* to respond to another panic on the Skeena when a constable shot murder suspect 'Kitwancool Jim' as he attempted to escape arrest. The troops' mission was to convey, with force, the government's message about the Queen's law to the Gitksan. The uprising had been grossly exaggerated, however, and 'C' Battery of the Royal Canadian Army returned to barracks after spending two weeks camped near the mouth of the Skeena with very little to do.[19]

All things considered, the line that Robson drew in his letters between the Queen's law and Aboriginal law seems sharper than the one that the Gitksan and the Tsimshian, whose ideas were being modified by missionary and other influences, had in mind. Several months earlier the Skeena chiefs had met and indicated a willingness to submit to governmental law enforcement, so long as their hunting, fishing, and gathering rights were respected. 'We are prepared to maintain [these rights] in our own way,' they said, 'or we are willing for the Government to maintain them for us by law, but we will not permit them to be interfered with.'[20] In short, the Queen's law was acceptable so long as it protected traditional property rights. And in the Haatq case it was acceptable so long as it was capable of accommodating Gitksan ideas about compensation. After all, Geddum-cal-doe's letter had simply described Gitksan law, according to which Youmans' death was not murder but a privileged act of retaliation; it can be interpreted as a request that the government regard this context as an explanation for Ha-at's behaviour that would justify clemency. The Metlakatlans went even further. Angry though they were about a number of matters, they had prefaced their complaint by noting that they knew that the Queen's laws were made 'for the benefit of all,' and that they had themselves benefited from such laws for years 'because they were justly administered amongst us.'[21]

As Clarence Bolt has argued, in the 1870s and 1880s many Tsimshian wanted what European religion and culture had to offer, and seemed willing to forgo much - but definitely not all - of their own culture and law if that were necessary. Disillusionment set in only as they gradually realized that, however much they changed, the government would keep them in a state of tutelage, refusing to recognize their title and their right to govern themselves as fully as non-Native communities did. For them, treating their communities as equals was as important as treating individuals equally was to Robson. David Leask, one of William Duncan's first converts, made this point when he said that the Tsimshian had developed well beyond the provisions of the Indian Advancement Act. Fitting within the Act, said Leask, 'would be like trying to put a small pair of shoes on feet too large for them.'[22] In 1889 a chief who converted to Methodism made a similar point. The Tsimshian, he said, disliked the government because 'they say the Native people are like little children and don't know anything. God does not call those small who keep his word.'[23]

Robson and his colleagues, however, were experiencing a resistance and an energy on the Northwest Coast that clearly alarmed them. Missionaries, miners, government agents, and Native people on the Skeena were all warning that violence and disorder could be the price of giving in to - or not giving in to - Native demands. Questions of law and sovereignty that were thought to have been settled two decades earlier by British governors, amply assisted by British gunboats, now seemed to require renewed and forceful attention.[24] Ignoring the serious divisions within the Gitksan community, the miners who wrote to Robson maintained that the Indians were threatening to drive them from the area, and that Ha-at's brother, Nee-qaut-sha-an, had sworn that he would kill the first white man he saw if Haatq were hanged.[25] One man who lived right at the Forks was in particular danger, they said, but 'as he is one of the survivors of the Bute Inlet massacre, he well knows the risk.' They then asked, 'is it right to desert these men – miners and traders – the pioneers of British Columbia, in their hour of need?'[26]

This reference to the Bute Inlet massacre, or the Chilcotin War of 1864, underscores the miners' conviction that the Queen's law had been established some time ago. Of course in theory – British legal theory – this was true. But it was not entirely true on the ground, especially in regions where the government had hitherto played only a peace-keeping rather than a law enforcement role, and where settlement and resource development pressures were only just beginning to build. The miners' plea therefore raises a number of interesting questions about what was being replaced, and about the extent to which the rhetoric of sovereignty matched the reality.[27] In what follows, therefore, some homicide cases involving Aboriginal defendants are examined from both the fur trade and the colonial eras, in an attempt to understand how the two legal cultures interacted during the first phases of contact, well before the troubles at Kit-au-max, and to assess the difficulties involved in doing justice across cultural and linguistic barriers. Of course, similar difficulties existed with respect to property and other offences, and – as the statement of the Skeena chiefs quoted earlier suggests – there is reason to believe that land and traditional rights were far more important to Aboriginal people than the occasional homicide prosecution. But it is homicide, and especially murder, that excites the deepest feelings about due process and just punishment, and which has the greatest potential for achieving symbolic significance. For this reason it is homicide that tends to leave the largest traces in the written, if not the oral, record of 'crime.'[28]

The fact that these records deal overwhelmingly with Aboriginal, rather than European, homicide defendants speaks volumes about whose law was on the defensive. Moreover, in the colonial period and the decades following Confederation, homicides by Aboriginal people against non-Aboriginals were committed against a backdrop of increasing appropriation of the former's land and resources by the latter. Even in the fur trade era it seems likely that these phenomena were linked. Traders were incensed by what they perceived as the Indians' penchant for stealing axes, horses, and other items of personal property, and nearly always responded, often violently. These same traders seem never to have considered that their own consumption, without permission, of wood, fish, and game animals may have appeared just as felonious to the chiefs and tribes whose traditional resources these were. Yet as early as 1778, the first European to set foot on the soil of what is now British Columbia had noted the strong feelings that the inhabitants of Nootka Sound had for their village sites, hunting and fishing grounds, and tribal territory generally. Captain James Cook wrote that he had never met a people 'who had such high notions of everything the Country produced being their exclusive property.'[29]

II

In so far as the written record is concerned, the first international homicide involving Europeans and the indigenous peoples of what is now British Columbia took place about a year after Cook's visit, in July 1789.[30] It occurred shortly after a Spanish naval expedition under Estaban Josef Martinez seized three American fur-trading ships at Nootka Sound. When Martinez boarded the *Princess Royal*, a Nootka chief, Callicum, approached in his canoe. Callicum was second only to Maquinna in authority, and he remonstrated with Martinez for interfering with the American and British traders in his territory, refusing an invitation to come aboard and calling Martinez uncomplimentary names.[31] There are a number of accounts of this incident, and details vary; but Martinez, enraged by Callicum's insults, either shot him or ordered one of his seamen to shoot him. He then demanded a quantity of sea otter skins before he would allow Callicum's companions to recover the body from the water. When Juan Fransisco de la Bodega y Quadra arrived on the coast three years later to carry out the provisions of the Nootka Convention, Maquinna spoke of Martinez with scorn, telling Quadra that he 'detested' the man's memory. But no action appears to have been taken against Martinez by the Spanish authorities.

It is hardly surprising, given the history of contact in the Pacific, that the first blood shed when Europe met the Northwest Coast was Aboriginal.[32] The second victim, however, was Joseph Navarro, a fourteen-year-old Spanish boy whose mutilated body was discovered in September 1792, after he had been missing for two days. It ultimately appeared that the perpetrators included the brother of another high-ranking chief, Wickininish, but although there are at least nine separate accounts of this incident, the motive remains unclear.[33] What is interesting is that Quadra left the task of seeing that justice was done to

Maquinna, and that his decision to do so was approved by the government in Spain. Whether Quadra knew enough about local law to be certain that Maquinna had the authority to carry out such a task seems doubtful.

Captain George Vancouver was also in the area at this time, charting the coast with the *Discovery* and the *Chatham*. Although he and Quadra got along well together, he appears to have thought that his Spanish counterpart did not prosecute the investigation with sufficient vigour. An anonymous crew member of the *Chatham*, writing of the Navarro murder, agreed. He recorded in his journal that 'Mr. Quadra was *too good* a man, he even treated the Indians more like companions than people who should be taught subjection.'[34]

There were of course other violent clashes between Europeans and the Native peoples of the west coast of Vancouver Island during the years of the maritime fur trade.[35] But it was not until the establishment of a land-based trade that relations among Europeans and the Aboriginal nations of the region became sufficiently regular to justify attempting some conclusions about patterns of 'law enforcement' in homicide cases. Beginning in 1805, a network of forts slowly spread south and westwards from the first post at McLeod Lake in New Caledonia (what is now northern British Columbia), and northwards from Fort George on the Columbia River. This process accelerated once the Hudson's Bay Company established themselves west of the Rockies after 1821,[36] and by 1832 there were at least eighteen of these posts, with more to come.[37]

Between 1818 and 1846 Great Britain and the United States shared a 'condominion' in the region, i.e., a joint occupancy that reflected their conflicting and unresolved claims to sovereignty. The arrangement implied that 'although both understood that law was command, neither would attempt to issue commands.'[38] Certainly there was no one in the far west to execute or enforce them if they were issued, save and except the British Hudson's Bay Company; but none of their traders spoke of the law that governed relations between trader and Indian as the Queen's (or the King's) law. Practical men all, they tended to equate the Queen's law with the power to enforce it, and therefore some of them believed that there was no law at all. Roderick Finlayson, for example, noted that the HBC held no courts for trials west of the mountains. The 'first time that English law was felt' on Vancouver Island, he said, was in 1850. That was when the first colonial governor summoned Chief Factor James Douglas before him to challenge Douglas' authority to sign a ship's register upon a change of captains – a function that HBC officers, prior to the establishment of the colony in 1849, had always performed.[39]

Still, senior HBC officers would have been vaguely aware that, at least in theory, some English law applied in Indian country prior to colonization, notably the Canada Jurisdiction Act of 1803 and the Regulation of the Fur Trade Act of 1821, imperial statutes that had been specially designed for the Indian country. They provided for the trial of fur trade offences in the Canadas, and the latter required the HBC to send capital cases there.[40] Indeed, some company men believed that these statutes even applied to international homicides committed by Aboriginal people against Europeans. Thus John Tod, explaining his role in the capture of the young Shuswap who killed Samuel Black at Fort Kamloops in 1841, said that he knew that the summary killing of 'Indian murderers' by traders 'was illegal, strictly, for I had seen at York Factory the British Parliament Acts [referred to above] with their regulations as to the committal and trial of offenders, and in consequence ... I never shared in their actual killing.' Tod conceded, however, that these statutes were 'practically useless' in the Indian country, even when both offender and victim were British, and that no attempt was made to apply them 'when the parties were Indians.'[41] In fact, no attempt was made to invoke them even when only one of the parties to a homicide was Aboriginal, and the official position of the Hudson's Bay Company was that they did not apply to such cases.[42] The Queen's law, therefore, was not the law of the Indian country.

So what law did govern when trader and Indian clashed? According to Tod, this time in a memoir that has not been published, 'the Mosaic law applied ... an eye for an eye; a tooth for a tooth, etc.'[43] John McLean, a somewhat disaffected former HBC employee, agreed: traders responded to aggression 'as the law of God allows, demanding 'blood for blood.'"[44] Peter Skene Ogden, who was in command of the New Caledonia district between 1835 and 1844, spoke not of God or Moses but as though he believed that the law of nature governed the fur country. Ogden was a son of Isaac Ogden, a puisne judge in Montreal, and he began his fur trade career with the American Fur Company and the North West Company. He earned a reputation for violence during the period of competition between the latter and the Hudson's Bay Company west of the Canadas, but then rendered years of valuable service to the HBC, finishing as a chief factor. He is supposed to have said that because the King's writ did not run in Indian country, 'many acts must be committed that would not stand ... strict investigation in the

Banco Regis.' 'My legal primer,' he proclaimed, 'says that necessity has no law; and in this place where the custom of the country, or as the lawyers say, the *Lex Non Scripta* is our only guide, we must, in our acts of summary legislation, perform the parts of judge, jury, sheriff, hangman, gallows and all!'[45]

The problem posed by these statements is that they seem to describe a regime of force, unrestrained by rules, yet seek to give that regime a legal name: the Mosaic law, the law of blood for blood, the law of nature, the unwritten law, etc. As Professor John Phillip Reid has suggested, we can choose to regard these as euphemisms for 'blind, absolute retaliation' if we wish – certainly the Hudson's Bay Company's critics did, and so did some of the company's own employees. But it may be useful to pause before we do.[46] After all, this is how generations of non-Aboriginal historians and popular writers once saw Indian law. Then legal anthropologists who listened to the elders, examined the surviving evidence carefully, and took a broader view provided a more thoughtful analysis. They pointed out that retaliatory violence is a form of social control, and that kinship and other relationships usually kept such violence – which was governed by customary expectations and principles of liability – within acceptable limits.[47] Perhaps there is more to fur trader retaliation, as well.

At least two questions present themselves. The first is the extent to which the fur traders' behaviour, whether they realized it or not, was influenced by Aboriginal legal norms. The second, much more difficult, question is: were the traders generally regarded as acting lawfully, or at least not unlawfully, by the tribes whose members they killed? Answers to these questions, which have already been addressed by Professor Reid in a published article,[48] require a brief consideration of some homicides that are well known to historians of the fur trade. A standard list would include those perpetrated by a group of Dunne-za (Beaver) at Fort St John in 1823 and by some Carrier at Fort George the same year;[49] by a party of Clallums upon an express canoe voyaging between Fort Langley and Fort Vancouver in 1828;[50] by a young Shuswap at Fort Kamloops in 1841, by a Babine at Fort Babine in 1843, and by a Sekani at Fort Chilcotin in 1844;[51] by a young Quesnel near Quesnel Forks in 1848;[52] and by a group of Newitty near Fort Rupert in 1850.[53] There are doubtless others,[54] but there is not space even to discuss those listed.[55] Accordingly, because Reid considers the Clallum, Shuswap, and Quesnel cases, only these will be examined – after a brief look at the Aboriginal legal context in which they occurred.

It is risky in the extreme to generalize about law, much less about the laws of a group of human beings as diverse as the Indian peoples of North America. However, the following attempt by Professor Reid is a succinct and useful one. There was a principle, he states, 'widely held among the Indian nations, of a duty – sometimes privileged, possessed by certain members of the nation, often kin folk of a specific lineage or of a defined degree – to retaliate in kind for the killing of a member of the nation or kin group. Often that principle was coupled with the doctrine of an individual liability upon the person who was the "cause" of the homicide, and a collective responsibility upon all members of his or her kin group, whether a household, an extended family, or a clan.' If the homicide were international, i.e., where the victim and perpetrator were of different nations, the collective responsibility 'attached to all members of the slayer's nation, not merely to the slayer's kin group. If the slayer was British, the liability might fall only on British people, depending on the international nuances of the victim's nation. Under the customs of some nations, however, all whites were considered liable, regardless of nationality.' Moreover, 'vengeance was not a privileged act' where international homicide was concerned, and 'what was legal under the first nation's customs was illegal to the second nation, and often caused international wars.'[56] Hence a rather difficult line had to be walked: there was both a need to respond promptly to aggression, lest further aggression be encouraged, and equally a need for caution and compromise to prevent a measured response from escalating into costly warfare. The latter need led to accepting compensation of some kind in lieu of, or in addition to, retaliatory vengeance, a practice that was firmly established among many of the nations on the Pacific coast when the trappers and traders arrived.[57] This permitted the deceased's family or other vengeance group to take into account mitigating circumstances, such as accident. However, the traders were newcomers, with limited regular intercourse with the local inhabitants, so the risk of accidental death was small. They were also vastly outnumbered. Hence, although traders were willing to pay compensation to avoid blood when they were at fault, if they saw themselves as the wronged party they were more inclined to put their faith in retaliation.

Thus when Chief Factor John McLoughlin learned in 1828 that a group of Clallums had killed Alexander McKenzie and four others of his party in order to obtain their clothes and arms, he organized a punitive expeditionary force. McKenzie had been en route to Fort Vancouver, McLoughlin's headquarters, with the dispatches from Fort Langley. The Clallums, in addition to killing the men, had taken the Indian wife of one of them as a slave. In these circumstances McLoughlin believed that 'the honour of the whites was at a stake,' and determined 'to make a salutary example.'[58] According to McLoughlin, all the Columbia tribes apparently offered to do the job for him. They had their own reasons for making such an offer, as Aboriginal people always did; but McLoughlin turned them down, concerned that accepting would put the HBC in the Indians' debt and lead them to think that 'we were unable without their assistance to protect ourselves.'

Clearly, McLoughlin believed that it was crucial to respond decisively and with deadly force, lest the numerous Indian nations of the Pacific slope conclude that the traders were easy pickings. By the time the expedition returned, this objective had been accomplished in spades. The HBC's men had bartered a captive for the woman who had been enslaved, killed between twenty-one and twenty-five people (including women and children), and destroyed two villages, thirty canoes, and all the stores of food and oil they could find.[59]

When McLoughlin reported to London, he acknowledged that some people might disapprove; but he defended his actions as carefully considered and quite necessary. The words he used in doing so are revealing. First, he described negotiations in which Alexander McLeod, the leader of the expedition, had told the Clallums that the HBC did not want to injure the 'innocent,' and that if they gave up the murderers no one else would be harmed. (By this time the HBC had already killed at least eight Clallums in an earlier attack.) When the negotiations broke off without result, McLeod opened fire on the first village. McLoughlin summarized the incident as follows: '[I]n my opinion the whole Expedition was most judiciously conducted, the woman was recovered, the murderers were punished & not a man of ours received the least injury, & *though the loss the murderers have suffered may appear great* ... I doubt if it is sufficient ... as though the report that *twenty one of their people were killed by us, & two of the murderers by the relations of those killed*, yet they are so devoid of feeling that this does not effect [sic] them so much as the burning of their Village & property & destruction of their canoes.'[60]

He then moved to the next item of business which, in case the owners in London had missed the point about how dangerous life could be west of the Rockies, was a report of trappers killed by the Blackfeet further south. But his language in the passage quoted is remarkable.

The HBC, it appears, killed many people, but none of them had been directly involved in the attack upon McKenzie and his men. The two 'murderers' were killed by relatives of those slain by the HBC, presumably to stop the company from inflicting further retribution upon the tribe and its possessions. Yet McLoughlin also speaks of the loss that the 'murderers' have suffered, apparently referring, not to the actual killers, but to the tribe as a whole. This mode of expression is from the Indian law of international homicide, and the passage reflects the tension between the common law view that liability is based upon individual responsibility for intentional acts (guilt) and the Aboriginal view that it is based upon collective responsibility for consequences. However, outside of war the Indian nations – who also committed massacres on occasion – tended to regard the law as requiring or authorizing only a life for a life, not the sort of literal overkill committed by McLoughlin's men.[61]

The attack upon the Clallums was not a typical HBC operation, either in scale or in execution.[62] As the cases described below suggest, most – although not all – company reprisals involved smaller sorties against individuals, and in New Caledonia the HBC had what was almost a one-man police force in the person of Jean-Baptiste Boucher, the notorious 'Waccan.'[63] The excesses of the Clallum raid may therefore be too slender a reed to muster in support of the proposition that the HBC was as inhumane in its dealings with Indians as the American traders were alleged to be.[64] There is, for example, a considerable body of evidence that, especially when settlement pressures began to increase, the Indian nations generally preferred the 'King George men' of the HBC to the 'Boston men.'[65] But the raid does provide a useful context for something James Douglas wrote years later in a dispatch, shortly after the colony of Vancouver Island was established.

Douglas was responding to Archibald Barclay, the secretary of the HBC, who had criticized him for not advising the governor and committee that the Newitty Indians had murdered three HBC deserters near Fort Rupert. The committee had therefore been unprepared when the Colonial Office informed them that Richard Blanshard, the first governor of Vancouver Island, had received a report (subsequently established as false) that HBC officers had encouraged the murders. Blanshard had sent HMS Daedalus to the scene, with a demand that the killers be produced. The Newitty said that they could not do so, and Blanshard refused their offer of blankets and furs as compensation. In a display of firepower that was to be characteristic of the colonial period, the navy then destroyed their village, along with whatever possessions the ship's crew could find. But the killers were not apprehended.[66]

In his dispatch to Barclay, Douglas expressed regret that he had not reported the murders, and assured Barclay that '[i]n all our intercourse with the Natives, we have invariably acted on the principle that it is inexpedient and unjust to hold *tribes* responsible for the acts of *individuals*; – that being without law or government every native should be responsible only for his own acts; and not for the acts of any other member of the tribe, unless they espouse the cause and take up arms in defence of criminals. I recommended that course ... but my advice was followed but in part; as the Tribe was attacked because they *could* not surrender the criminals.'[67]

Douglas may well have been telling the truth as he saw it, and the part about Aboriginal people being without law goes a long way towards explaining the mutual misunderstandings that characterized relations during the fur trade and after. Moreover, there is no doubt that Douglas disapproved of Blanshard's tactics. He would have preferred more negotiations and, if these failed, retaliation by a small force of company men with orders to secure the offenders; he did not like military expeditions which might ignite an Indian war, at least not when commanded by the likes of Blanshard.[68] But Douglas fudges the HBC's willingness, at least in the past, to retaliate against family members if the actual perpetrators could not be apprehended.[69] And the distinction he makes between whether one 'could not' or 'would not' surrender perpetrators is a fine one, which the company was not overly concerned about during the Clallam expedition. What the passage probably reflects most is Douglas' growing awareness that the ways of the past would not be acceptable to the new colonists, or to public opinion in England.[70]

The murder of Chief Trader Samuel Black by a young Shuswap in 1841 is the second case worthy of note.[71] It not only caused considerable excitement at the time, it also resulted in protracted legal wrangles over the deceased's estate between relatives in Scotland and Black's Indian children, who were regarded as illegitimate.[72] There are a number of more or less contemporary accounts of both the killing and its aftermath, most of which are cited by Professor Reid.[73] The following brief summary draws upon his composite version and upon the memoirs of two of Black's fellow traders.

It seems that Black and Le Tranquille, a Shuswap chief, had exchanged angry words about the latter's right to a gun, which an Indian named

Capot Blanc had left with Black. Le Tranquille said that Capot Blanc had promised it to him, but Black insisted that he needed more proof before he would turn it over. Five days after this incident Le Tranquille sickened and died, sending – if trader Alexander Caulfield Anderson is to be believed – 'a friendly and conciliatory message to his old friend, Mr. Black,' just before breathing his last.[74] At the funeral a few days later, an old woman who was a relative of the deceased spoke, berating a young man who by most accounts was Le Tranquille's nephew. She accused him of being a coward who, 'though he saw his uncle's remains before him and though he knew that his death occurred from the evil medicine cast upon him at their parting interview by Mr. Black, he had not the courage to avenge him.'[75] Humiliated, the young man left the funeral gathering and, a few days later, he turned up at Fort Kamloops and shot Black in the back after engaging him in general conversation. He then made his escape and remained at large for some time.

As with the Clallum case some fourteen years earlier, the HBC was determined to respond with force. A party was dispatched from Fort Vancouver, a reward was offered, and a notice went out to the effect that neither tobacco nor ammunition would be issued to the Indians until the 'murderer' was apprehended.[76] Eventually the HBC force, with the help of Chief Nicola of the Okanagans and his family, captured the young man, who was then transported to Kamloops for hanging. En route, however, they had to cross a river. Anderson describes what happened: 'The horses were swung across, the party crossed over a few at a time in a wooden canoe which was stationed there. At last the time of the murderer came, who was heavily ironed and accompanied by two guards [sic] had reached the middle of the river. Suddenly he threw himself on one side, upset the canoe and drifted down the current, singing his war song, and it may be supposed with little hope of escape. The son and adherents of Nicola galloped along the beach and the murderer was by them shot whilst floating in the water.'[77]

According to John Tod, however, this cooperation from Chief Nicola was a late development.[78] Prior to the capture Tod had replaced Donald McLean as commander of the HBC party, and he was highly critical of how McLean had handled the situation. McLean, said Tod, seized horses, destroyed property, and generally terrorized the region in order to force the Shuswap to give up the murderer. This went on for two months, to the great annoyance of the Indians who, in Tod's opinion, 'regretted [the murder] as much as the white man. It was a great mistake.' Although the homicide was international, such harsh and ineffectual tactics could only be justified against the nation of the perpetrator. But in a way it was Tod, not McLean, who was departing from the norm: when he took over he returned the horses and compensated the Indians – 'to their great amazement' – for their losses.[79] More importantly, he secured their assistance in the hunt. But it still took another four or five months to capture the young Shuswap, notwithstanding that by then he had become something of an outcast.

To the HBC, the killing of Black was an appalling act of murder. It is more difficult to assess how it appeared to the Shuswap and the Okanagan. Presumably, many of the former believed that Black had killed Le Tranquille through bad medicine, and that the woman who shamed Le Tranquille's nephew into acting was justified in asserting that he had a right, or was even under a duty, to avenge his uncle's death.[80] Such vengeance, however, would lead to further retaliation by the HBC, perhaps even to a war with the Shuswap that would interfere with trade – a prospect which must have dismayed the other nations who were affected. Chief Nicola of the Okanagans therefore told the Shuswaps that justice required that the young man die. But what, exactly, did he mean? Reid suggests that

Nicola's words should not be read in haste. He seems to be urging the Shuswaps to terminate the international conflict by killing Black's slayer themselves. More likely, however, he could not conceive that any Shuswap possessed the authority or privilege to kill another Shuswap and, therefore, had something else in mind. Perhaps he anticipated that an Okanagan ... might kill the manslayer, and he was asking the Shuswaps to overlook the slaying as a thing done in the dark. A stronger possibility is that he knew the most likely avenger of blood would be a Hudson's Bay Company employee and wanted the Shuswaps to accept the killing to avoid a war with the British.[81]

If Reid is correct, the capture and killing of Le Tranquille's nephew by a joint HBC/Okanagan 'posse' was an acceptable solution to the problem created by Black's death. It was 'one for one,' the actions of both sides were justified within their own legal systems, and an end to the killing was in everyone's best interests. It may not have been common law, but it was common sense.

The final example involves Donald McLean again, but this time as a central player rather than as a man whose lack of success resulted in his replacement.[82] In the spring of 1848 a young Quesnel named

Tlhelh shot and killed Alexis Bélanger, a half-Cree who had learned the Carrier language sufficiently well to have the HBC employ him as an interpreter in the New Caledonia district.[83] By 1848, however, Bélanger had passed in and out of the company's service a number of times, and had achieved a mixed reputation among both traders and Indians. According to his people, Tlhelh had resolved to kill a white man as revenge for the death of his wife; but why he chose to kill Bélanger is unclear. On one account, it was a random choice of a white man; another suggests that there was a reason Bélanger was the victim. Whatever the truth of the matter, Bélanger was steering one of five boats in the Stuart Lake brigade when, shortly after the brigade passed the Quesnel village, Tlhelh fired from a nearby cliff. He inflicted a mortal wound.

Although his superiors do not appear to have been especially unhappy about being rid of Bélanger, the company rule was that, if at all possible, no death should go unavenged. Donald McLean, who was in charge of Fort Alexandria at the time, was therefore dispatched with a force of sixteen men to capture Tlhelh. When McLean arrived at the Quesnel village he discovered Tlhelh's uncle and some other members of his family, but Tlhelh was gone. Through the interpreter, Waccan, McLean demanded to know his whereabouts. When the uncle replied that he did not know, McLean is reputed to have said, 'Then you shall be Tlhelh for today,' and shot him dead. The HBC men also killed a son-in-law who tried to help the uncle, wounding the latter's young wife and killing her baby in the process. The attitude towards Aboriginal peoples that such actions display, one writer has concluded, suggests that McLean must have been an American.[84]

But historians, Professor Reid argues, 'must be cautious when they describe such an event.'[85] The original homicide was international, and it was therefore open to the HBC, as the offended nation, to retaliate against a member of the offending nation, and especially against a member of the killer's family. Hence the killing of the uncle may not have been unlawful. It is unlikely, however, that the deaths of the young man and the baby could be so justified, because only one life was owed. In some situations a woman or a child who stood in the required kinship relation to an offender might satisfy the requirement that privileged blood be shed; but such was not the case here. And as Reid argues, although McLean may have cared little and known less about these sorts of distinctions, historians should.[86]

Thus it may be that, whether they realized it or not, the behaviour

AUGUSTANA UNIVERSITY COLLEGE
LIBRARY

of the HBC and other fur traders in the Indian country was influenced by Aboriginal legal norms as well as common law ones. It seems, in fact, to have been an uneasy amalgam of the two. But, well aware that their behaviour could be unlawful if the Queen's law applied, they may have been reluctant to acknowledge any Aboriginal influence, preferring instead to hearken back to the Mosaic law or to the law of necessity that rushes in to fill a legal vacuum. It would, after all, be somewhat unseemly to concede that Europeans appeared to be observing some of the same legal principles that the 'savages' were, especially because, on occasion, trader vengeance was far bloodier than that exacted by peoples whom Victorian social science regarded as primitive and inferior. Yet which explanation seems more likely: that the traders' blood-for-blood policy was based on the Old Testament, or that it reflected, at least in part, the law ways of the thousands upon thousands of Aboriginal people among whom they lived? Perhaps even the remorseless Donald McLean was acknowledging the truth of the latter explanation when, writing to his superior officer about sending Waccan to find Tlhelh, he said that he wished 'the glib-tongued speakers and ready-penned writers against the Company were placed for a few years in the unchristianized Indian country. They would, I suspect, change their sentiments. I know my own, and shall not easily be induced to change them.'[87]

The answer to the second question posed at the outset of this part, however, remains elusive. International law is always a mix of principle and power, and there was often more than one Indian nation – and therefore more than one point of view – involved when the Hudson's Bay Company exacted retribution. Perhaps the closest one can come to an answer is to say that, although HBC traders may generally have been regarded as acting lawfully by the tribes whose members they killed, the reasonable limits of blood vengeance were unclear and the mixing of common law and Aboriginal legal ideas could lead to results that were harsher or, on occasion, more lenient than Aboriginal law would have contemplated. Consequently, there would have been times when the extent of the company's revenge was resented. The settler regimes that were to follow the HBC, both north and south of the forty-ninth parallel, would produce more of this sort of exchange, but with an important difference. Their laws were part of an ambitious project which, unlike the policies and practices of the Hudson's Bay Company, was committed to the idea that the Queen's law extinguished all others.

III

Historians tend to need 'turning points,' events which can be flagged as representing at least a symbolic moment of change. In the legal history of British Columbia, the trial of Sque-is and Siam-a-sit for the murder of HBC shepherd Peter Brown is an ideal candidate to mark the transition from fur trade to colony. Although British sovereignty over Vancouver Island was confirmed by the Treaty of Washington with the United States in 1846, and although the colony of Vancouver Island was brought into legal existence by letters patent from the Crown in 1849, the English criminal justice system was not applied in a homicide case until Sque-is, a Cowichan, and Siam-a-sit, the son of a Nanaimo chief, were tried at Sne-ny-mo (Nanaimo) in January 1853.[88] This may have been partly because it took some time for many HBC officers to appreciate the legal change that colonization involved.[89] Another factor may have been that the company was still the government on the mainland, and the so-called club law of the fur trade continued to apply there until the colony of British Columbia was established in 1858. Alternatively, it may have been simply that there were no homicides until then.[90] Whatever the explanation, the trial represents the first, unequivocal application of English criminal law and procedure to an Aboriginal person accused of murder, and an equally clear rejection of the law that would otherwise have applied.[91]

At this distance in time the truth of what happened to Peter Brown is even more difficult to retrieve than it was at the time of the trial. There is no official record, and the population decline of the last century, especially the devastating smallpox epidemic which broke out in 1862 and which killed at least one-third of the Aboriginal population, has adversely affected the oral tradition. Nonetheless, the prosecution's case seems to have been more or less as follows.[92] In November 1852 Brown and his fellow Orkneyman, James Skea, were employed at Lake Hill station, near Fort Victoria, tending sheep. On the morning of the 5th it was Skea's turn to drive the sheep to pasture, and Brown's to remain at their cabin to do routine chores. As Skea left he noticed some Indians arriving, but that was not unusual. When he returned a few hours later, he found Brown lying, dead, near the doorway. He had been shot a number of times in the chest. Skea went for help, but a search of the area confirmed that whoever had killed Brown was long gone. Governor James Douglas soon received word, presumably from Aboriginal sources, that Sque-is and Siam-a-sit were responsible.

Douglas stopped all sales of gunpowder to the Indians and consulted the chiefs of the Cowichan and Nanaimo tribes, some of whom seemed prepared to cooperate. But when he realized that the relations of the men were not willing to turn them over, Douglas – much as Blanshard had done two years earlier – headed north with the brigantine *Recovery* and some small boats from HMS *Thetis*, Captain A.L. Kuper commanding.[93] The steamer *Beaver* towed them to Saanich and then westwards through Satellite Channel to Cowichan Bay. In all, the party consisted of over 150 men, including sailors, marines, and a contingent of the fort's own force, the Victoria Voltigeurs.[94] The weather was cold and wet.

At Cowichan Douglas' party waited ashore for the Indians because the chiefs would not board the *Beaver*. The description in his private papers of their arrival, announced by drums and the appearance of many canoes in the river, is evocative: 'They had a very imposing appearance as they pulled slowly towards us, chanting their war-like songs, whooping like demons, and drumming on their canoes by turns with all their might. They landed a little beyond and rushed the hill in a state of the wildest excitement, shouting and dashing their arms about, like people who expected to be immediately attacked. This was a most trying moment.'[95] No wonder the inexperienced troops had to be restrained from firing.

Although Sque-is maintained his innocence, the Cowichans handed him over when Douglas promised that there would be a fair hearing at Nanaimo. The governor then made a speech, urging them all to respect 'Her Majesty's Warrant,' and reminding them that resistance to the civil power 'would expose them to be considered as enemies.' He then distributed some tobacco, feeling well-pleased that the strongest tribe on the island had given up one of their own without bloodshed.[96] At Nanaimo, however, things turned out a little differently. Douglas rejected an offer of furs as compensation for the killing, and seized the Indians' village when it became clear that there would be no co-operation. Eventually a landing party found Siam-a-sit several miles distant, in a wood near a creek that came thereafter to be known as Chase River. They returned him to Nanaimo for proceedings that included a grand jury indictment and trial by petty jury.

There are different views of the significance of this trial. One writer, perhaps contrasting the proceedings with the lynch law that he associated with elements south of the border, has described it as democracy in action, the arrival of *Magna Carta* on the North Pacific Coast. Referring to the jury, which was composed of naval officers, he wrote that it was 'fitting ... that the prerogative of free men to have their guilt or innocence determined by their peers or equals should have been extended first to two uncivilized subjects of the Crown.'[97] Others, perhaps, may find a different significance in the fact that the first men to die on a gallows in British Columbia were Aboriginal, and may have more difficulty in seeing a jury of British sailors as the peers of Sque-is and Siam-a-sit, especially in the absence of any surviving explanation of why they killed Brown. At the very least, the fact that they pleaded not guilty suggests that there may have been some sort of justification for the deed, even if retaliation by the British was expected.[98]

Faced with this strange and new form of proceeding, the mother of Siam-a-sit begged Douglas to hang her husband instead, because 'he was old and could not live long ... and one for one was Indian law.'[99] In short, she recognized that the circumstances required that the blood debt be paid, and offered in satisfaction the life of a chief for that of a mere shepherd. But this proposal 'did not meet the ideas of the whites, backed by a British man of war with a file of marines.'[100] English law required that the killer die, the actual perpetrator, not someone put forward in his place. Blood for blood, as understood by most Aboriginal people, was not a principle that was capable of justifying HBC rule in what was now a British colony, especially one in which ownership of land and resources was about to become a critical issue. English law, not Salish, would govern relations between the two peoples at Nanaimo, and Douglas reported with some satisfaction that the execution had made 'a deep impression on [the] minds [of the Indians].'[101]

One of the sailors present clearly agreed. Writing to his father, Admiral Fairfax Moresby, John Moresby recounted that, when the condemned men died, the yells and cries that rose up from the assembled Indians were the most mournful 'it has ever fallen to the ears of men to hear.' He added: 'I little thought these savages possessed such feeling.'[102] Years later, when he had himself become an admiral, Moresby realized that the execution had made a deep impression on him, too. As a Victorian who could not see the legal norms that informed Aboriginal actions, he was probably unaware of the widely differing concepts of blame and responsibility that were involved in the case. But he knew that, in his youthful enthusiasm, he had missed at least one element of what had happened that day in 1853: 'I fear the pity of this, one of the myriad tragedies of the red man's collision with civilization, appealed to none of us at the time ... I can remember nothing but pleasure and excitement.'[103]

Three years after the executions of Sque-is and Siam-a-sit, a Cowichan named Tathlasut was also tried by a jury of naval personnel, on a charge of attempting to murder a man Douglas refers to as Thomas Williams, a white settler. Tathlasut was pursued by a military force three times the size of the one that had been sent after Sque-is and Siam-a-sit, and, like them, he was convicted and hanged on the same day.[104] On this occasion, however, it is clear not only that the Cowichans submitted because of Douglas' superior force, but also that some of them bitterly resented his actions and continued to feel aggrieved long afterwards. This contrast with the earlier case has puzzled at least one commentator, but the reasons for it are tolerably clear.[105] In the first place, there may be no contrast: the Nanaimo people probably did not accept the hanging of Sque-is and Siam-a-sit as well as some have assumed. Certainly the tribe proved difficult in another area, i.e., the matter of a treaty ceding their title to the rich coal-bearing lands of the district. Notwithstanding that the execution of Sque-is and Siam-a-sit took place on Protection Island, close by the spot where the first mine shaft was to be sunk, they resisted Douglas' attempts to secure such a treaty for a full two years.[106] But even if the hangings in Nanaimo were not resented as Tathlasut's was, the cases may have been different: Tathlasut had shot at Williams because the man had seduced, or attempted to seduce, his bride-to-be, and this was probably a lawful response to a gross insult, especially by someone from a different nation.[107]

Moreover, Thomas Williams was from a different nation in more ways than one. If he was a settler, he must have been the first in the region, because until the expedition to capture Tathlasut completed its task, the true size and fertility of the Cowichan Valley was not appreciated.[108] More importantly, 'Thomas Williams' was a rather fancy way of describing Tathalsut's victim. Usually – that is, when Governor Douglas was not intent on characterizing him as 'a British subject settled in the Cowegin country' – Williams was referred to as Tomo Ouamtomy (Omtamy), or as Tomo Antoine or, simply, Tomo.[109] The son of an Iroquois voyageur and a Chinook mother, Ouamtomy, like Waccan, served the HBC and the colony in a number of capacities, notably on expeditions sent out to assess Vancouver Island's resources.

Ouamtomy, together with J.W. McKay, whose name appears on a number of the land cession treaties of the early 1850s, was the first HBC man to explore the Cowichan River in 1851. Sent there by Douglas, they located good land along the river, 'with a view to opening [it] to settlers.'[110] But the Cowichan were not happy about European incursions into their territory (like most Aboriginal nations in British Columbia, they have never ceded their title by treaty), and Ouamtomy's interference with Tathlasut's intended wife would have been doubly offensive. In any event, he was a rough man, and years after his dispute with Tathlasut – the outcome of which led to his being known thereafter as 'One-armed Toma' – he was charged with the murder of his own wife.[111] Given all these factors, the Cowichan may not have regarded him as someone who automatically came under the protection of English law, and so resisted what they saw as the intrusion of British justice and military force into a lawful, perhaps even a privileged, act of vengeance against a wrongdoer from another nation.

But even if they did acknowledge a British interest, death was an extreme penalty for such an offence, whether or not the Cowichans accepted that Tathlasut was guilty of attempted murder rather than lawful retaliation. Moreover, it was extreme even in English law. As Judge Matthew Baillie Begbie pointed out in an 1869 case where an Indian had been convicted of attempting to murder a white man, by the mid-1850s the practice in England was not to carry out the death sentence 'unless life had actually been taken.' The prisoner in the 1869 case, Mootsack, is described as a boy, and the majority of the Executive Council advised Governor Musgrave that deterrence required that the execution be carried out. Musgrave, however, disagreed. He commuted the sentence, stating that he 'regarded it as dangerous to admit the principle that ... a different standard from that prevailing in the Mother Country should govern the Administration of Criminal Law in this Colony. Painful instances had already come under his notice as [sic] a disposition to regard as venial offences in the case of White men, acts which would have incurred Capital punishment in the case of Indians.'[112]

Of course, the principle of equality espoused by Musgrave also has its problems, and the alternative sentence of life imprisonment with hard labour was hardly lenient, especially as there was evidence that Mootsack was insane. But the point remains: the way Douglas characterized Tomo Ouamtomy for the purposes of Tathlasut's trial, and the failure to grant executive clemency when yet another military jury returned a verdict of guilty, conveyed a message. The execution, like the executions of Sque-is and Siam-a-sit three years earlier, was an emphatic statement about how the government would protect those it chose to define as settlers, whatever the reason for an attack upon them. On the surface, this looked not so very different from established HBC policy. But the anger of the Cowichan suggests that they were beginning to understand that the Queen's law, unlike that of the HBC, was interested in much more than blood and furs.[113] It displayed an even greater dedication to, and capacity for, the use of force, and it had rules about land as well as violence. Sending over four hundred men to arrest Tathlasut for wounding Tomo Ouamtomy was therefore a new kind of excess, and the ceremony it entailed had implications for Aboriginal law that the blood-for-blood policies of the fur trade era did not.

The difficulties involved in applying English criminal law and procedure to international homicide cases became even clearer as the colonial period progressed. There were no lawyers or judges west of the Rocky Mountains when Sque-is, Siam-a-sit, and Tathlasut were tried and executed; nor were the trials held in Victoria, where most of the colonists lived. But these things changed with the gold-rush of 1858. Thus in 1860 Alfred Waddington watched with horror the execution in Victoria of a young Tsimshian named Allache, and then went home to write out an accusation of 'judicial murder' against the court and the Attorney General. Allache was one of the hundreds, and often thousands, of 'Northern Indians' who regularly camped on or near the Songhees lands adjacent to the colonial capital. Under the influence of whisky and provoked by the deceased's repeated attempts to have sexual relations with his wife, Allache attacked him with a knife, inflicting a fatal wound. Despite a citizens' petition for clemency, the response from the executive – James Douglas, presumably – was that 'an example ... must be made, and the Indians taught to respect the laws.'[115]

No doubt the fact that the deceased was, in Waddington's words, a 'worthless, diseased young negro' influenced Waddington's opinion of the case. '[W]here is the white man,' he asked, who might not have acted as Allache had done if such a man had 'practised the same outrages on himself and his wife?' But Waddington cites additional reasons for his outrage, some of which apply to many subsequent cases. Allache was not represented by counsel, and no lawyer present offered to defend him. Nor did the presiding judge, Chief Justice David Cameron, assign counsel or even suggest that someone act. The interpreter was apparently incompetent, speaking neither English nor Tsimshian very well, only the Chinook Jargon – a pidgin language developed during the fur trade era.[116] There were no defence witnesses to explain the provocation, and (although Waddington did not, understandably, mention this) it would be more than thirty years before a person accused of homicide could testify under oath. Instead, Allache was 'condemned on an *ex parte* statement of facts' in a language he did not understand. No man, writes

Waddington, *'even though he be an Indian,'* should be tried and convicted under such circumstances.[117] A final consideration, quite astonishing if true, was that Allache was hanged by the very man who used to sell him whisky, and 'who was now to be handsomely paid, pardoned and liberated' for placing the noose. Waddington then describes the execution, in classic Victorian prose, as follows:

[A]s the clock struck eight, our poor Indian boy, his eyes streaming with tears, was brought out to the foot of the scaffold ... [A]ll was silent save a word of consolation from a Policeman who addressed him in English. The poor fellow stepped up the scaffold, and looked around, pale as death, and as the fatal rope was being adjusted round his neck, with all the strength of his lungs, and looking up to Heaven as a last appeal, he breathed forth one long, loud lamentable wail. Oh, what a wail was that, appealing as it did from the sentence of unjust men to an All Righteous Heaven. There was an indescribable accent in that wail, never to be forgotten by those who heard it – an accent of complaint but of resignation, bespeaking a feeling of injustice, which suddenly aroused every kinder instinct in the breathless crowd, and sent a thrill of horror to every conscience. Tears started from many a man's eyes, and a great many, perhaps one-half of those present, hastened away, unable to endure the sight any longer. The writer was of that number.

Other cases attracted much less criticism, especially where the victims were white settlers (or, if they were Aboriginal, where the execution of the Aboriginal prisoners was perceived as the removal of a threat that might soon be directed against non-Aboriginals).[118] Thus when Un-whan-uck, a Lemalchi Indian, was convicted of murdering settler Frederick Marks and his daughter, his execution was applauded, although the reason for the attack – and an earlier one upon a white man and a half-Cherokee at Bedwell Harbour on Pender Island – has never been satisfactorily explained.[119] This trial is an instructive example of the difficulties involved in attempting to impose English criminal law upon an indigenous prisoner.

Two interpreters were required, a white man to translate from English into the Chinook Jargon and an Indian to translate from the Jargon into Cowichan (more accurately, Halkomelem), Un-whan-uck's language.[120] There was no defence lawyer, nor, of course, were there any Aboriginal people on the jury. In addition to the superintendent of police, who described the murder scene on Kulman (Saturna) Island, and the wife of the deceased, who identified articles of clothing, there were three Aboriginal witnesses for the prosecution. These were all put through the ritual of establishing that they understood the nature of an oath, and all duly replied, through the interpreters, that they knew that punishment in Hell was the consequence of swearing falsely.[121] With Kottinah, a witness described as the prisoner's wife, special pains were taken to establish that she was not 'legally' married to Un-whan-uck. Otherwise crucial prosecution evidence would have been excluded because English law prohibited a wife from testifying against her husband in such a case. It still does.

After the prosecutor examined each of the five witnesses in chief, Chief Justice Cameron asked the prisoner if he had any questions to put. Of the testimony of Kottinah and another woman who had been present at the scene, Un-whan-uck said only that he had no questions but that the witness 'does not tell the truth,' or 'tells lies.'[122] The third witness testified about what an accomplice had said in Un-whan-uck's presence, and also that Un-whan-uck had said it was best not to talk about what happened on Saturna Island. Un-whan-uck again had no questions because 'the witness was there and saw it.' He also had no questions for the superintendent of police and Mrs Marks. When asked at the close of the case for the prosecution whether he had any witnesses or anything to say for himself, he said only that he had no friends to speak for him and that he did not wish to die. It took only a few minutes for the jury to find him guilty.

A week later Chief Justice Cameron presided over another trial, this one involving an indictment for murder arising out of the hunt for Marks' killers. Governor Douglas had dispatched HMS *Forward*, Lieutenant Horace D. Lascelles commanding, to seek them out, and the search quickly focused upon the Lemalchi of Kuper Island, a band notorious as raiders, even renegades.[123] The *Forward* laid siege to their village, and demanded that the suspects be given up. The Lemalchi refused, so a shot was fired over the village. Musket fire then opened up from the shore, and a volley 'raked [the] deck fore and aft,' killing a young seaman, Charles Gliddon.[124] The ship's guns then laid waste to the village, but the suspects escaped. Their capture took many more weeks, and required the assistance of HMS *Devastation*, the gunboat *Grappler*, and the Penelukut band, who had no reason to love the Lemalchi. But in the end eighteen Lemalchi were taken prisoner, and their leader, Otch-ee-wan (or Acheewun), was captured near Active Pass on Galiano Island.[125]

The trial of the three who were charged with the murder of Gliddon – Qual-ah-itton, Otch-ee-wan, and his brother She-nall-ou-luk – was not unlike that of Un-whan-uck. There was the same need for two interpreters, there was an all-white jury, and there were no defence counsel. But the prosecution's evidence was not as strong as the authorities might have liked. In the first place, Police Superintendent Horace Smith, who had been in charge of the capture, testified that no one on board ship could identify the prisoners because the distance was too great – a factor which, so long as the prisoners were members of the offending nation, would not have been a problem for Aboriginal law. And although Lemalchi witnesses testified that the three had fired at the ship, they also said that everyone fired one shot, and that a chief, Squakim, told them to. Again, the prisoners had no questions for any of these witnesses, although they contradicted some of the testimony and She-nall-ou-luk accused one of them of 'telling lies from first to last.' At the close of the Crown's case, Otch-ee-wan said that his heart was good towards the white people, and he and his brother maintained that they did not fire. Qual-ah-itton, however, seemed to admit that he did fire, but only upon being urged to do so by Squakim.

Chief Justice Cameron explained to the jury that it was not necessary for any of the prisoners to have fired the fatal shot, but the jury could not agree and had to be instructed again before they returned verdicts of guilty. Notwithstanding the chief justice's instructions, they accompanied their verdicts with a 'strong' recommendation of mercy because they were not convinced that any of the prisoners had in fact fired the fatal shot. In his report to the colonial government, Cameron expressed his regret that he could not agree with this recommendation.[126] In the result, they were all hanged, as was Un-whan-uck.

In November 1864 Chief Justice Cameron presided over a rather different sort of case.[127] Quoquilimot and Stashal, both men, and Tchchi-co-mat, a woman, were charged with the murder on Saltspring Island of Mary Smith, her young daughter, a young boy named Tax, and two men named Neach and Lo-lo-ax. All were Aboriginal: the prisoners were Chemainus Indians, and all of the deceased, including Mary Smith and her child, were Tsimshian. This made the case an international homicide within the Aboriginal world, but it also had this flavour for the colonial authorities because Mary Smith was married to a white man.

Samuel Smith, who ran a mill at Nanaimo, last saw his wife and

child, and their three companions, when they set off by canoe from
Nanaimo, heading for Victoria. He testified that his wife had money
and goods on board, which he identified when Quoquilimot and Stashal
were arrested. This time the prisoners had a lawyer, who acted for all
three of them, and the prosecution was represented by the Attorney
General. When Stashal was asked how he pleaded, he said that he was
guilty but the woman was not. Quoquilimot also said he was guilty,
and Tch-chi-co-mat said nothing. The court entered not guilty pleas
for all three. There was only one interpreter, a white man who translated
between English and the Chinook Jargon.

A number of Aboriginal witnesses gave evidence after the usual statements about their religious beliefs and the afterlife. (During this period
trying criminal cases involving Aboriginal people seems to have been
very much a matter of finding Christian Indians, or at least nominally
Christian ones, to testify against those who were not.) One, a policeman, told of confessions made by the two male prisoners, although
he admitted on cross-examination that he had not cautioned them. This
appears not to have mattered; there was other, circumstantial evidence
against them, and there were statements that the prisoners had made
before the committing magistrate. One wonders how much was lost
in the translation. Another witness said that he knew of no 'quarrel'
between the Tsimshians and the Chemainus, although on cross-
examination he added the word 'lately.'

The defence called no evidence, and because they had counsel there
is nothing in the record that indicates how they viewed the proceedings
except for their pleas at the outset. There is also no indication of what
their counsel said to the jury on their behalf. As a result, there is no
real evidence of the motive for the murders other than the obvious
one of robbery, and the possibility that some sort of tribal feud may
have been involved. While such an explanation may seem unlikely on
the evidence in this case, some Chemainus probably regarded both the
British and any Tsimshian associated with them as interlopers who took
much more than they lost. And because all members of an offending
nation were answerable for the deeds of individual members, homicides
by Aboriginal people might be related to past injuries that the rules
of a common law trial, hobbled by linguistic and cultural incompre-
hension, might never uncover; or, if uncovered, would classify as
irrelevant.

After the trial, the grand jury which had found a true bill against
the three prisoners appeared to be uneasy about applying the fine points

of English law, however crudely, to this sort of case. In their report to the chief justice they 'respectfully' called the court's attention to 'the difficulties attendant upon the application of our criminal code in cases for murder alleged to have been committed by Indians, and they would suggest that in future a Commission should be despatched by His Excellency to the locality of the offence with power to deal with such offences at once.'[128]

They clearly felt that speed was important – Siam-a-sit and Tathlasut had, after all, been tried and executed within a day of their capture – and they may even have been concerned about the predictable lack of defence witnesses when trials were held in Victoria. Perhaps they also wanted to see Chief Justice Cameron get into a canoe and leave the relative comfort of the city, as Judge Begbie, his counterpart on the mainland, did. Whatever the grand jury's concerns may have been, the trial jury took very little time in convicting the two men, although they acquitted Tch-chi-co-mat. Chief Justice Cameron sentenced Quoquilimot and Stashal to death a few days later, and advised Governor Kennedy that because the offence was an 'atrocious' one he could not recommend mercy. The executive council agreed, saying that it was 'not expedient to interfere with the course of the law.'[129]

Begbie, judge and later chief justice of British Columbia, doubtless presided over more trials in which Aboriginal defendants faced murder charges than any other judge. Some, like the prosecutions of the men hanged for their part in the Chilcotin War, are well known; others are not. Begbie's bench books and correspondence, much more than Cameron's sketchy notes and letters, detail the true 'difficulties attendant upon the application' of English criminal law in such circumstances. Unlike the Vancouver Island judge, he was a trained lawyer; he also had a much keener eye for the nuances of Aboriginal life and culture than had Cameron or, for that matter, any other judge of his era. His methods, as revealed in the records, are therefore worth examining, although space permits only a sparse selection.

Begbie's most famous case in the colonial period was no doubt the Chilcotin War trials, which are described in such detail elsewhere that they will only be summarized here.[131] The salient facts are that in April and May 1864 a number of Chilcotins, apparently under the leadership of a man known as Klatassin, killed twenty-one white men, most of whom were engaged in building a trail from Bute Inlet into the interior. The pattern of the killings indicated, as the men who were executed later told missionary R.C. Lundin Brown, that the perpetrators 'meant war, not murder.'[132] Two expeditions were sent to deal with the uprising, one to Bute Inlet under Chartres Brew, the man who established the colonial police, and a second from Fort Alexandria under the gold commissioner in the Cariboo, William G. Cox. Governor Frederick Seymour, who had been on the job for only a few weeks, also went to Bute Inlet. After the first batch of trials, he advised the secretary of state for the colonies that he might find himself compelled 'to follow the example of the Governor of Colorado ... and invite every white man to shoot each Indian he may meet.' Such a directive, said Seymour, 'would not be badly received here.' The secretary of state was not impressed.[133]

There were a number of factors that precipitated the uprising, but probably the most important, immediate cause was the one stated by Klatassin when he was sentenced. Just prior to the outbreak of small-pox in 1862, which probably killed two-thirds of the Chilcotins, a white man had predicted its coming. Then, in the spring of 1864, one of the men at the trail-building camp threatened a group of Chilcotins suspected of stealing flour with death, and took down their names. The man was of course speaking through an interpreter, so it is difficult to know precisely what was said. But causation in Aboriginal law is a much broader concept than it is in the common law of the nineteenth and twentieth centuries, where notions of remoteness, secular science, and economic practicality have eradicated all traces of an earlier, more mystical view. *Deodand*, the common law doctrine that physical objects which played a role in someone's death should be forfeit, was probably the last vestige to go when railway accidents abruptly brought about its abolition in 1846.[134] But taking down names remained a powerful and dangerous thing to do in front of people who believed that human beings could work through spirits to harm or kill others, and who saw writing as a form of magic. Klatassin told the court that the white man had said that they would die, and he repeated, three times, that the man had taken down their names. This, he said, was the cause of the outbreak.[135]

But there was also a less immediate, but no less important, cause of the Chilcotin War. Fur traders had never successfully penetrated Chilcotin territory, primarily because they had not been welcome. Nor was the missionary influence very strong. Moreover, the Chilcotins who were involved in the uprising were generally those who had the least contact with whites, and what contact they had was disconcerting. The miners who came through brought disease and, unlike the fur traders, they 'were there to take something of which the Indians had learned the value but for which the miner did not expect to pay the Indians.'[136] Moreover, the accusation of flour-stealing was linked to refusals to give food to Indians who were hungry, refusals by men who were in Chilcotin territory, eating Chilcotin fish and game. The Chilcotins therefore would have seen the Bute Inlet trail as bringing more of this sort of white man into their territories, and they had another reason to be concerned: the one real settler who was already there – and who was subsequently killed in the uprising – had occupied a traditional camping ground near Puntzi Lake by appropriating the spring and chasing off anyone who opposed him. It is hardly surprising, then, that in his trial notes for 29 September 1864 Begbie recorded the 'land quarrel' as a factor. He remained of that opinion.[137]

There are also some peculiarly ironic aspects to this bloody and unfortunate clash between cultures. One is that the trail-building project was headed and partly financed by Alfred Waddington, who had been so appalled by the hanging of Allache a few years earlier, and who himself died of smallpox in 1872. Another is that the sole non-Aboriginal casualty of the expeditions sent to capture the Chilcotin warriors was Donald McLean, the original pursuer of Samuel Black's murderer and the killer of Tlhelh's uncle. McLean – or Samandlin, as he is known to the Chilcotins – insisted on doing some reconnaissance on his own, and, ever confident, had taken off the bulletproof vest he often wore, because of the extreme heat that day.[139] He was ambushed and shot dead. A third is the elusive identity of the key figure, Klatassin, whom Begbie described as 'the finest savage I have met with yet, I think.'[140] Although spellings vary, this is the name by which the man is known in the histories of both sides in the Bute Inlet War. But in the Chilcotin language, Klatassin means 'We don't know who it is.'[141]

There seems little doubt that Klatassin and most of the others who faced trial had done more or less what they were alleged to have done. But if regarding the events as crimes means applying strict rules of evidence and due process, then – notwithstanding that the prosecution against one defendant, Chedekki, was withdrawn and a second defendant, Lutas, received a free pardon – there were some serious problems with the trials.[142] Aside from the usual difficulties concerning evidence and procedure, the most important one revolves around the admissibility of statements made by Klatassin and his companions to Gold Commissioner Cox. It now seems clear that, when Klatassin and seven others (Telloot, Tahpit, Chessus, Chedekki, Sanstanki, Cheloot, and Klatassin's son, Piell) arrived at Cox's camp on 15 August, they believed that they were coming to parlay with 'the big chief,' Governor Seymour, and to negotiate a peace of some kind. To this end, they brought presents for both Cox and Seymour. They appear to have been unaware that Seymour was not going to see them. However, after they had told Cox that there had been twenty-one warriors in all and had made incriminating statements about themselves, they were arrested – much to their surprise and indignation. Cox said that he had made it quite clear that the 'big chief' in question was Begbie, not Seymour, and that he had not tricked Klatassin into surrendering.[143]

But of course the possibilities for misunderstanding were vast. In addition to the language problem, it turned out that an aide of Cox's had shown Klatassin a photograph of Seymour. Both sides therefore saw the meeting in an entirely different light: the warring chiefs came to negotiate a peace, the colonial authorities came to arrest criminals. Because of these circumstances Begbie was concerned about the admissibility of the confessions, although he did admit them into evidence. After the trials, however, he interviewed Klatassin in his jail cell, hoping, presumably, to reassure himself that he had ruled properly. His reason for concluding that he had – i.e., that Klatassin eventually agreed that he would have had to surrender on terms at some point – seems unconvincing. Years later, Begbie conceded that Klatassin had been 'induced to surrender.'[144]

The six who appeared before Begbie did so in four separate trials, reflecting the fact that in addition to the main massacre there were three other attacks. Although Begbie's notes are somewhat ambiguous on the point, all six seem to have been represented by one lawyer, George Barnston, whose role leaves little trace in the record. Of more significance is the fact that when the trial of two of the warriors who had not come to Cox's camp took place at a special assize in New Westminster in July 1865, Attorney General H.P.P. Crease presided. Williams speculates that Begbie may have disqualified himself, and notes that it seems to be the only instance in British Columbia of a lawyer presiding over a court of assize rather than a judge. His conclusion that the chief law enforcement officer of the Crown could hardly be regarded as impartial in such a case is surely correct.[145] But the Chilcotin trials were really war by other means, and Begbie's report to the Executive Council, which had to decide whether clemency was in order, makes this clear. After making the comment quoted earlier about Klatassin's impressive demeanour, he stated: 'It seems horrible to hang five men at once –

especially under the circumstances of the capitulation. Yet the blood of twenty-one whites calls for retribution. These fellows are cruel, murdering pirates – taking life and making slaves in the same spirit in which you or I would go out after partridges or rabbit-shooting.'[146] It is noteworthy that one of the five, Telloot, had been convicted only of attempted murder, yet, like Tathlasut, he was sentenced to death. No white man was ever executed for attempted murder.

When the five were hanged on 26 October, Lundin Brown told each one: 'Jesu Christ nerhunschita coontse [Jesus Christ be with thy spirit].' Tahpit, the oldest, urged his fellows to 'have courage,' and then spoke to the Carrier Indians who were present and who were old enemies. 'Tell the Chilcoatens to cease anger against the whites,' he said. 'We are going to see the Great Father.'[147]

The problems identified in the early Vancouver Island trials, and in the trials of Klatassin and his companions, received more of Begbie's attention in succeeding years. Three of these cases will suffice to make the point. The first, *Regina v. Kalabeen and Another*, enjoys the distinction of being the first reported case in volume 1, part 1 of the *British Columbia Law Reports*. Selected by Paul Aemelius Irving, British Columbia's 'first official Law Reporter,' *Kalabeen* is the oldest reported case (1867), and one of the shortest, occupying only one page.[148] The report is of a simple motion made in the course of trial to exclude a statement made by one of the prisoners to the committing magistrate, Clement F. Cornwall. The ground was that the magistrate had not complied with the provisions of the relevant statute because he had not prefaced Kalabeen's statement with the required statutory warning. Cornwall conceded this, but testified that he had orally warned the prisoners, and Begbie ruled this sufficient.[149] Attorney General Crease prosecuted; H.P. Walker is shown as representing the prisoners on the motion.

However, the archival records paint a somewhat different picture of the trial. Kalabeen and Scothla, referred to as brothers, were convicted of murdering François Caban at Hat Creek.[150] There was, as always, an interpreter and an all-white jury. The evidence revealed that the motive for the murder was probably robbery, although the prisoners had failed to find the deceased's silver watch and money, which he kept in a second purse hidden in the pocket of a pair of trousers that he wore underneath his outer pair. More importantly, in his notes Begbie states that the prisoners were *undefended*. There is no mention of H.P. Walker or anyone else representing Kalabeen when the issue of the admissibility of his statement to Cornwall was argued, or for the remainder of the trial. Quite the contrary: in the 'remarks' appended to his notes, Begbie states: 'Had the prisoners been white men, *defended by counsel*, & tried separately, it is more than probable that Scothla would have got off [emphasis added].'

The reason Begbie said this is not difficult to discern. The strongest, indeed almost the only, testimony against Scothla was Kalabeen's statement to Cornwall, which alleged that Scothla was the actual killer. Not only was this statement defectively taken, but it was, as against Scothla, not evidence. It was inadmissible hearsay, an out-of-court assertion offered to prove the truth of what was contained therein. Nonetheless, it went before the jury – which it would not have done if Scothla had been tried separately. Begbie therefore 'pointed out' to the jurors that 'the legally admissible evidence was very scanty against Scothla: resting almost entirely on Kalabeen's statement to Se-in-shoot,' another Crown witness.

Se-in-shoot, who, significantly, appeared in court with a government silver-mounted staff, had testified that when the prisoners were at Cornwall's he had asked them what the matter was. Kalabeen responded, in Scothla's presence, that Scothla had killed 'the Frenchman.' Scothla had said nothing. But it was not clearly established that Scothla had heard the remark, which was a prerequisite to a jury finding that he had acquiesced in the truth of the statement (making it an 'adoptive admission' in legal parlance). Nor was Sessee-ask, who had been present when this was said, brought to court to confirm Se-in-shoot's testimony. There was also, according to Begbie, some 'discrepancy' in Se-in-shoot's evidence. Begbie therefore stressed these weaknesses in the Crown's case and urged the jury to 'dismiss from their minds entirely all preconceived notions.' They nonetheless convicted both prisoners after deliberating for only half an hour.

Begbie approved of this result, because before sentencing he had asked the two prisoners if they wanted to make a statement, and Scothla had confessed his guilt. Begbie was disturbed by their attitude: 'I have never seen an instance where there seemed such an utter absence of all ideas of any moral guilt, or offence, in taking human life,' he reported, and, as he had done in the Chilcotin cases, he added that they seemed to think that shooting a man was no different than shooting a grouse. (They did look downcast, however, when he reminded them – not necessarily correctly – that both whites and Indians punished murder with death.)

This was a case when the due process of English criminal law ran headlong into the clashing cultures of colonial British Columbia. If the jury had difficulty understanding Begbie's direction about the use they could make of Kalabeen's statement to Cornwall, how much more difficult would this be for an Aboriginal person? And which group of people would have found the rule more baffling? Clearly, Begbie decided that such rules might be rigorously applied when white men were in the dock, but not otherwise. Like the fur traders before him, he and his fellow colonists were vastly outnumbered, and the priority was deterrence. Judicial unorthodoxy was therefore required to prevent due process from interfering with results. Begbie knew that the statements that Kalabeen and Scothla made after verdict were irrelevant to the question of whether the convictions were legally valid. He must also have noticed that each blamed the other for initiating the plan to kill Caban, which made a joint trial even more awkward. So uneasy was he that he reported to the governor that he 'felt some difficulty in letting Scothla's case go to the jury at all.' Yet when he was summoned to the Executive Council to be questioned, he stated that he was firmly convinced of the guilt of both prisoners, so the death sentences were carried out.[151]

Begbie was also capable of showing mercy, however. Perhaps the most remarkable example begins in 1866 and concerns a young man named Chilpaken, whom Begbie visited in jail after his murder trial (just as he had done earlier with Klatassin). This interview led him to conclude that the deceased in the case may already have been killed by Chilpakin's companion when Chilpakin fired into the body, so he persuaded the Executive Council to commute the sentence.[152] And although the shine on this deed is tarnished somewhat when one considers that his accomplice had escaped and the Crown would need Chilpakin to give evidence against him,[153] this is not the end of the story. In 1868, Chilpakin and another young man, Tesch (alias Charley), were charged at Lillooet with the murder of Tien Fook several years earlier.

In this case there was counsel neither for the Crown nor for the prisoners. When asked to plead, Chilpakin and Tesch made statements that Begbie interpreted as confessing the act but citing extenuating circumstances.[154] He therefore registered not guilty pleas. At the 'express, reiterated and evident wish of the prisoners' their statements were repeated to the jury, and the evidence of an Aboriginal woman, Kitál-qualm, was taken as to their guilt and their age, and that of a settler,

William Chadwick, as to their age only. The gist of the evidence was that, under the influence of alcohol and grief at the death of Chilpakin's sister, the two boys – who were probably about twelve or thirteen at the time – decided to go out and kill a 'Chinaman.' They found one, and murdered him. According to Chilpakin, he attacked first, grabbing the man by the hair and stabbing him in the neck with his knife. Tesch then struck him on the head with an axe, and he 'cried out very loud.' This part of Chilpakin's statement concludes: 'I said he was long dying, and ran up and ripped him across the stomach.' The jury, needless to say, convicted.

Begbie found many difficulties in this case. There was, first of all, the usual matter of language: two interpreters were employed, one to translate from Lillooet into the Chinook Jargon, the other from the Jargon into English. Another important consideration was the age of the prisoners, and Begbie notes that there was no accurate way of ascertaining this. The prisoners had addressed the question by indicating what their heights were seven years earlier, and Kitálqualm had testified that they were both quite small boys at the time. Although Chadwick said that Chilpakin was as tall then as he was at trial, he told Begbie afterwards that he wanted both to hang. Begbie was reluctant to rely on his evidence. Legally this did not matter, because at common law anyone over seven could be convicted of murder; but it was relevant to whether there would be a hanging.

The third problem is more startling. No evidence had been led as to whether the deceased was in fact Tien Fook, the man named in the indictment. Begbie thought that this was an 'absolutely fatal' defect in the prosecution and he conceded that he ought to have directed a verdict of acquittal – especially because the evidence, if believed, amounted to proof that the man that Chilpakin and Tesch had killed was *not* Tien Fook.[155] 'If the accused had been a European,' Begbie concluded, just as he had in the Scothla case, 'and no amendment of the indictment prayed (as none was prayed), I should have felt bound to direct an acquittal.' Of course, no lawyer acted for the prosecution, so no one could have requested such an amendment; Begbie reported that he let the case go to the jury anyway because he was confident that Chilpakin and Tesch had committed the act and there would be a failure of justice otherwise. He also implies that, whatever the defects in the case, settler opinion was to the effect that the two could not be allowed to remain at large. In other words, the judge applied the criminal law by invoking a principle that many people think they would like to see applied uniformly: no one who is factually guilty gets off on a technicality, and 'technicality' is widely defined.

Begbie felt comfortable about his decision because, although the two prisoners were said to be 'dangerous characters' who had committed several murders, he seemed to think that Chilpakin, at least, had reformed in the intervening years. He also believed that inflicting capital punishment on boys who were 'barely of the age of puberty' at the time of the killing was unacceptable, and that the governor and Executive Council would agree. They did, commuting Chilpaken's sentence to seven years, and Tesch's to four, with hard labour.[156]

The last case, *The Queen* v. *Peter*, is also reported in the first volume of the *British Columbia Law Reports*, but only on a point of jury procedure.[157] The main interest of the more extensive, archival sources is the glimpse that they provide of the role of the Chinook Jargon in Aboriginal homicide cases. Peter, like Chilpakin and many others in colonial British Columbia, was charged years after the actual event, being indicted in 1869 for the murder of Patrick O'Brien Murphy in 1861. Although the jury convicted him, both Begbie and the Executive Council were concerned about the unsatisfactory nature of the evidence. The question of whether the sentence would be commuted was therefore suspended in the hope that further evidence might come to light.[158]

The only real new evidence was a sworn statement by one James Wise, who said that in the winter of 1861-2 he was at a party that Peter also attended.[159] Peter was 'about half drunk' and had been quarrelling with some Katzie Indians when he decided to speak to Wise about it. The conversation was in the Chinook Jargon, and literal translations reveal much about how this form of speech functioned.[160] Wise warned Peter to stay away from the Katzies, and Peter responded that Wise was his friend, that he liked the white man. He then said that he had a 'sick tum-tum' (was sick at heart) because he had 'mumu-mucked mastache' to a white man. This would usually be rendered 'mamooked mesachie,' and the difference may be attributable to the fact that Peter was drunk or that Wise was no expert speller of a language that had an unsettled spelling to begin with. In any event, it meant that Peter had done evil to a white man, and Wise inferred that he was speaking of Murphy. The next day Wise said to him, 'Peter, delate mika mahmeloose okuk old man?' which translates as 'Peter, truth, you kill that old man?' and Peter replied, 'Wake, halo.' 'No, no.' And that was it.

Much later, Wise spoke with Peter's woman when she 'was in liquor and angry with Peter.' Peter had been 'abusing her sometime before,' and she told Wise that 'alke [soon] he would kumtux [understand] that he [Peter] had mumumucked mastache to the old man.' She said the old man was Murphy. But when she was sober she always denied that Peter was guilty. 'Halo kumtux [no understand],' she told Wise when he asked her why she had accused Peter. Then she laughed and said it was all 'cultus wawa [worthless talk].' It was hardly a language of nuances, but the effect of Wise's evidence was clear enough, and Begbie concluded that it added little to what had transpired at trial. The governor agreed. After a long administrative silence, the sentence of death was commuted in June 1871 to imprisonment for life.[161] The last sentence to be reviewed by the colonial Executive Council, it has the air of a final bit of business that, in the gathering momentum towards confederation with Canada, was almost forgotten.

IV

One conclusion that emerges from the records surveyed in this essay is that during the colonial period it seems unlikely that Aboriginal people in British Columbia perceived the imposition of English criminal law upon homicide defendants, in and of itself, as their main grievance. Some in fact saw benefits in the Queen's law, especially when it coincided with their interests or was directed against old enemies; and there were nearly always individual Indians who were willing, for their own reasons, to help the authorities apprehend or convict fugitives. Examples include the Penelukut band's role in the capture of Otch-ee-wan and his followers; John Wesley Mountain's role in the arrest of Haatq; the Chemainus policeman who testified against Quoquilimot and Stashal; and Se-in-shoot, who carried his government staff into court to testify against Kalabeen and Scothla. Even in the Chilcotin case there is evidence that the Aboriginal wives of two of the victims told their husbands what was to happen, and that a Homathko boy named George carried the news of the first killings down river to warn the rest of the trail builders. George not only testified for the prosecution in the trials, but even served 'occasionally' as an unsworn interpreter.[162] American historian Patricia Nelson Limerick is therefore correct when she reminds those who think and write about Indian history to 'follow the policy of cautious street crossers: Remember to look both ways.'[163]

Certainly hanging must have seemed a grotesque punishment, but the result in many cases appears to have been seen as just (e.g., the trial of Quoquilimot and Stashal in 1864) or unjust (e.g., Tathlasut's trial in 1856 or the Chilcotin trials in 1864-5) more or less on the merits, and according to tribal law and interests. That the British would apply their own punishments to someone from another nation (assuming that they could get their hands on him) was hardly startling; this is what the HBC had done, and what any nation would do. It is true that the colonial authorities, unlike the fur traders, regarded trial by jury in the name of the Queen as an assertion of British sovereignty over new, albeit legally disadvantaged, subjects. But it is not clear that, in the colonial period at least, Aboriginal people outside the relatively few European population centres realized that this was supposed to replace, rather than merely supplement or coexist with, their own laws. One must look elsewhere, to governmental handling of the land question, to repression of cultural and legal institutions such as the potlatch, and to prosecutions for less serious, alcohol-related offences, to find where the sovereignty shoe really pinched.[164]

Had the colonial government recognized Aboriginal title and embarked upon a programme of purchasing land, no doubt Native people would have differed about the extent to which treaties should be made and land should be sold, just as they differed about the extent to which they should cooperate with law enforcement authorities.[165] In New Zealand, for example, the Treaty of Waitangi was interpreted as acknowledging Native title to the whole country, and when the implications of extensive land sales began to sink in the Maori quickly divided into two parties: the land sellers and their opponents. Eventually these tensions led to the formation of the King movement, the Taranaki War, and the war in the Waikato, in which some Maori sided with the government.[166] It may therefore be significant that, in British Columbia, the homicide cases that became grievances tended to be ones - e.g., Tathlasut, the Chilcotin trials, Haatq, Kitwancool Jim - that were directly related to, or occurred in the course of, conflicts over land. Because settlement required that the land be pacified before it was parcelled out, some of these cases remain sore points even today.[167]

Of course, the thesis that homicide law was not the most important grievance cannot be pressed too far. Not only must ongoing conflicts over land and resources be borne in mind, there is reason to believe that prosecutions against white men for criminal offences were not pursued with the vigour that characterized the trials canvassed here, and that this fact was resented.[168] Moreover, much less documentation has surfaced regarding white men who killed Indians, and there is but a trace of this sort of murder prosecution in the records.[169] Further, when English law was applied, not only to international homicides committed against settlers but to homicides committed within a particular Aboriginal nation, this constituted a marked and probably unwelcome departure from pre-existing norms.[170] Perhaps most important of all, it underscored a growing asymmetry in the legal system: increasingly, Aboriginal people were treated as being entitled to Governor Musgrave's equality before the law when criminal punishment was at stake, but not when it was a question of civil rights. As Robert Brown, the leader of the Vancouver Island Exploring Expedition, put it: 'The Indians have not been treated well by any means. There is continually an empty boast that they are British subjects, but yet have none of the privileges or the right [sic] of one. Their lands have never been paid for ... They are not taxed nor yet vote. They are confined in their villages to certain places. Nor are any means taken to protect their rights of fishing & hunting & yet if an Indian kills another in obedience to their laws ... he is immediately taken up to Victoria. Witness the case of How-a-matcha.'[171]

More than twenty years later, the Toronto *Mail* made a related point during the so-called 'Skeena War.' Taking issue with the prevailing view that the hostilities related solely to the killing of Kitwancool Jim, the *Mail* ventured the opinion that the underlying cause was the ongoing dispute over aboriginal land.[172]

In short, Aboriginal people may have been formally equal before the law in criminal matters, but this was insufficient to protect them in the circumstances in which they found themselves. Colonization always involves two parties of unequal power and sophistication, and as the Rev. Montagu Hawtrey, an early New Zealand colonist, once remarked, 'the only consequence of establishing the same rights and the same obligations for both will be to destroy the weaker under a show of justice.'[173] Certainly the cases discussed here indicate that Aboriginal people laboured under significant disadvantages in a common law trial. To take but one example, while all defendants had the right to an interpreter and to defence counsel, such rights were more apparent than real where Aboriginal defendants were concerned. There was, moreover, confusion in the mid-1860s about the extent to which Aboriginal witnesses could testify under oath, and the spousal competency rule applied in Un-whan-uck's case was only one of a number of evidentiary rules that did not protect Aboriginal defendants as they did non-Aboriginal ones.[174] Thus, many Aboriginal defendants had no counsel; had to hear evidence translated across one pidgin language and two 'real' ones; asked no questions in cross-examination; summoned no defence witnesses; and, probably, often faced Aboriginal witnesses for the prosecution who had motives based upon settling old scores that were, in terms of English law, irrelevant. Isolated by culture and language, these defendants were in effect being tried and, more often than not, condemned by an occupying power unwilling to impose fur trade justice per se but embarrassed (although not too embarrassed) by the unsuitability of English criminal procedure.

To speak of an 'occupying power' may seem unfair to the many persons in the law enforcement system – Begbie, for example – who tried to do their jobs honestly in the difficult circumstances in which they found themselves. But as Gilbert Malcolm Sproat said of the colonization process in the 1860s, the 'wrong of [European] intrusion, if it is a wrong, is quickly turned into a right,' and settlers 'are justified in defending their occupation against the original so-called occupiers, now transformed, by the course of events, from patriots into aggressors.'[175] The Chilcotin, Kalabeen, and Chilpakin cases show that the law was an important part of this defence: different standards did apply to Aboriginal defendants, standards that resulted in convictions where otherwise there might well have been acquittals. Moreover, these differences appear to be a feature of the imposition of colonial law, not merely a function of individual prejudice or competence.

This conclusion is not simply a product of comfortable, 20/20 hindsight. In 1873, for example, Indian Superintendent Powell wrote to a prominent local lawyer for his views on the subject of how the criminal law should be applied to Indians. The reply he received is interesting. Citing the Indians' lack of knowledge, both of English law and of the English language, the lawyer pointed out that, once in the dock, the Indian prisoner 'knows not where to turn for his defence, he knows not what the meaning of evidence is, and never thinks of trying to show by [illegible] circumstances which should plead in his favour. The law of evidence bears very hardly on him, he is not allowed to show circumstances, which to his mind are an all sufficient cause for his actions, because it is not evidence.' He goes on, after stating that English jurisprudence is 'unfitted' for the trial of Indian offences:

As the Indians in their tribal condition have established almost universally a system of recompense for almost all offences, why should not that system be carried out and only those offences brought before the Supreme Court which couldn't be dealt with in this manner? I would also suggest that in all cases of Indian offences care should be taken that the prisoner should have the means and opportunity of obtaining Evidence in his own defence and not left until the day of the trial to make out from adverse witnesses, a [illegible] defence.

The signature on this letter is difficult to read, but it appears to be that of Montague Tyrwhyt Drake. If so, he was the lawyer who would defend Haatq eleven years later, and find his most important evidence ruled to be 'not evidence' for a jury.[176]

An examination of the capital cases reviewed by the executive councils of the colonies of Vancouver Island and British Columbia in the years before 1871 tends to confirm that serious problems existed. Unfortunately, documentation for the entire colonial period may not be complete. The early years are especially elusive, because Executive Council meetings were secret and, on the mainland, Douglas operated without a formal advisory council. Even during the documented period (1864–71) there is at least one capital case, that of James Barry for the murder of Morgan Blessing in 1867, that does not appear to have been recorded in the deliberations of the council.[177] The possibility that there are more unrecorded cases makes conclusions based upon Executive Council deliberations somewhat tentative. Nonetheless, the colonial journals reveal that between the first reported case, *Regina* v. *How-a-matcha*, in August 1864, and the last before Confederation, *Regina* v. *Peter*, in June 1871, the colonial councils considered thirty-eight capital sentences involving thirty-seven men (one, Chilpakin, was convicted of two separate murders).[178] Thirty-three of the condemned were Indians, three were Chinese, one was Kanaka (Hawaiian), and the nationality of the remaining man is not stated.[179] None of the condemned in the reported cases was white, although three white men were convicted of murder prior to Confederation and one of these, James Barry, was hanged within the reporting period.[180] Thirteen of the death sentences – two Chinese, the man whose nationality is unclear, and ten Indians (counting Chilpakin twice) – were commuted.[181]

This means that of the twenty-six men (including Barry and the Chilcotin warriors) hanged in this period, twenty-three were Indians.[182] An observation that Begbie made in 1872, a year after Confederation, confirms the impression created by these figures. Referring to the reaction to a death sentence he had pronounced at Nanaimo upon one George Bell, he noted that the Indians 'were incredulous apparently, that a white man would be convicted or executed for a capital offence.'[183] Bell seems to have been the first white man convicted of murder on Vancouver Island, and Begbie's remark suggests that hanging a European was, indeed, a rare occurrence. It is therefore difficult to avoid the conclusion that the gallows, and the threat of the gallows, were primarily for Indians.

It is true that in early British Columbia, much like South Africa today, the white population was quite small in relation to the indigenous population, so it is to be expected that many more Indians would run afoul of the law than whites. It is also true that only a detailed examination of the facts of each case can provide the context necessary to come to an informed judgment about how the law was applied in it. But some of these cases are reviewed above, and the figures, which seem accurate enough, speak to the overall effect of legal colonization. They suggest that, whether intended or not, it amounted to that potent, discretionary mix of terror and mercy that historians have documented in other times and places.[184] In nineteenth-century British Columbia, moreover, there were between the Aboriginal defendants and their British prosecutors and judges very few of the cultural and social connections that tended to mitigate the law's harshness in the mother country. Apart from the occasional priest or crusading entrepreneur, there were no squires or well-connected relatives to put in a good word.[185] Instead, there was a wide gulf of linguistic and cultural ignorance and misunderstanding. The Aboriginal objects of the Queen's law were no more able to understand its nuances than Europeans were able to understand those of Aboriginal law; and many aspects of British due process – e.g., the non-compellability of the accused and the rules against hearsay or unsworn testimony – must have left them shaking their heads.

A final observation involves leaping forward in time, to this essay's starting point: the Indian troubles on the Northwest Coast during the 1880s, when Haatq killed Youmans and the Metlakatlans left to seek fairer treatment in Alaska. Twenty years after Robert Brown recorded his impressions about equality before the law, the Rev. Robert Tomlinson complained to the chief commissioner of lands and works about Dominion Reserve Commissioner Peter O'Reilly, who had announced that the law of trespass would no longer protect traditional hunting and gathering rights. Years before, said Tomlinson, William Duncan convicted an Indian who had 'trespassed upon the hunting ground of a Christian Indian from Metlakatlah,' and his decision had been upheld by the Supreme Court in Victoria. A few years after that, J.W. McKay, JP, made a similar ruling when the same Indian trespassed on someone else's hunting ground. According to Tomlinson, the attorney general of the day had, when consulted, instructed McKay to uphold 'the Indian law and punish the offender.'[186]

But O'Reilly had come to lay out reserves, and that changed everything. He informed the Indians that 'beyond any rights [they] would have in the reserves he was then marking out, the Government would not acknowledge any right to the exclusive use of any land as a hunting ground by any family or any tribe, and would not punish trespassers on these grounds.'[187] John Robson supported O'Reilly, telling Tomlinson that the government would 'not disturb' whatever hunting and gathering rights the chiefs might claim, 'at least until such time as the lands are required.' But, he added, 'as between themselves these alleged claims cannot be enforced by the Justices of the Peace. Indeed such matters can only be regarded as mere domestic arrangements of which the law cannot even take cognizance.'[188]

Tomlinson replied that Robson's first point appeared unintelligible to the chiefs. Who, they wanted to know, had the government's permission 'to require' Indian lands? Could any white man? If so, how was that 'consistent with the statement that the government will *not* disturb'? Indian hunting and gathering rights *are* being disturbed, reported Tomlinson, 'and those disturbing them claim they are being supported by the government.' For his part, Tomlinson wanted to know what he was supposed to do about the large number of white men in the area, 'whose only idea of law and justice seems to be to force the Indian back wherever the white man wants a footing.'[189]

For whom, Tomlinson seemed to ask, was the Queen's law, as conceived in Victoria, truly better? The government's attitude towards traditional rights denied such rights protection in the courts and allowed them to be eroded on the ground – a ground that was even then being surveyed away from Tsimshian ownership and control without any real acknowledgment of Indian title, just as it had been further south. Yet it was the land and the rights attached to it that mattered most, and the colonists threatened these in a way that the fur traders, whose harsh methods of retaliation were unencumbered by the trappings of British due process, had not. It is true that some Aboriginal people may have seen the threat posed by the Queen's law in a more positive light, and therefore welcomed some of its effects upon traditional structures that denied them wealth and power. But once the Queen's law and the criminal justice system that followed in its wake had become well-established, such people must have felt betrayed. Most of the land was gone, and the wealth and the power had gone with it.[190] Because the issues created by this transfer are unresolved, the colonial era, with all its conflicts over land and law enforcement, remains with us.

NOTES

Sections II and III of this essay are based to some extent upon research done at the Bancroft Library, University of California at Berkeley, in 1984, and upon material in two unpublished essays of mine written in 1986–7: 'Here before Christ: Administering Justice in the Western Fur Trade, 1670–1858' and 'Law before the Lawyers: Administering Justice on Vancouver's Island, 1849–1858.' Part of the latter was presented as a paper at the Canadian Law in History Conference at Carleton University in June 1987.

1 'Correspondence relating to the recent Indian troubles on the North-West Coast' B.C. *Sessional Papers*, 1885 (hereafter *BCSP*) 279 (Geddum-cal-doe to Provincial Secretary John Robson, 7 Sept. 1884). The Gitksan are a Tsimshian people, and the name means people (Git) of the Skeena river (Ksan). Tsimshian (or Tsimpsean) is derived from a word meaning 'inside the Skeena River,' and it includes the Nisga'a, the Gitksan, and the Southern and Coastal Tsimshian. Kit-au-max (or Gitenmaax), at the Forks of the Skeena, is now Hazleton.

2 Ibid. 281–2 (William F. Madden and thirty-eight others to the provincial secretary, 15 Sept. 1884)

3 Geddum-cal-doe to Robson, above n. 1. This letter was written by the Rev. D. Jennings and the Rev. A.E. Green at the request of the friends of Haatq, and it is consistent with the law of most Indian nations where the liability of hosts is concerned. Perhaps the most famous BC example is the problem caused by James Douglas in 1828 when he sought out and killed a young Fraser's Lake man thought responsible for killing two Hudson's Bay Company clerks at Fort George several years earlier. Because the man was hiding in the Stuart's Lake village when Douglas killed him, the Stuart's Lake people were expected to compensate the Fraser's Lake people for his death. For this reason the Stuart's Lake chief sought satisfaction from Douglas and the company, thus precipitating an incident that has loomed large in Douglas' legend ever since. See, for example, the brief account in G.P.V. Akrigg and Helen B. Akrigg *British Columbia Chronicle 1778–1846* (Vancouver: Discovery Press 1975) 255–6.

4 Ibid.

5 The information in this paragraph is taken primarily from the capital case file on *Reg.* v. *Haatq* (or Aht) in the National Archives of Canada (hereafter NAC), RG 13, vol. 1421, file 190, and the quoted passage is from the report of Mr Justice Henry Pering Pellew Crease to the Secretary of State, Ottawa, dated 18 Dec. 1884. Another source is William Henry Collison *In the Wake of the War Canoe* (Victoria: Sono Nis Press 1981 reprint, ed. Charles Lillard), who at 213 states that Billy Owen was the second son of Haatq to die in Youmans' employ, and that on both occasions Youmans denied Haatq's demand for compensation. In light of the evidence led at trial, this seems unlikely. More probable, however, is Collison's assertion that Haatq's tribesmen 'chaffed' him when they learned of Billy's death, perhaps provoking him to act.

6 Ibid.

7 See the trial judge's Notes and his report to the Secretary of State in *Reg.* v. *Haatq*, above n. 5. According to Jennings, above n. 3, Haatq's friends had made threats that he and Green refused to include in Geddum-cal-doe's letter to Robson, threats concerning the dire consequences of an execution: Jennings to provincial secretary, 16 Sept. 1884, *BCSP 1885* 280.

8 *BCSP 1885* 282–3 (Robson to the chief and people of Kit-au-max, 13 Oct. 1884). Robson, a member of the government led by William Smithe, became premier himself in 1889.

9 Ibid.

10 The trial judge's report, above n. 5. In so far as alternative remedies are concerned, Crease notes that Haatq's friends had complained that the provincial authorities had shown no interest in Indian deaths, 'but the moment a white man is killed instant steps are taken to avenge it.' For a discussion of how tribes, whether Aboriginal or white, protect their own, see section II, below.

11 Above n. 8. There is reason to doubt Robson on this point. Five of the twelve persons sentenced to death in Canada in 1884 were in BC, but in none of these five cases does it appear that a white man was executed for killing an Indian. The only possibility in terms of the date and the location of the hanging is *Reg.* v. *Edward Lemon (Lamont)* hanged in May 1884 at Victoria for killing an Indian described as 'Johnny.' But in the records, Lemon is himself described as a male Indian, so Robson seems to have been stretching the truth somewhat. See: Lorraine Godoury and Antonio LeChasseur *Persons Sentenced to Death in Canada, 1876–1976; An Inventory of Case Files in the Records of the Department of Justice (RG 13)* (Government Archives Division, NAC 1994), cases 0539, 0777, 1169, 1178, and 1333.

12 *Reg.* v. *Haatq* and Collison *In the Wake of the War Canoe*, above n. 5. Public opinion in Victoria was apparently against the commutation of Haatq's death

sentence: see Patricia Roy 'Law and Order in British Columbia in the 1880s: Images and Realities' in R.C. MacLeod, ed. *Swords and Phoughshares: War and Agriculture in Western Canada* (Edmonton: University of Alberta Press 1993) 55, 62, where Roy refers to the prisoner as 'Aht-ah.'

13 Ibid. 213–14

14 John W. Mountain is the John Wesley, son of Chief Mountain of Greenville, who was part of the Tsimshian delegation that met with Premier Smithe in Victoria in February 1887 to protest government land policy. He asked Smithe to make a treaty with his people, as the law of England and Canada required, and no doubt expected Smithe to remember his role in the You-mans case. But the premier denied that the law required any such thing, holding out no hope that the Indian title would be recognized: see *BCSP 1887* 255–7 (Report of conferences between the provincial government and Indian delegates from Fort Simpson and Naas River). A few months later Wesley's father, who was the second-highest chief on the Nass, appeared before the commission that inquired into Indian complaints on the Northwest Coast, and spoke 'with a sore heart': see *BCSP 1888* 430–1 (Papers relating to the commission appointed to enquire into the state and condition of the Indians of the North-West Coast of British Columbia). The commission had been instructed that Indian title was not within its mandate and that all talk of it should be discouraged. The senior chief Mountain, however, had a change of heart and became a supporter of the government: see NAC, RG 10, vol. 3699, file 16,682 (reel C-10122).

15 *BCSP 1885* 290–1 (Robson to David Leask). The Metlakatlans had complained about Andrew Charles Elliott, formerly premier of British Columbia (1876–8), who had by then descended to the offices of magistrate and Indian agent at Metlakatla. His views, including his firm conviction that the 'dangerous state' of affairs on the entire coast was 'almost entirely owing to the teaching of Mr. Duncan and Mr. Tomlinson,' are reproduced on 286–8.

16 Ibid.

17 See Jean Ussher *William Duncan of Metlakatla: A Victorian Missionary in British Columbia* Publications in History, no. 5 (Ottawa: National Museums of Canada 1974), Peter Murray *The Devil and Mr. Duncan* (Victoria: Sono Nis Press 1985), and Clarence Bolt *Thomas Crosby and the Tsimshian: Small Shoes for Feet Too Large* (Vancouver: University of British Columbia Press 1992). Further information on the disturbances at Metlakatla is in *BCSP 1883* at 203–6 (Papers relating to breaches of the peace and destruction of property on the Indian Reserve at Metlakatlah) and *BCSP 1885* at 317–21 (Depositions in the hearing of the charge against the Indians for riotously taking possession of a schoolhouse at Metlakatlah).

18 See n. 14, above. This commission appears to have been first promised in 1884, the year of Youmans' death: *BCSP 1885* 288 (Robert Tomlinson to Robson, 12 Nov. 1884).

19 See Ken Campbell 'The Skeena War' *The Beaver* 69/4 (1989) 34–40. For an imaginative account of the Gitksan view of events leading up to the decision to dispatch troops see Marius Barbeau *The Downfall of Temlaham* (Toronto: Hurtig 1973 reprint); originally published in 1928, this is a well-known anthropologist's fictionalized version of the story of Kamalmuk (Kitwancool Jim), the man whose death sparked the 'war.'

20 Tomlinson to chief commissioner of lands and works, 27 Feb. 1884, *BCSP 1885* 277–8 (citing the chiefs)

21 *BCSP 1885* 290 (David Leask to Robson, 22 Nov. 1884)

22 Bolt *Thomas Crosby and the Tsimishian*

23 Ibid. 88

24 In 1869 the region had been placed under English law when the colonial governor travelled to the Nass and the Skeena aboard HMS *Sparrowhawk* to intervene in a dispute between the Nisga'a and the Tsimshian arising out of another accidental death. Afterwards, the chief commissioner of lands and works commented on the contrast between how his government had settled that conflict and the 'bombardment and burning of Indian villages' that had been resorted to in the past. This time, the 'warring tribes were brought to relinquish their feud, and [were] bound over to live in future according to English law.' However, he added, it had to be 'borne steadily in mind, that as these tribes were specially placed by the direct act of the Head of the Executive under the operation of English Law, *that law must in future be enforced among them at whatever cost*' (emphasis added). See Joseph W. Trutch to officer administering the government, 22 June 1869, in *Papers Connected with the Indian Land Question, 1850–1875* (Victoria: Richard Wolfenden 1875) 68–70.

25 For a dramatic account of these divisions, see Barbeau *The Downfall of Temlaham*. The government was well aware of the tensions among the Nisga'a and the Tsimshian on the lower Skeena, ascribing them almost exclusively to denominational rivalry. Indeed, Attorney General A.E.B. Davie indicated that, were it not for the limitation period, he would have prosecuted William Duncan for treason. He told the federal minister of justice that he intended to have Duncan arrested and charged with sedition, instead: see Roy 'Law and Order in British Columbia' 63.

26 Above n. 2, 282 (for the Bute Inlet massacre, see text accompanying nn. 131–47 below). The problem for the authorities often lay in assessing who was to blame for clashes between colonist and Indian. As Trutch (above n.

24) put it in 1869, when disputes arose in remote regions of the colony white people often called upon the government 'to punish the Indians without its [sic] being proved that they are actually more blameable than those who accuse them.'

27 See, for example, Bolt *Thomas Crosby and the Tsimishian* and J.D. Darling 'The Effects of Culture Contact on the Tsimshian System of Land Tenure during the Nineteenth Century' (MA thesis, University of British Columbia 1955), concluding that Tsimshian land law survived the imposition of the reserve system in the late nineteenth century.

28 A somewhat similar, earlier essay is Cornelia Schuh 'Justice on the Northern Frontier: Early Murder Trials of Native Accused' *Criminal Law Quarterly* 22 (1979–80) 74, but it deals with a later period, east of the Rockies. Regional case studies outside British Columbia include Chief Thomas Fidler and James R. Stevens *Killing the Shaman* (Moonbeam: Penumbra Press 1985), Graham Price 'The King v. Alikomiak' in Dale Gibson and Wesley Pue, eds. *Glimpses of Canadian Legal History* (Winnipeg: Legal Research Institute, 1991) 213–35, and Hamar Foster, 'Sins against the Great Spirit: The Law, the Hudson's Bay Company, and the Mackenzie's River Murders, 1835–1839' *Criminal Justice History: An International Annual* 10 (1989) 23–76. The well-known case of Sinnisiak and Uluksuk has been chronicled in R.G. Moyles *British Law and Arctic Men* (Burnaby: The Northern Justice Society 1989) and Sidney L. Harring 'The Rich Men of the Country: Canadian Law in the Land of the Copper Inuit, 1914–1930' *Ottawa Law Review* 21 (1989) 1. There are also some relevant cases discussed in Sidney L. Harring 'The Incorporation of Alaskan Natives under American Law: United States and Tlingit Sovereignty, 1867–1900' *Arizona Law Review* 31 (1989) 279.

29 Gilbert Malcolm Sproat *The Nootka: Scenes and Studies of Savage Life* ed. Charles Lillard (Victoria: Sono Nis Press 1987; originally published London: Smith, Elder 1868) 59, quoting Captain Cook

30 The account which follows is from Tomas Bartroli 'The Earliest Recorded Murders in British Columbia,' Bancroft Library, University of California at Berkeley (hereafter 'Bancroft L.'), m F1088 B3, 5–15, 25–6, citing other sources.

By 'international' homicide I mean a homicide in which the deceased and perpetrator, like Youmans and Haatq, are of different nations, whether European or Aboriginal: see generally John Phillip Reid 'A Perilous Rule: The Law of International Homicide' in Duane H. King, ed. *The Cherokee Indian Nation: A Troubled History* (Knoxville 1979) 33–45. Thus, Shuswap/Okanagan and British/Shuswap homicides would be international ones, but Shuswap/Shuswap and British/British homicides would not.

31 The meaning of such words can be elusive. 'Nootka,' for example, is one of Captain Cook's mistakes: when he heard the word, he apparently thought that the speakers, who were telling him to 'circle about' to find a better anchorage, were answering his inquiry about who they were. The words that Callicum hurled at Martinez were 'pisce' and 'capsil' (there are various spellings), meaning 'bad' and 'thief.'

32 Twenty years earlier a Maori was the first to die in New Zealand when one of Cook's lieutenants shot him for refusing to pay for a bolt of cloth. His people elected to regard the death as *utu* (compensation, satisfaction) for his offence, and did not attempt vengeance: see Alan Ward *A Show of Justice: Racial Amalgamation in Nineteenth Century New Zealand* (Auckland: Oxford University Press 1974) 12.

33 Bartroli 'The Earliest Recorded Murders' 27–30

34 Ibid. 37. Vancouver ordered the execution of several Natives in the Hawaiian Islands who were suspected in a similar incident, notwithstanding doubts about their guilt.

35 See, for example, Robin Fisher *Contact and Conflict: Indian-European Relations in British Columbia, 1774–1890* (Vancouver: University of British Columbia Press 1977; 2nd ed., 1992) chap. 1.

36 Alexander Mackenzie of the North West Company reached the Pacific Ocean overland from Fort Chipewyan in 1793, but it was another twelve years before Simon Fraser established the post at McLeod Lake. John Jacob Astor's Pacific Fur Company founded Fort Astoria in 1811, which they sold in 1813 to the North West Company, who renamed it Fort George. The North West Company merged with the HBC in 1821, which established its new headquarters on the Columbia at Fort Vancouver.

37 See the map reproduced at the back of Glyndwr Williams, ed. *Hudson's Bay Miscellany* (Winnipeg: Hudson's Bay Record Society vol. 30, 1975).

38 John Phillip Reid 'Crosscultural Vengeance: Sources of Legal Principles in the Formulation of Mountain Men Vengeance against Indians in the Old Oregon Country' 2–3, to be published in Sweden in 1993

39 Roderick Finlayson 'History of Vancouver Island and the Northwest Coast' (Bancroft L., P-C 15, n.d.) 99–100. Finlayson became a chief trader in 1850 and ultimately a chief factor. He was a member of the council of Vancouver Island from 1851 to 1863, and became mayor of Victoria in 1878. This incident is also described by John Sebastian Helmcken in Dorothy Blakey Smith, ed. *The Reminiscences of John Sebastian Helmcken* (Vancouver: University of British Columbia Press 1975) 135–6.

40 See 43 Geo. III (1803), c. 138 (UK) and 1 Geo. IV (1821), c. 66 (UK), discussed in Hamar Foster 'Long-Distance Justice: The Criminal Jurisdiction of

Canadian Courts West of the Canadas, 1763–1859' *American Journal of Legal History* 34 (1990) 1–48. However, in the one case where the HBC considered sending a homicide on the Pacific coast east for trial, doubts were expressed about the applicability of these statutes west of the Rockies: see Hamar Foster 'Killing Mr. John: Law and Jurisdiction at Fort Stikine, 1842–1846' in John McLaren et al., eds. *Law for the Elephant, Law for the Beaver: Essays in the Legal History of the North American West* (Regina: Canadian Plains Research Centre 1992) 147–93.

41 'John Tod: "Career of a Scotch Boy"' *British Columbia Historical Quarterly* 18 (1954) 133, 196 (hereafter *BCHQ*). Tod joined the HBC in 1811 and served in New Caledonia from 1823 to 1832. He was promoted to chief trader in 1834, and after a stint east of the Rockies he returned to the Pacific slope, where he retired in 1852.

42 Testimony of Sir George Simpson, governor of the HBC in British North America, in *Report from the Select Committee on the Hudson's Bay Company* (London: House of Commons 1857) 1060, 1749, and 1752–3, confirming that a summary law of 'blood for blood' applied. The issue of the applicability of the statutes to homicides involving Aboriginal people is discussed in Foster 'Sins against the Great Spirit' and 'Forgotten Arguments: Aboriginal Title and Sovereignty in Canada Jurisdiction Act Cases' *Manitoba Law Journal* 21 (1992) 343–89.

43 John Tod 'History of New Caledonia and the Northwest Coast' (Bancroft L., P-C 27, 1878) 62. Most historians are of the same opinion. Bancroft, for example, described HBC law as 'justice without form [and] barely respectable, appearing oftener in elk-skin than in ermine, and quite frequently with gaunt belly and tattered habiliments' (*The Works of Hubert Howe Bancroft* vol. 32: *History of British Columbia 1792–1887* (San Francisco 1887) 419. As late as Haatq's trial in 1884, defence counsel said of the Gitksan: 'It is the Mosaic law they ignorantly follow, that admits money payment for any description of injury.' Or, as one prosecution witness put it: 'Youmans expected there would be trouble, but a person could always pay enough to save his neck. That is one good thing about Indians.' (*Reg. v. Haatq*, above n. 5.)

44 *John McLean's Notes of a Twenty-Five Year's Service in the Hudson's Bay Territory* ed. W.S. Wallace (Toronto: Champlain Society vol. 19, 1932) 323. McLean joined the HBC in 1821. He served in New Caledonia between 1833 and 1837, spending the rest of his fur trade career east of the Rockies. Dissatisfied with the way in which Sir George Simpson managed the business, McLean resigned in 1845 and published his *Notes* in 1849.

45 Quoted in Ross Cox *Adventures on the Columbia River* 2 vols. (London 1831) 2:

242–5. Cox was somewhat taken with 'the humorous, honest, eccentric, law-defying Peter Ogden, the terror of Indians, and the delight of all gay fellows,' for whom 'the study of provincial jurisprudence, and the signeurial subdivisions of Canadian property, had no charms.' Ogden served mainly in New Caledonia and the Columbia, and was one of the three members of the Board of Management that succeeded John McLoughlin, the so-called 'Emperor of the West,' in the Western Department.

46 John Philip Reid 'Principles of Vengeance: Fur Trappers, Indians, and Retaliation for Homicide in the Transboundary North American West' *Western Historical Quarterly* 24 (1993) 21, 34

47 On this issue there are many sources, notably the work of Hoebel, Bohannan, Hogbin, Malinowksi, etc. A particularly helpful book is Max Gluckman *Politics, Law and Ritual in Tribal Society* (Oxford: Basil Blackwell 1965).

48 See n. 46, above, and John Philip Reid 'The Hudson's Bay Company and Retaliation in Kind against Indian Offenders in New Caledonia' *Montana: The Magazine of Western History* Winter 1993, 5–17. Professor Reid has kindly made available to me a number of other soon-to-be published articles on related topics, and the discussion which follows draws upon them as well.

49 For reports of these incidents see *Minutes of Council of the Northern Department, 1821–31* (London: Hudson's Bay Record Society vol. 3, 1940) xxxvi, lxiv-v, 104, 107. The Fort St John case is also discussed in *John McLean's Notes* (above n. 44, 141–2) and Shepherd Krech III 'The Beaver Indians and the Hostilities at Fort St. John's' *Arctic Anthropology* 20/2 (1983) 35–45. At Fort George two *engagés* were killed; at Fort St John, the dead included four *engagés* and the man in charge of the post, Guy Hughes. James Douglas' retaliation against one of the perpetrators of the Fort George killings (see n. 3, above) constitutes an almost legendary episode in fur trade history, and there are a number of accounts of it, some of which are listed in Smith *Reminiscences of ... Helmcken* 130n.

50 See the *Fort Langley Post Journal*, Bancroft L., P-C22; the *Journal of Francis (Frank) Ermatinger, clerk, etc.*, Bancroft L., P-B216 (fm F1060.8.E8); and E.E. Rich, ed. *The Letters of John McLoughlin from Fort Vancouver to the Governor and Committee, First Series, 1825–38* (London: Hudson's Bay Record Society vol. 4, 1941) 57–8, 63–5. A number of people were killed, including clerk Alexander Mckenzie.

51 There are many accounts of Chief Trader Samuel Black's murder at Fort Kamloops, but very few of Postmaster William Morwick's at Fort Babine and clerk John McIntosh's at Fort Chilcotin. All three are described in A.G. Morice *The History of the Northern Interior of British Columbia* (Smithers: Interior Stationery 1978 reprint) 181, 211–17, 185, 243.

52 The victim was the notorious Alexis Bélanger: see Morice, ibid. 266ff.

53 There are also many accounts of this incident, which involved the killing of three HBC deserters. A recent one is in Barry Gough *Gunboat Frontier: British Maritime Authority and Northwest Coast Indians, 1846–1890* (Vancouver: UBC Press 1984) chap. 3.

54 For example, the killing of David Livingstone, the interpreter at Fort Babine in 1827 – reported in Morice *History of the Northern Interior* 147, 254–5 – and of a Canadian *engagé* at Fort McLoughlin in 1833 – reported in Alexander Caulfield Anderson 'History of the Northwest Coast,' Bancroft L. (1878), P-C2, 17ff., and in *The Journals of William Fraser Tolmie, Physician and Fur Trader* (Vancouver: Mitchell Press 1963) 252–3, 264. E.E. Rich states that there was a killing at Fort Dunvegan in 1824 as well: see *The History of the Hudson's Bay Company 1670–1870* vol. 2 (London: Hudson's Bay Record Society 1959) 474.

55 There are also a number of documented instances east of the Rockies, such as the Hannah Bay 'massacre' described in *John McLean's Notes* (above n. 44, 99–101), and even some where traders returned blood for lesser offences, such as the killing of six Stoney Indian horse thieves described by J.G. MacGregor in *John Rowand: Czar of the Prairies* (Saskatoon: Western Producer Prairie Books 1978) 101.

56 Reid 'Principles of Vengeance' 24–5

57 See Philip Drucker *Cultures of the North Pacific Coast* (New York: Harper & Row 1965) 72–4 and Stuart Michael Piddocke 'Wergild among the Northwest Coast Indians' (MA thesis, University of British Columbia 1959). Reid ('Principles of Vengeance' 27) states that the traders found the willingness of Indians on the Columbia to accept compensation unusual because this did not happen in many other parts of North America.

58 Or so reports Francis Ermatinger, above n. 50, 1, wherein he underlines the words.

59 Ibid. 12–21, and *The Letters of John McLoughlin, First Series* (above n. 50, 57, 65).

60 *The Letters of John McLoughlin, First Series* (emphasis added). The awkward phrasing is in the original.

61 In an unpublished paper (see above n. 38, 9–22), Reid argues that in fur trade accounts there is 'a persistent mixing of the concept of individual personal guilt from the European, Anglo-American tradition, with the concept of collective liability basic to North American Indian law,' and uses an example from 1832–3, when John Work was in command of the Snake Country expedition. A year earlier one of the trappers had been killed by three Snakes, and Work, who became a chief factor in 1846 and a member of the council of Vancouver Island in 1853, did not want his men 'to punish the innocent for the guilty.' But he allowed that three members of their family could be killed if the killers were not apprehended, thus expanding the Eu-

ropean concept of guilt towards the Indian concept of liability, but confusing it even further by substituting the number of killers as the relevant figure for the 'one for one' principle.

62 Ermatinger (above n. 50, 12, 19) reports that there were more than sixty men in the party, and that the 'Iroquois, Owhyees and Cheenook slaves painted themselves ... for battle.' When the killing began, the officers could not control it, hence the casualties among the women and children. One Iroquois *engagé* began scalping, and almost scalped a Clallum who was still alive.

63 See Morice *History of the Northern Interior* 147, 215, 253ff. Waccan was a 'half-breed' (presumably half-Iroquois) whose first wife was Carrier. He then married a trader's daughter, and became a sort of company 'enforcer' until his death during the measles epidemic of 1850. He was in charge of the expedition that shot William Morwick's killer (see n. 51, above).

   C.A. Bayley recites an incident in which an HBC agent, possibly Waccan, attended a potlatch in search of a man who had killed a company employee. After making a speech about the incident and about Indian law, he coolly shot and killed the suspect in front of the whole assembly. Although this occurred years after the original killing, '[j]ustice [was] satisfied, the business of the congregation proceeded and peace prevailed': 'Early Life on Vancouver Island,' Bancroft L., P-C3, 32–3.

64 See Reid 'The Hudson's Bay Company and Retaliation in Kind against Indian Offenders in New Caledonia,' where he may attach too much significance to the views of Peter Skene Ogden, a rather atypical trader who, like McLoughlin, remained south of 49° after 1846. The Clallum case does, however, support another of Reid's arguments: because the HBC had the resources and manpower to keep a large force 'in the field,' their vengeance was more swift and certain than that exacted by less disciplined parties of American trappers.

65 These terms – and the attitudes they represented – long survived the death of King George III in 1820 and the passage of the Boston trading ships from the scene. A number of contemporary accounts speak of American settlers obtaining HBC *capots* to wear as protection during the Indian wars of the 1850s. Although Governor Douglas sent powder and arms to the Americans and made it clear that this 'was not a fight in which the King George men would take sides with the red men,' HBC posts remained immune from attack during these wars, a circumstance which many Americans viewed with suspicion: see 'The Olympia Club Conversazione' recorded in Olympia, W.T., 9 June 1878, and William Fraser Tolmie 'History of Puget Sound and the Northwest Coast' Bancroft L., P-B 15, 13–15, and P-B 25, 43.

Edward Eldridge, who travelled to Fort Colville when gold was discovered there in 1855, states that he had been told that 'the Indians ... were very friendly to King George men ... far more so than to Bostons ... and [that] it would be better for us to represent ourselves as King George men whenever we met any Indians.' He reports that he was glad that his party had purchased their blankets at Fort Victoria, because 'had [the] Indians [we met] known us to be Bostons, we would have been put to a sleep from which there would have been no waking': Edward Eldridge 'Sketch of Washington Territory,' Bancroft L., P-A88 (Whatcom 1880) 15-17.

66 This is the incident referred to in the text accompanying n. 53, above. The following summer Blanshard dispatched a second ship, the *Daphne*, which destroyed a second encampment, including houses, canoes, and other property. This, plus the offer of thirty blankets for each murderer they captured, induced the Newitty to cooperate. They produced three bodies, one of which may have been that of a slave who was substituted when the real killer escaped: see Smith *Reminiscences of ... Helmcken* 312-23, and Gough *Gunboat Frontier* 43-5.

67 Douglas to Barclay, 16 Apr. 1851, in Hartwell Bowsfield, ed. *Fort Victoria Letters 1846-1851* (Winnipeg: Hudson's Bay Record Society vol. 32, 1979) 176 (emphasis in original). See also Anderson 'History of the Northwest Coast' 250ff., who states that 'punishment was inflicted only on the guilty; and then usually through the medium of the tribe, or with their approval or cooperation.'

68 It is noteworthy, however, that his reservations did not prevent him from adding that the *Daedalus'* actions had 'a salutary effect.' The Newitty were in 'a state of great alarm and have promised to deliver the murderers to the first Ship of War which arrives on the Coast.' Douglas' subsequent conduct as governor (see section III, below) suggests that he took this lesson to heart.

69 See, for example, the Snake country case described by Reid, above n. 61, and the Quesnel case, below, text accompanying nn. 82-7.

70 By April 1851, when he wrote to Barclay, English law had been notionally in force on Vancouver Island for two years. And by August, Douglas was governor in Blanshard's place, charged with overseeing the transition from a fur trade to a colonial regime. For an account of the sort of law that HBC officers applied to their own employees before and during the transition to the colonial legal regime, see Hamar Foster 'Mutiny on the *Beaver*: Law and Authority in the Fur Trade Navy, 1835-1840' in Gibson and Pue, eds. *Glimpses of Canadian Legal History* (above n. 28) 15-46.

71 In Reid 'Principles of Vengeance' 22, Black is incorrectly described as a chief

factor, a promotion that was unlikely even if he had survived the attack on his life at Fort Kamloops. Black, like Ogden, was initially blocked from joining the HBC upon amalgamation in 1821 because of his violent behaviour during the trade wars of the previous decade, and in 1832 Governor Simpson recorded that he 'should be sorry to see a man of such character at our Council board': see 'Simpson's Character Book' in Williams, ed. *Hudson's Bay Miscellany* (above n. 37) 193.

72 The lawyers were still wrangling in 1889, and the debate even included a learned discussion of the Statute of Merton, 1236, which rejected the canon law doctrine of legitimation by subsequent marriage: see Correspondence and documents relating to *Reid* v. *Keith*, Hudson's Bay Company Archives (hereafter HBCA), A.38/23-6, and George B. Roberts, 'Recollections,' Bancroft L., P-A 83, 11. Black was not the only HBC man whose British relatives balked at seeing estate moneys pass to children of fur trade marriages, *à la façon du pays*.

73 See n. 46, above. One account that Reid does not cite is in Anderson 'History of the Northwest Coast' 77-82. The most accessible published version of the incident is in Akrigg and Akrigg *British Columbia Chronicle* 325-8. All the versions differ in a number of details.

74 Anderson, ibid.

75 Ibid.

76 Ibid. It is perhaps worth noting that economic sanctions could be worse than blood vengeance from the Aboriginal point of view. For example, when Guy Hughes and his men were killed at Fort St John (above n. 49) the HBC closed both that post and Fort Dunvegan, causing extreme economic hardship to the Indians of the region.

77 Ibid. The place at which this occurred came to be called Savona's Ferry.

78 What follows is based on Tod's accounts in 'John Tod: "Career of a Scotch Boy"' 213-17 and 'History of New Caledonia and the Northwest Coast' 10-19.

79 Gilbert Malcolm Sproat described Tod as 'somewhat separated from his environment ... guided by natural probity. A reference to standards of truth and justice, as he conceived them, was the habit of his mind. This, naturally, drew some criticism' (see 'John Tod' 133-4 and Tod's own comments on the Canada Jurisdiction Act in the text accompanying n. 41, above).

80 Either by killing Black, or another British trader, or any white man he could find, depending upon whether the whites were (regarded as) a single nation or, like the Indians, several nations. As Reid points out ('Principle of Vengeance' 24, 26-7), the proper avenger depended upon whether the kinship system was patrilineal, matrilineal, or bilateral. Because the Shuswaps are a

Salish people, their system was probably bilateral and the young man was probably Le Tranquille's son, urged on by his widow. If the killer was his nephew, this suggests a matrilineal system and means that the woman who urged him to the act was Le Tranquille's sister.

81 Ibid. 25–6

82 McLean's career as an 'enforcer' was a somewhat notorious one, and he managed to end it by becoming, quite unnecessarily, the sole non-Aboriginal casualty of the Chilcotin War in 1864. His sons achieved an even greater notoriety when all three were hanged in 1881 for killing the constable at Kamloops: see Hamar Foster 'The Kamloops Outlaws and Commissions of Assize in Nineteenth-Century British Columbia' in David H. Flaherty, ed. *Essays in the History of Canadian Law: Volume II* (Toronto: University of Toronto Press and Osgoode Society 1983) 308–64.

83 The account that follows is taken from Morice *History of the Northern Interior* 266ff..

84 Ibid. 268. This is the sort of silly statement that no doubt prompts Professor Reid to argue that the HBC was no more humane than the American traders: see 'The Hudson's Bay Company and Retaliation in Kind against Indian Offenders in New Caledonia,' above nn. 48, 64.

85 Reid 'Principle of Vengeance' 30. Reid's suggestion (text accompanying n. 81, above) that Nicola could probably not conceive of one Shuswap having the authority to kill another in such circumstances is borne out by the aftermath to the Tlhelh case. Unsatisfied as long as Tlhelh was still at large, McLean bribed and bullied Neztel, another of Tlhelh's uncles, to kill Tlhelh. Netzel formed a party and eventually found his nephew, shooting and scalping him. But the old man was so disturbed by what he had done that he tried to shoot his companions and then begged them to kill him. According to Morice (*History of the Northern Interior* 270–3), half a century later the Quesnel still told, 'with unhidden glee, how, on his return ... Neztel whipped McLean's face with the scalp of his nephew.'

86 Actually, however much he cared, McLean may have known a fair bit: his first wife was part Indian and his second – whom he did not marry until after the Quesnel incident – was Salish, from Fort Colville. But the Quesnel were Carriers and therefore Athapaskan (not Salish, as Reid suggests), and there are differing opinions about the effects of intermarriage with the Gitksan and the Bella Coola on their kinship system: see Margaret L. Tobey 'Carrier' in June Helm, ed. *Handbook of North American Indians* vol. 6: *Subarctic* (Washington: Smithsonian 1981) 413, 418ff.

87 Morice *History of the Northern Interior* 271

88 In the early days Nanaimo was also called Wentuhuysen Inlet, after the

Spanish name, and Colville Town: see B.A. McKelvie 'The Founding of Nanaimo' *BCHQ* 8 (1944) 169.

89 See n. 70, above.

90 None, that is, that involved Europeans as perpetrator or victim, or both. At this point in time and for some time afterwards, homicides with no European connection were beyond the means of the colony to police.

91 The author, Alan Grove, and Susan Johnson (of the Department of History at the University of Victoria) are currently researching a study of the Sque-is and Siam-a-sit prosecution which should be completed sometime in 1995.

92 There are a number of contemporary, non-Aboriginal accounts, all of them sketchy. A recent and useful summary of the case may be found in Gough *Gunboat Frontier* 50–6.

93 See W. Kaye Lamb, ed. 'Four Letters Relating to the Cruise of the *Thetis*, 1852–1853' *BCHQ* 6 (1942) 189–207.

94 This was a sort of militia composed largely of Métis who were retired employees of the HBC: see B.A. McKelvie and W.E. Ireland 'The Victoria Voltigeurs' *BCHQ* 20 (1956) 221–39.

95 'Private Papers of James Douglas, first series' (Bancroft L. copy). The Peter Brown case is dealt with at 34–46 of the ms.

96 Ibid. 42ff., Douglas to John Tod, 7 Jan. 1853

97 B.A. McKelvie *Tales of Conflict: Indian-White Murders and Massacres in Pioneer British Columbia* (Surrey: Heritage House 1985 reprint; originally published 1949) chap. 10 'The Basis of Freedom' 57

98 There is a suggestion in John Moresby *Two Admirals* (London: John Murray 1909) 107 that the tribes had refused to surrender the accused because Brown 'had insulted the squaws of the Indians and had merited his doom.' Moresby was a young gunnery lieutenant on the *Thetis* when Sque-is and Siam-a-sit were hanged.

99 Bayley 'Early Life on Vancouver Island' 20. Bayley came to Vancouver Island in 1851 with his father and mother, and went to Nanaimo as the colonial schoolteacher, a post he held until 1856. Douglas also made him coroner, and he represented Nanaimo in the Legislative Assembly, 1863–5.

100 Ibid.

101 Douglas to Archibald Barclay, 20 Jan. 1853, in Lamb, ed. 'Four Letters' 205

102 Lieutenant John Moresby to Admiral Fairfax Moresby, 4 Feb. 1853, published in *The Week*, Saturday, 15 July 1911

103 Moresby *Two Admirals* 107

104 Gough *Gunboat Frontier* 67

105 The commentator is Gough, ibid.

106 John Flett Sabiston 'Reminiscences' British Columbia Archives and Records Services (hereafter 'BCARS'), Vertical Files, set 1, microfilm reel 124. Douglas was first instructed to extinguish title in the Nanaimo coal district in January 1853, i.e., the month that Sque-is and Siam-a-sit were hanged. He did not succeed in doing so until December 1854: Dennis Maddill *British Columbia Indian Treaties in Historical Perspective* (Ottawa: Research Branch, Corporate Policy, INAC 1981) 20–1. This aspect of the Peter Brown case will be explored further in the study referred to in n. 91, above, and I am grateful to Mr Grove and Ms Johnson for drawing my attention to the Sabiston papers.

107 In 1830 Francis Ermatinger's woman had run away with an Indian, so he sent Leolo, the interpreter, after them with instructions to cut off the tip of the man's ear. Leolo did exactly that. Chief Factor McLoughlin acknowledged that, because this would appear harsh 'to the civilized world,' it would have been better if he had 'resorted to some other mode of punishment.' But he nonetheless defended Ermatinger's action and noted that the Indians themselves 'would never allow such an offence to pass unpunished' (*The Letters of John McLoughlin from Fort Vancouver to the Governor and Committee, First Series*, above n. 50, 227). Obviously this was the view of Tathlasut and his people.

108 Gough *Gunboat Frontier* 67. After returning from the expedition to avenge the attack on Williams, Douglas wrote to James Murray Yale at Fort Langley that 'Cowegin is a fine valley, far more extensive and valuable as an agricultural country, than I had any idea of' (Douglas to Yale, 5 Sept. 1856, HBCA, b.226/b/12, fo. 109). According to Kenneth Duncan, *History of Cowichan* (n.d.), 2, and John Newell Evans, *Pioneers of the Cowichan Valley* (1938), 1, whose accounts are in Special Collections, McPherson Library, University of Victoria, the first white colonist in the Cowichan Valley was probably one John Humphreys, and although Humphreys may have been there in 1856, it is much more likely that he did not settle in the area until 1857 or 1858. However, at one point he did have a companion who, according to Duncan, may have been wounded by an Indian in 1856. Presumably, this was Williams.

109 John Hayman, ed. *Robert Brown and the Vancouver Island Exploring Expedition* (Vancouver: University of British Columbia Press 1989) 12, 26n, citing W.H. Olsen *Water over the Wheel* (Chemainus: Chemainus Valley Historical Society 1963) 17. See also Richard Somerset Mackie 'Colonial Land, Indian Labour and Company Capital: The Economy of Vancouver Island, 1849–1858' (MA thesis, University of Victoria 1984) 75ff., where the reference is to 'Toma' rather than 'Tomo.' On the 1864 Vancouver Island exploring ex-

pedition Brown and his party came across a number of names written on a stump by a previous group, and Brown noted in his journal that one of the names carved there, Thomas Anthony, was in fact 'our "Tomo"' (Hayman 65–6). All of the sources cited in this and the preceding note point to the conclusion that the only person in Cowichan in 1856 other than its aboriginal inhabitants was Tomo, and that he therefore must have been the 'Thomas Williams' shot by Tathasut. It is therefore all the more remarkable that Douglas, in the letter book copies of letters he wrote to HBC men who would certainly have known that Williams was Tomo, nonetheless referred to him as a white man or white squatter (see, for example, Douglas to Yale, 25 Aug. 1856, and Douglas to Blenkinson, 8 Sept. 1856, in which the word 'white' has been written over an erasure: HBCA, B.226/b/12, fos. 104, 110d). This suggests that Douglas was engaged in what today would be called a 'cover-up.' According to Olsen, Tomo and Douglas had a great deal of respect for one another, and he speculates that Douglas may have described Tomo as he did 'to conceal [from the colonial office] the fact that a warship and 400 men were sent out to apprehend an Indian who had shot a half-breed.' If this is true, it certainly helps to explain why Douglas seemed so concerned about being reprimanded by the colonial office for the raid (see Fisher *Contact and Conflict* at 56).

110 Joseph William McKay 'Recollections of a Chief Trader in the Hudson's Bay Company' (Bancroft L., P-C24) 11

111 He was acquitted because of insufficient evidence: see Hayman and Mackie, above n. 109, at 12 and 84, respectively. According to Olsen (*Water over the Wheel* at 14), Tomo held the coastal tribes in contempt – a factor which may have contributed to his difficulties with the Cowichan in 1856. In the course of the Vancouver Island exploring expedition of 1864 he was often drunk, and Brown described him as 'the one I am most afraid of as he is a madman in liquor.' Another colonist reported that the expedition's delay at Nanaimo was due partly to 'the Indian refusing to work with a half breed [Tomo] who ... has been constantly drunk during his stay here, and who the Indians are afraid of' (Hayman 65–6, 150n.). It therefore seems hardly surprising that Tathlasut's execution was resented, notwithstanding that Douglas reported that only his friends made any attempt to resist his capture: see Douglas to Tolmie, 6 Sept. 1856, HBCA, B.226/b/12, fo. 108–108d.

112 Minutes of the Executive Council of the Colony of British Columbia for 1 Dec. 1869 in James E. Hendrickson, ed. *Journals of the Colonial Legislatures of the Colonies of Vancouver Island and British Columbia 1851–1871*, 5 vols. (Victoria: Provincial Archives of British Columbia 1980) 4: 136–7. Musgrave does not

give examples, but Tathlasut's case is noteworthy in this respect as well. He was executed for wounding 'Williams,' whereas less than a year later Douglas arranged for a sailor who wounded a Stikine Indian at Victoria to pay compensation to his relatives: see Fisher *Contact and Conflict* 57. No white man was ever executed for attempted murder during this period, but another Indian was (see text following n. 146, below).

113 In this connection it may be worth noting that, prior to the colonial period, fur trade employees were under strict instructions not to interfere with Indian women, in order to avoid just the sort of situation that developed between Tathlasut and Ouamtomy: see Foster 'Killing Mr. John, etc.' (above n. 40) 177ff.

114 Alfred Waddington 'Judicial Murder' BCARS, NW p, 970.51, W118. The court must have been Chief Justice David Cameron, James Douglas' brother-in-law and a controversial figure because of his lack of formal legal training and his association with the HBC. It is unclear who the attorney general was in this period: see David M.L. Farr 'The Organization of the Judicial System of the Colonies of Vancouver Island and British Columbia, 1849–1871' (BA essay, University of British Columbia 1944) 24.

115 Ibid. It seems that Douglas took no formal advice regarding executive clemency: at least, there appears to be no formal record of the executive council of either Vancouver Island or British Columbia considering such questions until after his retirement. In the Sque-is, Siam-a-sit, and Tathlasut cases the executions took place on the spot, immediately after the verdicts, so there was no time for such niceties.

116 This was a composite 'language' with a very simple grammar and a limited vocabulary of Chinook, Nootkan, French, and English words; in short, a sort of *lingua franca* of the fur trade. See Robie L. Reid 'The Chinook Jargon and British Columbia' and F.W. Howay 'The Origin of the Chinook Jargon' *BCHQ* 6 (1942) 1 and 225. See also Frederick L. Long *Dictionary of the Chinook Jargon* (Seattle: Lowman & Hanford Co. 1909).

117 Emphasis in original.

118 For reasons of space and the availability of records, only a few cases will be discussed. Many more are referred to in Gough *Gunboat Frontier*, McKelvie *Tales of Conflict*, and Charles Lillard *Seven Shillings a Year: The History of Vancouver Island* (Ganges: Horsdal & Schubart 1986). It is also noteworthy that the authorities in Victoria exercised much more restraint in cases where no non-Aboriginals were involved. In 1863, for example, the police investigated a serious assault on the Songhees reserve only because they were requested to do so by the chief; and they declined to take any further action when they discovered that the assailant, a Cowichan, had compensated the

victim with twenty blankets and that everyone seemed satisfied: Sergeant's Daily Report Book (1863–6), entry for 24 Dec. 1863, BCARS GR 426, vol. I.

119 Ibid., Gough 139, and Lillard 152–3. Bill Brady, the white man in the Pender Island case, was killed and three Cowichans were hanged for the deed. A fourth, who was a woman, received life imprisonment. Lillard speculates that some of the apparently motiveless killings of whites by Indians in this period may have been related to the illicit liquor trade. As he points out, survivors 'certainly were not going to admit they were whisky traders.'

120 This and the information that follows are from the Colonial Correspondence of David Cameron dealing with *Regina v. Un-Whan-Uck*, Notes of Trial dated 17 June 1863 and letter to the Colonial Secretary dated 1 July 1863, BCARS, F 260, 8 (reel B1313). Halkomelem is the Salishan language spoken by the Cowichan people.

121 This ritual suddenly came to an end in 1864, when Chief Justice Cameron refused to allow Aboriginal witnesses to testify in two cases involving Ohiat, Sheshat, and Ahousat attacks on west coast shipping. The reason was apparently that the witnesses did not believe in punishment in the afterlife; perhaps it was the first case in which the prosecution was unable to find Aboriginal witnesses who could swear a Christian oath. However, imperial law did not, strictly speaking, require such a belief: see Douglas to Earl Grey, 16 Dec. 1851, Public Record Office, CO 305, no. 3 at 75–8, and 6 & 7 Vict. (1843), c. 22 (UK). Both Vancouver Island and British Columbia responded by enacting special laws permitting Aboriginal witnesses to give unsworn evidence if certain prerequisites were met.

122 After Kottinah gave evidence, the first witness had to be recalled because her evidence conflicted with that of the second.

123 Gough *Gunboat Frontier* 146 describes the Lemalchi as outcasts from other tribes.

124 Testimony of Superintendent of Police Horace Smith in *Regina versus Qualah-itton, She-nall-ou-luk, and Otch-ee-wan*, Colonial Correspondence of David Cameron (above n. 120). Much of what follows is based upon this source.

125 See Gough *Gunboat Frontier* 145–6 and McKelvie *Tales of Conflict* 87.

126 Cameron's jury instructions left open the possibility of a manslaughter verdict if the jury found that the prisoners were unaware of the navy's authority to act as it did; however, he told them that the prisoners' mere presence at the ambush was sufficient to convict them of murder if they did know. For a later case in which the executive decided that evidence implicating chiefs in the acts of men facing the death sentence was irrelevant,

see *Regina* v. *Anaits-che-sit (alias 'John')*, Minutes of the Executive Council of the Colony of British Columbia for 2, 13, 15, and 16 July 1869 (above n. 112) 4: 126, 128–30.

127 *Regina* v. *Quoquilimot, Stashal and Tch-chi-co-mat*, Colonial Correspondence of David Cameron (above n. 120)

128 Ibid., Report of the Grand Jury, 18 Nov. 1864

129 Ibid., and see Minutes of the Executive Council of the Colony of Vancouver Island for 28 Nov. 1864 (above n. 112) 1: 158. Arthur Edward Kennedy succeeded James Douglas as governor of Vancouver Island in 1863.

130 Many of these cases are referred to in David R. Williams '... *The Man for a New Country': Sir Matthew Baillie Begbie* (Sidney: Gray's Publishing 1977) esp. chaps. 7 and 9.

131 See, for example, Edward Sleigh Hewlett 'The Chilcotin Uprising: A Study of Indian-White Relations in Nineteenth Century British Columbia' (MA thesis, University of British Columbia 1972) and 'The Chilcotin Uprising of 1864' *BC Studies* 19 (1973) 50; and Tina Merrill Loo 'Law and Authority in British Columbia, 1821–1871' (PhD thesis, University of British Columbia 1990) 290. A recent, fascinating account of the local oral history of these events is in Terry Glavin et al. *Nemiah: The Unconquered Country* (Vancouver: New Star Books 1992).

132 R.C. Lundin Brown, *Klatassan and Other Reminiscences of Missionary Life in British Columbia* (London: Society for Promoting Christian Knowledge 1873) quoted in Hewlett 'The Chilcotin Uprising of 1864' 60. Among other things, Hewlett notes that at least one of the attacking party had blackened his face, and that some of the bodies were mutilated. Both actions were features of traditional warfare.

133 Seymour to Cardwell, 4 Oct. 1864, Public Record Office, Kew, CO 60/19, 298. Cardwell professed not to know what Seymour meant, saying that he expected him to adhere to 'the line of conduct hitherto pursued' (Cardwell to Seymour, 1 Dec. 1864, CO 398/2, 271).

134 J.H. Baker *An Introduction to English Legal History* 2nd ed. (London: Butterworths 1979) 322. Much more recently the relationship between these different world-views was dealt with, albeit in predictable fashion, in *Thomas v. Norris*, [1992] 2 CNLR 139 (BCSC). The case involved the tension between the common law of assault and a version of the Coast Salish initiation ceremony of spirit dancing.

135 Judge Begbie's Benchbook notes, BCARS, reel B5085, vol. 4, 203. See also Hewlett 'The Chilcotin Uprising of 1864' 62–3. Unfortunately, significant portions of the notes are in Begbie's archaic 'Gurney' shorthand. This has

posed problems for many researchers: see Williams 'The Man for a New Country' and Sydney G. Pettit 'Judge Begbie's Shorthand: A Mystery Solved' *BCHQ* 12 (1948) 293.

In an unrelated 1864 case, Chac-a-tum-Kah, a Bella Bella chief, was hanged for killing a white man because the whites had brought smallpox to his people: see Minutes of the Executive Council of the Colony of British Columbia for 15 Nov. 1864 (above n. 112) 4: 18. The deceased, a miner, had returned from the mines to find his Indian wife and child dead from the disease. Williams ('The Man for a New Country' at 116–17) reproduces Begbie's translation of part of the testimony of one of the Aboriginal witnesses: 'The deceased cried with us a good time; he then washed his face and lit his pipe. After smoking he went to his canoe and drank some whiskey out of a bottle.' Chac-a-tum-Kah then shot him.

136 Hewlett 'The Chilcotin Uprising of 1864' 51. This entire paragraph owes much to Hewlett's account.

137 Above n. 135, 197, and see Begbie's contribution to the *Langevin Report on British Columbia* (1872), cited in Williams 'The Man for a New Country' 116. The settler in question was William Manning. His partner, Alexander Macdonald, was killed in a separate exchange, along with two others and, possibly, Klymtedza, the Chilcotin wife of one of them. Manning's wife, Nancy, was probably also Chilcotin. She gave evidence for the prosecution at the trial, testifying that she had warned Manning but that he did not believe the Chilcotins would kill him. The roles of both of these women are discussed in Loo 'Law and Authority in British Columbia.'

138 See text accompanying nn. 71–87, above.

139 French was largely the language of the fur trade, and Glavin (*Nemiah* 44) suggests that 'Samandlin' may be how the Chilcotin pronounced 'Monsieur McLean.'

140 Begbie to Governor Seymour, 30 Sept. 1864, quoted in Williams 'The Man for a New Country' 115

141 Glavin *Nemiah* 96

142 Chedekki was sent to New Westminster, where there was supposed to be a witness who could identify him. Lundin Brown reports that he escaped en route and was never recaptured (Hewlett 'The Chilcotin Uprising of 1864' 71). Lutas was not tried until 1865, when he was given a pardon and sent 'back to his Tribe' because of his 'extreme' youth and because Governor Seymour felt that a sufficient number of lives had been taken in atonement: Minutes of the Executive Council of the Colony of British Columbia for 12 July 1865 (above n. 112) 4: 35. (Williams 'The Man for a New Country' 116 states incorrectly that Lutas was hanged.) Two others, Sanstanki and his son Cheloot, were not charged for lack of evidence.

143 Williams, ibid. 112, and Glavin *Nemiah* 107–8. Klatassin is alleged to have
said: 'We are seven murderers who are here to give ourselves up and I am
another.' Two of the ten still in the mountains were Ahan and Lutas. Ahan
was taken into custody in 1865 when he travelled down the Bella Coola
River with a large quantity of furs to offer as compensation for his role in
the uprising (Hewlett 'The Chilcotin Uprising' 71). He was tried along
with his young relative Lutas, and was hanged. Although Cox may have
felt he did not trick Klatassin, in his letter to Governor Seymour Begbie
states that Cox knew that Klatassin 'was completely in the dark as to the
consequences of his entering Mr. Cox's camp' (see letter referred to in n.
140 above). According to the report in the Victoria *Colonist* on 7 Sept. 1864,
the 'account given by our informant of the means by which Mr Cox obtained possession of the eight Indian prisoners ... does not look very
well.'

144 Williams 'The Man for a New Country' 115. Williams suggests that, although
the statements would probably not be admitted into evidence today, the
rules in the mid nineteenth century were less protective of defendants'
rights in this area. However, although it is true that in *Regina* v. *Baldry*
(1852), 169 ER 568 the Court for Crown Cases Reserved announced a relaxation of the rule excluding confessions, this did not produce a drastic
change: see *Cross on Evidence* (London: Butterworths 1979) 537.

145 Williams 'The Man for a New Country' 116. It was not illegal to issue a commission of assize to someone who was not a superior court judge,
however.

146 Begbie to Governor Seymour (above n. 140)

147 Hewlett 'The Chilcotin Uprising,' citing Lundin Brown

148 *Regina* v. *Kalabeen and Another* (1867), 1 BCLR 1 (BCSC), and the 'Memorandum' dated 27 Sept. 1895 at the beginning of the volume. The report series actually began in 1884: see Joan N. Fraser 'Case Law Reporting in
British Columbia' *Canadian Law Libraries* 18 (1993) 47.

149 As was so often the case, the same men who administered justice to Indians were the ones who made the laws and presided over the confiscation
of what they regarded as their lands: Cornwall later became a senator, a
lieutenant-governor of British Columbia, and, in 1887, the Dominion representative on the commission that inquired into the land grievances of the
Northwest Coast Indians: see text accompanying n. 18, above.

150 See *Regina* v. *Scothla and Carabine, alias Kalabeen*, BCARS, GR 1372, reel B-
1308, F142g, 20, containing Begbie's Notes of the Evidence, 'with remarks,' and Kalabeen's statement to Cornwall.

151 Minutes of the Executive Council of the Colony of British Columbia for 21
Nov. 1867 (above n. 112) 4: 91

152 Williams 'The Man for a New Country' 104

153 Minutes of the Executive Council of the Colony of British Columbia for 19 June 1866 (above n. 112)4: 61

154 Regina v. Chilpakin, Regina v. Tesch, alias Charley, BCARS, GR 1372, reel B 1308, F142H, 2, containing Begbie's notes and remarks

155 The killing of Tien Fook had taken place five years earlier, whereas that of the man whose death was proved at trial had occurred two years before that. This seems to suggest that more Orientals may have been murdered in this period than are revealed by court records.

156 Minutes of the Executive Council of the Colony of British Columbia for 22 June 1868 (above n. 112) 4: 101

157 The Queen v. Peter (1869), I BCLR 2 (BCSC). A juror took 'a fit' and had to be removed to his house, where the rest of the jury joined him. They returned a verdict from there when he recovered. Chief Justice Begbie ruled that affidavits from the sheriff and the attending physician were sufficient to negative any suggestion of improper communication and that, in any event, the application should have been made before verdict.

158 Minutes of the Executive Council of the Colony of British Columbia for 1 Dec. 1869 (above n. 112) 4: 136–7

159 BCARS, GR 1372, reel B 1308, F142H, 5, containing correspondence between Begbie and the governor's office, a letter from H.M. Ball, the stipendiary magistrate before whom Wise swore his statement, and the statement itself

160 It is not translated in the documents, which suggests that Wise assumed that anyone reading it would be familiar with the Jargon. I have used the dictionary referred to in n. 116, above, to translate, and I am indebted to Dr Barbara Harris, chair of the Department of Linguistics at the University of Victoria, for her most able assistance. Any errors that I have persisted in are, of course, my own.

161 Minutes of the Executive Council of the Colony of British Columbia for 14 June 1871 (above n. 112) 4: 172. The Roman Catholic priest at New Westminster also wrote to Governor Musgrave on Peter's behalf: see petition dated 15 Dec. 1869, BCARS, GR 1394, box 1, file 7.

162 See n. 137, above; Hewlett 'The Chilcotin Uprising of 1864' 56–7; and Judge Begbie's Benchbook notes (above n. 135) 192–3.

163 Patricia Nelson Limerick The Legacy of Conquest: The Unbroken Past of the American West (New York: W.W. Norton & Company 1987) 181

164 It was the policy of successive colonial and provincial governments from the 1860s on that Aboriginal people did not enjoy title to their traditional territories, and colonial legislation first passed in 1866 severely restricted

the right of Aboriginal people to pre-empt land. On the potlatch law see Douglas Cole and Ira Chaikin *An Iron Hand upon the People* (Vancouver: Douglas & McIntyre 1990). An example of cultural repression at the level of petty offences is the practice of cutting the hair of Indian defendants, male and female alike: see F.W. Howay, *British Columbia from the Earliest Times to the Present* vol. 2 (Vancouver: S.J. Clark 1914) 668.

165 For further discussion, see the review in *BC Studies* 91–2 (1991–2) 218 of the book by Cole and Chaikin referred to in the preceding note.

166 This all took place in the 1850s and 1860s, when the first colonies were being established in the Pacific Northwest. The parallels are explored in Hamar Foster 'Measures Essentially Unjust: English "Law" and Native "Custom" in New Zealand, Vancouver Island and British Columbia, 1769–1871' (MJur thesis, University of Auckland 1989).

167 The Haatq (Youmans) case, for example, is referred to by the trial judge in the Gitksan-Wet'suwet'en land claims litigation: see *Delgamuukw v. The Queen* (1991), 79 DLR (4th) 185 (BCSC) at 226 (reversed in part, 25 June 1993, BCCA). And on 28 October 1993 the BC government released the *Report of the Cariboo-Chilcotin Justice Inquiry,* authored by Provincial Court Judge Anthony Sarich, who recommended that the government grant a posthumous pardon to the men who were hanged in 1864. He also recommended that the Ministry of the Attorney General consult with the Ts'il-quot'in (Chilcotin) Tribal Council with a view to locating the remains and having them reburied with a suitable memorial.

168 See Governor Musgrave's comments in the text accompanying n. 112, above.

169 Robson, for example, speaks of a white man being hanged for murdering an Indian in his 1884 letter to the Kit-au-max, but there is no record of this: see n. 11, above.

170 Such applications of the law were delayed in the remote parts of the province. As late as the time of the 'Skeena War' the Attorney General advised that homicides not involving white men were 'best let alone in a country in which hitherto only the tribal laws of the Indians have prevailed' (Roy 'Law and Order in British Columbia' 67).

171 John Hayman, ed. *Robert Brown and the Vancouver Island Exploring Expedition* (Vancouver: University of British Columbia Press 1989) 44 (journal entry for 9 June 1864). How-a-matcha was convicted of the murder of another Indian, but the death sentence was commuted subsequent to Brown's journal entry: see Minutes of the Executive Council of the Colony of Vancouver Island for 15 Aug. 1864 (above n. 112) 1: 143.

172 Roy 'Law and Order in British Columbia' 68

173 'Exceptional laws in favour of the natives of New Zealand,' quoted in Alan Ward *A Show of Justice* at 34. This statement is also quoted, albeit not entirely correctly, by Chapman, J. in the leading New Zealand aboriginal title case, *The Queen v. Symonds* (1847), [1840–1932] NZPC Cases 387.

174 See n. 121, above, and accompanying text.

175 Sproat *The Nootka* 188. Sproat was an Indian Reserve commissioner between 1876 and 1880, and formed a very low opinion of the ability of settlers and their governments to deal fairly with Aboriginal people.

176 The letter to Powell, reciting the latter's request for advice, is dated 11 Nov. 1873 and may be found in NAC, RG10, vol. 3604, file 2521 (reel C 11063). When the sole defence witness in Haatq's case tried to state that Youmans had paid compensation for an accidental death before, the Attorney General objected that 'this is not evidence,' and the trial judge replied, 'Of course not' (*Reg. v. Haatq*, above n. 5).

177 Williams *'The Man for a New Country'* 134 says that Begbie made a report that was considered by the Executive Council, but cites no reference. For more details about the problems with sources for Executive Council proceedings see Hendrickson's 'Introduction' to vol. 1 of the *Journals of the Colonial Legislatures of the Colonies of Vancouver Island and British Columbia 1851–1871*, xxiii–iv.

178 See nn. 154, 157, and 171, above, and accompanying text. The death sentence in another case, *Regina v. Moyese*, had been pronounced in 1863, but Moyese escaped from jail and was not recaptured and executed until July 1865. His case is therefore included here, but his three Aboriginal co-accused are not: they were hanged in 1863, before the recorded deliberations begin.

179 The name of the last man is Mattie Rassid, who was convicted of sodomy. Although the case was 'a gross and clear one,' the death sentence was not carried out because by the 1860s this was 'unusual.' The Kanaka was Peter Kankan, whose case was considered along with that of Harry, an Indian. Both were executed (Minutes of the Executive Council of the Colony of Vancouver Island, 5 Mar. 1866, above n. 112, 1: 211, and of British Columbia, 27 Feb. 1869, 4: 114).

180 The three cases took place in 1861 (Robert Wall), 1863 (a man named Armitage), and 1867 (James Barry): see Williams *'The Man for a New Country'* 134, 142. Armitage was also hanged, but Wall escaped custody and fled (personal communication from Mr Williams, Oct. 1993).

181 Three of the Indians had killed white men, but the sentence of one of them, Meshek, was commuted only because Begbie had stated in court that his life would probably be spared. The Executive Council decided that,

although Meshek had since made a full confession, Begbie's statement precluded them from carrying out the sentence: see Minutes of the Executive Council of the Colony of British Columbia, 7 Jan. 1870 (above n. 112) 4: 139.

182 The three exceptions were Sed Gee, a Chinese, Peter Kankan (above n. 179), and Barry. Sed Gee's case is referred to in the Minutes of the Executive Council of the Colony of British Columbia, 2 July 1869 (above n. 112) 4: 126. Death penalty statistics are also discussed by Williams 'The Man for a New Country' 141–2 and Loo 'Law and Authority in British Columbia' 366.

183 Quoted in Williams, ibid. 139. The fact that very few white men were convicted of murder in this period does not mean that there were not homicides that went undetected or unsolved; nor does it mean that convictions for the lesser offence of manslaughter were always justified. Juries, not judges, decided what the proper verdict should be, and juries occasionally reduced one of murder to manslaughter when the defendant was white. For example, in the Gilchrist case described in Williams (ibid. 144), the jury, contrary to the evidence, brought in a conviction for manslaughter only. Waddington ('Judicial Murder') cites a similar case, alleging that, the day before Allache was tried, a well-paid lawyer and a sympathetic court managed to obtain a manslaughter verdict for a white man named Snelling that stood in stark contrast to Allache's prosecution.

184 See, for example, the essays in Douglas Hay et al., eds. Albion's Fatal Tree: Crime and Society in Eighteenth Century England (New York: Allen Lane 1975), especially Hay's 'Property, Authority and the Criminal Law' at 17–63, and E.P. Thompson, Whigs and Hunters: The Origin of the Black Act (Harmondsworth: Penguin 1977).

185 For example, the priest in the Peter case (above n. 157) and Waddington's protest in the Allache case (above nn. 111–14 and accompanying text)

186 Tomlinson to chief commissioner of lands and works, 27 Feb 1884, BSP 1885 277

187 Ibid. paraphrasing O'Reilly.

188 BCSP 1885 279 (Robson to Tomlinson, 29 Feb. 1884)

189 Ibid. 283–4 (Tomlinson to Robson, 20 Oct. 1884)

190 For some recent commentary upon how well the criminal justice system has served Native people in Western Canada see the Report of the Cariboo-Chilcotin Justice Inquiry (above n. 167) and the Report of the Aboriginal Justice Inquiry of Manitoba 2 vols. (Winnipeg: Province of Manitoba 1991). Today, Indian reserves comprise only 0.35 per cent of British Columbia: Richard H. Bartlett, Indian Reserves and Aboriginal Lands in Canada (Saskatoon: Native Law Centre 1990), 94.

4

The Road from Bute Inlet: Crime and Colonial Identity in British Columbia

TINA LOO

In the middle of August 1864, eight Chilcotin Indians walked into the camp of the men who had been pursuing them without avail for some four months and were promptly arrested without incident by Justice of the Peace William George Cox. Five were charged with the murders of eighteen Europeans, most of them labourers, who had met their ends while working on the Bute Inlet road in the spring of that year. The group were tried at the fall assizes in Quesnelmouth, found guilty, and sentenced to death. In writing to British Columbia's governor to report on the case and its disposition, Supreme Court Judge Matthew Baillie Begbie took a rare moment to reflect on the fate of the perpetrators of what had become known as the 'Bute Inlet massacre.' 'It seems horrible to hang five men at once,' he told Frederick Seymour, 'especially under the circumstances of the capitulation.' Begbie, it seemed, had reason to believe that the Chilcotin had entered Cox's camp under false pretences, believing that they had been invited to talk, when, to their surprise and consternation, they were taken captive.

Begbie's sentiments were strange ones coming from a man who established a reputation as the 'Hanging Judge' and whose record indicates that the majority of those he condemned to the gallows – without any such compunction as he offered in the case of the Chilcotin five – were native.[1] Were they indicative of a touch of squeamishness, perhaps? A momentary and idiosyncratic lapse in a man who was given to idiosyncracies? Or do the reservations Begbie expressed have a larger significance?

I think they do, for they can shed light on the nature of colonial identity in British Columbia. As we shall see, the Supreme Court judge's concerns point to the centrality of the rule of law and procedural justice in the colonial identity of European British Columbians. Crime, particularly serious crime – like murder – which attracts a good deal of commentary, can be especially revealing of who the law-abiding population think themselves to be. Lincoln Faller considers criminals a 'social resource' from which a community takes and sustains its identity, while Martin Wiener argues that because crime was 'the central metaphor of disorder' in the nineteenth century, responses to it adumbrate the contours of social order.[2] In discussing what happened at Bute Inlet, why it did, and what they should do about it, European British Columbians revealed as much about who they thought they were as they did of the event and its perpetrators. There was, as the sociologist Robert Miles put it, 'a dialectic between Self and Other in which the attributed characteristics of Other refract contrasting characteristics of Self, and vice versa.'[3]

This essay, then, is directed towards understanding those 'attributed characteristics' as a way of getting at colonial identity and the centrality of law in it. It also aims to understand how who European British Columbians thought they were influenced how they acted; or, put another way, how identity structures action. But in order to reach that high ground and to appreciate the view from the top, we need to start our journey at the beginning of the road from Bute Inlet.

I

'That respectable old fool Waddington.'[4] John A. Macdonald's description of Alfred Penderell Waddington could easily have served as an epitaph for him and perhaps many other British Columbians, for he represented both the circumstances and the spirit of many of the European immigrants to the gold colony. Of his respectability there was little doubt: Waddington was born in 1801, the sixth son of an English merchant and banking family, and after being educated at the Ecole Spéciale du Commerce in Paris and the University of Göttingen, he embarked on a series of business ventures, none of which was especially successful. With nothing to keep him in either England or Europe, his spirit of enterprise (and a little bit of money from his favourite brother Frederick) led him to California in 1850. San Francisco's gold-rush economy proved so buoyant that even the previously luckless Waddington failed to sink, and, indeed, the wholesale grocery firm he co-partnered prospered. When news of the Fraser River discoveries broke in 1858, Waddington joined the rush northward to open a branch of his business in Victoria, arriving as 'one of the oldest as well as the best educated' of the fortune seekers.[5]

Like some other English emigrants, Waddington found being back in British territory to his liking, and became an active participant in the political as well as the economic life of Vancouver Island and British Columbia.[6] Though he was elected to the island's House of Assembly in 1860, he resigned a year later to begin the project which earned him the second part of Macdonald's label – that of 'old fool' – and led him to Bute Inlet.

Just as 'Fraser River fever' threatened to turn into 'Fraser River humbug,' British Columbia's fortunes – not to mention those of merchants like Alfred Waddington – were given another, more sustained boost with the discovery of gold in the Cariboo.[7] Unlike the lower country diggings, however, those in the Cariboo were more difficult to get to, involving a lengthy and arduous journey.[8] In the absence of proper wagon roads, prospective miners had to make their way north from New Westminster along old fur trade brigade trails. Lying in bed one day, incapacitated by gout, Waddington's mind turned, as it so often seemed to, to contemplating his own fortunes.[9] He sent out for a map of the colony and a ruler and, using both, became convinced that it would be both quicker and easier to reach the Cariboo via an overland route from one of the inlets along British Columbia's coast, specifically Bute Inlet.[10] Prospective miners would travel by canoe or steamer 200 miles north from Victoria (their initial port of arrival) along the east coast of Vancouver Island to the head of Bute Inlet. From there, the gold-fields lay a mere 160 miles inland,[11] instead of the more than 300 rugged miles from New Westminster.[12]

Anxious to realize his idea and the fortune that would accrue to the person who could secure a government charter to build a road from Bute Inlet, Waddington lobbied the colonial government and made plans to establish the Bute Inlet Wagon Road Company and garner public support. If the newspaper reports are to be believed, Victorians proved no less susceptible to 'Bute Inlet fever' than they were to Fraser River malady.[13] Without doing anything except the most cursory survey, Wad-

dington, armed with a map that was little more than 'a waggish distortion of rivers and mountains,' claimed his Bute Inlet route was quite
literally the road to prosperity, and estimated it would bring £100,000
of foreign capital into the colony.[14] His enthusiasm won him a charter
in 1862 and both the confidence and hard currency of investors who
had likely seen a speculation or two in the gold-rush town.[15]

Construction began almost immediately, and by the end of 1862 almost thirty-three miles of the Bute Inlet road had been completed, a
rate of progress which only served to fuel Waddington's enthusiasm
and that of his investors further, and to worry the residents of New
Westminster, who stood to lose if Waddington's folly (as they saw it)
proved successful. Like the gold rushes themselves, however, the overblown optimism surrounding the Bute Inlet road soon gave way to a
harsher reality. 1863 saw Waddington's road crew repairing flood damage to sections they had completed the previous year and encountering
the formidable Homathko canyon, whose terrain proved less amenable
to 'improvement.'[16] Compounding Waddington's problems was the fact
that the government had begun two other roads to the Cariboo – one
from the head of Harrison Lake and the other from Yale – both of
which looked as if they would be completed before his. Though his
investors were dismayed and sold their shares to him at a loss, Waddington himself was undeterred, and sold his Victoria property to finance the next year's construction.[17]

If the newspaper reports and government investigations into the
events at Bute Inlet are to be believed, money had been an ongoing
concern of Waddington and his Wagon Road Company, and they attempted to limit their expenditures by hiring Chilcotin labourers to pack
their supplies and equipment to the construction site and by paying
them in trade goods rather than cash.[18] This practice proved to be a
point of contention with the Chilcotin, who wanted wages, and felt
that the road party should have provided them with a certain amount
of provisions.[19] Though they continued to work for Waddington's party,
their disaffection with their treatment likely contributed to a larger and
growing sense of uncertainty concerning their relationship with the
European population. Until the arrival of Waddington's party at Bute
Inlet, the Chilcotin had had little contact with the white population.[20]
Within a very short space of time, however, a number of changes manifested themselves which, taken together, may have been enough to
transform their disaffection into direct and violent action: not only did
the arrival of the whites at Bute Inlet in 1862 coincide with a smallpox

epidemic which decimated much of the coastal native population, but the construction of a road through the heart of their territory threatened to bring further encroachment.[21] Moreover, the retirement of James Douglas as the colony's governor in 1864 signalled the possibility of a further disturbing change: no longer could natives count on the old fur trader's paternalism to protect them.[22]

If any of this uncertainty and latent animosity existed, it was not apparent to the twelve men who, in the spring of 1864, laboured at the main road camp, forty miles from the head of Bute Inlet, or to the five members of the advance party who were busy two miles farther on.[23] Indeed, so comfortable and secure were the road makers in their relationship with the Chilcotin that 'among 17 men there was but one gun.'[24] Nothing transpired on the evening of 29 April to make Waddington's men think differently; so confident – and so tired – were they that '[e]ven the precaution ordinarily in the bush of having one to keep watch was dispensed with.'[25]

At daybreak, eighteen Chilcotin descended on the main camp, shooting at the sleeping men through their tents. As the tent poles collapsed, those whom the bullets missed were trapped and met their ends soon afterwards. A similar scene was being played out at the advance camp. Of the seventeen road men, three managed to escape and, though wounded, to make their way to the head of the inlet and then to Victoria to break the news of the 'Bute Inlet massacre.'[26]

As news of the killings greeted the readers of the British Colonist and the Daily Chronicle on 11 and 12 May, another party of Waddington's men led by Alexander Macdonald was making its way to Bute Inlet from the interior to work on the road from the opposite direction, oblivious of what had happened. Their progress was slow, and loaded down as they were with some twenty-eight horses carrying full packs, as well as a number of unburdened ones, they proved an easy target for the Chilcotin. Were it not for a well-timed warning from the native wife of one of the party of the ensuing attack, it is likely all of Macdonald's men would have been killed. As it was, three of the eight were, along with William Manning, a nearby settler, and the only one in the district.[27]

Though public reaction to the deaths of eighteen whites was swift and sure, concrete action was a little less so. The colony's distances and geography had already kept news of the killings from reaching Victoria and New Westminster, and they further hampered the government's response. Not only was there the problem of organizing and launching a campaign to the far reaches of the colony, but the costs associated with doing so threatened to break the colonial coffers.[28] Though Governor Frederick Seymour accompanied Magistrate Chartres Brew and twenty-eight special constables to Bute Inlet in mid-May to investigate the scene of the initial killings, it was not until the end of June that the 'Bute Inlet Expedition,' as it became known, was fully underway. Two parties, one starting from New Westminster and under Brew, and the other starting in the Cariboo and under the command of William George Cox, made their way to the Homathko in pursuit of the massacre's perpetrators.[29] A difficult and dangerous task itself, the job of capturing the Chilcotin was made even more problematic because of the absence of anything but the most vague descriptions of the alleged killers.[30]

As it happened, however, the Chilcotin solved this problem for the expedition: eight surrendered themselves to Cox's party on 15 August. Klatsassin, said to be their head, Telloot, Cheeloot, Tapitt, Pierre, Chessus, Chedekki, and Sanstanki were taken to Quesnelmouth, where they were tried at the September assizes, and five of them hanged.[31] 'Justice,' reported Frederick Seymour, had been done 'legally as well as faithfully.'[32]

II

In discussing the Bute Inlet killings, the perpetrators, and their own response, European British Columbians erected a series of dichotomies between reason and passion, civilization and savagery, and culture and nature, all of which served to construct the Indian 'criminals' – and, indeed, Indians in general – as 'others' against which they articulated their own identity.[33]

Descriptions of the massacre emphasized the extreme violence of the attack, underscoring the perpetrators' irrationality and savagery. Attracting particular comment was the mutilation of workers' bodies. When Brew's party arrived at the end of May to make their preliminary investigation, Victoria's *Daily Chronicle* reported that they found evidence of an 'indiscriminate attack,' and observed that '[t]he wretches, not content with depriving the poor fellows of life, hacked and mutilated the bodies in the most shocking manner ... the heads of some had been hacked off – others ripped open, and the fiends, in more than one instance, had quartered the bodies of their victims.'[34] Similarly, the New Westminster–based *British Columbian* alleged that the foreman, Brewster, had been 'horribly mutilated ... [his] left breast having been cut open and his heart torn out, and according to the statement of the friendly natives, barbarously eaten by the savage murderers'[35] in what Rev. Robert Christopher Lundin Brown described as an 'infernal repast.'[36]

If the massacre itself was savagely excessive and senseless, so too was the destruction of property that accompanied it. Indeed, stories of the Indians' wasteful destruction of property seemed as reprehensible and incomprehensible to European sensibilities as the killings themselves.[37] According to the British Columbian, '[t]he savages had wantonly destroyed everything they could not carry off, even to the few books in the possession of the unfortunate party ... [T]he ground was completely strewn with tea, coffee, apples, sugar and other stores, recklessly scattered about and trampled underfoot.'[38] The same sense of puzzled disgust underlay Seymour's description of the death of William Manning. The Indians had not, he noted, been satisfied with killing the settler and 'plundering' his stores, but had 'burnt buildings, hay stacks, all that could be destroyed, and even went to the trouble of breaking up the ploughs and agricultural implements.'[39] To reinforce their descriptions of this wilful wastefulness, the Bute Inlet stories often contrasted the Indians' actions with the more rational, calculating work ethic of the men killed. For instance, Waddington's road party and Macdonald's packers were 'brutally butchered' while they were 'sleeping the sleep of hard-working men,'[40] and William Manning's death was particularly unjust and undeserved because he, unlike the native inhabitants of the area, had 'improved' the land he occupied.[41]

If in discussing the killings at Bute Inlet European British Columbians emphasized the Indians' lack of restraint, their otherness and particularly their lack of reason were further accentuated in explanations of the massacre. In attributing motives to the Indians, European British Columbians identified three aspects of the native character which contributed to their criminality, all of which were consistent with the view of Indians as slaves to their emotions, 'impelled' – to use the Colonist's word – by their passions: the massacres were motivated by the Indians' fickle and hence treacherous nature, their superstitious proclivities, and, finally, their covetousness. With a few exceptions, most of the accounts of the massacre were at pains to emphasize that the Chilcotin had not been abused and, indeed, that they had been well-treated – 'rewarded liberally'[42] – and the recipients of 'presents of tobacco and other articles, besides food.'[43] Moreover, according to the survivors and to Waddington himself, there had been nothing in the Indians' behaviour toward the work party to lead them to suspect that relations had soured, much less that they had deteriorated to the point at which violent conflict was possible. In fact, as Seymour informed the Colonial Office, relations had been so good that Waddington's men had, 'with each returning spring, [become] more and more confident of a friendly welcome.'[44] It was this background of what appeared to be good relations that made the killings all the more treacherous and disconcerting to European sensibilities. White British Columbians had to be ever-vigilant, for as Frederick Whymper warned, '[t]hough civilization may have varnished his [the Indian's] exterior, beneath the crust the savage nature lurks, ever ready to break forth, like those volcanic mountains whose pure snow only hides the molten lava within.'[45]

As further evidence of the Indians' inconstant and changeable nature, Lundin Brown wove the conduct of native women into his Bute Inlet story, playing on the existing stereotype of female fickleness. He introduced his readers to 'Klymtedza,' the 'squaw' of one of the white packers in Macdonald's party, who out of loyalty and thankfulness to her husband for delivering her from the hardships of native life, and despite considerable danger to herself, warned the pack train of the imminent attack.[46] Though she escaped, Brown speculated that Klymtedza, in true tragic tradition, killed herself out of grief.[47] Not all women, and certainly not all native women, were so honourable. In contrast to Klymtedza's decision to stand by her man, Brown points to 'Nancy,' William Manning's native partner. Complicit in orchestrating the attack on Manning's farm and his murder, Nancy is presented as the quintessential designing woman: not satisfied or grateful in the least for the generous treatment she received from Manning, and recognizing that her immediate interests were best served by allying with Klatsas-sin's party, she betrayed her husband.[48]

If their fickleness pointed to a lack of reason, European British Columbians argued that the Indians' superstitious nature reinforced it and made relations all the more difficult. Actions on the part of whites that were considered innocent at best or thoughtless at worst – but certainly not malicious – were, in the eyes of the superstitious Indian, transformed into 'fancied slights' that precipitated a response well out of proportion to the offence. In formulating his explanation for the attack on Waddington's men, Lundin Brown recalled an incident in the fall of 1863 involving the theft of some flour from the supply store at the head of Bute Inlet. The Chilcotin were suspected, and when they refused to admit to the theft, the white man in charge of the stores took down their names and threatened them with sickness. His action had the intended effect of alarming the Indians, but rather than make them compliant, it precipitated the killings, for as Brown argued, the Indian was a superstitious creature, given to believing in the maleficent powers of what he or she did not understand. 'They have ... a very special horror of having their names written down,' he asserted. 'They look upon paper as a very awful thing.'

Writing is, they imagine, a dread mystery. By it the mighty whites seem to carry on intercourse with unseen powers. When they're writing, there's no telling what they're doing. They may be bidding a pestilence come over the land, or ordering the rain to stay in the west, or giving directions for the salmon to remain in the ocean. Especially is the Indian appalled when he sees his own *name* put on paper. To him the name is not distinct from the person who owns it. If his name is written down, he is written down. If his name is passed over to the demons which people his hierarchy, he is sure to be bewitched and given as a prey into the teeth of his invisible foes. So when those Chilcoaten saw their names taken down and heard themselves threatened with disease, they were only too ready to believe it.[49]

And, as Lundin Brown concluded, to kill.

'Covetousness' and 'cupidity' were the final characteristics European British Columbians identified as part of Indian criminality. The Chilcotin, it was argued, were attracted to the goods carried by the road party and were unable to resist the temptation to possess them, particularly given their impoverished state. Though magistrate Chartres Brew observed 'there was in camp a store of all the things most coveted by Indians: clothes, powder, balls, sugar, flour, [and] meat,'[50] Frederick Seymour thought 'the property of small value.' The 'rough clothes and poor provisions' should have 'offered but a small temptation to the commission of so terrible an outrage.'[51] And they would have, if the Indians had been at all calculating or possessed of reason. The fact that they were not and remained attracted to the road party's poor supplies and provisions, however, merely underscored the irrationality of the Indians further, as did the reckless way the Indians treated their 'plunder,' strewing the goods that had so tempted them over a wide area or destroying them outright.

III

Many of the elements in what might be called the discourse of savagery which ran through the accounts of Bute Inlet had a long, and in fact, ancient genealogy. The sheer animality of those deemed savage – something that encompassed the Chilcotins' other alleged traits: their inconstancy, covetousness, cupidity, profligacy, and passion – was a characteristic that had been used to distinguish the barbarian from the civilized since the Greeks. Christianity further reinforced the otherness of those who displayed these traits by designating them sins, and they continued to be part and parcel of what comprised savagery as well as providing a rationale for colonialism long before the Europeans ever imagined or came to realize their imperial aspirations on the Pacific Northwest Coast.

Particularly notable, however, were the repeated references to the Chilcotins' alleged cannibalism and Lundin Brown's observation of their reaction to the written word. Cannibalism, or as it was known until the fifteenth century, 'anthropophagi,' was and continues to be an especially resonant and enduring characteristic of savagery, one that has been used since at least the fifth century BC to distinguish 'us' from 'them.'[52] Long before the Chilcotin came to be placed beyond the pale of civilization because of their alleged anthropophagic practices, they were preceded by the Scots and Picts, the Jews, the Irish, much of the population of Africa and the Indian subcontinent, as well as the indigenous peoples of Central and South America, all of whom were also apparently 'man-eaters.'[53]

The power of the cannibal label to consign entire populations to a kind of moral exile and thus to serve as a rationale for self-proclaimed civilized communities to suspend their own morality in dealing with those deemed beyond the pale lay in a complex constellation of beliefs, some Christian and others not. As Anthony Pagden notes, cannibalism involved killing another human being, and so for Christians violated the sixth commandment. More than that, cannibalism also denied victims their right to be buried in a place of their choosing. This is a significant point because for Christians the day of judgment involves the resurrection of the body; hence burial and its attendant rituals are of crucial importance. Beyond these Christian dicta against cannibalism, however, are other, perhaps more basic beliefs which contributed to the revulsion that cannibalism elicited.[54] Humans were simply not to eat other humans, nor any creatures their own kind; rather, legitimate sustenance came only from those creatures who occupied the lower orders. Thus, Pagden argues, '[c]annibalism demonstrated that they [Indians] could not distinguish between the rigid and self-defining categories into which the natural world was divided.'[55]

Like cannibalism, the fear and fascination which writing was said to hold for Indians also had a long history. Though it's now the stuff of grade-B westerns, the Indians' reaction to and capacity to understand the written word represented a recapitulation of the centuries-old Greek definition of barbarism, which at its core was grounded in language.[56] Barbarians had been, to start, simply non-Greek speakers. Over time, however, different levels of savagery were distinguished by their different modes of communication, and transcription, or the writtenness of language, became the central feature of civility. A written language allowed the society which possessed it to reach beyond its grasp and to attain, it was thought, a certain level of intellectual and moral sophistication that came from the exchange of ideas made possible by and through the written word. Thus the absence of a written language, along with a dread fear of it, was an indictment of Chilcotin culture both present and future.

Though ancient, the historical context in which the discourse of savagery was articulated gave it a particular and added resonance. The ideology of liberalism, ascendant in the nineteenth century, provided new standards with which to measure the Chilcotins' alleged savagery, standards that, though new, worked to reinforce the very old images and beliefs that were embedded in the savage discourse that ran through the stories that were told about Bute Inlet. The killers' actions affronted liberal sensibilities because they were antithetical to what liberals believed constituted rational human nature; namely, the pursuit of individual self-interest. This pursuit, however, itself rested on an ability to look ahead and to calculate the course of action that would bring the greatest rewards. Because this often involved a denial of immediate pleasures and short-term gains, restraint, as well as calculation, was also a key characteristic of rationality. The Chilcotins' actions on Bute Inlet – not just the act of killing but the manner in which those killings were carried out – were evidence of their irrationality and only confirmed their otherness within a liberal frame of reference.

If the Chilcotins' actions were not enough to make them into an Other against whom European British Columbians defined themselves, they even looked different: the Indians' physical otherness was emblematic of the moral distance that separated savagery from civilization. 'A set of men and women more squalid and repulsive I have rarely beheld,' said Lundin Brown of the Chilcotin. 'Dark faces, big mouths, black eyes, narrow foreheads, long tangled hair black as night; their thin and sinewy frames with little on them save dirt and a piece of blanket or a deerskin.'[57] Frederick Whymper, an artist who had accompanied the ill-fated road party at the start of the 1864 season, but had left for Victoria before the killings, described the Bute Inlet natives as 'creature[s], half child–half animal' – a combination of innocence and danger – who had been degraded by their contact with European civilization, presumably because they lacked the self-discipline to resist its temptations.[58]

Like their alleged irrationality, natives' physical appearance was something that Europeans had commented upon since the first contact, and that had served to distinguish them as Other. Though there is some debate about when this occurred, by the nineteenth century at least the connection between the physical otherness of various cultural groups and the hierarchy of development and civility it suggested were buttressed by the emergence of anthropology and Darwinian ideas regarding the origin of the species. Both lent scientific credence to already existing beliefs about what became known as the 'great chain of being,' transforming a social and religious concept into a scientific one, thus providing another rationale for colonialism.

At the same time, anthropological language and concepts, what Martin Wiener calls the 'ethnological imagination,' were also being deployed by Victorian social critics to understand and colonize the 'dark continents' nearer to home: the slums and particularly the criminal rookeries of London.[59] Despite the racial differences, much of the language and many of the concepts of otherness European British Columbians used to describe and understand the Chilcotin killers were identical to those employed by English social critics of the Victorian period.[60] The 'intertextuality' of colonial and imperial discourses of crime suggests that an overarching language of otherness existed and could – at least to some degree – transcend the differences imposed by race and class, and more generally by the very different social contexts in which they operated. Placed side by side, descriptions of English criminals differed little from those of British Columbian ones. Mayhew's 'nomadic street people' bore a striking similarity to Lundin Brown's and Whymper's Chilcotin. 'There is,' Mayhew argued of the street people, 'a greater development of the animal than of the intellectual or moral nature of man'; 'they are more or less distinguished for their high cheek bones and protruding jaws ... for their lax ideas of property – for their general improvidence – their repugnance to continuous labour – their disregard of female honour – their love of cruelty – their pugnacity – and their utter want of religion.'[61]

Though English reformers like Mayhew could use the word 'tribal' to describe London's criminal class, European British Columbians had the 'real' thing: a group that, to white sensibilities, appeared indolent, dissipated, and prone to drunkenness or other kinds of excess; a group shackled by custom and who perpetuated cruelties in its name; and perhaps most significantly, a group that was distinguished by a separate language, rituals, and physiognomy. In British Columbia, the criminal class were quite literally 'savages': signifier and signified were collapsed – criminological imagination had met ethnographic reality, and the intersection of the two discourses on Bute Inlet only heightened and reinforced the sense of Indians as Other.

Finally, and perhaps more tangibly, the incident at Bute Inlet occurred at a time when racial attitudes, both in the colony and in the empire more generally, were hardening. As Robin Fisher argues, the 1858 Fraser River gold rush marked the beginnings of a shift in attitude on the part of Europeans toward the native population of the colony. No longer dependent on the cooperation of native peoples as the fur traders had been, miners and settlers like the unfortunate William Manning came to view them as obstacles to their own economic gain, which was part and parcel of the 'progress of the colony.'[62] Given this conflation, the Bute Inlet 'massacre' took on a larger allegorical significance in addition to its material one. The eighteen labourers who lost their lives at the hands of the Chilcotin were building a road through a 'trackless' wilderness: and not just any road, but one to the gold fields – literally, a road to prosperity – to be travelled by men possessed of the same vigorous spirit of enterprise that animated its promotor and developer, Alfred Waddington. In a sense, the Bute Inlet massacre stood for the European penetration of North America, embodying the violent clash of civilization and savagery, reason and passion, progress and backwardness, and culture and nature.[63]

As well, there were likely few in this British colony who could fail to draw parallels – justified or not – between the massacre at Bute Inlet and the Indian Mutiny just seven years before, an event which precipitated a hardening of attitudes towards indigenous peoples throughout the empire and influenced colonial policy for at least a decade afterwards.[64] In both cases a small group of English men and women found themselves in an alien land surrounded and outnumbered by an equally alien and potentially hostile population who did not, curiously enough, seem interested in availing themselves of the opportunity for moral uplift the white presence made possible.

IV

Having constructed the Chilcotin as savages and their actions as sense-less, European British Columbians should have been well-justified and comfortable in embarking on a policy of destruction: savagery had to be met with savagery. There was, as the *Colonist* put it, no place for 'maudlin sentimentality' in dealing with the Chilcotin. As the fate of Waddington's road party became known, demands for immediate action were not long in coming. The New Westminster–based *British Columbian* called for the citizens of the island and mainland colonies to unite 'in dealing out speedy justice, at whatever cost, to these sixteen devils done up in red skins,'[65] while the *Weekly British Colonist* expressed its 'hope that the ridiculous farce of bringing them down to New Westminster and trying them by jury will not be attempted in case of their appre-hension.' 'A summary examination, and a hempen noose for each from the nearest tree, in the presence of all the tribe, would have a hun-dredfold more effect on all the Indians of all the coast than the solemn and (to them) unintelligible mummery of a trial by jury.'[66] News of the attack on Macdonald's pack train reached Victoria a week or so later and led the same newspaper to harden its already rigid position: '[t]here are hundreds of bold hardy spirits who would at once volunteer to march against the savage murderers,' it reported. 'Let them not stay their hands till every member of the rascally murderous tribe is sus-pended to the trees of their own forests – a salutary warning to the whole coast for years to come.'[67]

And yet there were doubts about whether this was the proper and, indeed, the civilized, course of action. In emphasizing the Indians' other-ness, some European British Columbians became self-conscious and re-flective about their own behaviour, discovering, to their dismay, that despite their best efforts to distance themselves from the Indians, the gulf between them was not as wide as they wished. Not only was the man in the animal visible, but, even more disturbing, the animal in man was also ever-present, always threatening to obliterate the distinc-tion between them. For all their adamant assertions and tightly drawn distinctions between reason and passion and savagery and civilization, one of the most palpable sentiments evoked by the Bute Inlet stories was uncertainty.

Though the Bute Inlet stories laid great emphasis on the swift, sud-den, and unexpected quality of the attack, contrasting the Indians' pas-sionate nature with the more methodical, calculating, and reasonable response of the white expedition that pursued them, there was a sense in at least some of the accounts that the Chilcotin had carefully planned the massacre; and thus that they were not creatures 'impelled' into action, but a people possessed of a level of calculation and rationality. In his initial investigation of the killings, Chartres Brew learned from other natives that 'the murderers had been concocting their villainous scheme for some time, and had waited over a week for the arrival of Mr. Waddington, hoping by his death to break up the road undertaking. This, from what could be gathered from the Coast Indians, seems to have been their main object, rather than plunder.'[68] Victoria's *Daily Chronicle* muddied the distinction between reason and passion in the same way when it described the attack as 'indiscriminate'[69] and insisted that 'plunder was no doubt the main object they [the Chilcotin] had in view,' but then noted that 'the plan of slaughter ... seems to have been formed with military precision, each Indian selecting his man.'[70]

The larger dichotomy which animated the Bute Inlet stories – that of savagery versus civilization – was also not as fixed and rigid as European British Columbians would have liked, for they recognized that the man in the animal – the potential for civility – was never completely lost, and the line between the civilized and the savage was not absolute. On meeting Klatsassin, the Chilcotin chief said to be the instigator of the killings, Lundin Brown pointedly observed that his 'face, narrow at the forehead, wide at the centre; and high cheek bones indicated the characteristics of the North American savage.'[71] Nevertheless, despite the chief's savagery, the missionary could also not help but comment on 'his strong frame, piercing dark *blue* eyes, aquiline nose; and very powerful underjaw, [which] proclaimed the man of intelligence.'[72] 'One could hardly look at Klatsassan,' Lundin Brown concluded, 'without feeling that there was about the man something awful, and something winning – in fact, something *great*.'[73]

If the man in the animal was never completely absent, neither could the animal in the man – even the Englishman – be completely domesticated. The bloodthirsty sentiments expressed by some European British Columbians as news of the massacre broke proved disconcerting and disturbing for others. 'We are too apt,' the *British Columbian* argued, 'in the first flush of excited indignation, to cry out for the utter and indiscriminate extermination of the savages, dealing out to them Lynch Law instead of British justice ... [W]e hope to see the same impartial justice brought into requisition in dealing with the aborigines that we would desire to have meted out to ourselves.'[74] Not only did they fear

the outbreak of an all-out war between themselves and the more numerous Indians if such sentiments were acted upon, but they were also
disturbed by these utterances at a much deeper level. Calls for the enforcement of the law had been conflated with calls for revenge: 'speedy
justice' was transformed, almost without comment, into 'summary vengeance,' and with it the civilized into savages.

V

Notably, however, it was less the savagery of the Indian that some European British Columbians associated with the calls for the indiscriminate extermination of native peoples following the massacre, than that
of the American. In fact, rather than the Indian, it was the American
who served as the foil against which they structured their identity and
hence their actions.

The experience of Americans, particularly those who lived in the
West, stood as a cautionary tale for British Columbians. In the absence
of the familiar Old World distinctions provided by family, class, ethnicity,
religion, and occupation – just to name a few – there was little, it seemed,
to anchor social identity on the frontier. Mindful of this, European British Columbians were fearful that the alien environment they found
themselves in would transform them into the savages they so loathed
and from which they drew their identity.[75] They needed to look no
farther than the United States for an example of the dangers of 'going
Native.' California, and the 'californization,' to use the contemporary
phrase, of the white population implied both an accretion of American
prejudices and a razing of all the social distinctions that gave civility
meaning.[76] The restraints imposed by those distinctions held society
together, and without them, even Englishmen could slip into savagery.
Anglican Bishop George Hills noted the beginnings of such a process
at Yale in 1861. Like Indians, the miners there 'had become reckless,'
he observed. 'They were away from home-ties and restraints of society,
so they gave themselves up to do whatever they were tempted to do;
so gambling, drinking [and] sensual pleasures soon wasted their substance away.'[77]

Certainly Frederick Seymour was struck by the differences in the
way Americans and Englishmen conducted themselves. In commenting
on the Bute Inlet volunteers under William Cox, the majority of whom
were Americans, the governor observed that they were 'not much disposed to relish the restraint which I put upon them in carrying out

operations against the Indians,' and though they seemed both appreciative and respectful of the British authority he represented – giving him a hearty three cheers upon his arrival in camp – there was a marked difference in their comportment and that of the English volunteers. 'The men raised in the Gold Districts, mostly Americans, passed the greater part of the night in dancing or playing cards to an accompaniment of war whoops and the beating of tin pots,' he reported. In contrast, he continued: 'The New Westminster expedition, almost exclusively English, and comprising many discharged Sappers [Royal Engineers], spent the evening in the usual quiet soldier-like manner. No spiritous liquor was in either camp, yet the amusements were kept up in one long after total silence prevailed in the other.'[78]

The sentiments Seymour expressed regarding the Americans were given popular expression in the colony's mainland newspaper, which, after some thought, argued for a more measured, calculated, and, above all, discriminating response which was in keeping with not just white, but British, civility. '[T]here are those amongst us who are disposed to ignore altogether the rights of Indians and their claims upon us, who hold the American doctrine of "manifest destiny" in its most fatal form,' observed the more reflective *British Columbian*, '... and under the shadow of this unchristian doctrine, the cry for "extermination" is raised at every pretext. Very different, however, are the views and sentiments held ... by the British Government.'[79]

Meting out justice according to the law was thus what separated British Columbians from Americans, and a failure to do so would surely mark the beginnings of 'californization' and a descent into savagery. The rule of law not only stood as a bulwark of individual freedom, but it was also emblematic of European British Columbians' identity, of their membership in the community of civilized British nations. Adhering to the rule of law meant, as the *British Columbian* indicated, treating everyone who came before the courts similarly. Indeed, as Matthew Begbie recalled, since the colony's creation, Indians had been told 'that all men are on a level before the Courts of criminal justice.'

That they are amenable to the same Tribunals, for the same offences, triable by the same methods and ceremonies and liable to the same punishments as white men, exactly.

They have been told most emphatically that their own old methods of investigation and punishments and licenced retributions and compensations &c. are annulled; and that we are 'showing them a more excellent way.' They have been told that the same line of conduct is therefore expected of them as from the Whites and they have acquiesced and seen the logic of the proposition.[80]

While adhering to the rule of law may have confirmed their British civility against the savagery of American manifest destiny, doing so required British Columbians to deny the very differences they had so carefully drawn between themselves and the Indian savages in the Bute Inlet stories. As we have seen, in understanding the killings as a 'massacre,' British Columbians constructed the Chilcotin as a savage Other, and themselves as civilized. But in order to conform to the standards of *British* civility – an identity formed in opposition to the American Other – British Columbians had to behave as if those differences did not exist.

Doing so was no easy task. There was always the danger of slippage, of violating the rule of law and treating the 'savages' savagely. It was a danger that made some at the top of British Columbia's colonial hierarchy self-conscious; their own actions, as well as those taken in the government's name, towards the colony's native peoples thus took on a larger symbolic significance. That significance and the tensions between two different colonial selves – one constructed against the Indian which justified savage treatment, and the other against the American which required they adhere to the rule of law – were apparent in Frederick Seymour's efforts to organize and instruct the two expeditionary forces sent to pursue the Chilcotin. On the one hand, Seymour had authorized the creation of a military force in recognition of the state of 'war' that gripped the colony; on the other, he was well aware of the significance of the force's conduct and continued to insist that they treat the Indians according to the strict standards of the rule of law.[81] In his initial dispatch to the Colonial Office, the governor made it clear that what he and his officers sought in organizing the Bute Inlet expedition was 'the capture of the murderers and the *vindication* of the law,'[82] and 'to show what had not previously been seen in this part of the world[:] a Government calm and just under circumstances calculated to create exasperation.'[83] Thus, it is clear that Seymour considered the expedition's purpose as twofold: practical and symbolic. It was to both capture the killers and do so in a manner that would establish the merits and superiority of British justice over that practised by both the Americans and the Indians. That manner was strictly legal: Seymour insisted that the volunteers under Brew and Cox be 'sworn constables – for we wish to proceed *legally*.'[84]

This concern for comportment had the effect of placing some curious constraints on what was a military expedition. For instance, Cox, along with his volunteers, was instructed 'to proceed to the headquarters of Alexis, great chief of the Chilcoaten tribe, shew his warrant and explain that the Queen's law must have its course,' Seymour reported. 'He will support his application for redress by showing my proclamation offering a reward of £50 for the apprehension of each of the murderers.'[85]

Despite the naïvety or the arrogance of the assumption that the Chilcotin, when confronted with the irrefutable logic and reasonableness of British justice in this way, would simply comply and turn over their brethren, Seymour's plan worked. Or it appeared to. Eight Chilcotin did surrender to Cox's party in mid-August and, in doing so, vindicated the law. It was an epochal moment: just as 'those who hold with the Yankee doctrine of "indiscriminate extermination" were beginning to triumph over their opponents,' British justice proved itself.[86] More importantly, European British Columbians had proved themselves to be possessed of the civility they had claimed. 'Things are not as they were,' observed a self-congratulatory *British Columbian*. 'A few years, or, indeed, a few months, ago, who would have dreamed of the murder of a few whites by the Indians calling forth such a demonstration in the vindication of the law as this Colony has recently witnessed?'

One of Her Majesty's gunboats might possibly have been despatched somewhere, and we might have heard of a naval demonstration against an Indian village without the slightest reference to its inhabitants being concerned in the murder, with a flourish of trumpets over old and superannuated Indians and squaws, with a large percentage of papooses, who were killed or wounded in the grand and successful operation! How all of this has changed now. Not only were the most thorough measures taken for the apprehension of the murderers, but the most careful discrimination between the guilty and the innocent [was] observed ...

'We look therefore, upon this as a redeeming feature of the Bute massacre,' the newspaper concluded, 'that it has afforded the Government an excellent opportunity of most forcibly illustrating to the Indian tribes the great superiority of British Law.'[87] And, I would add, the episode served to validate their own identity.

Or did it? Questions about the circumstances surrounding the surrender of the Chilcotin were raised at the Quesnelmouth assizes which cast some doubt on just how much the law had been vindicated by the conduct of the Bute Inlet expedition. Just when European British Columbians were beginning to reassert their civility and superiority again, they discovered once more that the distinctions they had made were not as certain as they would have liked. Though the Chilcotin five were hanged, the uncertainty surrounding their execution precipitated a degree of self-criticism.

The Chilcotin, it turned out, may have come into Cox's camp under false pretences, believing that they would be granted a meeting with the governor, rather than be arrested and detained. Certainly, their capture came as a surprise to Alexis, chief of the Chilcotin, who told Begbie that 'Mr. Cox must have two tongues' upon learning of what happened.[88] Trickery on the part of Cox's party tarnished the law's victory, and raised questions about the justice of hanging the prisoners.[89] There had been questions about Cox's honour during the course of the expedition, making the possibility of his malfeasance less remote. According to the diary of a volunteer, it appeared 'that Mr. Cox, anxious to secure all the glory of bagging the murderers, sent a messenger to tell them [the Chilcotin] that Mr. Brew's party would kill them all ... whereas *he* only wanted to talk to them and make terms.'[90] So concerned was Matthew Begbie about the possibility of duplicity that he took the unusual step of speaking to Klatsassin privately after the trial but before the sentencing about what had transpired. After the interview, Begbie concluded that '[b]oth Mr Cox and Klatsassin leave me under the impression – in fact they expressly state – that the latter was completely in the dark as to the consequences of his entering Mr. Cox's camp.' 'It seems horrible to hang 5 men at once,' the judge concluded, 'especially under the circumstances of the capitulation.' But he resigned himself to necessity, observing that 'the blood of 21 [sic] whites calls for retribution. And these fellows are cruel, murdering pirates – taking life and making slaves in the same spirit in w[hi]ch you or I w[oul]d go out after partridges or rabbit shooting.'[91] The Chilcotins' otherness, it seemed, prevailed; the need for Terror outweighed the need for British Justice.[92]

VI

The morning of October 26th [1864] broke bright and frosty. With that feeling of heart-sickness which those who know who have had to approach the King of Terrors, and stand by when, with all its fearful ceremonial, the Law puts forth its hand deliberately and violently to take away life, I rose and hastened to the prison. The Indians were already at their prayers ... I then entered the cell, and asked if they were ready to receive the Holy Communion? They said they were most desirous. In celebrating, I said the principal parts of the service in their language; the rest in English. This, of course, they did not understand; but they knew the general meaning. They were very devout in receiving, and seemed cheered and encouraged by the Sacrament.

After the service the prisoners took breakfast, then the gaoler called them out, one by one, to be pinioned. As they went I shook hands with each one, bidding them farewell. First went young Pierre, who wept a little, thinking, no doubt of his young wife and child at home. Then there was Chessus, now a changed man, his face no longer fiendishly hideous as at first, but softened and beautified by the touch of Faith. The rest followed. Klatsassan was the last to leave. He grasped me warmly by the hand, and thanked me ...

I noticed ... someone offering Klatsassan a drink, and his refusing. I don't think he ... refused the liquor from any notion save a sense of impropriety of the thing, and a heroic kind of feeling, as if he thought it nobler to meet the worst with all his faculties about him, and face death manfully ...

The prisoners were then led on to the scaffold. There was a large crowd of Indians and white men round, but perfect silence and decorum reigned throughout; prayers were said in Chilcoaten; very short, of course; such is not the time or place for more than a brief commendation of the souls about to depart. I remember saying to each one, as in turn they were blindfolded, and the rope adjusted, and they were placed on the drops, '*Jesu Christ nerhunschita sincha coontese*' ('Jesus Christ be with thy spirit'). As I was going to repeat this to Taloot, a voice was heard; it was Tapeet. He first called out to his comrades to 'have courage.' Then he spoke two sentences to the Indians round the scaffold. They were of the Alexandrian tribe, and at feud with the Chilcoatens. Still, in such a moment such feelings must be forgotten. So he addressed himself to them, and said, '*Tell the Chilcoatens to cease anger against the whites.*' He added, 'We are going to see the Great Father.'

One instant more and the signal was given; the drops fell. All was done so quietly and so quickly that it was difficult to realize that the frightful work was over.

The remains were interred with Christian burial, after the Anglican rite, in a wood near Quesnelmouth, not far from the Cariboo road. A wooden cross with a rude inscription was set up to mark the spot where those poor fellows sleep.[93]

While Matthew Begbie may have had doubts about whether the Chilcotin had been treated justly, the Rev. Robert Christopher Lundin

Brown, the Anglican priest who ministered to the prisoners in their last days and the author of the above account – written several years later – did not. Though Lundin Brown admitted that the Chilcotin came to a melancholy end, he also considered it the only fitting one: justice demanded that such a heinous crime be met with the ultimate sanction of the law. Lundin Brown's eyewitness account of the fate of the Chilcotin five was also fitting in a different sense of the word: it was made to fit the needs and expectations of the teller and the audience who read it. True to a man of the cloth, Lundin Brown told a story of sin, repentance, and salvation, setting out a perfect, almost predictable and self-contained resolution to a tragic series of events that invoked a kind of moral closure on them. Here we have men described as 'cruel, murdering pirates' wholly repentant in the end, accepting of both their fate and a Christian God, who, through their embrace of him, and him of them, transforms the Chilcotin both physically (in the case of the once 'hideous' Chessus) and spiritually, and lends them comfort and fortitude to face the 'King of Terrors' in a composed manner. 'Composed' is the key here: for not only did Lundin Brown's Chilcotin face death with great calm, but both they and their story were actually *composed* – created – to leave no doubt in the minds of those who read the account as to the inevitability and justice of the Chilcotins' fate, and the justice of those who meted it out.

Lundin Brown's 'fitting' end belies the untidiness of the Bute Inlet story. For the parson, the road from Bute Inlet led directly and unwaveringly to salvation for the Chilcotin and exculpation for the Europeans and their system of justice. But those who travelled it discovered that the route was not at all straight and narrow, but rather hazardous, requiring them to negotiate between two identities and the conflicting actions they engendered. On the one hand, portraying the Chilcotin as savages established their own civility and – for some – justified treating the perpetrators, and perhaps all Indians, savagely. On the other, however, savage treatment raised doubts about European civility and in fact diminished it. The indiscriminate killing of native peoples was what Americans did. To separate themselves from the 'savagery' of their southern neighbours, European British Columbians insisted that Indians be treated equally before the law; that is, they distinguished themselves from the Americans by treating 'their' Indians differently than the Americans did theirs – which, ironically, meant treating them in a manner *similar* to Europeans.

In British Columbia, then, the rule of law was the linchpin of colonial identity, but that identity was never fixed or decided once-and-for-all. Instead, as the Bute Inlet route we have travelled shows, it was something that was fluid and contingent. European British Columbians were always, as Angela Harris put it, 'being and becoming,' their identities negotiated and renegotiated with and against the 'others' who lived among the western mountains.[94]

NOTES

An earlier version of this essay was booted around by the Early Canadian History Group at the University of Toronto. Thanks to its members, and also to John Beattie, Clifford Shearing, Carolyn Strange, and my co-editors, Susan Lewthwaite and Jim Phillips, for their insight and helpful comments.

1 See David Ricardo Williams '... *The Man for a New Country': Sir Matthew Baillie Begbie* (Sidney: Gray's Publishing 1977) or his shorter biography of Begbie in *The Dictionary of Canadian Biography* vol. 12 (Toronto: University of Toronto Press 1990).

2 Lincoln B. Faller *Turned to Account: The Forms and Functions of Criminal Biography in Late Seventeenth- and Early Eighteenth-Century England* (Cambridge: Cambridge University Press 1987) xi and Martin J. Wiener, *Reconstructing the Criminal: Culture, Law, and Policy in England, 1830–1914* (Cambridge: Cambridge University Press 1990) 11

3 Robert Miles *Racism* (London: Routledge 1989) 11. See also Peter Mason *Deconstructing America: Representations of the Other* (London: Routledge 1990). Echoing Miles, Mason notes that Europeans 'defined themselves and the culture they defended in a way resembling that of the photographic negative: by portraying everything that they were *not*, they created – by antithesis – an implicit image of what they in fact *were* – or rather, thought themselves to be' (44).

4 Cited in 'Alfred Penderell Waddington' *Dictionary of Canadian Biography* vol. 10 (Toronto: University of Toronto Press 1972) 698

5 Unless otherwise noted, all biographical information on Waddington is taken from his entry in vol. 10 of the *Dictionary of Canadian Biography*, Adrian Kershaw and John Spittle *The Bute Inlet Route: Alfred Waddington's Wagon Road, 1862–64* (Kelowna: Okanagan College 1978) 4–8, and Neville Shanks *Waddington: A Biography of Alfred Penderill Waddington* (Port Hardy: North Island Gazette 1975).

6 Richard Carr (father of Emily) was one of the most notable, and certainly

one of the most vocal, expatriate Britons to voice his distaste for California and to migrate to Victoria with the discovery of gold in British Columbia. See Maria Tippett *Emily Carr: A Biography* (Toronto: Oxford University Press 1979) 2–9. Matthew Begbie made a similar observation and claimed that a California sojourn rendered an otherwise respectable Englishman unfit for colonial service, and told James Douglas so. (Douglas himself was certainly not enamoured of his Yankee neighbours after his experience both at Fort Vancouver during a time when British sovereignty in the Oregon Territories was contested by the Americans and as governor of Vancouver Island, where he again had to fight off American incursions in the San Juan Islands.) 'I am afraid,' he told Douglas, 'that English sentiments are less prevalent than could be wished in Englishmen who have long resided in California. I do not mean to insinuate that such a residence diminishes – on the contrary, I believe, it often even augments – their natural loyalty & good affection to Her Majesty. But there is usually to be remarked among such persons an alteration in voice, in tone and manner, and an accretion of prejudices, which, I think, render them less fit, and contrast unfavorably with the tone[,] manner and prejudices of Englishmen habitually resident in the United Kingdom.' See Begbie to Douglas, Victoria, Vancouver Island, 18 May 1859, BCARS [British Columbia Archives and Records Services], GR 1372, reel B-1307, f 142b1/7.

7 'Fraser River fever' and 'Fraser River humbug' are both terms used by Waddington himself, in *The Fraser Mines Vindicated, or the History of Four Months* (Victoria: P. de Garro 1858), a defence of the economic prospects of the new colony.

8 See W. Champness *To Cariboo and Back: An Emigrant's Journey to the Gold Fields of British Columbia* ([London?]: n.p. 1865); M. Claudet, *The Handbook of British Columbia and Emigrant's Guide to the Gold Fields* (London: W. Oliver [1862]); Jules H. Féry *Map and Guide to the Cariboo Gold Mines of British Columbia* (San Francisco: F. Truette 1862); and William Carew Hazlitt *The Great Gold Fields of Cariboo ...* (London: Routledge, Warne, and Routledge 1862).

9 Chartres Brew 'Remarks on Mr. Waddington's Petition' undated ms, BCARS

10 Ibid.

11 Figure from 'Alfred Pendrell Waddington' *Dictionary of Canadian Biography* 10: 697

12 It was 363 miles from New Westminster to Williams Lake via the Brigade Trail and 329 via the River Trail. See Jo. Lindley *Three Years in Cariboo: Being the Experience and Observations of a Packer* (San Francisco: A. Rosenfield 1862) 3–14.

13 Edward Sleigh Hewlett 'The Chilcotin Uprising of 1864' (MA thesis, Department of History, University of British Columbia 1972) 91

14 'Waggish distortion' from 'The Bute Route' *Daily Evening Press* 16 June 1861, cited in ibid. The £100,000 figure is from Brew 'Remarks on Mr. Waddington's Petition.' Brew likely was mistaken, for the Bute Inlet Wagon Road Company's prospectus estimated the profits to be of the order of $100,000. See Bute Inlet Wagon Road Company Limited [Prospectus] (Victoria: n.p. 1863).

15 In return for building the road, the Bute Inlet Wagon Road Company was granted the right to levy and collect a toll for ten years (see ibid.). Waddington also hoped to profit from the sale of town lots in 'Waddington,' the settlement he envisioned being established at the head of Bute Inlet as a provisioning point for the journey overland.

16 Frederick Seymour told the Colonial Office that he 'never saw so difficult a country. The mountains in many cases rise simply at right angles to the plains. Glaciers are poised over narrow valleys of almost tropical heat, and the cascades fall from the summit of the precipice scarcely wetting the perpendicular wall of rock': Seymour to Cardwell, New Westminster, 9 Sept. 1864, CO 60/19, 150.

17 In refuting Waddington's claim that he had spent $63,000 on the Bute Inlet road, Brew argued: '[t]here is not work done to be seen [and] besides the cost of what work [was] done did not all come out of Mr. Waddington's pocket. I know persons who subscribed towards the outlay and a company was formed in Victoria to support Mr. Waddington's scheme. When the trail did not progress as rapidly or as easily as Mr. Waddington promised, faith in his representations was very much shaken, and the shareholders were satisfied to let Mr. Waddington buy them out for a trifle.' See Brew 'Remarks on Mr. Waddington's Petition' and 'Alfred Penderell Waddington' *Dictionary of Canadian Biography* 10: 697.

18 Brew to the Colonial Secretary, Waddington, 23 May 1864, BCARS, GR 1372, reel B-1310, f 193/14

19 Ibid.

20 Robin Fisher *Contact and Conflict: Indian-European Relations in British Columbia, 1774–1890* (Vancouver: University of British Columbia Press 1978) 107–9 and Hewlett 'The Chilcotin Uprising of 1864' chaps. 2 and 3

21 Fisher 107–9; Hewlett, chap. 5

22 Seymour to Cardwell, New Westminster, 31 Aug. 1864, Great Britain, Colonial Office, British Columbia Original Correspondence, CO 60/19, National Archives of Canada (hereafter NAC), MG 11, 95ff. As Seymour noted, 'on the departure of Sir James Douglas, who had been known by the Indians as a great Chief, the principal authority in this territory, for up-

wards of forty years, an impression was allowed to arise among them [the Indians] that their protector was withdrawn and would have no successor. The Fraser River Indians uttered many lamentations over their deserted condition and it became desirable for me to make myself known to the natives and show them that I had succeeded to all the power of my successor and to his solicitude for their welfare.' In an earlier letter to Cardwell discussing the causes of the 'massacre,' Seymour noted that '[o]thers throw out the conjecture that the proceedings previous to Sir James Douglas's departure [i.e., the ceremonies surrounding his retirement] may have induced the Indians to believe that the white men are without a head. Possibly so. We know that the more civilized tribes on the Fraser have been allowed to believe that they are now without a protector or a friend.' See Seymour to Cardwell, New Westminster, 20 May 1864, CO 60/18, 283.

23 Hewlett 123

24 Seymour to Cardwell, New Westminster, 20 May 1864, CO 60/18, 276

25 Ibid.

26 For a detailed account of the killings, see Hewlett 'The Chilcotin Uprising of 1864' chap. 5, and his article, 'The Chilcotin Uprising of 1864' BC Studies 19 (1973) 50–72.

27 Hewlett 'The Chilcotin Uprising of 1864' (thesis) 130–4; Rev. R.C. Lundin Brown Klatsassan, and Other Reminiscences of Missionary Life in British Columbia (London: Society for Promoting Christian Knowledge 1873) 17–36

28 For a breakdown of the expenses, see the ledger sheets enclosed in BCARS, GR 1372, reel B-1321, f 380/6.

29 Hewlett 'The Chilcotin Uprising of 1864' (thesis), 165–76

30 Birch to Cox, Colonial Secretary's Office, 14 May 1864, BCARS, GR 1372, f 379/22 noted that 'the Governor regrets that he cannot furnish you with the names or description of the offenders, but he is advised that their own tribe would easily identify them should they think fit. You are at liberty to offer such rewards as you may think fit to the Indians for the apprehension of the murderers.'

31 Only six were tried. Cheloot and Sanstanki were freed, and Chedekki, whom no witnesses recognized, but who it was said would be recognized by one of the survivors, was taken to New Westminster for identification and, if identified, to stand trial. Chedekki escaped while en route to New Westminster, and was never captured. See Hewlett 'The Chilcotin Uprising of 1864' BC Studies 19 (1973) 71.

32 Seymour to Cardwell, New Westminster, 9 Sept. 1864, CO 60/19, 180

33 For an excellent general overview, see Robert F. Berkhofer, Jr The Whiteman's Indian: Images of the American Indian from Columbus to the Present (New York: Alfred A. Knopf 1978).

34 'Horrible Massacre' *Daily Chronicle* 12 May 1864

35 'The Bute Tragedy' *British Columbian* 27 May 1864

36 Lundin Brown 16

37 This reaction also underlay European British Columbians' opposition to the potlatch. See Tina Loo 'Dan Cranmer's Potlatch: Law as Coercion, Symbol, and Rhetoric, 1884–1951' *Canadian Historical Review* 125 (1992) 125–65.

38 'The Bute Tragedy' *British Columbian* 27 May 1864. The Chilcotin had even left money strewn on the ground – further testimony to their profligacy.

39 Seymour to Cardwell, New Westminster, 9 Sept. 1864, CO 60/19, 154

40 Lundin Brown 13–14. Brown described the evening before the attack on the packers as follows, again emphasizing the Europeans' work ethic: 'they [the packers] had had a long day of it, and were glad enough ... to reach the place of bivouac. No one can realize, who has not felt it, the delight to the worn-out miner or packer of gaining a nightly resting place ... Sweet indeed is rest after labour' (20). And I would add, how unjust it was that these hard-working men be killed in the course of doing an honest day's work.

41 Brown emphasized the progress Manning's presence and actions represented: 'as the years rolled on, Manning replaced his tent by a good substantial log house; he extended his garden, and cleared more land; he procured a plough, and turned up the rich virgin soil, and the yellow corn waved by the bank of that far-off lake' (36).

42 Lundin Brown 36

43 'Dreadful Massacre' *British Colonist* 12 May 1864

44 Seymour to Cardwell, New Westminster, 20 May 1864, CO 60/18, 276

45 Frederick Whymper *Travel and Adventure in the Territory of Alaska* ... (New York: Harper's 1871) 36. Mariana Valverde discusses the use of the volcanic metaphor in the nineteenth-century discourse of moral reform. See *The Age of Light, Soap, and Water: Moral Reform in English Canada, 1885–1925* (Toronto: McClelland and Stewart 1991) 132.

46 Lundin Brown 21–6

47 Ibid. 34–5

48 Ibid. 38–9. Still later, during the trial, Nancy once again demonstrated what Brown and others would describe as female fickleness when she testified against her native compatriots, and asked for government support afterwards, for she was fearful of returning to her village given her actions. Seymour complied, but Nancy eventually returned home – to an unknown fate. See Cox to the Colonial Secretary, Quesnelmouth, 2 Oct. 1864, BCARS, GR 1372, reel B-1321, f 380/1; Colonial Secretary to Cox, New Westminster, 8 Oct. 1864, ibid.; and Cox to Colonial Secretary, Richfield, BC, 8 Nov.

1864, ibid., f 380/9. The names of both women are also significant and work to reinforce the archetypes they represent: honour, loyalty, and integrity are associated with a woman who has retained her native name, while the woman who compromised those around her has also compromised her own identity by taking on an Anglicized name. Indeed, many contemporary commentators thought that Indians who lived in close association with non-natives, like the Songhees, who lived around Victoria, were more degraded by the experience. An Anglicized name might thus also indicate a greater state of degradation.

49 Lundin Brown 9

50 Brew to the Colonial Secretary, Waddington, 23 May 1864, BCARS, GR 1372, reel B-1310, f 193/14. See also Whymper *Travel and Adventure in the Territory of Alaska* 36. Whymper contended that the killings were motivated out of 'a strong desire for plunder.'

51 Seymour to Cardwell, New Westminster, 20 May 1864, CO 60/18, 282

52 For a provocative overview and a critique of anthropologists' work on anthropophagi, see W. Arens *The Man-Eating Myth: Anthropology and Anthropophagi* (Oxford: Oxford University Press 1979). Looking at reports of anthropophagi over time, Arens contends that 'anthropology [through its uncritical treatment of reports of cannibalism] has often served as a reviver and reinventor of the notion of savagery' (166).

53 Ibid. chap. 1. The only work on cannibalism on the Northwest Coast is Christon Archer 'Cannibalism in the Early History of the Northwest Coast: Enduring Myths and Neglected Realities' *Canadian Historical Review* 61 (1980) 453–79.

54 Anthony Pagden *The Fall of Natural Man: The American Indian and the Origins of Comparative Ethnology* (Cambridge: Cambridge University Press 1982) 80–7

55 Ibid.

56 Ibid. 16, and chap. 2 generally

57 Lundin Brown 4

58 Whymper 36. The 'half child–half animal' description is very similar to that used by Rudyard Kipling's for the Hindu population of India ('half child–half devil') in 'The White Man's Burden.' See F.G. Hutchins *The Illusion of Permanence: British Imperialism in India* (Princeton: Princeton University Press 1967) 77. Christine Bolt also discusses the image of the Indian after the mutiny in *Victorian Attitudes to Race* (London: Routledge and Kegan Paul 1971) chap. 5.

59 Wiener *Reconstructing the Criminal* 33

60 Nicholas Canny discusses the similarities between the language the English used to describe the Irish and that used to describe the natives of North America, arguing that both were part of a discourse of colonization. See

'The Ideology of English Colonization: From Ireland to America' in Stanley N. Katz and John M. Murrin, eds. *Colonial America: Essays in Politics and Social Development,* 3rd ed. (New York: Alfred A. Knopf 1983). See also Mason *Deconstructing America* chap. 2.

61 Henry Mayhew *London Labour and the London Poor* (London 1862) 1: 2–3, cited in Clive Emsley *Crime and Society in England, 1750–1900* (London: Longman's 1987) 61

62 Robin Fisher *Contact and Conflict* chap. 4. Sylvia Van Kirk, in her study of native women in the fur trade, also points to the mid nineteenth century as a time when attitudes towards native peoples and peoples of mixed blood were hardening. See her *'Many Tender Ties': Women in the Fur Trade* (Winnipeg: Watson and Dwyer 1978).

63 Francis Jennings argues that phrases like 'trackless wilderness' and 'virgin land' are part of what he describes as a 'cant of conquest' – a language that disqualifies native peoples' claim to the land by denying their existence. See his *The Invasion of America: Colonialism and the Cant of Conquest* (Chapel Hill: University of North Carolina Press 1975).

64 See Bolt *Victorian Attitudes to Race* 201ff., Hutchins *The Illusion of Permanence* chap. 4, and Donovan Williams *The India Office, 1858–1869* (Hoshiarpur: Vishveshvaranand Vedic Research Institute 1983) 336. Thanks to my colleague, Edward Ingram, for guiding me through some of the literature on the mutiny.

65 'The Bute Massacre' *British Columbian* 14 May 1864. There was some question as to the number of Chilcotin attackers: this report identifies sixteen while others say eighteen.

66 'The Bute Massacre' *Weekly Colonist* 24 May 1864

67 'The Indian Murders' *Weekly British Colonist* 7 June 1864

68 'The Bute Tragedy' *British Columbian* 27 May 1864

69 'Horrible Massacre' *Daily Chronicle* 12 May 1864

70 'Additional Particulars' *Daily Chronicle* 12 May 1864

71 Lundin Brown 7, 98–9

72 Ibid. 98–9; emphasis added

73 Ibid. 102

74 'The Bute Massacre' *British Columbian* 18 May 1864

75 On this theme in colonial America, see James Axtell 'The Unkindest Cut, or Who Invented Scalping?: A Case Study,' 'The White Indians of Colonial America,' and 'Scalping: The Ethnohistory of a Moral Question,' all in his collection of essays entitled *The European and the Indian: Essays in the Ethnohistory of Colonial North America* (New York: Oxford University Press 1981).

76 Begbie to Douglas, Victoria, Vancouver's Island, 18 May 1859, BCARS, GR 1372, reel B-1307, f 142b1/7

77 'Extracts from Bishop's Journal, 1861' in Columbia Mission *Third Report of the Columbia Mission, 1861* (London: Rivington 1861) 19

78 Seymour to Cardwell, New Westminster, 30 Aug. 1864, CO 60/19, 167

79 'An Indian Policy' *British Columbian* 14 May 1864. The same article went on to criticize James Douglas' administration with respect to its Indian policy, and to call for the colonial government to formulate a more effective one.

80 Matthew Baillie Begbie, Memorandum on Indian relief legislation and Indian chiefs' jurisdiction, Cache Creek, 11 Sept. 1876, Canada, Department of Indian Affairs (hereafter DIA), Black Series, RG 10, reel C-10112, vol. 3638, file 7271

81 As Seymour told Cardwell, 'this was a war – merciless on their side – in which we were engaged with the Chilcoaten nation and must be carried on as a war by us'. Seymour to Cardwell, New Westminster, 9 Sept. 1864, CO 60/19, 178-9.

82 Seymour to Cardwell, New Westminster, 20 May 1864, CO 60/18, 290; emphasis added

83 Ibid. 179

84 Ibid.; emphasis added. However, from E.A. Atkins' recollection, it is apparent that the distinction Seymour drew between the less-restrained Americans and the decorous Britons was not complete. The following incident indicated that the New Westminster party were not completely imbued with the dour discipline one might expect. On locating the road party's camp, Atkins recalled that they 'found nothing but some Kegs of Black blasting powder and they were all busted and spilt on the ground. There was a laughable thing happened there[.] Mr. Bonson got a sun glas (it was a hot day) and though he had drawn a pice of the powder far enough away and was sitting on his Haunches holding the glass over it. I saw him so did Mr. Brough and we went to see what he was doing and got nicly sitting on our Haunches when the whole thing went up in a big Blase knocked us over on our backs and burnt some of Broughs whiskers.' See E.A. Atkins 'History of the Chilcotin War' BCARS, ms.

85 Ibid. 291

86 'The Indian Expedition' *British Columbian* 24 Aug. 1864

87 'Things Are Not as They Were' *British Columbian* 27 Aug. 1864

88 Begbie to Seymour, Quesnellemouth, 30 Sept. 1864, BCARS, GR 1372, reel B-1309, f 142f/16

89 Hanging often raised moral doubts, and authorities were always concerned

to make a good death. Even so, there were always some observers who failed to see the difference between capital punishment, which was legal, and homicide, which was not. One of these, interestingly enough, was Alfred Waddington. Shortly after his arrival in Victoria, he wrote and published a pamphlet entitled *Judicial Murder* (Victoria: Alfred Waddington 1860) in which he condemned the hanging of Allache, a native man found guilty of killing a Black man in a drunken altercation. More generally on the questionable morality of hanging and the need to make a good death, see Peter Linebaugh 'The Tyburn Riot against the Surgeons' in Douglas Hay et al., eds. *Albion's Fatal Tree: Crime and Society in Eighteenth Century England* (London: Allen Lane 1975) and his *The London Hanged: Crime and Civil Society in the Eighteenth Century* (London: Allen Lane 1991).

90 'The Chilcoaten Expedition: Diary of a Volunteer' *British Colonist* 17 Oct. 1864

91 Ibid.

92 'Terror' and 'justice' are elements identified as part of the ideology of the law by Douglas Hay: see his 'Property, Authority, and the Criminal Law' in Hay et al., eds. *Albion's Fatal Tree.*

93 Lundin Brown 118–21

94 Angela Harris 'Race and Essentialism in Feminist Legal Theory' *Stanford Law Review* 42 (1990) 584ff.

5

Violence, Marriage, and Family Honour: Aspects of the Legal Regulation of Marriage in New France

ANDRÉ LACHANCE AND SYLVIE SAVOIE

This essay falls within the framework of research into family life. For about thirty years now, researchers in Europe have been looking at the development of the family in terms of its composition and its educational, social, and economic functions. There have also been studies on contraception, sexual relations, and parent-child and husband-wife relationships. This essay is intended to shed light on some of these issues with regard to couples and families in New France.

Since the pioneer essays of Philippe Ariés, there have been important developments in the history of the family both in Europe and in North America. Although the leading research has been in demography, social and psychological studies are gradually beginning to make progress in this area as well.[1]

In Canada, works devoted to the history of the couple and the family are just beginning to appear. Monographs on the French regime have painted an idyllic picture of the pioneer family,[2] or studied the legal aspects of households,[3] but not many have focused on family attitudes or behaviour patterns. Only the studies in historical demography by Jacques Henripin and Hubert Charbonneau and the monographs by Marcel Trudel, Louise Dechêne, and John F. Bosher provide specific information on the Canadian family in the seventeenth and eighteenth centuries. Since the 1980s, however, historians and researchers in other disciplines have begun work in this new field, examining specific aspects of family life. Studies are now being done on childhood, midwives, fosterage, illegitimacy, family relationships, and matrimonial strategies which take into account the context of a new country and the influence of European traditions and habits.[4]

This essay deals with an area still largely ignored by Canadian historians: family violence and other family-related crime in seventeenth- and eighteenth-century Canada. Research into this topic is hampered by the fact that in this period families went to great lengths to hide anything that might taint their honour. The code of silence played a major role in the concealment of 'family secrets' and hatreds and divisions within the family unit. Behind a facade of respectability family members hid all the things they were not supposed to talk about and tried to keep to themselves, such as abusive treatment of wives and children and disagreements between husbands and wives and parents and children. In the circumstances, it has been difficult to uncover evidence of these kinds of acts in the usual manner and, as a result, the realities of family life at that time are largely inaccessible to us. Fortunately, the judicial archives of the Prévôté de Québec, the royal jurisdictions of Montreal and Trois-Rivières, and the Superior Council of Quebec (Conseil supérieur de Québec) have records of both criminal proceedings and civil cases concerning applications for separation as to property and applications for separation as to bed and board and as to property, and these offer a glimpse of some of the realities of family life in that era. The picture is far from complete, of course, since it was only as a last resort, after trying every means of private redress, that a couple or a family would swallow its pride and expose its troubles in public by appealing to the courts. This essay is concerned with conflict, disorder, scandal, violence, and crime, in fact with everything that disturbed the 'normal' functioning of the family in New France.

We have searched both the civil and criminal archives of the royal tribunals of first instance of Quebec City, Montreal, and Trois-Rivières. The territorial jurisdiction of these courts of justice matched the administrative area of the government where the court was located. The tribunals of first instance were known as 'royal jurisdictions' in Montreal and Trois-Rivières and as the Prévôté in Quebec City. Appeals from these courts were heard by the Quebec Superior Council. The council was the highest court in New France, and it had the power to make final decisions with sovereign authority in all civil and criminal cases. Theoretically it had territorial jurisdiction in all parts of New France, but since there were similar appellate courts in Louisiana (in New Orleans) and French Acadia (in Louisbourg), in practice it had jurisdiction only in Labrador, the royal posts, in Canada, in the Great Lakes Heartland, and in the area around the 'Western Sea.'[5]

Notarial deeds were also consulted with regard to separations.[6] In some cases, applications for separation as to property and the resulting financial arrangements were indeed found in the notarial archives.[7] One such case concerns Marie Josephe Aubuchon, who first entered into an amicable separation agreement drawn up by a notary although she later instituted legal proceedings in the jurisdiction of Montreal.[8] Catherine Frémont and her husband also agreed to a notarized separation as to property and as to bed and board.[9] Voluntary separations of this kind were theoretically not permitted and required confirmation by the courts to be valid, yet we were often unable to find any trace of such agreements in the records of the royal tribunals.[10] We also hoped to examine the archives of the Officialité de Québec, the ecclesiastical tribunal created by Msgr de Laval and officially recognized by the State in 1684. Unfortunately, the documents of this ecclesiastical court for the French regime seem to have disappeared.[11] Thus, our study is based mainly on the judicial records of the royal tribunals of first and last instance of Quebec, Montreal, and Trois-Rivières.

The geographical focus of our study is the St Lawrence valley. We have looked primarily at the first half of the eighteenth century, although we did use some data from the seventeenth century, and we have limited the subject-matter to couples and families. According to European and American as well as Canadian research, most families at that time consisted of a married couple and their children, sometimes a surviving grandparent, and in rare instances, an unmarried brother or sister. In Canada, the typical family was made up of a mother, a father, and four children. More complex families, such as those which included brothers and sisters of the spouses and/or elderly relatives, were far less common.[12] This study will examine the couple and the family with respect to acts which the society of that time considered breaches of the law, such as murder, physical abuse, verbal abuse, adultery, bigamy, and common law relationships.

THREATS TO MARRIAGE

But first, before studying family crimes, we must examine law and custom in regard to marriage in Canadian society in order to understand what was accepted and tolerated and what was not. In Canadian society, the married state was the norm for the majority of the adult population.

Indeed, marriage was the very foundation of society and, as such, it was promoted in every possible way. The colonial government took various steps to foster marriage, offering such inducements as the 'royal gift' to encourage young people to marry early and to persuade soldiers of the Troupes de la Marine to wed local girls and establish families in the colony.[13] As a result, from the end of the seventeenth to the middle of the eighteenth century, the marriage rate remained fairly high.[14]

Marriage was strictly regulated by Church and State and governed by standards established by both canon and civil law. First and foremost, a religious marriage was confirmation of a civil marriage. Without that sacrament, under the *ancien régime*, there was no marriage. Furthermore, such a union was indissoluble: 'the normal situation of husband and wife is to live together.'[15] Even when a secular court annulled the civil contract, the marriage sacrament remained intact. It was possible to have a marriage annulled, but only according to rules established by canon law.[16] While marriage remained a sacrament, it was seen increasingly as a contract influenced by the civil authorities.[17] Civil judges who 'in France during the seventeenth and eighteenth centuries challenged and reduced the jurisdiction of the Church in matrimonial matters' did so in the belief that marriage formed the basis of civil society.[18] The State began to assert and gradually to expand its jurisdiction over the institution of marriage.

In New France, every marriage created a new family unit which was regulated and organized in every detail according to 'custom,' regardless of the wishes of husband or wife.[19] The husband-wife partnership began not when the marriage contract was signed but when the marriage was solemnized in church.[20] Signing a marriage contract before a notary seems to have been a common custom throughout the colony.[21] Because of the influence of the *Coutume de Paris*, married couples lived in a community of property arrangement unless their marriage contract specified otherwise. The *Coutume de Paris*, officially imposed on the colony in 1664 with the creation of the West India Company, governed the organization of the family, the transfer of property, procedures for the recovery of debts, and landholdings.[22] The matrimonial regime of community property, which was the usual arrangement, included all moveables belonging to the husband and wife (furniture and moveable property) and immoveables acquired during the marriage (*acquêts*). Both spouses were liable for any moveable debts incurred by either of them prior to the marriage unless the marriage contract specified that each partner would pay any debts incurred prior to the marriage, in which case an inventory of property was to be drawn up. Private property (*biens propres*) – moveable property received from a parent, ground rent, immoveables owned on the day of the marriage or subsequently acquired by succession or gift – did not enter into the community property. Private property remained within the family of the spouse who owned it.[23]

This type of matrimonial regime was characterized by the supremacy of the husband and the legal incapacity of the wife. 'The husband is lord of the moveable property and immoveable *acquests*,' wrote the jurist Ferrière in the eighteenth century.[24] The husband could dispose of, sell, 'give away or pledge the community property provided his actions were intended to be for their common good.'[25] The marital authority of the husband and the economic and legal subordination of the wife to her husband, even in domestic matters, determined how community property worked. The woman retained the status of a minor and had no legal capacity even after she reached the age of majority at twenty-five. According to Diderot's *Encyclopédie*, 'it is a husband's responsibility to defend the rights of his wife in legal proceedings.'[26] A married woman could not institute legal proceedings without her husband's permission or, in cases where he refused permission, leave from the court. She was not entitled to start a business without the consent of the person who administered the community property.[27] A married woman did not have the right to enter into contracts or other forms of legally binding obligations or to sell, dispose of, or mortgage her inheritance without the consent and permission of her husband. Even when her private property entered into the community, she had no rights over the property of that community until it was dissolved, which in most cases meant until her husband died. As long as the community survived, 'a woman's right was merely a right to protest, a potential or customary right, and the husband by whose work and industry the property was acquired was its master.'[28]

A wife's legal status was determined by the *Coutume de Paris*. However, in New France, where husbands were often absent in the Great Lakes Heartland working in the fur trade or on trips to France, it was not uncommon for a married woman to look after her family and manage the family estate on her own.[29] In such cases, a husband would give his wife the authority to manage their affairs before he left. As master of the community, the husband could, unilaterally, take any administrative action or dispose of any community-owned moveables as he saw fit.[30]

TABLE 1
Applications for Separation under the French Regime

Royal jurisdiction	Separations			
	Property only		Bed and board	Total
Montreal	57	(86.4%)	9 (13.6%)	66
Quebec (Prévôté)	44	(69.8%)	19 (30.2%)	63
Trois Rivières	20	(100.0%)	0 –	20
Sovereign Council of Quebec	9	(64.3%)	5 (35.7%)	14
Total	130	(79.8%)	33 (20.2%)	163

APPLICATIONS FOR SEPARATION

Although women were considered 'persons with no legal capacity,' a woman whose husband proved to be a poor manager or who ignored his family's physical well-being was permitted to institute proceedings for separation as to property or for separation as to property and as to bed and board.[31] However, to do either, she needed her husband's permission or, failing that, leave from the court. In our examination of the archives of the Superior Council of Quebec, the royal tribunals of first instance of the Prévôté de Québec, and the royal jurisdictions of Trois-Rivières and Montreal, we found 163 applications for separation (table 1). Although there may have been more – assuming some proceedings were settled before a notary – we believe the figure we have given here is fairly realistic. This procedure was not common in New France, but it did provide a way out of difficult emotional or economic situations for some women. Msgr Saint-Vallier, the second bishop of New France, wrote in the ritual for 1701 that 'although the Marriage bond cannot be broken, married persons may be separated as to living quarters, as to bed and as to property, but only on the basis of a judicial decision.'[32]

Thus, the law did offer women a right of protection. It was, however, a right women turned to only as a last resort, since the courts did not consent to separation until all other recourse had been exhausted. A woman could apply either for separation as to property only or for separation as to bed and board and as to property if her husband was not properly carrying out his role and obligations as master of the community property. In such circumstances, some women were able to limit the damage to the community property by separating. Once a woman was legally authorized to pursue her rights, she could file an application for separation as to property on grounds that the community property was being squandered, that her dowry was in jeopardy, or that her husband was insane. She could also file an application for separation as to bed and board, which always included separation as to property in any event, on grounds of cruelty and mistreatment, or physical abuse and threats, or on the grounds that her husband was insane and flew into 'rages,' that he had attempted to kill her or had threatened to kill her. Legal separation did not nullify the marriage, but it did permit spouses to cease living together.

Five types of separation were practised: informal separation, where the spouses lived apart without legal authorization; voluntary separation agreed to before a notary; separation by marriage contract, which affected only the property of the parties; separation as to property judicially obtained; and separation as to bed and board, where the marriage was not dissolved but the spouses were legally authorized to live apart.

How then did applying for and obtaining a separation affect a woman's legal status? According to Diderot, a separated woman was a woman 'who does not live with her husband or who is mistress of her property.'[33] A woman separated as to property could administer her property and institute legal proceedings without her husband's permission.[34] She did not, however, have the right to dispose of, sell, or mortgage that same property without either her husband's permission or leave from the court.[35] 'A separated woman,' according to the jurist Ferrière, 'cannot be made guardian of her property without such permission because it is a man's job, and for a woman to do it would be unseemly.'[36]

Furthermore, a woman who obtained a separation did not have full legal capacity. She continued to be subject to marital authority. She still required her husband's consent with respect to major decisions concerning property, and she was merely allowed to administer her property, not to dispose of it as she saw fit. In reality, her administrative powers were limited – they extended only to her own property – and she often required her husband's agreement before she could act. The only appreciable advantage a woman gained by separation was that her husband could no longer dispose of her property and the revenues it generated with impunity. Since separation was considered a temporary arrangement, the intention was to 'protect the husband's prerogatives in case of reconciliation.'[37] If a reconciliation did take place, the re-

TABLE 2
Place of Residence of Couples Involved in Applications for Separation

Royal jurisdiction	Towns*		Outside the towns†		Total	
Montreal	23	(63.9%)	13	(36.1%)	36	(40.9%)
Quebec (Prévôté)	28	(82.4%)	6	(17.6%)	34	(38.6%)
Trois Rivières	9	(50.0%)	9	(50.0%)	18	(20.5%)
Total	60	(68.2%)	28	(31.8%)	88	(100%)

*Montreal, Quebec, and Trois-Rivières
†Lachine, Boucherville, Rivière des Prairies, Beauport, Sainte-Foy, Batiscan, Maskinongé, etc.

sponsibility for administering the community property reverted to the husband. According to attitudes of the time, allowing separated women to dispose of their property as they saw fit would be disadvantageous and even dangerous and could result in poor management or misuse of the property.[38]

Despite these legal obstacles, women did apply to the courts for separations. Who were they, and where did they come from? Clearly, most applicants lived within the royal jurisdictions of Montreal, Quebec, and Trois-Rivières. Although we have precise information on only 88 of the 163 applications (54 per cent), some major themes emerged from the data regarding applicants' place of residence (table 2). The geographic distribution of applications (excluding those of undetermined location) indicates that 68 per cent originated in the cities of Quebec, Montreal, and Trois-Rivières, and 32 per cent in neighbouring areas. Alain Lottin has noticed the same phenomenon, but only in the case of separation as to bed and board in the Officialité de Cambrai, 60 per cent of applications were filed by city dwellers.[39] Nancy F. Cott also found that most applications were filed by city dwellers, with three quarters of the applicants living in towns in Massachusetts and one quarter of them in Boston.[40] If we consider only the applications for separation as to bed and board brought before the royal jurisdictions, the applications came almost exclusively from the towns (nineteen from urban areas as opposed to one from outside the towns). It is as though living in an urban environment increased the grounds for separation.

Perhaps urban wives were more sensitive to abuse and could rely on greater support from their neighbours at separation hearings than women who lived in the country. It could be argued that a woman who lived in the city would be more likely to have neighbours who were familiar with her circumstances, because of the closer proximity of living quarters in urban environments. In some cases, witnesses at separation hearings testified that they were awakened at night by the sound of the husband beating his wife and the wife begging him to stop. According to A. Lottin, the crowded conditions and opportunities for escape available in cities gave rise to situations which led to separation. Also, people in rural areas tended to take longer to make up their minds about getting married than city people did.[41] Another possible explanation is that city dwellers were more familiar with separation procedures and, therefore, were more apt to separate. It should be noted that there were differences between urban and rural behaviour patterns due, from a demographic point of view, to geographic factors but also due to the fact that urban society was different and more diverse than rural society.[42]

WOMEN'S GRIEVANCES

The evidence submitted and the complaints filed by women enable us to analyse the conflicts between husbands and wives in qualitative terms. The grounds cited by applicants reveal why they sought separation as to bed and board or merely as to property. There were fixed limits to what a woman was prepared to tolerate in terms of divergent behaviour on the part of her husband. The charges alleged at separation hearings shed light on both the wife's grievances and the discord surrounding the couple's relationship.

The women's grievances reveal a real sense of anguish. Often, 'the poor supplicant is almost in despair, with no way of providing for her family's subsistence.'[43] Women applied for separation to avoid even greater misfortune. Generally, they acted before a complete collapse occurred, or before they became partially or totally insolvent. Some applicants, in particular those seeking separation as to bed and board, were attempting to escape from spousal violence and rage. Indeed, it was not unheard of for a judge, at the beginning of a hearing for separation as to bed and board, 'to prohibit [the husband], in clear and unequivocal terms, from physically abusing, disturbing or molesting [the supplicant] on pain of corporal punishment.'[44]

A woman seeking a separation as to property and a woman seeking a separation as to bed and board wanted more or less the same things. In both cases, the woman asked that her husband return with interest any sums she had brought into the marriage, that the property be seized, that an inventory be made, and that the property be divided. She also asked for compensation and that she be guaranteed payment of all amounts for which she had contracted jointly with her husband, that her personal belongings be restored to her, and that she receive support for herself and her children while awaiting dower. In the case of separation as to bed and board, the applicant also asked that she be allowed to live apart from her husband during the proceedings so as to avoid abuse and that her husband be prohibited from seeing her.

PRINCIPAL CATEGORIES OF COMPLAINT

At first glance, it would appear that the complaints and evidence follow a stereotype. They fall into three main categories: alcoholism, mistreatment (physical and verbal abuse), and family irresponsibility (inability of the husband to meet the needs of his family and his lack of involvement in family life). Such grounds were successfully raised in cases before the royal courts throughout the period studied. Were there other, undeclared reasons for marital incompatibility? Did the reasons cited by women come under valid grounds provided for under secular law? As grounds for separation as to property, the courts accepted squandering of property and insanity of the husband and, as grounds for separation as to bed and board and as to property, cruelty and mistreatment, the fact that the husband was insane and flew into 'rages,' and physical abuse and threats. Although there may have been other, underlying problems, the allegations in these categories – alcoholism, mistreatment, and family irresponsibility – were confirmed by witnesses, who were, in many cases, neighbours of the couple. The charges were usually interrelated, especially in cases involving separation as to bed and board and as to property.

A plaintiff seeking a separation did not plead adultery as a cause. Secular law at that time was opposed to a woman pleading her husband's adultery.[45] In our research, we found only four references to 'other women.' In one such reference, a witness stated: 'I have known Mr. St-Aubin for about eleven years and for the past four or five years his behaviour has been rather disgraceful. He chases after women and he drinks.'[46]

In the case of alcohol, the law agreed with women that it disrupted family life, since habitual drinking usually meant spending time in bars, debauchery, and gambling. One witness testified that 'the said Ledoux is completely dissolute,' that he had very often seen him drunk, and that, moreover, he was not in his right mind and was going mad.[47] Another witness stated that on three or four occasions he had seen a man named Buisson (whose wife was seeking a separation) 'pass by his house fully clothed and return without his clothes or shoes on, and the rumour was that he sold his clothes in order to drink.'[48] The behaviour (misconduct) of a husband described as violent, disturbed, and given to excess was bound to interfere with the economic stability of the conjugal unit and lead to poverty and violence. How important was alcohol abuse compared to other grounds for complaints by women? Although alcoholism was not the main cause of separation, it was often the catalyst, since it usually resulted in family irresponsibility and cruelty. Alcohol is mentioned in 16.8 per cent of the cases (25 references). In one case, Etiennette Alton's husband asked her for money to buy wine. When she refused, he hit her with a stick to express his displeasure.[49]

Often, or, to be more precise, in 23.5 per cent of cases (35 references), women who applied for separation as to bed and board and as to property complained of being physically abused by their spouses. Marie Boucher said that her husband, Nicolas Vernet, severely abused her. Her evidence was supported by witnesses who stated that she had to leave her house at night to escape his beatings.[50] Women were not the only victims of male violence in families; children too were physically abused. One witness at a hearing said that he 'heard [people say] that when the said Buisson was drunk he would beat his wife and children so badly they had to leave the house,' adding that he 'saw them come out crying and complaining of their plight.'[51]

Under the *ancien régime*, a husband had a right, albeit limited, of correction over his wife. It was accepted that just as a father was entitled to discipline his children, a husband was entitled to inflict corporal punishment on his wife, since legally a woman was considered a child. However, the society of the time did impose some restrictions on the husband's right of correction. To begin with, the punishment had to be justified by the wife's behaviour, but even then, it could not go beyond certain limits. In general, husbands were allowed to hit their wives so long as they did not use sharp or blunt instruments or cause any injuries. Wife-battering was an art and men who did not want to be seen in a bad light by those around them were obliged to follow certain rules.

They had to avoid hitting any sensitive area or vital organ, such as the head, breasts, or stomach; slaps, jabs, kicks, and punches on the backside were permissible provided they did not leave lasting marks.[52]

In the eighteenth century, the husband's customary right of correction over his wife gradually disappeared. In *Habitants et marchands de Montréal*, Louise Dechêne notes that there were no proceedings concerning spousal violence in the seventeenth century.[53] We found references to physical abuse in only nine of the applications for separation as to bed and board and as to property brought in the seventeenth century, but thirty-three such references in the applications brought in the eighteenth century. Moreover, the number of applications for separation as to bed and board and as to property more than tripled during that time. Does this mean that women and others in Canadian society were becoming less and less tolerant of abuse as the century progressed? While the figures seem to lead to that conclusion, the increase in both the population and the number of marriages during the eighteenth century should also be taken into account. Alain Lottin notes that in France, in the Officialité de Cambrai, separation as to bed and board was more common in the second third of the eighteenth century (1737–74) than in the first third (1710–36).[54] Jean-Louis Flandrin confirms that wife-battering could no longer be justified as 'a duty to correct, which disappeared gradually' during the eighteenth century.[55] However, canon law continued to assert that 'a wife is subject to correction on the part of her husband.'[56] In Canada, society still appeared to tolerate limited use of that right. For example, the royal judges in Montreal were far from offended by the paradoxical explanation offered by two husbands as to why they had beaten their wives. One, whose wife was on trial for assault, said he had done it to show that 'he was opposed to all violence,'[57] while the other, whose wife was on trial for theft, claimed he had done it to cure her of stealing.[58]

Separation applications were brought by women from all social levels. However, women who applied for separation as to property only were not typical: they seem to have been better educated and more self-assertive than those who applied for separation as to bed and board. In many cases, they were women who looked after their husbands' business affairs when they were away or who were in business with their husbands. In general, as the wives of businessmen, merchants, or civil or military officers, they were members of the upper class. Most women who applied for separations as to bed and board, in contrast, were the wives of artisans and tradesmen and were therefore, as in France and

New England at that time, regarded as members of the middle classes.[59] It should also be noted that separation as to bed and board was generally considered an extreme solution and, as indicated by the figures quoted above, it was fairly rare.

At hearings concerning separation as to bed and board, a husband accused by his wife of beating her defended himself by claiming his right of correction. In one case, a husband was indignant with his wife for complaining that he had struck her, saying that he 'reprimanded her only when she deserved it.'[60] In another case a husband pointed out that he had never abused his wife except 'when she made him lose his temper and drove him to it,' adding that although his wife appeared 'to have a few bruises today' on her face and body, it was 'not because he mistreated her,' since he had merely given her 'what she asked for – a slap across the face.'[61] Clearly then, in the eyes of husbands and society in general, the use of physical force could be justified on the grounds of the wife's conduct. For example, Françoise Duval, known as *Vinaigre*, stated that her husband 'beat her senseless' when he learned that she had prostituted herself with the skipper of a small boat in the port of Montreal.[62] Furthermore, if a woman who complained of physical abuse wanted to obtain a separation, she had to prove to the royal judges that her husband had indeed beaten her excessively. For example, Etiennette Alton had to produce a report signed by a surgeon as proof of 'the condition of the illness or injury' she claimed she suffered following abusive treatment at the hands of her husband.[63]

Limited violence was tolerated socially and did not lead to assault charges or to applications for separation as to bed and board on the grounds of abuse. However, neither a wife nor society could continue to condone abuse that went beyond the permissible limits, as illustrated by the case of Françoise Petit-Boismorel. Françoise, who apparently did not wish to separate from her husband but rather to stop him from beating her, laid a complaint of assault before the royal jurisdiction of Montreal against her husband, the royal bailiff Antoine Puyperoux, Sieur de la Fosse. Fleury Deschambault, the judge before whom the couple appeared, settled the case by ordering temporary separation as to bed and board. However, some time later Françoise and Antoine resumed living together and he began beating her again. This time, Françoise's brother, Etienne, had to intervene forcefully to stop Puyperoux from hitting his sister, who, the bailiff claimed, had failed to arrange for firewood to be brought into the house.[64] We do not know how this case was resolved.

In cases of separation as to bed and board and as to property where mistreatment was alleged, witnesses who testified at hearings before royal judges confirmed the women's allegations. They stated that certain men were known to beat their wives and leave their children stark naked,[65] or that on several occasions they had seen the men lose their tempers and physically attack their wives, hitting them with sticks and kicking and punching them.[66] In the case of Jeanne Duplessis Faber, wife of Sieur Bailly de Baieuville, an officer in the Troupes de la Marine, the witnesses were Jean-Baptiste Petit, a Montreal carpenter, and his wife, who lived in the apartment next door to the Baieuvilles. They stated at the hearing that they had been awakened at night by noise from the Baieuville apartment and that, when they listened through the partition-wall, they could hear Madame Baieuville crying and carrying on and saying to her husband, 'Leave me alone, I beg you, you'll kill me, I'll scream.' But Baieuville, jealous of the attention his wife had shown a visiting wig-maker, continued to beat her. She moaned and groaned and pleaded with him in a low voice, saying 'Leave me alone, please, I won't do it anymore. I'm sorry.' The Petits told the judge that the woman endured this abuse 'from eleven o'clock in the evening until about three or four o'clock the next morning.' They said that the following day they noticed she had 'scratches' on her face.[67]

When a man beat his wife at night to the point that her cries disturbed the neighbours, his violence towards her was regarded as serious enough to warrant intervention. Witnesses at hearings concerning applications for separation often described how they and others stepped in when the husband was beating his wife. In some cases, they managed to make him stop hitting her.[68] In other instances, the man continued to punch his wife and 'refused to listen to reason from neighbours or passers-by who witnessed the event.'[69] In addition, witnesses' statements were often tinged with indignation at the husband's disgraceful treatment of his wife and children. In their eyes, it seemed, there was no excuse for the husband's excessive physical abuse.

Family members also came to the aid of their daughters or sisters. Indeed, sometimes the father and/or brother of the victim took the initiative and became involved in the couple's quarrels. Such was the case of Marie-Renée Gauthier de Varennes, who had been abused for a number of years by her husband Timothée Sylvain, the King's doctor in Montreal. Her father, Pierre Gauthier de La Vérendrye, remonstrated with the husband a few times, but nothing came of it; Sylvain continued to beat his wife. Finally, Pierre Gauthier de La Vérendrye had had enough. With the help of his son, Gauthier de Varennes, he removed his daughter from the marital home and brought her back to live under the paternal roof. Ultimately, Marie-Renée was granted a separation as to bed and board by the royal court of the jurisdiction of Montreal.[70] Similarly, when Antoine Puyperoux, in the case mentioned above, beat his wife, Françoise Petit-Boismorel, her brother Etienne came to her aid.[71]

Clearly, married couples and their children did not live in isolation. In towns, they were constantly under observation, watched by people who lived in the same house, by their parents, by their neighbours, by the parish priest. They were continually aware of the image they projected, and they tried to appear dignified and honourable because their reputation and credibility in the community depended very much on how others saw them.[72] There was almost no privacy in the modern sense of the word. Their neighbours knew everything about them. They lived on the same street as people who might be called to give evidence about them. For instance, one witness was introduced as follows: 'For a year now he has been living in the aforementioned street practically opposite the house [of Marie-Madeleine Darragon and Julien Delière, dit Bonvouloir].'[73] In the towns, there was often nothing more than a thin partition-wall separating the residence of the witness from the residence of the defendant. As Jean-Baptiste stated at the hearing mentioned above, his wife awakened him and told him to 'listen to that Sieur Baieuville beating his wife,' which he did, through the partition.[74] In another case, the witness worked in the shop adjoining the complainant's house.[75] Thus, a couple's relationship was subject to constant scrutiny by the community, so that when a husband behaved badly towards his wife, either because he mistreated her or because of excessive spending, the whole neighbourhood knew about it. According to one witness, 'what the supplicant alleges is only too well-known by the public,'[76] while another stated that several people had been witness to the couple's marital disputes.[77]

Spousal violence was of concern to the whole community. The conduct of a man who 'held his wife by the hair' was 'upsetting to the whole lower town,' according to testimony at a hearing for separation as to bed and board.[78] A dispute between husband and wife created a scandal and cast a shadow over the idealized picture of marriage which the elite hoped to promote. For example, one witness in a case testified: 'her husband beat her [his wife] every day without fail in full view of everyone – the more affluent people of the town were scandalized.'[79]

Every now and then spousal violence led one of the partners to commit murder. In 1751, Nicolas de Launay, dit Lacroix, who lived in Pointe-à-la-Caille near Quebec City, killed his wife with an axe.[80] Marie-Josephe Ethier killed her husband in the same way, and then ran off with her lover.[81] In this last case, it appears the adulterer was behind the husband's murder. Unfortunately, the reason for the first murder is unknown. Except for one involuntary homicide where a husband killed his wife accidentally – his gun was 'at rest under his arm' when it accidentally discharged[82] – these were the only two cases of family-related murder we found.

Nearly one-third of husbands (30 per cent or 49 out of 163) whose wives applied for separation intervened during the legal proceedings. In cases of applications for separation as to bed and board and as to property or as to property only, attitudes varied. Some men refused to grant their wives permission to proceed, denied the facts presented in the complaint, as we have seen, or categorically refused and opposed the requested separation. Others reprimanded the witnesses. In the end, a few asked their wives to come back home, and the rest agreed to the separation.

Whether men did or did not agree to separations, their reactions described what they expected of their wives. A wife should not meddle in business matters without her husband's permission but should help him maintain and increase his property. A wife is obliged to behave according to her station and to abstain from foolish expenditures beyond her social class. One husband said he needed his wife with him 'in order to keep his expenses down.'[83] In addition, it is a wife's job 'to take good care of her family and to make sure her children are well brought up.'[84] The ideal wife was a virtuous woman whose behaviour was constant and beyond reproach. According to Msgr Laval, a woman should 'love her husband sincerely and affectionately, sharing all his concerns, both temporal and spiritual; always make an effort to win him over to God through her prayers, her good example, and other appropriate means; obey him, treat him with respect and gentleness, and be patient with him when he makes mistakes or is in a bad mood.'[85]

DECISIONS RENDERED

The decisions of the royal judges were influenced by the expectations of both wives and society and also by the role that women were tra-

TABLE 3
Results of Separation Hearings

Separation	As to property		As to bed and board		Total	
Granted	50	(38.5%)	16	(48.5%)	66	(40.5%)
Denied	1	(0.7%)	6	(18.2%)	7	(4.3%)
Unknown	79	(60.8%)	11	(33.3%)	90	(55.2%)
Total	130	(79.8%)	33	(20.2%)	163	(100%)

ditionally expected to play. The number of decisions we were able to find (73 out of 163, or 45 per cent – see table 3) is too small to enable us to confirm whether there was in fact a trend towards adopting more modern attitudes – for instance, making separations easier to obtain and reducing the level of toleration of violence and irresponsible behaviour on the part of the husband. Separation applications were denied in cases where the applicant failed to present enough evidence to prove the allegations against her husband or where the applicant's relatives were found to have been excessively involved in the disagreement. Of the fifty-one applications for separation as to property where the results are known, only one application was denied, but of the twenty-two applications for separation as to bed and board and as to property where the results are known, six (27.3 per cent) were not granted. The State, like the Church, seems to have been much more cautious about agreeing to separation as to bed and board. A. Lottin emphasizes that in laws were 'if not the cause, [at least] the catalyst of conflicts which led to separation.'[86] In some cases, husband and wife agreed to stop the proceedings, rent a house, and resume living together away from their parents. Relatives and family solidarity clearly interfered with marital relationships. Women often went back to live with their parents to avoid mistreatment. When relatives became too deeply enmeshed in a couple's household they were liable to exacerbate disagreements between husbands and wives. In any case, that was the opinion of the public prosecutor and it is also what the documents tell us.

Separation applications were also denied in cases where a woman criticized her husband's behaviour in ways considered unacceptable. If a woman protested against her husband's attacks in an aggressive manner, verbally or otherwise, she was not granted a separation. For example, 'the wife of the said Lenclus was just as violent towards her husband as he was capable of behaving towards her.' The result was that 'the woman Lapierre was ordered to go back to her husband, and both parties were directed to live together amicably or face a prison sentence.'[87]

If a woman admitted abusing her husband, she no longer deserved permission to separate. The wife of one defendant 'was in an extraordinary rage, fuming and swearing like a sailor, saying every stupid thing imaginable against her husband and her children.'[88] A woman who did not devote herself to helping her husband manage 'the family finances' and who squandered the community property could be sure her separation application would be denied, as happened in the case of the wife of a certain Mr Demers. 'It is really too bad about Demers,' said a witness at the hearing. 'He was a decent man and things were going well for him until he married that woman – he has been in financial trouble ever since.'[89]

The prosecutor would dismiss an application from a wife who caused quarrels, who provoked the husband, or who behaved improperly. In one case, a witness said, 'the arguments were always started by Marie Vendezeque and she was the cause of all the unpleasantness in the household.'[90] In such cases, the applicant would be prohibited 'from leaving the house or going anywhere without her husband's permission.'[91] In many cases where separation as to bed and board or as to property was denied, the wife was ordered to 'go back and live with her husband, and he was directed to treat her as a good husband should.'[92] Thus, if a woman wanted to apply for a separation, her conduct had to be beyond reproach. If she had ever given her husband the slightest reason to mistreat her, her application would be denied. She had to show that she had been patient, that she had not retaliated when her husband abused her, and that she had always behaved properly regardless of the circumstances. Consequently, separations were granted only in cases where the evidence was irrefutable and the grounds were very serious.

Most of the time, when the courts granted a separation they did so in order to maintain the social and economic function of the marriage and the family; that is, their purpose was to protect the property necessary for the family's survival. Protecting the rights of the wife as a person was often incidental. The courts did not grant separations as to bed and board and as to property except in extreme cases, because 'the separation of spouses breaks up the estate, disrupts lines of descent, and weakens the social order.'[93]

ADULTERY

In this context, 'the obligations of a husband and wife were to live together in holy matrimony,' each with a role to play according to the example set by Joseph and the Blessed Virgin.[94] Anything that might endanger the union of man and wife and its corollary, the family, was severely punished. Adultery, for instance, was regarded as a threat to the unity of both the couple and the family and to its principal function, the perpetuation and preservation of the human race. In dealing with this offence, society adopted a double standard.[95] A woman was not entitled to lodge a complaint if her husband committed adultery. Legally, she was considered a minor and therefore had no right of recrimination against her husband who, in the eyes of the law, was her superior. A man, in contrast, was entitled to sue his wife for the same offence. A woman who was found guilty of the crime of adultery was usually ordered to apologize to her husband, in addition to being deprived of her dower. Generally, the judge allowed the cuckolded husband various options with respect to the physical punishment of his wife. He could have her put away in a convent at his expense, send her to live with her family, send her back to France if she was an immigrant, or simply take her back. A man was also entitled to apply for separation as to bed and board on the ground of adultery. Women, however, were pro-hibited under civil law from applying for separation on the ground of adultery alone. A woman's application would be allowed by the court only if she could cite other grounds such as those discussed above. In any case, women did not seek redress in the courts except as a last resort. A woman tended to tolerate her husband's bad behaviour for a long time before turning to the courts, because to expose her situation publicly was to admit her marriage was a failure. The lover of a woman found guilty of adultery was usually banished from the colony, fined, and ordered to pay damages and interest to the husband. In addition, the courts frequently required lovers to provide care and support for any children born as a result of such relationships. According to Sara Matthews Grieco, 'discrimination in favour of the husband in adultery cases was based, in particular, on the value attached to the chastity of women in a patriarchal society, where property circulated mainly in the hands of men' and women were considered 'property which declined in value when used by someone other than the legitimate owner.'[96]

In our study of the case law, we found eight cases of adultery in Can-ada in the seventeenth century (1650–99), but only one in the eighteenth.

That trial involved Geneviève Maillet, her husband Pierre Roy, a sailor, and Pierre Sillon, known as Larochelle, also a sailor. As soon as he arrived in the colony, Pierre Sillon, aided and abetted by Geneviève Maillet, began passing himself off as Pierre Roy, Geneviève's husband. For a time, the pair succeeded in their subterfuge, living together openly and publicly for three months. However, when Sillon decided to go off on a fishing expedition without leaving any money behind for his mistress, who was pregnant with his child, the truth came out. Geneviève lost no time in coming before the intendant, Hocquart, claiming that 'her husband Pierre Roy known as Larochelle' had promised to pay her forty pounds out of his wages. When Pierre Sillon was pressed by the authorities to pay that sum, he admitted that although he and Geneviève Maillet had lived together as 'man and wife,' he was not her husband. The two lovers were tried for 'having abused the sanctity of marriage by living together publicly as husband and wife in an adulterous relationship.' They were found guilty. The court ordered Geneviève and Pierre to make an *amende honorable* in front of the 'main gates of the cathedral' and sentenced them both to be flogged 'in the usual public places and localities' in Quebec City. In addition, the court ordered that Madame Maillet be incarcerated in the Hôpital Général de Québec for three years. As for Pierre Sillon, he was banished from the colony for three years and ordered to take into his care – that is, 'feed, support and raise in the Catholic religion' at his expense – the child Geneviève was carrying.[97]

It should be pointed out, however, that there were probably numerous instances of adultery between voyageurs and Amerindians in the fur-trading areas. A white man travelling in the Great Lakes Heartland found it advisable in terms of survival to have an Amerindian woman at his side who could act as an interpreter and guide, prepare the skins, and so on. Voyageurs and traders often scandalized the missionaries by marrying 'according to the custom of the country,' that is, in accordance with Amerindian custom. An Amerindian common law wife, following her traditions, stayed in her marriage as long as her husband remained in the trading areas. When her white spouse returned to Canada's colony, she took the Métis children he had left behind and returned to live with her tribe.[98] The Canadian justice system never dealt with such cases of bigamy or adultery. Neither the justice system nor the colonial society of the time saw the Amerindians as a threat to the institution of the family, since the voyageurs usually came back to take care of their families in the colony.

Indeed, we found only one bigamy case in the eighteenth century. This is surprising in view of the fact that in the colony at that time it was extremely easy for a European to deceive the authorities into thinking he was free to marry. Being far away from his native country and not required, as he would have been in France, to produce papers regarding his civil status, an immigrant merely had to assert that he had not been married in France and, if necessary, to name a few witnesses currently in Canada who had known him in the mother country.[99] Although Robert-Lionel Séguin counted eight cases of bigamy in the seventeenth century, that number can be explained by the fact that the earlier period saw a greater influx of immigrants.[100]

The only bigamy case in the eighteenth century involved Jean-Julien Mainguy, dit Duplessis, who was originally from France. In 1726, in Charlesbourg, he married Marie-Josephe Valade, even though he was still bound to one Julienne Le Tessier, whom he had married in France in 1717 in a religious ceremony. Duplessis' Canadian wife had had three children by him by the time the bigamy was discovered and the marriage annulled.[101] There is no record of what became of the bigamist. Perhaps the reason why there were so few bigamy cases is that the men were far away from their mother country and the wives they had abandoned in France had no way of knowing where their husbands were.

Living in a consensual union was another crime which was seen as a possible threat to the institution of marriage in New France. Generally speaking, Canadian society was tolerant of common law relationships It was understood that in most cases people lived in such relationships because the authorities, as a result of parental opposition, refused to give them permission to marry. Parents did not want their child to marry into a family which was socially inferior or did not have a good reputation. Robert-Lionel Séguin found six instances of couples living common law in the seventeenth century.[102] In the eighteenth century, we found only two. One case involved Jean-Baptiste Joubert and Geneviève Gendron. The parish priest at Sault-Saint-Louis would not marry them because of the opposition of Joubert's parents, who claimed that Geneviève was 'an immoral girl who had just given birth to a baby who was not their son's child' and that her family was disreputable too. Indeed, in 1734, one of Geneviève's sisters, Marie-Anne, had been sentenced to be hanged for the murder of her newborn child. Ultimately, in the face of the young couple's determination and their *mariage à la gaumine* at the parish church in Montreal in 1740,[103] the priest from Châteaugay married them on 18 January 1741.[104]

FAMILY REPUTATION AND FAMILY HONOUR

As the Joubert-Gendron case shows, a family's honour and reputation within its social circle was of paramount importance and had to be defended at all costs. According to Arlette Farge, under the *ancien régime* 'honour was considered as essential an asset as life itself and had to be defended by any means necessary.'[105] In New France, where this concept of honour was accepted as a given, it formed the basis of an entire social system which relied, in particular, on the social impact of reputation and public gossip.[106] Everyone was always judging everyone else. They divided each other into two groups – those who had a good name and were respected in the community and those who 'were not worth much,' such as the itinerant schoolteacher Jean-Baptiste Caron. Sent to New France by order of the king for smuggling salt, Caron was subsequently accused in the colony of stealing clothes.[107] In criminal trials, judges often questioned witnesses about the accused's reputation, and the witnesses answered by telling the court whether the person was or was not well thought of within his or her social circle. For example, in one case a witness testified that the accused was known as 'a very honest man' and that if he had been a 'good-for-nothing,' he (the witness) would not have had anything to do with him, while in another case a witness stated that the accused 'did not have a good reputation.'[108]

New France was basically an oral society, a place where the spoken word reigned supreme. People could measure their status, recognition, and esteem in the community by what others said about them. There was no question but that words were a powerful tool for regulating behaviour. 'Public gossip' defined a person's honour and reputation, creating perceptions which could only be overcome by the most overwhelming evidence. It was very difficult to convince people that men and women in their neighbourhood whom they had previously respected were disreputable, just as it was almost impossible to rehabilitate a bad reputation. The following is a case in point. In the Gouriaux, Duval, and Dumesnil families, both the men and the women had on several occasions been found guilty of stealing. In addition, the women were referred to as 'floozies [women of little virtue] who will sleep with anybody.' Those families were marked, and no other family would associate with them except for those of similar ill repute. It was said of the Gouriaux family at the time that its members were 'reputed to be guilty of all sorts of vices, including stealing and other shenanigans,' and that they 'have always had a bad reputation.'[109]

In such a climate, any comment that was offensive, defamatory, or even just evasive could have a disastrous effect on a person's reputation. Questioning the virginity or the sexual honesty of a woman was an attack both on the woman herself and on any man associated with her. Accordingly, the most common insult against a woman was the epithet 'whore' or any of its variations, such as 'tart,' 'hooker,' 'floozie,' or 'loose woman.'[110] A woman's honour was based essentially on sexuality (pre-marital virginity and conjugal fidelity) and on motherhood,[111] and one of the primary duties of the husband and father was to defend the honour and reputation of 'his' women and his family. For instance, Antoine Poudret Jr, a baker, took on the role of defender of female honour when he assaulted the master mason, Jean-Baptiste Payette known as St-Amour, for calling his wife a 'bloody whore.'[112] In some cases, fathers went to court to claim compensation when a daughter's virginity was called into question. In July 1714, Henry Delaunay, master wheelwright, appeared before Rouer D'Artigny, a judge at the Prévôté de Québec, to ask that the honour and reputation of his daughter Barbe be 'repaired' following statements made in public by Jean-Baptiste La Grange dit Tou-louse, a domestic at the Hôtel-Dieu de Québec, to the effect that he had seen Barbe Delaunay with a man in a field 'in an indecent posture committing the crime of fornication.'[113] There were also assault cases where the whole family banded together to avenge the honour of the women of the clan, as in the case of Charles Leblanc of Côte St Michel near Montreal. Charles, his wife, and their two sons and two daughters all attacked the innkeeper Pierre Drouin, hitting him on the head with sticks, in revenge for his having insulted them by suggesting to one Joseph Roger, a lumberjack who was in love with one of Charles' daughters, Marie-Suzanne, that 'if he wanted to get her he should screw her.'[114]

The use of gossip to malign reputations and spread rumours was probably the most common form of self-regulation in Canada at that time. If a victim wanted to repair the damage to his reputation, he could always take matters into his own hands. There were more coercive forms of social control as well. One deterrent used to deal with flagrant breaches of established rules was, of course, to bring people before the courts. Another was the ritual of humiliation known as the charivari, where offenders were subjected to ridicule and mild forms of perse-cution. The charivari was a shrill musical parody organized by young people to show community disapproval in cases where a widow or wid-ower remarried too soon following the death of a spouse or where there was too big an age difference between husband and wife. The cacophony of sound which characterized these raucous events echoed the social disorder which was being condemned. A group of young people would get together, go to the house of the newly married couple, and 'serenade' them with mockery and insults. The performance would be repeated every evening until the couple agreed to buy some peace and quiet by giving money, food, or drink to the 'musicians.' An event of this nature occurred in Montreal in December 1717, following the marriage in late November of Pierre Chartier, a forty-seven-year-old bachelor and merchant, to twenty-four-year-old Catherine Catin. A group of young men, resentful at having been done out of a young woman their age by an 'old geezer,' expressed their disapproval by holding a charivari near the merchant's house. The newlyweds refused to pay them, so the 'musicians' came back every evening for over a month to 'taunt' the couple, ultimately forcing their way into the house. This last incident so provoked the husband that he had the principal assailants charged with verbal and physical abuse.[115]

CONCLUSION

In conclusion, it is clear that the men and women of New France were bound by the Church, the State, and society. The Church and the State, who had the power to grant or refuse permission for couples to separate, exercised scrutiny and control over the lives of married couples. Both Church and State intended by their interventions (laws, instructions, regulations) to protect the stability of the couple and the family, at that time the natural environment in which individuals spent the most essential part of their lives. The community, in particular neighbours, also watched what was going on in peoples' homes. They saw to it that married couples conformed to prevailing social and religious values. When scandals erupted or people behaved in a disgraceful manner, neighbours intervened to help put straying couples back on the right path.

The influence of the *ancien régime* in New France led to a society where married couples and families were always watching each other. Scrutiny by neighbours and gossip elicited by inappropriate behaviour constituted a first line of defence against disorder. It is important also to remember that for the popular classes – labourers, artisans, shopkeepers, and the like – defending the honour of their families in conflicts involving such issues as assault, petty theft, and deception was not only a means of self-defence and assertion, but an opportunity for self-affirmation.[116] It was only when gossip proved ineffective that society turned to more elaborate forms of control. Generally, people saw the courts as a last resort and went to great lengths to avoid that recourse. Under the social system of New France in the seventeenth and eighteenth centuries, compromise and self-regulation were considered preferable to public punishment.

NOTES

1 P. Ariès *L'enfant et la vie familiale sous l'Ancien Régime* (Paris: Seuil 1973) and 'La famille, hier et aujourd'hui' *Contrepoint* 11 (1973) 89–97; A. Armengaud *La famille et l'enfant en France et en Angleterre du XVIe au XVIIe siècle: Aspects démographiques* (Paris: SEDES 1975); D. Blake Smith 'The Study of the Family in Early America: Trends, Problems and Prospects' *The Family in Early America* 34 (1982) 3–28; A. Colomp *La maison du père* (Paris: PUF 1983). See also the special issues of *Annales Economie Société Civilisation* (hereafter *AESC*) (1972) and of *Revue d'histoire de l'Amérique française* (hereafter *RHAF*) 39 (1985) on the family and society; T.K. Kareven 'The History of the Family as an Interdisciplinary Field' *Journal of Interdisciplinary History* 2 (1971) 399–414; J. Parr, ed. *Childhood and Family in Canadian History* (Toronto: McClelland and Stewart 1982).

2 G. Poulin *Problèmes de la famille canadienne-française* (Quebec: PUL 1952) 9–27

3 J. Boucher and A. Morel *Livre du centenaire du Code civil: Le droit dans la vie familiale* 2 vols. (Montreal: PUM 1970)

4 J. Henripin *La population canadienne au début du XVIIIe siècle: Nuptialité, fécondité, mortalité infantile* (Paris: PUF 1954); H. Charbonneau *Vie et mort de nos ancêtres: Etude démographique* (Montreal: PUM 1975); M. Trudel *Montréal: La formation d'une société* (Montreal: Fides 1976) and *La Seigneurie des Cent-Associés* (Montreal: Fides 1983). The last devotes a chapter to the colonial family, describing its composition and structures in quantitative terms. Only L. Dechêne *Habitants et marchands de Montréal au XVIIe siècle* (Montreal and Paris: Plon 1974), after examining the composition of the households and the legal aspects which governed them, deals with the issue of family attitudes and behaviour patterns. J.F. Bosher 'The Family in New France' in R.D. Frances and D.B. Smith, eds. *Readings in Canadian History: Pre-Confederation* (Toronto: Holt, Rinehart and Winston 1986) 101–11 presents a general synthesis of this issue. The Collectif Clio *L'histoire des femmes au Québec depuis quatre siècles* (Montreal: Quinze 1982) also deals with the family from these perspectives, but puts more emphasis on the role of the woman within the family. The more re-

cent research, which has grown out of the fertile ground provided by demography, anthropology, and sociology and which illustrates the interest generated by the family in New France since 1980, should also be mentioned. See M.-A. Cliche 'Filles-mères, familles et société sous le régime français' *Histoire sociale – Social History* 21 (1988) 39–69 and 'L'infanticide dans la région de Québec, 1660–1969' *RHAF* 44 (1990) 31–59; D. Gauvreau 'Nuptialité et catégories professionelles à Québec pendant le régime français' *Sociologie et société* 19 (1987) 25–35, and 'À propos de la mise en nourrice à Québec pendant le régime français' *RHAF* 41 (1987) 53–61; H. Laforce *Histoire de la sage-femme dans la région de Québec* (Quebec: Institut québécois de recherche sur la culture 1985); J. Mathieu et al. 'Les alliances matrimoniales exogames dans le gouvernment de Québec, 1700–1760' *RHAF* 35 (1985) 3–32. We would also point out the many works in historical demography which have increased our knowledge about the family of that era: see especially H. Charbonneau et al. *Naissance d'une population: Les Français établis au Canada au XVIIe siècle* (Paris and Montreal: Presses universitaires de France and Presses de l'Université de Montréal 1987).

5 A. Lachance *Crimes et criminels en Nouvelle-France* (Montreal: Boréal 1984) 17–18

6 We examined the court documents of the royal tribunals of Trois Rivières, Quebec, and Montreal from 1668 to 1760.

7 Although the notarial archives have not been examined in a systematic manner, research on separations before a notary enables us to assess the importance of this phenomenon.

8 National Archives of Quebec (hereafter ANQ), Montreal, Pièces judiciaires, 7 July 1740

9 ANQ, Montreal, Greffe du notaire Gervais Hodiesme, minute 3576, 3 July 1760

10 Diderot says that 'voluntary separations are not recognized' and that 'every separation as to property and as to bed and board or even just as to property ... must be ordered by a court having full knowledge of the facts': *Encyclopédie* ... 36 vols. (Geneva: Pellet 1777–9) vol. 8: 675 and 30: 827.

11 Nothing remains of the files of the Officialité du régime français. On the subject of the jurisdiction of the Officialité see A. Corvisier *Sources et méthodes en histoire sociale* (Paris: Société d'Enseignement supérieur 1980) and A. Lottin 'Vie et mort du couple; difficultés conjugales et divorces dans le nord de la France aux XVIIe et XVIIIe siècles' *XVIIe siècle* 102–3 (1974) 59. The authors agree that the *officialités* gradually lost their jurisdiction over matrimonial cases, which were increasingly heard by secular judges in the eighteenth century. We do not know what happened in New France because of the lack of documents.

12 Dechêne *Habitants et marchands* 417

13 H. Charbonneau and Y. Landry 'La politique démographique en Nouvelle-France' *Annales de démographie historique* (1979) 43–5

14 Collectif Clio *L'histoire des femmes au Québec depuis quatre siècles* (Montreal: Le Jour 1992) 91; Charbonneau *Vie et mort de nos ancêtres* 150–66

15 A. Lottin *La désunion du couple sous l'Ancien Régime: L'exemple du Nord* (Paris: Editions Universitaires 1975) 24

16 Ibid. 137. The limited number of valid reasons (formal defect, lack of consent, bigamy, failure to reach puberty, impotence, non-consummation, and kinship) certainly limited the number of applications.

17 With respect to the trend towards marriage by contract rather than by sacrament, which was reinforced in the seventeenth and eighteenth centuries, see Armengaud *La famille et l'enfant* 22–8.

18 Lottin 'Vie et mort du couple' 59–60

19 Y.-F. Zoltvany 'Esquisse de la coutume de Paris' *RHAF* 25 (1971) 368

20 C. de Ferrière *Nouveau commentaire sur la coutume de la prévôté et vicomté de Paris* (Paris: Les Libraires associés 1770) 11

21 Dechêne *Habitants et marchands* 418–19. According to Dechêne, signing a marriage contract was a 'normal procedure.' A high proportion of 'people who married had marriage contracts.'

22 Zoltvany 'Coutume de Paris' 365

23 Diderot, *Encyclopédie* 8: 671

24 C. de Ferrière *Dictionnaire de droit et de pratique* (Paris: Desaint 1762) 1: art. 225

25 De Ferrière, *Nouveau commentaire sur la coutume* 22

26 Diderot *Encyclopédie* 21: 73

27 De Ferrière *Dictionnaire de droit* 1: art. 16

28 F.-J. Cugnet *Traité abrégé des anciennes lois, coutumes et usages de la colonie du Canada* (Quebec: Brown 1775) 91

29 Boucher and Morel *Le droit dans la vie familiale* 166

30 Diderot *Encyclopédie* 8: 674

31 Separation as to bed and board always included separation as to property. In this article, the expression 'separation as to bed and board' is used, rather than the more precise term 'separation as to bed and board and as to property,' in order to lighten the text.

32 *Rituel du diocèse de Québec publié par l'ordre de Saint-Vallier, évêque de Québec,* quoted in P.-A. Leclerc 'Le mariage sous le régime français' *RHAF* 13 (1959) 395

33 Diderot *Encyclopédie* 13: 965

34 Ibid. 30: 827

35 O. Martin *Histoire de la coutume de la prévôté et vicomté de Paris* 259

36 De Ferrière *Nouveau commentaire sur la coutume* 28

37 Ibid.

38 Ibid. 259

39 Lottin *La désunion du couple* 114

40 N.-F. Cott 'Eighteenth Century Family and Social Life Revealed in Massachusetts Divorce Records' *Journal of Social History* 10 (1976) 36

41 Lottin 'Vie et mort du couple' 67

42 L. Gadoury, Y. Landry, and H. Charbonneau 'Démographie différentielle en Nouvelle-France: Villes et campagnes' *RHAF* 38 (1985) 357–78

43 ANQ (Quebec), Pièces judiciaires et notariales [hereafter PJN], Nouvelle France [hereafter NF] 25, folio 110

44 ANQ, Quebec, Prévôté: registres, 1731

45 J. Portemer 'Réflexions sur les pouvoirs de la femme selon le droit français au XVIIe siècle' *XVIIe siècle* 144 (1984) 189–202

46 ANQ, Montreal, Pièces judiciaires, 25 May 1756

47 ANQ, Montreal, Pièces judiciaires, 15 Nov. 1741

48 Ibid. 17 July 1740

49 Ibid. 1691

50 Ibid. 25 Jan. 1757

51 Ibid. 7 July 1746

52 N. Castan 'Condition féminine et violence conjugale dans la société méridionale française au XVIIIe siècle' in *Le modèle familial européen: Normes, déviances, contrôle du pouvoir* (Rome: Ecole française de Rome 1986) 181

53 Dechêne *Habitants et marchands* 439

54 Lottin 'Vie et mort du couple' 65

55 J.-L. Flandrin *Familles, parenté, maison, sexualité dans l'ancienne société* (Paris: Hachette 1976) 127

56 Diderot *Encyclopédie* 21: 73

57 ANQ, Montreal, Pièces judiciaires, Affaire Gabriel Cordier, 4–15 Dec. 1744

58 Ibid., Affaire Antoine Laurent, 15 Jan.–21 Feb. 1734

59 Sylvie Savoie, 'Les couples en difficulté aux XVIIe et XVIIIe siècles: Les demandes de séparation en Nouvelle-France' (MA thesis, University of Sherbrooke 1986), 42

60 ANQ, Quebec, Prévôté de Québec, Registre, 1735

61 ANQ, Quebec, PJN, 1012, 14 July 1734

62 ANQ, Montreal, Pièces judiciaires, 21 Feb.–10 Mar. 1756

63 Ibid. 1691

64 Ibid. 26 Mar.–13 June 1714

65 Ibid.

66 Ibid. 8 July 1755

67 Ibid. 3 Dec. 1754

68 Ibid., Affaire Gendron, 1706
69 ANQ, Quebec, NF 25, PJN 961, 1733
70 ANQ, Montreal, Pièces judiciaires, 13 Jan.–25 Feb. 1738
71 Ibid. 1 Mar. 1716
72 A. Farge and M. Foucault *Le désordre des familles: Lettres de cachet des Archives de la Bastille* (Paris: Gallimard, Julliard 1982) 35
73 ANQ, Montreal, Pièces judiciaires, 1732
74 Ibid. 29 Nov. 1754
75 Ibid. 1732
76 Ibid. 7 July 1740
77 ANQ, Quebec, NF 25, PJN 961, 1733
78 ANQ, Montreal, Pièces judiciaires, 1714
79 Ibid. 7 July 1740
80 ANQ, Quebec, NF 11–37, Registre du Conseil supérieur de Québec, vol. 37, 122v–123v; NF 14–5, Pièces détachées du Conseil supérieur, 1730–60, no. 247
81 ANQ, Montreal, Pièces judiciaires, Affaire Marie-Josephe Ethier, 29 Oct. 1746–24 Mar. 1747
82 ANQ, Quebec, NF 25, PJN 928
83 Ibid., PJN, NF 25, f. 110
84 ANQ, Montreal, Pièces judiciaires, 1706
85 H. Têtu and C.-O. Gagnon *Mandements, lettres pastorales et circulaires des évêques de Québec* (Quebec: Imprimerie A. Coté 1887) 1: 57
86 Lottin 'Vie et mort du couple' 73
87 ANQ, Quebec, PJN, NF 25, f. 961, 13 Aug. 1733
88 ANQ, Montreal, Pièces judiciaires, 1719
89 Ibid. 1719; separation as to bed and board denied
90 Ibid. 1692
91 ANQ, Quebec, Prévôté: registres, 1749
92 Diderot *Encyclopédie* 30: 828
93 L. Trenard 'Amour et mariage dans l'ancienne France' *L'information historique* 43 (1981) 80
94 J.-B. de la Croix de Chevrières de Saint-Vallier *Rituel du diocèse de Québec publié par l'ordre de Saint-Vallier, évêque de Québec* 296
95 For more on this subject see K. Thomas 'The Double Standard' *Journal of the History of Ideas* 20 (1959) 195–216.
96 S.F. Matthews Grieco 'Corps, apparence et sexualité' in G. Duby and M. Perrot, eds. *Histoire des femmes en Occident, XVIe–XVIIIe siècles* (Paris: Plon 1991) 3: 91–2
97 Intendant Hocquart to the minister, 3 Oct. 1733, Archives Nationale de

France, Colonies, C 11^A, vol. 60, f. 48–9, 117. See also *Jugements et délibérations du Conseil souverain* 3 Nov. 1668, Affaire Isabelle Alure, vol. 1, 528–30, and Affaire Marie Chauvet, 21 Jan. 1669, vol. 1, 540–2.

98 Collectif Clio *L'histoire des femmes* 101. See also S. Van Kirk 'The Custom of the Country: An Examination of Fur Trade Marriage Practices' in L.H. Thomas, ed. *Essays on Western History* (Edmonton: University of Alberta Press 1976).

99 For more on this subject see 'Le cahier des témoingages de liberté au mariage 1757–1763' in *Rapport des Archives de la province de Québec* (Quebec: National Archives 1951–3).

100 See, for example, *Jugements et délibérations du Conseil souverain* vol. 1, 769–70, and vol. 2, 52–3, and R.L. Séguin *La vie libertine en Nouvelle-France au dix-septième siècle* (Montreal: Leméac 1972) 2: 505.

101 ANQ, Quebec, NF 2-21, Ordonnances de l'intendant Hocquart, 7 and 9 Mar. 1733, vol. 21, f. 29v–30v

102 Séguin *La vie libertine* 2: 504–5

103 'Mariage à la gaumine' was a folk custom originally from France for young people who wished to marry without their parents' consent, or without a proper wedding. They would attend a regular church service and announce during the service that they regarded themselves as husband and wife. The clergy said the custom was based 'on a strict and illegitimate interpretation of the Papal ruling that marriage required the Church's blessing.' See J. Bosher 'The Family in New France' in R.D. Francis and D.B. Smith, eds. *Readings in Canadian History: Pre-Confederation* (Toronto: Holt, Rinehart and Winston 1986) 105.

104 ANQ, Montreal, Pièces judiciaires, Affaire Joubert-Gendron, 25 June–18 July 1740

105 A. Farge 'Familles: L'honneur et le secret' in Philippe Ariés and Georges Duby *L'histoire de la vie privée: De la Renaissance aux Lumières* (Paris: Seuil 1986) 3: 589

106 On this subject see S.D. Amussen 'Féminin/Masculin: Le genre dans l'Angleterre de l'époque moderne' *AESC* 2 (1985) 269–87.

107 ANQ, Quebec, NF 25, PJN 1160

108 Ibid. NF 25, PJN 1655. See also PJN 1640 and ANQ, Montreal, Pièces judiciaires, 28 Oct.–5 Nov. 1722, 22 Dec. 1728–5 Jan. 1729, 14 May–7 June 1752; ANQ, Quebec, Procédures judiciaires, Matières criminelles, vol. 4, 40–9.

109 See, for example, ANQ, Montreal, Pièces judiciaires, 2 and 7 May 1731, 21 Feb.–10 Mar. 1756, 18 Feb.–1 June 1757, 23 Feb.–12 Mar. 1753; ANQ, Quebec, NF 25, PJN, 1736.

110 A. Lachance 'Une étude de mentalité: Les injures verbales au Canada au XVIIIe siècle (1712–1748)' *RHAF* 31 (1977) 233. See also P.N. Moogk '"Thieving Buggers" and "Stupid Sluts": Insults and Popular Culture in New France' *William and Mary Quarterly* 36 (1979) 524–47.

111 N. Castan 'La criminalité familiale dans le ressort du Parlement de Toulouse, 1690–1730' in A. Abbiateci et al. *Crimes et criminalité en France, 17e–18e siècles* (Paris: A. Colin 1971) 106

112 ANQ, Montreal, Pièces judiciaires, 1–3 Apr. 1727

113 ANQ, Quebec, NF 13-1, Matières de police, 1695–1755, 100 et seq.

114 ANQ, Montreal, Pièces judiciaires, 13 Feb.–12 Apr. 1736. See also 23–30 June 1729, 14–24 Sept. 1736, and 11 Sept. 1741–15 Sept. 1742.

115 ANQ, Montreal, Pièces judiciaires, 30 Dec. 1717 and 5 Feb. 1718. Pierre Chartier and Catherine Catin were married in Montreal on 27 November 1717: C. Tanguay *Dictionnaire généalogique des familles canadiennes* (Quebec: Sénécal 1871) 3: 28. See also ANQ, Quebec, PJN 803, 1728. For more on the charivari see C. Karnoouh 'Le charivari ou l'hypothèse de la monogamie' in J. Le Goff and J.-C. Schmitt *Le Charivari* (Paris: Mouton 1981) 35 et seq. and R. Hardy 'Le charivari: Divulger et sanctionner la vie privée?' in M. Brunet and S. Gagnon, eds. *Discours et pratique de l'intime* (Quebec: Institut québécois de recherche sur la culture 1993).

116 Farge 'Familles' 601

6

Women, Crime, and Criminal Justice in Early Halifax, 1750–1800

JIM PHILLIPS

This essay is principally concerned with two aspects of the relationship among women, crime, and punishment in eighteenth-century Halifax – the treatment of female offenders by the criminal justice system and women's experience as victims of male violence. It complements another paper on female offending in this period.[1] Both papers are guided by two lines of inquiry. First, they seek to chart the broad contours of aspects of crime and punishment in one early Canadian society, to analyse rates of offending and prosecution, the prevalence and nature of violence, and the ways in which the institutions of criminal justice responded to these. In that regard this paper demonstrates, first, that female offenders were treated no less rigorously than male offenders, and second, that from the evidence on the prevalence and nature of rape and murder charges, eighteenth-century Halifax was a very dangerous place for women, a society in which they were victimized by male violence at a high rate.

In themselves crime and punishment are important subjects for the historian, and the evidence presented here tells us a good deal about early Nova Scotia. But I wish also to use the records of crime as a prism through which to analyse both male attitudes to women and the related issue of women's experience in this society. The evidence is admittedly at times circumstantial, but I will nonetheless suggest that both the response of the criminal justice system to crime committed by women and the high level of violence directed at them were the respective consequences of the particularly authoritarian and violent nature of early Halifax society. Moreover, I also argue that there were significant links between these two principal factual conclusions, for together they demonstrate that women in this time and place were subject to harsh treatment both by official agencies and by significant sectors of the male population. It is somewhat unusual to combine a study of victimization with one of treatment by the criminal justice system, and more common to analyse the latter in conjunction with patterns of female offending.[2] But while the study of female offending is important and allows us insight into their past experience, and indeed the patterns of female offending in Halifax form a necessary backdrop in this paper to their treatment by the courts, I have taken this approach precisely because these other aspects of crime and punishment show us women's experience from a different angle, from the perspective principally of male attitudes to women. The history of crime and punishment is above all else a history of the complicated intertwining of deviance, authority, and social status. Crime, like the poor, may have always been with us, but who offends, who is victimized, and how fundamentally discretionary systems of justice treat these occurrences are crucial windows through which to view a particular society. I have argued elsewhere that the ways in which the English criminal justice system operated underwent subtle but important transformations when transplanted to the unique society that was eighteenth-century Nova Scotia,[3] and this essay is also to some extent concerned with the specifics of local adaptation and the social meaning of that system.

Before I deal with the principal subjects of this paper, however, something must be said about the city of Halifax itself and about the rate and nature of female offending there. Halifax was an unusual community even when measured against the diverse settlements of the first British empire; for current purposes, two related aspects of the city's early history deserve particular explication. First, it was marked by being essentially a naval and military town. Founded in 1749 by a British government anxious to provide a strategic counterweight to the French stronghold at Louisbourg, its development continued throughout the next half century to be fundamentally influenced by the same *raison d'être*. It was crucial to British operations against the French in the Seven Years War (1756–63), it represented a loyal enclave during the American revolutionary war, it received, if it did not retain, many thousands of loyalists after 1783, and it became prominent again late in the century as Britain worked out its new relationship with its former colonies to the south and when the struggle against Napoleon took on a North American dimension. Halifax was 'a city built for war,' one with 'an ongoing military establishment ... whose presence left a clear imprint on the community.'[4] The military role of the city gave it a distinctly military 'nature.' Prominent among its public buildings were the Citadel, with its barracks for over 2000 men, other barracks and fortified batteries scattered around the city, the dockyard, and the naval and military stores and ancillary buildings.

Prominent also among its inhabitants were the soldiers and sailors who thronged the streets, especially at night. Halifax grew from a city of c. 2500 on its establishment to c. 5000 in the early 1770s to almost 9000 at the end of the century.[5] But for much of this period there were also thousands of military personnel stationed there. Their numbers fluctuated with the tides of war and British perceptions of strategic requirements, but across the period as a whole they remained a substantial presence.[6] Those in the army could, to a limited extent, have their families accompany them on peacetime service abroad,[7] but naval and military establishments also brought with them less welcome guests, the 'great Concourse of dissolute abandoned Women, followers of the Camp, Army and Navy.'[8]

In a host of other tangible and not so tangible ways did the army and navy make its mark on eighteenth-century Halifax. Throughout this period the colony's economy generally was 'dominated by war' which 'played havoc with the orderly economic development of Nova Scotia.'[9] Merchants did well during conflicts, but were less successful at other times, demand being heavily reliant on public spending. For the ordinary inhabitants shortages and high prices were frequent occurrences in the boom and bust economy. As Governor Campbell noted in 1768, in arguing against a troop reduction, 'I am afraid the misery of an approaching winter will be severely felt' for many inhabitants were dependent on 'the circulating Cash spent by the Troops.'[10] Influxes of people brought different problems; while they injected spending power into the economy they also drove up rents and other prices and created short-term dearth of essential supplies.[11] Formal events, from the occasional reception of an important visitor like Prince William to the regular Sunday observances, saw military pomp and ceremony to the fore.[12] Less formal aspects of public life were also military-dominated. Halifax's large population of soldiers, sailors, and other transients both created and revelled in the city's low life, habituating the taverns and brothels that grew up in the area around the Citadel, carousing, fighting, damaging property, and, as we shall see, on occasion raping and killing.[13]

The second, and related, significant aspect of eighteenth-century Halifax, one that derived in part but not entirely from its military aspect, was what I would term the authoritarian nature of its governance. The entire colony of Nova Scotia, which did not extend much beyond Halifax and Lunenburg before the planter migrations of the 1760s, was governed without an assembly for the first decade, and even after the establishment of representative government power continued to rest largely in the hands of the governor and his council. In the city and in the out-settlements local government was, by imperial design, the preserve of unelected justices of the peace, not that of town meeting and city council as elsewhere in the New England colonies, and the gap between the capital and those out-settlements, in knowledge, understanding, and sympathy, was large.[14]

These features represent the tangible trappings of rule by oligarchy. In addition, for many visitors and commentators the city had the less tangible but equally significant 'feel' of an authoritarian community. Policing, judging by the frequency with which the guard was called out to deal with disturbances, was largely the preserve of the military.[15] Visitors, particularly those from New England, frequently remarked on the fact that, as one put it, 'the *government* of Halifax is *arbitrary.*'[16] It was a community marked by the authorities' unwillingness to brook indiscipline. Government was fundamentally touched by a garrison *mentalité*; 'no temptation would induce ... [New Englanders] to settle in ... Halifax,' Captain Seth Jenkins told the House of Lords in 1775, because 'they believe it to be a military government.'[17]

These two related features of eighteenth-century Halifax affected the operation, if not the form, of many inherited institutions, including those of criminal justice. I have argued elsewhere that the city's Anglophile elite saw the harsh English criminal law as a necessary bulwark of authority in what was in many ways a frontier society, and that the discretionary operation of the pardon system came to reflect distinctly local, military, values.[18] So too, I would suggest, did these values crucially influence women's experience of crime and criminal justice in the city. The authoritarian nature of the community meant that female offenders were treated just as harshly as men when they found themselves before the courts, while the military domination in the city made it a violent and dangerous place for women to live. But before these topics are examined in detail, one final point needs to be made by way of introduction – that women played a relatively minor role in the city's experience of crime and punishment, as measured by the rate at which they were prosecuted in the superior criminal courts.[19] What follows

TABLE 1
Male and Female Charges – All Offences

Type of offence	Men	Women	Total	Percentage of women
Offences against the person	159	18	177	10.2
Property offences	345	84	429	19.6
Other offences	133	10	143	6.9
Total	637	112	749	14.9

is only a general overview of female offending, designed to make just three principal points.

First, prosecutions of women for the range of offences represented here – primarily homicide, rape, serious assaults, burglary, robbery, and capital and non-capital larcenies – formed only a small minority of the total – 14.9 per cent (table 1).[20] Although the practice of underreporting and some jurisdictional wrinkles may somewhat deflate the 'true' figures for female participation in crime, and although account must be taken of the fact that women were always in the minority in the city because of the presence of military personnel, the fact remains that women's crime was of very low frequency compared to that of men.[21] Indeed, while in this regard Halifax was much the same as many other early modern communities, the absolute numbers for female offenders are if anything lower than in comparable jurisdictions.[22]

Second, female crime was of a different nature than male crime, in that women were more substantially represented in property offences than in offences against the person, and within the broad sweep of property offences women were charged much more often with grand larceny, petit larceny, and receiving than with the violent and/or capital property offences such as robbery, burglary, or capital larceny.[23] Only 14 per cent (12 of 84) of the women charged with a property offence were charged capitally, compared to 40 per cent (139 of 345) of the men. This gendered nature of offending is highlighted by the fact that, as table 1 reveals, some 75 per cent of women charged were accused of a property crime, compared to just over half of the men.

The third significant aspect of female offending in the city in this period was its uneven temporal distribution. Forty-eight, or only a little less than half, of the 112 charges against women represented in table 1 were actually laid in the years up to and including 1760, the other 64

TABLE 2
Male and Female Conviction Rates – All Offences

Disposition	Men		Women	
	Number	% of cases	Number	% of cases
Convicted as charged	250	39	47	42
Convicted on a lesser charge	66	11	10	9
Not convicted*	321	50	55	49

*Includes cases where the grand jury found no bill, those where the case went to trial
and resulted in a verdict of not guilty, and those where for some reason, usually the
failure of a prosecutor to appear at trial, the charge was abandoned.

being fairly evenly spread across the remaining 40-year period.[24] This
did not mean that the ratio of female to male prosecutions in the 1750s
was entirely out of line with the period in general, for the first decade
saw generally very high rates of prosecution, although it was a little
greater, at approximately 20 per cent. Why women were so much in
the minority, why female crime was of a different nature than male,
and why it was so unevenly distributed, are all complex questions with
which I deal elsewhere.[25] For current purposes I wish only to establish
these facts as a backdrop to an investigation of the treatment of those
that did offend and in particular to make clear that serious female crime
had both a low visibility and a generally non-violent nature.

Despite their relative docility, females who deviated from the straight
and narrow do appear to have been treated as harshly by the system
as men. Although the evidence is in some respects equivocal, in general
the men who sat on juries, presided in the courts, and wielded the
reins of executive clemency displayed little conviction that women who
offended should be treated much differently than men. Beginning with
jury decisions, both those of the grand jury, which decided whether
a case should go to trial, and the petit, or trial, jury, table 2 shows
that there was essentially no difference between men and women in
the rate of conviction. The point is that there was certainly no marked
trend for leniency.

Differential treatment was apparently a feature of capital charges, although in separating them out here I render the absolute numbers very
small and the comparison of percentages less reliable as a consequence.
Nonetheless tables 3 and 4 show that while a third of men charged
capitally were convicted of the full offence, only a fifth of women were:
three of the eight accused of murder, one of four for infanticide, one

TABLE 3
Female Conviction Rates – Capital Offences

Offence	Convicted as charged	Convicted on a lesser charge	Not convicted
Murder	3	2	3
Infanticide	1	0	3
Property offences	1	1	10
Arson	0	0	2
Total	5 (19)*	3 (12)	18 (69)

*Figures in parentheses are the percentages of total cases.

TABLE 4
Male Conviction Rates – Capital Offences

Offence	Convicted as charged	Convicted on a lesser charge	Not convicted
Murder	21	9	41
Rape	6	4	13
Burglary and robbery	36	22	33
Other property offences	14	6	28
Others*	3	2	4
Total	80 (33)	43 (18)	119 (49)

*Sodomy, coining, arson, and treason

of three for burglary, and none of the eleven accused of other capital property offences (including arson). It is significant, despite the absolute low numbers, that the conviction rates for a charge of murder were roughly the same for women as for men, so the difference is represented by juries being much more willing to convict men of capital property crimes than women. Squeamishness about courting the gallows where women were accused of capital property offences seems to have been common elsewhere in this period,[26] although it should be noted that on two occasions juries did convict on grand larceny charges women who had previously been convicted of that offence and received benefit of clergy; the women were sentenced to death. There is no way of telling if the jury knew of this possible consequence, although the prosecution and the court did.[27] It should also be stressed that distaste for the gallows clearly informed jury decisions in all cases, male and female, in a criminal justice system which relied so heavily on capital punish-

TABLE 5
Male and Female Conviction Rates – Non-capital Offences

Gender/Offence	Convicted as charged	Convicted on a lesser charge	Not convicted
Women			
Property offences	36	7	27
Other offences	6	0	10
All offences	42 (49)*	7 (8)	37 (43)
Men			
Property offences	94	22	87
Other offences	76	1	115
All offences	170 (43)	23 (6)	202 (51)

*Figures in parentheses represent percentages of total cases.

ment, and that the gap between the male and female figures is not that great. Nonetheless, there was clearly some small advantage extended to women.

The gender gap in conviction rates for capital offences meant, given the approximate equality in conviction rates for all offences, that for non-capital offences women were convicted slightly more often than men. Table 5 shows that almost half the women were convicted as charged, and more than half convicted either as charged or of a lesser offence.[28] In England in the same period men were more likely to be convicted; although the gender gap was not large, the difference between England and Nova Scotia, where women were more often convicted, was quite substantial.[29]

Data on reasons for non-conviction demonstrate that prosecutors, grand jurors, and petit jurors all acted consistently in their decision-making as between the genders. Grand jurors turned back indictments of men in 10.4 per cent of all cases, of women in 11.6 per cent. Petit jurors rendered not guilty verdicts for 25 per cent of male trials, 26 per cent of female ones. For those cases in which for some reason either the grand jury or the petit jury could not do its work and the charge was abandoned, the figures were 14.9 per cent of male charges and 11.6 per cent of female ones. Again, any tenderness towards defendants on the part of prosecutors benefited men, not women. It may well have been easier for prosecutors, public or private, to bargain with accused men for restitution or service than to make such deals with women. Whatever the cause, the principal point is that the evidence from the indictment and trial process clearly demonstrates that there was no general leniency shown towards female offenders. There was a marked reluctance to bring the full force of the law against women in only one area – capital property offences. In all other areas, including women charged with murder, any gender preference that existed actually worked against women.

Another prism through which the treatment of women can be viewed is sentencing practice. In most instances there was no discretion in sentencing, especially in capital charges. The judges could elect not to brand those found guilty of a capital offence which carried benefit of clergy (grand larceny and manslaughter), but throughout this period the practice of branding those convicted of grand larceny was consistently adhered to for both men (58 of 80 cases, or 72 per cent) and women (17 of 20 cases, or 85 per cent).[30] The higher percentage for women is a little misleading because female convictions were concentrated early in the period and before branding generally became less common,[31] but the point is that judges certainly did not shrink from its imposition.[32] Nor did they spare women the lash following convictions for petit larceny, the available sentences being prison or whipping, or both. Of the 38 men convicted of petit larceny,[33] 24, or 63 per cent, were ordered to be publicly whipped; for women, the figure was 82 per cent (14 of 17). Again, the apparent harsher treatment of women is substantially the result of the female convictions being concentrated earlier in the period, before the use of prison sentences instead of whipping became more common. But as late as 1791 the court sentenced Rebecca Hunt to be whipped when she was found guilty of petit larceny.[34] Whether women were whipped as often as or more often than men, the point is that they were not sentenced to this physical punishment less frequently than men. Women were whipped privately rather than publicly from about the mid-1780s,[35] and on occasion they were able to obtain remission of the sentence,[36] but given that men too were able to achieve this,[37] it is not possible to say that any marked tenderness was shown to convicted females.

Also under the topic of sentencing we should consider the exercise of the prerogative of mercy for those convicted of a capital charge, a central feature of the eighteenth-century system and wielded in Nova Scotia by the governor.[38] Here I use a sample of all capital cases from across the colony. The vast majority were Halifax cases, but, more importantly, the decision on whether to execute or pardon was a Halifax decision, irrespective of the origin of the case, and the pardon evidence thus provides insight into the decision-making of the Halifax-based governing oligarchy. Between 1750 and 1800 exactly 100 persons were condemned to death in the courts of Nova Scotia. Of these, 8 were women, and half of them were executed. Of the 92 men, only 43, a little less than half, suffered the same fate. Although we are dealing here with a very small sample of female convicts, this was a striking rate of execution for them. In eighteenth-century England, for example, only 18 per cent of condemned women actually met their fate on the gallows.[39]

The totality of the evidence makes it abundantly clear that women were certainly not treated more leniently than men and that, in some respects, particularly in the apparent nonchalance with which the authorities dispatched female convicts to the gallows, they were treated rather harshly. This does make Halifax somewhat unusual, comparative historical work suggesting that in general women have been less liable to conviction, and certainly much less liable to execution, than men.[40]

The causes of this distinctiveness are not readily apparent; they are certainly not easily revealed by the generally opaque formal records of the criminal justice process or by any contemporary commentary on female offenders. Two possible explanations must be considered, if only for the purpose of rejecting them. First, it is unlikely that there was a widespread perception that female offending was a significant social problem, that it was seen to pose a real threat to community stability. The numbers involved were very small; indeed they were negligible from the early 1760s, for only sixty-four women were prosecuted in forty years in all offence categories, a rate of less than two a year. Thus visibility can hardly provide an explanation for the attitudes of male actors in the system.

Second, it is equally unlikely that an answer can easily be found in gender relations that were radically different than in other societies at this time. If women were afforded significantly greater status in this society, one might expect them to be saddled with concomitantly greater responsibility, including responsibility for criminal actions. But there is no real evidence that this was the case. In one or two small ways there may have been differences between Halifax and other communities in the Anglo-American world in the status of women and in the attitudes of men to women's roles,[41] but generally it is reasonable to assume (and for the most part we unfortunately only have assumptions)[42] that women in this society were no more equal than elsewhere. They lived under the control of men – husbands, fathers, and employers of domestic servants – tied to the domestic world, expected 'to put wifely duty first' with marriage and family 'the focus of their existence.'[43] As one local newspaper put it, women were made to assist men 'in the toils of life,' their proper roles being to 'preside[th] in the house,' to '[take] care of ... family ... manage the household prudently and imbue children with wisdom and goodness.'[44] Indeed, as I argue elsewhere, the very absence of women from the criminal courts serves as testament to their subordination and the effectiveness of the informal social controls that governed their lives.[45] The answer to the puzzle posed by criminal justice practices cannot be found in the general structure of gender relations.

Having rejected these explanations, it seems to me more likely that part of the answer at least must be sought in the attitudes of the men who made the decisions in the justice system, and to discover these we must look again at the nature of politics and society in eighteenth-century Halifax. I have already argued that this was an authoritarian place, and important consequences flowed from this. In particular, the criminal justice system does appear to have been used as an active arm of government policy in the search for order and discipline. Prosecution rates were comparatively very high in Halifax,[46] and, in some contrast to eighteenth-century England, local authorities put great stress on supporting public prosecution.[47] Deviants could expect little sympathy from those with discretionary power, and thus Halifax was less likely than other societies to treat any particular group of offenders leniently.

Halifax, however, treated the least deviant group among military personnel, male civilians, and women at least as harshly as it did others, and perhaps more harshly than the military. Thus to an explanation based on the general authoritarian nature of the society we might add two further points. One is that the accepted reliance on the military may have induced both an occasional and grudging acceptance of crimes committed by its members, thereby driving down the male conviction rate. I am not suggesting here a kind of conscious preference, but a sense that crimes by soldiers were somehow to be expected and thereby in some way more tolerable. Second, and I think more importantly, the women who found themselves in the criminal court were what me might call 'doubly deviant.' They not only committed crimes but, in order to do so, stepped out into the public world of men. When they did so their offences assumed an importance greater than their numbers would suggest. The disobedience of those most expected to assume subordinate roles was more troubling than that of others, such as sailors and soldiers, whose offending was more expected. In this analysis the order sought in this authoritarian society was not simply the absence or punishment of crime, but the imposition, in part, of certain gendered values. Recent research on nineteenth-century punishment strategies relating to women has argued that they were driven by a perception of the female offender as not only criminally liable but also as peculiarly morally deficient: 'they offended not only against the law, but against their ascribed social and moral roles.'[48] Halifax may provide an earlier example of this same phenomenon.

This thesis is difficult to prove, and certainly cannot be supported directly. But there are a few scraps of evidence by which we can test it. First, it is worth noting the collective identity of the offender population.[49] The vast majority of the women brought to court, especially in the 1750s, were young, single, and unattached to families. Precise ages are very rarely given, but references in the depositions of witnesses to 'a girl,' 'a young girl,' 'a young woman, servant to such and such a person,' offer consistent evidence of the youth of offenders. Case files also allow me to establish that the majority of these young women were single – seventeen of the twenty-five known cases in the first decade, for example.[50] Class status can to some extent be measured by literacy, and few of those whose statements were taken by justices of the peace were able to sign their names. Not only were the majority of offenders single women, but many also lived apart from their families – they were not daughters of households. They were frequently domestic servants, like Ann Pentenny and Margaret Bryant, while others like Mary Pinfold, Rebecca Young, Martha Welsh, Rebecca Hunt, and Sarah Ross worked as prostitutes.[51] Halifax thus appears to have contained a substantial number of young, unattached, women, separated by choice or otherwise from their own families and living on the margins of society. They found it difficult to survive in the boom and bust economy and crime was always an option. My point is that the very 'independence' of this group, let alone their criminality, was an affront to respectable society. When juries and judges were confronted with female offenders, they thought of the rejection of gendered notions of respectability represented by the class from which many offenders came as much as of the particular crime for which an individual was charged.

Perhaps the best evidence of attitudes to female deviance comes from a closer examination of the cases of those women convicted of capital offences and sentenced to death. These represent relatively rare decisions by juries to convict women on capital charges, and they also provide the evidence for the most unusual aspect of this society's treatment of deviant women – the execution of half of those condemned. Of the eight women condemned in this period, three were convicted of murder and they were all hanged. Although the rates of pardon were generally lower for murderers than for those convicted of property crimes,[52] many male murderers did escape, and one would not necessarily expect all of the women to have been executed. But there was something in the particular circumstances of at least two of these crimes that would have encouraged execution. Martha Orpin, the first woman hanged in the colony, not only stabbed her youthful male victim, the eight- or nine-year-old son of a neighbour, an 'unnatural' act, she also did so out of her home and at night, and then concealed the body for some time. Perhaps most importantly, she did all this while her husband Edward, a middling merchant who had been one of the first settlers in 1749, 'had gone up the river trading.'[53] We know little else about the case, but it does seem that this apparently respectable woman, long before she committed a crime, had been where she was not supposed to be and perhaps was doing what she was not supposed to do; her place was in the home, waiting for her husband's return. There is much less information available for the case of Mary Collins, hanged for murder in 1783. Although she was convicted with two male Collinses, only one John Collins was pardoned. This suggests that Mary had acted to some degree independently. She was certainly not able to persuade either a jury or the governor that she had been susceptible to male influence; the latter's clemency went to John, 'his former life and conduct having been well spoken of' and 'some circumstances having appeared in [his] favour' at the trial.[54]

The same interpretation would obviously account for the fate of Margaret Whippy, perhaps the most remarkable female offender of the period and the only woman condemned for a property offence who was hanged. She was a principal member, if not the leader, of a gang of burglars convicted in 1768, and while four of the men involved were pardoned Whippy and another man were not spared. Unfortunately it has proved impossible to find out much about her, but she may have come from a reasonably respectable local family.[55] In sentencing her Chief Justice Belcher made it very clear that her sex made the leading role she had played in the crime a much worse offence.[56]

The cases of women pardoned provide a substantial contrast to these. They included two women convicted of grand larceny on more than one occasion, and therefore not eligible for benefit of clergy, one case of housebreaking and one of infanticide, and at least two of those pardoned were black.[57] It has been suggested that women generally escaped the gallows in the early modern period precisely because 'on the whole [they] did not present the kind of threat to the community, to property, to life, to social order, that men presented,'[58] and these cases certainly fit that description in a way that those of Orpin and Whippy do not. Moreover, if we see 'chivalric' mercy as a technique of power that 'upholds equally the ideals of feminine frailty and masculine heroism ... [and] reaffirms the class and race privilege of the men who wield the power to protect and the option to pardon,'[59] we have excellent candidates for this in poor, black women. Pardoning all of these women allowed the authorities to display mercy while executing the others condemned the crime and the fundamental breach of the essence of good womanhood that respectable women were supposed to embody. The case of Margaret Murphy, who strangled a co-resident of a Halifax brothel in 1791 and who had to wait only a week before being hanged, does not fit this analysis so well, but there may have been additional factors in her case.[60] Overall, therefore, and even given the difficulty of making such direct connections, it is tempting to look for an explanation for the decisions to pardon or execute women in the subordinate feminine roles women were supposed to adopt but which some so obviously did not. Eighteenth-century Halifax society, generally authoritarian to start with, was willing to convict many women and to execute in particular the more respectable of those condemned and/or those whose actions were considered to have posed a significant challenge to social as well as legal authority.

The remainder of this essay analyses a different, but I believe related, aspect of women's experience with crime in eighteenth-century Halifax – their victimization in violent crime, specifically murder and rape. Like the preceding sections, I believe this can tell us much about women's experience in the city, for the risks of physical harm were surely a central aspect of that experience. This section also, in examining the responses that women as victims of violent crime, particularly rape victims, could extract from the criminal justice system, reveals something more about the attitudes of the same male decision-makers who judged female offenders.

Research on contemporary murder trends and those in the recent past demonstrates two central features of women's experience of deadly victimization: in absolute terms they constitute a minority of homicide victims, around 35 per cent in most western societies, and they are more likely to be killed by intimates than by strangers, a pattern that is distinctly different from that of men who are killed. Unfortunately there is very little evidence on whether these modern trends have also been reflected in societies in the more distant past; what evidence there is suggests that the gender gap was even greater, while unfortunately we know practically nothing about the rate of women killing by intimates.[61]

Three features of homicide in eighteenth-century Halifax stand out. First, rates were comparatively very high. Among the cases brought to court there were 62 homicide victims in these years, more than one a year.[62] It is impossible to translate this figure into a precise per capita rate, given the problem of assessing the population, but a conservative estimate might put that rate at around 16 per 100,000 population per annum.[63] In contrast, modern Canada had a rate of 2.2 per 100,000 between 1951 and 1984, the third highest rate among developed democracies and one that includes cases in which no charges were laid, which my eighteenth-century sample does not.[64] One study of eighteenth-century England, also based on cases that went to court, estimates the rate per 100,000 as slightly over 0.5 per cent between 1760 and 1802.[65] Even taking into account the difficulties of measuring such matters with precision, it is clear that Halifax during its early decades saw an exceptionally high level of personal violence.[66]

This violence, of course, affected men as well as women. But the point is that it did affect women. That is, women in eighteenth-century Halifax lived in a violent society. But they also seem to have been disproportionately affected, in comparative terms, by that violence, and that is the second significant feature of homicide in this community that I wish to highlight. Of the 44 victims of homicides committed solely by males, 31 are identifiable, and of those 31, 22 were males and 9 were females – 7 adults and 2 children.[67] Thus women constituted over a quarter of all male homicide victims. Although this is a smaller percentage than that given above for contemporary western societies, in context it appears as a comparatively high number. Women were always a distinct minority of the population, often no more than a third given the military presence. Moreover, not surprisingly that military presence dominates the homicide landscape. More than half of the male victims in male homicide cases were soldiers or sailors, mostly slain in drunken brawls between servicemen, and the 9 female victims actually represent

almost half of the total number of civilian victims (19),[68] a very substantial rate of victimization.

The third notable feature of female homicide victimization was that
killing by intimate male partners was not as prevalent as one might
expect, and certainly not the principal cause of female homicide that
it is today. One must draw such a conclusion cautiously, for the sample
of cases gets very small at this stage, but in no more than two of the
seven cases involving adult women victims was an intimate responsible.
Catherine Seidler of Dartmouth was killed by her husband Gotleib in
1771. All we know about the case is that he was a German immigrant
who required an interpreter at his trial, and was hanged for the crime.[69]
Mary Russell was killed by a spurned suitor, a context similar to wife
murder, in 1798. Thomas Bambridge, a young farmer with lands on
the outskirts of Dartmouth, was keen on Russell, but neither she nor
her family welcomed his attentions. On the evening of 27 September
Bambridge armed himself with 'a long butcher's knife' and burst into
the Russell house, and when Mary refused to speak with him he walked
up to her and stabbed her to death in front of her family. He tried
to commit suicide but succeeded only in wounding himself. Two weeks
later Bambridge was tried and convicted of murder, and a week after
that a rope completed the job that his own knife had started.[70] I am
not suggesting that these were the only cases of female victimization
by intimates; there were likely many more which did not produce prosecutions and I know of one other Nova Scotia case, committed on the
South Shore, during this period.[71] But it is significant that in a substantial majority of the known cases prosecuted in Halifax women were
killed by non-intimates.

Indeed, in the other cases women were struck down in seemingly
casual ways when they encountered men easily given to violence and
little caring of the consequences. And in none of the non-intimate cases
was a conviction recorded. Unfortunately we do not have details of a
good many of these, but those that are available show a consistent pattern. The circumstances of the death of Mary Burt in 1761 were not
untypical. While sitting by the fire one night in the downstairs parlour
of a lodging house a little water fell on Sergeant John Taylor. He went
upstairs to see who had spilled it, discovered Burt in the room above,
and came back down a few minutes later with 'his hair ... loose and
tumbled, and his finger ... bleeding.' The next morning Burt, a lodger
in the house, told the wife of her landlord that Taylor had 'wanted

to kiss her' and had been 'very rude to her and used her very ill' when she refused. Burt's mouth was still bleeding at that time, and a substantial struggle had obviously taken place, Taylor getting in a good number of blows. Over the next few days she constantly 'complained very much of her side,' and five days after the fracas with Taylor she was found dead in the street. A coroner's inquest determined that she had died 'by the abuses she received ... by a person or persons unknown,' but then the story of Taylor's assault came out. He was found not guilty. There is much more one would like to know about the case, particularly the reaction, or apparent lack of it, from others in the house, but what seems to me to be significant about this story is the crudity of the sexual violence and the casualness of the violent reaction which accompanied its rebuff.[72]

Casualness indeed seems to have marked the actions of Sergeant John Bruff in 1791. Apparently in a drunken rage, he drew his sword one night and struck at Mary Moulton, 'an infant,' hitting her a mortal blow on the head. Bruff was able to get bail before his trial, a very rare event in this period, and was charged not with murder but manslaughter. When convicted he pleaded his clergy, which was allowed, but rather than a branding he was sentenced to a fine of one shilling and twenty-four hours in prison. Life, at least Moulton's life, was cheap.[73] It was also precarious for Bridget Eacott, attacked by sailors in her home when she refused to serve them liquor on the not unreasonable grounds that it was not a tavern.[74]

On a number of occasions female deaths went entirely unprosecuted. Early in the morning of 27 December 1796, for example, carpenter John Anderson was on his way to work with his apprentice when they noticed a body lying on the snow of Citadel Hill some twenty yards from their path. Anderson investigated and 'found it to be a female person, then laying dead and in a very indecent posture, on her back, her clothes thrown up over her breasts, her lower parts entirely naked.' The area around was covered with a good many footprints. The ensuing investigation revealed that the evening before the woman, not identified although it seems fairly clear from the evidence that she was a prostitute, had been very drunk and in the company of at least two soldiers, Privates Charles Collins and Richard Murphy, who had been seen pulling her towards a disused magazine near where she was found the next morning. That was the last anybody, or at least anybody whom the justices of the peace talked to, saw of her. The soldiers identified stated that they had simply left her in the street.[75] The authorities appear to have been content to leave it at this, not caring to look further into what was at least a gang rape and possibly a murder as well, although one must concede the possibility that they had simply left her unconscious and lying in the snow in late December. This anonymous victim was one of many women, and men also, whose bodies provided silent testimony to the violence of the city but about whose deaths no other evidence was ever forthcoming.[76]

Although the number of cases on which this analysis is based is small, it does seem reasonable to conclude that there was something unique both about homicide in general in eighteenth-century Halifax and about the homicidal victimization of women in particular. Unusually high levels of deadly violence pertained in the city, and women were killed both in unusually high numbers and in unusual ways. Moreover, it should be stressed that women were not only disproportionately affected as victims by this aggressive society – they appeared in court charged with homicides less often than in other jurisdictions.[72] In addition, of the twelve homicides charged against women, at least four were infanticide cases.[78] Halifax was, in short, a dangerous place for women, but it was not a society in which women themselves played much of a role in establishing the level of danger.

That danger was not limited to violence resulting in death, but also encompassed sexual assault. In these years 23 rape charges – 18 rape and 5 statutory rape – and 7 assault with intent to rape charges were heard by the courts (table 6).[79] The 23 rape charges represented 19 incidents (when multiple defendants are eliminated), or a rape charge about every two and a half years. Using the same population estimate as in the discussion of homicide above, this translates into a rape prosecution rate of about 4.7 per annum per 100,000 population. This is much higher than in England in the same period, where the rate was around 0.25 per annum per 100,000. The figure for all sexual assault cases, rape and attempted rape, is also a good deal higher than for England, where attempt charges were much more numerous; including the latter puts Halifax at about 6 per annum per 100,000, England at 0.8.[80] Halifax thus saw a rate of sexual assault prosecution that was almost ten times higher than England, and higher also than in any jurisdiction studied by other historians.[81] It might be possible to argue that this community prosecuted many more rapes than others did, but there is no evidence of that. Moreover, if a higher rate of prosecution represented greater concern about rape one would also expect to see such concern manifested in unusually high rates of conviction, and such was

TABLE 6
Rape and Assault with Intent to Rape Prosecutions

Disposition	Rape	Statutory rape	Total*	Assault with intent to commit rape
Guilty as charged	6	0	6	6
Guilty of lesser charge	4	0	4	n/a
Not guilty	3	4	7	1
True bill not found	1	0	1	0
Other	4†	1	5	0
Total	18	5	23	7

*Of capital charges – rape and statutory rape
†See the cases of William Gillislin and John Warburton discussed below. Both William Mulcahy (1768) and William Cary (1780) escaped from jail: RG 39, Series J, vol. 1, 58 and 370; RG 1, vol. 166, 52–3.

not the case. Thus it is likely that the comparative differences in prosecution rates reflected real differences in behaviour.

This level of sexual assault was not simply the product of the military presence, for only eleven of the nineteen known defendants in all three categories of offence in table 6 were soldiers or sailors, and the figures include the one prosecution in which there were three defendants for the same incident. This is actually a puzzling case, for Mary Pinfold died at the hands of these men, and although indictments for murder seem to have been prepared they were charged with rape and found guilty of a lesser offence.[82] This case is not included in the previous section on homicide victimization, although it perhaps should be, and if it was it would add further evidence to the argument presented there about a high level of victimization.

Other defendants, in the few cases in which such information is available, ran the gamut of relationships to the victim – employers of domestic servants, neighbours, and complete strangers. Examples of the first include Henry Heron, described obviously incorrectly in his indictment as 'a gentleman,' who was charged in 1752 with rape by his eighteen-year-old servant, Christian Melech, and possibly also another 'gentleman,' the improbable figure of Peter, Marquess de Conty and Gravina, a Sicilian nobleman who for some reason ended up in Halifax in the late 1750s (perhaps because of his predilection for young girls) and then landed in court. He was prosecuted for an assault with intent to commit a rape on one Jane Gleason, a girl less than ten years old.[83] Among other cases Thomas Flinn attacked a neighbour's child, James

Condon was accused by the woman of the house in which he boarded, and Timothy Keife and Benjamin Bristy attacked comparative strangers who came into contact with them.[84] Rape, like murder, appears to have been a crime easily and often committed, by soldiers and civilians alike, often, but not always, in the netherworld of city life.

The disposition figures in table 6 suggest that rape was an offence easy to commit and difficult to convict for; convictions on the capital charges of rape and statutory rape totalled only 6 of 23, or 26 per cent. Low levels of conviction for rape have been noted in all historical studies, and Halifax was no exception. Indeed, the conviction rate in Halifax was, in comparative terms, not 'low' at all.[85] Moreover, it was only marginally lower, on a very small sample, than the rate at which men were convicted on all other capital charges – 33 per cent. Thus the acquittal rate in rape had something to do with jurors' fear of sending an accused person to the gallows, not just their tolerance of sexual assault. In at least one instance it also had something to do with Governor Charles Lawrence's favouritism to the soldiery. In July 1757 William Gillislin and John Warburton, soldiers of the 55th Regiment, along with a good many comrades burst into a house and assaulted one Hannah Price. One of them 'drew his Sword, held it across her Neck, & Swore he would Cut her throat if she made any noise.' Apparently 'fifteen or sixteen' of the soldiers then 'lay with her.' Price identified Gillislin and Warburton, whom she apparently knew, and they were apprehended and charged with both rape and burglary. Lawrence thought them fit cases for a pre-trial pardon, they having 'behaved themselves as good Subjects in His Majesty's Service' and these events representing 'the first felony or crime charged against them.'[86]

Even when cases were brought to trial, the fact remains that it was difficult in the eighteenth century, in Halifax and elsewhere, to secure a conviction on a rape charge. The vast majority of such trials involved no third party witnesses, and the rules of evidence peculiar to rape placed hurdles in the path of a prosecutor. In this period proof of the offence required, inter alia, that the woman be shown to have complained almost immediately, that there had been both penetration and ejaculation, and that there had been demonstrable and substantial resistance. Moreover a rape trial was a humiliating experience for the woman, who not only had to prove the facts but was subject to attacks on her own character.[87] Unfortunately the lack of trial records prevents us from seeing how these procedural hurdles worked in particular cases; but they did establish a generally high standard for the prosecution to meet.

The impression left by the cases of unsuccessful or only partially successful prosecutions, which are the only ones for which details are available, suggests that a defendant was rather unlucky to find himself actually convicted of rape, for the cases reveal a substantial male reluctance – among prosecuting authorities and jury members – to believe a woman's story. We can discern this in part from the fact that none of the statutory rape charges stuck, for that required believing the testimony of a child.[88] We can also point to the case of Sergeant John Traynor, charged with assault with intent to commit rape in 1765 although the deposition evidence generated by the investigations of the justices of the peace clearly indicates forcible statutory rape, not the lesser offence, and yet somebody decided not to proceed on the full offence, perhaps because they did not wish the child to suffer the humiliation of a court appearance.[89] Whether it was the public prosecutor's own scepticism, or his or the victim's view of what jurors would think, does not matter. One complainant not prepared to let matters rest was the aforementioned Christian Melech, who told JP Charles Morris that her attacker and employer, Henry Heron, had first tried to persuade her to 'be good-natured' with him through an intermediary, a male servant, and had offered her a present in return. She refused the offer, and a few days later was dispatched alone to clean an empty house that Heron would shortly be moving to. He turned up and raped her there. She told a tale of substantial resistance, a brave attempt in the lonely circumstances in which she found herself: 'as she was at work ... her master came to her and took hold of her and flung her on the floor and endeavoured to force her ... she shrieked and struggling with him prevented him ... then he took hold of her and flung her into a hammock and then forced her and had carnal knowledge of her body and she shrieked and made all the resistance she was able but could not hinder him.' When it was over Heron apparently tried to buy her silence by offering to double her wages, give her an immediate present of a guinea, equivalent to over four months' wages, and provide for her 'stockings and cloaths' whenever she should want them. On her refusal he contemptuously defied her to complain, warning her, correctly as it turned out, that 'nobody would believe her oath.' She went to her mother and then to the justice of the peace. He was right; her oath was believed sufficiently to get Heron to trial, but he was found not guilty.[90]

Another example comes from a case prosecuted nearly forty years later, in which there appears from the investigating documents to have been very clear evidence of guilt. In October 1790 one Thomas Flinn was tried for the rape of twelve-year-old Susannah Swift, an 'apprentice girl.' The investigating magistrate heard from a deputy sheriff of his sitting in a house one afternoon and being interrupted by a little girl who came tearing in to report that 'there was an old man at McCurdy's playing fury along with Suzy.' He went to the house named, and as he neared his destination heard 'a screeching in the house.' When he got inside he saw Flinn 'in the room with the said Suzy, ... the girl was crying, and said that Thomas Flinn had thrown her on the bed and forced her.' Here was 'recent complaint' indeed, but even more damning evidence came from Flinn himself, who told two JPs that 'he had carnal knowledge of the body of the said Susanna, that it is the first time he was ever guilty of such an action, that he was somewhat in liquor at the time.' The crime took place in mid summer, and by the time the trial came around in October Flinn had obviously thought better of confessing, and pleaded not guilty. The jury found him guilty of assault only, not even of assault with intent to commit a rape.[91]

While these details of unsuccessful prosecutions make clear the great difficulties faced by complainants, there is unfortunately simply not enough information about successful ones to say why some men were convicted and, indeed, why three of the six convicted were actually executed. Two suggestions can be offered. First, two of the six convicted defendants were black, they were tried out of the same set of facts, and both were hanged. Race was likely a factor in the fate of Henry Graham and Anthony Johnstone in 1785, particularly given that they acted in concert and if, which I do not know, the complainant had been white.[92] Unfortunately there is insufficient evidence to offer more general conclusions about the role played by race in the courts.[93] Second, convictions in some cases may simply have resulted from the fact that the evidence against the accused was overwhelming, even more damning than in some of the instances already discussed which ended up in acquittals.

Drawing conclusions from the evidence presented here should be done with considerable caution, for the nature of the records and the poverty of the historiography of eighteenth-century Halifax, particularly that relating to women, make sweeping assertions difficult. Nonetheless, it is reasonably clear that there were distinctive features in the relationship between women and crime in eighteenth-century Halifax. While women appeared in the dock much less often than they did in other societies in approximately the same period, once they got there they were not generally the recipients of male 'chivalry' at any level, despite the rarity of their appearances. The brand of deviance represented by a social group of whom the utmost conformity was expected was dealt with vigorously. Not spared the official violence of the criminal justice system, women were also, as a collectivity, potentially subject to a large measure of unofficial violence, for it is necessary to assume that the curial records represent only the tip of a large iceberg of male violence. Their experience was in some measure defined by that violence, or its potential. Finally, it is worth speculating that the violent nature of the community and the repression of the court system likely reinforced existing informal social controls applied to women, adding to the restraints that prevented them from stepping outside the bounds that society defined for them.

NOTES

For their comments on an earlier version of this paper I thank the members of the Early Canada History Group at the University of Toronto. My co-editors are to be commended for their forthright criticisms of that version, and Rosemary Gartner and Carolyn Strange also provided very helpful insights. I am grateful to Rebecca Veinott and Cara Fraser for research assistance.

1 J. Phillips 'Women and Crime in Halifax, 1750–1800' (unpublished ms)
2 A recent work which considers both victimization and the treatment of female offenders is C. Backhouse *Petticoats and Prejudice: Women and Law in Nineteenth-Century Canada* (Toronto: University of Toronto Press and Osgoode Society 1991).
3 J. Phillips 'Securing Obedience to Necessary Laws: The Criminal Law in Eighteenth Century Nova Scotia' *Nova Scotia Historical Review* 12 (1992) 87–124 and 'The Operation of the Royal Pardon in Nova Scotia, 1749–1815' *University of Toronto Law Journal* 42 (1992) 401–47
4 D.A. Sutherland '*Warden of the North* Revisited: A Re-examination of Thomas Raddall's Assessment of Nineteenth-Century Halifax' *Transactions of the Royal Society of Canada* 19 (1981) 81, summarizing the eighteenth-century historiography. For the general history of the city in this period see, inter alia, T.B. Akins 'History of Halifax City' *Collections of the Nova Scotia Historical Society* 8 (1894); J.B. Brebner *The Neutral Yankees of Nova Scotia* (Toronto: McClelland and Stewart 1969); J.G. Reid *Six Crucial Decades: Times of Change in the History of*

the Maritimes (Halifax: Nimbus 1987); H. Piers *The Evolution of the Halifax Fortress, 1749–1948* (Halifax: Public Archives of Nova Scotia 1947).

5 This summarizes the data in *Censuses of Canada 1665–1871* (Ottawa: Queen's Printer 1876) xxiv and 69–70 and 'Early Descriptions of Nova Scotia' *Report of the Public Archives of Nova Scotia for 1933* (Halifax: Public Archives of Nova Scotia 1934) 21–51. These figures are approximate, for contemporary census data are not particularly reliable and nor was growth consistent.

6 It is difficult to arrive at firm figures for the military population at any given time. Wartime brought considerable movement in and out. For example, in 1757 and 1758 many thousands of soldiers and sailors were gathered in Halifax for an assault on Louisbourg. In contrast, in the spring of 1775 General Gage ordered all troops to Boston in response to the impending conflict with the rebellious colonies, apparently leaving just thirty-six men in Halifax: Akins 'History of Halifax City' 54 and Brebner *Neutral Yankees* 300. The peacetime establishment before and after the revolutionary war was c. 2000–3000 men: see R.A. Evans 'The Army and Navy at Halifax, 1783–1793' (MA thesis, Dalhousie University 1970) chap. 1 and 148; C.P. Stacey 'Halifax as an International Strategic Factor, 1749–1949' *Canadian Historical Association Report* (1949) 46–8; 'Journal of Benigne Charles de Saint Mesmin, 1793' *Report of the Public Archives of Canada* (1946) xxv.

7 Evans 'The Army and Navy at Halifax' 71

8 Report of the State of the Orphan House, May 1761, P[ublic] A[rchives of] N[ova] S[cotia], C[olonial] O[ffice Series] 217, vol. 18, 26. See also Governor Sir William Campbell's 1771 complaint that large numbers of 'idle, helpless and indigent women' were 'left in Halifax by regiments on their departure from the Province'; he wanted them to be 'obliged' to leave with the soldiery: Campbell to Bruce, April 1771, PANS, R[ecord] G[roup] 1, vol. 136. For other references to 'camp followers' see R. Williams 'Poor Relief and Medicine in Nova Scotia, 1749–1783' *Collections of the Nova Scotia Historical Society* 24 (1938) passim.

9 J. Gwynn 'Economic Fluctuations in Wartime Nova Scotia, 1755–1815' in M. Conrad, ed. *Making Adjustments: Change and Continuity in Planter Nova Scotia 1759–1800* (Fredericton: Acadiensis Press 1991) 60–1

10 Campbell to Dartmouth, 12 Sept. 1768, RG 1, vol. 43

11 Hughes to Germain, 27 Feb. 1779, RG 1, vol. 45; Akins 'History of Halifax City' 76; *Remembrancer* 1776, 267; Campbell to North, 18 Dec. 1783, CO 217, vol. 56, 117v

12 R.W. Jeffrey, ed. *Diary of General William Dyott 1781–1845* 2 vols. (London: Heinemann 1907) 1: 39–40 and 50–5; Akins 'History of Halifax City' 93

13 See T. Raddall *Halifax: Warden of the North* (Toronto: McClelland and Stewart

1971); Akins 'History of Halifax City' passim; Memorial of Robert Sanderson, 1760, CO 217, vol. 18, 73–80; *Nova Scotia Gazette* 18 Mar. 1788; PANS, RG 39, Supreme Court Records, Halifax County, ser. C, vol. 2, no. 18; vol. 8, no. 9; vol. 56, no. 71; Green to Board of Trade, 24 Aug. 1766, CO 217, vol. 21, 278–291.

14 For the structure of Nova Scotia government generally see Brebner *Neutral Yankees* and D.C. Harvey 'The Struggle for the New England Form of Township Government in Nova Scotia' *Canadian Historical Association Report* (1933) 15–22. The best study of Halifax-hinterland relations is E.A. Clarke *Canada and the American Revolution* (Montreal and Kingston: McGill-Queen's University Press 1994).

15 See the many depositions in RG 39, ser. C, vols. 1–82, passim.

16 Testimony of Brook Watson to the House of Commons in 1775, cited in R.C. Simmons and P.D.G. Thomas, eds. *Proceedings and Debates of the British Parliament Respecting North America, 1754–1783* 6 vols. (New York: Kraus 1982–6) 5: 490, emphasis in original. See also Josiah Throop of Cumberland's comment that Nova Scotia 'has ever been in a great measure a military and almost an arbitrary government': Memorial of Josiah Throop, 29 May 1777, Massachusetts Archives, vol. 142, 69.

17 *Proceedings and Debates of the British Parliament* vol. 5, 528. There is not space here for a lengthy excursus on this topic, but see also P. M'Robert *A Tour through Part of the North Provinces of North America ... in 1774 and 1775* (Edinburgh 1776) 20 and the comments of 'A Member of Assembly' in *An Essay on the Present State of the Province of Nova Scotia* (Halifax 1774) 6–7.

18 See respectively Phillips 'The Criminal Law in Nova Scotia' and 'The Operation of the Royal Pardon.'

19 These were the General Court (1749–54) and the Nova Scotia Supreme Court in Halifax (1754–1800).

20 The information in all tables in this paper, and that given elsewhere in the text and not otherwise referenced, is contained in my Halifax Crime File No. 1, compiled primarily from the records of the General and Supreme courts, RG 39, ser. J, vols. 1, 2, and 117, and ser. C, Halifax County, vols. 1–82. These provide a substantially complete summary of all cases prosecuted in the General Court and the Supreme Court between 1750 and 1800, except for 1761–4, for which proceedings are incomplete. I have not used Quarter Sessions Court records because they are only sporadically available. The data from court records have been supplemented by newspapers, official correspondence, and various other sources. The tables include only cases brought before the grand jury, not those known to the authorities but not brought to court.

21 I discuss these statistics in detail, and consider the various 'adjustments' that perhaps should be made to the figures, in Phillips 'Women and Crime.'

22 The literature on this is reviewed in detail in ibid. 4–6. The major comparative work includes J.M. Beattie 'The Criminality of Women in Eighteenth Century England' *Journal of Social History* 8 (1975) 80–115; M. Feeley and D. Little 'The Vanishing Female: The Decline of Women in the Criminal Process, 1687–1912' *Law and Society Review* 25 (1991) 719–51; A. Lachance 'Women and Crime in Canada, 1712–1748' in L.A. Knafla, ed. *Crime and Criminal Justice in Europe and Canada* (Waterloo: Wilfrid Laurier University Press 1981); and N.E.H. Hull *Female Felons: Women and Serious Crime in Colonial Massachusetts* (Champaign, Ill.: University of Illinois Press 1987).

23 For the content of the criminal law in this period, including the distinction between capital larcenies and grand larceny (which was nominally capital but for which an offender could claim benefit of clergy and escape the gallows on a first offence), see Phillips, 'The Criminal Law in Nova Scotia' 94–7 and 114–17.

24 As noted above, most cases from 1761 to 1764 inclusive are missing, and so it is not possible to tell precisely when the prevalence of women ended. It is the case, nonetheless, that this occurred sometime in the early 1760s.

25 See Phillips 'Women and Crime.'

26 As in Halifax, the conviction rate for men and women on charges of murder in eighteenth-century England was substantially the same. Also like Halifax, there was a significant gender gap in property crime: see J.M. Beattie *Crime and the Courts in England, 1660–1800* (Princeton: Princeton University Press 1986) 437.

27 Cases of Martha Welsh and Christian Regan: RG 39, ser. J, vol. 117, and ser. C, vol. 3, no. 94; RG 1, vol. 165, 102, 117, 119, 133, and 153–4

28 The vast majority of these, for men and women, were convictions of petit larceny following charges of grand larceny.

29 Again, Beattie's figures for conviction rates for both genders are higher than mine, because he works from trials, not from cases brought to court. But this did not affect the relative rates at which the genders were convicted. In fact in England women were more likely to be convicted as charged of non-capital property offences than were men (34.6 per cent compared to 24.7 per cent at assizes), but men were more often convicted of a lesser offence (40.5 per cent compared to 33.9 per cent). Overall, over 66 per cent of men were convicted and slightly less than 60 per cent of women. Approximately the same differential pertained in quarter sessions: Beattie *Crime and the Courts* 437.

30 These totals include both persons charged with grand larceny and found

guilty, and those charged with a capital property offence and found guilty of the lesser offence.

31 Although the case of Jane Wishart, the last woman to receive a branding, occurred in 1790: see RG 39, ser. J, vol. 2, 99.

32 It should perhaps be noted that four men were ordered to be publicly whipped in addition to being branded, whereas this additional sanction was never employed for women who received clergy. However, five women were branded and also sentenced to a short term of imprisonment.

33 Either after being charged with that offence, or after being charged with grand larceny or a capital larceny but convicted only of petit larceny.

34 RG 39, ser. J, vol. 2, 123

35 This was ordered in Hunt's case. But for most of this period women so sentenced had to suffer as did Mary Pinfold, who in 1757 was sentenced to 're-ceive 20 stripes on her bare back at the public whipping post': RG 39, ser. J, vol. 117.

36 See the cases of Eleanor Matthews (1753), Margaret Bryant (1754), Frances Cook (1759), and Jane Tolmy (1774): RG 39, ser. J, vol. 117, and ser. C, vol. 3, no 21; Lawrence to Board of Trade, 1 June 1754, CO 217, vol. 15, 70; RG 1, vol. 170, 125–6.

37 See, inter alia, the cases of Jane Sexton (1757), John Rock (1760), John Woodruff (1765), Patrick Trent (1766), William Graham (1768): RG 39, ser. J, vol. 117; RG 1, vol. 165, 31 and 382, and vol. 166, 22–3 and 48–9.

38 For a detailed account of the pardon process and for the figures used in this paragraph, see Phillips 'The Operation of the Royal Pardon' 411–24.

39 Beattie *Crime and the Courts* 532

40 In addition to the work of Beattie already cited, see N.E.H. Hull 'The Certain Wages of Sin: Sentence and Punishment of Female Felons in Colonial Massachusetts, 1673-1774' in D.K. Weisberg, ed. *Women and the Law: A Social Historical Perspective* (Cambridge, Mass.: Schenkman 1982); T.A. Green *Verdict According to Conscience: Perspectives on the English Criminal Trial Jury* (Chicago: University of Chicago Press 1985) 376; P.G. Lawson, 'Lawless Juries? The Composition and Behaviour of Hertfordshire Juries, 1573-1624' in J.S. Cockburn and T.A. Green, eds. *Twelve Good Men and True: The Criminal Trial Jury in England, 1200-1800* (Princeton: Princeton University Press 1988) 151; P. Lawson 'Patriarchy, Crime and the Courts: The Criminality of Women in Late Tudor and Early Stuart England' (unpublished paper, 1992) 27–8; H. Boritch 'Gender and Criminal Court Outcomes: An Historical Analysis' *Criminology* 30 (1992) 293–325. These studies all address the issue using a range of general offences. Complicating any analysis of the treatment of women, however, is the fact that accounts of specific offences, such as

witchcraft, petit treason, or infanticide, suggest either great leniency or considerable harshness and savage treatment of female offenders.

41 Aspects of Nova Scotia law, derived from Massachusetts, showed a greater regard for women's status than was the case in England. The examples of the availability of judicial divorce on gender-neutral grounds and of the partial abolition of primogeniture stand out: see K. Smith-Maynard 'Divorce in Nova Scotia, 1750–1900' in P. Girard and J. Phillips, eds. *Essays in the History of Canadian Law: Volume III – Nova Scotia* (Toronto: University of Toronto Press and Osgoode Society 1990) and 'An Act relating to Wills, Legacies and Executors' *Statutes of Nova Scotia* 1758, c. 11, s. 12.

42 We know very little about the history of women in eighteenth-century Halifax, or in Nova Scotia generally. As one reviewer has put it, Canadian scholars in the field have 'leaped from the fur trade to industrial society': M. Conrad 'The Rebirth of Canada's Past: A Decade of Women's History' *Acadiensis* 12 (1983) 146. There is a very limited discussion of eighteenth-century women, mostly those of the middle class, in G. Davies 'Literary Women in Pre-Confederation Nova Scotia' in Davies *Studies in Maritime Literary History, 1760–1930* (Fredericton: Acadiensis Press 1991) and B.R. Buszek 'By Fortune Wounded: Loyalist Women in Nova Scotia' *Nova Scotia Historical Review* 7 (1987) 45–62.

43 Buszek 'Loyalist Women' 50 and 58

44 *Nova Scotia Chronicle* 4–11 Apr. 1769. See also the same newspaper's warning to women that visiting with neighbours in the evening was acceptable, but only if they had first 'carefully attended the concerns of their families in the preceding part of the day': ibid. 13–20 Feb. 1770. Some insight into the domestic ordinariness of women's lives can be gleaned from the few extant contemporary diaries and correspondence; see, for example, the diary of Anna Kearney in MG 1, vol. 526A.

45 See Phillips 'Women and Crime' 36–9.

46 These are difficult to calculate precisely because of the uncertainties about population, but they likely came close to 200 per 100,000 per annum, a figure more than twice as high as in the urban (London) areas of Surrey in the same period: Beattie *Crime and the Courts* passim.

47 Phillips 'The Criminal Law in Nova Scotia' 112–13

48 L. Zedner 'Women, Crime and Penal Responses: An Historical Account' in M. Tonry and N. Morris, eds. *Crime and Justice: An Annual Review of Research* vol. 13 (Chicago: University of Chicago Press 1991) 320. See also N. Rafter 'Prisons for Women, 1790–1980' in ibid., vol. 5 (Chicago: University of Chicago Press 1983) and L. Zedner *Women, Crime and Custody in Victorian England* (Oxford: Clarendon Press 1991).

49 A more detailed analysis of the female offender population appears in Phillips 'Women and Crime' 39–45.

50 I have used indictment and deposition evidence here. Although the formalities of procedure meant that 'spinster' was sometimes used in an indictment even if the accused was married, just as 'labourer' or 'yeoman' was a standard term in indictments of men, in fact in Halifax indictments of married or widowed women stated that fact, and the validity of the term spinster is frequently confirmed by deposition evidence.

51 RG 39, ser. J, vol. 117, and ser. C, vol. 1, nos. 43, 44, 58, and 59; vol. 2, nos. 19, 36, and 37; vol. 3, nos. 50, 77, 82, 83, and 94; vol. 4, no. 33; vol. 63, no. 31; Lawrence to Board of Trade, 1 June 1754, CO 217, vol. 15, 68–9

52 Phillips 'The Operation of the Royal Pardon' 431

53 *The Diary of Elijah Estabrooks, 1758–1760* (Halifax: Privately published n.d. [1761]) 27. Other records of the case are at RG 39, ser. J, vol. 117; ibid., ser. C, vol. 3, no. 77, and vol. 9, unnumbered; Lawrence to Board of Trade, 16 June 1760, CO 217, vol. 18, 38–40; RG 1, vol. 165, 62. The Orpin family history can be reconstructed from E.C. Wright *Planters and Pioneers* (Hantsport, NS: Lancelot Press 1982) 214; PANS, Probate Records, RG 48, reel 417, O17 and O18; *Royal Gazette and Nova Scotia Advertiser* 1 and 22 Jan. 1793; Genealogical Notes, C.B. Fergusson Papers, MG 1, vol. 1845.

54 Parr to North, 13 Dec. 1783, CO 217, vol. 56, 117. See also Sydney to Parr, 8 Mar. 1785, ibid., vol. 57, 32; RG 39, ser. J, vol. 1, 430; RG 1, vol. 170, 350.

55 For this case see RG 39, ser. J, vol. 1, 55. My conclusion about Whippy's social status is based on the fact that the only Whippy or Whippey I have been able to trace in Halifax census, genealogical, land, etc. records is one Allen Whippey, who married a woman named Margaret in 1756: PANS, St Paul's Church Records, Marriages, reel 3. Alan Whippey appears in the civil side records of the Supreme Court, described as a fisherman with a house and land in the south suburbs: *Whippe v. Watson*, RG 39, ser. C, vol. 6, no. 48. He also served as both a petit and a grand juror in criminal proceedings, and the latter in particular indicates a person of some status: ibid., vol. 3, no. 110, and RG 60, Halifax, vol. 1.

56 For Belcher's comments see his draft sentencing speech in MG 1, vol. 1738, no. 111.

57 See the cases of Martha Welsh and Christian Regan, above, text accompanying note 27, of Mary Webb (1758, infanticide, at RG 39, ser. J, vol. 117, and ser. C, vol. 2, no 54; RG 1, vol. 163[3], 142, and vol. 165, 25; Belcher to Board of Trade, 12 Dec. 1760, CO 217, vol. 18, 85, and Board of Trade to Belcher, 10 June 1762, ibid., vol. 6, 86), and of Alicia Wiggins (1792, housebreaking, at Shelburne, at RG 1, vol. 169, 206; MG 1, vol. 950, no 533; M.

Robertson *King's Bounty: A History of Early Shelburne, Nova Scotia* (Halifax: Nova Scotia Museum 1986) 148.

58 J.M. Beattie 'The Royal Pardon and Criminal Procedure in Early Modern England' *Historical Papers* (1981) 21

59 C. Strange 'Wounded Womanhood and Dead Men: Chivalry and the Trials of Clara Ford and Carrie Davis' in F. Iacovetta and M. Valverde, eds. *Gender Conflicts: New Essays in Women's History* (Toronto: University of Toronto Press 1992) 151

60 For Murphy see RG 39, ser. J, vol. 2, 120, and ser. C, vol. 63, no 40; *Nova Scotia Gazette* 18 and 25 Oct. 1791; and *Nova Scotia Magazine* Oct. 1791, 633. Murphy apparently had a long record of petty crime and had not been long in Halifax; the latter may have meant that she suffered, as many did in the eighteenth-century criminal justice system, from her 'outsider' status.

61 The historical literature is very scanty and not always directly on point; see J. Sharpe 'Domestic Homicide in Early Modern England' *Historical Journal* 24 (1981) 29–48; N. Tomes 'A "Torrent of Abuse": Crimes of Violence between Working Class Men and Women in London, 1840–1875' *Journal of Social History* 11 (1978) 328–45. For more recent surveys see, inter alia, R. Gartner et al. 'Gender Stratification and the Gender Gap in Homicide Victimisation' *Social Problems* 37 (1990) 593–612 and R. Gartner and B. McCarthy 'The Social Distribution of Femicide in Urban Canada, 1921-1988' *Law and Society Review* 25 (1991) 287–311.

62 This total represents all murder, manslaughter, and infanticide charges brought against men and women. A total of 85 individuals (73 men and 12 women) were charged with homicide in these years, and the discrepancy between this figure and that for victims is the result of there being multiple defendants in some cases.

63 I have used an average population figure of 8000, far too high given that the city did not reach that level until the 1790s. But the overestimate is deliberate, for I want to make sure I more than account for the presence of military personnel. Even with them, however, the city would rarely have contained this many people before the 1780s.

64 R. Gartner 'Homicide in Canada' (unpublished paper) 33

65 Beattie Crime and the Courts 108

66 For reviews of the historical data on levels of violence in western societies see T.R. Gurr 'Historical Trends in Violent Crime: A Critical Review of the Evidence' *Crime and Justice* vol. 3 (1981), and L. Stone 'Interpersonal Violence in English Society, 1300-1980' *Past and Present* 101 (1983) 22–33.

67 Because of multiple defendants in some cases the 73 male murder and manslaughter charges noted above actually involved 47 victims. I have removed

from this sample three cases in which men and women were charged together, to arrive at the total of 44 victims of exclusively male homicide.

68 In 14 of the 22 male victim cases it was possible to tell whether the victim
was a soldier (8) or a civilian (6). I extrapolated this ratio to the full sample
of 22 male victims, so that the adjusted figures become soldiers 12, civilians
10, and females 9.

69 RG 39, ser. J, vol. 1, 105. Seidler was a shoemaker and one of the group of
German immigrants who came to the colony in 1751. In 1760 he married his
second wife, Catherine Wenigerkind – it is not known what happened to
the first: see Wright *Planters and Pioneers* 249.

70 RG 39, ser. J, vol. 2, 191; ibid., ser. C, vol. 79; *Nova Scotia Gazette* 2 Oct. 1798

71 Michael Hayes killed his wife in December 1785 in Port Mahone, and was
tried, convicted, and executed at Liverpool, Queen's County, in July 1786:
RG 1, vol. 170, 390; *The Diary of Simeon Perkins* 4 vols. (Toronto: Champlain
Society 1948–67) 2: 301, 315, 316, 322, and 323.

72 RG 39, ser. C, vol. 3, no. 99

73 RG 39, ser. J, vol. 2, 122, and ser. C, vol. 63, no. 37

74 RG 39, ser. C, vol. 77. See also the case of Catherine MacIntosh, who according to a coroner's inquest in 1758 came to her death 'by violent strokes
and abuses she received from James Richardson': ibid., vol. 2, nos. 56 and 57.

75 RG 39, ser. C, vol. 78

76 See the reward offered for discovering the murderers of Ann Dunbrack,
widow, in *Nova Scotia Gazette and Weekly Chronicle* 23 July 1782. See also the
case of Mrs Bennett, who was found dead in 1762 'with some marks of violence on her body.' When a coroner's inquest could get no information on
how she received them, it concluded that she died a natural death: RG 39,
ser. C, vol. 3, no. 121. See also for a variety of other coroner's reports on
women's bodies ibid., vol. 4, no. 44; PANS, Coroners' Records, RG 41, vols.
1 and 2, passim; *Nova Scotia Gazette and Weekly Chronicle* 2 Mar. 1773.

77 Twelve homicides were charged against women, which was 14 per cent of
the total of 85. The figure for eighteenth-century England was 22.3 per
cent: Beattie 'Criminality of Women' 85.

78 I say 'at least' four because this charge is recorded in the summary of proceedings as 'murder,' and in some cases additional documents reveal that
the victim was a bastard newborn. It is likely that others were also, but
there is no information to establish this fact.

79 The summary of court proceedings does not distinguish between rape and
statutory rape as such; 21 charges are recorded as 'rape,' one as 'rape of Elizabeth Hinkle, 10 years old' and one as 'rape of an infant.' I have chosen to

classify the last two as statutory rape, and to add to that category three other cases where the charge is recorded as simply 'rape' but where the deposition evidence makes it clear that the victim was under the age of consent (twelve). See cases of John Ferguson (1750), John Nightingale (1758), John Traynor (1765), Hugh Finlay (1773), and John Lackey (1799): RG 39, ser. J, vol. 117, vol. 1, 21 and 221–2, and vol. 2, 195; ibid., ser. C, vol. 4, no. 52, and vol. 81; 'An Act Relating to Treasons and Felonies' *Statutes of Nova Scotia 1758*, c. 13, s. 8.

80 I have derived the English figure from Beattie's finding of 29 rape indictments and 70 attempt rape indictments in Surrey between 1740 and 1802, and have used a slightly conservative average population figure for that county of 200,000, given that it grew from c. 135,000 in 1750 to c. 278,000 in 1801: Beattie *Crime and the Courts* 28 and 131.

81 Compare these figures with those for nineteenth-century Ontario in C. Backhouse 'Nineteenth-Century Canadian Rape Law 1800–92' in D.H. Flaherty, ed. *Essays in the History of Canadian Law: Volume II* (Toronto: University of Toronto Press and Osgoode Society 1983) 222, and for late nineteenth-century and early twentieth-century Toronto presented in the essay by Carolyn Strange in this volume.

82 See the cases of soldiers William Calfrey, Alexander McManus, and Robert Sarty: RG 39, ser. J, vol. 117; ibid., ser. C, vol. 3, nos. 77, 82, and 83. In fact, they were on conviction sentenced to death but received benefit of clergy, which suggests that they may in fact have been convicted of manslaughter, for the penalty for assault with intent to commit rape was the pillory plus a fine and/or imprisonment at the discretion of the judge: 'An Act Relating to Treasons and Felonies' *Statutes of Nova Scotia 1758*, c. 13, s. 8.

83 RG 39, ser. J, vol. 117; ibid., ser. C, vol. 1, nos. 70, 71, and 88; RG 1, vol. 163[3], 145 and 166; Hopson to Board of Trade, 6 Dec. 1752, CO 217, vol. 13, 415–16; *Halifax Gazette* 12 Oct. 1754; Akins 'History of Halifax City' 32 and 52

84 Flinn's case is discussed below. For the other cases see RG 39, ser. J, vol. 1, 7, and vol. 2, 121 and 176; ibid., ser. C, vol. 4, nos. 46 and 51; vol. 63, no. 36; and vol. 76.

85 Backhouse found that only 21 per cent of rape charges led to convictions in mid to late nineteenth-century Ontario, and the comparable figure for eighteenth-century England was 14.7 per cent: see Backhouse 'Nineteenth-Century Canadian Rape Law' 222 and Beattie *Crime and the Courts* 411. For other 'low' conviction rates see the essay by Carolyn Strange in this volume; R. Olson 'Rape – An 'Un-Victorian' Aspect of Life in Upper Canada' *Ontario*

History 68 (1976) 75–9; A. Clark *Women's Silence, Men's Violence: Sexual Assault in England, 1770–1845* (London: Pandora 1987) chap. 3.

86 RG 1, vol. 163 [3], 103. See also Lawrence to Foy, 3 Aug. 1757, ibid., 105, and Memorial of Robert Sanderson, 1760, CO 217, vol. 18, 75–75v.

87 The rules of evidence relating to rape, the problem of corroborating witnesses, and the defence tactic of attacking the victim's character are variously discussed in Backhouse 'Nineteenth-Century Canadian Rape Law' 213–26, Beattie *Crime and the Courts* 124–7, and the essay by Carolyn Strange in this volume. Note also that the statutory provisions on rape in local legislation gave complainants ten days to go to the authorities, else consent was assumed: 'An Act Relating to Treasons and Felonies' *Statutes of Nova Scotia* 1758, c. 13, s. 7. For other studies of the problems peculiar to rape trials see C.P. Nemeth 'Character Evidence in Rape Trials in Nineteenth Century New York: Chastity and the Admissibility of Specific Acts' *Women's Rights Law Reporter* 6 (1980) 214–25, C. Conley 'Rape and Justice in Victorian England' *Victorian Studies* 29 (1986) 519–36, and A.E. Simpson 'The "Blackmail Myth" and the Prosecution of Rape and Its Attempt in 18th Century London: The Creation of a Legal Tradition' *Journal of Criminal Law and Criminology* 77 (1986) 101–50.

88 For a discussion of this see Beattie *Crime and the Courts* 127–8.

89 RG 39, ser. J, vol. 1, 21, and ser. C, vol. 4, no. 52

90 RG 39, ser. C, vol. 1, nos. 70, 71, and 88; Hopson to Board of Trade, 6 Dec. 1752, CO 217, vol. 13, 415–16

91 RG 39, ser. J, vol. 2, 107, and ser. C, vol. 52, no. 86

92 For these cases see RG 39, ser. J, vol. 2, 27–8; RG 1, vol. 170, 381; *Nova Scotia Gazette and Weekly Chronicle* 19 July 1785. For executions for rape generally see Phillips 'The Operation of the Royal Pardon' 430.

93 The eighteenth-century records do not permit the identification of any person, accused or victim, as being a member of a native society, and while blacks appear occasionally, more frequently from the mid-1780s than before, in no other rape case does race seem to have been a factor. For a brief analysis of race and the pardon process, which demonstrates that statistically blacks fared little worse than whites in general, see Phillips 'The Operation of the Royal Pardon' 435–7.

7

Patriarchy Modified:
The Criminal Prosecution of Rape
in York County, Ontario, 1880–1930

CAROLYN STRANGE

Three centuries after jurist Matthew Hale cautioned that rape is a crime easy to charge but difficult to defend, recent feminist research has established that it is a crime easy to commit and extremely difficult to prove.[1] The sexual victimization of women and children by men, we now realize, is more extensive than police and court records would indicate. Furthermore, victims who do report offences to authorities may find the trial more traumatic than the assault itself.[2] Susan Brownmiller and others have argued that rape laws originated not out of a desire to protect women from sexual assault but rather to allow patriarchs to protect property interests in 'their' women. The grudging enforcement of rape laws in modern contexts, Brownmiller contended, reflects the survival of those ancient notions of women as male property.[3]

Men accused of rape have historically faced serious legal sanctions, including the death penalty, yet those penalties have rarely been enforced because defendants were acquitted or convicted on lesser charges, or, as was more often the case, because magistrates or grand jurors considered evidence for rape unconvincing. Feminist historians, particularly those who study the nineteenth century, have concluded that rape laws operated to protect only virtuous, chaste women who 'belonged' to men. Anna Clark's study of rape in late-eighteenth-century and early-nineteenth-century England and Carolyn Conley's work on the mid-nineteenth century, for instance, assert that the victim's sexual reputation, rather than her testimony of coercion or corroborative testimony from witnesses or medical experts, commanded judges' and jurors' attention.[4] In the Victorian era, as chastity and 'passionlessness' became the hallmark of ideal femininity, judges and defence lawyers freely challenged the credibility of rape complaints if they appeared to fall short of those standards of propriety. Because the Victorians equated chastity with feminine character, however, the very act of giving evidence of a sexual assault undercut complainants' credibility before the courts. This prosecutorial paradox has been cited as an explanation for notoriously low prosecution rates for rape and the preference of prosecutors and victims themselves to prosecute for the lesser offences of attempted rape or indecent assault. If rape laws symbolized the property value of female chastity, rape victims embodied damaged property that had lost its original value.

Ironically, feminists' concern with the courts' unwarranted scrutiny of victims's sexual respectability reproduces the very practice they condemn. The result is that we know much less about why some men *are* punished than about why so many women are disbelieved. Clearly, the question of the prosecutrix's chastity cannot be overlooked in analyses of rape; however, the trial of a rapist involves more than the 'second assault' of the victim, even in the most egregious examples of sexism in the courtroom. While patriarchal interests inform the laws governing rape, those interests are never translated directly into the criminal legal process, as some feminists contend.[5] Scholars influenced by post-structuralist theory urge a 'sceptical look at sexism,' one that recognizes the discriminatory treatment of women yet is equally cognizant of the mediation of sexism by a variety of social, economic, and political factors. Otherwise, as Loraine Gelsthorpe warns, 'we are left with "tidy" theories floating free from the reality of an "untidy" world.'[6]

Historical and current-day studies of rape have begun to explore 'untidy worlds' where classism and racism are as apparent as sexism in the prosecution of rape.[7] Criminologists Lorenne Clark and Debra Lewis found that, of those men charged with rape, it is 'low men on the totem pole' – primarily poor men and those from racial and ethnic minorities – who have historically faced a greater risk of conviction than men from dominant economic and social groups.[8] Even so, conviction and acquittal statistics have never conformed to predictable patterns of racial and class injustice, in part because racism and classism are themselves subject to modification. Not even the myth of the Black rapist has ensured that Black men have invariably faced conviction. In Reconstruction-era North Carolina, for instance, Blacks accused of rape occasionally received support from both the Black and white community, whereas poor white women, particularly those with chequered reputations, were frequently 'excluded from the societal protections to which all white women were supposedly entitled.'[9] Moreover, the myth of the Black 'jezebel' operated alongside that of the Black rapist, so that Black women assaulted by men of their race were not considered 'legitimate' victims.[10] The history of rape in the South suggests that historians might be more cautious about interpreting biases in the enforcement of the law. In spite of obvious prejudices against racial and ethnic minorities and the poor, the fate of accused rapists has not mirrored these injustices; rather, the disposition of rape cases is situated in a matrix of changing social and political relations as well as in shifting cultural dispositions toward alleged perpetrators and victims. Thus, while historians may claim that trial outcomes were predictable, especially in periods of overt racial oppression or in contexts of extreme class disparities, they were never predetermined.

Because rape trials are bound up in wider disputes over power and inequality they expose a great deal about those broader social tensions which may appear, at first, to be unrelated to heterosexual conflict. Much of what we know about the history of rape concerns nineteenth-century England and the United States and the peculiar cultural, demographic, economic, and social conditions associated with those places.[11] Not surprisingly, the character of individual regions is distinct and subject to changes over time. In turn-of-the-century Ontario, for instance, the Victorian ideal of femininity or the myth of the Black rapist may have had purchase but the nature of life in the young province was not, however, identical to 1830s Yorkshire or Louisiana in the 1900s. Karen Dubinsky has found that Ontario's rural depopulation crisis, coupled with the drive to settle and civilize the North, coloured the legal treatment of sexual violence in farming, small-town, and northern communities at the turn of the century.[12] In York County, dominated by Toronto (the county seat and the provincial capital), different economic, social, and political transitions were taking place at the turn of the century. Rapid urbanization, fuelled by industrial growth, made the county one of the most populous and 'modern' in the country. Focusing on the criminal prosecution of rape at the turn of the century in this county, then, is necessarily a journey into the ways the various players in rape prosecutions made sense of that changing world.

Both the nature of rape trials and rates of conviction changed significantly from 1880 to 1930 in York County in spite of the fact that no significant changes in policing practices or in statutory definitions of sexual assault took place. The proportion of men found guilty as charged ranged from a low of 7 percent in the 1890s to a high of 33 percent in the early 1900s. How might one explain the varying success of rape prosecutions? The legal purist might connect such fluctuations to the relative skill of Crown prosecutors and defence lawyers or to the strength of the evidence presented. Existing trial records indicate, however, that neither compelling testimony, medical corroboration, nor eyewitnesses ensured conviction; at the same time, some men, even those defended by skilful counsel, were convicted on the basis of uncorroborated, flimsy evidence. Arguments that point to the relevance of defendants' socio-economic status are more convincing. Virtually all of the men convicted of rape were drawn from the working poor or the unemployed. Their class position appears to support Clark and Lewis's argument that the criminal justice system unfairly targets poor men, yet all but a handful of *acquitted* men, like their convicted counterparts, were either unemployed or identified as labourers or semiskilled factory operatives. Men from Toronto's new ethnic and racial groups were also overrepresented among the convicted; however, their greater vulnerability to conviction was not evident until the 1910s and it appears to have subsided by the 1920s. These observations beg the question: how did jurors decide which men to condemn as rapists? In York County, the answers lie not only in the sexist, racist, and classist elements of justice but also in the changing climate of moral reform. Each of these elements coloured jurors' assessments of the character and credibility of alleged victims and offenders – the overwhelming preoccupation in rape trials.

In many respects, then, rape trials resemble all other civil or criminal trials: jurors and judges evaluate witnesses' characters to arrive at verdicts, sometimes even in the face of the evidence; lawyers, for their part, bolster their cases by raising doubts about the character of witnesses giving evidence for opposing counsel. There are frequent charges, nonetheless, that the preoccupation with women's chastity in rape trials ranges far beyond the usual challenges to complainants' credibility.[13] 'It is *being* raped that is punished,' feminists have complained, 'and it is being raped that is the crime.'[14] The forcefulness of this assertion has obscured the fact that rape trials are ultimately tests of male character as well. After all, the formal objective of the trial is to determine whether or not an offence occurred and, if so, whether the accused man committed the offence.

Although women's and men's characters have historically been judged according to gendered criteria that focus almost exclusively on women's sexuality (while taking into consideration a broader range of qualities to evaluate men), the characters of accused rapists, particularly those who were poor and/or members of racial and ethnic minorities, were also vulnerable to the depredations of crown attorneys and judges.[15] For men, habitual drunkenness, prolonged unemployment, poor relations with creditors, or the shirking of family responsibilities could all be read as evidence of low character. In turn-of-the-century York County, cultural codes of ethnicity and race also provided a shorthand means of assessing character, so that Black men and defendants from non-British ethnic groups were automatically suspect.[16] Thus, exploring the cultural representations of men of low character, rather than simply presenting demographic profiles of convicted men, is a more subtle means of capturing jurors' and judges' motivations and their culturally scripted interpretations of male character. Although poor men and those from minority ethnic and racial groups were certainly vulnerable to conviction in turn-of-the-century York County, those whom jurors perceived as men of low character – 'foreigners,' strangers, incest rapists, and fast-living youths – were the most likely to be convicted.

The similarities between rape prosecutions and other criminal trials also confirm general observations about the state's interest in convicting a proportion of indicted suspects in order, as E.P. Thompson noted, to convey the appearance, at least, of justice. If rape prosecutions involved nothing more than the expression of patriarchal interests, one would anticipate the conviction of no more than a few 'outsiders' deemed guilty of violating men's property rights in chaste women. In fact, men who attacked unattached, independent women, those who violated older widows or their own children, and even those who attacked sexually promiscuous women numbered among the convicted men in York County. Rape trials, like prosecutions by the Crown for any other offence, put the credibility of the state on the line. Occasional convictions are thus essential if the state is to maintain its legitimacy.[17] In eighteenth-century England, for example, infrequent but highly publicized hangings of upper-class offenders dramatized the state's adherence to natural justice and thereby lent symbolic weight to its claims to uphold the rule of law against charges that the wealthy enjoyed immunity from prosecution.[18] Similarly, the infrequent punishment of rapists has historically reinforced the impression that the state regards the sexual violation of females as a serious breach of the law and a crime worthy of severe punishment.

If the occasional stiff sentence of convicted rapists reinforced the

legitimacy of the law, it did not, however, undermine patriarchal assumptions about female chastity, just as the execution of a few noblemen
failed to erase the classist underpinnings of the law in industrializing
England. Douglas Hay's persuasive argument about the reinforcement
of class rule through the judicious and idiosyncratic use of mercy toward
the humble can be turned on its head and adapted to the analysis of
gender inequality; in other words, patriarchal sexual norms were obscured through the judicious and idiosyncratic punishment of rapists.
The 'rare spectacle of a titled villain on the gallows made a sharp impression' that the law operated for the poor as well as the rich; similarly,
the rare pronouncement of a life sentence or corporal punishment imposed on a rapist in turn-of-the-century York County could be, and
was invariably interpreted by judges and news media as, evidence that
the law truly avenged wronged women.[19] In fact, women who had been
sexually assaulted could take little comfort from the results of rape trials
in the county. In the end, as complainants and defendants alike learned,
only credible women were deemed worthy of protection, while only
men of low character were considered sufficiently dangerous to convict.

By concentrating on the factors that contributed to the changing and,
at times, relatively high rates of rape conviction in turn-of-the-century
York County, I am not suggesting that the law was an effective response
to sexual violence. For every complaint that resulted in a conviction,
countless others never appeared on police records: women believed attackers who threatened to kill them if they talked; girls were afraid
that their parents would punish them for bringing shame to the family;
or victims weighed the trauma of the trial and its publicity against the
option of recovering in private. Those few women who did see their
assailants convicted might have subsequently regretted their decision
to press charges after having to answer probing questions about their
sexual reputations and being made to relate every painful detail of the
assault in open court. Rather, I am asking why, in spite of sexist suspicions about the credibility of rape complainants, some men *were* convicted, and how, in the process, the patriarchal character of rape law
was obscured.

THE CHANGING CONTEXT OF RAPE PROSECUTIONS

Toronto's early position as a military garrison and, later, as the provincial
capital lent it importance that far outweighed that of most county seats.
In 1880, it was still an overgrown, ramshackle town of warehouses,

saloons, and steam-driven factories. Fifty years later it had become a minor metropolis filled with banking headquarters, department stores, and movie theatres. As the second-largest city in the country, it set the standard of civilization for Anglo-Canada, or so Torontonians boasted. In moral matters, Torontonians considered themselves superior not only to their French rivals in Montreal but to the citizens of the sinful cities to the south. In reform campaigns that outmatched the efforts launched in other North American cities, Toronto's city fathers and mothers began in the 1880s to consciously preserve a sense of small-town morality in civic affairs. The 'dangerous delights' of city life, particularly prostitution, gambling, and drinking, were their prime targets.[20] Journalist C.K. Clark was one of the few public figures to denounce police efforts to suppress organized vice. His ironically titled *Of Toronto the Good* claimed that the force's crack-down on brothels allowed immorality to flourish on an informal basis. Aside from Clark, however, there were few dissenting voices raised as women's organizations, such as the YWCA and the Local Council of Women, along with men and women in sabbatarian groups and moral and social reform organizations, gained influence in civic politics. By the 1910s, the social purity movement was in full swing and Toronto became the bellwether of the national campaign to bring about a new moral order in Canada. Through the 1910s and 1920s, the policing and legal reforms they had advocated – the suppression of brothels, the limitation of alcohol consumption and sales, the stricter enforcement of vagrancy laws against 'occasional prostitutes,' the establishment of separate courts for children and women – were largely instituted. By the onset of the Depression, the net of moral regulation had been cast more broadly and pulled more tightly than it had been fifty years earlier. This process of enveloping moral regulation may not have made the city a safer place for women but it does seem to have made it more dangerous for some men.

Toronto's moral uplifters expressed a genuine concern about women's sexual vulnerability in the city, particularly as thousands of young, single women migrated from farms and towns each year – many from rural York County – in search of waged work. Concern for their moral safety grew as the Anglo-Celtic majority apprehensively observed the rising proportion of Jews, Italians, Greeks, Slavic peoples, and Chinese concentrated in the city's impoverished downtown wards.[21] These newcomers very quickly replaced the Irish, the stock figures in colourful newspaper reports about Police Court characters, as the focus of public pronouncements about the 'source' of urban immorality.[22] The *Report of the Toronto Social Survey Committee* of 1915, instigated by the Local Council of Women's demands to investigate the city's alleged white slave trade, claimed that 'foreigners' capitalized on naive country girls new to Toronto; in the same breath, it also alleged that young women recklessly set their own courses toward immorality by bartering sexual favours for material gain. Even in official investigations of the sexual endangerment of young women, then, Toronto's moral overseers revealed their equally strong convictions about the promiscuity of young women. Throughout Toronto's transition from a large town to a big city, concerns about women's safety and attempts to decrease their vulnerability in the city were expressed through urban mythology about dangerous strangers, white slavers, and 'good times' girls. More important, the rise of prostitution as a master narrative in tales of the dangerous city cast all non-marital heterosexual encounters, even those that women claimed were non-consensual, in a suspicious light. Although campaigns demanding that immorality be uprooted may have encouraged the prosecution of rape in turn-of-the-century Toronto, the urban moral reform movement provided shaky support for rape complainants' credibility.[23] The prosecution of rape cases was swept up in these political, social, and cultural currents, and not simply funnelled into a single, patriarchal stream.

The changing nature of rape prosecutions is apparent through the contents of York County Supreme Court indictment files, which, in some cases, included Magistrate's Court transcripts, informations, and exhibits. In addition, the quarterly reports of the Clerk of the Assize (a précis of the proceedings and cases tried during each assize) supplement the indictments, which are incomplete in some decades.[24] Toronto's population dominance in the county is reflected in the urban-rural split: 102 of 118 indictments referred to attacks in the city. Slightly more than two prosecutions per annum might appear to offer a questionable sample, and, indeed, caution is called for in the interpretation of percentages based on small numbers. Some historical rape studies and recent reports on sexual violence have actually dealt with even smaller samples than the York County total, and those with large samples have tended to be based on depositions rather than indictments, or they have grouped a variety of offences together under a general category of 'sexual violence.' Although prosecution statistics offer only impressions, then, they may nevertheless chart changes over time within jurisdictions and they allow comparisons to be made between jurisdictions. Not only did the number of rapes prosecuted vary considerably in York County from 1880 to 1930, but the rate of men convicted as charged changed over time, averaging approximately 20 per cent. Combined with the conviction rate on lesser charges, the average proportion of successful prosecutions was almost 37 per cent – a figure comparable to or slightly higher than that for other historical jurisdictions. During the height of Toronto's urban moral reform campaign, however, the conviction rate was significantly higher than levels historians have documented in other periods and places.[25]

Information contained in indictment files suggests that the city police, the rural constables, justices of the peace, magistrates, and crown attorneys exercised enormous discretion in deciding how to deal with a man accused of rape. When women or parents entered a police station or a JP's home to claim that a sexual assault had occurred, law enforcement officials channelled those tales either back out the door or down the narrow corridor of legal definitions. Alleged rapes could be prosecuted under a variety of statutes, including rape, attempted rape, indecent assault, carnal knowledge, procurement, and seduction. Although some historians, along with contemporary feminist activists, reject artificial legal definitions of sexual offences in order to focus on the victim's experience of violation, seemingly abstract legal distinctions between rape and other forms of violent or manipulative heterosexual sex are nevertheless important for their very artificiality. A woman's experience of an unwanted sexual encounter may have been the same, whether the man was eventually charged with seduction or rape, but the state's choice to indict for rape rather than an offence with lower evidentiary requirements, or one in which the victim's age rather than her consent was at issue, was a significant symbolic gesture. An indictment for rape signalled the gravity of the offence above all other sexual crimes, and for that reason, this paper looks exclusively at prosecutions for rape.

Rape was defined as unlawful 'carnal knowledge' of a woman by a man, other than her husband, without her consent. Since 1870, the legal test of rape was simply 'any degree of [vaginal] penetration'; furthermore, the Crown was not required to establish ejaculation or the use of force in order to indict a suspect.[26] That definition remained in force after the codification of criminal law in 1892 and throughout the period in question. What made rape unique among sexual offences was its punishment: until 1873, rape was punishable only by death, and after that point it was subject to a maximum penalty of death *or* life imprisonment.[27] Because it remained a capital crime, rape could be tried exclusively in the Supreme Court, where judges had the power to impose sentences of death. The only other change in the legal framework of rape statutes came in 1921, when it became possible for judges to add whipping to a term of imprisonment.[28] Although the maximum penalties for rape were uniformly severe from the 1880s to the 1920s, the statutory minimum punishment of seven years provided considerable scope for sentencing flexibility. Furthermore, since many men were convicted on lesser charges that carried no *minimum* punishment, the potential outcome of a rape trial ranged from the remote possibility of a judge donning the black cap and imposing a sentence of death to, at the other extreme, the pronouncement of a suspended sentence and the release of a convicted man on his own recognizance.

THE PROFILE OF RAPE PROSECUTIONS

Between 1880 and 1929, 118 indictments for rape, involving 156 men (and one woman) were filed in York County (see table 1). Of the 16 cases in which alleged attacks occurred outside of the city, 5 were committed on its suburban outskirts. The distribution of cases over the fifty-year period did not grow at the same rate as the population. The 1890s stand out, for in that decade the number of indictments filed more than tripled relative to the 1880s. After the turn of the century, the rate levelled off to 3.5 per annum and then sank even lower by the 1910s and 1920s, by which point Toronto's population had reached close to one-half million. Unless one assumes that the actual incidence of sexual assault dropped off, an assumption impossible to prove and unlikely to be true, the dwindling number of rape trials might appear to signal local law enforcers' declining interest in trying alleged rapists. That hypothesis may be challenged, however, by two factors. First, the rate of conviction actually rose as the number of trials dwindled: in the 1910s, when only 24 men were tried for rape, one-third were convicted as charged and a further 29 per cent were convicted on lesser charges (see table 2). Second, it appears that indictments for a variety of other sexual offences that carried lower maximum penalties (particularly carnal knowledge and indecent assault) were used increasingly after the turn of the century as an alternative to rape, for which convictions had been extremely low in the 1890s. In the 1880s and 1890s, for instance, the Toronto police made no arrests for carnal knowledge but by the 1910s and 1920s, they arrested an average of ˙12 men per annum. The changing arrest rates for indecent assault are even more dramatic: from the 1880s to 1910, approximately 11 men were arrested

TABLE 1

Men Indicted for Rape and Results, York County, 1880–1929

Decade	NG	NGBD	NB	HJ	?	G	G < er	Total
1880s	7	2	1	0	1	4	2	17
1890s	25	11	5	5	0	4	4	54
1900s	13	4	3	2	1	8	4	35
1910s	8	0	1	0	0	8	7	24
1920s	6	4	1	0	0	7	9	27
Totals	59	21	11	7	2	31	26	157*
Per cent	37.6	13.4	7.0	4.5	1.3	19.7	16.6	100

*Includes all defendants named in 118 indictments
Key: NG = not guilty; NGBD = not guilty by direction of court, or case dropped by Crown; NB = no bill; HJ = hung jury and no indication of retrial; ? = unknown; G = guilty as charged; G < er = guilty of a lesser offence (e.g., attempted rape, indecent assault, common assault, carnal knowledge)

TABLE 2

Percentage of Men Guilty of Rape and Guilty as Charged and/or of Lesser Offences

Decade	Guilty of rape	Guilty as charged and/or of lesser offences
1880–9	23.5	35.3
1890–9	7.4	14.8
1900–9	22.9	34.3
1910–19	33.3	62.5
1920–9	25.0	59.3
Average	19.6%	36.7%

annually, but in the 1910s and 1920s, that number shot up to 45.[29] What these figures suggest, then, is that after the 1890s, the crown attorney's office, in conjunction with the police, opted for charges that carried lighter penalties but which were more likely to lead to convictions. Such a practice followed a middle road between, on the one hand, judicial impatience over flimsy cases and, on the other, criticism from the increasingly powerful social purity movement that the criminal justice system was turning a blind eye to sexual immorality.

An accused rapist's likelihood of conviction, then, varied considerably over the years in which Toronto emerged as an industrial metropolis. Similarly, the profile of convicted rapists changed as anxieties over the moral tone of urban life shaped the prosecution of rape. In the late-nineteenth century, with the rise of 'Toronto the Good,' crown attorneys amplified evidence of intemperance and vice in their attempts to secure convictions; by the 1910s, rising xenophobia rendered foreign-born men vulnerable to conviction, whether or not they were intemperate. In the postwar era, jurors and judges seemed to find cases that exemplified the dangers of big-city living most troubling. In the rural outskirts of York County, few men were accused of rape but their likelihood of conviction was significantly higher because local justices of the peace and constables apparently selected only the most compelling cases for prosecution. These conviction patterns do not, however, overturn the earlier observation about character as a determinant of defendants' fates. In country areas, for instance, both the complainant and the accused were likely known to the police and magistrates whose assessments of both parties' characters played a significant role in the selection of cases that were eventually tried. As the final section will argue, men who appeared to be of suspicious character, such as strangers and tramps, and those of demonstrably low character, particularly incestuous fathers, were treated with severity, no matter when they were tried or where the offence took place.

All but a few of the cases heard by York County Supreme Court juries were as much urban morality tales as trials of men charged with rape. The jury panels which were chosen to represent the county's rural and urban mix would understandably have gained the impression that rape was a distinctly urban problem.[30] Crown attorneys often intoned about the moral decline of the city when they argued cases but jurors more often than not assumed that urban women's lack of feminine modesty 'provoked' sexual immorality. In a typical trial, two teenaged men escaped conviction because the victim had seemed to be a willing participant in a casual sexual encounter. Domestic servant Emma Foam had been strolling with a friend on Yonge Street when she met John Noble, who invited her to a restaurant in the red-light district. There, he and Fred Pallen had raped her, she claimed. Prosecutor John Kerr faced long odds in his attempt to distinguish between the immorality of a casual sexual encounter and rape. He told the jury that 'Immorality is *rampant*' in Toronto, but he went on to say that the woman's 'fall' could not excuse the assault: 'young men like this must not think because immorality is *rampant* that they can *abuse* and *rape*.' The jury believed otherwise.[31] This case, representative of the majority of rape trials in which coercive sex was translated into a consensual liaison, suggests that juries were prepared to believe that women, particularly young 'working girls,' deserved what they suffered if they flirted with men. Neither Foam's friend's corroboration of her story nor the arresting officer's evidence of her dishevelled and hysterical condition when he made the arrest impressed the jury. Thus, Torontonians' growing concern with 'rampant' immorality by no means translated into an unreflective readiness to convict men charged with rape, particularly when the victim in question was evidently a 'fallen' woman. For men to be convicted, it was necessary that they be presented as serious threats, not so much to the victim or to other women as to the moral foundations of urban life.

In the 1880s, it was not sexual violence but drunkenness, gambling, and prostitution that commanded the greatest concern among those committed to improving the tone of city life. Grand jury reports from this decade consistently recommended the suppression of the liquor trade in districts where crime was rife. While commercial amusements would later bear the blame as the breeding grounds of urban immorality, saloons bore the brunt of criticism in the 1880s. As one grand jury complained, taverns were in the business of manufacturing 'drunkards and criminals': 'The excessive number of places where liquors are sold is thus a curse to the community and a great limitation of their number would bring hope and brightness into multitudes of homes where now there is broken heartedness and despair ...'[32] Newspapers featured daily reports on the endless stream of drunkards, pickpockets, and prostitutes who filed into the Toronto Police Court after police executed their nightly sweeps of the rowdier neighbourhoods. Reports of rape, in contrast, were rare and reserved. This was no longer the Toronto of the 1850s when details of the 'Sayer St. Outrage,' including witnesses' personal quirks and the frequent outbursts of spectators' laughter, were recounted for the entertainment of readers.[33] When reporting the conviction of Michael Ryan for rape in 1884, for instance, the *News*, normally the source of florid descriptions of courtroom tales, soberly stated that it had already printed as many details 'as decency permits,' even though it had simply said that Ryan had been charged for an 'outrage.' So while Torontonians could talk openly about drunkenness and vice in the 1880s there was no public discourse that articulated concerns about sexual violence towards women, particularly if they were married, widowed, or aged.

Until the end of the decade, sexual assaults most likely to lead to conviction were those that implicated the 'drunkards and criminals' of the grand jury's fears. Cases such as Michael Ryan's showed that the abuse of alcohol could lead not only to property damage but to serious assaults of innocent bystanders. Thirty-five-year-old widow Mary Gibson had been staying at the Kelly household in a notorious part of town populated by poor Irish and known for its drunken fights. So it was hardly unusual that all the occupants of the house had been drinking on an April evening, or that Michael Ryan and Arthur Christie had been 'ordered out' because they had grown belligerent. They returned at midnight and broke into the house to settle a dispute about money but set upon Mrs Gibson instead. The melee attracted the police, who heard her cries of 'murder!' and found Michael Ryan in the course of raping Mrs Gibson in a lane off Lombard Street, 'that classic locality,' the *Telegram* commented. That the original police charge of indecent assault was increased to rape signalled the seriousness of the assault, while the conviction of the 'tough looking youth' after only a few minutes' deliberation suggests that jurors were unwilling to overlook sexual assault, even if it occurred among the most despised of the urban poor.[34] Ryan's and later Christie's conviction and sentences of seven years sent a message that the criminal justice system could distinguish between the rowdy sociability of the poor and the brutal sexual assault of a woman, particularly as she was a visitor to the neighbourhood. The Crown's success did not, however, overturn patriarchal notions since the conviction and sentence were dramatic exceptions to the rule in the 1880s. The fate of Ryan and Christie did, however, provide the emerging temperance movement with a case to illustrate further the links between alcohol and crime.

Toronto Mayor William Howland, elected in 1886, represented the hopes and dreams of evangelical reformers and temperance advocates in particular. One of his first acts as mayor was to establish a Morality Department (officially known as the Staff Inspector's Department). The more than 300 per cent jump in indictments from the 1880s to the 1890s corresponds with the rise of this police branch. Staff Inspector Archibald and his morality squad took up Howland's challenge to expose and uproot immorality wherever it festered. As the mayor's flagship of urban moral reform, the department was a favourite target of C.S. Clark and the libertarian press, which was convinced that the police had become the tools of the WCTU and other wrong-headed ladies who meddled in civic affairs.[35] Clark believed that punishing men for rape could only backfire because the exposure of the crime invariably 'disgraces' the complainant 'forever.'[36] After observing a decade of elevated arrest statistics, he might well have worried that the Morality

Department had gone overboard, but the conviction rates for accused rapists would have assured him that sanity prevailed in the courtroom.

In a textbook example of the disjunction between ideology and the 'untidy world' of social practice, the conviction rate in the 1890s was significantly lower than at any other point in the period. Judges and juries, 'deluged' by an average of five or six rape cases per year, may have suspected that in addition to women's supposed tendency to make false accusations, the police and the Crown had begun to encourage flimsy or false reports of rape. Twenty per cent of the indictments in the 1890s resulted either in the Crown withdrawing the case or in the judge directing a verdict of not guilty. In a further 9 per cent of cases, grand juries were unwilling to declare true bills or trial juries were unable to reach verdicts. The zealousness of the police in prosecuting rape was met not with praise but with suspicion and even disapproval by the court. There were several occasions when the presiding judge rebuked the Crown for wasting the court's time (and testing the judge's patience). In a revolting 1899 case, the police had laid charges against eight young Irishmen and one woman for gang raping an old woman in her house in a neighbourhood known as a criminal haunt. The attack grew out of a conflict between neighbours and it appears to have been something of a latter-day charivari, although the 'music' in this instance was particularly 'rough.'[37] The victim, Jane Owens, testified that Maud Sullivan had led the attack, yelling, '"Go ahead and give it to her."' Sullivan further egged on the men by accusing them of being 'no good' if they failed to rape the old woman. There was some doubt, however, as to Owen's ability to identify the accused persons. Judge MacMahon, himself an Irish Catholic, was furious with the police who had tracked down the suspects through leads from eyewitnesses who later acted as Crown witnesses. In a column headed 'Pointers for the Police,' the *Telegram* reported that MacMahon's charge to the jury virtually directed them to acquit: '[H]e severely reprobated the habit detectives and police officers have not only in hounding down a man who had a conviction against him but of their superabundant and over-officious zeal in securing convictions.' The Crown had discovered, among other bits of damning character evidence, that one of the defendants, David Gordon, had been convicted four years earlier for throwing a snowball and had served sixty days for the offence; the *Telegram* sniffed at this vain attempt to discredit the 'now most respectable young man.'[38] More suspicious still, city detectives had sat at crown attorney Kerr's side throughout the trial, constantly 'suggesting things' to secure a conviction. 'His Lordship also took objection to the manner in which the police worked up evidence against prisoners,' the report continued. Not surprisingly, the jury returned a not guilty verdict after deliberating for one hour. The acquittal of the prisoners was met with applause.[39]

By the early years of this century, it appears that the police and the Crown had learned something about keeping their moral zeal in step with the willingness of judges and juries to convict. The number of rape indictments declined sharply in the 1900s and levelled off to approximately 2.5 per annum in the 1910s and 1920s. The percentage of men found guilty of rape returned to the level established prior to the introduction of the Morality Department and then climbed significantly in the 1910s when the social purity movement was at the height of its influence in city politics. Even more dramatic was the willingness of juries to convict on lesser charges (usually attempted rape or indecent assault) rather than to acquit or to fail to agree on a verdict as had so often been the case in the 1890s. In the 1910s, almost two-thirds of the indictments for rape resulted in convictions and half of those men were found guilty as charged. Unlike the Victorian juries who were reluctant to convict, Toronto juries after the turn of the century were relatively disposed to believe that indicted men had indeed committed a crime. Male sexual misconduct was treated more seriously as social purity advocates pressed the police to enforce a single standard of sexual morality on Toronto's citizenry. By the 1910s it was not just the Morality Department but a broad coalition of Protestant reformers and city politicians who demanded that the criminal justice system exercise its power to inflict punishment on men as well as women.[40]

These transitions on the sexual political stage were entwined with Anglo-Celtic Torontonians' perceptions of new immigrants. Unlike in the US South, where Blacks suffered the imposition of prejudicial justice, the 'strangers' within Toronto's 'gates' were identified by their unfamiliar languages, customs, and religions, all of which marked them as less civilized and potentially dangerous in the eyes of the smug host society.[41] For all its pretensions to upholding British traditions of fairness and justice, the criminal justice system in York County responded to these currents of xenophobia to the extent, in some cases, of eroding its legitimacy in the eyes of the daily newspapers. Men who were readily identified as 'the Other' were particularly vulnerable to conviction irrespective of the evidence, as the prosecution of David Hawes demonstrated. His 1901 trial was the only case in this period in which the cliché of sexual endangerment – the rape of a white woman by a Black man – was played out in a Toronto courtroom. Long a staple of fear-mongering in the US South, the tale of sexual victimization of white women was given a Canadian twist in this case. Seventeen-year-old Louisa LeBar, a domestic living in rural Manitoba, had travelled by train on a visit to her sister who lived outside of Toronto. While waiting in Union Station to board a connecting train, she claimed that porter David Hawes tricked her into boarding the government car, where he raped her. Many reported seeing the two together, apparently on friendly terms, but no one heard her call for help and the examining physician could subsequently find no medical evidence of penetration or violence. Uncorroborated complaints like LeBar's rarely led to an indictment, let alone the conviction of the accused man, but this case touched a sensitive nerve because it combined racist fears with contemporary warnings about the sexual enslavement of 'Canadian' girls in the big city. Furthermore, whether the encounter had been coercive or consensual it violated social prohibitions against miscegenation.

Although rape trials were scarcely ever reported in the dailies at the turn of the century, 'COLOURED MAN ON TRIAL' trumpeted that this was no ordinary case. Hawes' vulnerability to vigilante-style justice inspired two of the best criminal lawyers in the country, veteran E.F.B. Johnston and rising star T.C. Robinette, to take on the penniless man's case. Their considerable courtroom skills proved inadequate to the near-impossible task of acquitting the porter. Still, Torontonians could congratulate themselves for having tried rather than lynched the man. As the *News* coldly remarked, Hawes was lucky to receive a sentence of ten years for a crime for 'which, if it had occurred in the Southern States, he would undoubtedly have been tried very summarily and suffered immediate death at the hands of an angry mob.' Toronto newspaper readers were familiar with US lynching incidents because they were reported, usually on the front page, in all the dailies in the period.[42] As the *News* comment suggests, Canadians' pride in the superiority of British justice may have been mixed with a sense of envy toward their white Southern neighbours. Judge Fergusson claimed that he would have imposed the death penalty had it not fallen out of fashion in the British colonies.[43] He must have recognized, however, that a ten-year sentence for a poor man, already fifty, might, indeed, have spelled the death penalty.[44]

Even though he was an English-speaking Canadian resident, Hawes' race branded him as a dangerous 'Other.' In Toronto, however, the potential criminality of European 'foreigners,' who far outnumbered

Blacks, commanded more concern, particularly after the war broke out. Six of the seventeen defendants convicted of rape or lesser offences in the 1910s were men who fit the Toronto Social Survey Report's image of ethnic types most dangerous to young, 'Canadian' women. Prior to 1910, all of those indicted for rape, other than Hawes, had been white men of Irish or British extraction. This sudden appearance of 'foreigners' in the prisoner's dock caught the attention of jurymen, who continued to be drawn from the county's Anglo-Celtic majority.⁴⁵ As early as the Fall Assizes of 1911, grand jury reports began what came to be persistent comments about the rise of the 'foreign element' indicted for serious offences. Their suspicion of non-Christians and non-British citizens reached its zenith in the war years and the immediate postwar period. Six weeks after World War I erupted, for instance, German chauffeur Marion Otto was convicted on the lesser charge of attempted rape. Judge Britton had presented a charge supportive of the accused man's claims of innocence and admitted after the jury delivered its verdict that he had considered Otto to be innocent. Nonetheless, he did not exercise his discretion to impose a suspended sentence but consigned him to three months at the Central Prison on top of the eleven months he had already spent in jail while awaiting his trial.⁴⁶ Jurors openly vented their suspicions about the criminality of the foreign born. The grand jury's spring 1919 report, for instance, stressed the 'fact that the foreign element contributed largely to the ... serious cases ... [A]ny steps taken towards the deportation of these undesirables now within the country [would] be greatly in the interest of this country at large.'⁴⁷

In this hostile atmosphere, Yovan Yocock and Yako Toshilik found themselves on trial for the rape of sixteen-year-old Vera Kirkland. In Police Court, the young working girl spun a tale of urban villainy that could have been lifted from a social purity tract. In September 1919 she went out in search of a waitressing job in an ice-cream parlour on the southern fringes of Cabbagetown, near chopsuey houses, fortune-tellers' parlours, and bootleggers' hideaways. Instead of offering her a job, the parlour operators raped her, she claimed. There were no witnesses to corroborate the complainant's testimony and doctors at St Michael's Hospital found that her hymen was unbroken and that she exhibited no physical injuries. The accused men admitted that Kirkland had spent the evening in the restaurant, where three different men had bought her ice-cream, tea, and chocolates. If anyone had raped her, they conjectured, it must have been one of the others.

Consorting with foreigners in a rough end of town and accepting treats from strange men was normally defined as 'occasional prostitution' and frequently understood by the police in this period as evidence of sexual delinquency or vagrancy. The spectators who had disrupted the courtroom proceedings while Kirkland gave her evidence may have suspected that she was a less-than-credible witness. Indeed, the supposed victim exposed the baselessness of her claims on the day after the ice-cream parlour operators were sentenced to seven years in the Kingston Penitentiary for attempted rape. On 30 October, Toronto *Star* readers were greeted with the front-page story: 'GIRL RETRACTS STORY WHICH JAILED TWO MEN.' Kirkland had gone to the defence counsel, W.D.M. Shorey, to retract her evidence and to admit that 'her story told on the stand was not a recital of fact, but a dream.' While in the 1890s the police had weathered criticism for their indiscriminate zeal, this botched prosecution implicated the Crown and the bench. Agents of Toronto's criminal justice system were evidently prepared to try and convict foreigners for sexual offences on the word of unchaste, untrustworthy complainants. And finally, the outcome confirmed how easily the state could undermine its image as the upholder of natural justice by succumbing to prejudices against ethnic outsiders.[48]

As wartime immigration restrictions and deportations of 'undesirables' quieted Torontonians' alarm over the 'foreign element,' new fears about the amorality of 'modern' life began to manifest themselves in the prosecution of rape cases in the 1920s.[49] Jazz music, dancehalls, and cars put a new spin on old concerns about the temptations of city living and the dangers these pleasures might conceal. A flurry of by-laws passed in the 1910s and 1920s targeted commercial amusement places while the Ontario Temperance Act of 1916 modernized Mayor Howland's earlier attack on the saloon industry.[50] Police women, as well as men, patrolled the city's parks, dancehalls, movie theatres, and ice rinks in an effort to regulate the burgeoning youth culture. Although familiar patterns of sexual assault involving the rape of women by men they knew persisted, rape cases that seemed to illustrate the dangers of the fast life seemed to draw the greatest concern from the criminal justice system.

One of the recognizably modern features of rape prosecutions by the 1920s was the visible participation of women. In Toronto, feminists had lobbied the city for more than twenty years to appoint a woman magistrate to the Police Court so that cases involving girls and women might be heard, at least at the level of a preliminary hearing, by a person sympathetic to the special needs of victims and the peculiar problems of women offenders. In 1922 Dr Margaret Patterson, a long-time feminist and advocate of strict moral standards for men and women, headed Canada's second 'Women's Court.'[51] A variety of agencies and professional women, including the Big Sisters, nurses, social workers, probation officers, and doctors, appeared in Patterson's court as advocates of girls and women. In a 1924 case involving the rape of a fourteen-year-old girl by her stepfather, Charles Davey, a school nurse and Dr Edna Guest, the VD clinic physician at the Mercer Reformatory and a founder of the Women's College Hospital, presented evidence before Magistrate Patterson, who deemed the evidence against the man sufficient to commit him for trial. Dr Guest's gynaecological experience certainly left her better qualified than the general practitioners who routinely testified that medical evidence of rape complainants' vaginal lacerations and extensive bleeding was consistent with consensual intercourse.[52] Once before the Supreme Court, Davey was convicted and sentenced to ten years in the Kingston Penitentiary. Karen Dubinsky has argued that the Ontario public 'balked' at the state's implementation of feminist and social purity measures,[53] and the Toronto Women's Court, headed by a cantankerous suffragist with no legal training, certainly drew criticism from the legal fraternity. Nonetheless, the conviction figures for the decade suggest that the modest feminization of the prosecutorial process did not produce a mass of acquittals as occurred in the 1890s. Although there was a slight drop in the conviction rate from its peak in the 1910s, juries continued to find almost 60 per cent of men guilty.[54]

Both men and women could agree that sexual assault incidents that demonstrated the dangers of modern city life called for sanctions, even if the character of the woman involved was suspect. It took only thirty minutes for the jury to find married war veteran Keith Gordon guilty of raping Caroline Monteith, a single woman of thirty who still lived in her family home. Gordon, like many accused men, contended that he had engaged in consensual sex. He had driven Monteith from the Hillcrest Dance Hall near Yonge and St Clair Streets to the rural outskirts of the city after midnight. Emboldened by a few illegally purchased drinks, he asked: 'if we were going to have a bit of fun [meaning] I meant to have connection with her ... [s]he then lay back with her own free will and told me I could do it if I did not get her in the family way and I said I wouldn't. We then had connection. After she got up she told me she was bleeding. I said if you never were touched before you will surely bleed.' Gordon openly admitted this tale to the police after he had been arrested and cautioned. While he knew that he had committed several breaches of the Temperance Act and violated his marriage vows, he hardly felt that he had committed a serious crime.[55] The defence, ably conducted by experienced barrister Frank Slattery, presented the well-worn theory of consent: Monteith, after all, had returned to the city in his car after the incident and had avoided talking to her mother until the following day. Gordon and his lawyer were both shocked when the jury found him guilty as charged. Judge Kelly considered the verdict just and, more than that, he hoped that Gordon's conviction and his six-year sentence might serve as a warning against the moral pitfalls of dancehalls and the dangers of automobiles. The *Mail and Empire* related that '[h]is Lordship ... deplored the type of dance hall which the evidence had shown existed in the city, and said he heartily agreed with the view held by many that the automobile was a curse to the community.' While none of the four dailies had reported the trial, assuming, perhaps, that it would result in acquittal, all but the more highbrow *Globe* covered Judge Kelly's sentencing remarks. The *Star* reported that Gordon 'seemed stunned by the sentence' and 'reeled slightly in the box.'[56] His enjoyable sexual escapade, initiated in the sexually charged atmosphere of a dancehall, had been dramatically altered in the trial process into a parable about the dangers of fast living.[57]

Automobiles were once again at issue in the 1928 trial of two youths, twenty-one-year-old Arthur Punsheon and twenty-two-year-old Thomas Hayes, who were convicted of raping an eighteen-year-old Scottish domestic whom they had taken out 'on a motor ride.' There was plenty in Mary McPhail's behaviour to convince the jury that she had been a willing participant, as the men both contended. She admitted that she had met the pair in a Queen Street East restaurant and agreed to go for a ride but denied that she had drunk wine with them. The trio then drove to a secluded spot under the Bloor Viaduct, where the sexual encounter (consensual, according to Hayes and Punsheon) took place. Although medical evidence of bruises and lacerations supported her story of having been raped, doctors and juries often understood that a certain degree of physical roughness was to be expected in 'normal' intercourse, particularly with two men in the same evening. What seemed to weigh heavier on the mind of the judge, if not the jury, was the men's use of a car for immoral purposes. Mr Justice Logie used his discretion to order corporal punishment when he handed down sentences of seven years with twenty lashes each. In imposing the sentence, the *Star* reported, Logie made 'scathing remarks on the cruelty shown by [the men].' Defence counsel W.B. Horkins pleaded for mercy, especially for Hayes who was the sole support of his invalid mother, but Logie would have none of it, as the *Telegram* related: 'These two young men are in a class of evildoers which unfortunately is becoming too numerous. These curb-cruisers picked the girl up in their auto; they tried to induce and when they found they couldn't, they raped her.' Judges Logie and Kelly, men who had grown up before the advent of automobiles, spoke as if buggies and sleighs had never before provided men with the opportunity to whisk women away from safety. The speed of autos seemed to stand for youth out of control. It was men such as Gordon, Punsheon, and Hayes who revealed that dangers to the moral well-being of the community were not only external but implicated in the very forces of modernization.[58]

What had changed in Toronto rape prosecutions, from the days before the Morality Department to the rise of the social purity and urban reform movements, was that a man indicted for rape in the 1910s and 1920s was much more likely than one indicted thirty or forty years earlier to be convicted. The high acquittal rate in the 1890s, however, showed that Toronto juries and judges were reluctant to be stern judges of accused rapists if they heard more than one or two cases per assize. They were, however, relatively disposed to convict when the men who stood accused of rape looked or sounded unfamiliar to them. As the Crown increasingly opted to indict men on the less serious charges of indecent assault and carnal knowledge, some of the more dubious cases were sifted down to the lower courts. Despite the constellation of forces encouraging the conviction of men who sexually assaulted women, however, the rate of men convicted as charged never climbed above 33 per cent. The courtroom remained a forum where character, more than evidence, governed the outcome of rape cases.

CHARACTER AND CREDIBILITY

Although the cultural context of rape trials in Toronto changed over the late-nineteenth and early-twentieth centuries, the questions of character and credibility, central issues in all criminal trials, did not. Patterns of systemic discrimination in respect to gender, ethnicity, class, and race were evident in the broad contours of convictions and acquittals, but juries nevertheless determined guilt and innocence on a case-by-case basis, looking at 'this man and this woman in this situation,' in Clark and Lewis' terms. Chaste women and respectable men were the surest candidates for credibility, yet women with blemished characters were sometimes believed and, conversely, men with solid character references were not always taken at their word. The reputations and courtroom demeanour of alleged rapists and victims were not considered in isolation but balanced and weighed according to the moral preoccupations of juries and judges. That some of those criteria were patriarchal is undeniable: women who encountered danger after straying from the confines of domesticity and male protection were judged harshly because they had squandered their credibility. In the hands of Toronto's increasingly specialized defence lawyers, evidence of female independence was slickly twisted into evidence of promiscuity, yet no defence was a 'cinch,' as Susan Brownmiller has claimed.[59] As the previous section argued, men who seemed to represent the growth of the criminal class or the suspicious 'foreign element' in Toronto could be denied the generous benefit of doubt usually granted to accused rapists, particularly during periods of moral reform agitation. When the propertied men who served on grand juries agitated for corporal punishment in rape cases, as they did repeatedly in the early 1900s, they called for an extraordinary sanction designed, they declared, 'to safeguard the community.'[60] Crown prosecutors tried to tap into these concerns about public welfare by painting accused rapists as threats not so much to individual women but to the wider community. When this strategy worked, most persuasively with the prosecution of stranger rapists, the myth of the law as the avenger of wronged womanhood was reinforced and the state could reaffirm its role as the enforcer of natural justice.

No matter how skilful the defence lawyer, some men proved to be more difficult to defend than others. The Crown readily capitalized on cases that entailed the violation of widely held moral codes, and not simply the alleged violation of the prosecutrix. For this reason, the conviction rate for men accused of raping their blood relations was high. That these men were indicted for rape, a potentially capital offence, rather than incest, an offence that carried a maximum penalty of fourteen years in addition to whipping, signalled the gravity of the crime.[61] The youth of the victims, a factor that consistently produced higher conviction rates, was undoubtedly significant as well.[62] Six of the eight men indicted for incestuous rapes in Toronto between 1880 and 1929 were found guilty. Juries, judges, and the press considered this type of rape more as a sin than a criminal offence; the language they used to describe incest was filled with the same terms of pollution and disgust reserved for portrayals of interracial rape, homosexual offences, bestiality, and child molestation. When Judge Fergusson sentenced Black porter David Hawes, for instance, he described his rape of a white woman as a 'dirty case' that called for the death penalty. Crimes against fundamental taboos seemed to call for extraordinary responses from the criminal justice system. Whenever grand juries submitted reports for assizes that included 'grave offences' against 'females of tender years,' they invariably recommended corporal punishment. The fall 1894 report, for instance, advised the 'application of the cat during the term of imprisonment ... *freely* and *often.*'[63] Clearly juries' and judges' willingness to grant men credit had its limits.

Scathing sentencing remarks spat by judges at men accused of incest rapes reflected broader social norms about the inviolability of adult-child relations. 'FILTHY CASES AT THE ASSIZE' was the headline the *Empire* used in 1895 to describe the trial of John Mitchell for the rape of two of his daughters, aged fourteen and fifteen. The girls' mother had been dead for a year and the father had raped them both in their East End house while drunk. For Mitchell's 'heinous assault on his children,' Judge Street sentenced him to seven years at the Kingston Penitentiary. When Judge Riddell sentenced Charles Davey to ten years for raping his stepdaughter, he 'severely castigated' the man for committing a 'heinous offence.' Riddell noted that the punishment no longer called for the death penalty but he reminded Davey that 'the crime was still great.' The melodramatic descriptions of incest rapists and their high conviction rate and relatively lengthy sentences (none received fewer than five years) proclaimed that the state responded sternly to the violation of taboos against both incest and intergenerational sex. At the same time, the minuscule number of incest cases reflected the overall pattern of low and decreasing numbers of rapes prosecuted in Toronto. The trial of so few incest rapists, like the prosecution of only a few men annually in a city of almost 500,000 people, maintained the illusion that women and children had little to fear, particularly if they remained in the orbit of their male protectors. The court could afford to take a stern, righteous pose in part because it so seldom was called upon to do so.[64]

Like incest rapes, sexual assaults in rural York were treated differently by the court, which dealt overwhelmingly with tales of urban assaults. In spite of the social purity movement's characterization of the city as a site of sexual danger for young women, assaults which occurred in Toronto's rural outskirts were more likely than those which occurred in the city to result in conviction. Karen Dubinsky has argued that rural Ontario rapists, particularly those who had assaulted their own children, were convicted not because male sexual abuse was taken seriously but because Crown lawyers could manipulate stereotypes of rural backwardness and depravity. On another level, though, rural cases were more likely to result in conviction because they involved people who were known to the entire community. Even when the man was a stranger, the woman and her family were usually locals. Unlike city constables and police magistrates, local constables and justices of the peace were more likely to be familiar with the character of alleged victims and perpetrators and were accordingly reluctant to make arrests and commit men to trial unless the victim seemed more credible than the accused rapist.[65]

The sixteen cases of rape in York County that occurred either in rural farming areas, small towns, or the suburban fringes of Toronto reveal significant distinctions between urban and rural patterns of prosecution. While the average rate of conviction from 1880 to 1929 in the county was 36.7 per cent, men indicted for rapes committed outside of Toronto were convicted at a rate of 56.3 per cent. A particularly well-documented rural case illustrates how rural authorities' knowledge of alleged victims and rapists encouraged a higher rate of conviction in rural York County. The local constable's familiarity with the Clifford and Rushton families' reputations sealed Richard Rushton's 1895 conviction for the rape of Cassie Clifford in 1895. In Newmarket Constable Savage's opinion, the complainant was 'an innocent and childish girl' who had been 'brutally outraged.' Because he caught wind of the defence strategy to discredit the fifteen-year-old with testimony of her unchastity, Savage chivalrously boosted her credibility by soliciting character references from 'several leading ladies.' Cassie, a domestic servant, could bask in the reflected status of women whose lofty class positions confirmed their respectability. Of her former mistresses, Constable Savage reported, '[a]ll give her a good character in all respects and are very empathetic [sic] in their assertions as such.' For good measure, Savage added that her current employer 'is a very respectable lady.'

If respectable women could 'give' working-class people 'good character,' disreputable men could not take it away. Savage informed York County crown attorney that the case 'against Cassie will be very weak' because the witnesses engaged to damage 'the character of Cassie Clifford' lacked credibility. While Clifford had 'ladies' on her side, Rushton had 'a coloured man ... of the worst character ...' Rushton's reputation was not much better. He was a drinker who was often 'pretty full,' and even the local men treated him with caution. A man who had been drinking with Rushton on the evening of the attack had subsequently left town because he was afraid that 'Rushton wanted to get his hands on [him].' By the time of the trial, the scales of justice tipped in Clifford's favour thanks to the extraordinary efforts of the constable to bolster the credibility of an 'innocent' girl.[66]

In the city, police officers who were unlikely to know any of the individuals involved had neither the time nor the inclination to supply the Crown with evidence of the prosecutrix's virtuous reputation; consequently, Crown lawyers had to resort to different tactics to counter defence lawyers' attempts to impugn the character of alleged victims. The best a Crown prosecutor could hope for was a case that involved an alleged stranger attack. The stranger, like 'the foreigner,' is an archetypal symbol of danger, primarily for women and children but for men as well.[67] The turn-of-the-century 'tramp problem,' for instance, articulated the settled community's fears about shiftless men, living on the fringes of civilized society, ungoverned by social or moral codes.[68] Stranger rapists were least well equipped to establish their characters, as John Macpherson's 1925 case illustrated. The recent Scottish immigrant pleaded guilty to the charge that he had followed a young Finnish domestic to North Toronto, where she worked. After she stepped off the streetcar, he threw himself on her, 'blackening her eyes and knocking out some teeth.' Because little was known of her character (she had been in Canada only one month) there was nothing on which to base a defence of consent. MacPherson's history was better known. Although he had served gallantly in the war, his family had been destitute since they had moved to Canada because his incompetence and inability to cooperate with fellow employees had left him unable to find steady work.[69] Earlier in 1925 he had been arrested once for nonsupport and a second time for stealing a suit from Eaton's. Crown counsel Norman Sommerville asked the judge to impose a life sentence: 'It was an assault of an unprovoked and brutal character ... and he left this decent, innocent young girl in a serious condition.' MacPherson's sterling war record could not counteract his recent failures as a husband and provider, and his cowardly, public attack on the maid branded him as a danger to the entire community. Judge Lennox admitted that he was tempted to impose the death penalty but settled instead on a sentence of ten years along with twenty-one lashes. 'There is no other way to protect society from persons such as you other than by reasonably severe sentences,' he admonished the convicted man. In this case, unlike the Sullivan gang rape case in 1899, the police were congratulated for their dogged pursuit of the accused and the trial brought credit to the justice system as a whole.[70]

In areas of York County not yet part of Toronto proper, rape by a stranger or strangers could illustrate the dangers faced by communities so close to the city, yet without its safeguards for citizen safety. Unlike the well-to-do suburb of North Toronto, the Township of York, an area east of the Don River, had a long association with crime. In an 1899 report of an attempted gang rape on Eastern Avenue, for instance, the *News* invoked an image of Jack the Ripper's London when it claimed that the neighbourhood was 'practically at the mercy of thieves and toughs, particularly at nightfall.' East End citizens persistently called for greater police protection, but to no avail. So when Mrs Rachel Barrible claimed in 1903 that she had been raped by four men near Kingston Road and Woodbine Avenue, her misfortune seemed to substantiate East Enders' fears that their neighbourhood was inadequately policed. The first report of the crime in the *News* commented that the 'outrage emphasized the necessity of a more modern method of policing' that would include night patrols. When Mrs Barrible left the downtown hotel where she worked, she had crossed the river and entered a locale where deserted lanes and a wooded ravine provided her attackers with a suitably isolated setting for their repeated sexual assaults and beatings. Eventually she stumbled back to the road – her hair unpinned, her hat off, and her clothes 'all tore and hanging down' – and managed to tell a passing man what had happened. The men, it was later discovered, were not tramps or touts from the nearby Woodbine Racetrack but local youths with records for drunkenness, disorderliness, and gambling. Still, they were strangers to their victim and their 'gross, revolting and brutal' crime confirmed the need for greater police protection for the citizens of the East End, an area trying to shake its reputation as a haven for criminals.[71]

The stiffest sentence imposed for rape in this period was handed down to Michael O'Hara who preyed on at least two women. O'Hara, a gruff man who drifted from one dead-end job to another, used an ingenious ploy to lure his victims into danger. Posing as an undercover detective on the lookout for young couples violating laws against public sex, O'Hara prowled Rosedale Ravine at night until he found a pair whom he could frighten into complying with his order that the male partner leave. After he separated the young couple, promising the young man that he would escort the woman home, he raped her. On a September evening in 1919, he used this ruse with an accomplice who pinned Jean Argent's boyfriend to the ground while he, still claiming to be a police officer, demanded: '"Are you going to give it to me or go to jail?"' Fighting off her attacker, she boldly declared that she would prefer jail until he threatened to 'tear [her] to pieces' if she resisted. Argent bravely reported the attack to the police immediately, and they were eventually able to arrest O'Hara after he was found lurking in the park several days later. The jury took only a few minutes to find him guilty, and Judge Kelly commented that O'Hara's crime was the worst offence imaginable after murder. The judge could find nothing in the prisoner's favour since he had evidently 'ordered his life in the vilest manner.' Because the public, to say nothing of law enforcement officials, had been shocked by the crime, Kelly felt justified in stunning the prisoner by imposing a life sentence. Like Judge Lennox, who felt bound to protect 'society' from Macpherson, Kelly felt that the sentence was imposed on behalf of the whole community: 'No person was safe with such a man at liberty and because of the extreme gravity of the offence and the fact that the Government recognized that it could be punishable by death, ... the public must be protected and the community taught that offences of the kind must cease.' Unfortunately, Kelly's extraordinary sentence did not put a stop to rape, nor did it prevent O'Hara from striking again since a life sentence imposed by the court did not compel the penal system to incarcerate a prisoner until he died.

In 1927, parole authorities released O'Hara and he was back in court a year later, this time charged with raping young domestic Mary Moses and with impersonating a police officer. After accusing Moses and her boyfriend of 'monkey business,' he managed to convince Moses that she would go to jail if she resisted: 'he said I would not have a chance if I went to the Police Court ... He said, "My word would be taken first."' Had he actually been a detective, he would probably have been right. In this case, however, the recital of the Crown's evidence persuaded him that his best course would be to plead guilty. This time it was Judge Jeffrey who passed sentence. 'If there was ever a case of rape which deserved the extreme penalty, it is your case,' he thundered: 'O'Hara, men like you cannot be at large ... The public must be protected. No man or girl is safe so long as men like you are at large. You have failed truly and miserably.' O'Hara's parole had 'turned loose an animal in the guise of a man.' Jeffrey's sentence of fifteen years with twenty lashes fit with his characterization of O'Hara as an untamed beast who would respond to nothing but brutality. At the same time, wild animals were a danger to everyone: Judge Kelly had worried that 'no person' was safe from Macpherson while Jeffrey feared for the safety of *men* and girls if O'Hara were 'loose.' These rapists were men whose victims – 'decent, innocent girls' – symbolized the vulnerability of women *and* men to random, senseless violence from 'Others.' Consequently, their severe punishments did not supplant sexist attitudes but rather reinforced the myth that danger always lurks without, but never from within, women's trusted circles.[72]

Convictions of rapists could illustrate another aspect of patriarchal justice: the rule of 'fathers' over young males. Patriarchs (and no figures more aptly personified patriarchs than elderly judges) established behavioural norms which young men were expected to follow. At the turn of the century, codes of gentlemanly conduct, promoted in everything from 'Boys' Own' stories, social hygiene pamphlets, and Boy Scout rituals to Sunday school homilies, set standards for male behaviour that distinguished respectable men from ruffians. Just as even the poor could be respectable, so a poor or working-class man could behave as a gentleman by showing kindness and care to his loved ones. Young men who came from wealthy families, in contrast, were expected to uphold the code of gentlemanly conduct as a matter of course. Since rape was a quintessentially unchivalrous act, crown attorneys often tried to persuade judges and juries to weigh defendants' characters against those standards, particularly in the postwar period when heroes sometimes acted less than heroically on the home front.

Aside from the rape of small children by grown men, gang rape provided the most dramatic evidence that gentlemanly conduct was far from universal. In over one-quarter of the cases prosecuted in Toronto between 1880 and 1929, women claimed that more than one man had either raped them or assisted in the assault.[73] The conviction of these men, however, was far from assured. In fact, the conviction rate for gang rape was almost 10 per cent lower than for rape in general. Many of these incidents involved alleged assaults in which the woman knew one or more of the assailants. In the 1898 trial of teenagers William Crawford, John Barrett, and Alfred Granner, defence lawyer E.E.A. DuVernet attacked the complainant's character by extracting her admission that she had been out walking with Crawford on several occasions. Although her sister witnessed the alleged rape and neighbourhood men had come to her aid after hearing a disturbance in a vacant lot, the young men were found not guilty. In a 1902 case, a twenty-one-year-old cigar factory worker went out in a boat with two male friends. The men rowed over to a sand bar where they proceeded to rape her repeatedly, leaving her bleeding and unclothed in the middle of the bay. In spite of the testimony of the men who rescued her and corroborative medical evidence of her extensive injuries, William Garrett and Richard Greer escaped conviction. Far from interpreting these incidents as blights on male honour, it seems that juries perceived them as stories of youthful hijinks gone awry. As long as women's apparent consent to familiarity on earlier occasions could be established by the defence, patriarchal wrath would not be invoked.

In a 1904 gang rape trial that did result in a conviction, the Crown successfully mobilized the code of masculine honour to erode the men's characters, in part because they were strangers to the woman and because she was married and significantly older than them.[74] This was the East End case, already introduced, in which Frank Duffy, his younger brother Edward, and Thomas Whitesides (another man being tried a year later) stood accused of raping Rachel Barrible. She claimed that she had arranged to meet her husband, who worked in a stable near the Woodbine Racetrack. When she turned down Woodbine Avenue the men leapt upon her and dragged her to a deserted lot while they 'thumped' her and raped her twice each over a period of two hours. Whitesides eventually persuaded the others to let her go and he followed her to implore her not to talk: "'we will all get five years,'" he pleaded. Barrible, undaunted, told a passing man that the young men had 'served [her] bad.' Local constable Burns concentrated his search for the culprits on known miscreants in the neighbourhood. He knew all three of the men he eventually arrested because he was aware that they frequented a local hotel where their carousing and gambling had led to several arrests. Thus they were not troublemakers from the city but, perhaps more unsettling, young men of low character who gave the East End a bad name.

Thomas Whitesides' attempt to establish himself as Barrible's honourable protector opened up a line of attack for the Crown. For one thing, Whitesides confirmed that the rape had taken place, although he denied taking part. His story was that he had made Mrs Barrible's acquaintance on Queen Street and that they had gone for a walk on the night in question. Suddenly, three men attacked the pair, holding Whitesides at bay while they raped the woman. Whitesides' only role in the affair, he contended, was his thwarted attempt to save her. To crown attorney Guthrie, this defence of frustrated gentlemanly concern could not go unchallenged. He asked why, unless Whitesides had 'immoral purposes' in mind, he had taken the woman on a mile walk in November to a 'lonely, out of the way place where there are no people and no passers by.' The nineteen-year-old lamely replied that he often met girls on the street and went out for walks. Guthrie borrowed the defence's strategy of character assassination by needling the man about his loose conduct: 'Then you are in the habit of way-laying or going with women on the street that you don't know?' Whitesides replied that he thought nothing of the habit. Guthrie saved his sharpest criticisms for the defendant's alleged attempt to help the woman. He pointed out that if one man pinned the woman down while another raped her, it left only one for the strapping bricklayer to fight off. 'You would not be man enough to have your block knocked off to defend her?' he taunted. Guthrie continued to chip away at Whitesides' character, contending that he 'was no brave one' after all. Whitesides' credibility was equally in question because he had first lied to the police that he knew nothing of the event. Guthrie threw the last barb: 'If you had such a plain and simple manly story of defending a woman from the assault of blackguards, why didn't you stick up for her? Why did you tell [the police] you were not there at all?' With his 'manliness' in doubt, the nineteen-year-old not only failed to separate himself from his co-accused but provided enough evidence to convict them all. Although Frank Duffy, the alleged ring leader and the eldest of the three, received a sentence of ten years, Judge Anglin focused his remarks on Whitesides, the supposed hero who had entered the witness-box 'in a most cowardly manner [and] attempted to blacken the woman's character.'[75]

It was not until after World War I, however, that it became common for defence counsel to introduce their clients' 'manly' reputations as a defence strategy. In cases conducted prior to 1914, there had been no such objective tests for heroic behaviour. Holding a steady job and earning a reputation as a temperate man were certainly indications of respectability but they were nothing compared to earning medals for bravery in the service of King and country. The only problem, as the Whitesides case revealed, was that the defence's introduction of masculine virtues invited the Crown to demonstrate that accused rapists had fallen far short of those standards. When Judge Kelly sentenced Keith Gordon, a man who had enlisted 'at the first call to arms,' he took his war record into account: 'Every man who served his country in the war is entitled to the greatest consideration in many ways,' Kelly conceded, 'But on the other hand, one of their motives in going overseas was to protect our women.' The old men of the bench who had lived to see many brave young men sacrificed on the battlefields of Europe did not take kindly to the young men who tried to capitalize on their war records. Seventy-six-year-old Judge Lennox counselled John Macpherson, fifty years his junior, that any man who attempted to excuse his conduct by relying on his reputation as a soldier had been fighting for the wrong reasons: 'Unlike the young men who joined the army from a sense of patriotism and duty, you seem to have looked on the army as a pleasant and exciting mode of occupation.' Lennox concluded his sermon by providing a definition of military manliness: 'The essence of a soldier is that he should be chivalrous and a protector.' The last thing a real soldier would do was to prey upon the weak and innocent.[76]

The well-publicized convictions of men such as Macpherson or porter David Hawes clouded the general picture: most men, even those tried after the social purity movement's impact on the criminal justice system had been felt, left the courtroom with their characters intact. Women continued to fight an uphill battle to have their stories believed, in part because of their position as the chief Crown witness. Unlike accused rapists, who could always opt for silence, the prosecutrix was bound to testify (or face the risk of imprisonment for contempt of court) and she had to withstand a barrage of questions from defence lawyers as brilliant as T.C. Robinette. It was only when *men's* characters were subjected to the same scrutiny that the metropolitan press reported trials. Readers were thereby encouraged to believe that only 'filthy' or bestial men could rape, but also that the criminal justice system provided adequate protection of the public.

CONCLUSION

Studying rape convictions and acquittals over time contributes to an anti-essentialist position on sexual violence. Men have always raped women (and children, and animals) but responses to sexual violence, by victims and perpetrators, by the courts, and by the press, have varied considerably in different historical contexts. In turn-of-the-century Toronto, an emerging culture of sexual puritanism elevated the conviction rate, although never enough to verify the myth that rape was a charge easily levelled and impossible to defend. Men of low character were always more vulnerable to conviction than high-status men, and while class, ethnicity, and race were crucial components of character, they did not define its limits. Thus, even in periods of anti-immigrant agitation and xenophobic panics, the outcome of individual cases was not predetermined. Criminal trials are inherently 'untidy' processes even though they distil a morass of evidence and testimony into a tidy verdict: the cross-examination skills of the defence lawyer, the demeanour of a frightened fifteen-year-old on the stand, the Crown's persuasiveness in his summation, the jury's reaction to the judge's charge – none of these pivotal factors is quantifiable. Systemic injustice toward identifiable social groups (in this case, the poor, 'foreigners,' and female victims) was certainly evident, although never invulnerable to modification.

Ironically, the conviction of rapists in late-nineteenth-century and early-twentieth-century Toronto reinforced patriarchal myths about rape. Because the majority of the few men indicted annually were either acquitted or convicted on lesser charges, the supposed rarity of rape, particularly rape committed by relatives or men women knew well, was confirmed. Evidently, there was an informal threshold on the number of rape charges that Torontonians were prepared to accept. When the number of indictments rose to four or five per anum in the 1890s, juries simply refused to convict and judges lectured the Crown and the police about malicious prosecutions. The harsher judgment of 'foreigners' and stranger rapists showed that the state could treat women's fears seriously but, like the laws of the tribal patriarchs, it did so by dramatizing the general threat of outsiders, not only to women, but to the community at large. Likewise, elderly judges expended more energy castigating 'unmanly' young men for shirking their duty to protect women than in proclaiming the right of all women to be free from sexual violence.

What, then, might an 'appropriate' conviction rate or a 'just' conviction have looked like? Because the criminal justice system's patriarchal character did not translate into an acquittal rate of 100 per cent, it would be unrealistic to expect a hypothetical non-patriarchal culture to produce a conviction rate of 100 per cent for rape (or any other offence). The possibility of mistaken identity alone would always account for some acquittals. Even if sexist attitudes had been expunged from turn-of-the-century rape prosecutions, classism and ethnocentrism would still have operated: wealthy men from respectable families would have remained invulnerable to conviction, and foreign-born and destitute women would still have confronted prejudicial attitudes. Furthermore, although we can question the sexist, classist, and ethnocentric bases of character assessment in turn-of-the-century rape trials, it would be naive to expect that character, in an ideal world, would not continue to colour legal judgments. Legal historians and anthropologists have shown that all crimes, not just sexual assaults, are assessed largely in terms of 'the perceived significance and character of the victim and offender and the concomitant threat to the respectable members of the local community.'[77] This pattern of justice, often associated with premodern prosecutorial practice, not only survived the rise of regularized law enforcement in the nineteenth century: as contemporary scholars have shown, discretionary, character-driven justice survives today.

The historian's task, then, is to tease out the criteria of character assessment that have been applied in different historical and cultural contexts. Rape trials in turn-of-the-century York County offer highly transparent views on the ways that propertied, Christian, Anglo-Celtic men's standards of respectability and perceptions of danger were deployed. These hegemonic notions were hardly confined to the courtroom, however. The trial is merely the final stage of a long process that, first, discourages women from perceiving of sexual assault as a crime and, second, stymies the efforts of those who do decide to report offences to the police. In societies where the stories of the oppressed are seldom told and rarely listened to, it is not surprising that rape victims find little solace in the criminal justice process. A just verdict would hinge upon a just society, an ideal far from realized in our own time.

NOTES

The editors of this collection have been keen and close critics and I have benefited greatly from their assistance and from the advice offered by anonymous readers. Tina Loo was particularly helpful when the project looked as if it would never materialize. I also appreciate the efforts of Morag Carny, the former assistant justice records archivist at the Public Archives of Ontario, who facilitated my research by preparing a list of rape indictments.

1 The exact wording of Hale's comment reads that rape is 'an accusation easy to be made and hard to be defended by the party accused': quoted in Henry John Stephen, *Mr. Sergeant Stephen's New Commentaries of the Laws of England* vol. 4 (London: Butterworth's 1890) 78.
2 Critical literature on the prosecution of rape is vast. See, for example, Zsuzsanna Adler *Rape on Trial* (London: Routledge and Kegan Paul 1987), Susan

Estrich *Real Rape: How the Legal System Victimizes Women Who Say No* (Cambridge: Harvard University Press 1987), and Gary LaFree, *Rape and Criminal Justice: The Social Construction of Sexual Assault* (Belmont, Calif.: Wadsworth 1989).

3 Susan Brownmiller *Against Our Will: Men, Women and Rape* (New York: Simon and Shuster 1975) 369. Brownmiller's work has been criticized for its tendency to essentialize male violence against women. Brownmiller herself has, since the publication of the book, retreated from the essentialist position. See Steven Pistono 'Susan Brownmiller and the History of Rape' *Women's Studies* 14 (1988) 265–76. It remains, nonetheless, the standard feminist reference point for studies of rape. See, for example, Anna Clark *Women's Silence, Men's Violence: Sexual Assault in England, 1770–1845* (London: Pandora 1987) and Karen Dubinsky *Improper Advances: Rape and Heterosexual Conflict in Ontario, 1880–1929* (Chicago: University of Chicago Press 1993).

4 Many historians have cited the greater willingness both of grand jurors to return bills for attempted rape and of petit jurors to convict on lesser charges those few men who were tried for rape. See Clark *Women's Silence, Men's Violence* at 47; John Beattie, *Crime and the Courts in England, 1660–1800* (Princeton: Princeton University Press 1986) 124–32; Carolyn Conley 'Rape and Justice in Victorian England' *Victorian Studies* 29 (1986) 523–4. On Canada, see Constance Backhouse 'Nineteenth-Century Canadian Rape Law 1800–1892' in David H. Flaherty, ed. *Essays in the History of Canadian Law: Volume II* (Toronto: University of Toronto Press and Osgoode Society 1983) 200–47 at 222; and Ruth A. Olsen 'Rape: An Un-Victorian Aspect of Life in Upper Canada' *Ontario History* 68 (1976) 75–9 at 77.

5 See, for example, Adler *Rape on Trial* and R. Rowland *Rape: The Ultimate Violation* (New York: Doubleday 1985).

6 Loraine Gelsthorpe 'Towards a Sceptical Look at Sexism' *International Journal of the Sociology of Law* 14 (1986) 144. In her study of juvenile corrections, for instance, she found that boys and girls were treated differently but that '"sexist" beliefs, where they existed, were mediated by administrative and organisational factors' (ibid.).

7 Most of the literature on rape and inequality concerns race in the US South. On the unequal infliction of the death penalty against Black men convicted of rape, see Julia Schwendinger and Herman Schwendinger *Rape and Inequality* (Beverly Hills, Calif.: Sage 1983). This pattern has been particularly evident in cases of interracial assaults since the Civil War, although the exaggerated severity of sanctions toward Blacks has lessened somewhat in the late-twentieth century. Kristin Bumiller analyses a recent Minnesota case in which a white prosecutrix was labelled a racist after she complained that several Black men had raped her. The transposition of the racist myth in the

trial is examined in her 'Rape as a Legal Symbol: An Essay on Sexual Violence and Racism' *University of Miami Law Review* 42 (1987) 75–92.

8 Clark and Lewis argue that men with status can coax sex from women (by buying them presents, offering marriage, etc.) whereas men of low status have to use physical coercion to achieve the same ends. Although this typology is classist (upper-class men do employ brutality, and poor men can attract sexual partners without intimidation) it does help explain why juries are prepared to believe that a lower-class man is more capable of sexual assault than is an upper-class man. Lorenne M.G. Clark and Debra J. Lewis *Rape: The Price of Coercive Sexuality* (Toronto: Women's Press 1977) at 144.

9 Laura F. Edwards 'Sexual Violence, Gender, Reconstruction, and the Extension of Patriarchy in Granville County, North Carolina' *North Carolina Historical Review* 67 (1991) 250. Edwards relates the story of several white women whose poverty and history of sexual immorality (adultery, unwed motherhood, prostitution) rendered them unbelievable victims. In one 1869 incident, sixty men, including white public-office holders, petitioned the governor to pardon a Black man convicted of raping an unchaste white woman.

10 For a critique of (white) feminists' analyses of rape, see Angela Davis *Women, Race and Class* (New York: Random House 1981) at 182.

11 Jacqueline Dowd Hall *Revolt against Chivalry: Jessie Daniel Ames and the Women's Campaign against Lynching* (New York: Columbia University Press 1979) remains an authoritative source for the United States. See also Hall's 'The Mind That Burns in Each Body' in Ann Snitow, Christine Stansell, and Sharon Thompson, eds. *Powers of Desire: The Politics of Sexuality* (New York: Monthly Review Press 1983). In addition to Conley's article on rape, see her discussion of sexual assault in the context of other crimes in Carolyn Conley *The Unwritten Law: Criminal Justice in Victorian Kent* (New York: Oxford University Press 1991).

12 Dubinsky *Improper Advances* at 62. Dubinsky develops this idea in a chapter that explores the association of immorality and geographical isolation.

13 Empirical studies of rape trials, in comparison with other trials for nonsexual assaults, have revealed that defence lawyers are likely in both types of trials to discredit the credibility of complainants by casting aspersions on their reputations and by alleging that victims egged on the attack. David Brereton 'Are Rape Trials Different?' (paper presented to the Law and Society Association, Chicago, May 1993). I am grateful to David for giving me a copy of his fine paper.

14 Clark and Lewis *Rape*. The most recent change relating to the admissibility of evidence regarding the alleged victim's sexual reputation is currently found in the Criminal Code, ss. 276 and 277. Section 276, the rape shield

law which prohibited the introduction of evidence relating to the sexual activities of the complainant with persons other than the defendant, was struck down as unconstitutional, however, in *Seaboyer v. The Queen; Gayme and the Queen* (1991), 2 SCR. The former common law rules permitting the reception of evidence concerning the victim's sexual reputation were not, however, revived.

15 On gender- and class-encoded sexual respectability, see Anna Clark 'Whores and Gossips: Sexual Reputation in London, 1770–1825' in Arina Angerman, Geerte Binnema, Annamiebe Keunen, Vefie Peols, and Jacqueline Zirkzee, eds. *Current Issues in Women's History* (London: Routledge 1989) 231–48, and Ellen Ross 'Not the Sort That Would Sit on the Doorstep: Respectability in Pre–World War One Neighbourhoods' *International Labour and Working-Class History* 27 (1985) 39–59.

16 I found no evidence of Asian or Aboriginal men accused of rape in this period.

17 Some scholars suggest that the civil law might offer more effective remedies for some women. See Nora West 'Rape in the Criminal Law and the Victim's Tort Alternative: A Feminist Analysis' *University of Toronto Faculty of Law Review* 50 (1992) 96–118.

18 Douglas Hay 'Property, Authority and the Criminal Law' in Douglas Hay, Peter Linebaugh, John Rule, E.P. Thompson, and Cal Winslow *Albion's Fatal Tree: Crime and Society in Eighteenth Century England* (London: Allen Lane 1975) 17–63

19 Hay is concerned with the issue of class in this essay and provides little discussion of gender, nor does he focus on crime inflicted by the poor upon the poor. Nonetheless, his framework on class injustice is readily adapted to a feminist analysis of gender injustice.

20 Judith R. Walkowitz *City of Dreadful Delight: Narratives of Sexual Danger in Late-Victorian London* (Chicago: University of Chicago Press 1992). Walkowitz borrows the phrase to refer to the narratives of sexual allure and endangerment that abounded in London. Although Toronto did not produce contemporary tales that rivalled 'The Maiden Tribute of Modern Babylon' or Jack the Ripper stories, this sexualized and gender-encoded notion of urban dangers was reproduced elsewhere, particularly in social purity tracts.

21 Bureau of Municipal Research 'What Is "The Ward" Going to Do with Toronto? A Report on Undesirable Living Conditions in One Section of the City of Toronto – "The Ward" – Conditions Which Are Spreading Rapidly to Other Districts' 1918, City of Toronto Archives, SC 3

22 Long-serving Police Court Magistrate Denison characterized the Irish as hot-tempered, fun-loving, hard-drinking loud-mouths in his reminiscences

of his time on the magistrate's bench. Newspapers, particularly the *News*, gave lengthy descriptions of persons brought before Denison who often engaged in verbal sparring matches with belligerent Irishmen and women: George T. Denison *Recollections of a Police Magistrate* (Toronto: Musson Book Co. Ltd. 1920).

23 Toronto, *Report of the Social Survey Commission of Toronto 1915*, United Church Archives, Doc. HN29, M4TO. See also Carolyn Strange 'From Modern Babylon to a City upon a Hill: The Toronto Social Survey Report (1915) and the Search for Sexual Order in the City' in Roger Hall, Laura Sefton MacDowell, and William Westfall, eds. *Patterns of the Past: Interpreting Ontario's History* (Toronto: Dundurn Press 1988). These themes are further explored in Carolyn Strange 'The Perils and Pleasures of the City: Single, Wage-earning Women in Toronto, 1880–1930' (PhD thesis, Rutgers University 1991).

24 PAO, Catherine J. Shepard 'Preliminary Inventory of Court Records, R.G. 22.' The series description indicates that 'a fairly high percentage of the case files are missing for each year': PAO, RG 22, ser. 392, Criminal Indictment Case Files, York County, 1880–1929. (Files exist after 1929 but they have been restricted because of privacy regulations.) A comparison of the York County files and the Clerk of the Assize's reports, however, reveals relatively complete listings for York County for most years. I found a total of 100 indictment files for rape and a further 18 indictments after cross-checking the Assize files. It should be noted, however, that the reports became somewhat sporadic by the 1920s. It seems reasonably certain that the figures up to 1920 accurately reflect the number of indictments actually filed up to that point, after which a slight degree of underreporting might have occurred: PAO, Criminal Indictments Clerk: Reports, York County, RG 22, ser. 391, 1880–1930 (hereafter 'Reports').

25 John Beattie's study of Sussex and Surrey from 1660 to 1802 includes only 61 indictments (Beattie *Crime and the Courts* at 131). Clark and Lewis's now-classic study is based on 116 cases (Clark and Lewis *Rape* at 34). Historical conviction rates vary considerably and they have been calculated differently. Beattie's study of jury trial verdicts in Surrey (Beattie, at 411) shows that only 14.7 per cent of rape trials resulted in convictions for rape. Jim Phillips' work on late-eighteenth-century Halifax (elsewhere in this volume) reveals that 28 per cent of men indicted for rape were convicted. Carolyn Conley's evidence indicates a relatively high rape conviction rate of 41 per cent for men actually tried for rape. She notes, however, that the rate for felonies in general in Kent County was 71 per cent (*The Unwritten Law* 82). Anna Clark's statistics are much lower because she starts with a base of depositions: she found that only 7–13 per cent of rape allegations in late-eight-

eenth-century England resulted in convictions for rape (*Women's Silence, Men's Violence*). In mid- to late-nineteenth-century Ontario, Constance Backhouse found that an average of 21.5 per cent of prosecuted rapes resulted in convictions as charged (Backhouse 'Nineteenth-Century Canadian Rape Law' at 222). Karen Dubinsky's rates are much higher, but she has grouped together 'crimes of sexual violence' (including rape, attempted rape, indecent assault, and carnal knowledge). Not only do her figures document crimes with lower potential penalties (and consequently crimes for which juries were more likely to return guilty verdicts) but she also includes convictions on lesser charges. For rural and Northern Ontario, she found a correspondingly high conviction rate that rose from 38 per cent in the 1880s to 56 per cent in the 1910s, after which it remained relatively steady at 54 per cent in the 1920s (Dubinsky *Improper Advances* at 172–3).

26 Act Respecting Offenses against the Person, 33 Vict. (1870), c. 28, s. 65. For a thorough review of statutes governing sexual assault in Ontario and Canada, see Backhouse 'Nineteenth-Century Canadian Rape Law' at 204–13.

27 Act Respecting Offenses against the Person, 40 Vict. (1877), c. 28, s. 2

28 Act to Amend the Criminal Code, 11 & 12 Geo. V (1921), c. 25, s. 4. The whipping provision had been added to the punishment for attempted rape a year earlier in 10 & 11 Geo. V (1920), c. 43, s. 7. The maximum term of imprisonment for attempted rape throughout the period was seven years. Whipping had been allowed for several offences in the 1892 Code, including robbery, sodomy, and the 'defilement' of children under fourteen.

29 Arrest figures from Strange 'The Perils and Pleasures of the City' 381. Unfortunately, conviction statistics were published in aggregate form.

30 Of forty-six men chosen for the petit jury panel in 1880, for instance twenty-one were farmers, two were 'gentlemen,' and the remainder were skilled craftsmen (such as plumbers, stonecutters, and stove makers) and labourers (including a milkman and a box-maker). The men on the grand jury represented a more urban mix of merchants, professionals (accountants, agents) and skilled tradesmen (cabinet-makers, boat builders, watchmakers). Still, eighteen of forty-seven men were farmers. 'Reports' Winter 1880.

31 High Court of Justice, Criminal Assize Indictments, 'Pallen' and 'Noble,' 1900 (hereafter 'Indictments')

32 'Reports' Fall 1892

33 Constance Backhouse 'The Sayer Street Outrage' in Dale Gibson and W. Wesley Pue, eds. *Glimpses of Canadian Legal History* (Winnipeg: Legal Research Institute) 47–70

34 Indictments, 'Ryan' 1884; *News* 2 Apr. 1884 ; *Telegram* 24 Apr. 1884. Arthur Christie was not apprehended on the night of the assault and was tried one

year later. Both he and Ryan were sentenced to seven years in the Kingston Penitentiary. Indictments, 'Christie' 1885.

35 The Staff Inspector's Department was also mandated to enforce a wide range of by-laws that impinged on (largely male) working-class leisure pursuits, such as ball playing, gambling, public drinking, and commercial sex. Its efforts were often lampooned in the Toronto *News* and *World*.

36 Clark *Of Toronto the Good, a Social Study: The Queen City of Canada as It Is* (Toronto: Coles 1970 [1898]) 110–11. Clark referred to one of his many undocumented examples to show that two 'boys' had gone on to become respectable citizens, whereas the woman would never be married and her family would always be shunned.

37 Bryan Palmer 'Discordant Music: Charivaris and Whitecapping in Nineteenth-Century North America' *Labour/Le Travailleur* 3 (1978) 5–62. The fifty-year-old widow claimed that approximately six men, one of them wielding a club, and Maud Sullivan had broken into the small house the old woman shared in a back lot off Eastern Avenue. She claimed that one of the men had said: 'pull her God damned guts out.' During their vicious attack they indeed pulled out her womb, as Dr Arthur Jukes Johnson's medical examination confirmed. 'If the female was resisting it is quite probable that the uterus came out,' he matter-of-factly commented at the Police Court hearing.

38 What was not mentioned was the fact, brought out by the police at the preliminary hearing, that Gordon also had three prior convictions for theft and that one of his co-accused, Thomas Sullivan, had been convicted twice for assaulting women with intent to rob and had served three years at the Kingston Penitentiary for breaking and entering at night and stealing two horses: Indictments, 'Sullivan et al.' 1899.

39 *Telegram* 9 Nov. 1899. The story was also picked up by the *Mail and Empire* 9 Nov. 1899, which proclaimed: 'JUDGE M'MAHON SCORES POLICE ...' MacMahon was nonetheless unimpressed by the cheering spectators, to whom he delivered 'a severe lecture.'

40 The wartime scare over venereal disease and the feared relaxation in sexual morals produced elevated arrest statistics for female vagrancy but it also led to unprecedented rates of arrest for male brothel customers. Strange 'The Perils and Pleasures' at app. II.

41 James Woodsworth *Strangers within Our Gates, or Coming Canadians* intro. Marilyn Barber (Toronto: University of Toronto Press 1972 [1909]). Woodsworth rated Canadian immigrants in terms of their potential to assimilate in Canadian (i.e., Anglo-Protestant) culture. Blacks were at the bottom of his list.

42 In July 1914, the Attorney General's department received a request from the 'query department' of the *New York Times* about the history of lynching in Canada. F.V. Johns replied on 19 August 1914 that 'no lynching ever occurred in that Province or in that part of Canada now know as Ontario since it has been organized' PAO, RG 4, ser. 32, 1914, no. 1335.

43 The death penalty for rape was formally abolished in England in 1841.

44 Indictments, 'Hawes' 1901; *Telegram* 9 Nov. 1901; News, 11 November 1901. The press coverage, although significantly more extensive than usual, was actually free of the open racism that one might have expected. Again, it is possible that the desire to demonstrate Canadians' commitment to fairness and restraint outweighed indigenous prejudices against Blacks. Hawes was also apparently 'of previous good character'; as an elderly family man and a steady worker, he was a Black man who did not readily conform to racist stereotypes of sexual danger.

45 This assessment is based on a random survey of jurors' names. I was unable to find any names other than those of British, Irish, or Scottish derivation.

46 Indictments, 'Otto' 1914

47 'Reports' Spring 1919

48 Indictments, 'Yocock et al.' 1920; *Star* 30 Oct. 1920. The trial, attended by a rowdy group of spectators, seemed to derail from the start. Judge Latchford chastised observers who had behaved 'flippantly' and who seemed 'to enter a courtroom as they would a picture show or place of amusement.' Several spectators whose behaviour 'was not becoming to a court of law' were ejected. *Globe* 28 Oct. 1920.

49 On the use of deportation to rid Canada of 'undesirables,' see Barbara Roberts *Whence They Came: Deportation from Canada, 1900–1935* (Ottawa: University of Ottawa Press 1988).

50 Ontario Temperance Act, 6 Geo. V (1916), c. 50. This was not a prohibition act but rather a means to restrict the sale and availability of alcohol through licensing.

51 Dorothy Chunn 'Maternal Feminism, Legal Professionalism and Political Pragmatism: The Rise and Fall of Magistrate Margaret Patterson, 1922–34' in W. Wesley Pue and Barry Wright, eds. *Canadian Perspectives on Law and Society* (Ottawa: Carleton University Press 1988) 91–117

52 Indictments, 'Davey' 1924. Dr Guest was considered an international authority on the treatment of venereal disease in women. She testified that she detected signs of venereal disease and spoke bluntly about the girl's injuries, which, she considered, were likely caused by 'recent violent intercourse of an adult.'

53 Dubinsky *Improper Advances* at 29

54 Ibid. at 54. Dubinsky traces this backlash in rural and Northern Ontario as far back as the 1890s and suggests that it either remained evident or grew in force by the early twentieth century. Conviction rates in Toronto, however, tell a different story.

55 According to the Temperance Act, liquor could not be purchased between 8 p.m. and 7 a.m. on weekdays, or between 7 p.m. Saturday and 7 a.m. Monday. Liquor could be consumed only in licensed establishments (the dancehall was not licensed) or in a private home.

56 Indictments, 'Gordon' 1923; *Mail and Empire* and *Star* 14 Nov. 1923. It was not uncommon for rape trials to go unreported in the dailies. The sentencing of rapists rarely received more than a line or two of press coverage unless justices made 'a long address,' as Kelly did in this case.

57 Kathy Peiss uses 'heterosociability' to describe the forms of amusements that fostered and indeed encouraged the development of familiarity between men and women. Dancehalls, movie theatres, and amusement parks all fostered heterosexual contact, as urban reformers feared. See Peiss *Cheap Amusements: Working Women and Leisure in Turn-of-the-Century New York* (Philadelphia: Temple University Press 1986).

58 Logie expressed both his paternalism and his sympathy for a fellow Scot when he made the extraordinary remark: 'I think the one admission of Punsheon that he heard this unfortunate young Scotch girl call out "daddy, daddy," was enough in itself for a conviction.' Indictments, 'Punsheon and Hayes' 1928; *Star Telegram* 11 May 1928. Logie was sixty-two at the time of their trial and Kelly was sixty-five when he sentenced Gordon.

59 Brownmiller *Against Our Will* at 369. A poor legal defence was rarely the reason for an accused rapist's conviction in late-nineteenth-century and early-twentieth-century Toronto. The vast majority of cases appear to have been tried by competent, dedicated lawyers. The most successful was Thomas Cowper Robinette, an indefatigable advocate who defended thirty rape cases between 1896 and 1919, including nine gang rape cases. His clients' conviction rate (for rape or lesser offences) was only 33 per cent, compared to the average of 46.7 per cent in the 1900s and 1910s. This achievement was even more remarkable because most of his clients, like David Hawes, were poor and without influential friends, and many came from Toronto's ethnic minorities. On Robinette's reputation as a champion of underdogs and the leading defence lawyer in turn-of-the-century Ontario, see Jack Batten *J.J. Robinette: The Dean of Canadian Lawyers* (Toronto: Macmillan 1984) 18–23.

60 'Reports' Fall 1910. This excerpt regarding the recommendation for the lash

was forwarded by Assistant Provincial Secretary F. Johns to the Attorney General of Ontario for his opinion, but the minister's reply is not included in the file: RG 4, ser. 32, Attorney General Files, 1910, no. 1516.

61 John Mitchell was tried in 1895 on several counts, including incest, but he was convicted of rape only. No other indictments for incest in York County exist for this period.

62 On the sexual violation of children, see Dubinsky *Improper Advances* at 54–7. Further evidence of the historical tendency to treat these crimes more seriously is found in Guido Ruggiero *The Boundaries of Eros: Sex Crime and Sexuality in Renaissance Venice* (New York: Oxford University Press) at 93 and Nazife Bashar 'Rape in England between 1550–1700' in London Feminist History Group *The Sexual Dynamics of History* (London: Pluto Press 1983) 40.

63 *News* 11 Nov. 1901; 'Reports' Fall 1894. The lash was occasionally recommended in reference to the deterrence of rapists who preyed on women as well; however, the rape of children inspired the most vehement and consistent recommendations. Homosexual offences were not capital and thus were rarely tried in the Supreme Court. The formal language of indictments regarding homosexual offences, and the fact that statutory provision for whipping was retained from the pre–Criminal Code era, suggest that sodomy and gross indecency, unlike rape, signified 'unnatural' and 'abominable' sins.

64 Indictments, 'Mitchell' 1888; *Empire* 31 Jan. 1888; Indictments, 'Davey'; and *Telegram* 2 Jan. 1924. The ages of the girls ranged from thirteen to seventeen and most of the men were at least twenty years older than their victims. In one case that failed to produce a true bill, a man in his twenties was accused of raping his sixteen-year-old niece and the smaller age gap, as well as the fact that she had not complained until after she discovered she was pregnant, may have explained the grand jury's reluctance to believe the complainant. Indictments, 'McAdam' 1899.

65 Dubinsky *Improper Advances* at 129–31. In contrast to the image of 'depraved families' of the North and rural Ontario, Dubinsky argues, incest in urban areas was depicted as the product of the urban poor's overcrowded housing conditions.

66 Rushton, along with his drinking mate, William Long, had driven a buggy to the Clifford home in King township north of Toronto to ask if Cassie might like a job as a helper for Rushton's wife. Mrs Clifford consented and the trio rode off along the lonely roads that led from Cassie's home. As darkness fell, Rushton took her out of the buggy and raped her at the side of the road and then drove her to his home. The Rushtons claimed that Clif-

ford was laughing, carrying on, and 'blackguarding' when she came into their house (tossing up her skirt and joking that she wore no underpants). They had allegedly sent her back home because they were afraid that *her* behaviour would give them a bad name. Rushton was convicted of attempted rape and sentenced to five years at the Kingston Penitentiary. Indictments, 'Rushton' 1895.

67 On 'stranger rapes' elsewhere in Ontario, see Dubinsky *Improper Advances* at 37–43.

68 On 10 June 1910, Deputy Attorney General John Cartwright sent a circular to Ontario police magistrates urging them to sentence tramps to six months at hard labour (the maximum sentence allowed by law) with no option of fine payment. 'It is desired that men of this class who it is believed are responsible for a large number of burglaries and other crimes of violence should be driven out of the Province ...' PAO, RG 4, ser. 32, Attorney General Files, 1910, no. 766. See also James Pitsula 'The Treatment of Tramps in Late Nineteenth-Century Toronto' *Historical Papers* (1980) 116–32.

69 Macpherson lost his job as a motorman with the Toronto Transit Company after he ran a car into an open switch, and he was dismissed from the Massey Harris Company for fighting with another employee. This information came from a report prepared by an alienist who had been engaged by the court to assess his sanity.

70 *Telegram* 13 and 16 Jan. 1926

71 Indictments, 'Duffy et al.' 1904; *News* 12 Oct. 1899; *Star* 11 May 1904

72 Indictments, 'O'Hara' 1919 and 1929; *Mail and Empire* and *Telegram* 8 Nov. 1919; *Telegram* 25 Jan. 1929. Jeffrey incorrectly interpreted the statute governing the punishment of rape. He believed that O'Hara could not be whipped if he were sentenced to life imprisonment. In fact, the Act to Amend the Criminal Code, Geo. V (1921), c. 25, s. 299 stated that persons found guilty of rape were 'liable to suffer death or to suffer imprisonment for life and to be whipped.' Even still, he could legally have sentenced O'Hara to a longer term than fifteen years.

73 Karen Dubinsky argues that gang rape in this period was regarded with no special degree of revulsion because the victims of these assaults were most often young, single women on their own: *Improper Advances* at 43.

74 This approach was doubtless employed in many cases but the near absence of transcripts in the criminal indictment files makes this impossible to establish. In addition, trial coverage was virtually non-existent throughout the period and only a handful of cases were reported in sufficient detail to determine the Crown's or the defence's strategies. This was the only indict-

ment file out of the 118 cases in the period that included a transcript of the Assize Court trial. Indictments, 'Duffy et al.' 1904.

75 Indictments, 'Duffy et al.' 1904; *News* 11 May 1904
76 *Telegram* 14 Nov. 1923, 16 Jan. 1926
77 Conley *The Unwritten Law* at 204

8

Prosecution of Abortions under Canadian Law, 1900–1950

CONSTANCE BACKHOUSE

The procurement of an abortion was a criminal offence under Canadian law throughout the first half of the twentieth century. The anti-abortion statutes which had originated in the nineteenth century made it a crime to induce miscarriage, or to attempt to do so, at any stage of pregnancy, whether the patient was actually pregnant or not. It was also unlawful to sell or advertise any birth control device.[1] Early-twentieth-century legislators apparently saw little need to alter these laws; with the enactment of the Criminal Code in 1892,[2] Canadian abortion law solidified into a shape which would not change substantially until the late 1960s. The four criminal statutes that touched upon abortion between 1892 and 1950 would make no significant revisions to the law whatsoever.[3]

Throughout this period, abortion seems not to have posed much of a concern to members of the Canadian social purity movement, who made no organized demands for any concerted increase in legal attack.[4] The Canadian Methodist Department of Temperance and Reform did call briefly for the enforcement of existing abortion legislation in 1907.[5] And the Toronto Local Council of Women would recommend in 1913 that Canadian journals refuse medical advertisements for abortifacients.[6] But these were isolated demands which were never promoted with much tenacity.

Nor was there any considerable public voice calling for greater access to abortion. The Canadian medical profession appears not to have taken a public position on the validity of the law, but to have assumed that the existing legislation permitted exceptions to be made for therapeutic abortions induced by regularly licensed physicians.[7] The organized movement for birth control was late developing in Canada in comparison with the United States or Britain, and most of the major Canadian women's groups seem to have shunned the issue in the first half of the twentieth century. Demands for contraception would originate in the 1920s with a small group of British Columbia socialists. Conservative neo-Malthusians, led by individuals such as Alvin Ratz Kaufman, Mary Elizabeth Hawkins, and A.H. Tyer, took over the movement after the onset of the depression in the 1930s. There is evidence that, beginning in 1925, various individuals and organizations called unsuccessfully for the removal of the Criminal Code provisions prohibiting the advertisement and sale of birth control devices. However, the birth controllers were virtually unanimous in condemning abortion, and there is no evidence of a lobby for the decriminalization of abortion in the first half of the twentieth century.[8]

Canadian women who found themselves unwillingly pregnant were considerably less acquiescent. Despite the legal prohibitions, many desperate and determined women went to remarkable lengths to terminate their pregnancies. The legal files provide a wealth of detail about those who were caught and prosecuted. The surviving court records at the Archives of Ontario reveal forty-seven indictments on abortion-related charges in the province between 1900 and 1929 (after which the records are closed pursuant to statutory privacy provisions). Information on abortion cases across Canada can also be culled from various law reports published between 1900 and 1950.[9] Although many women and their abortionists doubtless escaped detection and prosecution, the legal records of those who were caught allow us to begin to speculate about the circumstances surrounding abortion in this period. There are some data about the class, family status, and age of women who sought abortions, and about the gender and occupational background of the abortionists. The legal materials reveal how difficult it was to locate an abortionist, the cost, the methods used, and the medical complications which often ensued. The prosecutions provide information about the types of charges laid, the legal intricacies of proof, conviction rates, and sentences. Two case studies, one from London, Ontario, and the other from Halifax, Nova Scotia, can serve as helpful illustrations.

THE 'LODGER EVIL' AND DESPOILED YOUNG WOMEN:
EMMA AGNES KILBOURNE, 1901

It was the fall of 1901, and Emma Agnes Kilbourne was pregnant. Unwillingly pregnant. The eighteen-year-old lived with her working-class foster mother, Julia A. Kilbourne, who ran a boarding-house at 345 Waterloo Street in London, Ontario. A dressmaker by occupation, Emma Agnes Kilbourne was unmarried. Her problems stemmed from a heterosexual[10] liaison she had with a teamster who boarded at her home.[11] It was yet another illustration of the much lamented 'lodger evil,' a phenomenon which, turn-of-the-century Canadian social reformers complained, placed far too many innocent young women at the mercy of predatory male boarders. Nothing but moral degeneracy, they wailed, could come of the indiscriminate social mingling of unmarried women and unrelated male lodgers in physically cramped, overcrowded quarters.[12]

The 'evil' lodger in this case, an unmarried man named William Mayo, seems to have been considerably less malevolent than popular rhetoric would have it. The overblown caricatures depicted by social reformers frequently bore less than passing resemblance to real life protagonists. William Mayo had no hesitation in admitting his responsibility, and he offered to marry Emma, trying, as he put it, 'to act the part of a man.' But Emma refused, for 'she did not want to get married,' especially to William, who had a reputation as a drinking man. Instead, she wanted desperately to be rid of the pregnancy.

Working-class women such as Emma Kilbourne seem to have been disproportionately visible in the abortion cases which came to public attention. Although the class status of those seeking abortion is not discernible from all of the forty-seven Archives of Ontario cases, the entries that do appear (such as dressmaker, cashier, tailoress, telephone operator, factory worker, wife of a bricklayer, and farmer's daughter) suggest working-class positions. Some have speculated that poorer women sought abortions more frequently than did middle- or upper-class women.[13] They may also have had less access to birth control.[14] Impoverished circumstances meant that many were forced to use dangerous, self-induced procedures, calling in physicians only after complications had become life-threatening. Affluent women must also have sought abortions, but they could afford more sophisticated medical services, which may have insulated them from some of the health complications which led to exposure. The social connections between middle- and upper-class women and medical and legal professionals may also have enabled them to falsify records and cover up their illegal abortions to a much greater degree.[15]

Emma Kilbourne's age also appears to be representative of the youthfulness of most of the women whose abortions attracted legal attention. Of the ten Archives of Ontario cases in which age is recorded, seven were twenty-one years or younger. All were younger than twenty-eight. Of the sixteen cases where marital status is listed, ten were single (like Emma) and six were married.

By early October, Emma's foster mother, Julia, had begun to suspect her daughter's condition. When confronted, Emma confessed but stood firm in her resolve not to marry William. Julia Kilbourne herself had no great affection for lodger William, a man she described as a 'dirty old skunk.' The two women decided to try to find a way to terminate the pregnancy. The first person they turned to was Jessie Clark, the Kilbourne's next-door neighbour. Clark, who ran a small child-adoption business for unwed mothers, advised turpentine and purchased some cotton root pills for Emma. When none of these worked, they resolved to find a physician who would induce a miscarriage.

The difficulties they experienced illustrate the degree of persistence and tenacity required to locate an abortionist during this period. Jessie Clark took Emma, disguised under the assumed name of 'Agnes Brown,' to visit a number of 'prominent doctors of the city.'[16] To some of the doctors, they complained that 'Agnes' was merely suffering from delayed menstruation, and sought to obtain medication 'to bring it on.'[17] To others, they confessed that the young woman was three months pregnant, and begged the doctors to get her out of her 'trouble.' On at least one occasion, they claimed that Emma was 'about six months gone,' that she had 'not felt any life' inside for some time, and that she 'thought the baby was dead.' Doctors George Wilson, Benjamin Bayly, Hutcheson Hogg, James Wilson, and James S. Niven refused all entreaties.

Yet the two women were not completely wide of the mark in searching for an abortionist among the ranks of male physicians. The Archives of Ontario cases reveal that 74 per cent of the individuals accused of procuring abortions were male, and many of these were physicians.[18] The women's continuing search finally brought them to Doctor Alexander Graham, an octogenarian who continued to run a busy obstetrical practice from an office at 380 Clarence Street.[19] He was apparently more forthcoming. A practising physician for thirty-three years, Dr Graham had originally lived in Newbury, where he had served as reeve, as well as on the local school board. In 1887, he had moved to London, where he resided with his wife, Annie, and two unmarried daughters, both teachers in London schools. Dr Graham examined Emma and determined she was five months pregnant. Jessie Clark would later testify that the doctor purported to have 'helped lots of girls,' and offered to procure a miscarriage for a fee of fifty dollars, '$25 down and the balance in four months with interest and $1 per trip to the house.'[20] Apparently advised by Dr Graham to seek financial assistance from the man responsible, Emma turned to her suitor.[21] William quibbled a bit about the price, but withdrew thirty dollars on Wednesday, 23 October, from the Ontario Loan and Debentures Company, explaining to the bank teller that the large withdrawal was necessary because 'he had been sick in the hospital for some time.' He gave Emma twenty-five dollars and an extra fifty cents for cab fare home.

At 7:30 p.m. that night, Emma Kilbourne and Jessie Clark left for Dr Graham's office. Anxious and frightened, Emma asked Jessie to wait outside, but to come searching for her if things seemed to be taking too long.[22] According to the testimony given at trial, Dr Graham cautioned Emma 'not to tell a living soul' what would take place inside his office that night. He instructed her to 'take off her drawers' and lie down on a couch. Then he inserted a 'long straight' instrument into 'her insides.' Dr Graham helped Emma to dress again, and warned her to go home quickly, advising that the 'child would come that night or in the morning.'

Jessie Clark took Emma home right away, for the young woman appeared to be 'pretty sick.' Her stockings and underclothing were 'wet' and she was having a great deal of difficulty walking. Despite the pain, Emma's first concern seemed to be to speak to William, to persuade him to sign a promissory note to Dr Graham for the remaining twenty-five dollars. William refused, insisting he would wait to see what happened to Emma before he paid anything further. When the promised miscarriage did not occur, Jessie Clark sent for Dr Graham on the morning of Thursday, the 24th. The doctor came to the Kilbourne home mid-morning and instructed the women to be patient, advising Emma 'to keep on her feet and go about her work.' Since Thursday was wash-day at the Kilbourne's, a burdensome chore in the large boarding-house, Emma was called into service at the washtub, where she managed to 'rub out two or three towels.'

That night Emma's pain grew so intense that Jessie stayed up with her until 3:00 a.m. Dr Graham paid another visit on Friday morning, and instructed Julia Kilbourne to keep him advised daily. Emma seemed to rally on Saturday, but worsened again by Wednesday, 30 October. That day Dr Graham told Emma that 'her womb was all crooked,' and he attempted to 'straighten' it, leaving her 'powders' to take orally for the pain. On Thursday and Friday, an anxious Dr Graham visited three times daily. Emma alternated between fever and chills and screamed with pain. Jessie continued to keep up her all-night vigil. William Mayo, whom Julia refused to permit into the bedchamber of her sick daughter, waited with rising alarm next door at the Clark residence. Impatient with the lack of progress, William finally marched down to Dr Graham's office, where he gave him 'a good calling down,' threatening that the doctor's medical diploma 'would be no good if anything happened [to] the girl.' On Friday, 1 November, Dr Graham apparently operated upon the patient two or three more times, with procedures sufficiently invasive to require chloroform. There was extensive bleeding, and skin-like clots emerged, staining the bed, quilt, carpet, and floor. By this point, Emma was frantic, and openly fearful of dying. She confessed to Julia and Jessie that she wished she had never tried to abort.

Truly alarmed, Julia Kilbourne and Dr Graham sent for other doctors. Dr John Wishart examined Emma briefly and concluded she was in no danger, but Dr James MacArthur, the second physician to come to the Kilbourne home, suspected that an illegal operation had been performed. Dr MacArthur announced that he 'thought there was going to be trouble in the case,' and ordered the patient removed to the hospital on Saturday, 2 November. Several hours later, in hospital, Emma Agnes Kilbourne delivered a female infant. The nurses wrapped the baby in a blanket and moved it to a warm place, but it lived less than twenty-four hours, dying around 4:00 p.m. the next day. The body had a visible scalp wound which was slightly curved, lacerated, and three inches in length. The cause of death was pronounced as 'premature birth.' Emma remained in hospital for three more days, and then discharged herself, against the advice of Dr Graham and the hospital nurses, who thought she should remain for at least another week or so. 'The girl evidently was anxious to get home,' observed the London *Daily News*.[23] Others speculated that the real reason was that she was desperate to seek respite from the detectives and physicians tenaciously pursuing her for a full confession.[24]

An inquest into the infant's death commenced before the coroner, Dr John M. Piper, at the London Police Station on the evening of 26 November. The news reporters present were quite protective towards

Emma Kilbourne, describing her more than once as an 'unfortunate girl' who had been 'brought into undesirable publicity.' Repeatedly the press emphasized that she was 'still [frail] from the effects of the birth of her child,' and obviously 'too weak to enter the witness box.'[25]

Undeterred, Crown Attorney James Magee, KC, called Emma Kilbourne to testify. Emma admitted that she had gone to Dr Graham as well as to other physicians to ask them 'to help her out of her trouble.' But she insisted that Dr Graham had refused to do so, advising her instead that 'she had better marry the fellow.' She denied that he had ever 'used any instruments' upon her, and attributed her miscarriage to lifting 'a heavy boiler of water off the stove that morning.' For good measure, Emma also added that 'she had the same day lifted a small, round coal stove out from the wall in order to polish it.' Julia Kilbourne backed up Emma's statements, although the press noted that 'like her foster daughter, she seemed possessed of a hazy recollection of things.'[26]

William Mayo took the stand and confessed that his sexual intimacy with Emma had resulted in her pregnancy. He told the coroner's inquest that he wanted to marry Emma, but she had refused, and 'he did not think it any use to talk to her, as women always have their own way anyway.' When Emma had asked to borrow twenty-five dollars, he had given her the money. Despite close questioning about what the sum was to be used for, William Mayo initially denied all knowledge. Then conceding that he feared Emma 'might go and poison herself,' he protested that he had warned Emma 'not do anything wrong with it, as he did not want to get into trouble.' 'He would rather she not go to the doctor if it was going to do her any harm,' he added. Increasingly shorn of credibility with every additional word, William Mayo ultimately professed that 'he did not know what was the matter with the girl until he saw her name in the paper.'[27]

Jessie Clark proved to be the Crown's key witness. Unlike Emma and Julia Kilbourne, she had apparently decided to make a clean breast of the situation. She described how she and Emma had canvassed a broad range of physicians in their efforts to locate one who would perform an abortion. She testified that Dr Graham had readily offered to comply with Emma's request. She admitted to waiting outside Dr Graham's office while the operation took place, peeking 'into the window of the office till the blind was pulled down.' She testified that Emma had taken the twenty-five dollars in with her, and when she came out, said: 'It's done.' In conclusion, she also advised that Emma and Julia Kilbourne had begged her to lie during the inquest, but that she had told them that 'if she was put on her oath she would [tell the truth].'

Shortly after the conclusion of the inquest, Dr Alexander Graham was charged with using an instrument with intent to procure a miscarriage, an offence punishable by life imprisonment. What made the case so unusual was that Emma Agnes Kilbourne also found herself one of the accused. She was charged with permitting an instrument to be used upon herself with intent to procure a miscarriage, an offence which carried a maximum sentence of seven years' imprisonment.

The first abortion statutes had focused exclusively upon the abortionist, rather than the pregnant woman. Not until the mid-nineteenth century did the law expressly provide that the women themselves could be charged.[28] Even after this clarification, it was exceedingly rare for police officers and Crown officials to bring the force of the criminal law to bear upon women seeking their own abortions.[29] Their reluctance may be credited to the sympathy generated by the plight of an unwillingly pregnant woman. The news reporters, for instance, had described Emma Kilbourne as an 'unfortunate' victim of circumstances. The customary decision not to charge the woman may also have hinged upon the importance of her testimony. Since most abortions were shrouded in secrecy, without written documentation or witnesses, it was extremely difficult to obtain sufficient evidence for a conviction. On rare occasions, the police resorted to using undercover methods of entrapment,[30] but most commonly they waited until medical complications forced abortion patients into the open. At that point, the authorities pressured women to testify against their abortionists. In many abortion trials, the key witness for the Crown was the abortion patient, whose testimony against her abortionist was probably traded for a promise of immunity from prosecution herself.[31]

Whatever remonstrations and threats the police detectives and Crown attorneys may have made to Emma Agnes Kilbourne, she seems to have been loath to testify against Dr Graham. She maintained throughout that there had been no operation, that Dr Graham had used no instruments of any kind, and that the miscarriage had been spontaneously caused by her heavy domestic exertions. She even appears to have tried to cover up Dr Graham's intervention by confessing that she had taken pennyroyal and cotton root compound, drugs that were often utilized by women seeking to induce their own abortions. To the last she stood firm, refusing to cooperate in implicating Dr Graham. Consequently she found herself charged alongside the doctor.

But this was not the only unusual feature of this case. Graham and

Kilbourne were also charged with the capital offence of murder, for 'kill[ing] and murder[ing] a female child theretofore born of the body of the said Emma Agnes Kilbourne.'[32] Murder or manslaughter charges were generally pressed against abortionists only when the pregnant woman died from medical complications. It was extremely rare to find such charges laid with respect to the death of the child concerned, unless the pregnancy had come to full term and the circumstances amounted to infanticide.[33] In this instance, the authorities may have been inspired to escalate the charge because of the late stage of pregnancy, which had resulted in the birth of an infant who lived for almost a day. It was also a clear signal of just how seriously the Crown Attorney intended to treat the accused pair. Ironically, the capital charge would also contribute to the downfall of the Crown's case.

The preliminary hearing into all of the charges was held in London, before Police Magistrate Francis Love, on 6 December 1901. The press noted that 'the aged doctor appeared to be cool,' while Emma Kilbourne 'entered the court room veiled so heavily her face could not be seen.' A crowd of 'three hundred men – mostly young men' thronged the police station to observe the proceedings, causing Magistrate Love to bar from the room all but court officials, witnesses, counsel, and the press. At the conclusion of the hearing, Magistrate Love held that there was sufficient evidence to bind the two accused over to the following spring's Criminal Assizes, and ordered Dr Graham and Emma Kilbourne remanded in custody to await trial. Friends and relatives came to their aid with sureties for bail, and Dr Graham was released from jail on 14 December 1901. Emma Kilbourne secured her release one week later.[34] The grand jury reviewed the Crown's evidence on 7 April 1902, and issued the 'true bills' necessary to push the case forward to trial.

Dr Graham had been diagnosed with diabetes, and had lost over one hundred and thirty pounds since the previous fall. Because of the 'precarious state' of his health, the trial was postponed until 16 September 1902. At the opening of the trial, the press exhibited acute curiosity over the appearance of the two accused when they took their seats on the prisoner's bench, 'as far apart as the narrow confines of the dock would permit.' The 'gray-bearded' Dr Graham was described as 'calm and even placid [in] a black frock coat [of] neat appearance.' Emma Kilbourne was reported to be 'quite healthy and plump', decked out in 'a light gray coat, buttoned closely across,' topped off with 'a black hat, with natural fruit and lace trimming.' Only 'the passing of her handkerchief across her mouth' gave any hint of emotion.[35]

The main line of attack of defence counsel Edmund Meredith, KC, was to undermine the credibility of the Crown's key witness, Jessie Clark. His intense cross-examination elicited the socially damning evidence that Jessie had herself been pregnant out of wedlock in the past. Meredith also intimated that Jessie Clark had been treated for venereal disease, that her child-adoption business was a 'baby-farming' or 'child-peddling' racket, and that her real motive for testifying against Dr Graham was malicious. Apparently Jessie Clark had been sued by the doctor some time earlier for failure to pay a medical bill, prompting Meredith to accuse her of being motivated by 'hate' or 'the hope of filthy lucre.' Meredith made much of the contrast between the discredited Jessie Clark and Dr Graham, an elderly reputable citizen who had 'held nearly every municipal position of honor.' Emphasizing that a conviction for murder would result in a sentence of death, Meredith insisted that Jessie Clark was clearly not the sort of woman 'upon whose word human life could be placed in jeopardy.'

The Crown's case faltered irretrievably when the medical witnesses indicated unanimously that the head wound on the infant was most likely suffered during the delivery in the hospital. Although the Crown hinted that physicians were naturally reluctant to testify against fellow practitioners in cases of this nature, the prosecution appeared doomed. When both Dr Graham and Emma Kilbourne held firm to their vehement denials, Crown Attorney Robert C. Clute, KC, was left with only his eloquence in the final charge to the jury: 'Life, infant life, is most sacred. The foundation of society depends upon its care and preservation, and he or she, married or unmarried, who attacks infant human life probably commits the grossest crime in the calendar. It is not simply our law, but also our churches that are attempting to stem this great evil. Its suppression depends in a great degree upon the courts. This case is now in your hands ... No greater trust was ever reposed in twelve men.'[36]

Judge William Lount was clearly unimpressed. Emphasizing the weaknesses in Jessie Clark's testimony, he cautioned the jurors on the danger of delivering a mistaken verdict of guilt, particularly in a capital offence where it would be impossible to 'call back the dead.' The jury took no more than twenty minutes to deliver verdicts of not guilty, on both the murder and abortion charges. The verdict was not surprising on the murder charges, where proof of criminal intent and the resulting penalty of death by hanging clearly presented substantial barriers to conviction. The Archives of Ontario sample discloses only two guilty verdicts out of twelve murder and manslaughter trials relating to abortion matters. Where the charge was procuring an abortion, advertising and selling abortifacients, or conspiracy to perform abortion, however, guilty verdicts appear to have been returned as often as acquittals during the first half of the twentieth century. On the procuring, advertising, selling, and conspiracy charges, twenty accused were found guilty, twenty were found not guilty, and three were registered 'nolle prosequi.' Dr Graham and Emma Kilbourne must have counted themselves extremely fortunate to have escaped further legal penalty.

The toll on their personal lives and reputations, of course, must have been immense. Dr Graham admitted at trial that his medical practice had fallen off dramatically. Despite the jury verdict, he would have faced ostracism within the medical community and the potential of disciplinary sanctions or expulsion from practice at the hands of his peers for 'infamous or unprofessional conduct.'[37] Before any such complications could transpire, however, Dr Graham's failing health intervened: he died one year after the trial.[38] Emma Kilbourne's life was also irreversibly affected. Indications are that she succumbed to external pressure and, despite her serious misgivings over William Mayo's reputation for alcoholism, married him midway through the proceedings.

LONELY WAR WIVES AND LAY ABORTIONISTS: ARDELLA VAUGHAN AND KATE TUDBALL, 1943

For Halifax Provincial Magistrate Robert E. Inglis, KC, the first case on the docket for 14 December 1943 was a preliminary hearing into charges against Kate Tudball. The accused was a married woman who resided in Westphal, a racially mixed, semi-rural hamlet on the south side of Lake Micmac in the County of Halifax.[39] The fifty-seven-year-old mother of nineteen children, Kate Tudball was not the usual sort of defendant tried in Police Court. The clerk read out the charge, which was typically long-winded and filled with arcane phraseology, but also more specific than most.[40] Kate Tudball stood accused that she did:

between the 25th day of March, A.D. 1943, and the 10th day of April, A.D. 1943, with intent thereby to procure the miscarriage of a woman, to wit, Ardella Vaughan of Spryfield in the said County of Halifax, unlawfully use upon her person an instrument to wit a long piece of needle-like metal and a rubber tubing through which the said Kate Tudball introduced into the womb of the said Ardella Vaughan a liquid consisting of alum and water with intent to procure thereby her miscarriage, contrary to Section 303 of the Criminal Code.

Those present in the courtroom must have been struck with the incongruity of an abortion trial centred upon such a maternal figure, a woman who had birthed nineteen children of her own. On the other hand, they may have sympathized that a mother with such overwhelming child-rearing responsibilities would respect and support other women's attempts to control their reproductive lives.

Unlike Emma Kilbourne, whose refusal to testify had resulted in her criminal prosecution, Ardella Vaughan did not stand accused of any crime. The price of her immunity was quite likely a detailed confession about the abortion. As the first witness called by Crown Attorney Ronald Manning Fielding, KC, Ardella Vaughan told the court that she was a twenty-two-year-old married woman, who resided on Green Road across 'the Northwest Arm' in Spryfield, in a boarding-house owned by her husband, Charles Vaughan.[41] The couple had only been married six months when Charles was called away from home in October 1942, probably for military service. Some months after her husband's departure, Ardella was embarrassed to discover that she was pregnant, and not with her husband's child.

Ardella Vaughan refused to divulge the name of her lover in court, although the circumstantial evidence was substantial. Shortly after her husband's departure, Ardella had struck up a relationship with Ira Matlock, a stoker for the Royal Canadian Navy, who was lodging in the Vaughan's boarding-house. It was to Ira Matlock that Ardella Vaughan had first confessed her pregnancy. He was the one who helped Ardella to plan the abortion, making all the initial arrangements and physically accompanying her to the home of the abortionist. He was the one who nursed Ardella Vaughan through her miscarriage and disposed of the foetal remains.[42] Although Ira Matlock was never explicitly identified as the male responsible for the pregnancy, he opted to cooperate fully with the legal authorities after the criminal investigation began, providing detailed information to the police and testifying for the Crown. Had he not, he would probably have found himself charged with procuring an abortion. It was not uncommon for criminal authorities to charge the male partners of the pregnant women, particularly where they were active in securing the services of an abortionist.[43]

Extramarital pregnancy carried great stigma throughout the first half of the twentieth century, as Emma Kilbourne could undoubtedly have attested in 1901, along with Ardella Vaughan in 1943. But much had also changed. World War I witnessed some relaxation of traditional sexual mores, accelerated by increasing opportunities for non-married sexual contacts in the automobiles and dancehalls of the 1920s. Economic pressures during the depression in the 1930s and an expansion in women's waged labour participation in the 1940s increased the pressures to curtail fertility. By the middle of World War II, women's waged labour became indispensable to wartime industry, leading some to speculate that the unprecedented mobilization of women might cause a breakdown in the established sex roles.[44]

With their husbands absent for extended periods during the war, it was not uncommon for young Canadian women to find themselves implicated in extramarital affairs. The strain of lengthy separation would be dramatically underscored by the burgeoning divorce figures, which almost tripled during the 1940s.[45] Many Canadians appear to have desired greater access to birth control during this period. Military men were routinely issued condoms, despite the continuing legal prohibition on the distribution of 'any article intended or represented as a means of preventing conception.' Such practices increased the supply and ultimately the demand for these products.[46] Yet despite the apparent interest in greater access to birth control, this would not culminate in any organized movement, or result in any legal reform, until the 1960s. The law stubbornly retained its nineteenth-century shape, forcing abortionists and their patients through excruciating criminal prosecutions despite the altered social and economic context.

Ardella and Ira appear to have decided to seek an abortion in April 1943. Ira had learned of an abortionist named Kate Tudball, and he and Ardella took a taxi and the ferry to her Westphal residence on 3 April. Under Crown Attorney Fielding's questioning, Ardella Vaughan described the encounter:

Q. When you arrived at the door what conversation did you have with the accused?
A. She answered the door. I asked her if she was Mrs. Tudball; she said yes; she asked me to come in and when we went into the room I just said to her, 'I guess you are the woman I am looking for to help me out' and she just asked me how far along I was.
Q. What did you say to that?
A. I told her I had my periods right along and I told her since January they were three or four days and they were usually a week and I thought I was pregnant because I couldn't keep a thing on my stomach and she asked me to come upstairs and she examined me.

Leaving Ira outside in the taxi, Ardella accompanied Kate Tudball upstairs to a bedroom at the end of the hall. There Mrs Tudball administered the initial treatment:

Q. You went into that room and what did you do?
A. She told me to lie down on the bed which I did and she examined me.
Q. Did you remove your clothing?
A. Yes, just my underclothing. She examined me and told me I was 2 1/2 or 3 months.
Q. What?
A. Pregnant.
Q. What then was said if anything?
A. There wasn't anything said, she just went over to her bureau.
Q. What did she do?
A. She had her back to me and she took this instrument from around her neck.
Q. What did that look like?
A. Like a long needle with a rubber tube on the end of it.
Q. What did she do?
A. She inserted the needle into me.
Q. Whereabouts into you?
A. Up into my womb, and took a mouthful of what I thought was water.
Q. Where was that?
A. On a stand by the bed.
Q. What was it in?
A. A cup.
Q. What did she do with that?
A. Took a mouthful of it and put it into the tube.
Q. What did she do after that?
A. After it went in the tube it just went inside of me I guess.
Q. Then what happened?
A. That was all, she turned her back to me and told me to get up. I was a little weak and it was kind of hard to walk at first and she went downstairs.
Q. Before she went downstairs did you have any conversation with her, did she ask you how you were?
A. I don't remember her asking, I told her I felt kind of weak, I sat on the bed 5 minutes before I got up.

After Ardella Vaughan reappeared downstairs, Kate Tudball informed her that the charge for the procedure would be fifteen dollars. This was substantially less than the ninety dollars charged in turn-of-the-century London by Dr Alexander Graham. Fees for illegal abortions during the first half of the twentieth century could vary enormously, from a few dollars to as much as $250. While some of the price disparity may have related to the formal qualifications of the abortionist, gender also appears to have been one of the most obvious distinctions. As in the labour market generally, women's work was typically valued at less than men's; female abortionists charged an average fee of thirty-five dollars and male abortionists an average of eighty-five dollars.47 On this occasion, however, Kate Tudball received an unexpected tip. The transcript continues:

Q. What did she say?
A. I don't remember her saying anything only I asked her what she charged and she told me $15.00. The smallest bill I had was a twenty and she had no change so I gave her the twenty.

The abortion was not yet complete, as Ardella Vaughan explained:

Q. Before you left the house did you know what was going to happen to you?
A. She told me to go home, to take a dose of salts and to walk around as much as I could, to exercise myself.
Q. What did she say would happen then; did she tell you anything that would follow then?
A. She told me that within twenty-four hours it would come.

But apart from a 'slight discharge of blood,' nothing happened. So Ira Matlock took Ardella back to Kate Tudball's two days later, where the procedure was repeated in exactly the same manner, at no extra charge. Ardella was bedridden immediately upon her return home, with pain so severe that against her vehement objections, Matlock called in Dr Ferguson Robert Little. Dr Little concluded that the patient was suffering from a miscarriage, although Ardella denied it. He prescribed some sulphanilamide pills to prevent infection and a sedative for the pain, and then left the Vaughan home. Shortly thereafter, Ardella Vaughan delivered what appeared to be a dead foetus. Ira Matlock disposed of the remains by burning them in the stove. On 11 April, Ardella was taken to the hospital by ambulance, where Dr Kenneth Colwell diagnosed her as suffering from 'pelvic abscess post abortal' and pulmonary tuberculosis. She would not be released until 18 June.

Ardella Vaughan's detailed description of the abortion procedure and eyewitness identification of the accused would have been crucial to the

Crown's chances for a successful prosecution. The need for such evidence was undoubtedly why the inducement of immunity was held out to entice so many women to testify against their abortionists. Why Ardella Vaughan chose to cooperate with the authorities, in marked contrast to her counterpart in the earlier London, Ontario, prosecution, remains a matter for speculation. Emma Kilbourne seems to have felt a certain loyalty towards Dr Graham, which prevented her from offering evidence against him. Ardella Vaughan seems to have wanted to deny her own complicity in the abortion, seeking instead to separate herself from Kate Tudball's medical practice and the resulting criminal law consequences.

The testimony that Ardella Vaughan was prepared to give against Kate Tudball raised a number of thorny legal problems. Women who consulted abortionists were technically 'accomplices' to the crime, and courts had traditionally greeted their evidence with suspicion. Hoping to accentuate these concerns, Kate Tudball's lawyer, O.R. Regan, KC, was scathing in his cross-examination of Ardella Vaughan. He opened with the question: 'When was it you started to blame this on Mrs. Tudball?' Ardella admitted that she had not pinpointed Kate Tudball until questioned by a detective in the hospital. This prompted defence lawyer Regan to demand:

Q. Up to that time you never blamed Mrs. Tudball had you?
A. No, I lied to the authorities at the hospital.
Q. Who did you blame it on?
A. I didn't blame it on anyone.
Q. But after being in the hospital for quite a while you thought it was time to blame it on somebody?
A. I blamed it on who did it.
Q. When you talked to the detective the first time?   ,
A. Yes.
Q. You never blamed it on anybody before?
A. No.
Q. Blamed nobody did you?
A. I told the hospital a different story when I went in.
Q. Did you blame anyone?
A. No.
Q. You just got that way yourself or Matlock – did you blame Matlock for it?
A. No I didn't.

Reminding the court that she had 'lied all the time' to the doctors who treated her, defence counsel Regan insinuated that Ardella Vaughan was falsely incriminating his client out of pure malice.

It was not uncommon to cast such aspersions upon accomplices. Surmising that such individuals might be embroidering the truth to divert attention from their own acts, judges had traditionally instructed juries that an admitted criminal was not entitled to much credibility on the witness-stand. Some jurists conjectured that abortion cases presented less danger in this respect, given the public embarrassment that enveloped such morally stigmatizing business. Alberta Supreme Court Chief Justice Horace Harvey had admitted as much in an abortion trial in 1912, when he pointed out that 'the evidence against the accused must necessarily implicate the accomplice and the horror of such an admission is such that the natural tendency would be to deny rather than declare the crime.'[48] Between 1900 and 1950, however, the degree of scepticism inspired by the testimony of a woman who was prepared to implicate her abortionist seemed to intensify. The early cases often permitted uncorroborated evidence from an accomplice to ground a conviction,[49] and the Quebec Court of King's Bench stated explicitly in 1914 that abortion trials were not among the group of cases where the evidence of 'the woman who underwent abortion must be corroborated.'[50] Later rulings required trial judges to caution juries about the perils of convicting in increasingly rigorous terms. By 1926, Canadian courts seem to have succumbed to the influence of English judicial rulings, which had categorically concluded several years earlier that in the absence of a warning by the trial judge, a jury was not entitled to convict on the uncorroborated testimony of an accomplice.[51] Defence lawyer Regan was clearly intending to put the court on notice that reliance upon Ardella Vaughan's testimony was seriously misplaced.

But there was ample corroborative evidence as well. RCMP Constable John R. Steinhauer had been dispatched to Kate Tudball's home with a search warrant on 29 April 1943, and he had emerged with a rich haul of incriminating objects. In the upstairs bedroom he had discovered seven needle-like instruments, a four-and-a-half-inch red-coloured rubber hose, another piece of rubber hose twelve inches long, a bag of crystal salts, and two glass tumblers containing water-like fluid. Chemical analysis had revealed that the crystal salts were 'alum,' an astringent capable of causing the contraction of membranes. The fluid in the glass tumblers was composed of a solution of alum and water.[52]

Evidence such as this suggested that Kate Tudball was what authorities liked to classify as a 'professional abortionist,' someone doing a volume business and attempting to earn a living by procuring miscarriages. It appears that not only was Kate Tudball well equipped to induce abortion, but that she had set aside an entire room in her home as a medical office for this purpose. There were a number of such individuals practising in the first half of the twentieth century. Some were women without formal medical credentials, but skilled in the arts of midwifery.[53]

The historical connection between midwifery and abortion has been less explored than the reproductive aspects of the profession. Historians have noted that female midwives dominated the practice of childbirth throughout much of the nineteenth century in Canada, but have uncovered little information about their provision of abortion services. Like Kate Tudball, most midwives were older, married women, who had borne children themselves, and worked in the field part-time to make money to help raise their families. Their numbers and influence began to decrease throughout the nineteenth century as male physicians and hospitals combined to create the 'scientific' new field of medical obstetrics, and a series of statutory enactments pronounced aspects of the practice of midwifery illegal. Although some midwives continued to practice throughout Canada well into the twentieth century, they did so from an increasingly marginalized position.[54] The trial of Kate Tudball apparently took no formal notice of the legality (or illegality) of her occupation per se. In the context of the prosecution of abortion charges, where the very act of procuring an abortion was expressly criminalized, there was no need to go beyond the events at hand to consider the status of midwifery itself.

Crown Attorney Fielding's task was to prove a causal connection between Kate Tudball's use of the rubber tubing and Ardella Vaughan's miscarriage. Dr Kenneth Colwell, a staff physician at the Victoria General Hospital, was of some assistance here:

Q. You have heard Doctor the evidence of Ardella Vaughan that a rubber tubing or catheter was shoved up into her womb and a liquid introduced into the womb, supposing that liquid were alum and water, what effect would that have?
A. I couldn't say definitely, I have my opinion.
Q. You heard her story that subsequent to two such treatments she had a discharge, would that be consistent with that treatment?

A. Yes.

Q. And a likely consequence of that treatment?

A. Yes.

Q. In fact the introduction of a catheter into the womb, have you had occasion to know in your training that is a method of abortion?

A. Yes.

This testimony was not entirely definitive, and defence counsel Regan rose with some eagerness, hoping to shed doubt on the causation issue:

Q. Can a woman have a miscarriage without being abortive?

A. An abortion and miscarriage are the same thing.

Q. It is not necessary to use a rubber tube in order to have an abortion?

A. No.

Q. Was her condition when you examined her consistent with a miscarriage?

A. Yes ... [S]he had a miscarriage and she was infected at the same time and there was evidence of infection outside the womb in addition to the miscarriage.

Q. How would that be brought about in your opinion?

A. By instrumentation most likely.

Q. Not necessarily so?

A. That's difficult to answer, it's only an opinion. We know that the vast majority of infective abortions are caused by instrumentation, particularly when the infection is extended beyond the womb.

Defence counsel Regan's next set of questions was intended to draw attention away from his client and implicate Dr Little instead:

Q. Do you recollect [Ardella Vaughan] said she passed this after taking the pills that Dr Little had prescribed?

A. Yes, she passed something – she had a discharge.

Q. That was after the pills were administered?

A. Yes.

Q. Would that bring about a miscarriage?

A. No.

Q. You cannot bring about a miscarriage with pills?

A. I don't think so.

Q. You say a woman cannot have a miscarriage by the taking of pills?

A. She would probably have a miscarriage if she took enough pills to get the poison out of the pills, and there's nothing I know of unless she takes enough to get poisoned.

Q. Of course you know that pills for abortions are widely used?
A. Yes.
Q. With good results?
A. No, I would say they wouldn't get good results.
Q. You want to say the sale of these pills are all a hocus-pocus and doesn't mean anything?
A. Yes I would say that.

Regan's line of questioning had not elicited much of use. But his obvious surprise over Dr Colwell's dismissal of the medication indicated just how widespread was the belief that pills could prompt a miscarriage. Some drugs were actually marketed for this purpose, surreptitiously to be sure, but with advertising claims that were unmistakably designed to tempt those seeking abortion. One such ad, published in the Toronto *Evening Telegraph*, read: 'Ladies – Dr De Voss' Capsules will cure suppressed menstruation from any abnormal condition, no case hopeless, price $2; extra double strength $3. Cure or money refunded; lady attendant. Dr. De Voss Medicine Co., 210 Queen East, Toronto.'[55] Although the authorities had sporadically attempted to prosecute those marketing such products, their record of success was mixed.[56]

The prosecution files are filled with references to various drugs women had ingested in the hopes of prompting their own miscarriages: ergot, yellow jasmine, tansy, pennyroyal, castor oil, and quinine. Most appear to have been ineffective, but some produced nausea and convulsions sufficient to induce an abortion.[57] Instruments were generally thought to be riskier, but more effective in producing the expulsion of the foetus.[58] One typical procedure was to dilate the cervix in order to reach into the uterus, and then to scrape out the contents. The legal records indicate that implements such as pointed sticks, wooden skewers, stove-pipe wire, buttonhooks, needles, uterine 'sounds,' laminary tents, and spoon-shaped surgical curettes were all employed.[59] One account even attested to the use of 'long finger nails.'[60] It was also common to introduce some sort of hollow tubing, catheter, or syringe into the womb, and then to attempt to flush out the foetus with mixtures of soap, castor oil, and Lysol.[61] Death was a possible outcome of any of these procedures, especially given the risks of laceration, perforation, and infection. Often the abortionist failed to expel the full contents of the womb, leaving behind tissue which could quickly become infected. There is little indication from the legal records that qualified medical practitioners were significantly more proficient or less likely to create health complications than were lay practitioners such as Kate Tudball. The sample of cases from the Archives of Ontario indicates that death resulted from abortions procured by physicians in six cases, and in at least one additional case, medical complications from a physician's operation required lengthy hospitalization. Non-physicians were responsible for seven deaths.

Defence counsel Regan had done his best to cast doubt upon the Crown's evidence, but there was more than enough to commit Kate Tudball for trial at the next sitting of the Supreme Court of Nova Scotia. On 22 March 1944, she was brought before Mr Justice William F. Carroll. There are no surviving judicial records of the trial, although the Halifax *Mail* reported that the ten witnesses called took up most of the day in court.[62] The prosecution seems to have put in its case largely unaltered from the preliminary hearing. Ardella Vaughan, whose name was discreetly left out of the newspaper account, testified that the accused woman had performed two operations upon her. While this had produced the desired abortion, she noted that it had also necessitated hospital attention of more than three months. Stoker Ira Matlock testified as to his role in obtaining the procedure. Doctors Little and Colwell gave their medical opinion that the patient had undergone an abortion. The RCMP officers itemized the various abortion instruments they had seized at Kate Tudball's home.

In view of the extensive incriminating evidence, defence counsel Regan advised his client to take the stand herself. Kate Tudball did testify in her own defence, but she was able to offer little except emphatic denials. According to the Halifax *Mail*, she flatly 'denied ever having seen the woman upon whom she was alleged to have performed the illegal operations.' Beyond this, Kate Tudball's only strategy was to remind the court that she was the mother of nineteen children, a point which she stressed unequivocally and repeatedly. None of this appears to have done any good, and after two and one-half hours of deliberation, the jury returned a verdict of 'guilty with a plea for leniency.'[63] The conviction would seem to have been a foregone conclusion, given the overwhelming evidence against the accused.

When it came time for sentencing, defence counsel Regan made the most of his client's advancing age and large family.[64] But the Tudball court records contain no petitions from friends, family, or community members attempting to persuade the judge to go lightly upon the convicted woman, such as were compiled on behalf of several other convicted abortionists.[65] And Judge Carroll, a sixty-eight-year-old Roman

Catholic father of five, was unconvinced.[66] He sentenced Kate Tudball to five years, a term within the typical range for this offence. The sample of cases from the Archives of Ontario reveals that penalties for procuring an abortion could range from a suspended sentence to ten years, while cases reported in the Canadian law reports show several offenders sentenced to life imprisonment or an indeterminate sentence.[67] Emphasizing the 'enormity' of the crime, Carroll confessed that but for the jury's recommendation for mercy, he would have sentenced Tudball to 'twenty years.' In closing, he lectured the prisoner: 'This offence you committed is really murder. You were instrumental in killing this woman's child. You are an old lady, and I hope this time in the penitentiary will benefit you.'[68]

Kate Tudball's lawyer immediately launched an appeal on a number of grounds. He protested that the conviction 'was against law, evidence and the weight of evidence,' that the accused had not been given 'the benefit of any reasonable doubt as to the law or the evidence,' that 'there was no evidence of corroboration,' that his client had been 'gravely prejudiced by the remarks and interjections of the trial judge during the progress of the trial,' and that the 'trial judge erred in not properly presenting the case for the defence to the jury.' Similar arguments had met with some success in other abortion appeals.[69] In addition, Regan argued that the jury verdict – 'guilty with a plea for leniency' – was ambiguous. The trial judge had erred, he claimed, in entering this as a finding of guilt, with a request for leniency at sentence.[70] The appeal was denied by the Nova Scotia Court of Criminal Appeal on 15 June 1944, without reasons, and Kate Tudball was duly dispatched to serve out her full term in the Kingston Penitentiary.

CONCLUSION

The first half of the twentieth century was marked by a certain legislative stability with respect to the law of abortion. The law was clear, and it did not deviate from its comprehensive and unrelenting prohibition of fertility control. The procuring of a miscarriage, by any 'means whatsoever,' could result in life imprisonment. Such legislative edicts coexisted uncomfortably with the reality of some women's lives. The social and economic circumstances shaping women's options and needs meant that there was always a demand for abortion services. Unwillingly pregnant women, like Emma Kilbourne and Ardella Vaughan, rebelled against the legal restrictions on reproductive control, and many sought to prevent childbirth with poisonous medications, sharp instruments, catheters, and syringes.

Legal records from inquests, police magistrates' courts, and criminal assize courts provide rich sources of historical documentation about the conditions under which women obtained abortions. Dr Alexander Graham and Kate Tudball typify the range of abortionists who found themselves under legal scrutiny for their actions. Dr Alexander Graham personifies the male physician-abortionists, who were prepared to provide their patients with pregnancy termination along with a range of other medical services. Kate Tudball exemplifies the lay practitioners, more evenly divided by gender, some of whom appear to have made a career out of offering abortions on a large-scale, volume basis.

Occasionally, the male suitors who had assisted their lovers with the termination of pregnancy also found themselves drawn into criminal proceedings. That William Mayo escaped prosecution for Emma Kilbourne's abortion probably relates to the availability of another Crown witness, Jessie Clark, who was willing to testify as to the circumstances of the procedure. Ira Matlock's full cooperation with the police investigation likely accounted for his immunity. The prosecution of pregnant women was extremely rare, but not impossible, as Emma Kilbourne's case illustrates.

The class-based nature of abortion prosecution is clearly apparent in these two cases. Working-class women who sought abortions, such as Emma Kilbourne and Ardella Vaughan, seem to have fallen under the grip of the law more frequently than their middle- and upper-class counterparts. The extent to which such women were willing to participate actively as Crown witnesses often spelled the difference between the success or failure of the prosecution's case. Crown attorneys were eager to trade promises of immunity with abortion patients in exchange for their testimony in court. Ardella Vaughan, who seems to have accepted this bargain, gave evidence which secured her abortionist's conviction, despite the rules of evidence which cast a fair degree of doubt over the credibility of accomplices, scepticism which increased during the fifty years under consideration. Emma Kilbourne was less accommodating, insisting to the end that no abortion had ever been performed. Her recalcitrance meant that she, too, faced criminal charges, but ironically, the very overzealousness of the Crown seems to have netted an acquittal for both Emma Kilbourne and her physician. The distinction in social position and professional standing of the accused abortionists may also have had something to do with the differential outcome. Dr

Alexander Graham was able to avail himself of his 'good name' and occupational stature in the community. Kate Tudball was merely a 'quack,' practising medicine without a licence.

Even in acquittal, however, Dr Graham seems to have scored a somewhat hollow victory. The very public prosecutions took an enormous toll on personal and professional lives. Kate Tudball, serving out her five-year sentence in the Kingston Penitentiary, and Dr Alexander Graham, dead less than one year after his trial, possibly of medical complications exacerbated by the trauma of prosecution, would serve as dramatic reminders to the community that abortion was contrary to law. Those who dared to subvert criminal prohibitions against abortion risked enormous consequences. Their trials and punishment signalled to the larger public that individuals who sought recourse to pregnancy termination could expect the full force of legal retribution.

NOTES

I am indebted to my research assistants, Anna Feltracco, Alexandra Hartmann, Anne Eichenberg, Jennifer Hall, Kevin Misak, and Dr Allen Robertson. Funding from the Law Foundation of Ontario and the Social Sciences and Humanities Research Council of Canada is gratefully acknowledged.

1 Prior to the enactment of the first criminal abortion statutes, many jurists had believed that the common law placed no sanctions upon abortion, particularly if procured during the early stages of pregnancy. But between 1810 and 1892, no less than seventeen separate statutes were passed by nine different legislative jurisdictions within the geographic area that would become twentieth-century Canada. The new abortion laws covered such issues as who could commit the crime, upon whom the crime could be committed, when the crime could be committed, the prohibited means of procuring miscarriage, and corresponding penalties. For a more detailed discussion of nineteenth-century abortion law, see Constance Backhouse 'Involuntary Motherhood: Abortion, Birth Control and the Law in Nineteenth Century Canada' *Windsor Yearbook of Access to Justice* 3 (1983) 61 and *Petticoats and Prejudice: Women and Law in Nineteenth-Century Canada* (Toronto: Women's Press and the Osgoode Society 1991) chap. 5; Shelley Gavigan 'The Criminal Sanction as It Relates to Human Reproduction: The Genesis of the Statutory Prohibition of Abortion' *Journal of Legal History* 5 (1984) 20; Bernard M. Dickens *Abortion and the Law* (Bristol: MacGibbon and Kee 1966).

2 The Criminal Code, 1892, SC 1892, c. 29, s. 179 made it an indictable offence, subject to two years' imprisonment for every one who 'offers to sell,
advertises, publishes an advertisement of or has for sale or disposal any
medicine, drug or article intended or represented as a means of preventing
conception or causing abortion.' It was a defence to prove that 'the public
good was served by the acts alleged to have been done,' although the section
noted that the 'motives of the seller, publisher or exhibitor shall in all cases
be irrelevant.' Section 272 made it an indictable offence, subject to life imprisonment, to unlawfully administer drugs or other noxious things, or unlawfully use any instrument or other means whatsoever, with the intent to
procure a miscarriage. Section 273 made it an indictable offence, subject to
seven years' imprisonment, for a woman who unlawfully used (or permitted
to be used) upon herself drugs or instruments with intent to procure miscarriage. Section 274 made it an indictable offence, subject to two years' imprisonment, to unlawfully supply drugs or instruments, knowing that these
were intended to procure a miscarriage.

3 The only substantial change was an enactment, in 1900, which authorized
the trial judge to exclude the public from the courtroom during an abortion
trial 'in the interests of public morals': see An Act further to amend the
Criminal Code, 1892, SC 1900, c. 46, s. 3; RSC 1906, c. 146, s. 645; SC
1915, c. 12, s. 7; RSC 1927, c. 36, s. 645. The other revisions were few and
of a minor nature. An Act further to amend the Criminal Code, 1892, SC
1900, c. 46, s. 3 made minor wording revisions to s. 179, and stressed that
where an accused was attempting to prove the defence of public good, there
must be 'no excess in the acts alleged beyond what the public good requires.'
An Act respecting the Criminal Law, RSC 1906, c. 146 made minor wording
and punctuation changes, and renumbered the abortion provisions: s. 179(c)
became 207(1)(c), s. 271 became 306, s. 272 became 303, s.273 became 304,
and s. 274 became 305. An Act to amend the Criminal Code, SC 1913, c. 13,
s. 8 made additional revisions to s. 207(1)(c), penalizing those who advertised instructions or medicines for 'restoring sexual virility or curing venereal diseases or diseases of the generative organs.' See also An Act respecting the Criminal Law, RSC 1927, c. 36, which made no revisions to the
relevant provisions. An Act to amend the Criminal Code, SC 1949, 2nd Session, c. 13, s. 1 renumbered s. 207(1)(c) as 207(2)(c) and made minor gram-
matical alterations to the section.

4 Mariana Valverde *The Age of Light, Soap, and Water: Moral Reform in English-
Canada, 1885–1925* (Toronto: McClelland and Stewart 1991) 167

5 United Church Archives, Victoria College, Toronto, Minutes and Annual
Reports of Methodist DESS, 1907, as quoted in Valverde *Light, Soap and Water*
53

6 National Archives of Canada, Ottawa, National Council of Women 'Report of Standing Committee on Objectionable Printed Matter' in 1913 *Annual Report* at 79–81, as quoted in Valverde *Light, Soap and Water* 62. On a comparative note, Judith R. Walkowitz has found that English feminists also attacked birth control literature and advertisements for female pills (abortifacient drugs), as part of a larger campaign to eradicate obscene books, music-halls, theatres, and nude paintings. Walkowitz attempts to explain the motivation of this feminist campaign as follows: 'To these moral crusaders, "pornographic literature", thus broadly defined, was a vile expression of the same "undifferentiated male lust" that ultimately led to homosexuality and prostitution ... Social purity feminists opposed artificial contraception, precisely because they believed that the separation of reproduction and sexuality would render all women "prostitutes"': 'Male Vice and Female Virtue: Feminism and the Politics of Prostitution in Nineteenth-Century Britain' in Ann Snitow et al., eds. *Powers of Desire: The Politics of Sexuality* (New York: Monthly Review Press 1983) 428–9.

7 See, for example, the reprints of British medical articles in 'Abortion Lawful or Unlawful' *Canadian Medical Association Journal* 26 (Mar. 1933) 364–5; 'Therapeutic Abortion and the Law' *Canadian Medical Association Journal* 39 (1938) 401–2; Shelley Gavigan 'On Bringing on the Menses: The Criminal Liability of Women and the Therapeutic Exception in Canadian Abortion Law' *Canadian Journal of Women and the Law* 1 (1986) 279–312. By way of contrast, several American physicians published books demanding greater access to lawful abortion during this period: see William J. Robinson *The Law against Abortion: Its Perniciousness Demonstrated and Its Repeal Demanded* (New York: Eugenics Publishing Co. 1933); Frederick J. Taussig *Abortion: Spontaneous and Induced, Medical and Social Aspects* (St Louis, Mo.: C.V. Mosby Co. 1936).

8 See Angus McLaren and Arlene Tigar McLaren *The Bedroom and the State: The Changing Practices and Politics of Contraception and Abortion in Canada, 1880–1980* (Toronto: McClelland & Stewart 1986) 12, 19, 59–70, 88, 92–7, 101–3, 116; Dianne Dodd 'Women's Involvement in the Canadian Birth Control Movement of the 1930s: The Hamilton Birth Control Clinic' in Katherine Arnup et al., eds. *Delivering Motherhood: Maternal Ideologies and Practices in the 19th and 20th Centuries* (London: Routledge 1990) 150 at 158; Gerald Storz and Murray Eaton 'Pro Bono Publico: The Eastview Birth Control Trial' *Atlantis* 8 (1983) 51–60; Wendall W. Watters *Compulsory Parenthood: The Truth about Abortion* (Toronto: McClelland and Stewart 1976) 122–6. Unlike their Canadian counterparts, a number of British women's organizations lobbied for legislative reform to permit greater access to abortions during the 1930s and 1940s. The Women Citizens' Association, the National Council of Women, the Women's Co-operative Guild, and the National Council for Equal Citi-

zenship all approved resolutions at annual conferences during the 1930s calling for 'greater female self-determination,' and in 1936, formed the Abortion Law Reform Association. After 1945, they were joined by the Federations of University Women, the Family Planning Association, and some sections of Townswomen's Guilds. For more details, see Dickens *Abortion and the Law* 115, 121.

9 Approximately fifty cases are reported in the series of law reports published across Canada during this period. These are only a small portion of the actual prosecutions. Statistics Canada has tabulated 980 cases between 1922 and 1950: see *Statistics of Criminal and Other Offences* (Ottawa: Statistics Canada 1973).

10 Several readers of this paper have suggested that I delete the word 'heterosexual' from this sentence, noting that the resulting pregnancy already establishes the heterosexual nature of the relationship. I have chosen to retain the reference, however, since I believe that in a culture which presumes heterosexuality as the norm, we need constant reminders that same-sex relationships exist and have always existed.

11 Accounts of this case are taken from the files in the Archives of Ontario: *The King* v. *Alexander Graham; The King* v. *Emma Agnes Mayo, otherwise called Emma Agnes Kilbourn*, RG 22, ser. 392, box 91, Criminal Indictment Case Files, County of Middlesex Assizes, High Court of Justice, April 1902. See also the files of the case in the D.B. Weldon Library, University of Western Ontario, Regional Room, Middlesex County Court Records, Middlesex County Crown Attorney and Crown Prosecutor Criminal Court Records, 1902, box 558. For press accounts, see London *Daily News* 26 Nov. 1901; London *Advertiser* 26–28 Nov. and 3 Dec. 1901; London *Daily Free Press* 26–28 Nov., 3–5, 7, 9, 11, 13, 20, 23 Dec. 1901, and 17–18 Sept. 1902. The spelling of some names is not uniform in the file: Kilbourn and Kilbourne; Mayo and Mayell. For Emma Kilbourne's address and occupation, see *London and Middlesex Directory* (Foster & Co. Publishers 1902).

12 For some discussion of the contemporary discourse on 'the lodger evil,' see Valverde *Light, Soap, and Water* 136–7, 195.

13 For some discussion of comparable English patterns, suggesting that working-class women resorted to abortion more frequently than others, see Angus McLaren 'Women's Work and Regulation of Family Size' *History Workshop* no. 4 (Autumn 1977) 70–81; Patricia Knight 'Women and Abortion in Victorian and Edwardian England' *History Workshop* no. 4 (Autumn 1977) 57. Leslie J. Reagan '"About to Meet Her Maker": Women, Doctors, Dying Declarations and the State's Investigation of Abortion, 1867–1940' *Journal of American History* 77 (1991) 1240 at 1246 discusses this syndrome in the

Chicago area, noting that 'working-class women may have had more abortions than did middle-class women.'

14 Various historians have debated whether middle-class women had greater access to birth control than their working-class counterparts, some suggesting they did, others suggesting the difference was not substantial: see Jane Lewis '"Motherhood Issues" in the Late Nineteenth and Twentieth Centuries' in Arnup et al., eds. *Delivering Motherhood* 3; Dodd 'Canadian Birth Control Movement' 155. See McLaren and McLaren *The Bedroom and the State* at 20–5 for a description of the birth control methods used by Canadians in the first half of the twentieth century: (hetero)sexual abstinence, prolonged nursing, rhythm, coitus interruptus, sheath, douche, pessary.

15 Reagan 'About to Meet Her Maker' describes this phenomenon based on American data, at 1246: 'Working-class women's poverty – in both wealth and health care – made it more likely that they, rather than middle-class women, would reach official attention for having abortions ... In addition, poor women, lacking funds, often used inexpensive, and often dangerous, self-induced measures and delayed calling in doctors if they had complications. By the time poor women sought medical attention, they had often reached a critical stage and, as a result, had come to the attention of officials. Affluent women avoided official investigations into their abortions because they had personal relations with private physicians, many of whom never collected dying statements, destroyed such statements, or falsified death certificates. If necessary, wealthier families might be able to pressure or pay physicians, coroners, the police, and the press to keep quiet about a woman's abortion related death.'

16 Other abortion case files indicate that some women attempted to secure the services of an abortionist through the mails. See, for example, *The King* v. *Dr. James W. Wheeler*, AO RG22, ser. 392, box 150, Criminal Indictment Case File, Supreme Court of Ontario, Counties of Stormont, Dundas and Glengarry, 1918.

17 Throughout the nineteenth century, most women appear to have believed that pregnancy had not been established until they felt foetal movements. Viewing themselves as merely 'irregular,' many believed themselves fully within their rights in attempting to 'bring on a period.' See Backhouse *Petticoats and Prejudice* 146; McLaren and McLaren *The Bedroom and the State* 38; Knight 'Women and Abortion' 64; Angus McLaren *Birth Control in Nineteenth-Century England* (London: Croom Helm 1978) 243–6.

18 The Ontario archival court files described above reveal that women were charged as abortionists in 25.5 per cent of the cases, men in 74.5 per cent. In thirteen of the twenty-three cases where the occupation of the abortionist

is noted, 'physician' is listed. Some of the other occupations included in this sample and in the cases reported in Canadian law reports between 1900 and 1950 are: druggist, electrotherapist, nursing home operator, boarding-house keeper, plumber, farmer, lawyer, department store manager.

19 Dr Graham must have been more than eighty years old, since the *History of the County of Middlesex* (Toronto and London: W.A. and C.L. Goodspeed n.d.) lists his date of marriage to Ann Stuart as 24 November 1836. Presuming him to have been at least sixteen years old at the time of marriage, his age at the time of trial would have been eighty-one years. The London *Daily Free Press* 5 Dec. 1901 refers to Graham as 'the aged doctor.' His residence at the time of the trial was 616 Richmond Street.

20 By way of comparison, physicians testified at the preliminary inquiry later on this case that the usual fee for medical attendance at a spontaneous miscarriage was $5: see 'The Charge Is Murder' London *Daily Free Press* 9 Dec. 1901, p. 6.

21 The designation 'suitor' was not used in the case reports, although this appears to be an accurate label in this instance. In Quebec, a man sexually responsible in an abortion case was sometimes described as a 'cavalier': see *Michel Brunet v. The King* (1928), 50 CCC 1 (SCC).

22 For more detailed descriptions of the mental qualms and apprehension that affected women seeking illegal abortions in the twentieth century, see Patricia G. Miller *The Worst of Times* (New York: Harper Collins 1993).

23 'Implicates Physician' London *Daily News* 26 Nov. 1901

24 See the statement of Crown Attorney James Magee, that the hospital 'was a place where she would be apt to talk,' in 'The Charge Is Murder' London *Daily Free Press* 9 Dec. 1901, p. 6.

25 'Stories That Do Not Agree' London *Advertiser* 27 Nov. 1901; 'Kilbourne Inquest Is Unfinished' London *Advertiser* 28 Nov. 1901. See also the reference to Emma Kilbourne as 'the unfortunate girl' in 'Murder Case for Friday' London *Daily Free Press* 5 Dec. 1901; 'The Charge Is Murder' *London Daily Free Press* 9 Dec. 1901.

26 'Kilbourne Inquest Is Unfinished' London *Advertiser* 28 Nov. 1901

27 'Implicates Physician' London *Daily News* 26 Nov. 1901; 'Sprung a Surprise' London *Daily News* 27 Nov. 1901

28 Provincial legislation in New Brunswick and Nova Scotia, passed in 1849 and 1851 respectively, was the first expressly to permit the authorities to charge women for procuring abortions upon themselves: An Act to consolidate ... the Criminal Law, SNB 1849, c. 29, art. 7; Of Offences against the Person, RSNS 1851, c. 162, s. 11. This rule was extended federally by An Act respecting Offences against the Person, SC 1869, c. 20, ss. 59–60, which

explicitly stated that women who administered poison or used an instrument upon themselves could be charged. An Act respecting Offences against the Person, RSC 1886, c. 162, ss. 47–48 expanded these provisions to apply to women who behaved in a more passive fashion. By 1886, it was an offence even for a woman to permit poison to be administered or to permit an instrument to be used upon her with the intent to procure a miscarriage. See also Backhouse 'Involuntary Motherhood' 71–82.

29 On the notable paucity of charges against women seeking to procure their own abortions in the nineteenth century, see the preliminary conclusions of Backhouse 'Involuntary Motherhood' 83–5. An extensive study of archival court records across Canada would be required before one could claim any statistical certainty in this matter. However, an examination of the reported cases and the Ontario archival records listed above suggests that during the period 1900–50 charges against the woman herself were few. One rare example is *Rex* v. *Holmes* (1902), 9 DCR 294 (DCSC), in which the jury refused to convict, which prompted the presiding judge to lecture the twelve male jurors on their failure to appreciate their responsibilities: see the account of this case in McLaren and McLaren *The Bedroom and the State* 42, citing Public Archives of British Columbia, AG (BC), Court Records, 1902: 20 (v. 92) and Nelson *Daily News* 10 May 1902. Another rare example is *The King* v. *Dr Allen McDonald and Hazel Eliza Lotan*, March 1928, Middlesex County Criminal Court Records, Summary Conviction Papers 1918–28, D.B. Weldon Library, University of Western Ontario, Regional Room, box 596, and Middlesex County Court Records, D.B. Weldon Library, University of Western Ontario, Regional Room, box 152. That Hazel Lotan was charged and convicted seems particularly unusual, since she and her abortionist, Dr McDonald, had cooperated fully with the authorities, offering complete confessions. Hazel Lotan received a sentence of six months' determinate and three months' indeterminate imprisonment at hard labour. Dr McDonald received two years at hard labour.

30 In the late 1940s, the Montreal municipal police instructed a female police officer to pose as a pregnant woman to gain entrance to the premises of an individual suspected of practising as a professional abortionist. The ruse failed, and Dame Kotyszyn was acquitted in *Rex* v. *Kotish/Kotyszyn* (1948), 93 CCC 138 (Montreal Court of Sessions of the Peace) of conspiring to procure an abortion, on the ground that the police woman had never intended to go through with the procedure and without two, there could be no conspiracy. This was upheld on appeal in *Rex* v. *Kotyszyn* (1949), 95 CCC 261 (Que. KB). Similar efforts on the part of the Quebec Provincial Police around the same period were more successful, with convictions for attempt-

ing to procure an abortion registered in *Rex v. Young* (1949), 94 CCC 117 (Montreal Court of Sessions of the Peace) and *Dame Delphine Sevigny-Roy v. The King* (29 Oct. 1948, no. 564 of the Record of the Court of King's Bench of the District of Montreal). Underscoring the difficulties of proof in abortion cases, Chief Justice Letourneau stated in the latter case: 'It is of no avail for the defence to speak of the odium of these police duties, simulations, trickery and traps which are connected therewith, for, if it were necessary for the police to count only upon the real accomplices, most of the offences would remain unpunished and it seems right that for a much greater good or, to be more exact, to restrain the crime as much as possible, these traps for vice must be admitted, particularly when it is a question of crime against morals and public order; to date we have not been able to find any other means of penetrating the mystery of accomplices, whether it be in connection with simple police or penal laws or, as in the present case, a real criminal act.' See also Mr Justice Armour 'Annotation: Police Traps and Incitements to Crime' (1933), 59 CCC 273.

Reagan 'About to Meet Her Maker' notes at 1262 that similar raids against suspected abortionists took place in the 1940s in Chicago: 'Rather than waiting for a death, the state attorney's office sent police to raid the offices of suspected abortionists where they arrested abortionists and patients and collected medical instruments and patient records.'

31 See infra, discussion of the evidence of accomplices. The legal status of women whose abortions prompted legal challenge perplexed early-twentieth-century legal reporters. Confusing the criminal and civil process, some reports of criminal abortion trials described the women as 'plaintiffs': see, for example, *Rex v. Sadick Bey* (1914), 25 CCC 259 (Que. KB) at 261. Others mistakenly utilized the traditional (and vindictive) appellation for rape victims in criminal procedure, 'prosecutrix': see, for example, *Rex v. Vye* (1925), 44 CCC 249 (BCCA). Both labels revealed that the women in these cases were not viewed as typical victims of crime, but as women with active interests in mobilizing legal process – a perspective most often opposite to the actual circumstances of the litigation.

32 The relevant homicide sections of An Act respecting the Criminal Law, SC 1892, c. 29 were found in ss. 218–20, 227, 230–1, 236, 271.

33 For a discussion of the legal response to infanticide, and the crossover between infanticide and abortion, see Constance Backhouse 'Desperate Women and Compassionate Courts: Infanticide in Nineteenth-Century Canada' *University of Toronto Law Journal* 34 (1984) 447; Backhouse *Petticoats* chap. 4; Marie-Aimée Cliche 'L'infanticide dans la région de Québec 1660–1969' *Revue d'histoire de l'Amerique française* (1990) 31.

34 George M. Reid, a London stationery manufacturer and printer, and John McNee, a London cigar manufacturer, each put up sureties of fifteen hundred dollars for Dr Alexander Graham's bail. William Kilbourne, Emma's unmarried brother of the Township of North Dorchester, and William Henry Chittick, the owner of the Dorchester Station Hotel, each put up sureties of one thousand dollars for Emma Kilbourne. John Kilbourne and Isaac Kilbourne of North Dorchester offered to join them, but their sureties were not required. Dr Graham put up his own surety of three thousand dollars, and Emma one for two thousand dollars.

35 See 'Graham Murder Case Drawing to a Close' London *Daily Free Press* 17 Sept. 1902.

36 'Dr. Graham and Mrs. Mayo are Not Guilty' London *Daily Free Press* 18 Sept. 1902

37 See, for example, *In re Robert Telford* (1905), 11 BCR 355 (BCSC), in which the British Columbia College of Physicians and Surgeons voted to erase Dr Telford's name from the register of medical practitioners despite his acquittal on criminal charges resulting from an abortion. The court ruled that the college was within its disciplinary power to prohibit Dr Telford from further medical practice. See also *Re Stinson and College of Physicians and Surgeons of Ontario* (1910), 2 OWN 298 (Ont. High Ct.), upheld (1911), 18 CCC 396 (Ont. Div'nal Ct.), in which the council of the College of Physicians and Surgeons of Ontario was permitted to hold an inquiry to determine whether Dr Albert W. Stinson of Cobourg should be erased from the medical register, despite his earlier acquittal on charges of procuring a miscarriage.

38 The *London and Middlesex Directory* (Foster & Co., Publishers 1904) lists Dr Graham's wife, Annie, as a 'widow of Dr. Alexander,' residing in his former residence at 616 Richmond Street.

39 Information about this case was taken from *The King* v. *Kate Tudball*, Public Archives of Nova Scotia, RG39 'C' vol. 751, no. 1745, Supreme Court of Nova Scotia, County of Halifax, Dec. 1943–Apr. 1944. Press accounts are found in the Halifax *Chronicle* 22 Mar. and 6 and 8 Apr. 1944, and Halifax *Mail* 21–23 Mar. 1944.

40 The wording of the charge often inspired technical legal arguments from defence counsel in abortion cases. In *Rex* v. *Campbell* (No. 2) (1946), 88 CCC 41 (BCCA), where the use of an instrument was charged, the court quashed the conviction (O'Halloran, J.A. dissenting), when it appeared that manual manipulation might have procured the miscarriage, noting: 'Section 303 is so unfortunately phrased that even if the crime of abortion is conclusively established by the testimony as it is here, nevertheless the accused may be

acquitted if the technical evidence of actual method employed is weak.' For other cases where the defence was raised successfully, see *Rex* v. *Cook* (1909), 15 CCC 40 (Ont. CA); *Rex* v. *Dale* (1939), 72 CCC 181 (BCCA); *Rex* v. *Poznansky* (1950), 97 CCC 208 (BCCA). For some examples of cases in which similar arguments were raised unsuccessfully, see *Rex* v. *Holmes* (1902), 9 BCR 294 (BCSC); *Rex* v. *Bachrack* (1913), 21 CCC 257 (Ont. CA); *Rex* v. *Doucette* (1949), 93 CCC 202 (Alta. CA).

41 The surviving records appear to reveal nothing further about Ardella or Charles Vaughan's occupational or class status.

42 Kate Tudball's defence lawyer could hardly contain his scepticism over Ardella Vaughan's continued refusal to name Ira Matlock as her lover, particularly in the face of his role in the clean-up. This was the exchange between the defence lawyer and Ira Matlock:

Q. At the time she was sick were there any women staying there?
A. Yes.
Q. Yet you had to clean up the mess?
A. Yes.
Q. Where were the ladies? ... Did they wait on their sister any?
A. Yes.
Q. But this particular job was done by you?
A. Right.
Q. Why did you do it?
A. I don't know why.
Q. Were you interested in getting rid of the stuff?
A. No.
Q. You burned it in the stove?
A. Right.

43 The extent of involvement varied from assisting in locating an abortionist to providing financial support for medical fees, supplying the medication, or actually operating upon the pregnant woman with instruments and syringes. For cases in which the male partners were charged, see *The King* v. *Edmund Bridant and Lillian Miller*, AO RG22, ser. 392, Box 267, Criminal Indictment Case File, Ontario High Court of Justice, County of York, 1907; *The King* v. *Walkem* (1908), 14 CCC 122 (BCSC); upheld [1908] AC 197 (PC); *In re Claude McCready* (1909), 14 CCC 481 (Sask. SC); *Rex* v. *Bachrack* (1913), 21 CCC 257 (Ont. CA); *Rex* v. *Inkster* (1915), 24 CCC 294 (Sask. SC); *Rex* v. *Pettibone* (1918), 30 CCC 164 (Alta. CA); *Rex* v. *Prentis-Arbuckle* (1925), University of Western Ontario, D.B. Weldon Library, Regional Room, Middlesex County Court Records, box 152; *Rex* v. *Vye* (1925), 44 CCC 249 (BCCA); *Rex* v. *Brooks* [1927], 4 DLR 458 (Ont. CA), rev'd *Brooks* v. *The King*

(1927), 48 CCC 333 (SCC); *Rex v. Dr. Allen McDonald and Hazel Eliza Lotan* (1928), University of Western Ontario, D.B. Weldon Library, Regional Room, Middlesex County Criminal Court Records, Summary Conviction Papers, box 596; *The King v. Thomas Navin*, AO RG22, ser. 392, box 94, Criminal Indictment Case File, Supreme Court of Ontario, County of Middlesex, 1928; *Rex v. Schwartzenhauer* (1935), 63 CCC 269 (BCCA), upheld *Schwartzenhauer v. The King* (1935), 64 CCC 1 (SCC); *Rex v. Stewart Clark* (1939), University of Western Ontario, D.B. Weldon Library, Regional Room, Middlesex County Court Records, box 169, Judges' Notebooks for Criminal County Court, vol. 2, Judge Wearing (June 1937–May 1946) at 110–18.

44 See Alison Prentice et al. *Canadian Women. A History* (Toronto. Harcourt, Brace, Jovanovich 1988) 295–302; Ruth Roach Pierson *'They're Still Women after All': The Second World War and Canadian Womanhood* (Toronto: McClelland & Stewart 1986) 15–16, 20, 149, 164, 179, 173, 187, 200; Ruth Roach Pierson *Canadian Women and the Second World War* (Ottawa: Canadian Historical Association 1983); Carolyn Gossage *Greatcoats and Glamour Boots: Canadian Women at War (1939–1945)* (Toronto: Dundurn 1991); James G. Snell, *In the Shadow of the Law: Divorce in Canada, 1900–1939* (Toronto: University of Toronto Press 1991) 262; Deborah L. Rhode *Justice and Gender: Sex Discrimination and the Law* (Cambridge: Harvard University Press 1989) 206.

45 Snell *In the Shadow of the Law* describes at 145 the impact of World War I on the dramatic rise in the divorce rate, noting at 156 that 'the transition to modern divorce began in the years following the First World War.' Prentice *Canadian Women* notes at 323 that divorce rates in Canada almost tripled at the end of World War II, a result 'of the dissolution of unhappy wartime marriages and those weakened by long separations; it may also have reflected the economic independence acquired by some married women during the war.'

46 Pierson *'They're Still Women after All'* 200; Rhode *Justice and Gender* 206

47 An examination of the Ontario archival cases listed above, as well as the abortion cases reported in the Canadian law reports between 1900 and 1950, found fees listed in only seventeen cases. The average fee was $58, with the lowest amount being the sum of $1 or $2 charged by a lay female practitioner in *The King v. Anna Reeder*, 1928, AO RG22, ser. 392, box 94, Criminal Indictment Case File, Supreme Court of Ontario, County of Middlesex, March 1928; and the highest being the sum of $250 charged by a man holding himself out as a physician in *Rex v. Young* (1949), 94 CCC 117 (Montreal Court of Sessions of the Peace). On a comparative note, it appears that medical costs for childbirth were generally somewhat lower. Re-

search on fees in Vancouver in 1921 revealed the following: $35 for a normal delivery, $50 with a haemorrhage, $45 with instrumental labour, and $35 if a miscarriage occurred. Even these fees were beyond the means of many families. See Veronica Strong-Boag and Kathryn McPherson 'The Confinement of Women: Childbirth and Hospitalization in Vancouver, 1919–39' in Arnup et al., eds. *Delivering Motherhood* 75 at 84.

48 *Rex v. Betchel* (1912), 19 CCC 423 (Alta. SC). See also *Rex v. Hayman* (1931), 57 CCC 189 (Man. CA), where Chief Justice Prendergast emphasized that accomplices in abortion cases were somewhat more credible than in other cases.

49 See *Rex v. Reynolds* (1908), 15 CCC 209 (Sask. SC); *Rex v. Betchel* (1912), 19 CCC 423 (Alta. SC); and *Rex v. Bechtel* (1913), 21 CCC 40 (Alta. SC); *Rex v. Sadick Bey* (1914), 25 CCC 259 (Que. KB) was even more direct at 261: '[T]here is really only one question which could be submitted on appeal, i.e., if in a case of abortion the evidence of the plaintiff – that is, of the woman who underwent abortion, must be corroborated. The law enumerates all the cases where the evidence of one witness must be corroborated and the present case is not in that enumeration.' See also *The King v. Walkem* (1908), 14 CCC 122 (BCSC); upheld [1908] A.C. 197 (PC).

50 *Rex v. Sadick Bey* (1914), 25 CCC 259 (Que. KB) at 261

51 See *Gouin v. The King* (1926), 46 CCC 1 (SCC); *Rex v. Hayman* (1931), 57 CCC 189 (Man. CA); *Rex v. Poznansky* (1950), 97 CCC 208 (BCCA). See also *Rex v. Schwartzenhauer* (1935), 63 CCC 269 (BCCA); *Schwartzenhauer v. The King* (1935), 64 CCC 1 (SCC); *Rex v. Synourizowa* (1930), 55 CCC 63 (Ont. CA); *Rex v. Picken* (1937), 69 CCC 61 (BCCA); reversing the conviction and ordering a new trial, [1938] 79 SCR 457; *Rex v. Doucette* (1949), 93 CCC 202 (Alta. CA). On the question of whether Quebec law should differ from that of the common law provinces on this issue (classified as a matter of evidence, not criminal law), see Mr Justice Greenshields of the Quebec Court of King's Bench 'Annotation: The Accomplice as a Witness' (1929), 53 CCC 1 at 13–14.

52 The chemical analyst at the preliminary hearing also noted that the water was not clean, but 'contained organisms ... similar to what you find in ponds [and] there was a little plant life in it too.'

53 For examples of cases in which lay female practitioners appear to have been operating an abortion business, see *Rex v. Petch* (1925) 45 CCC 49 (Man. CA), where the court made reference to 'habitual abortion-mongers'; *The King v. Marion Emily Bettes*, AO RG22, ser. 392, box 285, Supreme Court of Ontario, County of York, 1926; and repeat charges against Amelia Murray in *The King v. Amelia Murray* (1926), 59 NSR 119 (NSSC) and *The King v. Amelia Murray* (1932), PANS RG39 'C,' vol. 717, no. 917, Supreme Court of

Nova Scotia, County of Halifax. Not all of the 'professional abortionists' were female midwives, however. For examples of cases in which male doctors appear, see *Rex* v. *Cook* (1909), 15 CCC 40 (Ont. CA), where Dr Edgar M. Cook operated in his own private lying-in maternity home; repeat charges against Dr Michel Brunet, characterized during the proceedings as 'a public abortioner' in *Rex* v. *Brunet* (1917), 30 CCC 9 (Que. KB), upheld as *Michel Brunet* v. *The King* (1918), 30 CCC 16 (SCC) and *Michel Brunet* v. *The King* (1928), 49 CCC 257 (SCC) and *Michel Brunet* v. *The King* (1928), 50 CCC 1 (SCC); and *Rex* v. *Campbell* (1946), 86 CCC 410 (BCCA) and *Rex* v. *Campbell (No.2)* (1946), 88 CCC 41 (BCCA), where the court concluded that Dr Campbell, a registered naturopath, had 'equipped a nursing home for the purpose of carrying on this illegal business in rather a wholesale way.'

54 For discussion of the history of midwifery, see Wendy Mitchinson *The Nature of Their Bodies: Women and Their Doctors in Victorian Canada* (Toronto: University of Toronto Press 1991) 163–91; Leslie Biggs ' The Case of the Missing Midwives: A History of Midwifery in Ontario from 1795–1900' *Ontario History* 75 (1983) 21–36; James Connor 'Minority Medicine in Ontario, 1795 to 1903: A Study of Medical Pluralism and Its Decline' (PhD thesis, University of Waterloo 1989); Colin Howell 'Reform and the Monopolistic Impulse: The Professionalization of Medicine in the Maritimes' *Acadiensis* 11 (1981) 20–1; Judith Litoff *American Midwives 1860 to the Present* (Westport, Conn.: Greenwood Press 1978); Jane Donegan 'Midwifery in America, 1760–1860: A Study in Medicine and Morality' (PhD thesis, Syracuse University 1972).

55 'Business Personals Column' Toronto *Evening Telegraph* 19 July 1906, exhibit filed in *The King* v. *Edmund Bridant and Lillian Miller*, AO RG22, ser. 392, box 267, Criminal Indictment Case File, Ontario High Court of Justice, County of York, 1907

56 Lillian Miller, who appears to have been the 'lady attendant' behind the above advertisement, was convicted under s. 274 of supplying the means to procure an abortion on 29 January 1907, and sentenced to two years in the provincial penitentiary: *The King* v. *Edmund Bridant and Lillian Miller*, AO RG22, ser. 392, box 267, Criminal Indictment Case File, Ontario High Court of Justice, County of York, 1907. An earlier prosecution against F.E. Karn of 132 Victoria Street, Toronto, a distributor of proprietary medicines, *The King* v. *Karn* (1901), 5 CCC 543 (Ontario County Court), failed to convict the accused under s. 179(c) for selling and advertising 'Friar's French Female Regulator.' The promotional literature had advised: 'They will speedily restore the menstrual secretions when all other remedies fail. Should this function become deranged from any cause whatever, relief can always be obtained by using the tablets. The only certain and effectual em-

menagogue known. These tablets surpass all such compounds as penny-royal, ergot, tansy, etc. Thousands of married ladies are using these tablets monthly. No name is ever divulged, and your private affairs, your health, are sacred to us. Do not use the regulator during pregnancy.' The trial judge concluded at 544 that 'the words used must be taken in their natural and primary sense' and directed an acquittal. On appeal as *The King* v. *Karn* (1903), 6 CCC 479 (Ont. CA), the judges expressed some doubt whether the last sentence was intended to dissuade pregnant women or to act as a tongue-in-cheek encouragement. They concluded that the latter was as likely as not: 'Their object and operation in promoting and ensuring the regularity of the menstrual flow, which is, popularly at all events, supposed to be interrupted by conception, is so clearly and explicitly stated, that it might well be asked for what other purpose married ladies, or others who might desire to prevent pregnancy, would be likely to be using them monthly.' However, the Court of Appeal declined to order a new trial, and the acquittal stood.

57 For examples of such cases, see *Rex* v. *Walkem* (1908), 14 CCC 122 (BCSC), upheld [1908] AC 197 (PC); *The King* v. *Scott* (1912), 19 CCC 370 (Ont. CA); *Rex* v. *Bachrack* (1913), 21 CCC 257 (Ont. CA); *Rex* v. *Inkster* (1915), 24 CCC 294 (Sask. SC); *Rex* v. *Pettibone* (1918), 30 CCC 164 (Alta. CA); *The King* v. *Sophia Arvelin*, AO RG22, ser. 392, box 155, Criminal Indictment Case File, Inquest and Police Court, District of Thunder Bay, 1921; *Rex* v. *Prentis-Arbuckle* (1925), University of Western Ontario, D.B. Weldon Library, Regional Room, Middlesex County Court Records, box 152; *The King* v. *Marion Emily Bettes and Wallace L. Gilbert*, AO RG22, ser. 392, box 285, Criminal Indictment Case File, Supreme Court of Ontario, County of York, 1926; *Rex* v. *Schwartzenhauer* (1935), 63 CCC 269 (BCCA), rev'd [1935] 3 DLR 711 (SCC); *Rex* v. *Stewart Clark* (1939), University of Western Ontario, D.B. Weldon Library, Regional Room, Middlesex County Court Records, box 169, Judges' Notebooks for Criminal County Court, vol. 2, Judge Wearing (June 1937–May 1946) at 110–18; *Rex* v. *Poznansky* (1950), 97 CCC 208 (BCCA). In the last case, the evidence indicated that the woman seeking abortion had also 'been taking mustard baths and jumping off a fire escape for a month or so before her miscarriage.'

See also the medical analysis by W.A. Dafoe, MB, Fellow in Obstetrics and Gynaecology, University of Toronto 'The Types and Treatment of Abortions' *Canadian Medical Association Journal* 22 (June 1930) 793–7, where he notes at 794 that 'a few of the drugs taken by mouth are as follows, quinine, castor oil, ergot, tinct. cantharidis, guaiacum, salts, lead pills, and the patent preparations such as pennyroyal and Beecham's pills ... The results are not always satisfactory to the patient and sometimes end in definite poisoning. Most of the drugs act moderately on the uterine musculature, but lead has a definite killing effect on the syncytial and Langhans cells of the chorionic villi.'

58 Some abortionists offered both methods, but clearly felt an operation to be superior. See, for example, the letter sent to Mrs Helen Chorley by the accused in *The King v. Dr. James W. Wheeler*, AO RG22, ser. 392, box 150, Criminal Indictment Case File, Supreme Court of Ontario, Counties of Stormont, Dundas, and Glengarry, 1918: 'Dear Madam: Can send remedy for $10.00 but more satisfactory to come and see me – Costs $25.00. Immediate action is best as you have waited so long now. Cordially.'

59 For examples of cases in which such instruments were employed, see *Rex v. Pollard and Tinsley* (1909), 15 CCC 74 (Ont. CA); *Rex v. Cook* (1909), 15 CCC 40 (Ont. CA); *The King v. Louisa Cull*, AO RG22, ser. 392, Box 274, Criminal Indictment Case File, Supreme Court of Ontario County of York, 1916; *The King v. Sophia Arvelin*, AO RG22, ser. 392, box 155, Criminal Indictment Case File, Inquest and Police Court, District of Thunder Bay, 1921; *Rex v. Brooks* (1927), 61 OLR 147 (Ont. CA), rev'd *Brooks v. The King* (1927), 48 CCC 333 (SCC); *Rex v. Dr. Allen McDonald and Hazel Eliza Lotan* (1928), University of Western Ontario, D.B. Weldon Library, Regional Room, Middlesex County Criminal Court Records, Summary Conviction Papers, box 596; *Rex v. Schwartzenhauer* (1935), 63 CCC 269 (BCCA), rev'd [1935] 3 DLR 711 (SCC); *Rex v. Louise Garnet* (1943), University of Western Ontario, D.B. Weldon Library, Regional Room, Judges' Notebooks for Criminal County Court, vol. 2 (Sept. 1934–June 1945), box 169 at 264–9; *Rex v. Williams* (1943), University of Western Ontario, D.B. Weldon Library, Regional Room, Judges' Notebooks Criminal County Court, vol. 2 (June 1937–May 1946), box 169 at 300–5; *Rex v. A.* (1944), 83 CCC 94 (Quebec Magistrate's Court, Three Rivers); *Molleur v. The King* (1948), 93 CCC 36 (Que. KB); *Rex v. Doucette* (1949), 93 CCC 202 (Alta. CA).

60 In *Rex v. Buck et al.* (1940), 74 CCC 314 (Ont. CA), Hilda Picot stated that the accused had tried to cause an abortion 'with her hand, she had long finger nails and I guess she busted something as I bled just a drop or two.'

61 The manufacturers of products such as Lysol and Dettol were not above hinting at the contraceptive attributes of their wares, and advertisements published in women's magazines during the first half of the twentieth century contained statements such as these: 'It used to be that feminine hygiene was not discussed. It was taboo. But today it is recognized as modern science's safeguard to health ... very often to happiness.' For further references, see McLaren and McLaren *The Bedroom and the State* 22–3.

For examples of cases reporting the abortifacient use of such methods, see *Rex* v. *Holmes* (1902), 9 BCR 294 (BCSC); *Coroner's Inquest of Evelyn Smith* (1917), University of Western Ontario, D.B. Weldon Library, Regional Room, Coroners' Inquests, box 692, folder no. 991–1000; *The King* v. *Amelia Murray*, Public Archives of Nova Scotia, RG39, 'C,' vol. 717, no. 917, Supreme Court of Nova Scotia, County of Halifax, 1933; *Rex* v. *Schwartzenhauer* (1935), 63 CCC 269 (BCCA), rev'd [1935] 3 DLR 711 (SCC); *Rex* v. *Anderson* (1935), 64 CCC 205 (BCCA); *Rex* v. *Dale* (1939), 72 CCC 181 (BCCA); *Rex* v. *Tass* (1946), 86 CCC 97 (Man. CA), upheld (1946), 87 CCC 97 (SCC); *Rex* v. *Myrtle Graham* (1946), University of Western Ontario, D.B. Weldon Library, Regional Room, Judges' Notebooks for Criminal County Court, vol. 2 (21 June 1937–8 May 1946), box 169, at 394–8; *Rex* v. *Doucette* (1949), 93 CCC 202 (Alta. CA); *Rex* v. *Edgecombe*, [1949] 2 WWR 584 (BCSC), upheld (1949), 96 CCC 93 (BCCA); *R.* v. *Hrechuk* (1950), 98 CCC 44 (Man. CA).

For a medical analysis of how these methods could be self-employed, see Dr Dafoe 'Types and Treatment of Abortions,' who noted at 794: 'This is done by the patient assuming a squatting position with a mirror propped upon the floor in front of her and attempting to push the instruments into the cervical canal. Sometimes the instruments are boiled, but often this is not done. Strong douches of lysol, potassium permanganate, vinegar, mustard, carbolic acid and mercury bichloride are used, with the resulting caustic effects, followed by excoriation, ulceration and absorption.' Another Canadian physician would note: 'The extremes that these women may go to rid themselves of their pregnancies apparently know no bounds'; see Murray Blair, MD, CM, Department of Gynaecology and Obstetrics, Vancouver General Hospital 'A Conservative Treatment of Incomplete Abortion' *Canadian Medical Association Journal* 25 (Nov. 1931) 576 at 578.

62 'Kate Tudball Convicted on Two Charges' Halifax *Mail* 23 Mar. 1944, p. 3
63 For similar verdicts, see *The King* v. *Marion Emily Bettes*, AO RG22, ser. 392, box 285, Criminal Indictment Case File, Supreme Court of Ontario, County of York, 1926, where the jury recommended mercy on the ground of the age and ill-health of the accused. She was sentenced to four years, having had a previous conviction for similar acts. See also *The King* v. *Anna Reeder*, 1928, AO RG22, ser. 392, box 94, Criminal Indictment Case File, Supreme Court of Ontario, County of Middlesex, March 1928, where the jury strongly recommended mercy, and the accused was sentenced to a term of seven months determinate and one year indeterminate.
64 For similar arguments, which met with more success than in the present instance, see *Rex* v. *Betchel* (1912), 19 CCC 423 (Alta. SC); and *Rex* v. *Bechtel* (1913), 21 CCC 40 (Alta. SC). In that case defence counsel argued that the

male physician concerned would lose his licence to practice if confined for a lengthy period, and that he had a young wife without any means of support. Although counsel argued for a suspended sentence, the accused got three months without hard labour. The sentencing judge, Charles Allan Stuart, also referred to his initial doubts about the correctness of the verdict, which appears to have affected the sentence as well.

65 See, for example, the petitions mounted in *Rex* v. *Dr. Allen McDonald and Hazel Eliza Lotan* (1928), University of Western Ontario, D.B. Weldon Library, Regional Room, Middlesex County Criminal Court Records, Summary Conviction Papers, box 596.

66 For biographical details on the Hon. William F. Carroll, who served three terms as a Liberal MP, see PANS Biography Card File, Halifax *Chronicle-Herald* 26 Aug. 1964, B.M. Greene, ed. *Who's Who in Canada, 1943–44* (Toronto: International Press 1944) 1134.

67 Life imprisonment was assessed in a manslaughter case, in *Molleur* v. *The King* (1948), 93 CCC 36 (Que. KB). One abortionist was sentenced to prison in *Rex* v. *Edgecombe*, [1949] 2 WWR 584 (BCSC), upheld (1949), 96 CCC 93 (BCCA) for an 'indeterminate period' as a 'habitual criminal,' because of his past record of convictions for rape, procuring women to become prostitutes, living off the avails of prostitution, and previous employment by a professional abortionist.

68 For examples of other cases in which the judges condemned abortion in similar terms, see *In re Robert Telford* (1905), 11 BCR 355 (BCSC), where Lyman Poore Duff described the practice as a 'grave and visible menace to the social welfare' (at 366). See also *Rex* v. *Petch* (1925), 45 CCC 49 (Man. CA), where Charles Percy Fullerton noted: 'The defendant here has been convicted of a most serious offence. That Parliament so regarded it is shown by the fact that it fixed life imprisonment as the maximum punishment.'

69 See, for example, *Rex* v. *Kolomrjyc* (1926), 46 CCC 35 (Man. CA); *Rex* v. *Brooks* (1927), 61 OLR 147 (Ont. CA), reversed in *Brooks* v. *The King* (1927), 48 CCC 333 (SCC); *Rex* v. *Picken* (1937), 69 CCC 61 (BCCA), reversed in [1938] 3 DLR 32 (SCC). An examination of the results of the appeals for all the cases of procuring an abortion (including advertising and selling abortifacients and conspiracy to perform an abortion) reported in the Canadian law reports between 1900 and 1950 shows a fairly even balance in results. Fourteen convictions were upheld on appeal and eleven quashed. Three acquittals were upheld on appeal and two overturned. In cases of abortion-related murder or manslaughter, the results were markedly different. Two convictions were upheld on appeal and ten quashed.

70 A similar argument would be made in *Molleur* v. *The King* (1948), 93 CCC 36

(Que. KB). In that case, the accused abortionist had been convicted of murder, a capital offence, after the jury entered a verdict with a recommendation for mercy. A dissenting judge on the Quebec Court of King's Bench concluded that such a verdict was inconsistent with a finding of murder, and expressed doubt as to the accused's guilt. On appeal, the majority substituted a verdict of manslaughter and a sentence of life imprisonment on another ground.

9

Between the Old Order and Modern Times: Poverty, Criminality, and Power in Quebec, 1791–1840

JEAN-MARIE FECTEAU

INTRODUCTION: POLITICAL ECONOMY AND SOCIAL REGULATION

In the half century between the enactment of the Constitutional Act in 1791 and the Act of Union in 1840 Lower Canada saw its traditional methods of dealing with poverty and criminality come under heavy attack, reviled by critics and buffeted by economic, political, and social transformations. In particular, the great transition to capitalism is generally regarded as having occurred in this period. This transition was a complex and far-reaching phenomenon which profoundly altered social and economic ideas and practices. Historians have tended, wrongly I believe, to see both this transition to capitalism and the changes in social practices that it wrought as both teleological and linear. That is, the advent of capitalism itself has been seen as a long-term process characterized by the expansion of trade and the rise of the bourgeoisie, whereas it is better characterized as brutal and sudden.[1] The transition to production capitalism did not simply produce an increase in trade and salaried workers: it involved a series of large changes which during the first half of the nineteenth century fundamentally and concomitantly redefined the state, the system of production, standards of consumption, and the world-view of the hegemonic classes. Similarly and, again I argue, incorrectly, the principal reforms suggested in response to the crisis of the Old World are generally seen as stages in the process of modernization. This view dominates historiographic analyses of the development of methods of dealing with poverty and criminality.[2] The aims and objectives of philanthropists and other reformers, from Howard to Bentham, are seen primarily as harbingers of the modern world, at best distorted by the idealism of those first exponents of the modern social world.

This paper, using the example of Lower Canada, presents a radical rejection of that approach. It postulates that the crisis of the old system, which reached a critical stage during the period under examination, must be understood in its own terms. In particular, it must be understood as a crisis faced by reformers themselves, for their patterns of thought were deeply ingrained with the old logic of regulation which looked primarily to the community as the agency of control and which envisaged that control as extending to both poverty and criminality, indeed to all aspects of 'deviance.' The persistence of such patterns of thought meant that the social control model developed during this period was actually an idealized image of a lost society, a utopic model which, in the tormented and troubled consciences of the philanthropists, developed out of the necessity of finding radical methods for dealing with a crisis which they regarded as fundamental. Therefore internment in institutions, the therapeutic practice of moral treatment, the blurring of the distinction between poverty and criminality, should all be seen simply as typical methods of reform based on the ideal of total control of the individual and on a desire to reform the popular classes systematically and en masse. Yet if there was continuity in ideas, there was a radical discontinuity in practice. The 'totalitarian' ideal just described, which sprang essentially from the state, is in many ways the exact opposite of the regulation system actually implemented under capitalism, for that system was mainly based on a recognition of individual responsibility and resulted in a separation between methods of dealing with poverty and methods of dealing with criminality.

This analysis of changes in social regulation is primarily a history of the changing logic regarding regulation, an account of the meaning of philanthropic discourse as it was employed in the debate on the crisis of the old model during the transition to capitalism. It is not, however, an abstract account of such discourse, for its particular setting is Lower Canada and it discusses the principal concrete initiatives taken, such as the introduction of the first private charitable organizations and the rapid development of the practice of putting offenders in prison which presaged a process of systematic exclusion based on the offence. This latter procedure, in the end, attached very little importance to therapeutic ideals in the development of the modern prison.[3] A necessary backdrop to all of this, however, is an understanding of the contradictions of the traditional system, and thus I will first look briefly at the logic which informed the old regulation system, the overall structure of that system, the position of the state, and the forms in which the crisis of the old model was manifested. Of particular interest here is the structure of the criticisms directed towards the traditional system. The main body of the paper then examines the various changes made to the aid and repression systems and assesses the limits to and constraints of the transition of regulation methods in Lower Canada.

THE OLD REGULATION SYSTEM

By the end of the eighteenth century, Lower Canada's system of repression – how it dealt with poverty, for example – displayed the persistence of what may be referred to as feudal characteristics. The realities of crime, poverty, and mental illness were intertwined with a social logic which was largely focused on the community in all its forms. The municipalities, villages, trades, and religious orders were the benchmarks of society. An individual's place in the social hierarchy was ultimately determined by status, that is, the place which an individual held by right within the tightly regulated network of social hierarchies.[4] On the basis of that social logic, society left it to the different collective organizational structures to deal with any breaches of law and order which might occur. In the early Middle Ages, crime had been seen as a private matter, a disruption of acceptable relations between individuals; eventually, when the King's power was firmly established, criminal matters were submitted to his exemplary justice. Poverty, which simply described the natural condition of almost the entire working population, was handled in the same way. Particular instances of hardship were the responsibility above all of a person's peers, neighbours, or community. This model presupposed the stable reproduction of the various communities. However, monetization of the economy, feudal and dynastic wars, and biological disasters contributed to the creation of a growing class of excluded and marginalized people who depended for subsistence on transient urban employment, begging, or petty theft.

Against this backdrop the power of the state[5] expanded, especially after the great crises of the fourteenth century. The feudal state, or in some countries urban elites, gradually took steps to palliate the most obvious deficiencies of classic methods of feudal regulation by establishing institutions specifically designed to deal with the marginalized and the rejected. For instance, over the course of the sixteenth and seventeenth centuries general hospitals and almshouses were set up in France, and workhouses and reformatories began to appear in England and then, during the eighteenth century, in the American colonies and states. The state took over responsibility for developing an institutional system in order to centralize control over the poor and the transient.[6] That policy was intended to increase collective wealth by putting the unemployed poor to work and to segregate transients from the rest of society while compelling them to conform by forcing them to work. A similar change was made to the regulation of criminality, for, by basing the King's justice on the concept of exemplarity the state intended the brutal and public punishment of crime to act as a deterrent while establishing both the King's power and his ability to preserve law and order within society.[7]

State intervention was, however, somewhat less than successful, and efforts by public authorities to control disruptive phenomena which were beyond the self-regulating capacities of the local communities were usually a matter of too little too late. The 'absolutist' state was fundamentally a 'minimal' state, royal governments' attempts to extend their authority being frequently frustrated by financial weakness. Institutions of confinement, whether general hospitals, prisons, reformatories,[8] or workhouses, were fairly modest, except perhaps in the great metropolises like London or Paris. Indeed, if we discount the network of repressive institutions established from the sixteenth century onwards, responsibility for the care and treatment of individuals isolated within their communities because of illness, physical disability, or mental illness usually fell to the religious authorities, either to orders founded specifically for that purpose or to existing orders which set up new institutions.

This regulation model was fully adhered to in colonial situations, although it was adapted to the particular features of the colonial societies where it was implemented. Traditional charitable institutions were established in New France very shortly after the colony was founded – hôtels-Dieu in Quebec City (1639) and Montreal (1644), and two general hospitals in 1692. The hôtels-Dieu were mainly concerned with looking after the indigent sick, while the general hospitals took in invalids, the mentally ill, and beggars as well as a few paying residents. A short-lived poor office and some anti-begging ordinances completed this aid and control system by the 1680s. The King's criminal justice system was responsible for the final and exemplary punishment of a handful of infractions considered particularly harmful to public order.[9] What was noteworthy about this regulation model was the limited role of the institutions concerned. No more than a few dozen individuals a year benefited from the aid facilities or appeared before the criminal courts. One reason for this, clearly, was the small size of the colonial population. Perhaps more significant, however, was the pervasiveness of the feudal logic regarding aid, which made access, especially access to the religious institutions, a privilege[10] reserved for certain individuals excluded from the many community support networks.[11]

The situation did not change as a result of the British conquest, which left the charitable institutions virtually untouched. Despite some vague threats to suppress religious communities, the new colonial state not only tolerated the women's orders which administered Lower Canada's charitable institutions, but was soon engaged in subsidizing them. There were similar developments in the system of repression. A great deal of importance was attached to the transition to English criminal law, which created considerable legal and institutional turmoil. However, although the French system was quickly replaced by British institutions,[12] the fundamental operating logic of this aspect of the social regulation system remained unchanged. Between 1764 and 1791 more than half of those convicted in the criminal courts were of British origin, a substantial overrepresentation given that such individuals comprised less than 10 per cent of the population. Moreover, it is likely that about a quarter of those accused were soldiers.[13] The principal conclusion that should be drawn from such statistics is that post-conquest Quebec witnessed a boycott of the criminal justice system by its pre-conquest inhabitants. Since the criminal system controlled only the exceptional, the accidental, and the excluded, it was likely to incite, in time of crisis, a boycott on the part of the community, for it was a relatively marginal contributor to general social regulation. Thus, despite the conquest a remarkable continuity in the primary function of the system of repression and the population groups involved was maintained until the beginning of the nineteenth century.

CRISIS IN THE OLD SYSTEM AND REFORM DISCOURSE IN LOWER CANADA

The crisis in the regulation system described above was a long-term phenomenon. It could even be said that the logic regarding regulation carried within it the makings of a permanent crisis, inasmuch as the destruction of the old forms of community solidarity was an irreversible process. The inadequacies of the central state's intervention system, the phenomenon of superposing or stratifying systems of aid and repression – royal initiatives did nothing more than substitute or supplement traditional measures – only made the relative fragility of feudalistic regulation structures more obvious. How then can we explain the fact that pointed and intensely bitter criticism arose, for the most part, only in the second half of the eighteenth century, and continued unabated until modern institutions of repression and aid were established?

The transition from one regulation system to another is a complex phenomenon which involves far more than simple institutional reforms. What is crucial here is the fact that from the middle of the eighteenth century through the first third of the nineteenth century there was a shift in critical thinking with respect to the old institutions. What began with Fielding, Beccaria, and Voltaire as a critique of penal procedure became, especially with Bentham and also with Howard, a systematic model of punishment by confinement. A parallel to this development can be found in society's conceptions concerning treatment of the poor. By the late eighteenth century the mercantilist concept of the poor as an immanent and inevitable social category was evolving towards the idea of a collective and massive advancement and transformation of the popular classes, occurring within the parameters developed by the enlightened elites. In short, what had been a critique of institutional processes became a large-scale social project where penitentiaries, workhouses, and other institutions were regarded as the best instruments for transforming popular ways of living and thinking.[14] The critical discourse was both recurrent and supranational. It repeatedly demonstrated the inadequacies of the old poverty and crime control techniques in order to construct a totally different, comprehensive regulation model. The new model had three basic characteristics.

First, it recognized that control of poverty and repression of crime were basically two aspects of the same problem. Poverty and indigence led to pauperism, creating problems which could ultimately be ascribed to the entire working class.[15] Thus institutional differences, such as those between the reformatory and the workhouse, became functional variations, related more to specific conditions of internment, criminal or charitable, than to any fundamental distinction between clientele and programmes. In short, poverty, illness, and criminality were now apprehended as constituents of a socially disruptive phenomenon which was global in nature.

Second, the subsumption of the categories of poor and criminal under the general *problématique* of social danger involved a much more systematic assertion of authority over the populations concerned. The concept of 'moral treatment' revealed a readiness to influence minds and souls, to transform 'the inner life' of the individual. That type of logic involved much more methodical use of disciplinary control techniques and more rigorous management of institutions for confinement.[16]

Finally, it was possible to integrate such basic techniques into a general prevention policy which could be applied to all members of the working classes before resorting to the option of confinement. In that context, what was so surprising about the idea that recourse to the power of the state should be universal? The state alone was in a position to implement treatment and prevention measures capable of uniform and systematic application. As one Lower Canadian commentator stated in 1818: 'The Government was ... established to help the weak, provide for the poor and defend the oppressed: thus, of course, governments provide workshops or workhouses to help the weak, hospitals to provide for the indigent sick and law courts to defend the oppressed.'[17]

The preceding general comments enable us to put in perspective the criticisms which, especially from the second decade of the nineteenth century, were mounting against Lower Canada's institutions. The wave of criticism was all the more remarkable in that the targeted institutions were often fairly young or had at least been recently reorganized. Such was the case with the system of aid for foundlings, which the government of Lower Canada did not implement until 1801, and with prisons built after 1805 on the model proposed by Howard.[18] The age of an institution was not important to the reformers. Institutions came under fire when they appeared to be mere extensions of the old aid and repression system. Criticism focused on three basic features of the old system.

First, the charity model itself was condemned as an extension of charity dependent on the goodwill of the traditional elites, including the religious communities. Charity dispensed on an arbitrary basis too often went to those who least deserved it.[19] Similar criticisms were levelled at the aid granted to institutions which sheltered foundlings. The fact that those institutions were subsidized by the state was reinterpreted as 'taxing the virtuous to support the children of dissolute, uncaring individuals.'[20]

Contemporary criticisms involved also a condemnation of the amateurism on which the old system was apparently based. That was the defect held to account for the numerous deficiencies in the treatment of the physically or mentally ill and in the enforcement of law and order. The charge also applied to the religious institutions,[21] to the various benefactors,[22] and to the system used by the police to apprehend criminals.[23] Henceforth, those responsible for dealing with the poor, the sick, and the criminal were expected to evince both professionalism and a willingness to subordinate punishment to the demands of treatment. This expectation was particularly reflected in a third major critique, one directed especially at the English criminal law after 1815. Here criticisms were aimed not at procedural techniques but at the system of punishment, in particular at the indiscriminate application of the death penalty under the 'Bloody Code.'

Our criminal statutes have remained in a state of near stagnation, notwithstanding the example of the United Kingdom and the existence in the United States of America of institutions which the new provinces would find more suitable. The natural consequences of the state of the criminal statutes have been aggravated by a profound reluctance, on the part of both the executive and the inhabitants of the province, to implement an extremely harsh penal code ... To gain the support of public opinion, there must be some amendments with respect to the treatment of prisoners and the punishment of persons convicted of crimes.[24]

Thus, reform of the penal system was perceived as a precondition to bringing criminal behaviour under systematic control. The blind cruelty of punishment would have to make way for the clinical treatment of what was now perceived as a social illness.[25] Consequently, condemnation of the old model became synonymous with criticism of punishment: 'The high rate of crime in Lower Canada is primarily due to the complete absence of discipline in the prisons, to the iniquitous construction of buildings where prisoners are shut up together, and more particularly, to the inefficacy of the English Criminal Code introduced into this province.'[26] Arbitrariness, amateurism, inefficacy, and gratuitous violence: the delicate balance of measures on which the old system relied in dealing with indigence and criminality now appeared obsolete and irrational, a waste of collective resources. Reformers and philanthropists would have many issues to resolve as they set about devising, from scratch, an entirely new system to deal with poverty and crime. Henceforth, the door was open to any utopian scheme.

Between 1815 and 1840 plans for institutional reforms proliferated throughout Lower Canada. These included construction of a provincial public hospital, the opening of a penitentiary, and proposals for organizing a public mental health facility, a provincial reformatory, and workhouses in Montreal and Quebec. The zeal for reform, which is clearly evident in the discourse of the time, merits analysis as a separate issue before we begin our examination of actual achievements. It was widely assumed that, apart from the particularities specific to each type of institution, solutions to social problems exposed by pauperism and criminality necessarily had to include the internment of individuals. In other words, internment became an appropriate, multifunctional social intervention procedure for restraining disruptive forces in society. As a result, some striking homologies are found in the discourse justifying hospitals, mental health facilities, workhouses, and penitentiaries. These homologies, however, cannot be reduced to formal similarities brought about by the actual practice of confinement. Rather, during this period confinement, in its many different dimensions, was a social project. That project involved three fundamental aspects: preventive measures, a demand for knowledge, and a search for power.

Confinement really meant separation, the isolation of a given population from the whole range of social relationships. Such separation for preventive purposes was justified by the risk to society in general or a need to protect the relevant 'clientele.' Although such justification seems obvious in the case of hospitals,[27] at the time it also applied to all the other institutions of control, from mental health facilities,[28] to penitentiaries,[29] to workhouses.[30] The medical metaphor contained in the notion of 'moral treatment' is to be taken literally: as if, once the community bonds and the customary standards which structured them had broken down, people lost their natural immunity to crime and poverty. Since dissolution of the old ties was seen, albeit with some regret, as an irreversible process, an environment had to be re-created which, though artificial, would foster the learning of a new, predominantly urban, sociability. Isolation was therefore the primary condition for rehabilitation of the individual. Extensive use of isolation made it possible to think in terms of mass reform: 'The morals, particularly of the inferior order of society, are of the highest importance to the country and to the whole of its population and whatever tends to preserve them from being contaminated must necessarily tend to prevent the increase of crimes.'[31]

Putting people in institutions served another basic function: it guaranteed opportunities for systematic treatment, which was really a means of intervening which involved the development and use of knowledge. Thus, the relevant population was not merely 'treated'; people participated, through treatment, in the accumulation of knowledge. As a result, improved methods of therapy became possible. This requirement gave rise to contemporary rethinking about what a hospital should be. The author of 'Essai sur l'établissement d'hôpitaux dans la province du Bas-Canada pour les pauvres malades' envisaged a whole network of hospital facilities with a public hospital at the top of the pyramid:

[Hospices for the mentally ill, pregnant women, the elderly, those suffering from scurvy or venereal diseases, and facilities which provide home assistance should be] regarded as special rather than public institutions; government should extend, supervise or fund only the large hospitals ... The private institutions should be envisaged simply as *training grounds* for individuals who may eventually be worth transferring ... to the hospitals, *the nation's great reservoirs and laboratories*.[32]

Similarly Doctor Hackett, who was in charge of the mentally ill at the Montreal General Hospital, feared that the institution 'may have to continue to be what it was in the past – a repository for Lunatics – without allowing persons in the profession to apply methods recommended by practice and experience for recovery from this terrible illness.'[33]

Such expertise also implied distance, indeed a separation which clearly marked the difference between aid recipients or criminals and the specialist, between the individual philanthropist and the social body on which he operated. The aid relationship and the act of repression became transformation techniques; indigence as a generalized illness of the social body gave rise to philanthropy as a mass treatment machine.

This development, of course, raised delicate questions about power. Here I do not refer to the many forms of domination scattered within social relationships and which constituted the substance of social inequality, such as those Foucault has described so well. The question is more fundamental and concerns the source of the collective power to compel. Historiography has often neglected to deal with this central problem. The power to confine had to be based on legitimacy of some kind. Under the feudal regulation system the problem of legality rarely arose since the process of forced internment was based on the power of the King (*lettre de cachet*) or on the need to detain an accused prior to possible punishment. It became an issue when confinement took on a penal dimension. One of the most frequently used methods of legitimizing confinement was to criminalize certain acts and to make them punishable by incarceration.[34]

The advent of more 'democratic' forms of government, however, posed the question of penality in radical new terms. I am not suggesting here that Lower Canadian society became at some point a 'democratic' one in any absolute sense; rather, I use the term to represent a process whereby citizens increasingly played a role in state decision-making, a process in which the establishment of an Assembly in 1791 was central, and a process which continued up to and beyond the achievement of responsible government in 1848. As the rights of the citizen began to supersede the duties of the subject, the issue of legality raised by the generalization of confinement procedures became particularly acute. How could the massive internment of targeted populations without evidence, on a case-by-case basis, of a deficiency serious enough to warrant separation of the individual from the rest of society be legitimized in a society apparently increasingly concerned with the rights of individuals? That was the reef on which all good philanthropic intentions foundered. Apart from mental health facilities and penal institutions,[35] it was impossible to equip institutions in the aid network with sufficient power to compel, to ensure that they would have control over the individuals requiring treatment. Frustration over that significant limitation was expressed in 1836 by those in charge of the workhouse in Quebec City: 'What will be wanted is legal control over persons who, being able to work, do not support themselves, but become burdensome to their neighbours. If the House of industry could be placed within the limits of the Gaol, these vagrants might be committed and held to labour. Out of is [sic] there is no legal power of detention.'[36] The specific constraints imposed on internment because of the emerging political rights enjoyed by individuals illustrate the profound ambiguity of the philanthropic projects of the early decades of the nineteenth century.

From hospitals to penitentiaries, institutions for rehabilitation and repentance became the most popular panacea,[37] but at the cost of a fundamental ambiguity. Philanthropic and reformist discourse of the early nineteenth century appears in the traditional analysis as the harbinger of modern institutions of social control. At best, the founding fathers of charity and modern repression are charged with having 'idealized' the effectiveness and reforming potential of the institutions they advocated.[38] However, the difference between the philanthropic projects of the time and their future implementation reflected much more than the usual delay between ideals and reality. Between the initial discourse about hospitals, asylums, workhouses, and penitentiaries and actual conditions of operation and social validation of the institutional network in the second half of the nineteenth century, there was a fundamental change in circumstances and a radical modification of the earlier social ideals.

The reformist discourse was the contradictory product of the fears, nostalgia, and aspirations of leading citizens in the late eighteenth and early nineteenth centuries.[39] They believed their world was falling apart – that what had previously been an unfortunate exception had become the general rule, that poverty was indicative of a general decline and that crime had become a way of life for many. The discourse reveals a world obsessed by a fear of endemic pauperism, where indigence and deviance were both seen as social symptoms of a general disintegration of moral standards. It is not surprising, then, that the institutional utopia spawned by the philanthropists was a microcosm of a lost world. The ideals embodied in their institutional programme projected a society where the authority of a landlord or an entrepreneur was, in itself, all that was required to put the impoverished masses to work and to ensure formal ownership by the wealthy. In that climate, the increasing strength of democratic and industrial forces was seen as an obstacle or constraint rather than a promise. From the moment of its inception, the ideal asylum or penitentiary was a desperate attempt to re-create the traditional, deferential relationships which existed in the feudal world of peasants and artisans.[40] Once such 'ideal institutions' were established, however, they had to be reintroduced into a very different regulatory logic, a subject to which I will return later in the text.

In Lower Canada, arguments surrounding the establishment of a penitentiary provide a striking example of the ambiguity in the reformist discourse. Historiography generally describes the birth of the modern penitentiary as an effort to renovate and update the old prison for the purpose of repressing crime. Underlying that approach was the close connection which had been established between alleviating the criminal law's more severe provisions and replacing the death penalty with a prison sentence. In this approach, which is systematically described by Foucault, the penitentiary prevailed over corporal punishment in cases of offences against the person and, especially, in cases of offences against property. Prison became the alternative to corporal punishment which was discredited by the philanthropists. Thus reformist discourse represents a precursor of future change.

The problem with such an approach, however, is that initially penitentiaries were intended mainly for people who had never been subject to the severe penalties of the 'Bloody Code.' It was expected that penitentiaries would confine and treat petty criminals in general. Originally, the penitentiary was seen as the ideal way to systematize and standardize the mass treatment of minor offences, a task which had previously been assigned to houses of correction.[41] In Lower Canada the push to establish a penitentiary came initially from the perceived need to repress minor crime. The aim was stated clearly by a grand jury convened in Montreal in September 1826: 'The grand juries are convinced that it is time we had a spacious and well run *penitentiary* where people *convicted of minor offences* would be employed in such a way as to benefit themselves and to reduce the cost to the public of their confinement.'[42] This recommendation soon became a suggestion that anyone found guilty of an offence should serve a prison term: 'A general penitentiary for the entire province, in which the *convicted* would be forced to work, would be one of the most significant steps towards reducing crime and classifying offenders. ... If such an institution were set up ... then the existing prisons would be adequate for detaining those merely *charged.*'[43]

At a stroke, the criterion used to distinguish the clientele no longer depended on the seriousness of the offence but simply on whether there was a criminal conviction. The new approach enabled the philanthropists to broaden the scope of their notion of the perfect prison. There would be a functional division of duties, with the penitentiary as the institution assigned to handle offenders and the old prison used, as it had always been, for preventive detention. Henceforth, the penitentiary would play the central role within the panoply of institutions envisaged by the philanthropists. All that remained was for the dream to become a reality.

INSTITUTIONAL PARALYSIS AND SPECIFIC REFORMS, 1815–1840

As coherent and universal as reformist discourse professed to be, the realities of implementation involved a series of contradictions – advances and setbacks, experiments and failures, aborted legislation and minor readjustments. In this chorus of diffuse attempts, half measures, and uncertain innovations, the state played an ambiguous role. The reformists expected the state to be a leading player in the new system. Ultimately, the state alone had the means to implement a systematic policy of providing individual moral treatment and of reforming popular morals. However, action by the state in Lower Canada from 1815 to 1840 actually amounted to very little. The system of state support for hospitals, which consisted of grants, remained virtually unchanged, whether the hospitals cared for the poor or looked after foundlings. Pious plans for building an insane asylum were never realized. Moreover, since the population increased, there was, in real terms, a *decrease* in state funding for institutions.[44] The sudden shock of British immigration, which began about 1810 and hit its peak in the 1830s, did force the government to take action but always as the exception rather than the rule. For example, the first hospital for immigrants was opened in 1820, and although it soon came under state control, for most of that period it cared exclusively for immigrants. The same was true of the Marine and Emigrant Hospital which opened in Quebec in 1830.[45]

The penal system, too, remained relatively untouched. Aside from the limited legislation of 1824 which abolished the death penalty for three types of offences,[46] the criminal law remained virtually the same. The only modification to the police system was the addition of a night watch in the large cities beginning in 1818.[47] It was not until the rebellions and the Durham Report that the first professional, paid police force was set up in Lower Canada, and even then it was only temporary.[48] Although there was a sharp increase in cases coming before the criminal courts immediately after 1815, the numbers quickly stabilized. The most noticeable change was the relative decrease, between 1815 and 1840, in cases brought before the Court of King's Bench dealing with offences against the person.[49]

Thus state intervention in the area of social regulation showed remarkable continuity with the past. New institutions or measures were simply superimposed ad hoc on the old system. State actions were undertaken more or less on a contingency basis to provide relief to traditional institutions when they become overburdened. Hence, the logic underlying the role of the state in regulating social contradictions remained unchanged and, in fact, appears to have been the exact inverse of reformist discourse. When the state acted, it was not for reasons of prevention or expertise, but to solve, for the most part temporarily, specific problems as they happened to arise.

There were many reasons why the state was not particularly responsive to the pressing demands of the reformers. With the possible exception of Quebec and Montreal, the number of people in Lower Canada who actually needed assistance remained fairly modest, at least in the period prior to the crisis of the 1830s. Another factor was the ongoing battle between the Legislative Assembly and the Legislative Council.[50] The fact that the colonial government was strapped for funds was also significant. However, in the final analysis, there were structural reasons for the colonial government's relative lack of power during the first third of the nineteenth century. Three factors were involved.

First of all, the political system's colonial aspect was especially evident in the government's extreme subservience to imperial interests. The development of a genuine aid policy, in particular, met occasional resistance from the British authorities who continued to maintain tight control.[51] Second, the colonial government was confronted by a major crisis of authority in Lower Canada. Communication between the government and the people, which was painfully deficient in the colony to begin with, became even worse during the rebellions for political independence when the patriots set up a virtual parallel network of authority.[52]

Finally, the high degree of centralization in the decision-making process resulted in organizational deficiencies at the local level. The reluctance to establish municipal institutions, which are indispensable to any system which delegates some powers in order to deal with poverty and crime, clearly revealed administrative and political gaps in the colonial system. In the short term, that failing made it difficult to redefine the role of the state with regard to the regulation of aid and repression.

In summary, it is clear that philanthropic and reformist discourse had no direct impact on the various levels of administration in Lower Canada. Before the middle of the nineteenth century, the need for fundamental change in the methods of regulating poverty and crime only rarely reflected a firm political will. The relationship between knowledge and power, between the reformist ideal and the administrative power of the state, which was secured in England and in France by a small group of inspectors and social investigators such as Chadwick or Villermé, did not develop until very late in Canada.

Despite such structural problems, however, important changes did occur in practices related to aid and repression. Notwithstanding reformist discourse, the period from 1815 to 1840 presaged the fundamental parting which, in the capitalist mode of regulation, occurred between the control of poverty and the repression of crime.

CONTROL OF POVERTY: THE BIRTH OF THE PRIVATE SPHERE

'We must convince the people that the only way they can avoid the ill-effects of poverty is to develop habits of industry and moral restraint; they should not expect any help except in the form of charity, which should be more than sufficient once such habits are commonplace.'[53]

On the periphery of the grand plans for public institutions advanced after 1815 another discourse gradually evolved. It developed as a parallel discourse because it entailed a fundamental retreat from the philanthropic ideal of mass treatment. This discourse was basically anti-state. Typical was an 1829 newspaper editorial which argued: 'The distribution of aid to the indigent should be part of the charity work of individuals. When such individuals perform this eminently religious duty, prudence can guide them to choose which gifts to give to which unfortunate people, to ensure that their charity benefits the recipients. When governments perform such acts of generosity, the results are almost always harmful.'[54]

In addition, this parallel discourse emphasized the importance of individual *will* as the driving force in the provision of aid and in the behaviour of the poor. What appeared at first to be a reactionary battle waged by some traditional elites against large-scale philanthropic projects gradually became, especially under the growing influence of Malthusian thought, a true liberal political economy of charity. Anti-state sentiment did not simply reflect the fear of a return to monarchical arbitrariness: it expressed a societal choice, favouring entrepreneurial freedom and equal opportunity over attempts to interfere with the free play of private transactions through the systematic organization of public assistance to able-bodied citizens. In that context, the control of poverty was based not on the urge to treat, but on the principle of scarcity, on the necessity of allowing for the free play of market forces by limiting organized assistance to people excluded from the game, namely the indigent sick or disabled, elderly people, infants who had been abandoned and were at risk, and widows or single mothers with dependent children.[55]

This is the context in which a new type of charitable institution which appeared in Lower Canada at the end of the first decade of the nineteenth century must be considered. Such institutions had several characteristics in common: they were resolutely private, they were intended for a specific clientele, they often attempted to be non-denominational and multi-ethnic,[56] and they were generally established on an ad hoc basis by members of the urban elites, in particular the wives of merchants or seigneurs. Another noteworthy characteristic shared by these diverse associations was a determination to establish fairly permanent structures, exemplified by the presence of institutions providing care or shelter.[57] In the end, they did prove to be the precursors of modern-day charities. The difficulties encountered in establishing and maintaining such institutions and the small number of clients they served show

how fragile the process of change was. Indeed, such institutions systematically turned to the state for assistance. In the early 1830s the government adopted a policy of providing annual grants to major, recently established private institutions on the basis of annual requests for funds made to the Legislative Assembly of Lower Canada at the beginning of each session.

During the transition period, private aid organizations still looked to government to ensure their long-term existence. Other institutional officials would likely have agreed with the comment by the directors of the workhouse in Montreal when, arguing in support of their request for public funds in 1823, they pointed out that financing by public subscription was 'an absolutely precarious and uncertain procedure which, moreover, would not provide any stability.'[58] However, when the state denied such institutions the right to any public funds, it symbolically sanctioned the break between the aid organizations and public responsibilities, thereby settling the issue once and for all. In Lower Canada, this symbolic turning-point came in 1836, when a committee of the Legislative Assembly responded to the many requests for funds by charitable associations:

This committee duly notes that most of the applications which have been made to this Honourable House, and which are the subject of this report, were made on the part of various societies which were formed under special circumstances, with the undoubtedly very praiseworthy aim of helping the poor and disadvantaged of all kinds. These different societies, initially supported by voluntary contributions from private citizens, have gradually begun to turn to the legislature for help ... The committee is of the view that although these various institutions and associations deserve much praise, they must be informed that they cannot, in future, rely on grants from the legislature and should limit their charity and their expenditures to funds which they can raise through voluntary contributions and the generosity of individuals.[59]

Thus, during the 1820s and in particular during the social crisis of the 1830s, at the level of day-to-day practices, principles began to emerge which would form the basis of the private sphere of action in matters of assistance. In the growing separation between public and private, groups made up of private individuals clearly developed into major players, an indication of how dynamic civil society had become.[60] In the area of aid to the poor, the implications of 'democratic' legitimacy and the constraints of the market produced a fundamental division between the duty to be charitable and state responsibility.[61]

THE REPRESSION OF CRIME: CHANGING THE PRISONS

The primary role played by private charities in controlling poverty had no counterpart in the repression of crime. In addition, by the middle of the nineteenth century, as poverty and crime increasingly came to be seen as separate issues, the state was universally recognized as having primary jurisdiction in the area of law enforcement.[62] More precisely, the lines of responsibility which were drawn not only gave public authorities the power to compel, they also delineated the conditions in which that power would be implemented. This is why the role of the state was crucial, not only in establishing a police and penitentiary system, but also in the setting up and the management of a network of mental institutions.

However, the state could not take meaningful action until some changes were made to the prison system. The control of crime would have to be rationalized in compliance with the legal and systemic constraints consistent with liberal democratic ideas and a free market. In short, the philanthropic dream of producing generalized and systematic treatment for offenders met the hard realities of liberalism. In Lower Canada, the process of transforming the prison system took place in two distinct periods. The first fundamental change occurred during the second half of the 1820s when prisons in Lower Canada began to exhibit some of the features of modern prisons. In a dual process, prisons became both the chief instrument of penal repression and a place for large-scale detention. In the space of a few years, without any significant changes to the legal or administrative systems, prisons became the place where great masses of transients and vagrants were summarily detained. Statistics indicate the extent of this phenomenon.[63] From 1815 to the end of the 1830s, the prison population increased twentyfold. This dramatic rise in intake occurred in four main stages: from 1814 to 1817, 1825 to 1827, 1830 to 1833, and 1836 to 1840 (see table 1). The data also show a relative decrease in the francophone population, a major increase in the percentage of female prisoners, and a significant rise in the number of young people admitted.[64]

The growth of the prison population between 1830 and 1833 also had a qualitative dimension, and here too the consequences were fundamental. During those years, the Quebec prison became a predominantly penal institution, housing mainly people who had been convicted of offences punishable by a prison term. This development was all the more remarkable given that Canada did not implement systematic re-

TABLE 1
The Quebec Prison, 1814–1840: Number of Entries in the Register

1814	1817	1825	1827	1830	1833	1836	1840
65	347	350	520	570	834	824	1992

TABLE 2
The Quebec Prison, 1814–1834: Reasons for Incarceration by Category
(multi-year groupings)

Year	Offences against the person	Offences against property	Offences against public order	Total
1814-17	229 (31%)	211 (29%)	293 (40%)	733 (100%)
1823-25	266 (34%)	265 (34%)	258 (33%)	789 (100%)
1832-34	307 (15%)	397 (20%)	1329 (65%)	2033 (100%)

placement of the death penalty by incarceration for most crimes until the advent of Black's laws in 1841.[65]

This basic change in the function of the prison system is easier to understand if we analyse the principal reasons for detention. There was a veritable explosion in the number of people sentenced to prison for vagrancy and other minor offences against public order (see table 2). The same trend can be demonstrated in the Montreal prison figures.[66] Thus the prison dynamic in Lower Canada was fundamentally and permanently altered when justices of the peace, using their power of summary conviction, began systematically to incarcerate the large numbers of transients and vagrants who appeared during the years of massive immigration.[67]

The second fundamental change in the prison system occurred in 1843 when the Canadian government decided that only people sentenced to more than two years in prison should be sent to the penitentiary. That decision dealt a death blow to philanthropic ideals and it established the prison hierarchy which still exists today. The most sophisticated branch of the system and the one most suitable for long-term detention was henceforth assigned to handle offenders who had committed the most serious crimes. Prisons, in contrast, continued to be a repository for vagrants and petty criminals, providing temporary asylum for a transient, volatile, changing population. The ideal of systematic treatment for petty criminals was transformed into a policy of short-term detention, while the penitentiary became an instrument of heavy-handed repression in the battle against serious crime. The underlying assumption was that it was legally impossible to impose a long prison sentence on an individual convicted of a minor infraction.[68] In the liberal view of the law, long-term incarceration could be justified only in cases where serious crimes had been committed.[69] Similarly, the legitimacy of confinement was increasingly based on control over dangerous individuals at the expense of rehabilitative ideals.

In liberal discourse, this major realignment took the form of weighing the implications of freedom against the constraints involved in moral treatment. In 1836 Amury Girod, a committed reformer and follower of Fellenberg, dampened the reformist enthusiasm for incarceration with this statement:

Society decides ... if one of its members has become a public enemy because of his crimes: he is ostracized or otherwise punished by society; but society is the judge and arbiter only of *his external actions*; it has nothing to do with and knows nothing of his inner self, his beliefs, his conscience. I do not wish to conclude from this that society should take no interest in the moral reform of criminals. I simply want *to say that every man, free or not, has the right to have God alone judge his thoughts, his conscience, and his opinions.* It is clearly desirable to be able to reform the hearts of perverse men, and we must use every legitimate means to do so. But the chances of success, it seems to me, are slimmer than we have been led to believe ... Man in society must submit to the law, which is an expression of the general will, and *society has the right to expect that of its members.* So long as a man submits to the law he has fulfilled his duty to society. If society succeeds in turning a criminal offender into a moral and virtuous being, so much the better; but I have not yet seen that happen.[70]

The appeal for moral treatment necessarily involved the idea of influencing the soul and reflected a traumatic and totalitarian obsession with changing people from the inside. Isolating people in a penitentiary was essentially a strategy to prick the conscience and reform the heart. Liberal discourse sounded the death-knell of this ideal by arguing on behalf of freedom for the inner self, the source of individual will and responsibility. According to the liberal view, depriving individuals of their liberty does not mean teaching them about liberty. In practice, imprisonment in a market-based regulation system inevitably leads to exclusion from the operating logic of the marketplace and, as a result, was merely punitive. Individuals were judged by their actions. They were expected to answer to their peers only in regard to the outward manifestations of their will. From this perspective, crime was, and is, less a sign of collective decadence than an individualized form of social aberration. During the great liberal transition, individuals were held responsible for their own acts, good or bad.

CONCLUSION: THE LAW OF THE MARKET

Democracy and the market are not *deus ex machina* which in themselves provide a full explanation of the organization of charity and modern repression. Rather, they are two forms of social relationships which expanded dramatically during the nineteenth century and provided a logic of social construction radically different from that of the previous centuries. At an accelerated rate after 1840, this expansion was marked mainly by a redistribution of responsibilities in the area of social control. A line was drawn in the form of a caesura, validating the separation in progress at the time between charity and repression. The chief modus operandi of control under capitalism was to individualize/normalize behaviour. When this procedure became a criterion for social differentiation, it was possible to speak in terms of a capitalistic regulation system. Henceforth, overall control of the masses was acceptable only through the normative evaluation of individual acts. The modern network of instruments of control and repression was built on the basis of differentiated behaviour. Thus, insanity and criminality were defined as behavioural categories based not on a social condition, but on criminal or irrational *acts*.

As for poverty, once it was relieved of the stigma conferred on it by an obsessive fear of pauperism, it was simply perceived as neediness – a low point on the scale of success, one of life's liabilities. Poverty was no longer considered an innate characteristic of the masses but was identified rather with accidents of fate, personal misfortunes, isolated incapacities, or particular blunders. Poverty was privatized, not only because civilian volunteer organizations were assigned to deal with it but, more importantly, because it now appeared as a possible form of existence for individual members of society. Thus a world was ushered in where individual destiny appeared to be the product of anonymous, unavoidable market forces. Poverty was the expression of failure, whereas crime was evidence of miscalculation. The private sphere claimed sole responsibility for the management of the failures, whereas the state's prison system punished the miscalculations. The gap between charity and punishment was ever expanding.

In practice, however, institutional life and prison life had much in common; in both cases, the vague impulse to provide treatment soon gave way to rather brutal segregation procedures. In spite of everything, poverty and crime still testify to society's inability to keep its promises to work towards individual and collective advancement. In the daily fight for survival, in the stochastic ferment of deviant acts, and in the undercurrent of minor oppressions and great injustices, charity still operates as a technique of domination, and repression continues its process of exclusion.

NOTES

This paper is part of a wider inquiry into the poverty and crime control processes in the colony of Lower Canada during the transition to capitalism in the first half of the nineteenth century. For a more detailed analysis see J.-M. Fecteau *Un nouvel ordre des choses: La pauvreté, le crime, l'Etat au Québec, de la fin du 18e siècle à 1840* (Montreal: VLB 1989). I would like to thank the editors of this volume, and particularly Jim Phillips, for a very thorough reading of the text that helped improve the argument.

1 Problems of methodology raised by a historical analysis of the transition are discussed in J.-M. Fecteau *Régulation sociale et transition au capitalisme: Jalons théoriques et méthodologiques pour une analyse du 19e siècle canadien* (Quebec: PARQ 1986).
2 See the references below to the work of Rothman, Ignatieff, and Teeters.
3 This paper could deal in more detail with the specifics of the evolution of Lower Canadian institutions, comparing their destiny to the classic analyses of Rothman, Ignatieff, and Foucault, cited below. But I have chosen to examine the general characteristics of the transition of the regulation system, and will refer only briefly to these other authors. While this paper has been influenced by them, it is also, of necessity, critical of their approaches.
4 While family networks also clearly played a fundamental role in training and protection, this is an aspect of social regulation which is analytically distinct from the community methods of grouping and socialization, and that aspect of the issue will not be dealt with here.
5 Given the fundamental political changes which have accompanied the transition to capitalism, I should explain the concept of state used in this paper.

Here the concept of state is not that of a simple administrative machine which enjoys supreme political legitimacy, nor have I broadened it arbitrarily to include all the relations of power which exist within a given society. I use the term to mean the political place where relationships of domination are 'condensed': it consists of a group of institutions which determine and guarantee the stable reproduction of the system of social regulation. In addition to what Weber has termed the legitimate monopoly of violence conferred on the state, it also includes a monopoly on the collective action of reproduction, 'collective' referring here to a given social formation within a dynastic or national context.

6 The literature abounds on this issue. See especially the fascinating study by M. Dean *The Constitution of Poverty: Toward a Genealogy of Liberal Governance* (London: Routledge 1991).

7 On this subject, in addition to the classic M. Foucault *Surveiller et punir* (Paris: Gallimard 1975), see the detailed analysis in P. Spierenburg *The Spectacle of Suffering: Executions and the Evolution of Repression from a Preindustrial Metropolis to the European Experience* (Cambridge: Cambridge University Press 1984).

8 The use of reformatories as public instruments in the fight against begging and repeated misdemeanours is especially interesting. For more on this subject see J. Innes 'Prisons for the Poor: English Bridewells, 1555–1800' in F. Snyder and D. Hay, eds. *Labour, Law and Crime: An Historical Perspective* (London: Tavistock 1987).

9 See A. Lachance *Crimes et châtiments en Nouvelle-France* (Montreal: Boréal 1984).

10 For example, referring to the hôtels-Dieu, Dr Perrault stated in 1819 that 'the majority of patients admitted to these institutions are servants ... of the rich': *Journaux de la Chambre d'Assemblée du Bas-Canada* (hereafter *Journaux*) 1819, 85.

11 Aside from the repressive zeal which governed the early years of operation of the general hospitals and workhouses, Europe also witnessed small numbers actually interned. Innes, for example, demonstrates that the annual rate of incarceration in British bridewells was one for every 3000 inhabitants: Innes 'Prisons for the Poor' 105.

12 See, in particular, correctional facilities mentioned as early as 1768 in Quebec City: Archives nationales du Québec (hereafter ANQ), T011-0001/2248.

13 These figures are from Fecteau *Un nouvel ordre* 128. The figure for soldiers accused is for 1791–1815, but this likely was a consistent feature of the English offender population from the conquest onwards. See also on the subject of a 'boycott' of the English criminal courts D. Hay 'The Meanings of the Criminal Law in Québec, 1764–1774' in L.A. Knafla, ed. *Crime and Criminal Justice in Europe and Canada* (Waterloo: Wilfrid Laurier University Press 1981).

14 This process has been fully described, especially for the United States, by D. Rothman *The Discovery of the Asylum* (Boston: Little, Brown 1971), and for England by M. Ignatieff *A Just Measure of Pain* (New York: Columbia University Press 1978).

15 This systematic amalgam between crime and poverty was expressed in a particularly clear fashion by a parliamentary committee of Lower Canada on the penitentiary in 1836: 'Laziness had dragged him [the criminal] into debauchery, from debauchery to misery, from misery to crime, and from crime into prison': Rapport du comité spécial sur le rapport des commissaires-enquêteurs (pénitencier), in *Journaux* 1835-6, app. FFF.

16 Administrators of the old system were neither willing nor able to adapt to this more rigorous approach. Dean describes the logic of confinement within which new institutions functioned: 'The workhouse ... went beyond the re-formation of the social order. In doing so, however, it became less a place for the reform of individuals than the site of the metamorphosis of the idle into the industrious, or dross into sterling, as Bentham might say. It is neither a protected workshop in which the Poor learned the skills for the supersession of their condition nor a reformatory in which they became normalised individuals, but a kind of switching mechanism. In it, the Poor would remain the Poor. That was their earthly lot. They would be transformed, but not as individuals so much as categories. The mercantilist workhouse, unlike later the prison, asylum, and reformatory ... did not attempt to act on the "soul" of the individual. It both gave rise to and was founded on the theory of associationism which sought an "ideological" technique of power, a *semi-technique*, which would educate its objects in an orderly and respectful course of life by connecting mental representations of virtue, industry, and obedience with happiness, and vice, idleness, and insubordination with pain': Dean *Constitution of Poverty* 64.

17 'Essai sur l'établissement d'hôpitaux dans la province du Bas-Canada pour les pauvres malades' in *Gazette de Québec* 30 Nov. 1818. It is in this context also that Bentham, in his *Constitutional Code* of 1830, allocated to the state a whole range of regulatory functions, from the repression of crime to the provision of aid, including various measures of prevention. On this see G. Procacci *Gouverner la misère: La question sociale en France, 1789-1848* (Paris: Seuil 1993).

18 See respectively 41 Geo. III (1801), c. 6, and 45 Geo. III (1805), c. 13.

19 This explains an anonymous letter to the editor objecting to the organization of soup-kitchens, an initiative which tended only to 'demoralize poor people' for 'everyone was poor and no one wanted to work': *Le Canadien* 5 Sept. 1819.

20 *Rapport du Comité spécial du Conseil législatif* (hereafter *Rapport*) 1824. The *Gazette de Québec* 6 Feb. 1815 also criticized 'this institution which, while it rewards the dissolute by absolving them of the care of their children, is ineffectual in preventing crime.'

21 See this comment published in *Canadian Courant* 31 Mar. 1819, regarding the Soeurs de l'Hôtel-Dieu in Montreal: 'Sublime motives are likely to pervade the bosom of an enlightened practitioner of the "healing art" as to prevail in the more contracted minds of the inmates of a cloister, whose hearts may fairly be supposed to have been rendered by precept, and habit, equally impervious to the joy of actual social virtue, as to the vices, in the world.'

22 'The most general and reasonable of all objections to Charitable Institutions is founded on the uncertainty of the contributors, with regard to the real necessities of those who are relieved by their bounty ... We therefore conceive it to be one of the duties of those who have occasion to observe, and ample opportunity to assure themselves of the reality of many more scenes of distress, that it is in their power individually to relieve, to point out the proper object of charity to those, who have means of relieving them': *Gazette de Québec* 30 Nov. 1818.

23 As evidenced by this caustic comment by an 'Ami du Bon ordre' in 1821: 'There are still people who were appointed as constables for the year about to end who are a disgrace to decent people ... Let us ... endeavour to attain the goal cherished by all, no longer to allow the big snake to eat the little one': *Le Canadien* 3 July 1819.

24 Représentations du grand jury de Montréal, Sept. 1826, in *Journaux 1827*, 72–3

25 'It is not enough to punish but it ought to be an object to mend, and proper treatment may bring and has brought the most abandoned to a conviction of the happiness and ease almost infallibly attending honest conduct with common industry and thus may be reclaimed to society many of its lost and valuable members': *Gazette de Québec* 20 Jan. 1823.

26 Rapport du comité spécial de la Chambre sur le rapport des commissaires enquêteurs (pénitenciers), *Journaux 1835–6*, app. FFF.

27 One of the chief criticisms levelled at the religious communities in Lower Canada which were assigned to care for the sick was their refusal to look after people with contagious diseases, a refusal motivated by the restrictive conditions written into their constitutive charter: 'The plea of charity and humanity on which all pretensions to the indulgence prayed are founded, must be qualified by the consideration that the Hôtel-Dieu of Montreal, in common with other religious establishments making similar professions of charitable observation, refuses to admit infectious cases, or any that they

may deem such, which greatly detract from their pretensions to usefulness':
Anonymous opinion (probably J. Sewell, chief justice of the province) included in a letter from Dalhousie to Bathurst, 4 May 1826, National Archives of Canada, Colonial Office Series (hereafter CO) 42, vol. 209, 114.

28 'It is almost impossible in private families, where one of the members
suffers from a mental disorder, to provide the constant supervision required
by such a condition with regard to the safety of the individual concerned
and the well-being and security of the family and society in general': *Rapport* 9.

29 'There is reason to believe that such an institution [penitentiary] would produce the advantages mentioned for the community, since it would prevent
moral depravity among the lower classes by removing persons who, because
of the immoral lives they lead, are likely to corrupt those around them':
Pétition des juges de paix, à l'Assemblée du Bas-Canada, *Journaux* 1827, 75.

30 'The experience of last winter has demonstrated to the Committee the advantage of confining all paupers who are entirely dependent upon the public
charity, instead of allowing them to be fed at large': Rapport du Comité de
gestion de la maison d'industrie de Montréal, *Montreal Transcript* 3 Oct. 1837.

31 Address by the Chief Justice to the Grand Jury, Québec, Sept. 1825, *Gazette
de Québec* 10 Oct. 1825

32 *Gazette de Québec* 24 Dec. 1818 (emphasis added)

33 *Rapport*, app. D, no. 3

34 See Innes 'Prisons for the Poor' 70, where she refers to the juridical vague-
ness surrounding conditions of internment in workhouses and reformatories. An earlier method was to list powers to imprison in the incorporating
charter of an institution of detention.

35 With asylums the power to compel was limited by the power of the family to
prevent confinement, except in cases of dangerous insanity.

36 *Gazette de Québec* 14 Oct. 1836

37 To the point that, occasionally, the legislature appears to have confused the
two. In 1833, the Legislative Assembly of Lower Canada discussed the function of a building then under construction in Quebec. Initially, it had been
intended to be used as a hospital but now three possibilities were envisaged:
it could be made into a hospital, a workhouse, or a penitentiary. After hearing from the architects, it was decided to use the building as originally intended: *Journaux* 1832–3, testimony of 6 Mar. 1833. In a fascinating summary of the issues of the day *Le Canadien* 25 Nov. 1833 affirmed that 'there
are sick people to care for and doctors to train just as there are criminals to
punish and correct, poor people to feed and lazy people to put to work.'

38 'Yet we look back on the discoverers of the asylum with pride, placing them

in our pantheon of reformers. We applaud the promoters of change, and are horrified with the results of their efforts ... Proposals that promise the most grandiose consequences often legitimate the most unsatisfactory developments. And one also grows wary about taking reform programs at face value; arrangements designed for the best of motives may have disastrous results': Rothman *Discovery of the Asylum* 294–5.

39 This fear is the fear mentioned in contemporary texts. It may very well have been fear directed specifically at the marginalized and at vagrants prowling about the better neighbourhoods and on the outskirts. But basically, this was the anguished cry of a generation gradually disintegrating under the combined shock of revolutions and democratic ideologies, values which had formed the basis of the social order since time immemorial. It was a fear which transcended 'party' lines, uniting reformers and conservatives. For the generalized nature of this concern see Fecteau *Un nouvel order des choses* passim.

40 See the brief but important comment by J. Lea 'Discipline and Capitalist Development' in B. Fine et al., eds. *Capitalism and the Rule of Law* (London: Hutchison 1979) 90–9. The problem posed here basically concerns the role attributed by the analysis to the critical discourse which developed in the West between 1750 and 1830. The teleological nature of the prevailing analysis of this discourse is discussed, in the case of the 'founding fathers' of political economy and, more specifically, in the case of Adam Smith, in K. Tribe *Land, Labour and Economic Discourse* (London: Routledge 1978) and especially in the same author's *Genealogies of Capitalism* (Atlantic Highlands, NJ: Humanities Press 1981). This fundamental criticism became a serious issue in the historiography of social regulation with the publication of Dean *The Constitution of Poverty* and of J. Minson *Genealogies of Morals* (London: Macmillan 1985).

41 See the classic study by N.K. Teeters *The Cradle of the Penitentiary: The Walnut Street Jail at Philadelphia, 1773–1835* (Philadelphia: Temple University Press 1955).

42 *Journaux* 1827, 73 (emphasis added). The justices of the peace, in a parallel petition, speak of a house of correction and penitence: 'There is good reason to think that such an institution would provide the above-mentioned benefits for the community, since it would be a means of *preventing moral depravity among the lower classes*': ibid. 75 (emphasis added).

43 Resolution of the Legislative Council, *Journaux* 1828–9, 380 (emphasis added)

44 Between 1815 and 1840, 39 per cent of public expenditures for assistance and health were in the form of grants to religious institutions. These institutions always served the same type and the same number of clients. For ex-

ample, during the nine years between 1815 and 1823, the Hôtel-Dieu in Montreal admitted, on average, 13.6 patients per week. The weekly rate of intake at the Hôtel-Dieu in Quebec was 5.3. These averages are calculated on the basis of statistics from *Rapport*, appendix A.

45 The funds were allocated under 10 & 11 Geo. IV (1830), c. 23.

46 Theft committed in a store, on a navigable river, or in an inhabited dwelling-house: 4 Geo. IV (1824), c. 4, 5, and 6

47 Under 58 Geo. III (1818), c. 2

48 A. Greer 'The Birth of the Police in Canada' in Greer and I. Radforth, eds. *Colonial Leviathan: State Formation in Mid-Nineteenth-Century Canada* (Toronto: University of Toronto Press 1992)

49 For example, the statistics for criminal cases heard by the Court of King's Bench in Quebec show that, for the period 1815 to 1819, the proportion of crimes against the person compared to crimes against property was 40 per cent. In the period from 1835 to 1839, the proportion decreased to 11 per cent: Fecteau *Un nouvel ordre des choses* 236.

50 The resulting paralysis played a significant role in delaying the enactment of certain statutes, notably those regarding the workhouse in Montreal. With respect to the revision of the criminal law, *Le Canadien* 17 Sept. 1834 clearly saw a connection between the adoption of reforms and the political battle: 'Revising the Criminal Code is a huge undertaking, so huge that we despair of seeing it successfully completed until a new system of government, designed to establish peace and security, allows the legislature, which enjoys the public's confidence, to devote its energy to these improvements which until now it has had to use to combat monopolies and despotism.'

51 The legislation which imposed a tax on ships bearing immigrants is a case in point. It was enacted in 1834 – 4 Will. IV (1834), c. 31 – but did not receive imperial sanction for almost a year.

52 On this point see J.-M. Fecteau 'Mesures d'exception et règle de droit: Les conditions d'application de la loi martiale au Québec lors des Rébellions de 1837–1838' *McGill Law Review* 32 (1987) 465–95.

53 *Gazette de Québec* 1 Jan. 1818

54 *La Minerve* 1 June 1829

55 For further information on this basic change in the clientele targeted for assistance in England, see F. Williams *From Pauperism to Poverty* (London: Routledge & Kegan Paul 1981).

56 For example, the Montreal General Hospital was established as a non-denominational institution: 'No clergy or other official character are [sic] inserted as honorary governors, in order to avoid the jealousy attendant on

selection': Dalhousie to Bathurst, 20 April 1822, CO 42, vol. 191, 174. As an example of avoiding ethnic problems, note that the administrative committee of the Female Compassionate Society, founded in 1820, included three francophones among its twelve members. This trend continued until the middle of the 1830s at least.

57 Two examples are the hospice for orphans, opened in 1832 by the Association des dames canadiennes pour les objets de charité, and the Institution pour les filles repenties (Magdalen Institute), founded by Madame Gamelin in Montreal in 1831.

58 *Journaux* 1823, 103–4

59 *Journaux* 1835–6, 197. See also *Gazette de Québec* 12 Oct. 1836: 'Societies usually have a beneficial effect in turning the public mind to matters of general interest: but they, not unfrequently, have the result of throwing the burden entirely on the revenue of the province ... Any societies which may be formed among us for philanthropic purposes would be more likely to succeed, if it were made part of their undertaking to guard against the recurrence of such results ... Too much has been expected from government or the Legislature. All that can reasonably be required of it is to afford legal facilities for the inhabitants of the different localities to do, conjointly, what they cannot so well do individually. Money not derived immediately from those who reap the benefit is not well looked after.'

60 In the case of Lower Canada, however, this division never became permanent and it took original forms. First, despite all the declarations of intent, the policy of annual grants continued until the twentieth century for a limited number of important institutions, although it covered only a very small proportion of their expenses. Second, in the case of francophones in Quebec, by 1850, the church was beginning to take over from civilians who were clearly incapable of organizing and financing aid organizations. But that is quite another story.

61 For a fascinating yet controversial theoretical explanation of this fundamental phenomenon, see F. Ewald *L'Etat providence* (Paris: Grasset 1986) 15–140.

62 However, this does not mean that there was absolute separation from private initiatives, which were very important, especially in the area of institutions for juvenile offenders. Indeed, Garland has successfully argued that in the second half of the nineteenth century in England, the private and public sectors could be remarkably complementary: see D. Garland *Punishment and Welfare: A History of Penal Strategies* (Aldershot: Grover 1985).

63 These data are taken from an analysis of the register of the Quebec Prison: ANQ, E-0017-001/2248–2270.

64 The proportion of francophones declined from 50 per cent to 25 per cent between 1814 and 1834; that of women rose from 10 per cent to 35 per cent in the same period, and that of prisoners under twenty-five years of age rose from 22 per cent in 1824 to 49 per cent in 1832.

65 4 & 5 Vict. (1841), c. 24 to 27. In Quebec the abolition laws of 1824, mentioned above, had only a minimal effect on prison terms.

66 A brief look at the registers of the Montreal prison shows a similar but less extreme pattern, perhaps because there are no data for the period prior to 1826. The average monthly incarcerations, by category, for the Montreal prison were as follows:

Year	Offences against the person	Offences against property	Offences against public order	Total
1827-28	4 (15%)	10 (38%)	12 (46%)	26 (100%)
1832-34	9 (18%)	16 (32%)	26 (52%)	51 (100%)

These figures are based on the number of incarcerations for a non-consecutive twelve-month period in 1827–8 and for a seven-month period in 1832–4.

67 The major evidence of this change is the comparison between penal incarceration and preventive (pre-trial) incarceration. At the Quebec prison, penal incarcerations constituted between 10 and 25 per cent of the total intake from 1823 to 1825 and between 65 and 75 per cent from 1832 to 1834.

68 This appeal to legality, as a constraint to the application of treatment or repression policies, was fundamental and marked a major transition toward modern methods of repression. There is a hint of what was to come in a letter to the editor published in *Gazette de Québec* 20 Nov. 1826, which referred to the increasingly systematic incarceration of transients in the common jail: 'It seems to me that it matters not whether the legislation begins by running amuck against drunkenness in miserable wretches, their starving wives and children, already reduced to a condition when their example is rather favourable to general sobriety than otherwise or whether it is directed against witchcraft, or popery, or lewdness, or gaming, or swearing, or idleness, or laziness, or any other heinous sin or vice ... That the criminal law of England shall continue to be administered in the Province as heretofore is good, but that innovations in matters of so much importance, if required, should have the sanction of the local legislature at least seems to me to be indispensable to the security and welfare of the subject.'

69 The long-term confinement of young offenders appears to be the most significant exception to this rule.

70 *Rapport*, app. FFF. Three years earlier Tocqueville wrote: 'Citizens subjected to the law are protected by it; they cease to be free only when they become wicked.' He added, with regard to the chances of reforming a criminal in prison: 'If he has not become better at heart, at least he is more obedient to the laws and that is all society has a right to ask of him': G. de Beaumont and A. de Tocqueville *Système pénitentiaire aux Etats-Unis et son application en France* (Paris: Gosselin [1833] 1845) 138, 151.

10

Rebel as Magistrate:
William Lyon Mackenzie
and His Enemies

PAUL ROMNEY

On 6 December 1834, the *Toronto Recorder* published a sensational charge against the mayor. Some two weeks earlier, it reported, the mayor had sentenced two prostitutes to a fortnight's hard labour in the district jail and had ordered them to be shut up without access to fire. The jail was a new brick building, and presumably less of a hell-hole than most Upper Canadian prisons. Still, it was not centrally heated, and to confine prisoners without fire during the cold days of late November was a cruel punishment if not an unlawful one. As for hard labour, that could only mean breaking stones, and who but a monster would sentence women to such an ordeal? This, though, was the man who had sentenced a mother of young children to the stocks for throwing a shoe at him in court.

The *Recorder*'s informant was the jailer himself. His charges were embarrassing, and the mayor denied them at once. The crucial evidence was the warrant committing the prostitutes to prison – the mayor's official directions to the jailer concerning their sentence. The mayor stated that he had sent a clerk to the jail to check the wording of the warrant. The clerk had found that an order to keep the prostitutes from fire had been added to the warrant and then crossed out. The mayor alleged that the jailer had added the words to the warrant in order to embarrass him. When required to produce the document, the jailer had crossed out the words in order to disguise the forgery.

The Mayor's Court happened to be in session. The grand jury had just been discharged, but the mayor recalled them and presented them with evidence of the forgery. The jurors agreed that the document had been criminally altered but did not name a culprit. In the absence of legal proof, the government rejected the mayor's demand that the jailer be suspended or dismissed. And there the matter rested. The fuss subsided, other news filled the papers, and a few weeks later the mayor was voted out of office. William Lyon Mackenzie's brief spell as a political executive and magistrate was at an end.

At the time of his election as Toronto's first mayor, in April 1834, Mackenzie had come for many Upper Canadians to personify political opposition to the provincial government. This was a recent event. The attack on his printing-shop in 1826 had marked him as a foe of the regime, but only one of several. His election to the legislature in 1828 was a portent, but he did not rank with leading oppositionists such as John Rolph, Marshall Bidwell, William Warren Baldwin, or even Baldwin's young son Robert. He gained stature through his combative journalism and zest for political organizing, but it was the events of 1832–4 that brought him to the fore: his repeated expulsions from the House of Assembly, his mission to England as spokesman for the discontented of Upper Canada, and his apparent influence on the British government's decision in 1833 to dismiss the province's attorney general and solicitor general.[1]

Neither Rolph nor the Baldwins had taken part in politics since 1830, and Mackenzie's new eminence was confirmed when the Reformers who controlled the city council chose him as mayor over his fellow-alderman Rolph, who promptly resigned in pique. For the sometime druggist and bookseller it was a moment to savour, but he was more than ever a marked man. Pro-government newspapers could be relied on to pounce upon any error or indiscretion, real or fancied, that he might commit in his unaccustomed roles as political executive and magistrate. A struggle for authority ensued as Mackenzie and his fellow Reformers set out to show themselves worthy of their new responsibilities while shocked Tory politicians and publicists laboured to prove them wrong.[2]

Luckily for the Tories, along with the mayoralty Mackenzie had inherited the problems which had persuaded the provincial government to create that office. Several years of heavy British immigration had distended Toronto from a village into a raw, muddy town which needed watering, sewering, paving, and policing – necessities which the cholera epidemic of 1832 had exposed in traumatic fashion. These functions entailed taxation on a scale which could legitimately be levied only by an elected authority. They also constituted an administrative burden requiring closer supervision than occasional meetings of the district magistrates could provide. Reformers might deplore the oppressions of the provincial government, but in order to make the new civic government effective Mackenzie and his fellow councillors would have to impose their power upon the citizens of Toronto more palpably than colonial officialdom ever had.

Inevitably, Mackenzie's conduct as a magistrate attracted special attention. Quite apart from the timeless fascination of crime, Mackenzie's leading part in the Reformers' attacks on the administration of justice rendered him especially vulnerable to any imputation of partiality or oppression in his own judicial performance.[3] Such imputations, justified or not, could easily be manufactured by a determined press. Administering a municipal police meant fining or imprisoning people for a variety of acts which were either habitual, such as beating their wives and children, or incidental if not essential to their livelihood, such as creating a public nuisance, selling liquor without a licence – and, of course, selling their bodies.[4] However beneficial these intrusions might be to injured individuals or the public at large, they were liable to be perceived as oppressive by their targets. But more dangerous to Mackenzie from the political point of view was the large discretionary element in the power of the magistracy. The summary power to convict and punish was distasteful to Reformers even in the hands of an elected judge,[5] but even at the city quarter sessions, or Mayor's Court, where trial by jury prevailed, discretionary sentencing might be a source of political embarrassment.

Like another essay in this book, then,[6] this is a story about the travails of an Upper Canadian magistrate. Both men were handicapped in the execution of their office by political animosities, and in both cases their difficulties owed much to their isolation. Robert Weir, active as a politician and militia officer in support of the government, was isolated in a rural area predominantly peopled by men and women hostile to the authority he represented. Mackenzie, though acting on the province's most crowded stage, was isolated in the spotlight of publicity as that authority's pre-eminent foe. Both men were surrounded by enemies, and both found that the execution of their judicial duties was complicated by their predicament.

II

It was no accident that Mackenzie and his enemies came to blows over the jail. It was a district institution, financed by the government-appointed district magistrates and operated by another government official, the sheriff. Thus Mackenzie, as the city's chief magistrate, was forced into a cooperative relationship with a group of men drawn from the elite to which he was politically opposed. The tension inherent in this relationship was aggravated by the fact that the city, which had no control over the jail, was obliged under its act of incorporation to pay the district magistrates a large sum for its use.[7] It did not help matters that the sheriff, William Botsford Jarvis, had borne a special responsibility for the terms of that legislation in his capacity as MPP for Toronto's pre-corporate incarnation, the town of York.

The institution thus made into a point of political friction was one over which Mackenzie and the district magistrates had already come to blows. In 1830, in his capacity as MPP for the county of York, he had chaired a select committee of the House of Assembly which had investigated the jail in response to a petition of the prisoners. An imposing brick structure, standing next to the courthouse on a grassy square in the centre of town, the jail had been opened only three years earlier,[8] but it evidently suffered from most of the defects typical of Upper Canadian jails. Three female lunatics, confined in the basement on straw bedding, created an appalling stench which pervaded the prison along with their incessant howling and groans. These shared the jail with thirteen criminals, most of whom were confined on the ground floor, and nine debtors, most of whom occupied the upper floor; one of the latter was accompanied by his wife and five children. Most of the criminals were subsisting on one pound of bread (costing three halfpence) a day and went for weeks without a change of linen; one asserted that his bedclothes had not been washed for six or eight months. Some of the debtors were even worse off: those confined on mesne process, unlike those imprisoned in execution, could not demand subsistence from the arresting creditor, and two of them had allegedly gone for days without eating.[9] The jail was badly built and the privy was blocked. The committee observed that the prisoners were kept in idleness, though several of them were mechanics, and they reproved the magistrates for confining young offenders with hardened criminals when space was available for their segregation. The insane were treated worse than the most hardened criminal, they noted, and suggested that their condition might improve if they were removed to the hospital, confined in strait-jackets, and treated gently.[10]

Little had changed for the better four years later. The city council's standing committee on police and prisons inspected the jail in April 1834, to be followed a few weeks later by the grand jury of the first Mayor's Court. The committee reported that the jail's unhealthy condition was aggravated by its insecurity, which precluded the prisoners from being let outdoors for exercise. It recommended the building of a more secure wall, the provision of extra water-closets, and the employment of guards to watch over the prison yard while the prisoners were taking the air. It alleged that district grand juries had made repeated presentments on the matter but nothing had been done. The presentment of the city grand jury differed only in detail. Both reports were influenced by a recent break-out from the jail, which had induced the jailer to subject some or all of the other criminal prisoners to twenty-eight days of solitary confinement.[11]

Mackenzie forwarded the grand jury report for the attention of the lieutenant-governor, Sir John Colborne, who referred it to the district authorities. In reporting this to Mackenzie, Colborne rashly remarked that the magistrates' attention had repeatedly been directed to the subject over the past three years – a comment which soon appeared in Mackenzie's newspaper along with an editorial chiding the magistrates for their negligence and remarking that Colborne's answer showed that he was 'investigating this nuisance.'[12] Goaded by this embarrassing publicity, both the sheriff and the magistrates wrote lengthy reports in self-exculpation.[13]

Jarvis dealt with the presentment point by point, the burden of his remarks being that all the evils complained of were irremediable. The prisoners' straw bedding was verminous because the prisoners were verminous when committed; there was a shortage of bedsteads and blankets because the prisoners destroyed them; the walls, whitewashed annually, were filthy because the prisoners 'filthed' them; the privies had been replaced with ordure tubs because the prisoners had blocked up the water-closets, flooding the jail. There was not enough money to remedy these defects or to build a secure fence. The building was well ventilated, but as long as the law required lunatics to be lodged in the basement their stench would continue to pervade the premises. The jailer did his best to keep liquor out of the prison but could not entirely prevent it without a fence to keep outsiders away from the windows.

Apart from all this, however, the jail was simply too small for the number of prisoners it now had to accommodate. Jarvis recommended that it be closed and its desirable central site sold to provide funds for a new establishment.

The magistrates' reply was delayed for several weeks. This was either a calculated snub to the lieutenant-governor or evidence of the leisurely style of government by quarter sessions; but in any case they had little to add to the sheriff's response. They pointed out that they were obliged by statute to repay the money borrowed for building the jail and court-house before incurring extraordinary expenses, however pressing, and ended by lamenting that the long and laborious service of the more senior justices had not sufficed to shield them against the governor's disapprobation. This letter also appeared in the *Advocate*, which commented: 'Their worships read His Excellency a pretty round lecture at the conclusion of their letter, pretty much in the impudent style of the Tory assembly and council to Lord Goderich.' Apparently this small coup aroused memories of Mackenzie's success two years previously in procuring the dismissal of the provincial law officers, which had set colonial conservatives fuming against the imperial authorities. At least, it provided a handy excuse for reviving such memories, and a general election was imminent.[14]

Between the penning of the magistrates' letter and its appearance in the *Advocate*, however, a disaster struck the city and the jail. On 31 July the jailer informed Mackenzie that one of the prisoners was sick with the cholera. He urged the mayor and council to free as many of them as possible. It is not known whether the city magistrates[15] acted on this recommendation, but later that day the council authorized the board of health to spend up to £15 in order to furnish fresh bedding to 'the criminals' while the cholera lasted. Perhaps the terms of the resolution were intended to distinguish the criminals from the debtors and lunatics as being the city's responsibility, though it is unlikely that all of them had been committed by the city courts. For his part, Sheriff Jarvis assumed a very real responsibility for the debtors by releasing them from custody, a step which made him liable for the debts of any that absconded.[16]

In the short term at any rate, the cholera was good for the jail and its custodians. When Mackenzie published the justices' letter in September, it appeared alongside a presentment of the grand jury of the Mayor's Court which accepted their explanation and Jarvis's as 'quite satisfactory' and declared the premises to be 'in as clean and wholesome a state as it could reasonably be expected with so many inmates.' Educated by the epidemic, the jurors advised that a well be dug in the courtyard in order to end the prison's dependence on Toronto's polluted bay. Commenting on the presentment, the *Advocate* ascribed the jail's cleanliness to the fact that the city had had the cells cleaned and whitewashed, as well as providing fresh bedding, at the onset of the epidemic. 'The complaint of the grand jurors last June was very just,' it affirmed, responding to the magistrates' insinuation that the jurors had been politically motivated.[17]

III

One action of the September grand jury which particularly vexed the mayor was its endorsement of the jailer's petition to the city council for a supplement to his salary. Charles Barnhart had first petitioned for this benefit in April, and the June grand jury had declared his salary of £100 a year 'a mere pittance compared with what the respectability, arduous duties and responsibility of that officer demand.'[18] Mackenzie agreed, and so did the sheriff. But who was to pay? The magistrates suggested that, since many of the prisoners were serving sentences of hard labour imposed by the city magistrates, the extra salary should come from the city. Barnhart himself backed the magistrates, declaring that the city courts had more than doubled his work by sentencing more than 120 persons to jail in addition to more than 200 who had been committed overnight or until sober. But the city already owed a large tribute for the use of the jail and courthouse, and Mackenzie was not inclined to hand out a further subsidy to the district authorities, whose housekeeping he called 'at best a burlesque on the very name of economy.'

In any case, to say that Barnhart's office deserved a higher salary was not to say that its present incumbent did. 'Barnhart is unworthy the office altogether, much more an additional income,' declared the *Advocate*. 'His place is now as good as £160, and we are not much pleased with his mode of doing its duties.'[19] The jailer, undaunted, began to assert that Mackenzie had personally promised him £100 from the city funds. He also presented the corporation with an account for 'extra services,' which seem to have consisted mainly in the provision of supplementary rations for convicts whom the mayor had sentenced to break stones.[20]

No doubt the squabble owed something to political animosity. It was later reported that, at the very time Barnhart was arguing with Mackenzie about his salary, the sheriff had given him leave 'to go to the country and harrangue [sic] at public meetings, and distribute handbills throughout the west riding of a most abusive nature.' The west riding of the county of York was the constituency which Mackenzie was contesting. It included the village of Streetsville, where Barnhart had relatives.[21]

It seems likely, though, that there was more to it than politics – an extra ingredient hinted at in Barnhart's reference to all the extra work the city authorities were causing him. Toronto had been incorporated in order to establish a more effective local government, and the new governors had thrown themselves energetically into their work. For several weeks the council had met daily to appoint new officers, ponder regulatory by laws, and initiate public works. Mackenzie, with his special responsibility as chief magistrate for instituting a more vigorous police, had been particularly active. Soon after his election, he had toured the slums in company with his chief of police and had found 'the obscure parts of the city' thronged with 'persons unlicensed selling beer, whiskey and other strong liquors, and affording place & room for gambling and vice in its blackest shapes.'[22] No doubt he had urged his companion to special vigilance in the suppression of these evils, and he himself held a daily police court in order to enforce an assortment of moral and sanitary regulations. (It was for this that the mayor, alone of the city council, received a salary.)[23] A concern with crime entailed a concern with punishment, and the new broom swept into the jail, exposing shortcomings by the dozen.

Mackenzie's energy meant more work for the jailer and a greater expense for the district magistrates. This arose not only from the greater number of committals but from Mackenzie's insistence on sentencing convicts to labour. In doing so he relied on a provincial statute of 1810, which had stated the need for houses of correction in the province and, until such institutions were built, had enacted that the common gaol of each district should also serve that purpose, 'any Law or Usage to the contrary in any wise notwithstanding.'[24] The house of correction, or bridewell, was an institution which in England dated back to the sixteenth and seventeenth centuries. In those days crime was not normally punished by imprisonment, and the gaols were populated chiefly by prisoners awaiting trial, convicts awaiting execution of their sentence, and debtors. The special purpose of bridewells was the incarceration of able-bodied paupers or vagrants, who were not to be kept in idleness but put to productive labour. By the middle of the eighteenth century, petty criminal offenders might also be sent there. By that time the bridewell's original purpose had been superseded in some measure by the development of the workhouse system; but this was a creature of the poor law, and the first provincial parliament, in receiving the law of England into the province, had specifically excepted the elaborate and expensive apparatus of the poor law. The designation of the district gaols as houses of correction in 1810 was consistent with that earlier decision.

It is unknown to what extent, if any, the law of 1810 was ever implemented, but in 1834 it appears to have been universally neglected.[26] It was, therefore, an innovation when Mackenzie invoked that statute, and a necessary education of the public when he apprised the grand jury of the first Mayor's Court of 'the description of employment by some called hard labor to which prisoners are subjected in the Jails of England and Wales.' He specified a wide assortment of occupations for men and women respectively,[27] but for the most part he resorted to only one of them. He ordered up a supply of stone to be broken by men sentenced to hard labour, and in June the council resolved to pave King Street with the product of their labours.[28]

Stone-breaking at the jail went well with municipal economy and municipal improvement. It was outdoor work, however, which necessitated the provision of guards and a secure fence, and it was arduous work, which meant providing extra rations for the underfed labourers.[29] Again – who was to pay? The city, which was already paying more than £1000 a year for the use of the jail? Or the district magistrates, who were paying off a heavy capital debt partly incurred in building it? It might seem just that the city should pay for the extra expenses incurred in an undertaking ordered by its mayor for its benefit. On the other hand, it could be argued that both securing of the prison yard and the provision of a more nutritious diet than three ha'p'orth of bread a day and a pitcher of bay water were ordinary obligations of the district magistrates, which they should fulfil in any case and were certainly not prevented from fulfilling by their statutory obligation to repay their debt.[30]

The quarrel between Mackenzie and the jailer reached a climax towards the end of the year. The general election was over. In Toronto the sheriff had lost by a whisker. Mackenzie had won handily in West

York, but municipal elections were impending when, on 20 November, he and Alderman James Lesslie sentenced two young women from the United States to a fortnight in jail, ordering them to be kept apart from the male prisoners. Apparently the women were prostitutes, who had been drawn to Mackenzie's attention by complaints about the riotous and disorderly conduct of their clients. Later that day, doubting whether the order to segregate the prostitutes would be carried out 'in such a way as would not turn the prison into a brothel,' the mayor went to the jail and found the women at large among the debtors. In his complaint to the lieutenant-governor, he repeated without comment Barnhart's claim to have given his turnkey strict instructions in conformity with the sentence. He also reported that he had visited the jail the previous night to find the turnkey staggering drunk.[31]

Sir John Colborne again sought explanations from the sheriff. He received them in the form of letters from Jarvis, Barnhart, and one of the debtors. Barnhart reported that the prostitutes had been committed with orders that 'they *were not* to be allowed *any fire* whatever,' but they had become so cold that his turnkey had sat them down for a few minutes at the stove in his room. Stephen Fuller, the debtor, declared that he himself had put in a word for them with the turnkey after hearing one of them crying from illness and thirst. While out of their cell they had been kept strictly apart from the male inmates, but Mackenzie, rejecting all excuses, had stormed out after directing them to be shut up without fire or light, although at that time they had neither bed nor bedding. For his part, Sheriff Jarvis stated that the women had been committed 'with directions to inflict a greater degree of punishment than is usually awarded to Felons of the male Sex.' In addition to the orders regarding their confinement, he noted, they had been sentenced to hard labour, which could only mean stonebreaking. As for the failure to segregate them, he observed: 'the prison now has confined within its walls 55 persons, besides the families of the Jailor and Turnkey, and when it is known, that of that number 5 are insane persons, and that only two flats of the prison are habitable, (except as kitchens) the crowded state of the jail will readily account for these females not being confined in cells.'[32]

In view of what was to happen, Mackenzie's reaction to these statements is remarkable. In a letter dated 'Dec. 2nd, 11 p.m.,' he complained bitterly that nothing had yet been done in response to his complaint about the turnkey's drunkenness and disregard of an order of the city magistrates. 'Had the jail been under the control of the city authorities,' he declared, 'the facts I communicated would undoubtedly have resulted in the removal of the under jailer from a situation he filled with no advantage to the community – as it is, I have subjected myself to a censure from the sheriff ... and to the perusal of a letter from a person of the name of Fuller ... the language of which ought, I think, to have satisfied Mr. Jarvis that it was unfit to be sent to the Lieut[enan]t Governor.'

Mackenzie proceeded to correct Barnhart's and the sheriff's misrepresentations of the sentence. The women had been sentenced to *labour*, not 'hard labour,' and previously in passing that sentence he had specified such tasks as cleaning the cells and washing the prisoners' linen. The sheriff, then, had no grounds for charging that he and Lesslie had sentenced the women to break stones. Nor had they ordered them to be deprived of fire. 'What we contemplated was, that they should be put in that ward up stairs where women have hitherto been placed, so that the prison might not become a common brothel.' Fuller's allegation he dismissed as 'an invention of some person to me unknown.'[33]

It is striking that this letter, like Mackenzie's original complaint, was aimed not at Barnhart but his drunken turnkey. It gives no sign that Mackenzie interpreted the countercharges regarding the sentence as anything but misunderstandings – not untainted with an intention to insult, perhaps, but nothing worse. The lack of animus against the jailer is the more significant because, since the first complaint, he had twice been guilty of disobedience towards the city magistrates – once towards Alderman Lesslie and the other time towards Mackenzie himself. Both times he had delayed acting on orders to release a prisoner, his excuse being that he had already locked up the prisoners for the night. The second offence had occurred on the very evening of 2 December, and Mackenzie had sent the lieutenant-governor a complaint about Barnhart's contempt from the courtroom itself. Yet the letter under discussion, dated only three hours later, made no mention of Barnhart's contumacy, focusing instead on the government's failure to support the city magistrates by dismissing the drunken turnkey.[34] And the next morning, when the sheriff apologized to the court for his subordinate's contempt in refusing to release the prisoner as ordered, the court excused the jailer's offence.[35]

Within a few days, Mackenzie would change his focus entirely. Barnhart, not the turnkey, would become his target; he would now see Jarvis's, Barnhart's, and the debtor Fuller's charges as a conspiracy to ruin his reputation; and he would begin to bombard the government with demands that the jailer be suspended on suspicion of the crime of forgery. What caused this turnabout?

IV

It appears that Mackenzie, piqued by Barnhart's assertion that the women had been committed with orders to keep them from fire, sent a clerk of the court to the jail to examine the warrant of commitment. Appended to the order to segregate the women from the male inmates, the clerk, John Elliott, found the words 'to keep from fire.' The words were scratched through with a thick pen-stroke, but Sheriff Jarvis told Mackenzie that he himself had seen them before their deletion. The mayor decided that someone had added the words in order to discredit him and later obliterated them to avoid detection. He was sure it must have been Barnhart, to whom as jailer the warrant had been directed.[36]

The reference to the grand jury followed on 5 December, apparently at the sheriff's behest, and on the following day the *Recorder* published its report, which took the form of three letters from the jailer.[37] Now the matter was public and political – not to mention criminal – and Mackenzie too went to the press. He had just sold his own paper, but the new owner readily published his allegation that Barnhart had forged the warrant or got someone else to do so. As for the charge that he had sentenced the prostitutes to hard labour, Mackenzie now said that Elliott had written the word 'hard' in the warrant but he, Mackenzie, had deleted the word at once and rebuked Elliott for using it in a sentence passed on women. There was no excuse, therefore, for the sheriff's reference to stone-breaking. The mayor concluded that Barnhart's forgery, Jarvis's misrepresentations, and the allegations of the debtor Fuller constituted a conspiracy to libel him by 'representing the chief magistrate of this city as a cruel monster who had ordered women to be kept in prison and deprived of fire *in Canada* in the month of December, an order which I never heard of any Magistrate giving on any occasion.'[38]

With a municipal election impending, the people's tribune might well fear exposure as a tyrant magistrate, an imposer of cruel and unusual punishments on women fallen into his power, the more so if the women were Irish Catholics, as their names (Mary Brown and Biddy Milligan) suggest. The municipal franchise was very broad and extended to many poor Irish Catholic householders. These might well be susceptible to any hint of ethnic or religious bias against them. In Mackenzie's ward,

St David's, the Catholic vote was especially important, and earlier in the year the Tories had cited several of his judicial actions in order to pin such a bias on him. When Ellen Halfpenny, described in an Irish Catholic, pro-Reform organ as 'a common scold, drunken and disorderly,'[39] was set in the stocks, the Tory *Patriot* hastened to identify her as 'an Irish Roman Catholic' and hint that Mackenzie had been influenced by the fact.[40] Halfpenny figured in the *Patriot*'s columns for several weeks thereafter, usually in outraged capitals. Now the same paper, affecting impartiality, declared: 'If his Lordship did not order the girls to be kept without fire, in common justice, he should not therewith be charged; but since he put a woman in the Stocks, he has been considered capable of any and every cruelty towards the fair sex.'[41]

A scandal of this sort might be just the thing to turn Catholic voters against a puritanical Presbyterian. Mackenzie was already feeling the heat resulting from a clash between a gang of Catholics and some constables during the general election, in which one of the rioters had been killed. Before the New Year he would be forced to commit his own police chief on a charge of murder in order to mollify his Catholic supporters.[42] He did not need another scandal and might well have wished to outface the charges about the prostitutes even if they were true. The question arises, therefore, why we should believe Mackenzie rather than his accusers.

The forged warrant survives,[43] and it might be possible to solve the conundrum by forensic analysis. The document was examined by the Ontario Centre of Forensic Sciences, but the test was inconclusive. Handwriting analysis is difficult when the amount of writing is small, and in this case we have only the words '& to keep from fire.' These are crammed into a narrow space and crossed out with a thick penstroke which, while it does not render the writing illegible, obscures its form and flow. The centre could say only that the hand was not Barnhart's, a fact evident to the lay eye and irrelevant to the idea that he committed or procured the forgery. Neither Mackenzie nor Elliott, the two writers of the warrant, could be identified or excluded as the writer of the contentious words; nor could it be determined whether or not the writing represented an attempt to imitate another's hand.[44] In short, the analysis left the problem exactly where it was, forcing us to rely on circumstantial evidence.

This, luckily, is fairly straightforward. It provides many arguments in Mackenzie's favour, but two are decisive. One is the fact that he first denied the charges, on 2 December, at a time when the warrant was in the jailer's hands. The warrant was the crucial evidence, and there was nothing to be gained by lying to the lieutenant-governor if his adversaries could produce it and prove him wrong. Secondly, one man who must have known if Mackenzie was lying was the clerk Elliott. Elliott had written most of the warrant, he had copied the certificate of conviction from it, and it was he whom Mackenzie had sent to the jail to check the warrant after learning of Barnhart's and the sheriff's charges.[45] Elliott testified before the grand jury. What he told them is not recorded, but we can be sure that, if he had contradicted the mayor, the Tory press would have served it up for breakfast, lunch, and dinner.

But might not Elliott have lied to protect the mayor? Here too the circumstances favour Mackenzie. It happens that Elliott had recently petitioned the city council to appoint him as city clerk, and only a week after calling Elliott as a witness in this matter the mayor opposed his petition on the ground of incompetence.[46] If Elliott was the sort of man to lie on Mackenzie's behalf, he was surely the sort to demand Mackenzie's support for his application as a *quid pro quo*. At any rate, it would have been rash of Mackenzie to oppose his application on such insulting grounds. It is reasonable to suppose that, when Mackenzie did so, he had no reason to fear any embarrassing disclosures from the affronted clerk. We can safely assume that the order to keep the prisoners from fire was not entered on the warrant by Mackenzie, either as a record of the sentence or as a clandestine amendment of it.[47]

The same goes for the charge that the women had been sentenced to break stones, which first came up in Sheriff Jarvis's letter of 27 November. Mackenzie had first replied that the two women had been sentenced to *labour* and Jarvis should have known what that meant, since on previous occasions, in sentencing women to labour, he had specified the task of cleaning cells. Later he had added that the clerk had mistakenly written 'hard labour' in the commitment but that he, Mackenzie, had deleted the word at once.[48] Both of these claims are circumstantially verifiable, at least with respect to Mackenzie's statement of his intentions regarding the sentence. In explaining hard labour in June to the grand jury of the Mayor's Court, Mackenzie had specified as women's tasks 'washing, mending, and making clothes, picking wool and feathers, knitting stockings and caps, 10 hours per day.' Stone-breaking headed the longer list reserved for men. At the June sessions Margaret Cotter, convicted of larceny, had been sent to prison for a month to clean the cells. About that time Ellen Halfpenny, the Woman in the Stocks, had also been sentenced to clean the cells to purge her contempt at the Police Court.[49] As for Brown and Milligan, Mackenzie had described them as being sentenced to 'labour' in his initial complaint of 23 November, four days before Jarvis had stated that they had been sentenced to hard labour. This is confirmed by the certificate of conviction – which, as Mackenzie had noted, was invariably prepared by copying the warrant of commitment.

There is no evidence, then, that the sentencing magistrates intended Brown and Milligan to break stones. But does that mean that there is no excuse for Sheriff Jarvis's misconstruction of the sentence? The one possible excuse lies in the very few women who were sentenced to labour. The Mayor's Court minutes, and a partial search of the newspapers for reports of Police Court proceedings, revealed only the cases of Cotter and Halfpenny. In neither case was the word 'labour' used in the sentence, which instead specified the form of work to be imposed. By contrast, men were frequently sentenced to terms of labour, and though here too the sentence normally specified the type of work (most often stone-breaking), the Police Court reports record several sentences to terms of 'hard labour' and one of 'labour.'[50] Thus Jarvis, seeing the word *labour* in the commitment, may have made no difference between that and *hard labour* and may automatically have associated it with the sort of task Mackenzie had been imposing on male prisoners. In 1834, after all, sentencing to terms of labour was a novelty in Upper Canada.

This, then, is the case for believing in Jarvis's good faith; but even if we accept it, we cannot do so without observing that he was remarkably quick to believe that Mackenzie had sentenced the women to break stones. Nor was he the only one. When Mackenzie's letter of 23 November was published in the newspapers, the word 'hard' was inserted before labour, thus making Mackenzie say that the women had been sentenced to that punishment.[51] This falsification too can be excused, if we suppose the word to have been inserted in the belief that it had been left out in error. If so, however, it was the work of someone else who was all too ready to convict Mackenzie of tyrannical conduct in office.

Perhaps people felt, with the *Patriot*, that a man who could sentence a woman to the stocks was capable of any iniquity.[52] It is worth noting, though, that the excesses in question were quite inconsistent with Mackenzie's own ideas as to the proprieties of punishment. He might inveigh against the prevalence of vice, but he was reluctant to chastise it unduly. In the very letter in which he had reported to Government House on conditions in the seedier parts of the city, he had complained that the statutory penalty for selling liquor without a licence (a £20 fine or three months' imprisonment) was too stringent; a fine of £5 would administer salutary correction without causing the offender's total ruin. Likewise, when he wrote to the lieutenant-governor about conditions at the jail, he declared: 'Even the captive in a dungeon has his rights, and ought not to be used as I have seen some such used in the dist[ric]t Jail.'[53] No more than the Assembly report of 1830 was this the voice of someone likely to inflict the brutalities imputed to Mackenzie.

In any case, it is no more likely that Mackenzie sentenced the women to break stones than to be kept without fire and light. This conclusion adds interest to the affidavit sworn just before Christmas by two city councilmen, George Gurnett and James Trotter. The two Tories stated that they had been in court when Brown and Milligan were sentenced, and that, to the best of their recollection, the women had been sentenced 'to be kept at hard labor in the Jail without fire and candle.'[54] In the month that had passed since the trial, this testimony was the first that Barnhart had managed to procure in his favour from anyone claiming to have been in court at the time, and it was almost certainly a lie. Apart from anything else, the candle is a bit too much of a good thing. The words on the warrant – the words Mackenzie and the jailer accused each other of writing – are '& to keep from fire.' There is nothing about a candle. In order to accept the affidavit we would have to suppose that Mackenzie and Lesslie, having sentenced the prostitutes to be kept without fire and candle, actually omitted part of the sentence from the commitment. It seems more likely that they were not sentenced to be kept 'without candle' – and probably not without fire either.

Who conjured up this candle? It is not mentioned in the initial reports of Jarvis or the jailer, but the debtor Fuller had described the mayor, as he stormed out of the jail, commanding the jailer to confine the women 'without fire or light.' Later Fuller embroidered this story in an affidavit submitted to the government along with that of Gurnett and Trotter. He now described Mackenzie as berating the turnkey for his drunkenness and complaining because 'the women I ordered to be kept without fire and candlelight' were at large among the debtors.[55] A story in which Mackenzie issued an order on the spot had become one in which Mackenzie referred to an order already given. But the same objection applies to Fuller's deposition as to the councilmen's: if Mackenzie did give such an order, why doesn't it appear in the warrant?

These candles, however, were only part of a veritable candelabrum.

Accompanying Fuller's and the councilmen's affidavits were others by two more debtors, the turnkey, Charles Sloan, and Biddy Milligan. All of these featured candles. In separate depositions, both debtors claimed to have heard Mackenzie direct the jailer to keep the women 'from fire and candlelight.' Milligan swore that she had been sentenced to be kept 'without any fire' and that, at the jail, Mackenzie had ordered her and Brown to be confined 'without fire and candlelight.' Sloan testified that he had seen the words 'to keep from fire' on the commitment and that the mayor had given the orders to which the other deponents testified.[56] It is necessary to consider how these statements may have come into being.

We cannot absolutely preclude the possibility that Mackenzie gave the order he was alleged to have given at the jail, or something like it. Right at the start of the row, Jarvis had given overcrowding as a reason why it might be impossible to segregate the women from the debtors.[57] Perhaps it *was* possible to segregate them, but only by confining them in a room without a stove, and perhaps also without a window. Mackenzie, enraged, may have refused to accept that excuse and repeated his instructions to segregate the women – instructions which were later construed, more or less maliciously, as a positive order to deprive them of fire and light. He may have done this or he may not – but if he did, it may have given Barnhart the inspiration for an audacious forgery. This hypothesis does not account for the candle, of course, but it may not be necessary to try very hard to account for a candle which took so long to appear in the record.

Even on the most indulgent construction, moreover, we confront evidence – not conclusive, perhaps, but highly suggestive – of a criminal conspiracy against Mackenzie acting in his capacity as the duly elected chief magistrate of Toronto. The original forgery must have entailed conspiracy if Barnhart procured it instead of executing it himself. The initial accusations against Mackenzie may have amounted to a criminal conspiracy to libel him. The subsequent affidavits in support of Barnhart appear to have added the ingredient of perjury. It is not suggested that all the possible culprits were in it from the start, or even that all of them plotted with one or more other conspirators at some point, though there must have been some sort of collusion inside the jail at least. This conspiracy was a matter of different people, from different motives, opportunistically conniving to discredit Mackenzie by means which ranged from the merely dishonest to the outright criminal. We need to consider what this implies with respect to prisons, politics, and the administration of justice in Upper Canada.

V

One can easily imagine why the witnesses at the jail might have taken part in a conspiracy to discredit Mackenzie. Biddy Milligan and Charles Sloan had their own special grudges to satisfy. The three debtors had every reason to oblige the jailer, condemned as they were to indefinite terms in his custody. So much is obvious without looking for political motives – which is just as well, since the prisoners, with one exception, have left no record of their allegiances, if any. The exception is Stephen Fuller, who pops up in official records a week after Mackenzie's rebellion in 1837 complaining about his 'sudden and irregular' dismissal from his lieutenancy in a volunteer militia company formed at the outbreak of the insurrection under the command of Sheriff Jarvis. The link with Jarvis may be coincidental, and the reasons for his dismissal are not specified, but there is nothing to suggest that he sympathized with Mackenzie. Fuller comes across, rather, as someone who aspires to service as a minion of the establishment. A month later we find him trying to cash in on what he says is a promise by the lieutenant-governor to approve his appointment as captain of his own volunteer company.[58]

This being so, it is noteworthy that his affidavit was one of only two which actually contradicted the documentary evidence by representing Mackenzie as having *sentenced* the women to be confined 'without candle.' The other, of course, was that of the Tory councilmen, Trotter and Gurnett. Trotter was small beer: an innkeeper who was to serve for decades as a city councilman while holding an appointment as one of the city's two tax assessors. Gurnett, however, was an epitome of those Upper Canadians who made their way by serving the elite. He had first come to public notice as a participant in the outrage at Ancaster in 1826, just a few days before the attack on Mackenzie's printing-shop, when masked invaders had dragged John Rolph's brother George from his house in the middle of the night and proceeded to tar and feather him. The next year he founded the *Gore Gazette*, and his journalism so impressed the provincial elite that in 1829, when Sir John Colborne found it politic to close down the newspaper published by the King's Printer, they paid him to move to the capital in order to fill the gap. There he ran the *Courier of Upper Canada* until his appointment in 1837 to the plum job of clerk of the peace of the Home District. This sinecure gave him time to preside for many years, as alderman and as mayor, in the Toronto Police Court before being appointed in 1851 as the city's first full-time police magistrate.[59]

The point is that the case of the forged commitment smacks of earlier affairs like the tar-and-feather outrage and the wrecking of Mackenzie's shop. Those incidents occurred in 1826, after the government and its supporters had been humbled in the general election of 1824 and the subsequent controversy over the alien question. The general election of 1830 had provided a brief respite for the Tories without changing the temper of provincial politics. The repeated unconstitutional expulsions of Mackenzie from the tenth provincial parliament were punctuated, in 1832, by the murderous assault of a gang of thugs led by William Kerr, an MPP, justice of the peace, and employee of the government. By 1834 the Tories were again politically insecure. The shocking dismissal of the provincial law officers for their role in Mackenzie's expulsion had been followed by Mackenzie's election as mayor, the Reformers' general election victory, and the loss of Sheriff Jarvis's seat in Toronto.

It is notorious that none of the perpetrators of the earlier scandals suffered much, if any, harm to his career. Samuel Jarvis (the sheriff's cousin), who had led the attack on Mackenzie's shop and later attempted to justify it in print, was soon made deputy superintendent of the Indian Department. John Lyons, another 'types rioter,' was appointed registrar of the Niagara District. A third, Charles Richardson (who was also instrumental in another scandal of 1826, the persecution of the opposition MPP John Matthews), soon became clerk of the peace of the same district. The heavy damages assessed against the rioters had been paid by public subscription. George Rolph had recovered minor damages from two of his assailants, but most had escaped scot-free, like Gurnett, to prosper from their energetic loyalty. Kerr paid a fine of £25 – no great matter for a man of some wealth.[60]

Such examples of indulgence on the part of the colonial executive and judiciary were accompanied by a constant hubbub of denunciation which branded the more radical critics of the provincial establishment as disloyal. Together they fostered a climate of public opinion which stripped Reformers, Mackenzie above all, of the protections comprised in the rule of law. In such a state of opinion, a forgery designed to discredit Mackenzie, and a little perjury to the same end, might appear to the zealously loyal as venial wrongs if not acts of positive virtue. A grand crime like forgery was beyond the jurisdiction of the Mayor's Court, and the city magistrates referred it to the Attorney General for prosecution at the assizes. When, however, the latter declined to take action in the matter, Mackenzie knew better than to institute a private prosecution in a court where the grand jury would be largely composed of members and familiars of the metropolitan elite, and where Sheriff Jarvis would exercise a well-known influence over the selection of jurors.[61]

What had become a feud between Mackenzie and the jailer would still figure in the proceedings of the Home District assizes, but at Barnhart's initiative. The jailer pursued his claim to a salary from the city only to find the Tory-dominated council of 1835 as unyielding as its predecessor. His suit came to trial in 1836 and was decided in the city's favour. Barnhart's only witness (so it was reported) was his *former* turnkey Sloan, who had refused to testify until his old job was restored. (There is no evidence that Mackenzie, or the case of Brown and Milligan, had had anything to do with Sloan's departure from the jail.) Mackenzie, who testified for the corporation, found himself facing that staple of vexatious prosecutions, a complaint of perjury. Under the headline 'Perjury – A Conspiracy to Ruin Mackenzie,' the *Correspondent and Advocate* reported 'a grand conspiracy of certain officials,' George Gurnett among them, against the former mayor. The plot came to nothing, but Mackenzie recalled it a year later after exposing an attempt to pack the jury against him in a libel suit in the Niagara District. He claimed on that occasion to have been alerted to the possibility of hanky-panky by this earlier experience at the Home District assizes.[62]

VI

The affair of the forged commitment was one small but characteristic incident in the history of Mackenzie's relations with the provincial elite and their minions. Likewise, Mackenzie's intervention in the affairs of the jail was but one episode in a continuing story. As his term ended the mayor, assertive to the last, drew the district magistrates' attention to the ragged condition of the men sentenced at the Mayor's Court in December to break stones in the winter's cold. Several of them lacked such necessities as shoes, headgear, and even trousers, while none had more than one shirt. Citing their indebtedness, the magistrates refused to supply the prisoners' wants or to increase their rations.[63] Perhaps it was for this reason that Mackenzie's successors gave up sentencing criminals to hard labour.[64]

Even so, the prisoners' treatment remained a scandal, and within a year Mackenzie's view of it was to receive powerful reinforcement from none other than the judges of the King's Bench. In December 1835, in a letter to the lieutenant-governor, they called for legislation to establish uniform standards for the treatment of prisoners confined on criminal charges in any district jail, but their argument was based on the deficiencies of the Home District regime. Granting that, in some districts, the authorities might lack sufficient funds to meet all their obligations, the judges declared 'that there can be no claim upon those funds entitled to take precedence of the indispensable charge for providing whatever may be necessary for preserving prisoners from absolute suffering.' Bread and water was an inadequate diet and should be supplemented with meat and vegetables. Any necessary bedding and coarse warm clothing should also be furnished. The judges made clear that their initiative was prompted by the presence in the Home District jail of prisoners who were 'in a state of suffering from the want of what we regard as the absolute necessaries of life.'[65]

To this imposing indictment the magistrates responded with an expansive view of the problem of the jail. They dwelt on the huge increase in the local population; the expense of caring for the insane; the special outlay entailed by the recent cholera epidemics; the district's indebtedness; the inequity of the legislation which made them responsible for prisoners, four-fifths of whom were committed by the city authorities. Turning to the little matter raised by the judges, they reported that the prison allowance was calculated on the assumption that prisoners could procure supplementary rations 'with their own means or the assistance of friends.' Whenever a case of special need was pointed out, the sufferer received extra provision. Nevertheless, the magistrates had now augmented the basic ration with 'a daily issue of soup, at a cheap rate and of a good and wholesome quality.' As to clothing, however, they were adamant: '[T]hat the apparent condition of some of the prisoners in the gaol may have given rise to an apprehension that they were in a state of suffering, the Magistrates cannot presume to deny; without more particular inquiry, it may probably have been confined to such of them as from their own intemperate conduct and continued insubordination it may have been found necessary to keep within more than usual restriction.'[66] This passing admission that prisoners were sometimes segregated in cold quarters has an obvious relevance to the case of the prostitutes committed by Mackenzie.

The magistrates had already committed themselves to building a new jail, after a recommendation to that effect by the assize grand jury in April 1835. Before the assizes, the sheriff had had to ask the city council to post constables at the jail during the assizes. 'It will probably be the means,' he wrote, 'of preventing the escape of persons now confined under charges of a most serious nature.'[67] Government House had referred the grand jury's presentment to the magistrates with a pointed suggestion that they hold a special meeting to discuss it, and the magistrates had duly appointed a committee to consider ways and means. This committee rejected the idea of selling the existing jail and courthouse lot, which was the only open space left in the centre of the city, in favour of applying to the legislature for an increased power of taxation. Once a new jail was built, they suggested, the old one might be transferred to the city authorities to be used as a bridewell.[68]

In March 1836, however, the magistrates seized on the judges' letter as an opportunity to urge that the city be made to build its own prison. This obligation was incorporated in the city's amended charter of 1837, which reduced its annual payment for the use of the district jail to £400 but required it to build its own within five years. Neither this nor the opening of the Kingston Penitentiary made much difference to the magistrates' building plans, however, for the simple reason that their existing building was full of holes. In January 1836 the sheriff had reported that there had lately been frequent escapes from every floor of the jail. The only remedy was a new building 'of durable materials.'[69] In November 1836, apparently despairing of statutory authority to increase taxes, the magistrates decided to finance the project by selling the courthouse square after all. Having obtained legislative permission to contract for the new edifice, they set about selling off the square, only to discover that it was a trust which was not theirs to sell. From this embarrassment they were relieved by an act of 1839, which retrospectively authorized them to sell the property and apply the proceeds as security for a loan to finance the project. The new stone edifice, very evidently built with an eye to security, was opened in 1840.[70]

In November 1836, too, Charles Barnhart's salary was at last raised to £125, and the following summer it was increased to £200 for as long as city prisoners and lunatics continued to be confined in the jail.[71] The problem of the lunatics was resolved by the opening of the new jail, which allowed the old one to be converted temporarily into an insane asylum,[72] but that of the city prisoners proved more intractable for the simple reason that the city took no steps to build its own jail. In 1842 a district committee opined that it would 'be in no haste to do so, so long as the District Council patiently submit to an annual Loss in the Charge, Care, and Support of the City Prisoners.'[73] The city council had been firmly in Tory hands since the rebellion, and the jail was now the responsibility of an elective district council with a majority of Reformers, but the problem of institutional friction was unaltered. Negotiations continued sporadically until 1845 (George Gurnett figuring prominently on both sides as clerk of the peace and alderman), when the two sides at last agreed that the city should continue to use the jail for five more years on payment of £600 a year.[74]

As late as 1839, Barnhart was still trying to obtain reimbursement from the city for the expenses he claimed to have incurred five years earlier. 'I think it no more than candid & honorable,' he told the mayor, 'to inform you, that I intend to publish this letter, together with your, or the Councils answer to it; with many other papers now in my possession.'[75]

VII

In December 1835, in a discussion of Toronto's charter of incorporation, the city's Reform newspaper declared: 'The most vicious part of the present system appears to be, the Aldermen being obliged to sit as police magistrates in judgement upon that class of persons upon whom they are in a great measure dependant for their seats, and no one can be insensible to the effect this is likely to have on their decisions.'[76] We have seen that this opinion may well have been justified, but also that it was the not the worst way in which politics impinged on the administration of justice in either the city or the province. In a society so deeply divided, neither an appointed nor an elective judiciary could command general respect or be free of political taint. In the 1820s, a number of *causes célèbres* had evoked complaints of a political bias in the administration of justice. However sincere they may have been, and however justified, they were not the less strident because opponents of the provincial establishment saw the discrediting of the legal system as a means to political reform. In 1834, likewise, Mackenzie's opponents could not stop to assess his judicial conduct impartially when unrelenting abuse might be the means to his political defeat.

NOTES

The author is grateful to J.M.S. Careless, Susan Houston, and Victor Russell for commenting on an earlier version of this paper.

1 Mackenzie's career is related in *Dictionary of Canadian Biography* (hereafter DCB) 9: 496–510.

2 Paul Romney 'A Struggle for Authority: Toronto Society and Politics in 1834' in Victor L. Russell, ed. *Forging a Consensus: Historical Essays on Toronto* (Toronto 1984); Paul Romney 'William Lyon Mackenzie as Mayor of Toronto' *Canadian Historical Review* 56 (1975); Frederick H. Armstrong 'William Lyon Mackenzie, First Mayor of Toronto: A Study of a Critic in Power' ibid. 48 (1967)

3 Paul Romney 'From the Types Riot to the Rebellion: Elite Ideology, Antilegal Sentiment, Political Violence, and the Rule of Law in Upper Canada' *Ontario History* 79 (1987)

4 Mackenzie's own newspaper, *The Advocate* (formerly *Colonial Advocate*), and the other Toronto newspapers reported frequently on proceedings in the city Police Court.

5 Commenting on the new charter, Mackenzie himself had decried 'the power to arrest and summarily to inflict a disgraceful punishment on certain classes of alledged [sic] offenders without the shield of a jury': *Advocate* 20 Mar. 1834, quoted in Edith G. Firth, ed. *The Town of York, 1815-1834* (Toronto 1966) 300.

6 See the following essay by Susan Lewthwaite.

7 Under 4 Wm. IV (1834), c. 23, s. 22, the city was obliged to pay the magistrates each year for district purposes a penny in the pound on the assessed value of city property. In 1834 this amounted to more than £1100.

8 Eric Arthur *Toronto: No Mean City*, 3rd ed., rev. Stephen A. Otto (Toronto 1986) 46, 47, 61

9 Insolvent debtors imprisoned in execution were entitled to claim maintenance of five shillings per week under a provincial statute of 1805 (45 Geo. III, c. 7). This privilege was not extended to those confined on mesne process until 1834: 4 Wm. IV, c. 3.

10 *Journal of the House of Assembly of Upper Canada* (1830), Appendix, 162, reprinted in Firth *Town of York* 281-3

11 City of Toronto Archives (hereafter CTA), RG1 A (Journal of the Common Council – hereafter Council Journal), 21 Apr. 1834; *Advocate* 8 May, 5 June 1834. The periodic presentments of the grand jury of the Home District quarter sessions are recorded in Archives of Ontario (hereafter AO), RG22, ser. 94 (Minutes of the Court of General Quarter Sessions for the Home District – hereafter Quarter Sessions Minutes).

12 National Archives of Canada (hereafter NAC), RG5 A1 (Upper Canada Sundries – hereafter Sundries), vol. 142, pp. 77497-500 (Mackenzie to W. Rowan, 9 June 1834); CTA, RG1 B (Toronto City Council Papers – hereafter Council Papers), Rowan to Mackenzie, 9 June 1834; *Advocate* 12 June 1834

13 Council Papers, W.B. Jarvis to W. Rowan, 17 June 1834, and Grant Powell to Rowan, 26 July 1834, both enclosed in Rowan to Mackenzie, 30 July 1834

14 *Advocate* 11 Sept. 1834

15 Each ward of the city was represented on the council by two aldermen and two councilmen. The mayor was elected by the council from among the aldermen. All of the aldermen were magistrates ex officio.

16 Council Papers, C. Barnhart to Mackenzie, 31 July 1834; Council Journal, 31 July 1834. On Jarvis see DCB 9: 411–12.

17 *Advocate* 11 Sept. 1834

18 Ibid. 5 June 1834; ibid. 1 May 1834

19 Ibid. 11 Sept. 1834; Council Papers, Mackenzie to W. Rowan, 5 June 1834, Jarvis to Rowan, 17 June 1834, Grant Powell to Rowan, 26 July 1834

20 *Correspondent and Advocate* (Toronto) 24 Dec. 1834; CTA RG7 C (Mayor's Letterbook), Mackenzie to Chairman, Home District Quarter Sessions, 30 Dec. 1834

21 *Correspondent and Advocate* 11 Apr. 1836. NAC, MG30 C40 (Barnhart Papers) consists largely of genealogical material relating to the Barnhart family.

22 Sundries, vol. 141, pp. 76923–6 (Mackenzie to W. Rowan, 7 May 1834)

23 *Canadian Correspondent* (Toronto) 19, 26 Apr. 1834; Council Journal, 12 Nov. 1834

24 50 Geo. III (1810), c. 5

25 Joanna Innes 'Prisons for the Poor: English Bridewells, 1555–1800' in Francis Snyder and Douglas Hay, eds. *Labour, Law and Crime: An Historical Perspective* (London 1987); Richard Burn *The Justice of the Peace and Parish Officer*, 3rd ed. (London 1756) 145, 384–6 (s.v. 'Commitment' and 'House of Correction'); 32 Geo. III (1792), c. 1

26 J.M. Beattie *Attitudes towards Crime and Punishment in Upper Canada, 1830–1850: A Documentary Study* (Toronto 1977) 14. Mackenzie cited the statute in his charge to the grand jury of the Mayor's Court in June: *Canadian Correspondent* 9 Aug. 1834.

27 *Canadian Correspondent* 9 Aug. 1834

28 *Advocate* 15 May 1834; Council Journal 19 June 1834

29 Sundries, vol. 142, pp. 77497–500 (Mackenzie to W. Rowan, 9 June 1834)

30 Under UC stat 4 Geo. IV (1823), c. 24, which authorized a loan of £4000 for building the goal and courthouse, all monies not required for the ordinary expenses of the district were to be used to liquidate the loan. UC stat. 6 Geo. IV (1825), c. 4 authorized a further loan of £2000 and provided that not less than £150 a year was to be paid in liquidation thereof. See also below, 343–4.

31 Sundries, vol. 147, pp. 80482–5 (Mackenzie to W. Rowan, 23 Nov. 1834)

32 Ibid., vol. 147, pp. 80549–57 (Jarvis to Rowan, 27 Nov. 1834; Barnhart to Jarvis, 26 Nov. 1834; Fuller to Jarvis, 26 Nov. 1834); emphasis in original

33 Ibid., vol. 148, pp. 80668–78 (Mackenzie to Rowan, 2 Dec. 1834)

34 Ibid., vol. 148, pp. 80680–5 (Mackenzie to Rowan, 2 Dec. 1834); ibid. pp. 80782–8 (Mackenzie to the Board of Aldermen, 8 Dec. 1834)

35 Sundries, vol. 148, p. 80678 (Mackenzie to Rowan, 3 Dec. 1834)

36 Mackenzie to Board of Aldermen, 8 Dec. 1834. This letter was printed in *Correspondent and Advocate*, 11 Dec. 1834.

37 This material was reprinted in *The Patriot and Farmer's Monitor* (Toronto) 12 Dec. 1834. The first letter was dated 26 November, but internal evidence suggests that all the material was published on 6 December, as does Mackenzie's failure to react to any offensive material in earlier numbers of the *Recorder*. I have been unable to find copies of the *Recorder* for these dates. The *Union List of Canadian Newspapers Held by Canadian Libraries* records them in the holdings of the National Library of Canada, but the library could not find them.

38 Sundries, vol. 148, pp. 80778, 80789–91 (Mackenzie to Sir John Colborne, 8 Dec. 1834); *Correspondent and Advocate* 11 Dec. 1834

39 *Canadian Correspondent* 28 June 1834

40 *Patriot*, 20 June 1834

41 Ibid. 12 Dec. 1834. Gender seems to have been the main issue: in December the Mayor's Court put a male thief in the stocks without arousing adverse comment (*Correspondent and Advocate* 11 Dec. 1834). On the 'MOTHER OF A FAMILY IN THE STOCKS' (*Patriot* 24 June 1834) and other cases where the Tories tried to exploit Mackenzie's actions as a magistrate in order to turn Catholics against him, see Romney 'Struggle for Authority' 24–5 and 'William Lyon Mackenzie as Mayor of Toronto' 423–4.

42 Paul Romney 'The Ordeal of William Higgins' *Ontario History* 67 (1975); Romney 'Struggle for Authority' 32

43 AO, Mackenzie-Lindsey Papers, Mackenzie clippings, envelope no. 6035. The certificate of conviction is attached to the warrant.

44 Report of G.W.K. Brohier, Head, Document Section, Ontario Centre of Forensic Sciences, 15 Dec. 1975 (copy in author's possession)

45 As Mackenzie told the Board of Aldermen in his letter of 8 December, 'The practice of the Court is to make out a commitment under the hands and seals of the Magistrates present, which commitment is handed by the Clerk of the Court to the Constable to take to the jailor [*sic*] ...

'Commitments are usually drawn up by the Clerk. I always examine them before I affix my signature, and if any error or omission is found it is corrected. In the present case I amended the document by adding, "you are further enjoined and required to keep them in a part of the prison to which the male prisoners have no access." We [Mackenzie and Lesslie] then signed it and handed it to Mr. Elliott who copied from it the conviction, which we also signed and sealed.

'Mr. Elliott after he made out the conviction and compared it with the commitment handed the letter to Constable Skellington who carried it over to the jail.'

46 *Toronto Recorder*, reprinted in *Kingston Chronicle and Gazette* 27 Dec. 1834. Elliott was secretary of Mackenzie's Toronto Political Union in the summer of 1837 and was present when Mackenzie is first known to have proposed a rebellion, but he took no part in the rising. In 1842 he was appointed clerk of the Home District by the Reform-dominated district council: see Eric Jackson 'The Organization of the Upper Canadian Reformers' in J.K. Johnson, ed. *Historical Essays on Upper Canada* (Toronto 1975) 106, and Ronald John Stagg 'The Yonge Street Rebellion of 1837: An Examination of the Social Background and a Re-assessment of the Events' (PhD thesis, University of Toronto 1976) 506.

47 Another witness before the grand jury was the other sentencing magistrate, James Lesslie, whose probity was acknowledged even by the *Toronto Recorder* (17 Jan. 1835). On Lesslie see DCB 11: 516–19.

48 See above, pp. 333–4, 335.

49 CTA, RG7 F (Proceedings of the Mayor's Court) 4 June 1834; *Canadian Correspondent* 28 June, 9 Aug. 1834

50 I searched the *Patriot* and the *Canadian Correspondent* from June to November. The words 'labour' and 'hard labour' do not appear in any Mayor's Court sentence in either June or September. The December sentences, passed during the controversy described here, include those of two women sentenced to 'such labour as the magistrates shall direct' and five of men sentenced to terms of imprisonment 'at hard labour breaking stones.'

51 *Patriot* 12 Dec. 1834

52 The *Patriot* may have been responsible for altering the letter. There is no way of knowing whether the alteration had appeared in the *Recorder* first, or whether, if so, the newspaper or its correspondent Barnhart was responsible.

53 Sundries, vol. 141, pp. 76930–5 (Mackenzie to W. Rowan, 7 May 1834); ibid., vol. 142, pp. 77497–500 (same to same, 9 June 1834)

54 Sundries, vol. 148, pp. 80981–81001 (Jarvis to Rowan, 23 Dec. 1834)

55 Ibid.

56 Ibid.

57 See above, p. 333.

58 NAC, RG5 C1 (Provincial Secretary's Correspondence), vol. 9, file no. 1192, pp. 5007–8 (Stephen J. Fuller to J. Joseph, Civil Secretary, 14 Dec. 1837);

NAC, RG9 IB1, vol. 22, Fuller to Col. O'Hara, Acting Adjutant General of Militia, 20 Dec. 1837; ibid., Fuller to Lt. Col. Strachan, Military Secretary, 19 Jan. 1838

59 On Gurnett see Paul Romney *Mr Attorney: The Attorney General for Ontario in Court, Cabinet, and Legislature, 1791–1899* (Toronto 1986) 112, 114, 154–5, and DCB 9: 345–7.

60 Romney *Mr Attorney* 82–157 passim; Romney 'From the Types Riot to the Rebellion'; Paul Romney 'Reinventing Upper Canada: American Immigrants, Upper Canadian History, English Law and the Alien Question' in Roger Hall et al., eds. *Patterns of the Past: Interpreting Ontario's History* (Toronto 1988). On Matthews see my article in DCB 6: 496–9, reprinted in Robert L. Fraser, ed. *Provincial Justice: Upper Canadian Legal Portraits from the Dictionary of Canadian Biography* (Toronto 1992); on Kerr see DCB 7: 466–7 and Charles Lindsey *The Life and Times of Wm. Lyon Mackenzie*, 2 vols. (Toronto 1862) 1: 245–9.

61 Mackenzie Lindsey Papers, Mackenzie correspondence, R J Jameson to Mackenzie, 8 Dec. 1834; Mayor's Letterbook, Mackenzie to Jameson, 8 Dec. 1834; Sundries, vol. 148, pp. 80778–91 (Mackenzie to Colborne, 8 Dec. 1834); ibid., pp. 80924–7 (Mackenzie to W. Rowan, 19 Dec. 1834); ibid., pp. 80974–6 (same to same, 22 Dec. 1834); Council Papers, Rowan to Mackenzie, 15 Dec. 1834; ibid., same to same, 20 Dec. 1834. On the composition of grand juries and the sheriff's influence over the selection of jurors, see Romney *Mr Attorney* 107, 114, 119, 291, 294–5.

62 Council Papers, Letter of S. Washburn, 16 Jan. 1835; ibid., Petition of C. Barnhart, 2 Feb. 1835; ibid., Washburn to C. Daly, 3 Apr. 1835; Council Journal 9 Feb. 1835; *Correspondent and Advocate*, 11 and 14 Apr. 1836; ibid. 4 May 1836; *The Constitution* (Toronto) 1 Nov. 1837

63 *Correspondent and Advocate* 24 Dec. 1834; Council Papers, Communication of S. Washburn, 31 Dec. 1834; Quarter Sessions Minutes, 31 Dec. 1834

64 *Correspondent and Advocate* 14 Apr. 1836

65 *Journal of the House of Assembly* (1836), appendix no. 44

66 Ibid.

67 Council Papers, Jarvis to the Mayor, 2 Apr. 1835

68 *Journal* (1836), app. no. 44

69 Ibid.; 7 Wm. IV (1837), c. 39, ss. 3, 4

70 Quarter Sessions Minutes, 22 Nov. 1836; 7 Wm. IV (1837), c. 40; 2 Vict. (1839), c. 44. There is a picture of the new jail in Arthur *Toronto: No Mean City* 79.

71 Quarter Sessions Minutes, 22 Nov. 1836, 15 July 1837

72 Richard B. Splane *Social Welfare in Ontario, 1791–1893: A Study in Social Welfare Administration* (Toronto 1965) 204

73 Council Papers, J. Scarlett, W. Thompson, and J.R. Gamble to the Mayor, 10 Sept. 1842

74 Council Journal, 5 Sept. 1842, 5 May 1845, 14 July 1845; Council Papers, J. Scarlett and J.W. Gamble to Aldermen Gurnett and Dixon and Geo. Walton, Esq., 23 Jan. 1843; ibid., Clerk of the Peace, H.D., to Charles Daly, 12 Feb. 1845

75 Council Papers, Barnhart to John Powell, 14 Feb. 1839

76 *Correspondent and Advocate* 24 Dec. 1835

11

Violence, Law, and Community in Rural Upper Canada

SUSAN LEWTHWAITE

On 18 December 1839 John Thomson, a farmer in Burford township, located southwest of Brantford, Ontario, appeared before John Weir, a local justice of the peace, to complain that Allan Muir, one of his neighbours, 'did with an Axe and other instruments maliciously ... cut down and destroy a gate and also did Break a Lock from off [my] Barn.'[1] This act of property damage, apparently trivial, is the kind of offence generally ignored by historians of crime and criminal justice in Ontario, who have preferred to discuss such topics as elite ideology, serious crime, the introduction of the penitentiary, or the development of policing, particularly in urban milieus after 1841. But this trespass case formed part of a longer series of disputes between several people in the township. While the events in Burford established no judicial precedent, they are indeed worthy of the historian's attention because they reveal a great deal about the social history of criminal justice in rural Upper Canada.[2] I will use the Burford story to examine three main themes: the social tensions in rural Upper Canadian society and the resulting undercurrents of violence;[3] the workings of the legal system at the local level;[4] and popular attitudes towards justices of the peace and the law more generally.[5] The story demonstrates that members of rural communities actively pursued their own interests, and that they could thwart the attempts of magistrates to regulate their behaviour.

After John Thomson's deposition complaining about the gate-breaking was sworn to and signed, the magistrate John Weir issued a warrant to have Allan Muir brought in to be tried for petty trespass.[6] Weir gave the warrant to his son, Robert, and told him to take it to the constable, who lived a few miles away. The constable was not at home, so Robert Weir, who had been appointed a special constable,[7] executed the warrant himself after having been so directed by George Whitehead, another magistrate. Robert Weir found Muir at William Cruden's house; Cruden was a close neighbour of the Weirs. There was trouble during the arrest, and John Weir witnessed the entire proceedings. According to him, four men – Cruden, William Bennett, John Treanor, and Robert McInnes – tried to prevent the arrest. Two of them had large butcher knives in their hands; the group had been slaughtering pigs.[8] John Weir tried to get them to 'desist such outrageous conduct' and help the constable, 'which they utterly refused, and set my commands as a Magistrate, the Constable and Every one else at defiance at the same time using most approbrious [sic] and insulting Expressions.' Robert Weir was finally able to get his prisoner to a nearby inn called the Burford Exchange. John Weir briefly went to his house to collect some papers and books; these were likely magistrates' manuals. When Weir was ready to arrange for Muir's bail the prisoner refused, answering that 'he felt very comfortable where he then was' and Weir went home.

A sitting of the local magistrates was arranged for the following day at Lewis Charles's inn several miles away. Weir chose this location 'being myself unwilling to have any thing further to do with these persons who live in my neighbourhood and who are very violent persons.' As they were preparing to set off, the prisoner's brother, Robert Muir, 'descried prisoner to come away from the Constable and not allow himself to be taken before the Magistrates.' Robert Muir further taunted his brother: 'I would see the Magistrates damned sooner than I would go before them.' Allan Muir tried to escape from the constable but was prevented from doing so. During this altercation, Muir behaved in a 'most outrageous,' 'very contumacious and abusive' manner, repeatedly calling Magistrate Weir 'a damned old scoundrel.' According to witnesses, Muir refused to proceed, and both of the Weirs remonstrated with him to no effect. To guarantee Muir's company on the journey, John Weir told his son to tie Muir up. Robert Weir tied a rope around Muir's waist and attached the other end of the rope to his horse's neck. Finally they set off. After a 'very short distance,' according to Weir, Muir was released and allowed into the sleigh.[9] At Lewis Charles's Inn, Weir and two other magistrates convicted Muir

of trespass for breaking the gate and the lock. Weir told the other magistrates about the events surrounding Muir's arrest on the preceding
day. They decided that the matter should be brought before the quarter
sessions in January 1840.

The manner of Allan Muir's arrest excited considerable local controversy. By early January, Muir and William Cruden had decided to
initiate a campaign of complaint against John Weir, and to try to have
him removed from the bench. Accordingly Muir wrote to the provincial
secretary's office complaining about the 'outrage' committed on him by
the Weirs. His account of the arrest differed considerably from that
of John Weir and his supporters outlined above.[10] Describing the circumstances of his arrest, Muir alleged that Robert Weir told him that
he had a warrant for his arrest, but refused to show it to him, despite
repeated requests. Muir's failure to cooperate during the arrest was thus
blamed on the constable, who had acted illegally: 'I refused to go with
him unless he shewed me the warrant.' When Muir did not submit,
Robert Weir assaulted him. Magistrate Weir also behaved improperly,
according to Muir; he encouraged Robert Weir's violent behaviour and
refused to take Muir's bail.[11] Consequently Muir was kept in custody
at the Burford Exchange all night, during which Robert Weir kept him
sitting on a chair for six hours and refused to let him stand up.[12] Muir
cast doubt on the authority of Robert Weir, who 'is not a regularly
appointed constable, but if appointed to act at all, it must have been
specially for the purpose of arresting me for the offence complained
of.' On the day when they were to proceed to Lewis Charles's Inn,
about eight miles away,

I told him I could not walk so far as I had a bad knee and that he must take
me some of the way. R[obert] Weir was on horseback and his Father in a Sleigh.
Robert Weir said I must walk – I told him I could not on which he seized
me by the collar of my coat and kicked me on the leg there several times.
John Weir was standing within two or three yards of me and must have seen
the treatment I received, and no doubt he did for he said 'take a rope and
tie him and drag the scoundrel along.' A rope was brought and tied round
my arm by John Weir and his son Robert who mounted his horse after having
twisted the other end round his horses neck, and then moved off at a trot
dragging me after him, and I was obliged to run as fast as I could to keep
up with the horse, and out of the way of John Weir who was driving the sleigh
behind me. Whilst I was being dragged in this way I stumbled, when John Weir
called out to Robert not to go so fast on which he went to the side of the

road and John Weir passed on and when he got in front told Robert he might take the rope off if I would go without it which was not done, but as the rope slackened I got it off my arm. I was dragged upwards of a quarter of a mile in the way in which I have described – after I got the rope off my arm John Weir asked me to to get into his sleigh as they were going so slow. I did so for my knee was very bad and I could scarcely walk.[13]

All of this amounted to 'an outrage committed on me' by the Weirs.

The day before Muir sent his letter of complaint about John Weir to the provincial secretary's office, William Cruden had written to the same official complaining generally about Weir's conduct as a justice of the peace.[14] He did not mention the Muir arrest, no doubt so he would appear to be an independent memorialist. There is little doubt, though, that the two had coordinated their efforts. Cruden used language very similar to that used by Muir, and implied a long-standing grievance: 'my feelings have been greatly outraged by the conduct of John Weir a Justice of the Peace and tho' many things have taken place of a character calculated to annoy & outrage my feelings, I have abstained from taking notice of his acts until now.' Cruden went on to accuse Weir of fining him an untoward sum, £5, for an assault on an 'apprentice' which Cruden denied had occurred. Cruden's labelling of Julia Higgins, his nineteen-year-old servant girl, as an 'apprentice' was undoubtedly an attempt to inflate his social status in the eyes of colonial officials.[15] Cruden said that Weir had not handed over the £5 to the clerk, and intimated that Weir regularly kept such funds. The nature of these complaints was guaranteed to get the attention of the authorities; Weir had punished him excessively, and was guilty of wrongdoing in his disposal of the fine. An inquiry was bound to ensue.

But John Weir had not acted alone at the trial in which the Crudens were convicted for assaulting Julia Higgins; another magistrate, George Whitehead, was involved.[16] Yet Cruden complained about Weir alone and not Whitehead. This fact suggests that Muir and Cruden cooperated in their efforts to beat the charges against them resulting from the attempted rescue and Muir's efforts to resist arrest. In his complaint, Cruden further alleged that Weir had cast aspersions upon Mrs Cruden's character in the 'BarRoom of a low Tavern.' According to Cruden Weir called Mrs Cruden a bitch, and said she was drunk and had had a 'connexion' with another man while intoxicated. Undoubtedly these accusations were intended to cast Weir's judgment further into doubt. In addition to the blows to Cruden's honour and Mrs Cruden's virtue implicit in Weir's alleged remarks, Cruden insinuated that Weir was known to frequent undesirable establishments of public entertainment, hardly a suitable pastime for a respectable magistrate. Cruden concluded by asserting that Weir's 'generally known overbearing and tyrannical character' had finally caused him to come forward. Again, the wording was calculated to capture the attention of colonial officials.[17] Tyrannical magistrates did not foster attachment to the laws and could endanger the legitimacy of the entire regime.[18] After Cruden's initial complaint against Weir had been forwarded to the colonial authorities, he mobilized support among his friends and neighbours. He circulated a petition objecting to Weir's activities as a magistrate and was able to persuade close to 240 other local men to affix their signatures to it.[19]

The provincial secretary's office became the repository of statements from several persons regarding Weir's conduct.[20] These documents show that the trespass incident formed only the most recent manifestation of an ongoing dispute between several local inhabitants and John Thomson. When asked to account for his actions, Weir described his relations with his neighbours. He reported that his first contact with the Crudens had been over the assault on their servant girl, Julia Higgins, who had been found during the night of 12 February 1839 so badly beaten that she was unable to walk. Weir 'found her in the most wretched condition literally naked filthy and full of bruises so much so one would hardly suppose her a human being.' According to her deposition, Julia Higgins had been flogged, beaten and kicked, had had her hair pulled, and had been struck with such items as a rope, a hand spike, fire-tongs, and a poker, during the time she had lived with the Crudens.[21] Several witnesses testified to her frequent abuse, particularly at the hands of Mrs Cruden. George Whitehead, the other presiding magistrate, referred to this affair as 'the most Brutal and unfeeling conduct toward a helpless ignorant orphan as disgraces the annals of any court calendar.'[22] The £5 fine, according to Weir, 'was applied to the payment of the Doctor who attended her and the remainder was Paid to the persons in whose House she was[,] she being a long time confined before she could walk or assist herself in any way – Consequently did not appear on the Town Clerks Books.' He denied that there had been any irregularities with the rest of the fines he had assessed and collected, which had 'been but few.'[23] According to Whitehead, 'the Magistrates without hesitation ordered the amount of the fine to be paid over to the Girl which was done.' Whitehead professed to be 'at a loss what Mr Cruden alludes to when he speaks of your [Weir's] Tyrannical conduct.'[24] The case of brutality seems to have been proven against the Crudens, and Weir's handling of the case appears humane and the steep fine justified; nevertheless, Weir was put on the defensive.

Until Thomson's arrival several months later, Weir had little contact with the Crudens after their conviction for assaulting Julia Higgins. Thomson, 'a respectable person,' then called on Weir as a magistrate several times seeking help in complaints against Cruden. Preferring not to get involved, Weir at first advised that the two men should seek to settle their disputes through arbitration: 'I told him they had better Leave all their differences to three respectable persons or even to one in preference to going to Law.' Cruden would have none of it, and the local magistrates convicted him three times for petty offences in cases initiated by Thomson. 'I think his Excellency the Governor General will see that the Tyrannical and overbearing conduct complained of by Mr Cruden has grown out of those Cases,' Weir concluded, and he referred the governor-general to Thomson's statement, which he submitted with his letter defending his actions.

Thomson's statement reveals a great deal about the nature of social relations in Burford township.[25] In response to an advertisement in *The Patriot*, Thomson had bought Cruden's farm in September 1839. Thomson paid Cruden in cash, and later had to sue Cruden for the $46 change owing him from the transaction. Cruden asked permission to stay for a short time in an old log house on the farm to sell off his livestock and some wheat and oats. Thomson agreed, but told Cruden that he could remain there for no longer than six weeks. After the six weeks had elapsed, Thomson was surprised to find that instead of selling his stock as promised, Cruden had bought more, and put them in the barn. When Thomson asked Cruden to remove his belongings from the barn, Cruden 'said he would just clear the Barn when he pleased, and told me he would let me know that I had nothing to do with the Barn or Farm or any thing belonging to them.' At this, Thomson resolved to take action:

and being an entire stranger and unacquainted with the local law, I called on Mr Weir the Magistrate, soliciting his advice and assistance. Mr Weir told me that he did not think a Magistrate could do any thing in the case, and advised me to apply to an attorney which I did and acted upon his advice. [In the] meantime Cruden collected a number of persons together who daily annoyed me on my premises, he also broke down and destroyed my fences, broke open the stable in my absence and turned my Horse into the stage road, and in company with a person named Allan Muir barricaded my gate so that no passage was left to the main road, they also removed a fence so that a young orchard on my Farm was exposed to the depradations of Crudens cattle. When I went for the purpose of driving the cattle of [sic] the Farm, Cruden accompanied by Allan Muir, Robert Muir, Robert McInnes, William Bennett & Mrs Cruden met me in a field in front of my Barn. Cruden then threatened me and presented a pistol at me, swearing, he would send me to Hell, Robt McInnes took the Pistol from Cruden and Mrs Cruden gave him a large bludgeon with which he threatened to batter out my brains.

When Thomson sought help from Weir, 'he said he was sorry for me as I was a stranger, but he did not wish to act as Cruden was a neighbour, he told me I had better go to Mr Whitehead and he would take the matter up, and no doubt I would have justice done me, but as Mr Whitehead resided at a distance of five miles, and I considered my person in danger, I insisted on Mr Weir taking my information and granting me a summons, which he then did, and I had Cruden and his wife bound over to keep the peace.'

Cruden and his friends continued to annoy and threaten Thomson. Allan Muir accosted Thomson when he was alone at the barn, and accused him of saying that an uncle of the Muirs had been hanged in Scotland, a story Cruden had apparently spread. Muir added menacingly: 'we can get rid of folks in this country without hanging them, and you had better take care.' On Christmas Eve, Thomson's horse was stabbed. After Christmas Cruden and eight other men tramped around removing hay and straw for three days, damaging Thomson's property. When Thomson told Robert Muir to stop hammering and splitting a board off one of the sheds, 'he told me, he was employed by Cruden and would do as he ordered him.' Thomson told him to leave, upon which 'Cruden and his party collected round me, fortunately the noise was heard at Mr Weirs House and two of his sons came to the Barn, Mrs Cruden came out of a tavern on the opposite side of the road with a bottle in her hand. She came up to me, put her clenched hand in my face twice, and said, By God, I'll knock your teeth down your throat; she appeared to be intoxicated, Cruden challenged me same time to fight him.'

Late in December a rack was removed from Thomson's cattle shed. One of Cruden's men walked around with a pistol sticking out of his pocket. When Thomson asked what he was doing there with a pistol, Robert McInnes said 'he was engaged by Cruden and would do as he ordered him. When I pointed out to any of them that the law would not justify them, in coming on my premises & annoying me, they told me, that Cruden would stand between them and all danger.' On 1 January 1840, the Crudens confronted Thomson in the barn; Mrs Cruden brandished a large stick, and Cruden a pitchfork. 'They began to abuse me and swore I would not be twelve months in Canada, as they would make the neighbourhood to [sic] hot for me.' When Thomson responded that he was sorry he had met with persons who had no regard for their character, a scuffle broke out. Cruden then 'came up with his fists in a pugilistic attitude saying, Damn you I[']ll knock you down.' Mrs Cruden assisted her husband, but Thomson managed to get away from them and they followed him out of the barn, still armed. Somehow he was able to escape, and Thomson complained 'to Mr Whitehead and Mr Weir and the case was fully gone into and Cruden fined.' Thomson concluded: 'The whole transaction appears to me to have been a pre-concerted plan for the purpose of defrauding me out of my property, and disgusting me at the country, and I believe I am correct in saying, there is not a respectable person in the neighbourhood, but what takes the same view of it.'[26]

Muir's act of vandalism to Thomson's property therefore represents but one incident in a long-standing series of disputes between Thomson and his neighbours. Weir had become involved, albeit reluctantly, on several occasions before the controversial arrest which led to the collection of evidence upon which their story has been reconstructed here. His fractious neighbours had finally pushed Weir too far, though, and he found himself in serious trouble because of his actions during Muir's arrest. He had been brought to the attention of the colony's administrators in a far from favourable light. And in the court case which ensued, the threatening behaviour of the Burford men was not seen as sufficient cause to excuse the conduct of the Weirs. John and Robert Weir, not Muir or Cruden or any of the others, were on trial.

At the summer 1841 assizes, Chief Justice John Beverley Robinson presided in a civil action for trespass, assault, and false imprisonment which Muir brought against the Weirs. Robinson had some trouble reconciling the evidence presented by the witnesses, which he described as 'conflicting' and 'extremely contradictory.' He reported that 'the Jury gave a verdict, with £16 damages from which it seemed to me, that in their view of all the circumstances, they thought it right to look with some indulgence on the conduct of the defendants, and especially perhaps the elder Weir.' Robinson described Weir as 'a well known person in the District, having resided in the same place between 20 & 30 years, and being an old Magistrate, a wealthy farmer of steady character, and as I have always had reason to suppose a man generally respected.' The others involved in the case were 'spoken of by the witnesses as lawless and disreputable characters.' What follows is Robinson's view of the case, as expressed in his report:

I explained to the Jury that where a Magistrate is called upon to act in a remote country place, against such lawless characters as the two Muirs were stated to be, it is his duty not to suffer his authority to be treated with contempt, and the law to be overborne; because if he were remiss in that respect, his fellow subjects should not receive that protection in their persons and property which the law gives them a right to look for. If therefore it was true that the Plaintiff Muir being strongly suspected of acts of malicious mischief committed against his neighbours, and positively charged by one man with such an offence, shewed a disposition to defy a Magistrate, and peace officers; and if in consequence of others abetting him in his resistance he were encouraged to conduct himself with insolence, and to refuse submitting to the warrant, the magistrate was well justified in compelling him, by such means as were necessary, to go with the party as their prisoner, – that if they had merely bound Muir and conveyed him in the sleigh, or compelled him to walk – not treating him unreasonably, there would have been no ground of complaint – but that if he was made fast to the horse in the manner described and thus dragged along, though but for a short distance, I considered such a course altogether unjustifiable. – It might have occasioned a serious, and even a fatal injury to the man; and at any rate *it had an inhuman and revolting appearance; and was, in my opinion, a culpable excess of authority.*[27]

    The Jury, I suppose, agreed in this view of the case ... On the whole case I thought there was reason to regret that Mr Weir (the elder) under the influence probably of considerable provocation – acting in a country place – remote from assistance that he could depend upon, and against turbulent persons disposed to resist his authority, adopted, in the agitation of the moment, or at least assented to a proceeding which he could hardly have thought justifiable, upon slight reflection – but he quickly checked himself, and seemed to carry the apparent harshness no further than he may, on the instant have been warrantable ...

John Beverley Robinson considered the award of £16 damages a 'temperate verdict.'[28] The reaction of the Weirs was not recorded. Weir was forced, then, to pay damages to Muir. The chief justice of the colony expressed the view that Weir had committed a 'culpable excess of authority.' Those involved in the incident at Muir's arrest were found not guilty of assault and attempted rescue at quarter sessions, and Muir's initial trespass conviction was overturned.[29] When a new commission of the peace was issued in 1842, Weir's name was not on it.[30]

This account of events in Burford township sheds light on many issues relating to dispute resolution, the uses to which the criminal law was put, and popular attitudes towards the law in rural Upper Canada which I want to discuss here. Perhaps the most obvious point which the Burford story reveals is the weakness of the formal mechanisms of the law and its administration in a 'remote country place.' When faced with determined opposition to his authority, John Weir responded with the only option he felt he had left – the use of force.[31] Yet his order to tie Muir to the horse was regarded as beyond the scope of his authority; this view was shared by the group of local men who complained about Weir's actions as a magistrate and the chief justice of the colony, John Beverley Robinson.

That Weir's authority was so limited in the post-rebellion period is particularly interesting. John Weir was a Tory and had run in an Oxford County by-election in 1832 but was defeated by a radical candidate. Both John Weir and his son Robert had held commissions in the militia during the rebellion; John Weir was a major, Robert a lieutenant. Many inhabitants of Burford township were 'wholly disaffected, or so indifferent to the cause of the Government, as to remain inert in its support.' In the rebellion in western Upper Canada there was widespread support for the rebels in Burford and the neighbouring townships, and afterwards several inhabitants fled to the United States, 'and those still left behind mob the loyal men who turn out, to endeavour to intimidate them from doing their duty.' Areas of western Ontario remained disaffected after the rebellion; local justices were unable to secure information about the activities of traitors in the region because the inhabitants refused to reveal what they knew.[32] This is the climate in which John Weir was attempting to carry out his duties. A large segment of the local population refused to cooperate with him, and there was little he could do about it.

We see from the Burford story that John Weir expressed reluctance to take action against Cruden. He claimed that he preferred to avoid involvement because Cruden was a neighbour. Perhaps he was simply afraid. In a society in which most men – and some women, such as Mrs Cruden – were often armed, and regularly drunk,[33] recourse to the law may not always have been the most prudent course of action. In such a rural township as Burford, people depended on hunting, chopping wood, and farming to survive; these activities required tools or implements, which were readily turned to use as weapons. Butcher knives were wielded at the arrest; Thomson was threatened with pistols, a pitchfork, and a bottle; and Julia Higgins was struck with fire-tongs and a poker. The men who tried to prevent the arrest of Allan Muir had been slaughtering hogs and drinking 'freely.' Small wonder that John Weir was reluctant to act against such persons by himself. He was not alone: '"when I became a magistrate," recounted George Munro, "I used to go away to the woods when I heard there was a fight at a bee, and keep away till the blood had cooled down."'[34] Justices of the peace and the victims of assaults or threats may have decided to ignore the breach of law, simply because it could be dangerous to take action against local offenders.

The Burford story demonstrates that there were a variety of options available to Upper Canadians involved in disputes. In the Burford example, a series of disputes involving threats, assaults, trespasses, and damage to property were taken before several levels of both civil and criminal courts. Criminal cases of assault and civil cases of trespass were tried summarily by justices of the peace, who also bound the Crudens over to keep the peace. Magistrates tried cases of assault and attempted rescue at quarter sessions, where appeals of convictions from summary trials were also heard. A civil case was referred to in which Thomson sued Cruden to get the $46 change owing from his purchase of Cruden's farm. Arbitration was recommended; inaction was also suggested. The case of *Muir v. Weir* regarding the 'outrageous' arrest was tried at the civil assizes. A number of choices – extralegal, civil, and criminal – could be made by people who sought to resolve disputes, and the Burford experience demonstrates that ordinary Upper Canadians availed themselves of various options depending on the nature of the disputes in which they became involved and what they hoped to achieve by bringing their problems before legal officials.[35]

Where minor offences were concerned, it is likely that civil and criminal law intermingled in the minds of Upper Canadians. Some disputes could be taken before either kind of tribunal. Historians tend to write about civil and criminal law as if they were clearly distinct and separate from one another. But it is by no means clear that such distinctions were made by contemporaries.[36] The structure of the courts and the duties of judicial personnel reinforced a popular perception that the law was integrated, rather than clearly and narrowly categorized as civil or criminal. Throughout most of the Upper Canadian period, justices of the peace tried minor cases of both civil and criminal law. They tried administrative offences and minor criminal cases, particularly assaults. They sat in judgment in cases of petty trespass, a civil matter, after 1834. As commissioners of the courts of requests, they also heard minor civil causes. Even after 1833, when commissioners of the courts of requests were no longer required to be JPs, over half of the commissioners remained justices of the peace,[37] and petty sessions and courts of requests were often held concurrently.[38] District courts and courts of quarter sessions were also held at the same time. Some district court judges were JPs, and sometimes those same men acted as chairmen of quarter sessions. The same judges presided at the superior civil and criminal courts, the assizes, and the civil and criminal sessions were held concurrently. In addition, the same list of jurors served at concurrent civil and criminal courts. At all levels, then, the dichotomy between civil and criminal law would not have been particularly obvious to the ordinary person using these courts. At least where minor cases were concerned, the boundaries between civil and criminal law were possibly blurred; 'law' was probably all one to them.

The Burford story also demonstrates another aspect of the administration of the criminal law in Upper Canada: legal officials encouraged people to solve problems by means other than recourse to the courts. John Weir told Thomson that 'he had better leave all their differences to three respectable persons or even to one in preference to going to Law.' In rural areas prosecution could be particularly inconvenient and expensive if several people were required to travel some distance to attend court. The time and trouble could cause much hard feeling between neighbours. It was in the interest of the local JP to arrange or to encourage some alternative means of dispute resolution, particularly if the situation seemed likely to result in divisiveness in his neighbourhood.[39] There are signs that arbitration may have been relied upon at times to deal with disputes or that attempts were made to reconcile the two sides before proceeding further. D.B. Stephenson, a Prince Edward County JP, noted in his informations book that a number of cases were 'settled by parties' and did not proceed to trial. At least five of forty-five assault cases, four of twenty-nine relating to trespasses, and two of five regarding violations of labour regulations recorded in Stephenson's book were resolved in such a manner.[40] In Georgina township a Mr Joliffe was 'bound to keep the peace with the family for six months and signed a bond to abide by an arbitration.'[41] The practice of arbitration was probably widespread, but because it did not result in the production of documents, it remains largely hidden behind the looming presence of the better-documented criminal courts.

Even when complaints were acted upon, the action taken was frequently of the most minimal sort. A variety of options, which were more clearly integrated into the framework of criminal justice administration than arbitration or ignoring the transgression, were also available to victims and magistrates seeking resolutions to all but the most serious disputes.[42] Rather than proceeding to a criminal trial, the perpetrator of threatening or violent acts could be bound over in recognizance to keep the peace. This was what happened to the Crudens after Cruden had threatened Thomson with a pistol, swearing he would send him to hell, and on the same occasion threatened to batter Thomson's brains out with a bludgeon supplied by Mrs Cruden. The recognizance to keep the peace defused the hostility which could arise from a formal prosecution. Instead of requiring the transgressor to pay a penalty or suffer a punishment, the recognizance in effect gave the accused a second chance. He had to pledge a required amount, and find sureties to support his pledge, to secure his future good behaviour. Put more simply, he was in effect promising to behave in future, and if he failed to keep that promise, he would be required to forfeit a hefty sum. Recognizances could be effective in situations where relations between neighbours could be damaged by more formal proceedings. They demonstrated that there was no overt desire to punish the transgressor, but nevertheless conveyed the message that his behaviour would no longer be tolerated. For similar reasons, recognizances to keep the peace were sometimes used to try to curb the violence of husbands against their wives.[43]

When cases proceeded to criminal trials, many offences were characterized as minor ones when the charges could have been more serious. Innumerable cases of 'petty assault' which were tried summarily by justices of the peace, the lowest officials in the judicial hierarchy, could have been charged as acts of more serious violence. Some of the cases involving the Crudens demonstrate this point. The assaults on Thomson, and particularly the treatment of Julia Higgins, seem more sinister than 'petty.' There are numerous similar examples in which JPs tried summarily cases involving assaults with weapons or assaults causing injury. The following occurred in the Newcastle district: Andrew Thomson struck Joseph Faulkner behind the neck with a sickle and kicked him; Alexander Coulter, a constable, was hit with a club; a barber whacked a labourer with an axe-helve; Josias Hughes was fined for striking John Goodliffe over the arm and shoulder with a poker.[44] Each of these incidents could have resulted in serious injury to the victim, or even death. Many of these cases involving violent assaults with weapons could have been tried at higher tribunals. The desire to minimize the disruption of community relations which might result from the expenses and hostility involved in a court case, and the convenience of a local hearing, meant that the burden of enforcing the criminal justice system fell on the lowest rung in the ladder of that system, the justice of the peace, if acts of violence were to be brought into the judicial system at all.[45]

Evidence suggests that other types of cases were also undercharged; that is, they could have been tried as more serious offences, but were tried as lesser ones. For example, some cases of trespass could have been tried as more serious property offences. The Picton magistrate D.B. Stephenson took an information on a trespass case in September 1839, wherein the defendant carried away a pair of boots from the victim's shop. Similarly, on 30 April 1838, the same JP took information in another trespass case which involved the theft of a promissory note valued at over £2.[46] These offences could have been tried as larcenies, and the perpetrators could have been sent to jail. Again, victims and magistrates had a great deal of discretion in deciding how individual cases ought to be pursued. The nature of the offence was not the only criterion in these decisions. Other issues, such as the character of the persons involved, or the possible harmful effects to the community of formal prosecution, might have led victims and magistrates to undercharge the offence. The cost and trouble involved in taking cases to the assizes or quarter sessions were undoubtedly taken into account as well.

We have seen the ways in which Cruden and his friends apparently terrorized John Thomson. The people involved rarely acted alone; usually there were an intimidating number of them together. Moreover, they seem to have believed themselves immune from prosecution. When Thomson threatened to take them 'before the law,' he was laughed at. One of them boasted that 'Cruden would stand between them and all danger.' Burford township did not provide the only setting for such powerful local groups who believed themselves beyond the reach of the law. Michael Cross has described the activities of one such group, the Shiners, in the Ottawa Valley in the 1830s.[47] A group known as the 'swampers' operated east of Brantford, along with 'another desperate gang ... who met on public and market days and had it out with clubs and axe handles, often joining forces to club quiet citizens right and left.'[48] In north Durham township during the pioneer period, a group of local Orangemen called the 'Cavan Blazers' were said to be the 'social regulators.' One early settler of that region later commented that the Blazers' methods had a positive side: 'Now-a-days it is all law, law, law. If any little dispute occurs between neighbours, or if someone is acting in a manner injurious to the community, the magistrate and constable must be called in. 'The Blazers' settled all such matters in the early days without delay, without cost, and with less of ill-feeling than follows upon legal proceedings now. Not only that, but they made the punishment fit the crime in the case of men whose offences could not be reached in the ordinary way.'[49]

Some of these groups of less than law-abiding persons were outright criminal gangs. In the countryside, where authority figures were distant from one another and the township constabulary was less than efficient, criminal gangs could operate with relative ease. One such group was the Markham Gang, active northeast of Toronto in the late 1830s and early 1840s. In Bayham township, now in Elgin County, a gang of skilled marksmen, the Ribbles family, operated in the early 1830s and seem to have been involved in the murder of a constable there.[50] In some rural areas, then, local groups could rival the formal system of justice. For a time at least, these groups could wield a considerable amount of power.[51]

In Burford, the point at which the law and the populace interacted did not always result in peaceful compliance. Legal officials themselves were not immune from attack. We saw in Burford that special constable Robert Weir was threatened by four men and probably assaulted during the attempted arrest of Allan Muir. Again, Burford was not the only scene of violence against officers of the law. There were at least fifty incidents in which constables or bailiffs were assaulted or threatened in the Newcastle district from 1813 to 1840, a considerable number in a predominantly rural district.[52] Although over half of those charged with assaulting judicial officers in the execution of their duty were convicted, several others were acquitted. There was no guarantee that a prosecuting constable would succeed in his case. The punishment for such an offence was a fine, and it ranged from a minimal amount to several pounds. Unfortunately, we do not have information beyond the barest details for many of these cases. However, we do know that weapons were often used. Sticks, axes, clubs, guns, and whips were wielded against legal officials, or used to threaten them. In the most serious case, for which a six-month prison sentence was meted out and the convicted person was fined £2 plus costs, farmer Patrick Fox struck a bailiff, Clark Spalding, with a sword and tried to kill him.[53] Women were not absent from the list of attackers either; for instance, Mary Halloran was fined for threatening a constable and a witness with an axe.[54]

We know what the legal officials were trying to do in only eleven of these cases. In seven, the assaults were on constables attempting to levy distress warrants or writs of execution from the courts of requests; in other words, they were seizing property to settle debts or pay fines.[55] One case arose out of an attempt to bring in a couple charged with violating liquor licensing regulations.[56] Another occurred when a constable told a defendant to keep quiet in the courtroom.[57] In two cases, the constable was assaulted by men he was trying to arrest on felony charges. In one of these he was wounded so badly that 'his life was despaired of'; in that case the culprit 'absconded.' In the other one the assailant was illegally rescued from the clutches of judicial officials.[58]

Historians of crime and criminal justice in England have discussed the difficulties of local legal officials there. According to John Brewer, the extraordinary sensitivity of the seventeenth- and eighteenth-century English to any form of official interference made the execution of law a hazardous undertaking. Court records 'abound with indictments for assaults on magistrates, constables, churchwardens and bailiffs.'[59] Joan Kent has also discussed the violence or abuse which sometimes prevented constables from fulfilling their police duties.[60] Forced to mediate between 'two concepts of order,' that of state law and that of their village community, the local constable had to perform a delicate balancing act. If he tried to carry out his orders, he could find himself subject to local pressures, including violence.[61] Similar patterns seem to hold true for Upper Canada as well. We can see that 'two concepts of order' were at work in Burford township, and special constable Robert Weir found himself caught between the two when he tried to arrest Allan Muir.

English historians have pointed to another weapon available to the populace in their battles against the forces of state order: 'vexatious lawsuits' undertaken against constables or other officials in retaliation for their actions.[62] Upper Canadian judicial officials were exposed to this hazard of office as well. In the Burford case, Allan Muir initiated a lawsuit against the Weirs for the 'outrage' committed on him at his arrest. Their case was not viewed as 'vexatious' by the chief justice, John Beverley Robinson, however; as we saw, he considered Muir to have a legitimate grievance. Magistrates, constables, and other legal officials, such as sheriffs and bailiffs, could not act without limits. Their behaviour was scrutinized by those with whom they came into conflict. If their actions were seen to be excessive or in violation of their powers, their detractors did not hesitate to use the courts against them. In the Newcastle district, there were at least twenty such cases in quarter sessions and assizes between 1815 and 1840.[63] Some were classified as 'neglect of duty' or 'misdemeanour in conduct of office' charges. A presentment was found against a constable at the January 1818 quarter sessions for 'taking leather the property of John Randall without legal authority.' Probably an overzealous constable had found evidence of stolen goods without a search warrant. Not all of these cases were considered to be 'vexatious' and without foundation; some resulted in convictions. In January 1815 Philip Waldron of Percy township was fined £2 for neglecting his duty as a constable. Dennis Riordan was fined £2/10 upon conviction of misdemeanour in his office as constable in April 1821. Constable Samuel Potter was fined 25s upon his conviction for extortion at quarter sessions; he had 'got 11s 6d from the prosecutor by pretending to be a constable executing a process issuing out of the Courts of Request[s].'[64]

Although it must have been difficult to achieve convictions in cases initiated against constables or magistrates, many ordinary people nevertheless initiated cases against such legal officials. Perhaps they did not care if they won the case or not, but sought to humiliate the magistrate or constable, or cause him some considerable trouble. Their sense of grievance must have been real in some cases for them to risk having to pay the costs of trial if they lost, which they must have known was a likely outcome. Still, an unfavourable outcome for the prosecutor was not inevitable.[65]

There were other ways of registering protest against the decisions of judicial officials in addition to assaulting them or suing them. If members of the community felt strongly that a person had been convicted and fined unjustly, they sometimes banded together and chipped in to help the person pay the fine. Anne Langton noted in March 1840: 'We had a begging petition to-day ... this was on the levy of a fine with costs for selling whiskey without a licence. Every one seemed disposed to open their purse-strings, for though the man, of course, was wrong, his case seemed hard, because the fining magistrate is a tavern-keeper. Law is rather curiously carried on in this irregular country.'[66]

In Port Hope in the 1830s, hundreds of local men subscribed small sums (generally 2s 6d or 5s) to help pay a £212 damage assessment which arose from a case at the civil assizes.[67] Participation in such schemes was one way of protesting the court's decision and mitigating its effect on the convicted person. Another was to take such initiatives as harbouring fugitives. For some months the Moodies had a house guest who was hiding from the sheriff's officers; 'a warrant was out for his apprehension, which he contrived to elude during his sojourn with us,' remarked Susanna.[68]

Ordinary Upper Canadians regularly participated in another form of protest against their legal officials: complaint. The relationship between the ordinary person and the government was much more complex than might be expected in a system which has been described as 'totally un-representative.'[69] The farmers in the back township of Burford thought nothing of appealing directly to the highest officials to seek help in solving their local legal problem. Both Cruden and Muir wrote to the provincial secretary's office to complain about the actions of the magistrate John Weir. Thousands of people affixed their signatures to similar letters throughout the Upper Canadian period. Some even wrote to the colonial secretary in London, if they considered the colony's officials remiss in dealing with their complaints. Officials were inundated with petitions, letters, memorials, requests, and demands for investigations. Although Upper Canadian officials did not intervene directly in the Burford case, the inhabitants succeeded in bringing an unpopular magistrate to the lieutenant-governor's attention.[70]

Another factor which must be considered here is the role of the trial jury. In the Burford case, the local magistrates did convict Allan Muir, and had convicted Cruden on more than one occasion for minor of-fences, albeit apparently reluctantly. The outcomes of cases brought be-fore trial juries were more favourable to the local troublemakers. Upon appeal at quarter sessions, the conviction for trespass which began the Burford story was overturned; the jury found Muir not guilty. The four men charged with attempted rescue were all found not guilty at quarter sessions. At the civil assizes, the jury found that John and Robert Weir had acted improperly and assessed damages which they were re-quired to pay to Muir. Perhaps the members of the jury were sym-pathetic to the Crudens and their friends, or interpreted the evidence in some unexpected way. In the reform press of the 1820s and 1830s, one of the most often cited grievances involved jury selection. Reformers alleged that sheriffs routinely 'packed' juries with government suppor- ters. Despite this allegation, juries could not be relied upon to support the government. On occasion, the trial jury could be intransigent in protecting local interests and expressing local opinion.[71]

For example, at the Newcastle district assizes in 1824, the Port Hope collector of customs appeared as the chief prosecution witness in a civil case against William McIntosh. The case involved a violation of customs regulations; McIntosh had not reported his vessel at port as required by law. Smuggling may have been involved or suspected, and if so the offence could been tried in the criminal courts. The *Colonial Advocate* reported that 'The case was generally considered as a very hard one on the defendant, and had excited a good deal of feeling in the country.' In his summing up, Mr Justice Boulton instructed the jury 'to discard from their minds every thing like hardship on the part of the defendant, to consider merely the abstract question, whether a breach of the Rev- enue Law had been committed; and as this was admitted even by the defendant's counsel, to find for the Crown.' The jury deliberated for half an hour, and returned a verdict for the defendant. Justice Boulton was not pleased:

On this verdict being announced, the Jury was required by the Court to *assign their reasons* for finding such a verdict. This was objected to as altogether without precedent, by the defendant's counsel; but he was overruled by the Court, and the foreman then gave the reason why the jury found as they did.

After this, his lordship addressed the jury at great length, pointing out to them that their verdict was against law and evidence; that however hard the case, they should not let that influence them; that however improper the conduct of the custom-house officer had been, they should put it out of sight, and try the one question only – that of the infraction of the law ...

This went on for some time, and the defendant's counsel tried to in- terject, but was ordered to sit down. After several attempts to get him to sit down, the judge finally ordered the sheriff to take him out of court, but he refrained from doing so. Boulton resumed addressing the jury, 'pointing out the propriety of altering their verdict.' The jury re- mained unmoved. The defendant's counsel requested the judge to ac- quaint the jury that they could find a special verdict if they so chose. 'This he did; when the Jury retired with pen and ink; and after an absence of three hours, returned with a written paper, setting forth their reasons for ... their former verdict.' The defendant's counsel requested that the verdict be recorded. The judge replied, 'The Jury evidently labours under a mistake, as to the issue.' He 'went on,' and was interrupted by the defendant's counsel, who insisted the verdict be recorded. 'His Lordship requested him not to interrupt the Court, and was going on to address the Jury again, when the Foreman informed him that he could not satisfy his conscience in no [sic] other manner than by the present verdict ... and that he would starve to death before he would alter his verdict.'[72] Finally Boulton gave up. The verdict was recorded. Trial juries, then, were not always intimidated by august personages, and could defy them openly in protection of local interests. In the above case at the assizes, the jury was probably composed of men of some local standing. Even they acted to further the local interests rather than those of the central authorities.

In this paper I have identified several characteristics which describe the way the inhabitants of Burford used the law, and which seem to hold true elsewhere in rural Upper Canada. The Burford story revealed a number of factors: the probable integration of civil and criminal law in the minds of ordinary people, at least with regards to less serious offences; attempts to ignore offences or to use arbitration to settle disputes rather than proceed to trial; the use of recognizances to keep the peace; the undercharging of offences; the existence of informal authority structures attempting to enforce local codes of order; and the ignoring, suing, criticizing, or attacking of legal officials. The laws were used by ordinary Upper Canadians in a variety of ways. Also, trial juries may have been influential in protecting local interests from central authorities.

The Burford story also unearths an undercurrent of violence in everyday life in the township, which authorities representing the formal legal system seem to have been powerless to stop. The need to examine rural societies in greater detail is evident, particularly because agrarian grievances were important factors in the formation of political opposition in Upper Canada, and the myth of bucolic agrarian life was so dear to the hearts of colonial administrators and immigration propagandists. Settlers, particularly those in frontier townships, lived lives of great hardship and frustration. The gap between expectation that the 'myth of the poor man's country' engendered, and the boredom, isolation, illness, incessant labour, and desperation which accompanied settlement,[73] created tensions peculiar to rural areas. Resentment of those with property and social pretensions, such as the local magistrate, may have been behind the hostility to John Weir, and even to the 're-spectable' John Thomson.[74] Hardship and a sense of grievance could easily spill over into violence such as that in Burford; desperation might explain the actions of the Crudens, the Muirs, and their friends.[75] These attitudes may have hardened in the aftermath of the rebellion.

And what does the Burford story reveal about popular attitudes to-wards the law? The picture is, not surprisingly, somewhat contradictory. On the one hand, the law was sometimes used by the Burford inhab-itants to further their own interests; they used it when it was to their advantage, as Muir's suing Weir at the civil assizes demonstrates. On the other hand, as Robinson described their actions in his report on the case, they behaved in a generally 'lawless' fashion. They did not react favourably when 'the law' was invoked against them. Their view of the formal judicial system seems ambivalent, if not overtly hostile. Moreover, Muir and Cruden exhibited some consciousness of their rights under the law. Muir complained about the 'outrage' of his arrest, and his view was upheld by the chief justice. Cruden complained about the 'tyrannical and overbearing' character of Magistrate Weir. Whether they initiated their campaign against Weir out of spite and personal dislike, out of resentment over events which occurred during and after the rebellion, or out of a genuine sense of grievance at Weir's actions as a magistrate we will never know for certain. What we do know is the result: Weir's behaviour was castigated, he was found guilty of using excessive force, and his name was omitted from the commissions list in 1842, probably to his relief.

The operation of the legal system in Upper Canada, then, seems to have been a more flexible process than is often perceived. Historians have assumed that power granted by the state through its appointment of magistrates was meaningful in the localities.[76] Family Compact–appointed magistrates acted as agents in the townships, enforcing government interests and reporting back to the centre. According to this view, the Family Compact resembles a powerful octopus, with its tentacles reaching into every corner of the colony, into even the most remote rural township.[77] But this is not the picture revealed to us in the Burford story; the tentacles did not reach there. When we look at the way the law operated in Burford, state-sanctioned authority re-sembles a jellyfish rather than an octopus. When removed from its ele-ment, the puffed-up compact ideology, based on leadership by 'superior men,' floundered and deflated. In Burford, formal state law and formal legal institutions could be manipulated according to the vagaries of community power. Cruden and Muir were the powerful figures here; Weir may have been the authority figure representing the formal legal system, but he was only marginally powerful. In between fell Thomson, seeking solutions to disputes through the local magistrate, but unable to find them when faced with determined community opposition.[78]

The people of Burford were far from the powerless individuals described by some historians of Upper Canada.[79] They knew what their interests were, and they were active, forceful, clever, and even violent in furthering them. The Burford story demonstrates that, without popular support, local officials found it difficult if not impossible to carry out their duties without reprisal. Members of the community helped to shape their own destinies; they were not simply impotent in the face of the state-sanctioned authority of the local magistrates.

NOTES

For their comments on an earlier version of this paper I thank my co-editors, Jim Phillips and Tina Loo, as well as John Beattie, Bob Lewthwaite, Peter Oliver, Paul Romney, the members of the Early Canadian History Group and Legal History Group at the University of Toronto, and especially Howard Baker and Jerry Bannister.

1 Archives of Ontario (hereinafter AO), RG8-23, Provincial Secretary Records, Pre-Confederation Correspondence, box 1, 26 May 1832–23 Jan. 1840, file entitled 'January 8, 1840,' deposition of John Thomson, 18 Dec. 1839. The documents relating to this case are all located in this file, and the full reference will be omitted hereinafter. When quoting from the documents, I have regularized the spellings of names and the punctuation; otherwise they are quoted verbatim.

2 J.A. Sharpe has noted that an understanding of the 'social milieu,' the interpersonal relations that preceded formal court action, is essential to understanding crime and, by extension, the operation of the criminal justice system: *Crime in Early Modern England, 1550–1750* (London and New York: Longmans 1984) 73.

3 Several historians have explored the issue of violence in Ontario history in recent decades. However, they have tended to concentrate on urban violence, labour-related violence, violence by political elites, and sectarian violence; often two or more of these categories overlap in individual studies.

Some authors who purport to examine violence in 'Upper Canada' actually focus on the post-union period. This study differs in its exploration of rural violence in agrarian communities before 1841. The literature on violence in early- to mid-nineteenth-century Ontario includes F.H. Armstrong 'The York Riots of March 23, 1832' *Ontario History* 55 (1963) 61–72; Ruth Bleasdale 'Class Conflict on the Canals of Upper Canada in the 1840s' *Labour/Le travailleur* 7 (1981) 9–39; Michael Cross 'Stony Monday, 1849: The Rebellion Losses Riots in Bytown' *Ontario History* 63 (1971) 177–90; Cross 'Violence and Authority: The Case of Bytown' in D.J. Bercuson and L.A. Knafla, eds. *Law and Society in Canada in Historical Perspective* (Calgary: University of Calgary Press 1979) 5–22; Cross 'The Shiners' War: Social Violence in the Ottawa Valley in the 1830s' *Canadian Historical Review* 54 (1973) 1–26; Cross 'The Laws Are like Cobwebs: Popular Resistance to Authority in Mid-Nineteenth Century British North America' in T.G. Barnes et al., eds. *Law in a Colonial Society: The Nova Scotia Experience* (Toronto: Carswell 1984); G.S. Kealey 'The Orange Order in Toronto: Religious Riot and the Working Class' in G. Kealey and P. Warrian, eds. *Essays in Canadian Working Class History* (Toronto: McClelland and Stewart 1970); W.T. Matthews 'The Myth of the Peaceable Kingdom: Upper Canadian Society during the Early Victorian Period' *Queen's Quarterly* 94/2 (Summer 1987) 383–401; Paul Romney 'From the Types Riot to the Rebellion: Elite Ideology, Anti-legal Sentiment, Political Violence, and the Rule of Law in Upper Canada' *Ontario History* 79/2 (June 1987) 113–44; John Weaver 'Crime, Public Order, and Repression: The Gore District in Upheaval, 1832–1851' *Ontario History* 78/3 (Sept. 1986) 175–207; Carol Wilton '"A Firebrand amongst the People": The Durham Meetings and Popular Politics in Upper Canada' (unpublished paper, April 1992).

4 As Donald Akenson points out, historians should 'look ... at customary law, that is, the actual practices which prevailed at the local level': *The Irish in Ontario: A Study in Rural History* (Kingston and Montreal: McGill-Queen's University Press 1984) 105.

5 While historians have written a great deal about elite ideology in Upper Canada, they have neglected popular attitudes towards the law. Greg Marquis notes this lacuna in 'Doing Justice to "British Justice": Law, Ideology, and Canadian Historiography' in W.W. Pue and B. Wright, eds. *Canadian Perspectives on Law and Society: Issues in Legal History* (Ottawa: Carleton University Press 1988) 44, 59. Marquis also cautions historians not to neglect the countryside: ibid. 59.

6 Muir's actions were characterized legally as trespass. Under 2 Wm. IV [1834], c. 4, 'An Act to provide for the summary punishment of Petty Trespasses, and other offences,' individual magistrates were given the jurisdic-

tion to try cases involving petty trespasses and assaults. The punishments they could assess were limited to £5 fine, or £5 damages in trespass cases involving damage to property. Appeals to quarter sessions were possible. Magistrates did not always try such cases alone, however; often they acted together in small groups of two or three. The ways in which magistrates carried out their duties under this act are discussed at greater length in my PhD dissertation, 'The Justices of the Peace in Upper Canada' (University of Toronto, forthcoming, 1994) chap. 5.

The following account of events appears in two written statements by John Weir to S.B. Harrison, n.d., 1840, except where noted. Weir's description of Muir's arrest was supported by Robert Weir, John Thomson, and the innkeeper of the Burford Exchange, John Wilmine, each of whom signed depositions on 27 January 1840. The documents upon which this account is based are all located in the file in the records of the provincial secretary, the full reference for which was provided above in note 2. The file was initiated when two persons, William Cruden and Allan Muir, wrote to that official to complain about the actions of Magistrate John Weir and his son Robert Weir, the special constable. John Weir responded to the accusations against him, and he secured substantiating statements from his supporters and friends. At least two differing views of the events described are thus contained in the file – those of the Weirs and their supporters, and those of their detractors. The point of entry into this account of the Burford story is the arrest of Allan Muir on the trespass charge with which this paper began. The ways in which John Weir's behaviour is described are of particular interest here.

7 It is not clear whether Robert Weir was appointed a special constable specifically to execute this warrant, or whether he had been appointed previously. We shall see that Allan Muir implied the former. According to John Weir, however, Robert had acted as such 'on several previous occasions.'

8 John Beverley Robinson's report on the case provided the explanation for the presence of the knives; he also noted that they had been drinking freely: 23 July 1841.

9 Details of this account of events on the day following Muir's initial arrest appear in Weir to Harrison, n.d.: depositions of John Wilmine, Robert Weir, and John Thomson before George W. Whitehead, 27 Jan. 1840.

10 Muir's account appears in Allan Muir to S.B. Harrison, 8 Jan. 1840.

11 Robert Weir and John Wilmine supported John Weir's statement that Allan Muir had refused to enter into recognizance: depositions dated 27 Jan. 1840.

12 According to Robert Weir and John Wilmine, both of whom were apparently at the inn on the evening in question, Muir had taken a bed at the Burford Exchange; depositions dated 27 Jan. 1840.

13 According to John Weir, Allan Muir had said nothing about his lameness at the time.

14 William Cruden to S.B. Harrison, 7 Jan. 1840

15 John Weir seems to have been aware of Cruden's motives; he describes Julia Higgins as 'an apprentice as *Mr. Cruden says* but never apprenticed to him[;] she was apprenticed to the slag making business from the poor House in London' and had been enticed away by Mrs Cruden (italics in original). As Sean Cadigan has pointed out, 'the image of the master encouraged identification between the different status groups of Upper Canadian society, from labourers ... to Executive Councillors.' By bringing attention to his 'apprentice,' Cruden identified himself as a master, probably expecting that the colonial officials would identify more closely with him and pay greater heed to his complaint. Sean T. Cadigan 'Paternalism and Politics: Sir Francis Bond Head, the Orange Order, and the Election of 1836' *Canadian Historical Review* 72/3 (1991) 321–2.

16 Cruden stated that the heavy fine was inflicted by Weir, contrary to the opinion of the other magistrate, who thought 5s a sufficient penalty. Cruden's recollection does not seem to agree with that of Whitehead, as we shall see. William Cruden to S.B. Harrison, 7 Jan. 1840; George W. Whitehead to John Weir, 1 Feb. 1840.

17 Muir and Cruden may have used the services of a lawyer to help them formulate their complaints, but I have found no clear evidence that they did so.

18 The role of the magistrate was considered essential in the preservation of order, according to elite ideology. The popular image of the law was created and sustained in large measure by justices of the peace. Moreover, JPs were supposed to provide leadership in their localities, and particularly to rule by example. Donald McMahon has observed in his discussion of John Beverley Robinson, 'To fix the fairmindedness of the law firmly in the public mind could only legitimate it ... in the face of all critics.' Magistrates who did not fulfil these functions, according to the ideas of men like Robinson, posed a threat to the legitimacy of legal and political institutions, and to a hierarchical social structure based upon character, property, and intelligence (in the absence of a hereditary landed aristocracy). Donald J. McMahon 'Law and Public Authority: Sir John Beverley Robinson and the Purposes of the Criminal Law' *University of Toronto Faculty of Law Review* 46/2 (1988) 390–423. See also David Howes 'Property, God and Nature in the Thought of Sir John Beverley Robinson' *McGill Law Journal* 30/3 (1985) 397 for Robinson's views on meritocracy; Patrick Brode *Sir John Beverley Robinson: Bone and Sinew of the Compact* (Toronto: The Osgoode Society and University of Toronto Press 1984); Robert Fraser '"All the Privileges Which Englishmen Possess": Order, Rights, and Constitutionalism in Upper Canada' in Robert Fraser, ed.

Provincial Justice: Upper Canadian Legal Portraits (Toronto: The Osgoode Society and University of Toronto Press 1992) xxi–xcii.

19 The petition and affixed signatures are not located in this file, but the number is referred to in S.B. Harrison to William Pitman, Esq, 7 Apr. 1840. The full petition, complete with several pages of signatures which indeed number close to 240, can be found in Upper Canada Sundries, vol. 240, Inhabitants of Burford to the Lieutenant-Governor, 7 Feb. 1840. The petition itself is illegible but most of the signatures can be read. William Cruden's name leads the petition's signatories. Interestingly, those who signed the petition did not seek those of elevated social standing to lead the signatures; self-described farmers and tradesmen compose the entire list. The large number of signatures Cruden was able to obtain suggests that there may have been a political connection here. Weir was a Tory, and Burford was strongly radical in sympathies; Charles Duncombe had lived in Burford prior to the rebellion. Cruden probably called upon local opposition forces for support. See Colin Read and R.J. Stagg *The Rebellion of 1837 in Upper Canada* (Ottawa: Champlain Society with Carleton University Press 1989) lviii, 428.

20 The colonial officials concluded that no inquiry was necessary; 'the charges in question properly appertain to the disposal of the legal tribunals of the Country': Harrison to Cruden and Harrison to John Weir, 15 Feb. 1840.

21 Examination of Julia Higgins before John Weir and William Whitehead, in the presence of the Crudens, 13 Feb. 1839. When asked her age at the examination, Julia Higgins said 'she has understood from Mrs. Cruden that she is nearly twenty years of age.'

22 George W. Whitehead to John Weir, 1 Feb. 1840. Whitehead had been so outraged by this incident that he found it impossible to believe that William Cruden should dredge it up; he wrote: 'It would have been much better for Mr. Cruden had he burned his communication before forwarding it to the Government office.' Should Cruden persist in his insinuations and accusations against Weir, Whitehead continued, he would recommend that the local magistrates have Cruden bound over to the assizes to stand trial for 'a foul and wicked conspiracy.'

23 Weir to Harrison, n.d.

24 Whitehead to Weir, 1 Feb. 1840

25 John Thomson to John Weir, n.d., 1840[?]

26 Thomson to Weir, n.d.

27 Emphasis added

28 John Beverley Robinson to Harrison, 23 July 1841

29 The four men who attempted to rescue Muir were indicted at the January 1840 quarter sessions, and bound over to the April sessions to answer two

charges: assault upon the special constable and attempted rescue. All were found not guilty by the jury. Muir appealed the initial trespass conviction, which was overturned at the January 1840 quarter sessions, where Muir was found not guilty. AO, RG22, ser. 61, vol. 9, London Quarter Sessions Minute Books, 1839-40.

30 R. Cuthbertson Muir *The Early Political and Military History of Burford* (Quebec: Cie d'imprimerie commerciale 1913) 74. It is possible that the author was a descendant of the Muirs described in this account. Weir may have requested that his name be omitted from the new commission of the peace, but I have found no evidence to suggest that this was the case.

31 The impotence of appointed legal officials was by no means unique to Burford township. Michael Cross has described a similar pattern in 'The Shiners' War.' Violence was not the only option chosen by a powerless JP; a Bytown magistrate, G.W. Baker, offered his resignation in June 1835, 'in light of the futility of attempting to check the Shiners with the feeble forces available': ibid. 2.

32 The results of the election of 1832 are described in Brian Dawe *'Old Oxford Is Wide Awake!' Pioneer Settlers and Politicians in Oxford County, 1793-1853* (Woodstock, Ont.: private printing, 1980) xxx. Militia list in Muir *The Early ... History of Burford* 277. References to disaffection in Burford cited in Read and Stagg, eds. *The Rebellion of 1837 in Upper Canada* 424-5, 427; difficulties of local justices in Colin Read *The Rising in Western Upper Canada, 1837-8: The Duncombe Revolt and After* (Toronto: University of Toronto Press 1982) 137. For post-rebellion disaffection in Western Ontario see Fred Landon *Western Ontario and the American Frontier* (Toronto: McClelland and Stewart 1967) 165-7, 172.

33 For alcohol consumption, see M.A. Garland and J.J. Talman 'Pioneer Drinking Habits and the Rise of the Temperance Agitation in Upper Canada prior to 1840' Ontario Historical Society *Papers and Records* 27 (1931); Matthews 'Myth of the Peaceable Kingdom' 390-1; Weaver 'The Gore District in Upheaval' 183-4; Cheryl Krasnick Warsh, ed. *Drink in Canada: Historical Essays* (Montreal and Kingston: McGill-Queen's University Press 1993). Many contemporary commentators noted that drunkenness was rampant.

34 Quoted in Edwin C. Guillet *Pioneer Days in Upper Canada* (Toronto: University of Toronto Press 1933) 133

35 Civil actions, if successful, generally involved payment of compensation for damages or injury; criminal actions, if successful, resulted in some form of punishment of the perpetrator. Criminal sanctions were probably more humiliating than civil, although both could be costly. Political interests were sometimes factors in prosecutorial decision-making; Paul Romney has noted that 'defects in the system of criminal prosecution could occasionally be

avoided by recourse to civil actions ... [In the case of the types riot] civil proceedings had seemed preferable to the aggrieved party because criminal proceedings in the appropriate court were subject to the control of a political partisan, the attorney-general': Romney 'From the Types Riot to the Rebellion' 131.

36 Early legal history was written by lawyers, who may have imposed their own legalistic classifications upon their writings about the past. The underdeveloped nature of the field of Canadian legal history is also responsible; much legwork is still required in both civil and criminal justice administration before a more integrated picture can be compiled. For civil courts in Upper Canada see J.H. Aitchison 'The Courts of Requests in Upper Canada' *Ontario History* 41 (1949); Howard Baker 'Small Claims, Communal Justice and the Rule of Law in Kingston, Upper Canada, c. 1785–1819' (LLM thesis, York University 1992); William N.T. Wylie 'Arbiters of Commerce, Instruments of Power: A Study of the Civil Courts in the Midland District, Upper Canada, 1789–1812' (PhD dissertation, Queen's University 1980); Wylie 'Instruments of Commerce and Authority: The Civil Courts in Upper Canada 1789–1812' in D.H. Flaherty, ed. *Essays in the History of Canadian Law: Volume II* (Toronto: The Osgoode Society and University of Toronto Press 1983) 3–48. The social historian should be aware of the advantages of examining and cross-linking records from both civil and criminal courts; the Burford story would not be nearly so revealing if it were incomplete.

37 The lists of names of Home District justices of the peace and commissioners of the courts of requests for the period 1834 to 1840 were compared.

38 Early Augusta township courts of requests minutes were occasionally interrupted by accounts of trials involving violations of liquor licensing regulations: AO, Solomon Jones Papers, MU1623.

39 Arbitration was often used in civil cases; see Baker 'Small Claims, Communal Justice and the Rule of Law' chap. 5. Several examples can be found in the Augusta township courts of requests minutes, AO, Solomon Jones Papers, MU 1623. The paperwork for a case in which arbitration was used to settle a dispute over debt and landownership can be found in AO, the Smith and Chisholm Papers, MU 2847, V, Justice of the Peace Records, env. 7, 1829–56; the file title is dated '10 May 1834.' Certain religious organizations encouraged arbitration to minimize the potential hostility between disputants; see, for example, Cecilia Morgan 'Gender, Religion, and Rural Society: Quaker Women in Norwich, Ontario, 1820–1880' *Ontario History* 82 (1990) 273–87.

40 AO, RG 22, ser. 86, Picton General (Quarter) Sessions, Miscellaneous Records, 1834–9, Informations book of D.B. Stephenson

41 AO, MS18, William Johnson diary, 5 Jan. 1844
42 These options have been explored at length in the early modern English context in Robert B. Shoemaker *Prosecution and Punishment: Petty Crime and the Law in London and Rural Middlesex, c. 1660–1725* (Cambridge and New York: Cambridge University Press 1991).
43 Examples can be found in the records of the Newcastle district; for instance, in April 1836, Thomas Lockhart of Smith township, farmer, was bound over in recognizance to keep the peace, particularly towards Mary Lockhart, his wife: AO, RG22, ser. 32, Cobourg General (Quarter) Sessions of the Peace, Filings, box 4, env. 2, 1836(1).
44 AO, RG22, ser. 39, Cobourg General (Quarter) Sessions, Convictions by Justices of the Peace, box 1; Andrew Thomson and Henry Cryderman defendants, env. 1 (1834); Thomas James, env. 4, 1836(1); Josias Hughes, env. 7, 1837(2)
45 J.M. Beattie has pointed out that these factors discouraged prosecution in early modern England; he emphasizes the importance of the decisions of victim-prosecutors: *Crime and the Courts in England 1660–1800* (Princeton: Princeton University Press 1986) 21, 35–48. Similar factors in the Upper Canadian setting are discussed in Lewthwaite 'Justices of the Peace.'
46 AO, RG22, ser. 86, Picton General (Quarter) Sessions, Miscellaneous Records, 1834–9, Informations book of D.B. Stephenson at dates cited
47 Cross 'Shiners' War'
48 J.J. Hawkins 'Early Days in Brantford' in AO, 'Some of the papers read during the years 1908–1911 at Meetings of the Brant Historical Society' (n.d.), 51
49 W. L. Smith *The Pioneers of Old Ontario* (Toronto: George N. Morang 1923) 320. A playwright from Cavan township recently produced a play about the Blazers. According to local legend, the Blazers burned to the ground a Catholic shanty settlement in the township in the 1820s. Playwright Robert Winslow says that the Blazers were so effective at discouraging Catholic settlers in Cavan that there are virtually no Catholics in the township to this day. Typescript 'The Cavan Blazers,' third draft, 1991. I thank Robert Winslow for giving me a copy of his script. See also Brian Greer 'The Cavan Blazers' in Quentin Brown, ed. *This Green & Pleasant Land: Chronicles of Cavan Township* (Millbrook, Ont.: Millbrook and Cavan Historical Society 1990) 34–8.
50 Reference to the Ribbles family in John D. Blackwell 'Crime in the London District, 1828–1837: A Case Study of the Effect of the 1833 Reform in Upper Canadian Penal Law' *Queen's Law Journal* 6/2 (Spring 1981) 552
51 English historians have described the activities of organized gangs of crimi-

nals (usually robbers); see, for example, Ruth Paley 'Thief-takers in London in the Age of the McDaniel Gang, c. 1745–1754' in Douglas Hay and Francis Snyder, eds. *Policing and Prosecution in Britain, 1750–1850* (Oxford: Clarendon Press 1989) 302–40; Beattie *Crime and the Courts* 252–63. For local groups which could rival formal systems of justice, see E.P. Thompson *Whigs and Hunters: The Origin of the Black Act* (New York: Pantheon Books 1975). Smuggling was one of the primary activities which involved the complicity of local people in resistance to attempts to regulate their behaviour; see Cal Winslow 'Sussex Smugglers' in E.P. Thompson et al. *Albion's Fatal Tree: Crime and Society in Eighteenth Century England* (New York: Pantheon Books 1975): 'They all say that there is no force in the country, the smugglers will do as they please,' 145. Upper Canadian smugglers behaved similarly; see Akenson *Irish in Ontario* 104–5.

52 In several of these cases, the assaults occurred when a constable or bailiff attempted to seize property to settle debts or pay fines or costs arising from some legal action. Again, the civil and criminal law are intertwined in such cases. Frequently a civil action preceded the seizure of property; criminal action followed the assault on the official.

The population of the Newcastle district was approximately as follows: 1824, 9292; 1830, 14,850; 1835, 25,000; 1840, 30,000. AO, RG22, ser. 134, General (Quarter) Sessions of the Peace, Cobourg (Newcastle District) Quarter Sessions Minute Books, 1824 and 1830. The 1835 and 1840 estimates are from Morgan Jellett *Index to the By-laws ... of Northumberland and Durham* (Cobourg 1857) 37–9. The district was about 1100 square miles in area. Settlement was densest in the townships along the lake front.

These fifty-odd incidents were complained of to magistrates, and prosecutions were initiated against the perpetrators. It is likely that there were more. Factors which discouraged prosecution were noted above. Constables may have had further disincentive to prosecute their attackers: by announcing their inability to carry out their duties smoothly, they risked falling into disrepute with local magistrates. Similarly, they may have risked ridicule and a loss of legitimacy in the eyes of their neighbours. In other words, it was not in their interest to advertise the difficulties they experienced. I owe this insight to Susan Beattie.

It should be noted that Newcastle District was regarded by officials as essentially 'loyal.' Despite its difference in character from Burford township, which was reportedly openly disaffected, similar trends in judicial administration occurred in both places.

53 AO, RG22, ser. 31, Cobourg General (Quarter) Sessions Case Files, box 1, env. 6

54 AO, RG22, ser. 39, Convictions by Justices of the Peace, box 1, env. 6. John

Beattie has noted that a number of women were brought to court in Surrey for assaulting officers in the course of their duty. Defence of family and personal interests occasionally included defiance of authority, according to Beattie: J.M. Beattie 'The Criminality of Women in Eighteenth-Century England' *Past and Present* 8 (1975) 88.

55 These seven cases are in AO, RG22, ser. 31, Cobourg General (Quarter) Sessions Case Files. The following description of these cases contains the name of the defendant, the year in which the case was tried, the outcome of the trial, and the location of the material relating to the case. Jediah Irish, 1813, £5, box 1; David White, 1818, £10, box 3; Peter Bice, 1819, 5s and two weeks imprisonment, box 3; Alexander and Sally Allen, 1830, no bill, box 9; John, Simon and Stephen Lee, 1832, 5s each, box 10; Timothy and Mary Donaghue, 1838, Timothy guilty and bound over to keep the peace, Mary not guilty, box 12; Lewis Drew, 1839, not guilty, box 13.

56 Flora and John Taylor, 1836, no bill, box 12

57 John Walker, 1839, 10 days in jail: RG 22, ser. 39, Convictions by justices of the peace, box 1, env. 10

58 Thomas Sheehan, 1830, RG22, ser. 31, General (Quarter) Sessions Case Files, box 9. The other case was Joel Stone, 1830, no bill, box 9; the file is mistitled 'William Robertson.' The information that Sheehan absconded was noted in RG 22, ser. 29, Quarter Sessions Minutes, Apr. 1831.

59 John Brewer 'An Ungovernable People?' *History Today* 30 (1980) 22

60 Joan Kent *The English Village Constable, 1580–1642* (Oxford: Clarendon Press 1986) 253–61

61 Keith Wrightson 'Two Concepts of Order: Justices, Constables and Jurymen in Seventeenth Century England' in John Brewer and John Styles, eds. *An Ungovernable People: the English and Their Law in the Seventeenth and Eighteenth Centuries* (London: Hutchinson 1980) 40–4; Joan Kent 'The English Village Constable, 1580–1642' *Journal of British Studies* 20/2 (1981) 28–9; J.A. Sharpe *Crime in Early Modern England* 76–7; Kent *The English Village Constable* 253–61

62 Brewer 'An Ungovernable People?' 22; Kent *The English Village Constable* 261–3; Douglas Hay 'Prosecution and Power: Malicious Prosecution in the English Courts, 1750–1850' in Douglas Hay and Francis Snyder, eds. *Policing and Prosecution in Britain, 1750–1850* (Oxford: Clarendon Press 1989), 343–95

63 There were likely many more. The only ones I have included here specified such charges in the quarter sessions minutes. There were many other cases in which individuals who were constables were defendants.

64 These cases appear in RG22, ser. 29, Cobourg General (Quarter) Sessions Minutes, at the dates cited. The details of the Potter case are in ser. 31, Quarter Sessions Case Files, box 4.

65 Ruth Paley observes of mid-eighteenth-century London thief-takers: 'Legal knowledge was a very powerful weapon indeed; coupled with a readiness to resort to physical violence it was not difficult to create a general impression of virtual immunity from the sanctions of the law': 'Thief-takers in the Age of the McDaniel Gang' 313. This statement could be applied equally to the activities of Cruden and his friends in Burford, as could the following statement about early-nineteenth-century New South Wales, Australia: 'The non-elite in the colony also had a more intimate knowledge of the law than most. While prepared to mimic, mock and break the law, they also used it extensively against their masters, in civil litigation': David Neal *The Rule of Law in a Penal Colony: Law and Power in Early New South Wales* (Cambridge: Cambridge University Press 1991) 24.

66 Anne Langton, cited in H.H. Langton, ed. *A Gentlewoman in Upper Canada: The Journals of Anne Langton* (Toronto: Clarke, Irwin 1950) 122

67 Upper Canada Sundries, vol. 128, 70614-26, n.d. [1833]. The subscribers express regret at the result of a recent Newcastle King's Bench trial, at which two prominent citizens were found guilty of libel. About 440 persons signed these forms, some of which were printed up, and paid either 5s or 2/6 towards the £212 damages.

68 Susanna Moodie *Roughing It in the Bush* (Toronto: McClelland and Stewart 1962) 177-80. Her husband was appointed a sheriff shortly after this incident.

69 J.K. Johnson *Becoming Prominent: Regional Leadership in Upper Canada, 1791–1841* (Kingston and Montreal: McGill-Queen's University Press 1989) 64-5

70 The subject of complaints against magistrates is dealt with at greater length in Lewthwaite 'Justices of the Peace.'

71 This will be discussed in greater depth in John Beattie and Susan Lewthwaite 'Trial by Jury in Upper Canada' (forthcoming). Paul Romney has explored this topic in the Upper Canadian context in 'From Constitutionalism to Legalism: Trial by Jury, Responsible Government and the Rule of Law in the Canadian Political Culture' *Law and History Review* 7 (1989) 121-74.

72 *Colonial Advocate*, 4 Nov. 1824. For the English trial jury, see Thomas A. Green *Verdict according to Conscience: Perspectives on the English Criminal Trial Jury, 1200–1800* (Chicago: University of Chicago Press 1985); J.S. Cockburn and T.A. Green, eds. *Twelve Good Men and True: The Criminal Trial Jury in England, 1200–1800* (Princeton: Princeton University Press 1988).

73 A poignant expression of utter demoralization can be found in an anonymous diary of a Georgina township resident of the 1830s: 'Affairs along the lake show very much the same, misery and poverty being the usual habitans': AO, Log book and diary formerly in the possession of Sanderson

Brown, 1821–31, Women's Canadian Historical Society, ser. H, Historical Documents, H-1, diary entry dated 7 Nov. 1830.

74 Popular resentment of social pretensions was remarked upon by numerous contemporary commentators and might be considered a rural form of class conflict. This theme is explored in greater depth in Lewthwaite 'Justices of the Peace' chap. 3.

75 Paul Romney has pointed out the significance of the interests of agrarian smallholders in formulating political opposition in Upper Canada; he notes, for example, that the seizure of land for non-payment of debt probably went further to alienate farmers from the regime than any other aspect of the law: *Mr Attorney: The Attorney General for Ontario in Court, Cabinet, and Legislature, 1791–1899* (Toronto: The Osgoode Society and University of Toronto Press 1986) 77–80. For the importance of agrarian reform ideas, see also S.D. Clark *Movements of Political Protest in Canada, 1640–1840* (Toronto: University of Toronto Press 1959) and *Church and Sect in Canada* (Toronto: University of Toronto Press 1948). For the mythology of bucolic agrarianism in Upper Canada, see Robert Wolfe 'The Myth of the Poor Man's Country: Upper Canadian Attitudes to Immigration, 1830–7' (unpublished MA thesis, Carleton University 1976).

76 S.F. Wise, in a piece which remains influential, characterized Upper Canadian government under the Family Compact as 'a complex network joining officials at the capital to interest groups in every locality,' a system of alliances between the bureaucratic elite and local elites and their followings, cemented by patronage; 'Upper Canada and the Conservative Tradition' in *Profiles of a Province: Studies in the History of Ontario* (Toronto: Ontario Historical Society 1967) 26–7. The power structure described by Wise may have been true of the larger towns, where the presence of formal legal officials was more heavily felt and the proximity of courts and jails reinforced the authority of those officials, but it probably does not apply to the countryside.

77 In fairness, this monolithic view of the Family Compact has been toned down a bit in recent years. For example, S.J.R. Noel labels justices of the peace as 'agents of the central government,' but cautions that although the Family Compact dominated government at the centre, that by no means guaranteed that its political domination would extend to the local level in an unbroken line of command: *Patrons, Clients, Brokers: Ontario Society and Politics, 1791–1896* (Toronto: University of Toronto Press 1990) 49, 98–9.

78 There were a number of places in Upper Canada into which formal mechanisms of authority did not seem to penetrate. Michael Cross describes the Ottawa Valley in the 1830s as one such place, which he characterizes as a 'frontier,' 'a place which is distant from the forces of social order': 'The

Shiners' War' 12. The town of Brantford, near Burford, was another such place: 'the law abiding whites, few in number and helpless, had many trials to bear in what was really a turbulent, and, at times, lawless frontier village': Hawkins 'Early Days in Brantford' 51.

79 Read and Stagg, for example, write that 'the voice of the common man was muted indeed': *The Rebellion of 1837* xxii.

12

Crime and Punishment in Middlesex County, Ontario, 1871–1920

HELEN BORITCH

Responding to crime and punishing criminals are central and enduring tasks of every social order. At the same time, what is defined as a crime, and which behaviours and offenders are judged most severely, mirror social values and are historically specific. It is these dual aspects of crime – its constancy as a social phenomenon, and the changing nature of society's responses to it – which make the complex realm of criminal justice one of the most important means of shedding light on the larger social structure in which it is embedded. On the one hand, studies of crime and punishment in specific historical periods provide insights into the key values and defining characteristics of a society at a particular stage in its development. On the other hand, at a broader level, the history of criminal justice can serve as a conceptual device with which to examine the more elusive phenomenon of social change. Through the process of reform and innovation, every generation attempts to re-make its criminal justice system to conform to changing conceptions of crime, criminals, and punishment. Consequently, looked at over time, criminal justice records represent an important means of discerning change, as well as continuity, in the relationship between social values and social structure.

This study of crime and punishment in Middlesex County, Ontario, for the period 1871 to 1920 seeks to contribute to the growing body of historical research on criminal justice in Canada in several ways.

Using data drawn from the local prison registers, the analysis focuses broadly on those who made up the criminal population: their crimes, their social characteristics, and their treatment by the judiciary. The temporal framework for the study, the decades spanning the late nineteenth and early twentieth centuries, represents a departure from previous research, which typically has concentrated on the mid nineteenth century. The first objective, then, is to provide a collective portrait of the criminal population and an overview of the factors related to the severity of punishment for an, as yet, unexamined period. The second objective is to highlight patterns of continuity and change in the essential features of criminal justice over time. These issues are addressed in relation to the time span encompassed in this particular study, and also in the comparative context of research on earlier time periods. In order to provide a backdrop for the study, some of the dominant aspects of criminal justice in the mid nineteenth century, as well as the characteristics of the period under study, are briefly reviewed.

RESEARCH ON CRIME, CRIMINAL JUSTICE, AND REFORM

Although the last decade has seen a tremendous growth of historical research on crime and criminal justice in Canada, here as elsewhere, research has relied primarily on aggregate-level data to describe broad trends and transformations in crime and criminal justice over time. This concern is evidenced in a variety of ways, including research focusing on long-term trends in crime rates and studies detailing the origin and development of police forces, prisons, and other legal institutions.[1] As a result of this research, we are gaining a better understanding of the general contours of the development of criminal justice in Canada. Yet, as various authors note, one major limitation of this institutional focus or 'view from the top down' is that we still know little about the affected population of criminals or their treatment by the criminal justice system.[2]

Increasingly, like their counterparts in Great Britain, the United States, and Australia,[3] Canadian social historians have begun to make use of primary nineteenth-century data sources to study the criminal population, and to relate offender characteristics such as birthplace, sex, age, and occupation to the type of crime committed, and to the form and magnitude of punishment.[4] These studies differ considerably in terms of whether the level of analysis consists primarily of detailed biographies of the careers of individual offenders, or of more broadly based statistical surveys of the criminal population and criminal justice. However, as Graff points out, at whatever level of analysis, studies delineating 'disproportionate representation and disproportionate rates of conviction offer key insights into the mechanism of social differentiation, social visibility, social distance and community prejudice.'[5]

More specifically, while there is disagreement regarding a number of issues, a common theme which emerges from this research is the various ways in which the basic facts of social stratification during the early stages of industrialization and urbanization were reflected and reinforced in the day-to-day operations of the criminal justice system in the mid nineteenth century. In this regard, it is apparent that neither all offences nor all offenders were given equal treatment by the criminal justice system. Public order offences such as drunkenness and vagrancy, rather than violent or property crimes, predominated as the most common offences for which offenders were apprehended and prosecuted. Moreover, individual offender traits such as gender, occupation, and ethnic affiliation were systematically related to the type of crime for which an offender was arrested, as well as the severity of punishment meted out by the courts during this era. The disproportionate representation of certain groups, including the lower classes, Irish immigrants, and women, among those apprehended and dealt with most severely offers concrete examples of the larger structure of inequality during the early to mid nineteenth century.

In comparison, we know much less about the treatment of crime and criminals during the later stages of urbanization and industrialization. Consequently, a statistical analysis of crime, criminals, and punishment during the decades spanning the late nineteenth and early twentieth centuries would seem to be a logical chronological extension of existing research. In addition to broadening the temporal scope of existing research, this shift in focus makes it possible to assess whether the patterns documented in research on the mid nineteenth century with respect to the nature of crime, the social characteristics of criminals, and the factors related to the form and magnitude of punishment persisted or underwent significant changes during this later era.

Beyond this consideration, the decades from 1871 to 1920 encompassed in this study are of particular interest because of the profound economic and social changes in Canadian society brought about by rapid urbanization and industrialization, and also because of the many changes which occurred in the criminal justice system. As the weight of the economy shifted from agriculture toward industry and finance, the parallel processes of rural depopulation and urban expansion served to alter radically the demographic character of Canada. While some of the basic essentials of the urban system in central eastern Canada were established by the middle of the nineteenth century, it was in the late nineteenth and early twentieth centuries that the process of urban growth was most dramatic. Between 1881 and 1921, the urban population of Canada increased in absolute terms from 1.1 million to 4.3 million and, in proportionate terms, from one-quarter to one-half the total population.[6]

While, at one level, cities were regarded as the physical embodiment of progress, at another level, urban growth increasingly came to be seen as a major threat to traditional cultural patterns and expectations. By the 1880s and 1890s, as it became widely accepted that the social problems of modern society, including disease, poverty, and crime, were reaching crisis proportions, major reform efforts were launched to redeem the urban environment and purify city life. Over the course of the late nineteenth and early twentieth centuries, many different urban-related problems were sheltered under the umbrella of urban reform.[7] Yet, for the predominantly middle-class advocates of reform, much the most serious problem was the moral and social degradation of the urban poor as evidenced in the proliferation of houses of prostitution, gambling dens, saloons, opium dens, and other places offensive to bourgeois sensibilities.[8] While seeking to alleviate the real social problems engendered by poverty and slums, reform, nonetheless, clearly reflected the class presumptions of its advocates. Consequently, as various social historians note, the progressive rhetoric used to promote reform tends to obscure the fundamentally conservative intent of many reforms, the limited interest in achieving substantive changes, and the overriding concern with perpetuating 'a stratified society based upon traditional patterns of deference and morality.'[9]

At the level of criminal justice specifically, changes were instituted at every level of the system as part of the reform agenda. Embracing the time-honoured arguments of economy, effectiveness, humanitarianism, and a renewed emphasis on rehabilitation, advocates of reform sought to expand and intensify crime control efforts in a variety of ways. At the broadest level, the establishment of municipal police forces from the mid to late nineteenth century in most major Canadian cities and the opening of several new federal penitentiaries in the space of a decade from the 1870s to 1880s were significant developments.[10] More specific changes over the course of the late nineteenth and early twentieth centuries included legislative enactments to allow for indeterminate sentences, suspended sentences, and eventually probation; the diversification of the court system to include special courts and procedures for females and young offenders; and the establishment of separate correctional institutions intended to carry out comprehensive rehabilitation schemes for different types of offenders.[11]

Not surprisingly, what we know of criminal justice during this period, particularly in Ontario, comes largely from studies which have examined changes in discrete parts of the system and the consequences for the specific target groups of concern. There is, in this regard, a significant body of research which has analysed transformations in the means used to control particular problem populations and which includes studies detailing the origins and impact of new procedures for regulating juvenile offenders;[12] changes in the laws relating to prostitution and, more generally, the treatment of female offenders in the criminal justice system;[13] the creation of family courts as alternatives to the police courts for the handling of domestic cases;[14] and the emergence of an integrated system of social welfare institutions.[15] Consistent with critical assessments of the urban reform movement generally, much of this research focuses on the disparity between reform pronouncements and actual accomplishments. While advocates of various reform measures invariably promoted them as more humane, effective, and economical, they served mainly to enlarge the scope of official control efforts while continuing to serve the same traditional functions as earlier practices. As a consequence, the system retained its traditional emphasis on punitiveness and deterrence over rehabilitation as a primary objective.[16]

Important as this research is, the concern with reforms directed at specific types of offenders has tended to divert attention away from a more broadly conceived analysis of the criminal population and operations of the criminal justice system during this era. For despite the establishment of new courts and intermediate correctional facilities, the vast majority of offenders continued to be tried in police courts, sentenced to relatively short terms in prison, and incarcerated in local county jails. Focusing at this level of the criminal justice system, therefore, allows for the most comprehensive portrayal of the nature of crime, the social characteristics of criminals, and the punishment process in the late nineteenth and early twentieth centuries.

At the same time, the police courts and county jails which made up the lowest level of the criminal justice system did not operate in isolation from developments in the larger system, and the decisions made by the lower courts had implications beyond this level. For example, police magistrates had sole jurisdiction over most cases that came before them and their sentencing decisions were, therefore, a primary determinant of whether an offender was incarcerated in the county jail or transferred to one of the intermediate institutions established during the late nineteenth century. The few existing descriptive accounts of police courts during this period suggest that reforms and the renewed emphasis on rehabilitative goals had a negligible effect in changing traditional assumptions about crime and criminals, or methods of dispensing justice in the lower courts. But as Homel concludes in his study of the Toronto Police Court, 'only a statistical analysis of sentencing over a lengthy period' can determine whether the reform process was accompanied by the system becoming more or less punitive over time as measured, for example, by rates of convictions, prison sentences, and the treatment of offences and offenders traditionally dealt with most harshly.[17] This broad survey of trends in crime, criminals, and punishment in Middlesex County from 1871 to 1920 makes it possible to address systematically the issue of whether these decades represent a distinct period of transition, or one of fundamental continuity, in criminal justice.

THE PRISON REGISTERS OF MIDDLESEX COUNTY

Data for this analysis were constructed from the records of the Middlesex County Jail in Ontario which have been preserved for the period from December 1867 to September 1920.[18] Located in southwestern Ontario, Middlesex County and its administrative centre, the city of London, exemplify the processes of urbanization and industrialization which characterized the late nineteenth and early twentieth centuries. By the time of its incorporation as a city in 1855, London was one of the nine largest cities in Canada and the trade focus of a rich agricultural area. Spurred by the rapid growth of agriculture, London was simultaneously establishing itself as a growing and prosperous centre of industry, commerce, and transportation. In the mid to late nineteenth century, railway development contributed a further impetus to London's continued expansion, consolidating its place as the economic hub of southwestern Ontario.[19] As census data reveal, these developments served to alter radically the urban/rural distribution of the population in the period from 1871 to 1921 as the urban population of the county increased, in proportionate terms, from 18.5 per cent to 63.1 per cent, and London's population rose from 15,315 to 59,784. This demographic shift changed the occupational composition of the county as the proportion of its population employed in secondary and tertiary industries increased from 39.5 per cent to 66.9 per cent from 1871 to 1911.[20]

As the lowest level of the prison structure in Ontario, the county (common) jails held those arrested and awaiting the disposition of their case, convicted offenders serving sentences of two months or less, and convicted offenders awaiting transfer to other institutions.[21] In Middlesex County, as elsewhere, virtually all offenders first passed through this jail, regardless of final case outcome or place of incarceration. In addition to recording demographic information on offenders and their criminal histories, the jail registers provide an overview of the progress of cases through different levels of the criminal justice system. As various researchers have noted, despite the methodological problems involved in their use, the wealth of information they contain make them an invaluable resource for social historians interested in questions pertaining to the criminal population and criminal justice.[22]

Still, like all criminal justice data, jail registers are limited to crimes for which someone was arrested. Consequently, these data cannot be used to answer definitively questions about the true amount of crime in society, or the characteristics of all criminals. The number of prison committals does, however, provide an indication of the responses of the criminal justice system to crime, considerable information on those directly accused of having committed a crime, and judicial decisions in relation to these individuals.

Overall, the number of prison committals fluctuated considerably on a yearly basis, ranging from a low of 281 in 1869 to a high of 962 in 1889. As shown in the figure on page 394, the rate of prison committals per 100,000 population from 1868 to 1919 reveals the same pattern of sharp increases and steep decreases. For the period as a whole, there is no straightforward pattern of increase or decrease in prison committals. Rather, the rate increased to approximately the late 1880s, declined to the turn of the century, increased again to the start of World War I in 1914, and then dropped off. There is, by this simple measure at least, no indication of a uniform increase in concern with, or response to, crime for the period as a whole.

Although changes in prison committals, or any measure of crime, represent one important means of understanding a society's responses to social and economic upheavals, this is not the major issue of concern

Middlesex County Jail: rate of committals, 1868–1919

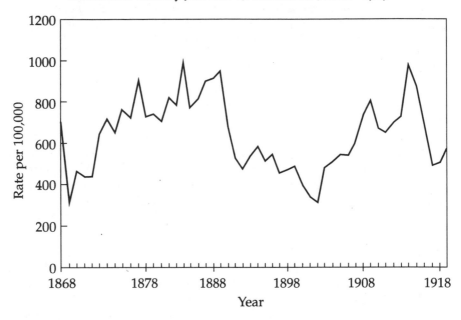

here. Instead, the prison registers are used primarily to understand the day-to-day operations of the criminal justice system – the types of crimes which preoccupied the courts and the social traits of criminals and their treatment at various decision-making levels. For this purpose, a sample of cases was selected for detailed analysis. To facilitate comparisons between prisoners and the general population, all committals which occurred in each of the six census years encompassed by the registers (i.e., 1871, 1881, 1891, 1901, 1911, and 1920) were selected, resulting in a sample of 3044 cases. Because an offender could be committed for more than one offence, as well as more than once in any given year, it is important to note that the unit of analysis is necessarily cases rather than individuals.

Much of the information contained in the registers had to be reclassified into broader categories before any useful analysis could be undertaken. In particular, the sheer number of different offences, occupations, and residences recorded for prisoners made collapsing these variables into more general categories among the most important first tasks. Although specific offences are examined to some degree, for most of the analysis the 91 separate offences and reasons for committal listed in the registers during these years were recategorized into three major offence types: violent offences, property offences, and public order offences.[23] Similarly, in order to provide a rough proxy of social class, the 194 different occupations were reclassified into broad groups consistent with previous research: i.e., professional, lower white-collar, skilled tradesman, semi- and unskilled workers, and unemployed.[24] Residences of prisoners were recoded into two major categories: those within Middlesex County and all others. Methodological issues, and decisions made with respect to other variables, are dealt with as they come up in the analysis.

THE NATURE OF CRIME

One of the most important contributions of recent historical scholarship has been to challenge the long-held assumption that urbanization and industrialization were accompanied by a dramatic increase in crime. Rather, the cumulative evidence across most Western nations strongly suggests that official rates of violent and property crime actually declined steeply over the nineteenth century and rose only moderately in the twentieth century. Moreover, throughout the nineteenth and early twentieth centuries, the vast majority of arrests were for various crimes against public order and morality.[25]

As shown in table 1, the types of crimes which led to committal to Middlesex County Jail, and which constituted the case load of the courts from 1871 to 1920, conform to this general pattern. That is, for the period as a whole, the category of violent crime was the least frequent in occurrence, comprising only 12.3 per cent of all prison committals.[26] Moreover, both the proportion of prisoners charged with violent crimes and the per capita rate for these offences declined steeply over time. Whereas violent crimes made up 29.2 per cent of all committals in 1871, the proportion dropped to only 3.0 per cent by 1920. This decline is, in large part, due to the steep decrease in common assault – the most frequently occurring violent crime, constituting 58.2 per cent of all charges in that category. The proportion of prisoners charged with common assault dropped steadily and precipitously from 15.2 per cent of all committals in 1871 to only 1.9 per cent in 1920.

Several explanations have been advanced for the overall decline in violent crime, particularly assault, throughout North America during this period. Prominent among these is the thesis that urbanization was

TABLE 1

Rates and Proportions of Prison Committals for Specific Offences, and by Offence Type: Middlesex County Jail, 1871–1920

	1871	1881	1891	1901	1911	1920	1871–1920
VIOLENT CRIMES							
Common Assault							
Rate/100,000	65.4	65.5	34.0	29.1	29.8	8.4	
% of all crime	15.2	9.2	6.3	8.3	4.5	1.9	7.2
Total	54	61	35	30	29	9	218
All Violent Offences							
Rate/100,000	125.9	97.8	72.8	45.6	44.3	13.1	
% of all crime	29.2	13.7	13.5	13.1	6.7	3.0	12.3
Total	104	91	75	47	43	14	374
PROPERTY CRIMES							
Larceny							
Rate/100,000	86.0	131.1	63.1	64.0	95.8	81.4	
% of all crime	19.9	18.4	11.7	18.3	14.4	18.6	16.6
Total	71	122	65	66	93	87	504
All Property Offences							
Rate/100,000	127.1	186.9	105.8	91.2	128.8	120.7	
% of all crime	29.5	26.3	19.7	26.1	19.4	27.6	24.2
Total	105	174	109	94	125	129	736
PUBLIC ORDER CRIMES							
Drunk/Disorderly							
Rate/100,000	47.2	213.8	195.1	125.1	361.6	133.8	
% of all crime	10.9	30.0	36.3	35.8	54.5	30.6	34.9
Total	39	199	201	129	351	143	1062

Vagrancy							
Rate/100,000	81.1	121.4	103.8	35.9	62.8	45.9	14.3
% of all crime	18.8	17.1	19.3	10.3	9.5	10.5	
Total	67	113	107	37	61	49	434
All Public Order Offences							
Rate/100,000	146.5	378.2	304.7	165.8	432.7	265.7	54.6
% of all crime	34.0	53.2	56.7	47.5	65.2	60.7	
Total	12?	352	314	171	420	284	1662
MISCELLANEOUS OFFENCES*							
Rate/100,000	31.5	48.3	54.4	46.5	57.7	38.4	8.9
% of all crime	7.3	6.8	10.1	13.3	8.7	8.7	
Total	26	45	56	48	56	41	272
Total	355	662	554	360	644	468	
Middlesex population	82,595	93,081	103,034	103,125	97,065	108,865	

*Miscellaneous offences included all other offences and reasons for committal. The majority of these consisted of persons committed for insanity, contempt of court, as witnesses, or prisoners staying overnight while in transit to another institution.

accompanied by a reduced tolerance of interpersonal violence, which was reinforced through a variety of social control measures, including mandatory schooling, new standards of discipline in the workplace, and the growth of urban police forces from the mid nineteenth century.[27] At another level, it is likely that reforms in family and welfare laws during this era are, at least, partly responsible for the declining volume of prison committals for common assault and related behaviours, such as threatening, indecent, or obscene language.[28] As various authors have noted, the lower criminal courts in the mid nineteenth century played a primary role in mediating various types of private quarrels and intrafamilial disputes, many of which figured as assault cases.[29] The establishment of family courts in the late nineteenth and early twentieth centuries was prompted, in large part, by a desire to find an alternative and more efficient means of regulating working-class families, thus relieving the criminal justice system of this burden.[30] Although the prison registers do not provide information on the specifics of assault cases, it is reasonable to speculate that family members (particularly women) made increasing use of these non-criminal tribunals to resolve problems, thereby avoiding the publicity and unpleasantness associated with the criminal courts.[31]

In marked contrast to violent crime, the proportion of offenders charged with property crimes generally was more stable, averaging 24.2 per cent of all committals for the period, and ranging from a high of 29.5 per cent in 1871 to a low of 19.4 per cent in 1911. There was greater variability in the rate per 100,000 on a yearly basis, but no overall pattern of increase or decrease. Similarly, the proportion of prisoners charged with the most common property offence, larceny, followed the same path, averaging 16.6 per cent of all committals for the period as a whole, and varying only within narrow boundaries from year to year. While it might be expected that the incidence of various types of fraud increased with the growth of cities,[32] these data reveal no such distinct trends and, in this regard, echo and extend to subsequent decades the findings of Katz, Doucet, and Stern for mid-nineteenth-century Hamilton.[33] Although it is true that the proportion of offenders charged with various types of fraud almost doubled from 2.8 per cent of all property crime committals in 1871 to 5.4 per cent in 1920, the small number of cases involved (three in 1871; seven in 1920) provides very weak support for the existence of any strong trend.

Against the backdrop of a small and decreasing proportion of prisoners committed for violent offences, and the relatively uniform proportion of persons charged with property offences over time, committals for offences against public order and morality stand in sharp relief. For the period as a whole, the category of public order offences made up more than half (54.6 per cent) of all prison committals. Of these offences, drunk and/or disorderly behaviour made up the majority of cases (34.9 per cent), followed by vagrancy (14.3 per cent) and various other offences against public morals (5.4 per cent). These latter offences consisted primarily of prostitution-related offences (i.e., being a keeper, inmate, or client of a house of ill fame) and liquor law violations. As equally important as the predominance of these offences is the marked fluctuation in both the committal rate and the proportion of offenders charged with public order crimes, which ranged from a low of 146.5 per 100,000 and 34.0 per cent respectively in 1871 to a high of 432.7 per 100,000 and 65.2 per cent respectively in 1911.

During the nineteenth century, the massive scale of geographic mobility of individuals and families in Ontario, as well as North American society more generally, contributed to the emergence of large transient populations in urban centres.[34] Those charged with vagrancy were thus a diverse group, reflecting both the punitive and more benevolent aspects of criminal justice. Vagrancy statutes were used to control and punish transients, prostitutes, and other problem populations in cities, but as well it was common practice for police stations and county jails to function as quasi-welfare institutions providing care and housing for tramps, indigents, and both elderly persons and children without families.[35] The proportion of prisoners charged with vagrancy was highest in the nineteenth century and declined in the twentieth century, a probable reflection of the increasing pressure on prison authorities to use alternatives to prison to deal with specific problem populations and those whose only crime was poverty.[36] In contrast, the opposite trend is evident for drunkenness, which constituted an increasingly larger proportion of prison committals over time. Moreover, it is noteworthy that the growing concern with intemperance throughout this era, which eventually culminated in the enactment of the Ontario Temperance Act in 1916, had only a partial effect in reducing the proportion of these committals from 54.5 per cent in 1911 to 30.6 per cent in 1920.

The preponderance of these offences, together with increases and decreases in committal rates on a yearly basis, tells us much about the cultural values, conceptions of criminality, and enforcement practices which dominated throughout the nineteenth and early twentieth centuries. Beginning in the late nineteenth century, Canadian reformers increasingly saw squalor, vice, and crime among the lower classes as one of the undesirable effects of rapid industrialization and urbanization and a serious threat to the fabric of society. Moreover, the prevailing ideology which saw drunkenness, immorality, and indigence as self-evident causes of criminality served to justify an aggressive enforcement policy towards public order offences as one of the most effective strategies in the prevention of more serious crimes.[37] It is, then, changes in police initiative and enforcement practices in this domain which are primarily responsible for the overall sharp fluctuations in the volume of prison committals over time. The visibility of public order offences made their enforcement particularly sensitive to public pressure. In turn, the police were facilitated in responding to these demands since, without the requirement of a complaining witness and with vague legal definitions, it was possible to increase greatly the number of these arrests through deliberate proactive enforcement policies.

The crime patterns observed in Middlesex County across the late nineteenth and early twentieth centuries are suggestive of both continuity and change in social control efforts over time. In so far as public order offences predominated as the most common form of crime, there is an overall similarity between the nature of crime as observed in this period and as noted in research on the mid nineteenth century. At the same time, the pattern of prison committals changed in significant ways across the span of time studied. At the beginning of this era, in 1871, the proportion of offenders charged with violent, property, and public order offences was roughly similar. However, over time, the expansion of social control measures, such as mandatory schooling and urban police forces, together with the development of new means of arbitrating interpersonal disputes contributed to an overall decline in the number of offenders charged with violent crimes. The concern with various types of property crime, especially larceny, remained a relatively stable feature of criminal justice throughout the period. In contrast, the increasingly more fervent agenda of moral reform as the era progressed served to increase sharply the proportion of prisoners charged with public order offences from 34 per cent in 1871 to 60.7 per cent by 1920. The result was that the pre-eminent focus of the criminal justice system on the activities and sins of the lower classes was further entrenched and expanded during this period.

THE PRISON POPULATION

Throughout the nineteenth century, reformers were convinced that crime was primarily the result of the existence of an identifiable criminal class, markedly different from the general population. According to the dominant ideology, criminals were members of a dangerous, self-perpetuating class composed disproportionately of Irish immigrants, urban residents, and, as previously noted, those whose lives were marked by intemperance, illiteracy, and idleness. While there is ongoing controversy as to the accuracy of this portrayal of criminals, and the adequacy of criminal justice records to address the issue of a criminal class, the available evidence suggests that offenders with these social traits were disproportionately represented among those arrested, convicted, and punished most severely in mid-nineteenth-century Canada.[38] In this part of the analysis, the primary concern is to determine the degree to which these social traits continued to be defining characteristics of the prison population in subsequent decades.

The extent to which the criminal population was representative of the general population is an issue of major importance both to the question of the validity of the concept of a criminal class and, more generally, to the issue of whether certain groups were singled out for differential treatment. However, the scope of such comparisons is necessarily limited because of the inherent problems in the available data sources, namely the prison registers and census data.[39] Consequently, while some relatively direct comparisons can be made between the prison and Middlesex populations for certain variables (e.g., ethnicity and sex), in other cases the comparisons are more speculative (age, occupation), and for some variables (intemperance), no comparisons can be made.

In the past, as in the present, the overwhelming majority of those arrested and committed to jail were men (see table 2). Compared to the general population, which was roughly equally divided by sex in each year and for the period as a whole (50.2 per cent male and 49.8 per cent female), males predominated in the prison population (87.4 per cent) throughout the era. Moreover, there is a notable pattern of a declining number of women in the jail population over time. The proportion of female prisoners decreased from 18 per cent in 1871 to a low of only 5.1 per cent in 1911. It then rose again, reaching 10 per cent in 1920.[40] This drop in the number of female criminals is not unique to Middlesex County but has been observed more generally in Ontario, as well as in the United States and England, during this period.[41] It

TABLE 2

Social and Demographic Characteristics of the Middlesex County Jail Population, 1871–1920

	1871 %	1881 %	1891 %	1901 %	1911 %	1920 %	1871–1920 %	Total
Sex								
Male	82.0	81.9	82.3	94.2	94.9	90.0	87.4	2661
Female	18.0	18.1	17.7	5.8	5.1	10.0	12.6	383
Marital Status								
Married	33.1	35.8	35.0	28.2	39.4	28.5	34.1	1026
Single/Widowed	66.9	64.2	65.0	71.8	60.6	71.5	65.9	1982
Age								
16 & under	7.3	9.1	5.4	4.8	3.7	9.0	6.3	197
17–25	36.3	31.3	27.3	31.4	17.4	31.7	27.2	852
26–35	29.9	21.6	23.6	24.0	31.5	22.8	24.4	764
36–45	10.7	20.7	15.7	17.5	21.3	22.5	17.8	559
46 & over	15.8	17.2	28.0	22.3	26.0	14.0	24.3	761
Birthplace								
Canada	38.2	44.5	54.9	63.8	66.6	68.3	56.2	1687
England	24.2	17.9	15.9	10.7	12.4	10.7	15.2	456
Ireland	21.3	23.6	17.5	13.2	7.3	2.8	14.5	436
Scotland	5.9	5.4	6.1	3.9	5.3	3.7	5.2	155
United States	7.3	7.1	4.3	6.7	6.8	10.5	6.7	207
Other	3.1	1.5	1.3	1.7	2.0	4.0	2.1	62
Residence								
Middlesex County	90.9	90.0	88.5	86.1	83.9	85.7	87.5	2495
Other	9.1	10.0	11.5	13.9	16.1	14.3	12.5	358

Occupation							
Professional	0.6	0.2	0.9	1.7	0.3	0.6	0.6 / 19
Lower white collar	12.6	9.5	11.9	13.2	8.1	8.5	10.3 / 311
Skilled tradesman	24.4	20.7	20.2	23.2	25.3	13.2	21.1 / 637
Semi- & unskilled workers	55.6	65.2	61.4	58.6	62.7	75.0	63.6 / 1917
No occupation*	6.7	4.4	5.6	3.4	3.6	2.6	4.3 / 130
Race							
White	97.8	93.0	94.2	93.8	91.4	92.4	93.5 / 2813
Other	2.2	7.0	5.8	6.2	8.6	7.6	6.5 / 196
Moral Habits							
Temperate	48.2	39.9	48.2	48.0	25.6	48.7	41.7 / 1254
Intemperate	51.8	60.1	51.8	52.0	74.4	51.3	58.3 / 1754
Education							
Literate	94.4	85.3	83.0	92.1	94.0	97.2	90.4 / 2722
Illiterate	5.6	14.7	17.0	7.9	6.0	2.8	9.6 / 290
Prior Committals							
None	55.3	55.6	41.6	51.5	45.5	50.0	51.1 / 1551
One or more	44.7	44.4	58.4	48.5	54.5	40.0	48.9 / 1485
Number of Charges							
One only	88.8	90.9	90.1	87.5	93.2	90.2	90.5 / 2754
Two or more	11.2	9.1	9.9	12.5	6.8	9.8	9.5 / 290
Total	356	665	554	360	644	468	3044

Note: Percentages may not add up to 100 because of rounding. Category subtotals may not add up to totals because of missing observations.

*Those recorded as having no occupation included in some years children, students, the elderly, 'married women,' and 'spinsters.' As such, it is not a homogenous category and cannot be interpreted to represent those deemed to be chronically unemployed.

is a pattern which, to a large extent, reflects the success of various new social control policies enacted for the purpose of reducing the criminalization, if not the criminality, of women during this era. Among the most important of these changes was the development, and increasing use, of various types of community-based informal controls to regulate younger and 'pre-delinquent' women, with the explicit hope of reducing the number of women processed through the criminal justice system.[42] The few women who continued to be subjected to formal controls experienced an increasingly diversified and intensified legal process characterized by the enactment of new laws and maximum penalties to deal with prostitution, the creation of separate courts for female offenders, and the establishment of a separate women's prison, the Mercer Reformatory, designed to rehabilitate wayward women and girls.[43]

On certain dimensions, most notably marital status, race, and age, there is an overall, although by no means perfect, correspondence between the prison and the general population. For the period as whole, both the Middlesex population (96.5 per cent) and the prison population (93.5 per cent) were predominantly white. There is, however, a trend toward an increasingly larger proportion of non-white individuals committed to jail, which rose from 2.2 per cent in 1871 to 7.6 per cent in 1920. Similarly, paralleling the distribution of single or widowed persons in the general population (62.3 per cent), most prisoners also were unattached (65.9 per cent). Moreover prisoners, like residents of Middlesex more generally, were relatively young and, although there is considerable variation in the ages of prisoners throughout the period, the majority (57.9 per cent) were thirty-five years old or younger. Census data are not directly comparable, but point towards those sixteen or under being among the most underrepresented segment of society in the prison population. In every year, this age group made up the smallest proportion of prisoners, and the enactment of the Juvenile Delinquent Act in 1908 does not appear to have had an appreciable effect in changing this group's representation in the prison population. So, while the finding that the proportion of these prisoners dropped to its lowest point of 3.7 per cent in 1911 seems consistent with the purported aim of reformers to divert young offenders from the criminal justice system, it is noteworthy that the proportion increased again to 9.0 per cent by 1920.

A closer look at the attributes most commonly associated with criminality in the mid nineteenth century reveals some interesting patterns. For the period as a whole, those most likely to be committed to prison were not only Middlesex County residents (87.5 per cent), but, more particularly, urban residents of the city of London (68.4 per cent). This is because the public order offences of drunkenness and vagrancy which made up the majority of arrests were almost exclusively an urban phenomenon. The public visibility of these offences made such manifestations of urban disorder not only open to public scrutiny but an enforcement priority of police forces throughout the nineteenth and early twentieth centuries. In London, Ontario, the police force was created in 1855 and, like other North American police forces, concentrated its efforts on these offences.[44] In turn, these concerns and enforcement practices probably served to reinforce in the minds of social reformers the self-evident link between urbanization and crime.

The analysis of data on prisoners' birthplace is consistent with the results of research on the national origins of prisoners in the mid nineteenth century. Those born in Canada remained underrepresented among the prison population, while Irish immigrants continued to be significantly overrepresented. At the same time, as the proportion of those born in Canada increased in the general population, there was a corresponding increase in Canadian-born prisoners and a decrease in the overrepresentation of Irish-born prisoners. Whereas in 1871, those born in Canada made up 68.3 per cent of the Middlesex population, but only 38.2 per cent of the prison population, by 1920, the corresponding figures are 79.2 per cent and 68.3 per cent respectively. In 1871, those born in Ireland made up 8.9 per cent of the population but 21.3 per cent of prisoners; by 1920 they constituted only 1.4 per cent of the population and 2.8 per cent of the prison population.

It is important, however, to consider the overrepresentation of Irish immigrants in the prison population in the more general context of differences in the national origins of prisoners. For while the dominant ideology focused on Irish immigrants as a major source of crime, this study confirms the findings of prior research that immigrant status was more important than national origin in this regard,[45] except for those born in Scotland, whose proportion in the prison population was roughly representative of the general population. Those born in England and the United States were also significantly overrepresented in the prison population throughout this period. Moreover, while the overrepresentation of English-born offenders generally decreased in parallel fashion to the decline in the overrepresentation of Irish-born offenders, the overrepresentation of American-born significantly increased over time. In 1871 those born in the United States made up only 2.6 per cent of the population but 7.3 per cent of the prison population; by 1920, the corresponding figures are 2.1 per cent and 10.5 per cent.[46] In sum, despite the popular stereotype of the criminal propensities of the Irish, in both this and earlier periods, the influence of national origin on the composition of the prison population applied more generally to those not born in Canada.

Throughout the nineteenth century, intemperance and illiteracy were inevitability equated with criminality, and these beliefs were given formal recognition in prison authorities' efforts to record this information. Undoubtedly, many of the habitual drunkards who were routinely arrested for drunkenness were well known to jail officials and automatically recorded as intemperate, but by no means did this practice apply more generally to offenders. First, for the period as a whole, slightly more than one-half (58.3 per cent) of all prisoners were recorded as intemperate. However, this overall average is somewhat inflated because of the very high proportion of those recorded as intemperate (74.4 per cent) in 1911 (a few years prior to the Ontario Temperance Act) when the rate of prison committals for drunkenness soared to its highest point. For the most part, in other years, the proportions of those deemed temperate and intemperate were roughly equal. Despite the prevailing view which saw intemperance as a root cause of criminality, jailers clearly exercised a measure of restraint and discrimination in their determination of offenders' drinking habits.

Second, consistent with the observation that the population as a whole in nineteenth-century Ontario was overwhelmingly literate, so too was the prison population.[47] While the proportion of those who could neither read nor write generally was higher in the prison population (10.6 per cent) than in the population as a whole (4.1 per cent for the years 1891–1920), nonetheless the vast majority of prisoners were literate. Moreover, with the establishment of mandatory schooling in the late nineteenth century, the incidence of illiteracy among prisoners decreased steadily over time, parallelling its decline in the general population.

Third, despite popular beliefs to the contrary, the prison population did not consist predominantly of career criminals as measured by the number of prisoners who were recidivists or charged with multiple crimes.[48] For the period as whole, roughly equal proportions of prisoners were first-time offenders (48.9 per cent) and repeat offenders (51.1 per cent). On a yearly basis, there is some indication that the level of recidivism decreased over time, but the trend is not especially pronounced. It is also apparent that a very few offenders were committed to prison for more than one offence. Throughout the period, only 9.5 per cent of all prisoners had multiple arrest charges pending, and this proportion generally was stable on a yearly basis.

The overrepresentation of the lowest occupational groups which characterized the prison population in the mid nineteenth century was even more pronounced during the late nineteenth and early twentieth centuries.[49] For the period as a whole, 63.6 per cent of prisoners were semi-skilled or unskilled workers. More specifically, the two most frequently recorded occupations were labourer (38.7 per cent) and domestic servant (9.3 per cent). Comparable census data on the Middlesex population are available only for 1871 and 1881, but it is noteworthy that 38.5 per cent of prisoners compared to only 11.4 per cent of the workforce consisted of labourers, while 10.5 per cent of the prison population compared to only 5.9 per cent of the workforce were in domestic service. Moreover, the disproportionate representation of semi- and unskilled workers in the prison population increased over time, rising from 55.6 per cent in 1871 to 75.0 per cent in 1920. Reflecting the various specific dimensions of Middlesex County's economy during this period, the other most frequently listed occupations included farmer (4.1 per cent), cigar-maker (2.9 per cent), carpenter (2.7 per cent), and shoemaker (2.0 per cent).

Although certain characteristics typified the prison population as a whole, it is nonetheless the case that prisoners did not constitute a homogenous group. There were important differences in the social traits of prisoners charged with the major types of offences, which generally are consistent with research on offender characteristics in mid-nineteenth-century Ontario.[50] In particular, recidivism was a defining characteristic of public order offenders: while 12.6 per cent of those charged with violent offences and 18.0 per cent of those charged with property offences had been committed previously to prison, among public order offenders, the proportion of recidivists was 69.4 per cent. Consequently, the different social traits associated with public order offenders go a long way toward explaining the continued overrepresentation of certain groups in the prison population over time. While factors such as marital status, residence, race, and literacy did not differentiate public order offenders from other types of offenders, several other social traits clearly distinguished these offenders and were associated with recidivism.

. First, compared to men, women were more often charged with public order offences (57.4 per cent and 78.1 per cent respectively) and less often charged with either violent (14.7 per cent and 5.2 per cent respectively) or property crimes (28.0 per cent and 16.6 per cent respectively).[51] Consequently, particularly in the nineteenth century when their numbers in the prison population were highest, women were somewhat more likely than men to be committed to prison more than once (57.6 and 50.2 per cent respectively for the years 1871–91).[52] Second, national origin played a role in differentiating types of offenders, but it was not as significant as popular stereotypes would have predicted. That is, the proportion of Irish immigrants charged with public order offences was highest (73.3 per cent) as expected, but virtually identical to the proportion of Scottish-born charged with these offences (72.9 per cent). The corresponding proportions for those born in Canada (55.9 per cent), England (60.9 per cent), and the United States (59.7 per cent) were both somewhat lower and roughly similar. American-born offenders were more likely than other groups to be charged with property offences (33.0 per cent) and English-born had, by a small margin, the highest proportion (15.0 per cent) of violent offenders. Third, as might be expected, occupation played some role in differentiating types of offenders. Professionals (46.7 per cent) and white-collar workers (47.0 per cent) were less likely than skilled workers (62.4 per cent), semi- or unskilled workers (61.7 per cent), or the unemployed (62.7 per cent) to be charged with public order offences. Fourth, public order offenders tended to be significantly older than either violent or property offenders: 25.7 per cent of public order offenders were forty-six years old or older, compared to 19.2 per cent of violent offenders and 10.6 per cent of property offenders. Finally, almost by definition, a significantly larger proportion (76.7 per cent) of these offenders, but by no means all, were deemed intemperate compared with violent (52.2 per cent) or property (31.4 per cent) offenders.

In sum, this collective portrait of the prison population during the urban reform era reveals little change from the mid nineteenth century in the predominant social characteristics of offenders. Throughout the nineteenth and early twentieth centuries, the same pattern of differences by sex, age, country of origin, and occupational status served to distinguish the prison population from the general population, as well as different types of offenders. Moreover, in this period as during the earlier stages of urbanization and industrialization, the offender population bore only a loose resemblance to contemporary conceptions which linked the Irish, intemperance, illiteracy, and idleness as the major causes of crime. To a large extent, the pre-eminent focus on public order offences ensured that the most visible and socially marginal members of society would continue to be overrepresented in the offender population. However, arrest and committal to prison was only the first stage in offenders' progress through the system. It is in the analysis of case outcomes that change or constancy in the differential treatment of certain types of offences and offenders is revealed most clearly.

PUNISHMENT: CONVICTION AND TYPE OF SENTENCE

As previously discussed, a central feature of criminal justice reform in the late nineteenth century was reform advocates' renewed emphasis on the importance of rehabilitative goals over punitive attitudes in the treatment of crime and criminals. Presumably, consistent with this ideology the primary concern was not simply to punish the overt act; rather sentences were to be determined after consideration of the social context of the crime and the prospects for reforming or curing offenders. Against the larger backdrop of calls for greater uniformity in the sentences meted out by various magistrates, sentencing was, nonetheless, to be individualized and guided by a careful consideration of the background, character, and habits of the offender.[53] The establishment of special courts and procedures for trying women and young offenders was regarded as a major development in diversifying the court system to meet more adequately the special needs of different types of offenders.

Yet, the available evidence suggests that, notwithstanding the reform rhetoric, traditional ideas of criminality and methods of dispensing justice continued to dominate the court system during this era. As various writers note, in large part this was because the primary burden of dispensing justice continued to fall on the lower criminal courts, particularly police courts, which seemed relatively impervious to implementing innovations.[54] By and large, the magistrates who presided in these lower courts continued to focus on the overt act and were never unduly concerned with the causes of crime or the prospects for rehabilitating offenders. As in previous decades, the principal social function of these courts was to underscore continually the line separating the respectable from the disreputable classes, in the minds of those who made the rules as well as those who violated them.[55] Justice as meted out in police courts did not involve a careful consideration of the details of a case in order to render a judgment; in the majority of cases, especially involving public order offences, the fact of arrest generally was sufficient for a finding of guilt. Consequently, these court proceedings were notoriously swift and unencumbered by legal technicalities.

To study judicial behaviour during this era, then, is to study the basement level of the criminal justice system, where the summary offences which made up the vast majority of cases were processed. Throughout the period under study, 82.4 per cent of all cases in Middlesex County were disposed of in these lower courts, either by police magistrates or by justices of the peace. Only a small minority of cases (12.9 per cent) were transferred to the next level of county courts, and very few cases (2.2 per cent) were decided at the highest level of the assizes.[56]

Between 1871 and 1920, 51.1 per cent of offenders were convicted, 1.7 per cent were acquitted after a trial, and a further 2.1 per cent were deemed insane and sent to the asylum. On a yearly basis, the proportion of those convicted fluctuated, declining from 60.7 per cent in 1871 to 46.0 per cent in 1891, increasing to 60.6 per cent in 1901, and falling again to 50.9 per cent by 1920. On this measure alone, there is no straightforward pattern to indicate a trend towards either harsher or more lenient outcomes over time. However, what is perhaps most striking about this period, and consistent with earlier eras,[57] is the large proportion of prisoners who were simply discharged by the courts: 37.8 per cent of all prisoners in this study. To some extent, the high rate with which offenders were released may suggest the difficulty of successfully prosecuting certain types of cases. But it is as, or more, likely that this figure reflects a criminal justice system in which, for a significant proportion of offenders (particularly those charged with various public order offences), the process of arrest and a few days spent in prison awaiting a court hearing were deemed sufficient punishment to show that the demands of order and discipline were being met.

Once convicted, judges had few sentencing options and, consequently, dispositions were essentially identical to those in earlier decades. That is, with few exceptions, offenders were given a jail sentence, with or without the option of paying a fine. In the case of offenders sentenced to Middlesex County Jail, judges could add hard labour to the sentence. At the same time, new legislative enactments which allowed for other sentencing options, such as indeterminate sentences, were rarely used by judges. To meet the goals of both punishment and rehabilitation, reformers advocated indeterminate sentences for a wide range of offenders including youth, habitual criminals, drunkards convicted a third or fourth time, and any woman sentenced to Mercer Reformatory for 'lewdness' or more than once.[58] Yet in the years when this option was available (1881–1920), only 2.6 per cent of convicted offenders were given indeterminate sentences and the vast majority of these were young offenders under the age of twenty-five (76.1 per cent) convicted of property offences (82.6 per cent). The use of indeterminate sentences primarily for youthful property offenders meant that less than half of the offenders given these sentences were recidivists (47.8 per cent), very few were women (8.7 per cent), and only a minority were deemed intemperate (21.7 per cent).

Overall, a slightly larger proportion of offenders were given the option of paying a fine (51.0 per cent) than were given straight jail time (42.9 per cent). But there were consistent differences across offence types in this regard. In particular, offenders convicted of property crimes were less likely to be given the option of paying a fine (10.3 per cent) than were violent offenders (39.6 per cent) or public order offenders (72.9 per cent), who were more often given this option. There was, as well, a marked trend toward the increasing use of the fine option as the era progressed. In 1871, 57.6 per cent of offenders were given straight jail time while 30.9 per cent were given a fine option; by 1920, the comparable figures were 38.8 per cent and 60.3 per cent. On the surface this might indicate that the system was becoming somewhat less punitive. However, from the perspective of the prison population, the increasing use of the fine option had little substantive impact since the average offender was no more able to avoid a prison term by paying the typical fine of a few dollars in the latter than in the earlier part of the period. Indeed, prisoners seemed to fare worse over time as an increasingly smaller proportion of offenders were able to exercise this option. While, for the period as a whole, 30.3 per cent of convicted offenders paid their fines, the proportion declined from 40.2 per cent in 1871 to 23.3 per cent in 1911. The year 1920 provides an exception to this general trend as 46.1 per cent of prisoners paid their fine; however, many of these individuals were charged for violation of the Ontario Temperance Act and, in view of the enormous fines levied by the courts and paid by defendants, these cases and offenders are singularly atypical of the period as a whole.[59]

There were, of course, systematic differences among offenders in terms of the ability to pay a fine. A larger proportion of offenders charged with violent offences (43.9 per cent) paid their fines than did property (23.3 per cent) or public order (29.1 per cent) offenders. The greater ability of violent offenders to pay their fines is a probable reflection of the fact that, as a group, these offenders tended to rank somewhat higher on various measures of social status than did other types of offenders. In this regard, the social attributes of those who paid their fines are fairly predictable, and consistent with their socio-economic status. Men (30.9 per cent) paid fines more often than women (23.6 per cent),[60] and married offenders (35.1 per cent) more often than single or widowed offenders (28.2 per cent). There were also differences by national origins and occupation in this regard. Those born in Canada (34.6 per cent) and the United States (33.3 per cent) were significantly more likely to pay their fines than those born in England (19.1 per cent), Ireland (25.6 per cent), or Scotland (21.6 per cent). As would be expected, professionals (100 per cent, total = 1) and lower-white-collar workers (49.1 per cent) paid their fines more often than did skilled (29.1 per cent) or semi- and unskilled workers (29.6 per cent). As well, a larger proportion of literate (31.1 per cent) than illiterate (21.2 per cent) offenders paid their fines.

Judges' addition of hard labour to the sentences of those incarcerated in Middlesex County Jail is consistent with the harsh view of intemperates and the 'undeserving poor' during this era, as it was reserved almost exclusively for public order offenders. Of these offenders, 74.9 per cent were given hard labour compared to 16.7 per cent of those convicted of property offences and 6.2 per cent of those convicted of violent offences. Moreover, the moral failings of women charged with public order offences were punished more severely than those of men, as they were more often sentenced to hard labour (84.4 per cent and 73.4 per cent respectively).

Throughout this era, the vast majority of offenders (92.0 per cent) faced one of two case outcomes: they were either discharged with no sentence, or convicted and given a prison sentence with or without a fine option.[61] Table 3 presents offender attributes as they relate to one or other outcome (prison/no prison) in each of the major offence categories. First, it is evident that the harsher outcome of a prison sentence was determined, in large part, by the nature of the offence. Consistent with previous research,[62] offenders charged with violent crimes were considerably less likely to receive a prison sentence (34.8 per cent) than were either property (56.3 per cent) or public order (53.5 per cent) offenders. Moreover, despite some fluctuations on a yearly basis, there was an overall stability in these differential case outcomes by offence type. Clearly, by the standards of the time, and consistent with the continued reluctance of the courts to deal with the types of common assault which made up the bulk of violent offences, judges did not regard these offences as particularly serious. More often than not, the criminal justice system dealt with these offenders by giving them a few days in prison to 'cool off' and then releasing them back to the community, either outright or with the payment of a fine or bond to keep the peace.

A closer look at differences in case outcomes in relation to various offender attributes reveals that traditional assumptions about the innate criminality of certain groups strongly influenced the severity of case outcomes throughout this era. Consequently, as in the mid nineteenth century, and across all offences, defendants who shared the constellation of social attributes which defined the most socially and economically marginal segments of society were dealt with most severely by the criminal justice system. Those offenders most often given a prison sentence were typically female, single, semi- or unskilled workers, intemperate, and illiterate. And, although the findings do not speak to the issue of the relative influence of individual variables, or the extent to which they undoubtedly overlapped, they highlight the way in which inequality in the larger society was systematically reinforced in judicial decisions throughout this period. Not only was the highest occupational category of professionals virtually never charged with violent or property offences, but all of these offenders were released. Similarly, for public order offences, professionals (85.7 per cent) and white-collar workers (61.3 per cent) were more often discharged than were skilled (46.7 per cent) or semi- and unskilled workers (40.0 per cent). And, as in the mid nineteenth century, recidivists and those with more than one arrest charge continued to be judged severely, and were given prison sentences more often than first-time offenders or those with only one arrest charge.

At the same time, looking at each offence type separately, one can discern significant differences in the social characteristics of offenders most often sentenced to prison, particularly in terms of age and country of origin. Among violent offenders, younger offenders were more likely to receive a prison sentence than older offenders, but the opposite pattern characterized public order offenders. Interestingly, although Irish immigrants were overrepresented among public order offenders, they were not treated more harshly for these offences than were those born in other countries. In contrast, few Irish immigrants were charged with property offences, but they were somewhat more often given a prison sentence than other groups in this crime category. Finally, among violent offenders, Irish immigrants were, by a small margin, least likely to be given a prison sentence. Although they were few in number, the system

TABLE 3
Probability of Conviction and Prison Sentence by Year, Offence Type, and Offender Characteristics

	Violent			Property			Public Order/Morality		
	Prison %	No prison %	(Total)	Prison %	No prison %	(Total)	Prison %	No prison %	(Total)
Year									
1871	38.5	61.5	(91)	62.9	37.1	(105)	80.5	19.5	(118)
1881	27.1	72.9	(85)	53.2	46.8	(171)	49.9	50.1	(345)
1891	41.9	58.1	(74)	55.3	44.7	(103)	46.8	53.2	(314)
1901	43.9	56.1	(41)	64.7	35.3	(85)	65.5	34.5	(165)
1911	21.4	78.6	(42)	51.7	48.3	(118)	49.3	50.7	(418)
1920	33.3	66.7	(12)	54.3	45.7	(129)	53.5	46.5	(284)
1871–1920	34.8	65.2	(345)	56.3	43.7	(711)	54.5	46.5	(1644)
Sex									
Male	34.1	65.9	(328)	55.9	44.1	(658)	52.8	47.2	(1379)
Female	47.1	52.9	(17)	60.4	39.6	(53)	57.4	42.6	(265)
Marital Status									
Married	30.3	69.7	(175)	52.0	48.0	(200)	45.7	54.3	(503)
Single/Widowed	40.4	59.6	(166)	58.1	41.9	(508)	57.2	42.8	(1135)
Age									
16 & under	0.0	100.0	(8)	54.7	45.3	(106)	28.3	71.7	(60)
17–25	41.5	58.8	(123)	55.4	44.6	(294)	47.5	52.5	(364)
26–35	35.7	64.3	(84)	59.1	40.9	(176)	58.7	41.3	(426)
36–45	29.0	71.0	(62)	56.4	43.6	(78)	56.0	44.0	(368)
46 & over	32.8	67.2	(64)	53.6	46.4	(56)	55.8	44.2	(419)
Birthplace									
Canada	34.7	65.3	(196)	54.8	45.2	(456)	52.2	47.8	(866)
England	34.5	65.5	(55)	60.8	39.2	(97)	56.6	43.4	(244)

Ireland	30.9	69.1	(55)	66.7	33.3	(51)	44.5	55.5	(292)
Scotland	46.2	53.8	(13)	47.8	52.2	(23)	46.5	53.5	(101)
United States	57.1	42.9	(14)	55.7	44.3	(61)	44.2	55.8	(113)
Residence									
Middlesex	35.1	64.9	(325)	54.8	45.2	(549)	44.8	55.2	(1357)
Other	38.5	61.5	(13)	57.8	42.2	(102)	51.6	48.4	(213)
Occupation									
Professional	0.0	100.0	(2)	0.0	100.0	(6)	85.7	14.3	(7)
Lower white collar	26.4	73.6	(53)	56.8	43.2	(74)	61.3	38.7	(124)
Skilled worker	35.4	64.6	(79)	54.0	46.0	(126)	46.7	53.3	(364)
Semi- & unskilled worker	37.8	62.2	(201)	59.3	40.7	(469)	40.0	60.0	(1075)
No occupation	20.0	80.0	(5)	33.3	66.7	(36)	38.9	61.1	(72)
Race									
White	35.3	64.7	(312)	56.6	43.4	(668)	46.4	53.6	(1521)
Other	34.5	65.5	(29)	52.4	47.6	(42)	44.9	55.1	(118)
Moral Habits									
Temperate	27.2	72.3	(169)	54.4	45.6	(485)	58.1	41.9	(382)
Intemperate	43.0	57.0	(172)	61.0	39.0	(223)	42.7	57.3	(1255)
Education									
Literate	34.2	65.3	(304)	56.2	43.8	(648)	47.1	52.9	(1476)
Illiterate	43.2	56.3	(37)	58.1	41.9	(62)	39.3	60.7	(163)
Prior Committals									
None	29.0	71.0	(183)	54.3	45.7	(462)	58.8	41.2	(674)
One or more	41.0	59.0	(161)	60.1	39.9	(248)	37.8	62.2	(968)
Number of Charges									
One only	30.0	70.0	(297)	46.0	54.0	(550)	47.7	52.3	(1585)
Two or more	64.6	35.4	(48)	91.3	8.7	(161)	13.6	86.4	(59)

Note: Category subtotals may not add up to total because of missing observations.

appeared to deal particularly harshly with violent offenders born in the United States.

The analysis of the case outcomes reveals one further important insight into the punishment process during this era. The extent to which the social characteristics of offenders were related to the severity of case outcomes was most evident for violent and public order offences. For these offence categories, case outcomes differed widely in relation to offender characteristics. In contrast, property offenders were treated in a surprisingly impartial and even-handed manner by the judicial system. Unlike other offenders, they were punished for their crimes, not their social status or other attributes. All of the social traits which appear to play a role in mitigating or accentuating the severity of punishment for other types of offenders had virtually no influence in these cases. By and large, property offenders were treated in a uniformly harsh manner, irrespective of their position in the social hierarchy. Overall, they were convicted and sentenced to prison at a high rate, and were least likely of all offenders to be given the option of paying a fine. Combining these findings with the overall constancy of prison committals for property crime during this era tends to underscore the continuing dominance of some of the key values which shaped criminal justice during the early stages of industrial capitalism: the protection of property and 'the primacy of commodities in an acquisitive age.'[63]

PUNISHMENT: PLACE OF INCARCERATION AND SENTENCE LENGTH

In terms of court outcomes, it would appear that traditional assumptions about criminality and the selectively harsher treatment of certain types of offenders continued to be defining characteristics of criminal justice during this period as in the mid nineteenth century. Still, it was primarily in the area of changes in the philosophy and structure of the province's correctional system that reformers hoped to achieve the goal of rehabilitating offenders. In Ontario, these ambitions led to a new phase in penal policy during the last quarter of the nineteenth century as various intermediate institutions were built to fill the gap between the local county jails and the federal penitentiary. The concern with youthful offenders led to the establishment of a wide array of institutions including boys and girls' reformatories and training schools, as well as industrial farms for young adult males sentenced to two years or less.

The adult penal system also saw major changes. At the lowest level, the common jails, including Middlesex County Jail, continued to house men and women sentenced to prison terms of two months or less, while those sentenced to two years or more continued to be sent to the Federal Penitentiary in Kingston. However, by 1874, male prisoners sentenced to periods of two months to two years were to be sent to Central Prison, and by 1879 women receiving such sentences were to be transferred to Mercer Reformatory, both in Toronto. Although prisons at all levels were expected to maximize their efforts to rehabilite offenders, these intermediate institutions were promoted by reformers as the most important facilities for implementing comprehensive rehabilitation schemes.[64]

As with most reforms to the criminal justice system, there were significant discrepancies between the rhetoric of reform and the implementation of reform ideas at the level of the various correctional institutions. For example, Oliver's research on Central Prison indicates that this institution paid minimal lip service to rehabilitative goals, focusing instead on deterring criminals through detention and harsh punishment.[65] However, if rehabilitation was most noticeable for its absence in many new institutions, authorities nonetheless continued to believe that they were exemplary environments compared with the situation in the province's local county jails. Prison inspectors continually decried the deplorable state of many county jails and their failure to accomplish even the limited tasks of classifying and segregating prisoners – regarded as an indispensable first step towards rehabilitation.[66] Implementation of more elaborate rehabilitation programmes related to education, work skills, or religious instruction was erratic and limited at best, or non-existent at worst. Problems related to overcrowding caused by the continuing committal of aged, infirm, indigent, and insane persons, together with ageing buildings of unsuitable design and untrained prison personnel, were never surmounted.

Yet because the majority of prisoners were sentenced in police courts and given relatively short prison terms of less than two months, most offenders continued to be incarcerated in local county jails. Throughout the late nineteenth and early twentieth centuries, only a small proportion of convicted offenders were sentenced to the various intermediate institutions, while the vast majority never moved beyond the confines of the local jails. The fate of offenders in Middlesex County illustrates these points well. From 1871 to 1920, 71.1 per cent of all convicted offenders received sentences of two months or less, and only 28.9 per cent were sentenced to longer terms. In terms of place of incarceration,

5 per cent were sentenced to the Federal Penitentiary, 11.8 per cent to Central Prison, 8.4 per cent to Mercer Reformatory, and 2.7 per cent to various institutions for youthful offenders. Thus, fully 78.2 per cent of convicted offenders, unless they had the option and were able to pay the fine, served out their sentences in the county jail.

Since neither Central Prison nor Mercer Reformatory existed in 1871, an examination of sentencing practices after 1881 provides a more accurate picture of the distribution of prisoners across various institutions. It is particularly noteworthy that, between 1881 and 1920, a significant proportion of adult prisoners given prison terms of two months to two years were not sentenced to these intermediate institutions. Among convicted males receiving these prison terms, 52.2 per cent were sentenced to Central Prison, but 43.8 per cent were sentenced to the county jail.[67] To some extent, the practice of holding males in the county jail was due to the overcrowding of Central Prison, a major problem for the prison by the late nineteenth century.[68] Unlike Central Prison, however, Mercer Reformatory seldom operated at even full capacity during this era[69] and, yet, judges sentenced only 42.9 per cent of eligible women offenders there, while the majority (57.1 per cent) continued to serve their sentences in the county jail. Consequently, not only did judges continue to sentence most offenders to prison terms of less than two months, but they also stubbornly resisted transferring a significant proportion of eligible prisoners to either Central Prison or Mercer Reformatory.

Although, at the broadest level, judges did not appear to take full advantage of new correctional facilities, it is, nonetheless, possible that the repeated arguments of inspectors and prison officials that longer periods of incarceration were necessary to rehabilitate offenders may have served to increase the sentences meted out to offenders. As previously noted, although indeterminate sentences were seldom meted out by the courts, this sentencing option was part of the more general belief that efforts at reforming criminals were futile so long as the system continued to operate on a 'revolving door' syndrome. The routine practice of sentencing offenders (especially for public order offences) to a few weeks in prison only to have them back before the courts shortly after release ran contrary to reform aspirations for rehabilitation. Particularly in the case of repeat offenders, drunkards, and those with dissolute lifestyles, the courts were urged to mete out the maximum sentences provided by law.[70] Consequently, it seems important to examine whether there were any notable trends in sentence length during this period. While conviction has been used as the primary measure of punitiveness in research on the mid nineteenth century, sentence length provides an alternative and somewhat different way of assessing the severity with which different offences and offenders were judged.

Because the general crime categories of violent, property, and public order crimes contained offences of varying degrees of seriousness, this analysis of sentence length is limited to the three most frequently occurring crimes during this era: larceny, drunk and/or disorderly behaviour, and vagrancy (see table 4). On the basis of average sentence lengths, it is clear that larceny was regarded as a particularly serious crime. For the period as a whole, offenders convicted of larceny received an average sentence of 235.8 days, compared to 103.1 for vagrancy and 22.8 for drunk/disorderly behaviour. Moreover, there was an overall trend toward increasingly longer sentences for larceny, from 106.6 days in 1871 to 443.6 days by 1920. By way of comparison, sentences for drunkenness, the mainstay of the system, remained stable, averaging approximately three weeks throughout the period. Because vagrancy laws were used to deal with a wide range of social problems, involving street prostitutes, transients, the indigent of all ages, and, generally, those deemed to be 'undesirable,' this offence shows the most variation in sentence length over time. Generally, sentences were higher in the nineteenth than in the twentieth century. As other social welfare agencies gradually were established to deal with the various problems encompassed by vagrancy statutes, both the number of arrests and average sentences for vagrancy declined.

Overall, then, it would appear that judges' compliance with penal authorities' continued requests for longer sentences were met only with respect to larceny. But, it is noteworthy that these offenders were, in some significant respects, least likely to conform to the stereotype of the type of criminal most in need of a lengthy prison sentence and rehabilitation. That is, as a group, property offenders were least likely to be intemperate or repeat offenders. While those arrested for drunk and disorderly conduct were most likely to fit this stereotype, sentences for these offenders remained both short and constant throughout the period.

A consideration of sentence length in relation to various offender attributes reveals some interesting patterns, particularly when compared with the findings for conviction and prison sentence. Although the analysis does not permit an estimate of the relative influence of specific offender traits, it is nonetheless suggestive of important differences in

TABLE 4
Average Sentence Length (days) for Selected Offences by Year and Offender Characteristics

	Larceny			Drunk/Disorderly			Vagrancy		
	Average sentence	(s.d)	Total	Average sentence	(s.d)	Total	Average sentence	(s.d)	Total
Year									
1871	106.6	(165.1)	48	22.8	(20.1)	37	47.5	(23.8)	52
1881	127.6	(159.7)	65	18.4	(10.4)	84	165.6	(245.6)	65
1891	162.0	(316.3)	33	21.2	(29.0)	87	126.8	(151.1)	55
1901	513.3	(572.5)	38	19.1	(11.7)	92	105.8	(99.4)	13
1911	214.6	(286.5)	43	25.1	(30.7)	168	30.5	(32.4)	30
1920	443.6	(439.9)	29	28.3	(73.2)	97	54.4	(28.6)	7
1871–1920	235.8	(360.0)	256	22.8	(37.3)	565	103.1	(163.4)	222
Sex									
Male	247.9	(374.0)	229	21.6	(36.6)	515	78.5	(157.8)	145
Female	133.0	(179.3)	27	36.7	(42.2)	50	149.4	(164.6)	77
Marital Status									
Married	224.8	(292.2)	68	22.2	(25.5)	164	108.8	(152.6)	34
Single/Widowed	240.9	(382.9)	187	23.2	(41.2)	401	102.0	(165.6)	188
Age									
16 & under	297.0	(463.1)	37	83.2	(157.6)	5	405.3	(643.5)	7
17–25	247.3	(386.6)	101	35.6	(69.5)	90	118.0	(130.9)	57
26–35	205.6	(267.1)	66	21.0	(25.2)	178	87.9	(122.7)	50
36–45	217.8	(359.5)	32	18.1	(14.1)	137	110.5	(134.6)	44
46 & over	201.6	(284.1)	19	20.0	(22.8)	155	63.4	(52.2)	64
Birthplace									
Canada	284.1	(414.7)	158	22.5	(36.0)	328	110.1	(231.4)	68
England	96.1	(111.7)	39	18.7	(14.7)	76	119.7	(143.1)	51

Ireland	169.5	(247.7)	20	19.9	(20.9)	94	83.7	(113.7)	61
Scotland	73.7	(38.5)	8	37.4	(66.0)	40	51.5	(30.4)	10
United States	248.7	(320.7)	23	31.5	(76.4)	22	92.3	(89.9)	28
Residence									
Middlesex	227.2	(360.9)	205	22.9	(37.6)	505	109.3	(180.3)	168
Other	213.0	(370.0)	26	25.6	(38.1)	50	84.3	(98.7)	40
Occupation									
Professional	–	–	–	–	–	–	–	–	–
Lower white collar	359.2	(508.2)	19	19.1	(28.2)	36	95.7	(80.2)	7
Skilled worker	239.4	(311.7)	40	20.2	(22.3)	137	82.9	(75.6)	35
Semi- & unskilled worker	238.3	(360.5)	191	27.7	(43.3)	332	112.6	(185.5)	151
No occupation	77.6	(68.7)	5	20.8	(17.3)	8	99.2	(89.2)	29
Race									
White	236.1	(360.6)	241	22.9	(37.8)	525	104.9	(165.6)	215
Other	231.0	(361.9)	15	23.3	(30.9)	40	47.9	(27.0)	7
Moral Habits									
Temperate	289.2	(415.2)	161	54.6	(106.9)	32	115.7	(204.5)	103
Intemperate	145.4	(212.6)	95	21.0	(27.4)	533	92.1	(116.5)	119
Education									
Literate	243.6	(360.1)	229	22.8	(37.9)	523	95.2	(121.4)	182
Illiterate	169.5	(358.8)	27	23.6	(29.4)	42	138.8	(285.1)	40
Prior Committals									
None	248.9	(372.0)	158	28.9	(37.3)	158	76.9	(91.5)	66
One or more	214.8	(340.6)	98	20.6	(21.8)	407	114.1	(184.7)	156
Number of Charges									
One only	120.1	(185.2)	161	22.6	(37.2)	528	102.6	(165.7)	215
Two or more	431.9	(481.1)	95	27.2	(40.0)	37	115.7	(61.1)	7

Note: Category subtotals may not add up to total because of missing observations.

the treatment of various offenders. Sex would appear to have played an influential role in judges' sentencing decisions. Although women received shorter sentences than men for larceny (133 and 247.9 days respectively), they received slightly longer sentences for drunkenness (42.2 and 36.6 days respectively) and substantially lengthier prison terms for vagrancy (149.4 and 78.5 days respectively). The harsher sentences meted out to women for these offences reflect the use of vagrancy statutes and drunk and disorderly charges as the primary means of criminalizing street prostitutes.[71]

While there were virtually no differences between residents and non-residents of Middlesex County in case outcomes for either larceny or drunkenness, there is some indication that Middlesex County residents received somewhat longer sentences for vagrancy than did non-residents (109.3 and 84.3 days respectively), although the differences are not great. There were, as well, no differences between whites and non-whites for larceny or drunkenness and, although whites received longer sentences for vagrancy (104.9 and 47.9 days respectively), there were too few cases involving non-whites to draw strong conclusions in this respect. Marital status per se was not an influential factor in sentence length, but there is generally a pattern of more severe sentences for younger offenders across all three offences. In addition to the creation of new court procedures and correctional facilities for youth, it would seem that a further manifestation of the concern for youthful offenders during this era was the imposition of long sentences.

Country of origin and occupation were variously related to sentence length. As with conviction, Irish immigrants were not singled out for particularly harsh treatment for any crime, but differences in outcome for other groups varied significantly by offence type. In the case of larceny, those born in Canada and the United States received the longest sentences; for drunkenness, those born in Scotland and the United States received somewhat longer sentences; and, for vagrancy, those born in Canada and England were given the longest sentences. Occupation had some influence on sentence length but, for public order offences, differences across groups were not as pronounced as might be expected. That is, semi- and unskilled workers received marginally longer sentences for drunkenness than did other groups, and notably longer sentences for vagrancy.

In contrast, the lowest occupational group received considerably shorter sentences than did lower-white-collar workers for the offence of larceny (238.3 and 359.2 days respectively). Although the prison registers do not provide details of the crimes committed, the explanation for this finding probably lies in the different types of larceny committed by the two groups. It is likely that many, if not most, of the larcenies committed by the lower social classes consisted of fairly petty crimes in which the victims were probably of the same social status. In contrast, it seems reasonable to speculate that a significant proportion of larcenies committed by white-collar workers were occupationally related (i.e., employees stealing from employers). In an era increasingly reliant on a developing market economy, and the rise of large corporations, such breaches of the normative principles of employment were undoubtedly viewed as particularly serious crimes and treated accordingly.

The relationship between intemperance and sentence length is also interesting. As previously noted, the designation of offenders as temperate or intemperate was probably made solely at the discretion of the jailer and, therefore, this classification may not accurately reflect the drinking habits of the offender population. Nonetheless, the designation was not without consequence for it clearly was related to sentence severity. Throughout this era, while intemperates were more often convicted and sentenced to prison than were temperates, it was temperate offenders who were given the longest sentences. Moreover, the pattern of temperates being sentenced to longer prison terms than intemperates was evident across all offences: larceny (289.2 and 145.4 days respectively), drunkenness (54.6 and 21.0 days respectively), and vagrancy (115.7 and 92.1 days respectively). So, it would seem, despite the conventional wisdom which saw intemperance as one of the root causes of criminality, and which led to the greater probability of drunkards being convicted and sentenced to prison, this same failing appeared to mitigate the severity of the prison term imposed. Perhaps, in the minds of judges, temperates lacking the excuse of drunkenness as a mitigating factor were deemed more responsible for their crimes and deserving of harsher treatment. Recidivism and the number of arrest charges pending also affected sentencing in the expected fashion but, here too, the influence of these variables on sentence length is less pronounced than it is for conviction and type of sentence. Compared with first-time offenders, recidivists received somewhat longer sentences for larceny (248.9 and 214.8 respectively) and considerably longer sentences for vagrancy (114.1 and 76.9 respectively). Differences between offenders with only one arrest charge and offenders with two or more arrest charges pending were most evident in the case of larceny. Offenders with multiple charges received on average a sentence of 431.9 days compared to 120.1 days for offenders with only one arrest charge.

Overall, the most notable change in this aspect of sentencing patterns is the trend toward increasingly longer sentences for the offence of larceny. More generally, the analysis of sentence length suggests that the relationship between social inequality and the severity of punishment is most evident with respect to apprehension and conviction. Once past these stages, somewhat different considerations appeared to influence judges' sentencing behaviour, as evidenced, for example, in the harsh treatment of temperates and of white-collar offenders convicted of larceny. Although the criminal justice system was selectively punitive to different types of offenders, it was not uniformly punitive to the same offenders at successive decision-making points.

CONCLUSION

This broad survey of crime, criminals, and punishment highlights the dual facets of change and constancy which characterize criminal justice in every era. Definitions of crime and ideologies of criminality vary, leading to different agendas for reformers in each historical epoch. But, at the same time, certain essential features of the system appear to remain as constants. In the past, as in the present, changing responses to crime and criminals occur within the context of the enduring relationship between social class and official criminality. Whether the focus is on public order offences, as it was in the period studied, or property crimes, as it is now, the disproportionate representation of those at the bottom of the social hierarchy among those processed through the system does not vary. Consequently, while patterns of crime, the characteristics of criminals, and the severity of punishment changed in various ways from 1871 to 1920, there is a fundamental continuity with earlier periods in the dominant features of criminal justice.

In the late nineteenth and early twentieth centuries, as in the mid nineteenth century, the prison population bore only a loose resemblance to contemporary conceptions of a criminal class. Irish immigrants were certainly overrepresented, but by no means were all criminals either intemperate or illiterate as prevailing beliefs dictated. Nor were the vast majority of offenders recidivists. As a group what they shared most clearly were various manifestations of social and economic marginality.

Several other findings bear repeating. Public order offenders provided the major focus of urban police forces, and consequently the major clientele for the criminal justice system, throughout this era. It is with these offenders that differential treatment on the basis of various social attributes is most clearly evidenced. In contrast, in the case of property crimes, the singular focus remained the act, rather than the characteristics of the offenders. The proportion of prison committals for these offences remained relatively constant throughout the era, and these offenders were treated uniformly more harshly at every stage of the judicial process. To some extent then, the simple preponderance of public order arrests masks the concern with, and response to, property crime in an emerging industrial capitalist society. In a different way than for public order offences, the treatment of these offences is an equally important defining element of criminal justice throughout the nineteenth and early twentieth centuries.

Overall, confirming the findings of previous research, reforms in the ideology and practice of criminal justice institutions would not appear to have been accompanied by marked changes in patterns of case outcomes. By and large, traditional assumptions about criminality and the selectively harsher treatment of certain types of offences and offenders which dominated in the mid nineteenth century continued to characterize criminal justice in this later period. There was no overall trend of greater leniency as measured by convictions and sentences. Throughout this era, at least for Middlesex County, there was little change from the mid nineteenth century in terms of the crimes dealt with by the criminal justice system, the social characteristics of criminals, the severity of punishment, or the place of incarceration.

NOTES

1 The following are representative of research on different topics. On crime trends see H. Boritch and J. Hagan 'Crime and the Changing Forms of Class Control: Policing Public Order in "Toronto the Good," 1859–1955' *Social Forces* 66 (1987) 307–55; P. and P. Brantingham *Patterns of Crime* (New York: Macmillan 1984); T. Thorner 'The Incidence of Crime in Southern Alberta, 1878–1905' in D.J. Bercuson and L. Knafla, eds. *Law and Society in Canada in Historical Perspective* (Calgary: University of Calgary Press 1979); T. Thorner and N. Watson 'Patterns of Prairie Crime: Calgary, 1875–1930' in L. Knafla, ed. *Crime and Criminal Justice in Europe and Canada* (Waterloo: Wilfrid Laurier

University Press 1981). On the development of municipal policing see H. Boritch 'Conflict, Compromise and Administrative Convenience: The Police Organization in Nineteenth-Century Toronto' *Canadian Journal of Law and Society* 3 (1988) 141–74; T.J. Juliania, C.K. Talbot, and C.H.S. Jayewardene 'Municipal Policing in Canada, a Developmental Perspective' *Canadian Police College Journal* 9 (1984) 315–84; G. Marquis 'A Machine of Oppression under the Guise of the Law: The Saint John Police Establishment, 1860–1890' *Acadiensis* 16 (1986) 58–77; G. Marquis 'The Contours of Canadian Urban Justice, 1830–1875' *Urban History Review* 15 (1987) 269–73; A.K. McDougall 'The Police Mandate: An Historical Perspective' *Canadian Police College Journal* 12 (1988) 10–47; N. Rogers 'Serving Toronto the Good: The Development of the City Police Force, 1834–1880' in V. Russell, ed. *Forging a Consensus: Historical Essays on Toronto* (Toronto: University of Toronto Press 1984). On Canadian prison history, particularly Kingston Penitentiary, see R. Baehre 'Origins of the Penitentiary System in Upper Canada' *Ontario History* 69 (1977) 185–207; J.M. Beattie *Attitudes towards Crime and Punishment in Upper Canada, 1830–1850* (Toronto: University of Toronto Centre of Criminology 1977); C.J. Taylor 'The Kingston, Ontario Penitentiary and Moral Architecture' *Histoire sociale – Social History* 12 (1979) 385–408. On the development of other legal institutions see R.C. Macleod, ed. *Lawful Authority: Readings on the History of Criminal Justice in Canada* (Toronto: Copp Clark Pitman 1988); R. Splane *Social Welfare in Ontario, 1791–1893* (Toronto: University of Toronto Press 1965). For a review of research on these topics, see also J. Phillips 'Crime and Punishment in the Dominion of North of the North: Canada from New France to the Present' in L. Knafla and C. Emsley, eds. *Crime History and Histories of Crime: Studies in the Historiography of Crime and Punishment* (Westport, Conn.: Greenwood Press 1994).

2 J. Fingard 'Jailbirds in Mid-Victorian Halifax' in P. Waite, S. Oxner, and T. Barnes, eds. *Law in a Colonial Society: The Nova Scotia Experience* (Toronto: Carswell 1984); Macleod *Lawful Authority* esp. 1–8; H. Graff 'Crime and Punishment in the Nineteenth Century: A New Look at the Criminal' *Journal of Interdisciplinary History* 7 (1977) 477–91

3 For Great Britain see D. Jones, ed. *Crime, Protest, Community and Police in Nineteenth-Century Britain* (London: Routledge and Kegan Paul 1982); G. Rude *Criminal and Victim: Crime and Society in Early Nineteenth-Century England* (Oxford: Oxford University Press 1985); J.J. Tobias *Crime and Industrial Society in the Nineteenth Century* (London: Botsford 1967). For the United States see L. Friedman and R.V. Percival *The Roots of Justice: Crime and Punishment in Alameda County, California 1870–1910* (Chapel Hill: University of North Carolina Press 1981); E. Monkkonen *The Dangerous Class: Crime and Poverty in Columbus Ohio,*

1860–1885 (Cambridge, Mass.: Harvard University Press 1977). For Australia see S. Nicholas, ed. *Convict Workers: Reinterpreting Australia's Past* (Cambridge: Cambridge University Press 1988).

4 To date the most commonly used records for this purpose are local jail records, particularly those for Ontario: see Fingard 'Jailbirds in Mid-Victorian Halifax'; Graff 'Crime and Punishment'; H. Graff 'Pauperism, Misery, and Vice: Illiteracy and Criminality in the Nineteenth Century' *Journal of Social History* 11 (1966) 245–68; M.B. Katz, M.J. Doucet, and M.J. Stern *The Social Organization of Early Industrial Capitalism* (Cambridge, Mass.: Harvard University Press 1982); J. Weaver 'Crime, Public Order and Repression: The Gore District in Upheaval, *1832–1851*' *Ontario History* 78 (1986) 175–207.

5 Graff 'Crime and Punishment' 481

6 See G. Stetler's introduction to the collections of articles on urban reform in the nineteenth century in the special issue of *Urban History Review* 1 (1975) 2.

7 Ibid. See also the collection of articles on urban reform in the 1976 special issue of *Urban History Review*, P. Rutherford 'Tomorrow's Metropolis: The Urban Reform Movement in Canada, *1880–1920*' *Historical Papers* (1971) 203–24, and P. Rutherford, ed. *Saving the Canadian City: The First Phase 1880–1920* (Toronto: University of Toronto Press 1974).

8 Rutherford 'Tomorrow's Metropolis' and *Saving the Canadian City*; M. Valverde *The Age of Light, Soap, and Water: Moral Reform in English Canada, 1885–1925* (Toronto: McClelland and Stewart 1991)

9 J.C. Weaver 'Tomorrow's Metropolis Revisited: A Critical Assessment of Urban Reform in Canada, *1890–1920*' in G.A. Stetler and A.F.J. Artibise, eds. *The Canadian City: Essays in Urban and Social History* (Ottawa: Carleton University Press 1977) 394. See also Valverde *The Age of Light, Soap, and Water*; R. Allen 'The Social Gospel and the Reform Tradition in Canada, *1890–1928*' *Canadian Historical Review* 49 (1968) 381–99; Rutherford 'Tomorrow's Metropolis' and *Saving the Canadian City*; L. Kealey, ed. *A Not Unreasonable Claim: Women and Reform in Canada, 1880's to 1920's* (Toronto: Women's Press 1979).

10 See note 1 above and J.A. Edmison 'Some Aspects of Nineteenth-Century Canadian Prisons' in W.T. McGrath, ed. *Crime and Its Treatment in Canada* (Toronto: Macmillan 1976).

11 On various legislative enactments during this period see generally T.R. Morrison 'Their Proper Sphere: Feminism, the Family and Child-Centered Reform in Ontario, *1875–1900*' *Ontario History* 63 (1976) 45–74; Splane *Social Welfare in Ontario*. On probation see P. Oliver and M.D. Whittingham 'Elitism, Localism, and the Emergence of Adult Probation Services in Ontario, *1893–1972*' *Canadian Historical Review* 68 (1987) 225–58. On the establishment

of separate courts for youth and women see A.E. Jones and L. Rutman *In the Children's Aid: J.J. Kelso and Child Welfare in Ontario* (Toronto: University of Toronto Press 1981); L. Gordon 'Doctor Margaret Norris Patterson: First Woman Police Magistrate in Eastern Canada – Toronto, January 1922 to November 1934' *Atlantis* 10 (1984) 95–109. On the establishment of specialized correctional institutions see C. Strange 'The Criminal and Fallen of Their Sex: The Establishment of Canada's First Women's Prison, 1874–1901' *Canadian Journal of Women and the Law* 1 (1985) 79–92 and 'Unlocking the Doors on Women's Prisons' *Resources for Feminist Research* 14 (1986) 13–15; D.G. Wetherell 'To Discipline and Train: Adult Rehabilitation Programmes in Ontario Prisons, 1874–1900' *Histoire sociale – Social History* 12 (1979) 145–65; P. Oliver 'A Terror to Evil-Doers: The Central Prison and the "Criminal Class" in Late Nineteenth-Century Ontario' in R. Hall et al., eds. *Patterns of the Past: Re-interpreting Ontario's History* (Toronto: Dundurn Press 1988); see also Oliver's essay in this volume.

12 J. Hagan and J. Leon 'Rediscovering Delinquency: Social History, Political Ideology and the Sociology of Law' *American Sociological Review* 42 (1978) 587–98; S. Houston 'The "Waifs and Strays" of a Late Victorian City: Juvenile Delinquents in Toronto' in J. Parr, ed. *Childhood and Family in Canadian History* (Toronto: McClelland and Stewart 1982); J. Leon 'The Development of Canadian Juvenile Justice: A Background for Reform' *Osgoode Hall Law Journal* 15 (1977) 71–106; N. Sutherland *Children in English-Canadian Society: Framing the Twentieth-Century Consensus* (Toronto: University of Toronto Press 1976)

13 C. Backhouse 'Nineteenth-Century Canadian Prostitution Law, Reflections of a Discriminatory Society' *Histoire sociale – Social History* 18 (1985) 387–423; J.P.S. McLaren 'Chasing the Social Evil: Moral Fervour and the Evolution of Canada's Prostitution Laws, 1867–1917' *Canadian Journal of Law and Society* 1 (1986) 125–66; L. Rotenberg 'The Wayward Worker: Toronto's Prostitute at the Turn of the Century' in J. Acton, P. Goldsmith, and B. Shepphard, eds. *Women at Work: Ontario 1850–1930* (Toronto: Canadian Women's Educational Press 1974); H. Boritch 'Gender and Criminal Court Outcomes: An Historical Analysis' *Criminology* 30 (1992) 239–325; Valverde *The Age of Light, Soap, and Water*

14 D. Chunn *From Punishment to Doing Good: Family Courts and Socialized Justice in Ontario, 1880–1940* (Toronto: University of Toronto Press 1992) and 'Regulating the Poor in Ontario: From Police Courts to Family Courts' *Canadian Journal of Family Law* 6 (1987) 86–102; J.G. Snell 'Courts of Domestic Relations: A Study of Early Twentieth Century Judicial Reform in Canada' *Windsor Yearbook of Access to Justice* 6 (1986) 36–60

15 For a broad overview of this process see Splane *Social Welfare in Ontario*. For

accounts of particular developments see R.C. Smandych and S.N. Verdun Jones 'The Emergence of the Asylum in 19th Century Ontario: A Study in the History of Segregative Control' in N. Boyd, ed. *The Social Dimensions of Law* (Scarborough: Prentice Hall 1986); P.A. Bator 'The Struggle to Raise the Lower Classes: Public Health Reform and the Problem of Poverty' *Journal of Canadian Studies* 14 (1979) 43–49; J. Pitsula 'The Emergence of Social Work in Toronto' *Journal of Canadian Studies* 14 (1979) 35–42; S. Speisman 'Municipal Parsons and Municipal Parsimony: Volunteer vs Public Relief in Nineteenth Century Toronto' *Ontario History* 65 (1973) 33–49.

16 The extent to which punishment and deterrence overshadowed concerns with rehabilitation is, perhaps, most evident in Oliver's study of Central Prison for Men established during this period (see note 11 above).

17 G. Homel 'Denisons's Law: Criminal Justice and the Police Court in Toronto, 1877–1921' *Ontario History* 73 (1981) 184. See also T. Thorner and N. Watson 'Keeper of the King's Peace: Colonel G.E. Sanders and the Calgary Police Magistrate's Court, 1911–1932' *Urban History Review* 12 (1984) 45–56; H.M. Wodson *The Whirlpool: Scenes from Toronto Police Court* (Toronto: n.p. 1917); Chunn *From Punishment to Doing Good* 56. See also the reminiscences of Colonel George T. Denison III who presided over the Toronto police court for forty-four years, in *Recollections of a Police Magistrate* (Toronto: Musson 1920).

18 The Middlesex County Prison registers are located in the Regional Collection of the University of Western Ontario, London, Ontario.

19 F.H. Armstrong and D.J. Brock 'The Rise of London: A Study of Urban Evolution in Nineteenth-Century Southwestern Ontario' in F.H. Armstrong, H.A. Stevenson, and J.D. Wilson, eds. *Aspects of Nineteenth-Century Ontario* (Toronto: University of Toronto Press 1974)

20 Occupational data for 1921 are excluded as they are not directly comparable with prior census data.

21 Wetherell 'To Discipline and Train'

22 Graff 'Crime and Punishment in the Nineteenth Century'; Katz, Doucet, and Stern *The Social Organization of Early Industrial Capitalism*; Weaver 'Crime, Public Order, and Repression'

23 Violent offences included all forms of assault, rape, abduction, threatening, robbery, shooting, stabbing, murder, and manslaughter. Property offences included larceny, trespassing, damaging property, burglary, and breaking and entering. Public order offences included drunk and disorderly behaviour, vagrancy, prostitution, gambling, and liquor law violations.

24 For discussions of methodological issues, and classification schemes with respect to occupations in the nineteenth century, see T. Hershberg et al.

'Occupation and Ethnicity in Five Nineteenth Century Cities: A Collaborative Inquiry' *Historical Methods Newsletter* 7 (1973) 174–216; M.B. Katz 'Social Class in North American Urban History' *Journal of Interdisciplinary History* 9 (1981) 579–605 and 'Occupational Classification in History' *Journal of Interdisciplinary History* 3 (1972) 63–88; Katz, Doucet, and Stern, *The Social Organization of Early Industrial Capitalism*.

25 For Canada see Boritch and Hagan 'Crime and the Changing Forms of Class Control' and Brantingham *Patterns of Crime*. For other countries see V.A.C. Gattrell 'The Decline of Theft and Violence in Victorian and Edwardian England' in V.A.C. Gattrell, B.P. Lenman, and G. Parker, eds. *Crime and Law: The Social History of Crime in Western Europe since 1500* (London: Europa 1980); T.R. Gurr 'Historical Trends in Violent Crime: A Critical Review of the Evidence' in N. Morris and M. Tonry, eds. *Crime and Justice: An Annual Review of Research* (Chicago: University of Chicago Press 1981); R. Lane 'Urban Homicide in the Nineteenth Century: Some Lessons for the Twentieth' in J.A. Inciardi and C.E. Faupel, eds. *History and Crime: Implications for Criminal Justice Policy* (Beverly Hills: Sage 1980); A.R. Gillis 'Crime and State Surveillance in Nineteenth-Century France' *American Journal of Sociology* 95 (1989) 307–41; E. Monkkonen *Police in Urban America, 1860–1920* (New York: Cambridge University Press 1981); C. Tilly et al. 'How Policing Affected the Visibility of Crime in Nineteenth-Century Europe and America' (The Center for Research on Social Organization, Working Paper no. 115, n.d.).

26 Murder and manslaughter were relatively infrequent crimes. In the six years studied, there were fourteen committals for murder, four for manslaughter, and seven persons were committed as accessories to murder. However, it is important to note that these figures do not represent incidences of these crimes as frequently several suspects and witnesses were arrested in a given case. On this same point see Weaver 'Crime, Public Order and Repression' 27.

27 R. Lane 'Urban Police and Crime in Nineteenth-Century America' in N. Morris and M. Tonry, eds. *Crime and Justice: An Annual Review of Research* (Chicago: University of Chicago Press 1980); Gurr 'Historical Trends in Violent Crime'; Monkkonen *Police in Urban America*

28 Taken together, these offences constituted 72 per cent of all violent offences from 1871 to 1920.

29 Fingard 'Jailbirds in Mid-Victorian Halifax'; Marquis 'Saint John Police'; Katz, Doucet, and Stern *The Social Organization of Early Industrial Capitalism*. The extensive role of police courts as arbiters of intrafamilial disputes in the nineteenth century is not unique to Canada. For the United States see Friedman and Percival *The Roots of Justice*, and for England see N. Tomes 'A

"Torrent of Abuse": Crimes of Violence between Working-Class Men and Women in London, 1840–1875' *Journal of Social History* 11 (1978) 328–45.

30 Chunn *From Punishment to Doing Good*

31 It is interesting to note in this regard that the offence of 'wife assault' appears for the first time in the registers in 1901, and the practice of specifically distinguishing this form of assault continues until 1920. To some extent, at least, the establishment of family courts and the official recognition of wife assault as a distinct crime in the prison registers suggest an increased concern with the prevalence of these offences, and the traditionally lenient treatment of offenders. The acceptance of wife abuse as a male prerogative, and even comic relief, in the mid nineteenth century is reflected in the depiction of one such accused in the *London Free Press* 3 Aug. 1869: 'A man imprisoned for cruelly beating his wife, poked his nose through the cell bars and exclaimed "I thank God I'm not locked up for any mean, dirty crime, like getting drunk."'

32 For a discussion of the relationship of fraud, or 'theft by trick,' to industrial and urban growth in the nineteenth century, see Monkkonen *The Dangerous Classes*, esp. 92–100.

33 Katz, Doucet, and Stern *The Social Organization of Early Industrial Capitalism* 207

34 For discussions of geographic mobility and transience in nineteenth-century Ontario see D. Gagan 'Geographical and Social Mobility in Nineteenth-Century Ontario: A Microstudy' *Canadian Review of Sociology and Anthropology* 13 (1976) 152–64; M. Katz 'The People of a Canadian City, 1851–52' *Canadian Historical Review* 53 (1972) 402–26. For the United States see S. Thernstrom and P. Knights 'Men in Motion: Some Data and Speculations about Urban Population Mobility in Nineteenth Century America' *Journal of Interdisciplinary History* 1 (1970) 17–47.

35 For Canada see J. Phillips 'Poverty, Unemployment and the Criminal Law: The Administration of the Vagrancy Laws in Halifax, 1864–1890' in P. Girard and J. Phillips, eds. *Essays in the History of Canadian Law: Volume III – Nova Scotia* (Toronto: University of Toronto Press and Osgoode Society 1990); J. Pitsula 'The Treatment of Tramps in Late Nineteenth-Century Toronto' *Historical Papers* (1980); Boritch 'Conflict, Compromise and Administrative Convenience'; E. Bradwin *The Bunkhouse Man* (New York: AMS Press 1968). For the United States see Monkkonen *The Dangerous Classes*; Friedman and Percival *The Roots of Justice* esp. 84; S.L. Harring *Policing a Class Society: The Experience of American Cities, 1865–1915* (New Brunswick, NJ: Rutgers University Press 1983).

36 For a detailed discussion of tramps and vagrants in Ontario jails, see the testimony and recommendations in the *Report of the Commission Appointed to En-*

quire into the Prison and Reformatory System of Ontario (Toronto 1891). The commissioners reaffirmed the contemporary distinction increasingly made between the 'deserving' and 'undeserving' poor by recommending hard labour and stiffer sentences for 'able-bodied' tramps, but arguing strongly against the 'inhuman system of committing homeless and destitute men, women and children to common gaols, many of whom are from old age or physical incapacity unable to earn a living' (220). Undoubtedly, the commissioners had in mind cases such as John and Sarah Lynch and their four children, aged one, two, eight, and nine, who were all committed to jail in October 1881 on vagrancy charges. They were 'convicted' and stayed in the jail for three months.

37 Beattie *Attitudes towards Crime and Punishment*; J.J. Bellomo 'Upper Canadian Attitudes toward Crime and Punishment, 1832–1851' *Ontario History* 64 (1972) 11–26; Katz, Doucet, and Stern *The Social Organization of Early Industrial Capitalism*; Marquis 'The Saint John Police'; Boritch and Hagan 'Crime and the Changing Forms of Class Control'

38 Fingard 'Jailbirds in Mid-Victorian Halifax'; Graff 'Crime and Punishment in the Nineteenth Century' and 'Pauperism, Misery, and Vice'; Katz, Doucet, and Stern *The Social Organization of Early Industrial Capitalism*; Rogers 'Serving Toronto the Good'; Weaver 'Crime, Public Order, and Repression'

39 While prison registers were fairly consistent in reporting the same broad categories of information on offenders from year to year, the specific way in which these data were recorded changed over time. In general, the effect of these variations in record-keeping practices was to limit the scope of analysis with respect to particular variables. For example, over time, the terms used to describe the educational levels of prisoners differed enough (e.g., elementary/imperfect; superior/very well, well) that this variable was coded simply as literate/illiterate. Census data for Middlesex County also are limited, in the first instance, because they do not contain information on certain key variables of interest (e.g., intemperance) and, in the second instance, because other types of information (e.g., occupation, age) were compiled only sporadically, or in an aggregate form that changed from one census to the next.

40 Looked at in terms of the six years studied here, the major decline in the male-female ratio appears to occur rather abruptly between 1891 and 1901, when the proportion of female offenders decreased from 17.7 per cent to 5.8 per cent. However, a closer examination of the data suggests that this impression is somewhat misleading since there was a relatively high proportion of female offenders in the particular year 1891 and a correspondingly low proportion of females in 1901. When the proportion of female offenders

is traced on a yearly basis for the entire span of time encompassed by the registers (1867 to 1920), there is an overall long-term trend of a steady decline in the number of females, punctuated by fluctuations in particular years. For a discussion of this point see Boritch 'Gender and Criminal Court Outcomes.'

41 Boritch and Hagan 'A Century of Crime in Toronto'; Boritch 'Gender and Criminal Court Outcomes'; M.M. Feeley and D.L. Little 'The Vanishing Female: The Decline of Women in the Criminal Process' *Law and Society Review* 25 (1991) 719–57

42 On the work of various organizations, particularly women's groups, see L.J. Miller 'Uneasy Alliance: Women as Agents of Social Control' *Canadian Journal of Sociology* 12 (1987) 345–61; A. Klein and W. Roberts 'Besieged Innocence: The "Problem" and the Problems of Working Women – Toronto 1896–1914' in Acton et al. *Women at Work*; D. Pederson 'Keeping Our Good Girls Good: The YWCA and the "Girl Problem," 1870–1930' *Canadian Woman Studies* 7 (1987) 20–24; Morrison 'Their Proper Sphere'; Valverde *The Age of Light, Soap, and Water*; Kealey, *A Not Unreasonable Claim*.

43 See notes 11 and 13 above.

44 C. Addington *A History of the London Police Force* (London: Phelps 1980)

45 See, for example, the discussion of the national origin of offenders in Hamilton in Katz, Doucet, and Stern *The Social Organization of Early Industrial Capitalism*, and also the inmate profile of the Central Prison in Oliver 'A Terror to Evil-Doers.'

46 While there is no way of distinguishing Canadians of American descent from American nationals in the prison population, there is some reason to believe that the latter group was a special target of concerted enforcement practices. This would seem to be especially true in relation to American prostitutes plying their trade in Canadian cities, especially in the nineteenth century. In this regard, American-born women were significantly more overrepresented in the prison population than American-born men. For example, in 1871, 30.2 per cent of female prisoners were born in the United States, compared to 2.4 per cent of male prisoners. Moreover, with the exception of one woman charged with theft, all of these women were charged with vagrancy or prostitution-related offences (i.e., being a keeper or inmate of a house of ill fame). Many of these women, like Eliza Caldwell who was arrested five times for vagrancy in 1871 alone, were also repeat offenders. Similar findings with respect to the overrepresentation of American-born women in the prison population are reported for nineteenth-century Hamilton by Katz, Doucet, and Stern in *The Social Organization of Early Industrial Capitalism* 224. See also the remarks of Staff Inspector Archibald of the

Toronto Morality Department on his attempt to rid the city of American prostitutes in Boritch and Hagan 'Crime and the Changing Forms of Class Control.' On the overrepresentation of American-born men in Central Prison see Oliver 'A Terror to Evil-Doers' 228.

47 H. Graff 'Respected and Profitable Labour: Literacy, Jobs and the Working Class in the Nineteenth Century' in G.S. Kealey and P. Warrian, eds. *Essays in Canadian Working Class History* (Toronto: New Hogtown Press 1976). See also Graff 'Pauperism, Misery and Vice.'

48 The analysis of recidivism was complicated by the different ways in which prior committals were defined and recorded over time in the prison registers. More specifically, in some years multiple arrest charges were recorded as separate committals; hence, for example, an offender committed on a given day for three offences would be noted as having two prior committals. Sorting out the 'true' number of prior committals was accomplished by matching names and other offender information. It was then possible to determine if an offender was a first-time offender or not in each year in the study. Unfortunately, it was not possible to determine accurately the number of times an offender might have been committed during the intervening years not included in the analysis. Consequently, a gross measure of recidivism is used based on whether the offender was a first-time offender or had one or more prior committals.

49 The simple fact that an occupation was recorded does not necessarily imply, of course, that the individual was actually employed at the time of arrest. Furthermore, since prisoners could give false information about their occupations (within the bounds of credibility), there is reason to view individual occupational histories with some scepticism. However, to argue therefore, as some historians have done (see Fingard 'Jailbirds in Mid-Victorian Halifax') that attempts to quantify the relationship between class and criminality on the basis of recorded occupations are meaningless seems an unreasonable retreat to an extreme position. All historical data have potential limitations and inaccuracies and, consequently, there are problems associated with statistical representations of the criminal population on this dimension as others. However, I tend to share the view of those social historians who believe that 'half a loaf is better than no bread at all' and that such problems constitute obstacles rather than insurmountable impasses. Presumably, since prisoners could report any occupation, it is significant that, in this study, the vast majority of prisoners reported their occupation, or were recorded, as semi- or unskilled workers. Moreover, these results are consistent with various other historical studies dealing with the same issues. These findings tend to reinforce the conclusion that, for the purposes of portraying broad

trends in the social characteristics of criminals, occupational data are, on the whole, reliable indicators of social class.

50 See, in particular, Katz, Doucet, and Stern *The Social Organization of Early Industrial Capitalism*; Graff 'Pauperism, Misery and Vice'; Weaver 'Crime, Public Order and Repression.'

51 Probably Middlesex County Jail's most famous female prisoner was twenty-four-year-old Phoebe Campbell, who was committed in July 1871, for the murder of her husband in Nissouri township. The circumstances of the murder were particularly grisly. Phoebe was accused of killing her husband with an axe while he slept in their one-room cabin, and in the presence of her two infant children. The alleged motive for the murder was Phoebe's involvement with a nineteen-year-old neighbour, Thomas Coyle, who also was committed for murder. Phoebe's outspoken manner, the nature of the crime, and the alleged motive, all ensured that the case received widespread coverage in the press. After deliberating for half an hour, the assizes jury found Phoebe guilty and she was hanged on 20 June 1872. In a subsequent trial, on 9 October 1872, Thomas Coyle was acquitted.

52 Although the measure of recidivism used in the study, and described in note 48, is useful for distinguishing first-time offenders from repeat offenders, it does not adequately convey the extent to which women (the vast majority of whom were charged with public order offences) were more serious recidivists than men in the nineteenth century. While it was noted that this measure was used primarily as a result of inconsistencies in the recording of multiple arrest charges, this was a problem which affected only a minority of cases. Consequently, while the exact number of prior committals recorded for a small proportion of prisoners may be inaccurate, these data are nonetheless valuable in highlighting broad differences between women and men. In this regard it is noteworthy that in the nineteenth century, 36.4 per cent of female prisoners had been committed more than eleven times to prison and, of these women, 16.0 per cent had been committed twenty-six or more times. The comparable figures for men are 19.6 per cent and 0.5 per cent. Offenders such as Bridget Moore provide an illustration of the more extreme cases which contributed to the overall pattern of greater recidivism among female offenders. Bridget, twenty-nine years old, first appears in the register on 6 January 1871 for being vagrant and drunk. It is recorded as her twenty-fourth committal to prison. She is subsequently arrested four more times for vagrancy and once more for being vagrant and drunk in 1871, the last time on 17 December. Each time, she is sentenced to two months in jail so that in the period between January 1871 and February 1872, she spent twelve months in jail. The 1881 register shows two more

arrests. Now forty, she is first arrested on 21 April for vagrancy and following her release on 20 July is rearrested for vagrancy on 24 July, to give a total of sixty-one committals to jail. She does not reappear in the 1891 register.

53 Wetherell 'To Discipline and Train'

54 See note 17 above. Nor are these conclusions limited to the Canadian context, as similar arguments are made with respect to the operation of police courts in the United States during this period in Friedman and Percival *The Roots of Justice*.

55 P. Craven 'Law and Ideology: The Toronto Police Court 1850–1880' in D.H. Flaherty, ed. *Essays in the History of Canadian Law: Volume II* (Toronto: University of Toronto Press and Osgoode Society 1983)

56 During the years under study, only a few offenders (4.2 per cent) were released on bail. Since there is no mention of any subsequent court hearings for these offenders, it is presumed they forfeited their bail and, having in effect paid a fine, were not pursued further by authorities.

57 In Hamilton, between 1879 and 1881, 28 per cent of those arrested for assault were discharged, while 51 per cent of those charged with theft were released: Katz, Doucet, and Stern *The Social Organization of Early Industrial Capitalism* 235. Similarly, Weaver's data for the Gore district from 1832 to 1852 reveal that 43.5 per cent of those charged with common assault and 26.9 per cent of those charged with larceny were discharged. A further 13.5 per cent of offenders charged with larceny were released after being acquitted at trial: 'Crime, Public Order, and Repression' 40.

58 See the commissioners' recommendations in *Report of the Commissioners Appointed to Enquire into the Prison and Reformatory System of Ontario* esp. 218–21 and 104–7.

59 While there was a general increase in the amount of fines levied by the courts over time, the majority of offenders (61.6 per cent) were fined $10 or less throughout the period. In 1911, before the enactment of the Ontario Temperance Act, the highest fine levied was $61.50. In contrast, in 1920, seventy-nine persons were charged with breaches of the act and forty-six offenders were given fines ranging from a low of $203 to a high of $525.35.

60 As a further observation, the imposition of the fine option in relation to women charged with prostitution-related offences provides a revealing illustration of the way in which particular assumptions about sex and class shaped the process of justice. Throughout this period, and especially in the nineteenth century, women charged with vagrancy were virtually never given the option of paying a fine. In the hierarchy of prostitution, these women represented the bottom level, those who plied their trade in public

places and who were, therefore, continually vulnerable to arrest. In contrast, women arrested for being a keeper or inmate of a 'house of ill fame' were both presumably of a somewhat higher social standing and more protected from continual prosecution. For these women, it was common practice for judges to levy enormous fines by the standards of the nineteenth century (often $50 or more). Nonetheless, these fines were obviously in keeping with their means (or the means of their brothel keepers) since they generally were paid.

61 The remaining small minority of prisoners received a diverse set of dispositions which included being committed to the insane asylum, hospital, or house of refuge, being handed over to the military, being deported, or being executed (two). As well, from 1891 on, a few prisoners (thirty-nine) were given suspended sentences.

62 See note 57 above.

63 Katz, Doucet, and Stern *The Social Organization of Early Industrial Capitalism* 40

64 See note 11 above.

65 Oliver 'A Terror to Evil-Doers'

66 Wetherell 'To Discipline and Train.' See also the review of the state of Ontario's prisons in *Report of the Commissioners Appointed to Enquire into the Prison and Reformatory System of Ontario*. It is, no doubt, a reflection of the conditions of Middlesex County Jail that it was not unusual to come across cases where prisoners would manage to come up with the money to pay their fines with only a few days of their sentences left to serve. Despite the hardship which such fines posed for the average offender and his family, gaining release from prison must have been a stronger consideration.

67 It must also be noted that a small number of men (twenty-seven) sentenced to less than two months were transferred to Central Prison. As well, twelve men sentenced to terms of less than two years were transferred to the Federal Penitentiary.

68 See Wetherell 'To Discipline and Train' 151.

69 Splane *Social Welfare in Ontario*. See also the testimony of Mercer Reformatory officials in the *Report of the Commissioners Appointed to Enquire into the Prison and Reformatory System of Ontario* esp. 751.

70 Oliver 'A Terror to Evil-Doers' 227. See also the *Report of the Commissioners Appointed to Enquire into the Prison and Reformatory System of Ontario*. With respect to habitual drunkards, the commissioners reaffirmed the testimony of witnesses who argued that 'to effect a cure it is absolutely necessary that the drunkard should be kept under restraint until the craving for strong drink has been subdued ... Three months may be sufficient in some cases to work this great change, six months may be sufficient in others; but in many

cases at least a year would be necessary and in not a few cases even more than a year' (107). The commissioners also recommended that 'professional tramps,' as opposed to 'honest tramps who desire to obtain employment,' be treated with more severity and 'if they will not settle down to some regular steady employment, be treated as dangerous and sent for a term of not less than six months to the Central Prison' (114). With respect to female offenders, the commissioners echoed the opinion expressed by the Mercer deputy-superintendent, Mrs Lucy Anne Coad, that the sentences served by most women were ineffectual since 'it is almost impossible to do anything in the way of reformation with those who are sent to us for a few months' (749). They recommended 'that all those who are sent to this institution more than once, or for lewdness or other serious offences should be committed under indeterminate sentences or committed for long terms; the power to liberate on parole those who have given satisfactory evidence of reformation being vested in some provincial authority' (218).

71 See Backhouse 'Nineteenth-Century Prostitution Law'; Boritch 'Gender and Criminal Court Outcomes'; McLaren 'Chasing the Social Evil'; Rotenberg 'The Wayward Worker.' While many street prostitutes were arrested for vagrancy, and drunkenness statutes provided an alternative means of criminalizing prostitutes, there is no means of distinguishing female prostitutes among those arrested for either offence. Only the small minority of women arrested for being an inmate of a house of ill fame can be clearly identified as prostitutes. For this reason, researchers studying prostitution in the past have had to make the decision as to whether to use more or less inclusive measures of prostitution. For example, Backhouse in her study of prostitution in nineteenth-century Toronto includes all women charged with either vagrancy or drunkenness. However, at least in this analysis, the markedly longer sentences meted out to women than to men charged with vagrancy, and the more similar sentences for drunkenness, would tend to suggest that vagrancy statutes were the more common means of criminalizing prostitutes.

13

Prison as Factory, Convict as Worker: A Study of the Mid-Victorian St John Penitentiary, 1841–1880

RAINER BAEHRE

A product of early nineteenth-century penal reform, the St John Penitentiary was a significant architectural fixture of St John (now Saint John), in the colony of New Brunswick. The prison, which existed from 1842 to 1880, was built on a six-acre site one and a half miles from the city centre across Courtenay Bay and slightly east of Little River Road in the parish of Simonds and consciously situated beyond the pale of respectable and law-abiding mid-Victorian society. Like its inmate population – the mid-Victorian 'criminal class' – the prison was geographically and socially marginalized. To most New Brunswickers, this major provincial institution existed only in their imagination though etched sharply in their minds. While few of the thirty thousand townsfolk of this bustling mercantile and industrializing centre and fewer still of the agricultural and timber colony's more distant inhabitants ever paid the penitentiary a visit, nevertheless, as one newspaper journalist observed in the 1870s, there were 'few, indeed,' who were unaware of its presence.[1] Its social function escaped no one. Likening the penitentiary to 'a great sewer which cleanses and purifies a City,' another journalist saw it as drawing 'beneath the surface those moral lepers whose presence would contaminate society.'[2]

Like other social welfare 'asylums' in early nineteenth-century St John, the penitentiary was based on American and British models adapted to colonial conditions. It originated, in part, as an inspired experiment in social control and reconstruction – a moral engine in the hinterland of the empire helping to drive forward the machinery of mid-Victorian progress. Modest in its physical proportions, it served both the inhabitants of St John and the province, and consistently rivalled the city's other major social welfare institutions – the Provincial Lunatic Asylum and the St John Almshouse – in terms of its physical size, number of annual inmates, capital investment, and operating expenses.[3]

Punishment has always had a moral dimension and the introduction of certain forms of convict labour in early nineteenth-century penitentiaries was no exception.[4] A host of studies have clearly demonstrated that 'hard labour' was intrinsic to aspirations of punishing and reforming the convicted criminal. In replicating the productive process of the emerging industrial marketplace, the penitentiary was not only a place of incarceration and secondary punishment, but an instrument of resocialization. Partly because 'idleness' and ignorance were seen as the root of much crime, the penitentiary's disciplinary regimen and its own institutional productive capacity were intended constantly to occupy convicts and to impart 'skills.' Such convict labour also served the economic function of underwriting the costs of operating the institution and of preparing released prisoners for a capitalist labour market. In this sense, as Melossi and Pavarini have provocatively argued, the penitentiary – as a disciplinary institution – represented 'a model of the ideal society,' belonged to 'a new policy of social control,' and operated as a 'factory of men.'[5] By the same token, it is widely recognized that the penitentiary as factory failed as a reformative instrument.

Informed by the above historical sociology[6] and divided into four main parts, this paper is a case study of how convict labour underlay the history of a particular British North American penitentiary. First, it examines the origins of the St John Penitentiary, about which very little information exists. To explain its adoption I will discuss the trans-Atlantic cultural and North American transmission of reform ideas, the artful hand and imprint of the British Colonial Office, and more immediately local factors which brought government attention to the issues of crime and moral order.[7] A second section, the bulk of the paper, explores the physical and operational nature of the St John Penitentiary and the extent to which its regime achieved a factory mode of production. In particular, the nature of the convict as worker and the sharply divided attitudes towards convict labour are discussed. A third section examines convict labour as punishment and demonstrates how work and institutional discipline were intimately interrelated. Finally, after examining the penitentiary as a manufacturing establishment and its attendant problems of production, I argue that its shortcomings in this respect undermined the reform ideal itself. Convict labour in the context of other developments at the St John Penitentiary sheds additional light on the general failure of the nineteenth-century penitentiary and on the frustration of reform efforts to resocialize and rehabilitate the convict as a free worker.

ORIGINS OF THE ST JOHN PENITENTIARY

Between 1820 and 1840 wide-ranging legal and penal reforms occurred throughout British North America as prevailing public and corporal forms of punishment became outmoded and as the imperial and colonial governments searched for effective 'secondary punishments.'[8] In this period New Brunswick joined ranks with Nova Scotia and the Canadas in dramatically reducing the number of capital offences and abandoning many traditional forms of punishment. Most notably, the colony led the way in 1831 in abolishing benefit of clergy, eliminating the death sentence for any forms of theft, and severely curtailing the use of corporal punishments. This was followed by a further reduction in capital offences during the following decade.[9]

These legal changes reflected the marked shift towards more reasonable and just legal, judicial, and penal processes which had begun in Britain during the second half of the eighteenth century and which accelerated in the post-Napoleonic era. Reform was motivated in part by a growing fear that the traditional moral and social order was in jeopardy, and in part by a new belief that the natural state of man, long thought immutable, could be altered by manipulating the individual and his environment. These ascendant beliefs in society's ability to control crime and related matters reflected romantic and evangelical idealism as well as secular utilitarian thought and new forms of scientific and medical knowledge.[10] This general attack on the old order challenged the long-standing belief in fatalism and providence, and propelled a powerful movement towards institutional reform by bringing together like-minded industrialists, scientists, lawyers, and other middle- and upper-class reformers. Some of them began to play a growing role in the Colonial Office and colonial politics during the 1830s, and they directly and indirectly influenced the course of New Brunswick's legal, social, and institutional reforms.

The penitentiary was central to New Brunswick reformism. In the 1820s and 1830s local penal and judicial 'professionals' carefully sought out and compared institutional models of reform adopted elsewhere. The most popular blueprints for punishing and reforming the criminal surfaced in the United States and took two principal forms: the Auburn, or congregate system, adopted in New York State, and the Pennsylvania, or separate system, initiated at Philadelphia.[11] Under both prison regimes convicts were physically separated from one another, forever kept silent except when spoken to, and put to productive hard labour. But under the Philadelphia system work was initially not compulsory and considered a privilege. When they did work, convicts, often unskilled, were completely isolated from one another at all times. Workers under the Auburn system, while prohibited from communicating with one another except through a keeper, worked together in conformity with prevailing factory practices. The Auburn system was adopted in most of North America, including New Brunswick, and was popular largely because of its more productive use of convict labour. It was cheaper to supervise and vastly more profitable.

The New Brunswick government's provincial and municipal prison reform ventures were strongly influenced by developments in the mother country. The colony, based as it was within the structures of imperial government, could not and did not act unilaterally. By the mid-1830s the British government, influenced by William Crawford's famous 1835 report which supported American penitentiary developments, especially the Philadelphia system,[12] had decided to rationalize prison practices, at home and throughout the empire. The most tangible product of London's interest came in 1836, when Colonial Secretary Lord Glenelg, an active evangelical Anglican reformer, forwarded *Reports on Gaols and Houses of Correction in England and Wales* to all the British North American colonies, and told colonial administrators of the most recent trends in prison reform and the direction set by the British government. It was anticipated that all British colonies would follow suit, and they were pressed to do so.[13]

Imperial influence was also less directly exercised. A minority of serious criminals in the empire had commonly been sentenced to banishment, transportation to a penal colony, or incarceration on a convict hulk.[14] Support for colonial penitentiary initiatives came during the hearings of the Transportation Committee of 1837–8, which signalled the beginning of the end for this mode of punishment. Critics of transportation wanted the courts to exchange this sentence for others involving 'severe' imprisonment and hard labour.[15] The penitentiary promised substantially more hope for making the punishment fit the crime and for reforming the criminal. A colonial penitentiary would also shift more of the financial burden of the administration of criminal justice to the colonies. In 1841 New Brunswick, when it wanted to transport several convicts, was told in the future to pay the costs of transportation, clothing, and provisions for any convict it wanted transported.[16] This practice rapidly fell into decline in favour of long-term prisonment at home.

The penitentiary system urged for New Brunswick differed significantly from its institutional antecedents, such as houses of confinement and bridewells. Detailed attention was now paid to the physical structure, aptly called 'moral architecture,' of the penitentiary.[17] Order and symmetry were evident in all aspects of the complex of buildings which constituted it, in the arrangement of cell blocks which separated prisoners, and in the elimination of all unnecessary contact. Penal reformers placed great faith in their new-found ability to classify prisoners, to separate them, to enforce discipline, and to use religious instruction and hard labour as reformative tools. Penitentiaries were to be arranged to promote constant vigilance, so that inmates would always 'feel' themselves watched. This controlling 'gaze,' endorsed by the Boston Prison Discipline Society, was an extension of the vital importance of the need for 'unceasing vigilance in government' and reflected as well significant aspects of emerging factory discipline.[18] The underlying intent was moral reordering and not merely the enhancement of state control for secular purposes. Variations of these themes made a substantial doctrinal impact on St John society and on social reform in the city, especially on the temperance movement, and influenced penal policy also.[19]

The decision by New Brunswick politicians to build a prison on the penitentiary model in the 1830s was therefore a reflection of international developments. But it also emerged in the context of indigenous needs and local politics. The commitment to a penitentiary came slowly, and only as local circumstances warranted. The original city charter of 1775 had given the mayor and councillors authority to build bridewells, houses of correction, or workhouses 'for preventing Idleness and Disorders, and for punishing Rogues, Vagabonds, and other Idle and Disorderly Persons.'[20] Successive New Brunswick governments ignored these options until the 1830s. Local jails sufficed as lock-ups, and for a long time more was not thought necessary until criticisms of the jails proved overwhelming. Overcrowding, chaotic and arbitrary administration, idleness, and unhygienic conditions were the main focus of attention. As early as 1803, a St John grand jury found the local jail in a state of terrible disrepair. Filth had accumulated in the basement creating an 'intolerable stench' which contemporary medical wisdom regarded as a miasmic condition contaminating the air and spreading disease. Conditions continued to deteriorate to the point where the 'apartments' set aside for criminals had broken windows and floors were covered in 'large quantities of snow and ice.' The grand jury also worried, quite rightly given the physical state of the jail, that prisoners would find it easy to escape. The place had become so dirty and so overcrowded that the jail keeper's family was forced to live in the kitchen. It was 'a most disgraceful nuisance reflecting dishonor on this city and county and impeaching its justice and humanity.'[21]

Little of this changed until the 1830s. Although local governments responded by making minor repairs or by replacing these edifices with others of similar design, modified forms of obsolete institutions failed to address these inherent flaws. The shortcomings of New Brunswick's county jail system were addressed only in 1841 when Colonial Secretary Lord Stanley and Lieutenant-Governor Colebrook discussed a summary of New Brunswick jail reports based on the *Blue Books*.[22] In addition to noting structural shortcomings that made inmates suffer from excessive heat in the summer and intense cold in the winter, Stanley pointed out that these overcrowded facilities had no clearly defined prison regimen, no employment or education for convicts, no opportunity for exercise, no bedding or clothing allowance, little evidence of discipline, and no regulated diet.[23]

The mid-1830s first saw suggestions that the problem could be solved by the city building its own house of correction. This represented the response of city officials to currents of penal reform as well as to pressure from the Colonial Office to modernize the penal system. St John sent an official envoy, G.J. Dibblee, to Boston, the home of the widely lauded Boston Prison Discipline Society, to examine the latest American model prisons. Dibblee forwarded his findings to the mayor and to future prison commissioner Robert Hazen, a prominent and reform-minded St John lawyer. Hazen soon was joined on a newly formed, provincial Prison Board by fellow members of the local elite, including George D. Robinson, a St John patrician, alderman Henry Porter of King's county, 'a puritan liberal,' who was known as an able, conscientious, and scrupulous magistrate; Noah Distrow, a wealthy merchant; and Robert Payne, of whom little is known.[24] What appealed to this group of reformers and civic notables about an independent house of correction was that it would bring 'order, regularity, [and a] chance of moral improvement to the convict.'[25]

The decision to create a house of correction along penitentiary lines for the city of St John appears to have been adopted without acrimony. This contrasts with Upper Canada, where the Kingston Penitentiary had numerous detractors, especially among local tradesmen.[26] Plans for the construction of the St John house of correction were formalized in 1836 through legislation in which the provincial government authorized £3000 for its construction, and through the House of Correction Act of 1836, which gave magistrates the power to send both minor offenders and long-term felons there for purposes of correction.[27] Government soon allocated a further £10,000, and newspapers advertised for tenders.[28] But in 1837 the Colonial Office withheld assent to the legislation.

Several reasons can be cited for London's hesitation. Houses of correction had fallen into disfavour in England as early as the later eighteenth century for economic and 'moral' reasons.[29] As extensions of local jails they suffered from similar shortcomings, especially 'moral contagion' caused by the lumping together of debtors, lunatics, vagrants, minor criminals, and felons. Such conditions made 'correction' unlikely and, it was presumed, increased rather than reduced the incidence of crime. The Colonial Office expressed several specific reservations about the St John project. First, the New Brunswick government had not sent a plan of the building to England. Keen to rationalize colonial jails throughout the empire to make them conform to newly developed British standards, imperial officials insisted on a high degree of institutional uniformity. Second, London feared that this legislation might not leave final authority over prison management to the lieutenant-governor, an appointee of the British government, and that local political interference would render the facility ineffective. The colonial secretary believed this would not protect the best interests of all those affected by the institution. Finally, this legislation appeared to promote a provincial system of local houses of correction in each county which would accommodate criminals and debtors, felons and misdemeanants, and this remedy was seen as too expensive and generally unsuitable. Instead, the Colonial Office offered to sanction a single penal institution to serve the entire province. Thus, when Lord Glenelg in 1838 forwarded information from the secretary of the London Prison Discipline Society to Lieutenant-

Governor Sir John Harvey, describing the state of jails and prison discipline in various colonies, he insisted that New Brunswick conform to new developments in penal policy in the mother country.[30]

Imperial pressure had its effect. Legislation of 1838 provided for a house of correction to be built in St John entirely separate from the city jail. In 1839 a statute was passed, 'to provide for the government and regulation of the House of Correction,' which marked a clear move to central control, with the governor in council retaining the authority to appoint and review a board of commissioners.[31] Yet the road to construction of a modern prison in St John was temporarily blocked by a combination of external factors. The 'Great Conflagration' of 1839 destroyed the recently built local jail and large sections of the city.[32] Although construction was begun in 1840, further delay in realizing the project occurred that same year when the Colonial Office expressed reservations about the proposed legislation and suggested alterations to the building plans, administration, and rules and regulations, using prisons of the West Indies as models of management. Further modifications were suggested in 1842.[33] Finally, the colony adopted a modified Auburn plan as re-evaluated by sympathetic British penal experts, though England itself followed the Philadelphia-based separate system.[34]

The new prison was completed in 1842 at a cost of £13,501, of which £8078 was contributed initially by the provincial legislature; the city, the principal user of the institution, was expected to pay the balance. The municipal government, however, was unable to meet its responsibilities in the midst of an economic downswing and near-bankruptcy. Further delays in construction would have been inevitable had not the province then agreed to fully fund and administer the institution. Appropriately, it was renamed the Provincial Penitentiary, thus becoming a provincial institution, not a municipal one.[35] In this way most of the imperial government's wishes, especially central control, were met. And yet the 'House of Correction' idea never entirely disappeared, as we shall see, and in its incarceration of minor offenders the St John Penitentiary differed dramatically from other early Canadian penitentiaries, like Kingston.[36]

The adoption of the penitentiary in New Brunswick can be explained only partly by reference to broad ideological changes in law and penal reform. One needs also to place its origins in the context of local social and economic developments. The early nineteenth century, and especially the 1830s, was a time of rapid economic expansion and social change in New Brunswick. St John was 'a microcosm of the economic and demographic changes that were altering the social fabric of the province.'[37] The city's population in 1841 was roughly 20,000 in a province of 160,000; its numbers more than doubled by 1880 when the penitentiary finally closed. The influence of the staple trades – timber, lumber, shipbuilding, fish, and agricultural produce – prevailed.[38] Despite economic expansion, growing prosperity, and the emergence of a dominant mercantile class, the city harboured its share of filthy slums, economic 'hard times,' and social disorder. As early as the 1830s the spread of disease, the presence of destitution, increases in crime, and a dose of xenophobia deriving from disproportionate Irish immigration united provincial and municipal politicians of diverse leanings in a new interest in 'advancement,' land reform, and the reform of government institutions.[39] St John was especially affected by pauper immigration, as many newcomers arrived with little or nothing.

In the period prior to the founding of the penitentiary concerns about social disorder were reflected in several statutes regulating public nuisances. An act 'to establish a House of Correction within the Counties of York and Charlotte,' passed in March 1830, was not acted upon because the small number of jail inmates did not warrant large capital expenditures.[40] In 1831 a bill was passed 'to provide for setting and keeping to hard labour persons adjudged to that punishment,' but local jails lacked the facilities to put this into effect.[41] Provincial magistrates consistently observed that many jail inmates were recent immigrants, mostly Irish, with a reputation for rowdiness, disorderliness, and lawlessness,[42] although the statistics indicate no epidemic of serious crime. Prior to the opening of the penitentiary, a return of the number of prisoners confined in all the county jails listed a total of just 149 prisoners, of whom 95 were debtors. Moreover, no more than twenty prisoners had ever been confined in any district jail at any one time.[43] A St John police force was not formed until 1849, seven years after the opening of the penitentiary.[44] Yet in explaining the need for a penitentiary in 1842, Lieutenant-Governor Harvey related its implementation to a general increase in crimes, especially 'some of an aggravated and alarming description.'[45] There was, then, a perception of increasing crime and public disorder prior to the construction of the penitentiary.

The 1830s and 1840s saw other institutional responses to the apparent crumbling of public and moral order. During the cholera scares of 1832 and 1834 legislation was passed introducing quarantine procedures and establishing temporary cholera hospitals. At the same time the growing presence of dependent women and their children prompted the city fathers to found a Female House of Industry. The committal of increasing numbers of lunatics to the local jail resulted in 1836 in the opening of British North America's first lunatic asylum, while the growing presence of beggars and aged peoples prompted the establishment in 1838 of a revamped almshouse.[46] These remedies – correcting the criminal, hard labour, and rounding up social nuisances – were, in effect, collectively incorporated into the legislation which established the St John Penitentiary and represented the transformation of punishment and the growth of state control.[47]

Thus the reformist sentiment which reshaped New Brunswick's penal system was propelled – as in New England and Great Britain – by the influence of a reform-minded middle-class elite concerned about the need to preserve public morality, property, and social order.[48] This response also points towards the process of state formation in a broader sense. In the European experience, the appeal of the reformed prison during the 1820s reflected an international movement towards centralization and state monopolization of violence. This, Spierenburg argues, was 'a necessary prerequisite for the emergence of the prison, a spatial solution for public order problems.'[49] The New Brunswick government, determined to control social disorder by legal, bureaucratic, and institutional means, exercised increasing authority over those individuals who contributed to the breakdown of order. The St John Penitentiary must be understood as a local variant of this wider government-promoted programme of social control.

PRISON AS FACTORY, CONVICT AS WORKER

The St John Penitentiary was not built on the well-known radial plan with wings extending from a central rotunda and shared little of the elaborate physical architecture of some contemporary counterparts. It consisted of three main buildings set up in a quadrangle with an L-shaped building on one side. The longest wing was 120 feet long and 45 feet wide with thirty cells back to back on each of the three floors, all facing a wide corridor, with a watch-tower and an armed guard on the roof. Each cell, constructed of granite, was 7 1/2 feet long, 4 1/2 feet wide, and 7 1/2 feet high. A rear brick addition held forty cells for female convicts. Directly across the quadrangle stood a building to house the keeper and guards, which also served as a hospital, storeroom, and office. In the middle of the quadrangle to the rear stood the workshops and storehouses. The main workshop, initially used for making bricks, eventually stood four storeys high, 100 feet long, and 25 feet wide. To one side was a wooden drying house, 40 feet long and 20 feet wide, and on the other side was a building for storing manufactured goods. The grounds of five to six acres on which the buildings stood were surrounded by a wooden pallisade fence.[50]

In its attempt to resocialize the convict the penitentiary regimen was based on the belief that 'society' had demonstrated 'the value of labor, not only as a means of support, but as an auxiliary of virtue.'[51] The 'main end and object' of the St John Penitentiary, according to its commissioners, was 'the amelioration of the morals of its inmates, and the encouragement of industry.'[52] The central element of the rehabilitative and economic success of the penitentiary was legitimated in the biblical doctrine 'Thou shalt labour,' and in the systematic application of the work ethic. To achieve these ends St John penal reformers implemented the Auburn system in the belief that it best favoured the inculcation of moral and ethical values.[53] Local interests were also drawn to the possible financial benefits of Auburn to the penitentiary. Prison work was seen as a method of reforming the criminal but, as importantly, was expected to reduce the operating costs of the institution, and perhaps, as several American penitentiaries had demonstrated, even to show a profit.[54] The Auburn-style workshops proved more productive by reproducing the workplace of the manufactory, while the Philadelphia system did not.[55] Equally, New Brunswick's reformers endeavoured to resocialize prisoners by exposing them to the realities of the industrial workplace, and in so doing to make them self-sufficient. In general, therefore, the penitentiary's rules and regulations resembled those of a model factory of the day,[56] emphasizing order, silence, obedience, and continual labour.

Of course the factory, unlike the penitentiary, never became what Erving Goffman has called a 'total institution.'[57] Like most similar institutions, the St John Penitentiary operated under a formal set of rules which applied to both inmates and staff.[58] The keeper was obligated to enforce hard labour (Rule 5), which convicts had to perform 'diligently' and 'to the best of his or her ability' (Rule 28). All prisoners 'unless prevented by sickness' were to be employed up to ten hours per day, with time allowed for meals. Exceptions were Sundays, Christmas Day, Good Friday, and other days allotted 'for fasting or thanksgiving' (Rule 8). No gambling, drinking, tobacco, vandalism, or indecency was permitted (Rules 15, 23, 25, and 27). Inmates were to remain silent unless spoken to by staff, be 'of quiet and orderly behaviour,' and to 'strictly and *implicitly* obey orders' (Rules 26 and 28).[59]

The daily routine largely conformed to these rules. In particular, the extent of convict labour at St John was significant. Male and female prisoners were responsible for much of its original construction. Between 1842 and 1844 male convicts produced bricks, some of their product being sold to the city to help build the almshouse situated across the road from the penitentiary. Over the next six years prison labour played an integral part in the construction of the workshops, two buildings containing a staff residence, a hospital room, and a storeroom, and another addition which became the female prison.

Once the penitentiary workshops were in place, the pattern of daily work remained ostensibly the same. A description from the mid-1860s is typical. Except for Sunday – a day of sermons and rest – work dominated. In summers work began at six and was interrupted only by breakfast at eight and dinner at one. Then work continued until six, when supper was served. During the winter months, work began at seven, after breakfast, and ended at sunset. Meals were taken in cells, requiring that convicts march in military order – probably lockstep – to and from their cells.[60]

Initially, the St John Penitentiary functioned more as a manufactory, a collection of small craft-based workshops, than as an industrial factory, with large-scale division of labour. In addition to brick-making, convicts worked for tradesmen assigned to the penitentiary and spent their time performing blacksmith's work, shoemaking, tailoring, and coopering. Carpentry and brush-making were soon added. Gender roles were apparent in the work of the female convicts who washed the barrack bedding, spun wool, knitted, and wove clothing. Convicts also carried out farm work, thus helping to defray operating costs further. Much of their time was spent performing maintenance duties. But productive labour, in the sense of products for sale on the open market, was regularly undermined because of the shortage of tradesmen and fluctuating demand for prison-made goods.[61]

With the gradual but steady industrialization of the workplace in colonial society, the nature of work at the prison changed considerably. Though more traditional and menial tasks continued to be performed, there also began a discernible shift away from strictly manual to more machine-dependent tasks. This transformation was first apparent towards the end of the 1840s when an emphasis began to be placed on industrial production and less on artisanal labour and handicraft production, as technology began to revolutionize many crafts. This movement towards industrial prison production and manufacturing technology, as evidenced in the use of steam-powered lathes, was influenced by changes in the external labour market and by the city's growing number of factories. It reflected, too, the migration of many artisans to other parts of British North America and the United States. The early changes to the nature of convict labour in the late 1840s can thus be interpreted as an institutional adaptation to new economic realities brought about by the demise of mercantilism and to a decline in the colony's traditional reliance on staple exports, such as timber and fish.

In 1848 the prison commissioners sought to increase the pace of change and called for an expansion and diversification of prison manufacturing. To further 'useful employment' the board promoted the introduction of a steam-operated carding machine and cloth manufactory. Steam power was intended to replace the two horses used at the brick mill, and it powered the lathe used to make agricultural tools and corn brooms. Industrial expansion, it was argued, would be 'of great advantage' to the province. Henceforth convicts would be instructed 'in the knowledge of various manufactures, inasmuch as upon their restoration to society they may carry the knowledge so required into the remote parts of the Province.'[62]

These aspirations were achieved only gradually, if at all. As the provincial economy recovered in the early 1850s, and following the election of a pro-artisan Common Council, the penitentiary commissioners put an end to any further expansion of prison manufacturing. They were likely alert to potential opposition from free labour, and endeavoured as a result to slow down the expansion of prison manufacturing. Although in 1852 a bone mill to grind bone into dust for fertilizer was added to the prison workshops, the experiment was short-lived. Towards the end of the 1850s the commissioners decided to close the brick manufactory. They reasoned that brick-making was a seasonal activity performed by the least fit criminals. Instead, they suggested using the traditional method of putting convicts to work breaking stones for road construction. A proposal to introduce a machine to produce draining tiles never came to fruition because of a lack of money and suitable tradesmen.[63]

Although the extent of manufacturing was limited by numerous considerations and handicraft production did not disappear, some prison industry remained viable and the prison workshops continued to reflect many characteristics of a mid-Victorian factory. There were separate workshops with a capacity to employ approximately sixty men and women. The first floor contained a blacksmith shop and an engine-room, the latter housing a twenty-five-horsepower steam engine which drove the machinery – metal lathes and planing machines used for meeting the institution's need for iron artefacts. The second floor was a manufactory for pails, tubs, and clothes-pins where the entire production from the cutting of logs to sanding the finished product was carried out. Several other forms of production took place on the third floor. In one part, convicts manufactured hay rakes, washboards, and scrubbing brushes. In another part, shoemakers plied their trade. Finally on the fourth floor there existed a broom factory and paint shop. Women worked in a separate workshop, a room forty feet square located on the top floor of the female prison. There they prepared wool – picking wool, carding, spinning, weaving – and made the prison clothing and bed sheets. Four or five women operated the kitchens. A prison matron supervised this work. The manufacture of brooms, tubs, and pails for sale outside the penitentiary continued up to the closing of the institution in 1880.[64] By that date the penitentiary had emerged full-blown as an important manufacturer of a wide range of consumer goods.

In fact, by the 1870s the penitentiary ranked among the city's largest manufacturing establishments. The daily average number of convicts in 1875 was 98, and approximately 60 persons were employed in the workshops alone. In contrast, four nail and tack factories in the city employed a total of 272 men, or an average of 68 workers each; ten city foundries boasted a combined workforce of 426, or roughly 43 workers each; twenty-seven lumber mills in the immediate vicinity hired 2225 workers, or 82 each; three cotton mills had 215 hands, three sash and blind factories a combined total of 210, and one tobacco manufacturer had 45 employees. All other city industries boasted only 30 workers or less.[65]

There were those who praised the quality of convict labour, including Warden John Quinton, who administered the prison from 1842 to 1875.[66] Quinton argued that prison-manufactured brooms were of higher quality than others on the market and available at a cheaper price.[67] James G. Moylan, Canada's secretary director of penitentiaries, reflected upon the closing of the prison on 'the workman-like and skilful manner in which the varied and extensive list of articles was turned out.' St John convicts had been put to work making 180 bedsteads, cell and other furniture, iron-gratings, doors, and tools for the Dorchester Penitentiary. Moylan complimented both convicts and staff for completing their assigned tasks quickly and well.[68]

Not all prison inmates made ideal workers, and many were very bad indeed. Like the Halifax Penitentiary, but unlike Kingston and all post-Confederation penitentiaries, St John, before and after Confederation, was forced to accept short-term, often repeat offenders sentenced to hard labour, in addition to the more useful prisoners sentenced for two years or more.[69] The type of convict labourer sent to the institution was beyond the warden's control, and local magistrates greatly exacerbated the problem by sending some prisoners who were guilty of no more than non-payment of fines. Quinton was privately convinced that the police courts of St John were regularly sending individuals whom the local jail did not want and some of these were useless as workers. A few examples of the many in Quinton's diary give credibility to his claim. In one six-month period in 1870, Quinton was forced to receive many persons whose incarceration was questionable, including a woman holding a small infant who was committed for non-payment of a fine. An almshouse inmate, who left that institution briefly, returned and was suspected of having contracted smallpox. He was refused readmission, taken to Police Court, and sent to the penitentiary on a trumped-up charge of vagrancy. Two children aged eleven and twelve, one missing an arm and the other with only a stump for a thumb, were picked up for petty offences and sent to the penitentiary. There was also a drunken vagrant charged with being a public nuisance. Filthy, vermin-ridden, and in rags, he arrived at the prison only to be released two days later when someone paid his fine. Meanwhile he had been fed, clothed, and cared for. 'We have too much of this nonsense, quite too much,' Quinton recorded.[70] Thus the prison served as a dumping ground for persons whom Quinton and others regarded as 'the refuse' of the city – 'the ne'er-do-well vagrants and drunkards, from the slums and back lanes ... incapable of earning a month's expenses in a year,' prostitutes of the 'lowest kind,' and the 'old, decrepit, and utterly broken-down characters, totally unfit and unable – were they even fit to work.'[71]

Not only did such inmates not belong in a penitentiary, they were barely trainable or useful in light of their physical state and short internment. The costs of their maintenance were absorbed by the institution, without any profitable return on their labour. Remarkably, a few did become moderately good workers. Most were kept busy, but their labour was marginally useful and questionably reformative.

Despite all efforts to make convict labour work as a reform technique, wider concerns undermined its role. Convict labour at St John was inevitably drawn into the ongoing international debate about its merits. In Upper Canada convict labour was a contentious issue from the op-

ening of Kingston Penitentiary, when its detractors expressed grave reservations over convicts in competition with free labourers.[72] When
Gladstone, as colonial secretary, asked in the 1850s whether transported
convicts might be employed on the projected railway linking Quebec
City and Halifax, he was told that the Nova Scotian government viewed
such a proposal as 'distasteful'; New Brunswick for its part was worried
that such a use of prison workers would cause 'great jealousy and
alarm.'[73] In large part such sentiments proceeded from the anxieties
of tradesmen. But anticonvict labour sentiment was also rooted in other
cultural and social values. As the Victorians increasingly distinguished
the respectable from the work-shy, they not only amended poor relief
practices but also developed a strong aversion to giving criminals any
benefit which the common, honest workingman did not have.[74] Convict
labour was justified if it reduced government expenditures, but it was
vilified if it affected free workers. Thus, from the late 1850s New Brunswick limited the extent of convict labour, in particular by refusing to
expand the penitentiary's manufacturing capacity and by rejecting the
system of contract labour.

After Confederation the St John Penitentiary was administered by
the federal government, and similar concerns about convict labour influenced federal penal policy. The struggle between its supporters and
detractors resurfaced during the economic crisis of the 1870s when unemployment rose and governments sought to cut costs. The objections
of the Canadian Labour Union and the Canadian Trades and Labour
Congress, as well as the fiasco at the Ontario Central Prison which
Joseph Berkovits discusses elsewhere in this volume, are telling illustrations of the sensitivities which the issue elicited in this period.[75] As
an alternative to 'state-use,' contract labour was employed in many jurisdictions as the standard system of organizing prison work. In the
contract system private tradesmen trained and supervised inmates,
whose products were sold on the open market.[76] This method had several apparent advantages. Prison staff were relieved of some of the daily
responsibility of supervision, and capital costs were largely borne by
the contractor as no expensive machinery or facilities had to be purchased by the penitentiary. However, after mid-century, state inspectors,
prison commissioners, and many wardens condemned contract labour:
it undermined prison discipline and the goal of reformation by interfering with the religious and secular instruction of convicts, it limited
the learning of a trade, and it did not provide as much of a financial
return to the state as might be possible under a well-supervised, entirely
state-run system.[77]

By Confederation federal penal officials were advocating the gradual abandonment of the contract system.[78] They foresaw two long-term options. Penitentiaries might embark on different forms of industry which could be carried out within the institution and exclusively under prison staff supervision, with products to be used by other government agencies. Or they could employ convicts on public works such as canal construction or land drainage projects in the remoter regions, also under government supervision. The first option was already being pursued at the St John Penitentiary, where the contract system had only tentatively taken hold. In 1858 the prison commissioners had recommended that the government consider the adoption of the system of contracting for the labour of the prisoners, which had proved successful in the Province of Canada and the United States. This system was instituted in 1863, when prisoners were contracted to J.P. Mackay & Fisher, but their labour amounted to only $248 compared with $13,287.50 from the sale of prison manufactures. This short-lived experiment was soon discontinued, and in 1867 it was reported that 'No labor of any description is hired to contractors.'[79] When the inspector of penitentiaries suggested in 1877 that productivity be increased at St John, with convicts manufacturing the cloth used in penitentiaries, making uniforms for the militia and Mounted Police, and doing casting for the rolling stock on government railways, the recommendations fell on deaf ears.[80] Even the state-use system excited opposition, and the federal government refused to risk alienating capital or free labour by expanding prison industry.

The new arrangements brought about by Confederation also led, in the case of the St John Penitentiary, to considerable legal and political wrangling on a number of issues, mostly financial. In the late 1860s the federal government decided to build a single, regional penitentiary in the Maritimes, and not thereafter to support the existing institution at St John. New Brunswick politicians insisted that the Confederation accord included a promise by Canada to maintain the existing St John Penitentiary. This meant complete and continuing federal responsibility for the maintenance and costs of all its prisoners. The issue was apparently resolved in 1871 when Ottawa, while insisting that the institution should be a provincial responsibility in so far as it catered to short-term prisoners, did agree to absorb the outstanding provincial bonds which had financed its construction. But in 1875 Ottawa ignored provincial objections and legislated to exclude from its responsibilities within three years all offenders sentenced to less than two years and to prohibit them from being sent to a penitentiary![80] Shortly thereafter the old St John Penitentiary was designated a provincial prison by federal order-in-council and the Dorchester Penitentiary was scheduled for opening, a move which saddled New Brunswick with what its politicians termed 'a white elephant' and threw 'a most vexatious and unforeseen burden and tax' upon New Brunswickers.[81] In the words of the chairman of Common Council of the City of St John, the federal action caused 'a crisis in the administration of the Criminal Law,'[82] for the province and its municipalities were now expected to pay for the costs of incarceration for any prisoner not sentenced to a penitentiary term. Protests fell on deaf ears, however, and this imbroglio illustrates further the fact that political and fiscal expediency, as much if not more than a concern about maximizing the rehabilitative aspects of the institution, shaped the penitentiary's history.

The low priority allotted to the rehabilitation of penitentiary convicts by politicians is further indicated by the absence of a Canadian representative at the International Prison Congress at London in 1872, where the issue of convict labour was addressed and contract labour was vilified. Having acquainted themselves with the proceedings, the Directors of Penitentiaries (Acting Chairman J.W. King, F.X. Prieur, and Secretary James G. Moylan) summarized its main findings and informed the federal government that 'industrial labour is alone in conformity with the true principles of penitentiary science.'[83] They argued also that it enhanced institutional order and made prison operations more economical. More importantly, they reminded the politicians that convicts should be made to work not for the sake of punishment, but as a means to reform, and that this end would be achieved if the teaching of trade skills was combined with moral and religious instruction. This was only possible if convict labour within the penitentiary was used. Moreover, if society was to be protected once prisoners were released, ex-convicts needed to have a trade and the opportunity to earn an honest living. Thus despite Quinton's own 'lost confidence' in prison manufacturing and his recommendation in 1869 that the contract system be introduced with labour and machinery hired out to private operators,[84] international reform views shared by the Directors of Penitentiaries provided ongoing legitimacy for continuing the 'state use' manufacturing system at the St John Penitentiary.

DISCIPLINING THE CONVICT

In light of the fact that 'hard labour' was intended to have both punitive and reformative qualities, it is not surprising that work discipline and institutional discipline were regarded as intimately interconnected. To meet the ends of 'reform,' physical and psychological coercion were frequently used to manage the convict labour force. The Board of Commissioners ordered from the beginning that a prisoner found guilty of destroying prison property, refusing to work, or being otherwise disobedient be put in solitary confinement and whipped. With the board's authorization, the keeper could impose solitary confinement for a period not exceeding three days, later extended to nine days, and with a diet of bread and water only.[85] The original 1842 draft of the rules and regulations included a provision for punishment by whipping, and although this clause was stroked out, the keeper retained the prerogative to punish prisoners in this manner, though formal whipping was used infrequently. In an 1847 memorandum to the provincial secretary, the lieutenant-governor insisted that prison discipline, especially the separation of hardened from minor criminals, the system of silence, solitary confinement, and the punishment of bread and water, be carefully observed. The commissioners responded that discipline had always been kept up.[86]

The rigorous enforcement of prison discipline was largely attributable to Warden John Quinton. In contrast to the Halifax Penitentiary, where enforcement depended at times on the disposition of the warden, there is no strong evidence to suggest a breakdown in discipline at any time during the entire forty-year history of the St John institution. There may have been occasional lapses in conforming to the rules and there are hints of a prisoner subculture to circumvent them, but these were isolated incidents.

There are no documents written by convicts about Quinton or about their reactions to prison work and prison discipline. There do exist two detailed letters written by a former tradesman and keeper, R. Bartlett, which graphically depict the high level of brutality in the enforcement of discipline. These letters also indicate how punishment was meted out both formally and informally. In the first letter, Bartlett, who had left his position at the penitentiary in disgust and begun work at a Massachusetts prison, described the case of an English sailor guilty of assaulting a policeman. The sailor had received a sentence of eighteen months but had obtained a good character reference from his captain and his sentence was reduced to six months. A favourite jail keeper of Quinton's disliked the convict intensely, and he contrived to place the sailor in 'the black hole' for three days and nights. To aggravate the convict's condition, several other keepers threw in several pails of water to make it impossible for the sailor to lie down on the floor without becoming soaked. Consequently, the convict contracted a severe cold and 'a terrible swelling of feet and legs' to the extent that they no longer looked 'human.' This condition rendered the convict incapable of working for several weeks.

This mode of discipline, according to Bartlett, was not unusual. He claimed to be able to recite a litany of comparable cruelties. He had witnessed daily beatings. One such beating involved the same keeper who had brutalized the unfortunate sailor. Using a broom handle with stiff leather thongs tied to the end, the keeper, utterly winding himself before he stopped, beat another convict into submission. Quinton followed behind 'saying, damn him, give it to him.' Barlett further remarked that a horse-whip was often used to beat recalcitrant female prisoners.[87]

In his second letter Bartlett wrote that he considered one prisoner to have been murdered by the keepers. After being placed in 'the black hole' for three days for refusing to work and claiming to be sick, this convict, in desperation, asked for a doctor; he was told 'Die and be damned.' Upon his release from solitary confinement he died within twenty-four hours. Worse, according to Bartlett, he was not alone in having been 'murdered by slow degrees.' Although Bartlett offered the names of at least five prisoners and keepers who would support his testimony, he recognized that convicts had no credibility in a court of law and would come forward only if given guarantees that they could be 'secured from Quinton's brutality afterwards,' and that staff were too intimidated by fear of losing their jobs to testify.[88]

An intermediary passed Barlett's letters on to Samuel Tilley, provincial secretary, who appears to have done nothing with them.[89] Perhaps Tilley believed Bartlett's allegations to be exaggerated or the result of a personality conflict between a disgruntled employee and the warden. More likely, Tilley reflected prevailing public opinion on penitentiary convicts. As members of the criminal class, convicts needed to be harshly disciplined and to have their will broken before reformative action became possible. In any event, like Tilley, prison officials did not tolerate any resistance to the imposed regimen, and convict labour was always enforced with particular rigour.

Though 'malingering' can be seen as a way for convicts to protest prison conditions and oppressive working conditions, for the most part they had no recourse: they had to endure and obey. Failure to comply with the demands of their overseers led to further punishment. A convict's ultimate disobedience, of course, was to attempt to escape. In such an event penitentiary guards were instructed to shoot, and over the years several convicts were shot, and one was killed.[90] To ensure security and as punishment, recaptured escapees or intractable prisoners were shackled and placed in 'the black hole.'

The use of physical punishment at the St John Penitentiary did wane towards the end of the prison's history, though it was never entirely abandoned. A careful examination of Quinton's diary for 1869 to 1872 supports this claim. The warden was insistent that any transgression, including failure to work or not performing labour properly, be dealt with swiftly in order to minimize the convict's ability to disrupt the institution. But, at least officially, the use of extreme forms of punishment was by then an infrequent occurrence. Nor in the post-Confederation era, when the penitentiary was regulated by federal officials, were prisoners who refused to work or who flagrantly violated the rules beaten into submission. Rather they were placed in solitary confinement. Quinton's successor still listed formal lashings as forms of punishment, though he claimed to have dispensed them only on rare occasions. In 1877 the inspector of penitentiaries contended that 'the dungeon and the cats are resorted to only in extreme cases, and when other means of correction are found to be inefficacious.'[91] What perhaps had earlier appalled keeper Bartlett was the nature of the penitentiary system itself, which he incorrectly attributed to the brutality of the warden. While personality clearly entered into the equation, a certain level of brutality was intrinisic to the penitentiary system. In fact, it represented the last resort for maintaining order. Its dispensation was intended to be rational and just, and to be in the long-term interests of the convict and society; its level of acceptability depended on the eye and influence of the beholder.

In a discussion of the nature of an ideal warden, the inspector of penitentiaries in 1876 called for more than 'a mere martinet, – a man of iron will and rule.' Enforcing rigid discipline by means of drill, he would turn convicts into 'mere automata, or animated pieces of mechanism.' Convinced that such an authority figure would subdue only the outer and not the inner man, the inspector argued that the best qualifications for warden had to include 'a fair education, good judgment, sound common sense, experience of life, and especially of men of the criminal class, even temper, a high sense of justice and self-respect, firmness of character coupled with a humane disposition and probity in a very high degree.'[92] No warden at St John appears to have lived up to these expectations.

Similar qualities were anticipated of prison staff. According to a federal inspector in the 1870s, convict labour would be a futile exercise unless prison staff demonstrated 'great tact, perfect patience, [and] irreproachable conduct.' They must be model human beings who could inspire 'a love of labour' and be able 'to render it both profitable and pleasant.' Under the existing system, he concluded: 'The convict is compelled to labour, because the law declares that he shall be made to labour – a routine is laid down and is followed.'[93] But, he continued, little effort was made to study the convict's character, his background, interests, tastes, inclinations, or abilities. There was little understanding of his future prospects, what would maximize his chances of avoiding subsequent crime and make him 'an honest member of the community.' Admitting that such comprehension required 'a degree of capacity' which few prison staff possessed, he was highly pessimistic that the convict's full rehabilitation could ever be achieved. Such personal shortcomings helped explain 'the routine manner in which everything is done' and the lack of specific proposals for realizing the ideals of prison reform.

This routine, and especially the mechanical nature of convict labour, worried some federal officials. In 1873 the federal prison directors, after observing labour practices at leading American penitentiaries, stated that: 'They freely admit having found the discipline strict and Draconian; but, in passing through they could not divest themselves of the feeling that they were looking at machines rather than human beings, so steady and regular, so involuntary and automatic did all their movements appear.'[94] Such rigid discipline and strict precision in the prison workplace indicated that the penitentiary regimen worked. But did it reform? The directors doubted that this system, 'so repressive, so devoid of all sympathy, and so replete with severity,' fulfilled the object of reformation. While they firmly believed that the dehumanization of convicts did not exist to the same extent in Canadian penitentiaries, the evidence from the St John Penitentiary confirms the findings of Calder's study of convict life in late-Victorian Canadian penitentiaries, that there existed unavoidable parallels in all such institutions.[95]

PRISON PRODUCTION AND PROFITABILITY

Regardless of how hard prisoners worked or how strict discipline was maintained, production and profitability depended on several other factors. In particular, the history of the penitentiary's business operations is central to understanding the failure of convict labour as a reformative tool. No private enterprise could have survived the inherent flaws and handicaps which affected production at the St John Penitentiary.

Industrial production at St John consisted of woodenware, tubs, pails, clothes-pins, and other items for sale in the open market. Sales at St John tended to fluctuate, sometimes wildly, and officials wondered why there was not a greater return on capital investment and labour.[96] The answer is that, as a factory operation, the St John Penitentiary had problems, in addition to a poorly skilled and often unfit labour force, which were potentially common to any other business: poor management and inadequate accounting procedures, undercapitalization, fluctuating markets, a shortage of productive capacity, excessive shrinkage of inventory, and fire. Each factor will be considered in turn.

In addition to the wretched physical condition of some convicts who were never incarcerated long enough to learn a proper skill or trade, Inspector Moylan believed that there occurred a 'great wear and tear of tools and machinery in the hands of convicts' as well as 'waste.' He was convinced that one could not expect forced labour to be as productive as free labour, regardless of how closely the prisoners were supervised by trade instructors.[97]

Management problems took several additional forms, including a lack of management supervision and accountability. Authority over internal management rested with the warden, but his statutory powers were limited. Before Confederation he was responsible to the overseers of the penitentiary, the Board of Commissioners, consisting of the mayor and four to eight additional members appointed by the governor in council. While the board's statutory responsibilities included defining policy, keeping accounts, purchasing, hiring, visiting the institution, and holding regular meetings, the commissioners 'seldom' visited, inspected, or reported in detail on its affairs, and delegated all financial dealings to the board's secretary, an accountant, who worked directly with the warden.[98] Consequently, it was often difficult for anyone to find out what, why, and where money was being spent. A government report in 1858 noted the complacency of the board, but with no result. In 1865 Lieutenant-Governor Arthur Hamilton Gordon wrote to Provincial Secretary Tilley requesting that the Commissioners of Public Institutions answer his questions on prison funding and maintenance costs over the previous five years. He also demanded to see the required annual reports and returns which described the state of the prison and offered statistical information.[99] The request to Tilley was the result of Quinton's not having been able to supply the information. But the fault was not Quinton's alone; the commissioners of the St John Penitentiary in the 1860s, who inspected infrequently and never on a surprise basis, continued to leave the day-to-day practical management of the institution to the warden.

Such lackadaisical practices were starkly revealed when Confederation brought all penitentiaries under the federal government. Prime Minister John A. Macdonald noted in 1868 that he had been 'compelled' to appoint three directors to deal with a general state of 'disorganization' in the prison system.[100] Upon first inspection, federal inspectors found that there was no regular system of checks and local audits at the St John Penitentiary, and its books were in disarray, thereby compounding the problems of accountability. The Directors of Penitentiaries and Secretary of State Hector Langevin were also exasperated by the fact that the St John administrators were paying high prices for goods of inferior quality. When little or nothing was done to remedy this practice, Terence O'Neill, the chairman of the directors, delivered a blunt order to Quinton demanding an explanation and told the warden that all information would be forwarded to the Department of Justice.[101] O'Neill's meaning was clear. Whether this problem was a case of fraud, corruption, or mere negligence, such irresponsible contracting had to stop.

Two measures were taken to protect the federal government's interest. First, Quinton was required to post a security bond. The warden was insulted by this demand, and he denied any wrongdoing. All contracting and purchasing had been handled, not by the warden, but by the penitentiary's accountant at a downtown office. Subsequent events suggest that the problem was here. Second, the federal government discontinued the practice of making the accountant responsible for purchasing, the task being assigned to an outsider, Chief Keeper Patchell, whom the government hired. Quinton had no influence over this hiring – there was another keeper whom he thought should have been promoted – and he soon found himself at loggerheads with the new chief keeper on several management issues. Convinced that Patchell was deliberately trying to usurp his position and undermine his credibility, Quinton did not like or trust him and countered by charging that Patchell's work was sloppy. He also alleged that the new chief keeper was shortchanging contractors on their shipments to the penitentiary, and he protested, but the federal government paid him little heed.[102]

The federal authorities must have had some doubts about Quinton's ability as prison warden. Complaints by former keeper Bartlett had described Quinton's management as 'a standing disgrace to the Province' and stated that 'no man can stay there as underkeeper that has any mind or spirit of his own, or the humanity that such men should have.' Moreover, no mechanic would stay employed there because Quinton had sanctioned the hiring of 'minions,' favourite convicts, and incompetent tradesmen to direct the workshops. During the last two years of his employment at the prison, Bartlett contended that Quinton was 'seldom' in the shops 'unless some of the Commissioners and some gentleman came to visit the place.' He regarded the warden as 'too Pompous and big to bother his head with such mean things. All he seemed to care about was seeing the prisoners was well punished.'[103]

But Bartlett's condemnation of Quinton flies in the face of other evidence. Except for his evident commercial inabilities, Quinton seems to have been regarded as at least a satisfactory warden. The Directors of Penitentiaries consistently found the institution clean and orderly; the cells were described as 'scrupulously' clean by one visitor. Quinton frequently defended his employees, and warden-employee relationships following the Bartlett episode never again appeared to be a cause for public concern. But the directors did blame Quinton for mismanagement of the prison's manufacturing. In 1872 they complained that more money might have been made from convict-made goods 'if the Warden had used the necessary degree of exertion which might be expected from an efficient and active officer.' They 'strongly' recommended the retirement of the sixty-six-year-old Quinton in favour of a more 'vigorous and energetic man.'[104] Two years later the old warden was replaced by Charles Ketchum. A bitter Quinton reflected in his diary on how he had survived thirty-three years as warden 'until a Grit Government decided I should be superannuated to make a place for one of their suckers.'[105]

Yet the penitentiary's lack of profitability can ultimately not be laid at Quinton's door. Despite the installation of a new warden and accountant it still failed to make higher profits. The director of penitentiaries appeared more sympathetic to the same difficulties faced by the new prison warden, and he explained that Quinton's replacement had used every power within his means to run the prison economically and efficiently; the prison staff were victims of 'circumstances beyond their control.'[106]

Despite such sympathetic mutterings, the federal government did little to bolster employee morale at the prison in the early 1870s. If salary can be used as an index of motivation, neither Quinton nor his staff had much reason to do more than fulfil their basic obligations as employees. The warden was paid pitifully. His annual salary of $600 was $400 less than that paid to the most lowly guard in a similar American institution. But at least he was paid regularly. Several times Quinton complained that prison guards suffered hardship when they had to wait months before receiving their pay.[107] It is little wonder that Quinton was privately cynical about whether provincial or federal politicians really cared about prison conditions and employee relations, or whether the penitentiary would ever fulfil its original promise. In practice, cost-cutting measures appear to have had perpetual priority over institutional needs.

Moreover, without consultation, the directors decided to alter the pattern of work and to force all guards to rotate their shifts regularly, including making them do night shift. Until then, the staff had agreed to a mutually satisfactory shift arrangement. The new system forced them to work extra shifts without pay and disrupted their private lives without apparent benefit to the operations of the institution. Depending on abilities, staff rather than tradesmen were assigned to supervise specific trades and tasks. This system helped to undermine the efficiency of manufacturing operations. Also, on occasion the directors would order purchases, such as timber, without understanding local markets or conditions, thereby causing unnecessary work and aggravation for the penitentiary staff. Evidently, the problems of management at the St John Penitentiary extended beyond the limitations of the warden but existed at all levels.[108]

In addition to shortcomings of management, there were continuing economic problems which undermined the profitability of the penitentiary. Manufacturing at the institution had always been promoted with the hope that the proceeds from convict labour would make it, if not self-sufficient, at least more economical. Nevertheless, from the beginning, the penitentiary was forced to rely heavily on government grants. This compounded the difficulties of successfully conducting business transactions. The parsimony of government made it difficult to pay suppliers on time and to invest in capital equipment when needed. Consequently, all the business operations suffered from undercapitalization. The directors in 1868 confirmed what a provincial committee reporting on the penitentiary had noted a decade before, that raw materials for manufacturing purposes were being purchased on credit and creditors were not being paid until the goods were sold.[109]

Borrowing money to meet prison manufacturing costs had been the practice since the introduction of the workshops. Government expected related expenditures, such as for raw materials and equipment, to be paid from profits, which were never sufficient. This 'hand-to-mouth' form of financing was both inefficient and expensive, with interest charged on outstanding accounts carrying the penitentiary further into debt. Suppliers were also antagonized. A letter to Tilley from the Boston manufacturers of a steam engine gives some idea of the problem. Although the company had delivered this machine in 1861, they were still looking for payment four years later, and they were willing to accept half the balance in order to close out the account. There remained a long list of outstanding debts at the penitentiary's closing.[110]

Prison sales were often adversely affected by market conditions. The cost of raw materials for manufacturing, especially broom corn and fuel, was consistently high. Sometimes these commodities were in short supply, for example because of strikes, which delayed workshop production. At other times demand for prison produced products slackened. This was especially so during the onset of depression in 1873. The St John Penitentiary was harmed by the consequent dumping of surplus goods, which resulted in declining sales, lower prices, and overall less revenue from prison manufactures.

Manufacturing at the St John Penitentiary was also hampered by its capacity to employ its labour force, the prison population. The daily average prison population ranged between 51 and 72 in the first decade of industrial production. Then, rising steadily, it reached between 74 and 162 during the 1870s. There were, however, only 60 to 65 jobs in the workshops. The remaining prisoners were kept occupied in maintenance and make work projects, and sometimes were left idle, contributing little to revenue. Quinton for one believed that the lack of manufacturing capacity seriously hampered production and profits.[111]

Other problems which undermined the profitability of prison labour included damage to inventory, principally through a lack of proper storage facilities. Mice nibbled at the stored brooms, making them unsaleable. Moisture and long-term storage caused the wires holding the brooms together to rust. And raw materials were often found to be of poor quality. Fire took its toll on several occasions. In 1855 a drying shed burnt to the ground causing a loss of £442. Three years later this building was reduced to ashes, at a cost of £250. A hydrant and fire-hoses were then introduced. The destruction of storehouses in 1863 came as a blow when stock and inventory valued at $2689 was reduced to ashes. This fire 'seriously crippled' manufacturing operations. In 1865 and 1870 the dry house burnt to the ground. Another substantial loss came during the famous Great Fire of 1877, a widespread conflagration which burnt much of the downtown core to the ground. In comparison with the rest of St John, the penitentiary escaped lightly. Nevertheless, property consisting of stock and furniture amounting to $2250 was reported lost. Each fire reduced profits and caused unanticipated delays.[112] The problems of realizing a profit from prison industries were apparently endless.

Yet from the point of view of prison officials, the merits of convict labour could not be judged entirely on the basis of profitability. James Moylan took this position in 1877, when he reviewed the state of manufacturing at the St John Penitentiary and at other federal penitentiaries. He thought it reasonable to expect prison industry to be as profitable as a private business, but he also argued that a complete 'remodelling [of] the whole Penitentiary' was necessary to achieve this goal. Ideally, he asserted, wardens should be hired for their business aptitude, the penitentiary accountant retrained in financial procedures, more highly skilled trade instructors, foremen, and mechanics employed, and political patronage eliminated in the making of penitentiary appointments. None of this, he thought, was likely to happen. Yet, if not for profit, Moylan asked rhetorically, why should manufacturing at the St John Penitentiary, or anywhere else, be promoted? He explained:

First – Because all the machinery and material necessary was handed over here with the Penitentiary, at the time of Confederation; and I take it, the Government of the day instructed that manufactures should be continued. Secondly – They afford work to the majority of the convicts for whom it would be no easy matter otherwise to find employment. Thirdly – They habituate those employed to industry, and prepare them, when liberated, to earn a livelihood at similar work. I might add fourthly, but not primarily, to endeavour to realize some profit, were that possible, with the means at hand.[113]

Despite Moylan's reaffirmation of the value of continuing industrial production, the matter had become a dead letter by the mid-1870s. The decision to build a single, federal institution at Dorchester to replace the Halifax and St John penitentiaries led to a recommendation that nothing be done at St John except maintain minimum operations. In 1878 Moylan commented that the administration of the St John Penitentiary was being carried out 'as well as could be expected.' He could barely blame the warden for the overcrowded conditions. There were far more prisoners than cells or workshops to accommodate them, and as a consequence many prisoners were 'full of sores and loathsome diseases' and placed on the third floor of the cell block in an open space, on 'make-shift bunks, packed side by side.'[114] With the transfer of convicts from St John to Dorchester imminent in 1880, Moylan rejoiced as he observed the institution shutting down. He thought this penal establishment was now and had always been entirely inappropriate for its purpose: 'It might have answered well enough for a common gaol – and a very common one at that – but it was utterly unsuited for a Penitentiary. There was not a solitary object or feature in the place, physically speaking, calculated to cheer, to elevate, or to produce a softening influence upon the hapless *détenu* during his dreary term of confinement. All was grim and dismal.'[115] In short, the failures of management and labour at the St John Penitentiary were rationalized away.

CONCLUSION

The idea of the prison as factory which competed with private industry and where the convict was trained as a skilled worker in a competitive wage-labour market had only a limited role in nineteenth-century New Brunswick. Recent literature on convict labour elsewhere in this period has noted the early nineteenth-century preoccupation with it as coincident with the contemporary need to create a disciplined working class in an emergent industrial order. Some authors have suggested its failures resulted from pressures exerted by organized free labour and by manufacturers.[116] Yet the St John example clearly demonstrates that any alliance of capital and labour in opposition to the ideals of penal reform, especially the reformation of convicts through labour, is insufficient to explain the penitentiary's failure to reform. The St John Penitentiary failed as a factory not merely because of hostility to the idea of reforming convicts by prison labour, but also because it demonstrated its inability to survive as a business. It succumbed to undercapitalization, ineffective management, an unskilled, unfree, slave-like, and poorly motivated labour force, and structural economic and ideological changes that together undermined the original beliefs in, and the underlying legitimacy of, convict labour.

Though a study of the American experience suggests that nineteenth-century crime control policies, including the deployment of the penitentiary, may have worked in reducing serious crime,[117] late nineteenth-century critics of the penitentiary system were unconvinced. They saw no clear evidence of a decrease in crime or the rehabilitation of convicts, and were apparently impervious to the idea of providing criminals with the competitive skills to raise their social condition. While penitentiary officials often understood the obstacles that undermined the potentially reformative nature of the penitentiary, politicians appeared to have paid their concerns little heed. It is understandable why the retributive aspects of punishment overwhelmed rehabilitative ones. Convicts were still expected to work, but neither productively nor competitively; they were actively discouraged from becoming truly skilled labourers. In practice convict labour mostly satisfied the disciplinary needs of the institution and, to a far less extent, the more abstract preoccupations of living in a free world.[118] Convict labour did contribute to the lowering of institutional costs. But most of all it enhanced the punitive qualities of incarceration. The ideal of truly reforming the criminal by means of hard labour played a secondary role, and the failure of the penitentiary to reform the convict thereby became self-fulfilling. To paraphrase David Rothman, public convenience triumphed over social conscience.[119]

NOTES

Earlier versions of this paper were presented at the Atlantic Law and History Workshop, University of New Brunswick, October 1989, and at the Annual Meeting of the Social Science History Association, Chicago, November 1992. The author gratefully acknowledges financial support from a Dean's Grant, Brock University, and a Vice-President's Research Grant, Memorial University of Newfoundland.

1 'Inside the Prison Walls' *Daily Telegraph* (St John) 14 Dec. 1875
2 Ibid. 20 Sept. 1866
3 *Livingston's Handbook and Visitors' Guide to Saint John* (Saint John: H. Chubb 1869)
4 See, generally, David Garland *Punishment and Modern Society: A Study in Social Theory* (Chicago: University of Chicago Press 1990).
5 Dario Melossi and Massimo Pavarini *The Prison and the Factory: Origins of the Penitentiary System* (Totowa, NJ: Barnes and Noble 1981) 143–4. Other studies which have attempted to place the penitentiary within the broad context of social disorder, social control, a new disciplinary discourse, industrialization,

and capitalism include Michael Ignatieff *A Just Measure of Pain: The Penitentiary in the Industrial Revolution, 1750–1850* (New York: Pantheon Books 1978) 174–206; Michel Foucault *Discipline and Punish: The Birth of the Prison* (New York: Pantheon 1977); David J. Rothman *The Discovery of the Asylum* (Boston: Little, Brown 1971); Glen A. Gildemeister *Prison Labour and Convict Competition with Free Workers in Industrializing America, 1840–1890* (New York and London: Garland 1987).

6 My approach is, in part, indebted to Oliver Zunz, ed. *Reliving The Past: The Worlds of Social History* (Chapel Hill: University of North Carolina Press 1985) 5–9.

7 Similar influences are evident in Upper Canada during this period. See Rainer Baehre 'Imperial Authority and Colonial Officialdom of Upper Canada in the 1830s: The State, Crime, Lunacy and Everyday Social Order' in Susan Binnie and Louis Knafla, eds. *Law, State, and Society: Essays in Modern Legal History* (Toronto: University of Toronto Press 1994).

8 On the adoption of the penitentiary in British North America, see P. Tremblay 'L'évolution de l'emprisonnement penitentiaire, de son intensité, de sa fermeté et de sa portée: Le cas de Montréal de 1845 à 1913' *Canadian Journal of Criminology* 28 (1986) 47–69; Jean-Pierre Wallot 'La querelle des prisons (Bas Canada) 1805–1807' *Revue d'histoire de l'Amérique française* 14 (1960–1) 61–86, 259–76, 395–407, 559–85; Rainer Baehre 'From Bridewell To Federal Penitentiary: Prisons and Punishment in Nova Scotia before 1880' in Philip Girard and Jim Phillips, eds. *Essays in the History of Canadian Law: Volume III – Nova Scotia* (Toronto: University of Toronto Press and Osgoode Society 1990); Russell Smandych 'Beware of the "Evil American Monster": Upper Canadian Views on the Need for a Penitentiary, 1830–1834' *Canadian Journal of Criminology* 33 (1991) 125–47; John D. Blackwell 'Crime in the London District, 1828–1837: A Case Study of the Effect of the 1833 Reform in Upper Canadian Penal Law' in J.K. Johnson and B. Wilson, eds. *Historical Essays on Upper Canada: New Perspectives* (Ottawa: Carleton University Press 1989); J.M. Beattie *Attitudes towards Crime and Punishment in Upper Canada, 1830–1850: A Documentary Study* (Toronto: University of Toronto Centre of Criminology 1977); Rainer Baehre 'Origins of the Penitentiary System in Upper Canada' *Ontario History* 69 (1977) 185–207; Frank Anderson 'Prisons and Prison Reform in the Old Canadian West' *Canadian Journal of Corrections* 2 (1960) 209–15.

9 *Statutes of New Brunswick* 1831, c. 14; 1840, c. 64; 1842, c. 31. The general context of these changes is described in J.W. Lawrence *The Judges of New Brunswick and Their Times* (Saint John: Macmillan 1888) 382–3.

10 Recent discussion of this ideological interrelationship includes Maxine Berg

'Progress and Providence in Early Nineteenth-Century Political Economy'
Social History 15 (1990) 365–75; James E. Crimmins 'Religion, Utility and Politics: Bentham versus Paley' in Crimmins, ed. *Religion, Secularization and Political Thought: Thomas Hobbes to J.S. Mill* (London and New York: Routledge
1990); Robert Weiss 'Humanitarianism, Labour Exploitation, or Social Control? A Critical Survey of Theory and Research on the Origin and Development of Prisons' *Social History* 12 (1987) 331–50; Richard Johnson 'Educational Policy and Social Control in Early Victorian England' *Past and Present*
49 (1970) esp. 96–7.

11 Rothman *Discovery of the Asylum* 79–198; W. David Lewis *From Newgate to Dan-
nemora: The Rise of the Penitentiary in New York, 1796–1848* (Ithaca: Cornell Uni-
versity Press 1965). For the origins of these systems see Pieter Spierenburg
'From Amsterdam to Auburn: An Explanation for the Rise of the Prison in
Seventeenth-Century Holland and Nineteenth-Century America' *Journal of
Social History* 20 (1977) 455–78.

12 *British Parliamentary Papers*, no. 593 (1834), xlvi, 349

13 Extract from Lord Glenelg's Circular, addressed to Sir John Harvey, 5 July
1837, *Journal of the House of Assembly of New Brunswick* (hereafter *Journals*)
1837–8, 44; Cunard, from Joint Committee, thanks to Glenelg for the Documents upon the State of the Prisons in England and Wales, ibid. 1836, 637;
1840, 16; Despatch Relative to the State of Prisons, no. 7, Downing Street,
1 Oct. 1841, ibid. 1842, n.p.

14 J.B. Hirst *Convict Society and Its Enemies: A History of Early New South Wales* (Sydney: Allen and Unwin 1983) 9–27; A.G.L. Shaw *Convicts and the Colonies: A
Study of Penal Transportation from Great Britain and Ireland to Australia and Other
Parts of the British Empire* (Melbourne: Melbourne University Press 1977)
127–45, 249–94

15 W.P. Morrell *British Colonial Policy in the Age of Peel and Russell* (London: Frank
Cass 1966) 387; Sean McConville *A History of English Prison Administration*
vol. 1: *1750–1877* (London: Routledge and Kegan Paul 1981) 187–97, 381–5

16 *Journals* 1841, 199

17 C.J. Taylor 'The Kingston, Ontario Penitentiary and Moral Architecture'
Histoire sociale – Social History 12 (1979) 385–408

18 *Fourth Report of the Prison Discipline Society, 1829* 63; Foucault *Discipline and Punish*
195–228

19 T.W. Acheson *Saint John: The Making of a Colonial Urban Community* (Toronto:
University of Toronto Press 1985) 115

20 The Charter of the City of St John, appendix 2, *Acts of the General Assembly of
Her Majesty's Province of New Brunswick (New Brunswick Acts), 1786–1836*

21 Minutes of the Court of Quarter Sessions, 9 Sept. 1803 and n.d. [March 1805], New Brunswick Museum (hereafter NBM)

22 The importance of the *Blue Books* as a source of information for the formation of the Canadian state is discussed at length in Bruce Curtis 'The Canada "Blue Books" and the Administrative Capacity of the Canadian State, 1822–67' *Canadian Historical Review* 74 (1993) 535–65.

23 Summary of the Reports on the County Gaols in the Province of New Brunswick, transmitted by the Lieutenant Governor in his Despatch, no. 46, dated 11 Aug. 1841, *Journals* 1841–2, 52

24 See Acheson *Saint John* 45, 51, 84, 88, 106, 181, 187, and 221–2; P.R. Lindon 'Robert Leonard Hazen' *Dictionary of Canadian Biography* vol. 10 (Toronto: University of Toronto Press 1972) 341–2.

25 G.J. Dibblee to Robert F. Hazen 28 Jan. 1839, Hazen Correspondence, box 1, shelf 36, packet 3, NBM

26 Smandych 'Beware of the "Evil American Monster"'; Bryan Palmer 'Kingston Mechanics and the Rise of the Penitentiary, 1833–1836' *Histoire sociale – Social History* 13 (1980) 7–32

27 *Statutes of New Brunswick 1836*, c. 41 and 50; Cunard, from Joint Committee, thanks to Glenelg for the Documents upon the State of the Prisons in England and Wales, *Journals* 1836, 637; Extract from Lord Glenelg's Circular, addressed to Sir John Harvey, 5 July 1837, ibid. 1837–8, 44

28 *Statutes of New Brunswick 1830*, c. 20; 1831, c. 14, 15, 17, and 18; 1836, c. 41 and 50; New Jail Calculations, St John Jail, 21 July 1836, and J. Peters, Clerk of the Peace, to Hazen, 11 Dec. 1837, Hazen Correspondence, S-36, F12-11, NBM

29 First, these institutions were designed for that minority of prisoners sentenced to a period of hard labour, mostly the idle poor or petty criminal, to discipline them and to teach them proper work habits. In practice, a high turnover of inmates, low productivity, and an inability to enforce sustained labour undermined their efficacy and contributed to public disillusionment. Even contractors who hired bridewell convicts had become critical of their utility. Moreover, in jurisdictions where crime was relatively uncommon, a house of correction made little sense because of the extra expenses involved. See Ignatieff *A Just Measure of Pain* 33–5 and J.M. Beattie *Crime and the Courts in England, 1660–1800* (Princeton: Princeton University Press 1986) 301–10.

30 Extract from Lord Glenelg's Circular, addressed to Sir John Harvey, 5 July 1837, *Journals* 1837–8, 44

31 *Statutes of New Brunswick 1838*, c. 16; 1839, c. 30

32 Acheson *Saint John* 218

33 *Journals 1840*, 16; Despatch Relative to the State of Prisons, 1 Oct. 1841, ibid. 1842, n.p.

34 McConville *History of English Prison Administration* 351

35 *Statutes of New Brunswick* 1841, c. 44

36 In an official visit in 1867 by the prison inspectors of the former Province of Canada to the prison, it, like the Halifax Penitentiary, was said to differ little from the larger jails of Quebec and Ontario: Return to an Address ..., *Sessional Papers* 1868, no. 40, 3.

37 Acheson *Saint John* 5

38 Graeme Wynn *Timber Colony: A Historical Geography of Early Nineteenth Century New Brunswick* (Toronto: University of Toronto Press 1981). Recent re-evaluations of the provincial economy include Beatrice Craig 'Agriculture in a Pioneer Region: The Upper St John River Valley in the First Half of the 19th Century' and T.W. Acheson 'New Brunswick Agriculture at the End of the Colonial Era: A Reassessment' both in K. Inwood, ed. *Farm, Factory and Fortune: New Studies in the Economic History of the Maritime Provinces* (Fredericton: Acadiensis Press 1993). New Brunswick in the 1860s and 1870s is considered within a regional context in D.A. Muise 'The 1860s: Forging the Bonds of Union' and Phillip A. Buckner 'The 1870s: Political Integration' in E.R. Forbes and D.A. Muise, eds. *The Atlantic Provinces in Confederation* (Toronto: University of Toronto Press 1993).

39 W.S. MacNutt *New Brunswick: A History, 1784–1867* (Toronto: Macmillan 1963) 225–314

40 *Statutes of New Brunswick* 1830, c. 20

41 *Statutes of New Brunswick* 1831, c. 28

42 Donald Akenson has been highly critical of the historical stereotyping of Irish immigrants. See 'Ontario: Whatever Happened to the Irish?' *Canadian Papers in Rural History* 3 (1982) 222–5. Recent studies of anti-Irish sentiment include T.M. Punch 'Anti-Irish Prejudice in Nineteenth-Century Nova Scotia: The Literary and Statistical Evidence' and A.J.B. Johnston 'Anti-Irish Ideology in a Mid-Nineteenth-Century British Colony' both in Thomas Power, ed. *The Irish in Atlantic Canada, 1780–1900* (Fredericton: New Ireland Press 1991).

43 Summary of the Reports on the County Gaols in the Province of New Brunswick, transmitted by the Lieutenant Governor in his Despatch, no. 6, 11 Aug. 1841, *Journals 1841–2*, 52

44 Greg Marquis '"A Machine of Oppression under the Guise of the Law": The Saint John Police Establishment, 1860–1890' *Acadiensis* 16 (1986) 59

45 Misc. S36, F9, No. 9, NBM; Provincial Secretary to the Commissioners of

the Provincial Penitentiary, New Brunswick Executive Council, Penitentiary Correspondence and Returns, 1842–54, MG 9, A1, vol. 95, 72, Public Archives of New Brunswick (hereafter PANB)

46 Acheson *Saint John* 26–7, 138–46; Geoffrey Bilson *A Darkened House: Cholera in Nineteenth-Century Canada* (Toronto: University of Toronto Press 1980) 106–8; Daniel Francis 'The Development of the Lunatic Asylum in the Maritime Provinces' *Acadiensis* 6 (1977) 27–8; Judith Fingard 'The Relief of the Unemployed Poor in Saint John, Halifax, and St John's, 1815–1860' *Acadiensis* 5 (1975) 51–2

47 *Statutes of New Brunswick* 1830, c. 20; 1831, c. 14, 15, 17, and 18; 1836, c. 41 and 50

48 Weiss 'Humanitarianism, Labour Exploitation, or Social Control' 349–50

49 Spierenburg 'From Amsterdam to Auburn' 456; P. Spierenburg *The Spectacle of Suffering: Executions and the Evolution of Repression from a Preindustrial Metropolis to the European Experience* (Cambridge: Cambridge University Press 1984); P. Spierenburg, ed. *The Emergence of Carceral Institutions: Prisons, Galleys and Lunatic Asylums, 1550–1900* (Rotterdam: Erasmus Universiteit 1984)

50 See *Report of the Commission Appointed to Enquire into the Management of the Light Houses, the Provincial Penitentiary, the Provincial Lunatic Asylum, and the Marine Hospital* (Fredericton: Queen's Printer 1858) 12–36.

51 *Fourth Report of the Prison Discipline Society, 1829* 60

52 Commissioners to John S. Saunders, Provincial Secretary, 10 Dec. 1847, New Brunswick Executive Council, Penitentiary, Correspondence and Returns, 1842–54, MG 9, A1, vol. 95, 95–8

53 Descriptions of the Auburn penitentiary are included in Rothman *Discovery of the Asylum* 96–7; Lewis, *From Newgate to Dannemora* 81–110; *First Report of the Prison Discipline Society, 1826* 15–17.

54 G.J. Dibblee to Robert F. Hazen, 28 Jan. 1839, Robert F. Hazen Mayor's Correspondence, box 1, shelf 36, packet 3, 1839, NBM. See also John Conley 'Prisons, Production and Profit: Reconsidering the Importance of Prison Industries' *Journal of Social History* 14 (1981) 257–75, 'Revising Conceptions about the Origin of Prisons: The Importance of Economic Considerations' *Social Science Quarterly* 62 (1981) 247–58, and 'Economics and the Social Reality of Prisons' *Journal of Criminal Justice* 10 (1982) 25–35.

55 Interestingly the prison treadmill was never used at St John, probably because, though this device was widely used in Great Britain, its critics in the 1830s felt that the treadmill promoted work for its own sake, but not 'manufacture.' See David H. Shayt 'Stairway to Redemption: America's Encounter with the British Prison Treadmill' *Technology and Culture* 30 (1989) 908–39.

56 For example, see 'A Factory and Its Discipline, 1846' an excerpt from 'Man-

ufacturing Industry of the State of New York' *Hunt's Merchants' Magazine* 15 (1846) 370–2, in W. Pursell Carroll, ed. *Readings in Technology and American Life* (New York: Oxford University Press 1969); 'Factory Rules' in Sidney Pollard and Colin Holmes, eds. *Documents of European Economic History* (London: St Martin's Press 1968).

57 Erving Goffman *Asylums* (Garden City: Anchor Books 1961) 184–6

58 Rules for the Penitentiary, 17 Sept. 1842, MG9, A1, vol. 95, 3–10, PANB

59 Rules and Regulations to be observed in the Provincial Penitentiary, Broadsides, Oversize, P1, NBM (my emphasis)

60 *Daily Telegraph* 20 Sept. 1866

61 Report of Visiting Commissioners of the Provincial Penitentiary, 31 May 1843, MG9, A1, vol. 95, 20–5, PANB

62 Report of the Commissioners of the Provincial Penitentiary, *Journals* 1849, app., 74

63 Report of the Commissioners of the Provincial Penitentiary, *Journals* 1855, app., 27; ibid. 1856, app., 62; Report from Commissioners to inquire into the management of the Provincial Penitentiary, ibid., app., 143

64 Various reports of the St John Penitentiary included in federal penitentiary reports: Canada *Sessional Papers* 1868–81

65 *St John and Its Business: A History of St John* (St John: n.p. 1875) 99–110

66 The thirty-three-year stint of Quinton, a former police chief of St John and grandson of a chief justice, is inseparable from the history of the institution. Appointed on the opening of the penitentiary and the second choice among thirty applicants, Quinton remained warden until 1875, when he was removed from office by Inspector Moylan. He wrote a family history, still available in typescript: see John Quinton, Narrative family history, 1762–1866, Quinton Family Papers, MG29, C11, NBM.

67 Saint John Penitentiary, Warden's Diary, 9 Jan. 1870, Microfilm reel F-700, PANB

68 Fifth Annual Report of the Inspector of Penitentiaries, 1880, *Sessional Papers* (1881) 13

69 Sixth Annual Report of the Directors of Penitentiaries, 1873, ibid. 1874, 14

70 Quinton Diary, MG29, C11, 3 Feb., 4 and 18 April, and 8 May 1870, NBM

71 Sixth Annual Report of the Directors of Penitentiaries, 1873, *Sessional Papers* 1874, 17

72 Dorothy E. Chunn 'Good Men Work Hard: Convict Labour in Kingston Penitentiary, 1835–1850' *Canadian Criminology Forum* 4 (1981) 13–22

73 Shaw *Convicts and the Colonies* 318

74 This application of the principle of 'less-eligibility' as it pertained to prisons

had been the subject of considerable debate in England during the 1830s: see McConville *History of English Prison Administration* 145.

75 H. Clare Pentland *Labour and Capital in Canada, 1650–1860* (Toronto: James Lorimer 1981) 13–21

76 A discussion of 'the contract system' as it applied to the Kingston Penitentiary is found in 'Sixth Annual Report of the Board of Inspectors of Asylums, Prisons, 1866' *Sessional Papers* 1868, 178–9.

77 The main concerns are summarized neatly in Second Annual Report of the Inspector of Penitentiaries, 1877, ibid. 1878, 6–11.

78 Sixth Annual Report of the Board of Inspectors of Asylums, Prisons, 1866, ibid. 1868, 178–9. Before Confederation, boards of commissioners were overseers of colonial penitentiaries. When the Province of Canada joined the Dominion, a Board of Inspectors of Asylums and Prisons was inherited by Canada, and it briefly shaped federal thinking. From 1868 to 1875, federal penitentiaries were regulated by the Directors of Penitentiaries. In 1875 the office of Inspector of Penitentiaries headed by a single individual was established.

79 'Provincial Institutions' *Journals* 1858, appendix dlvi; 'Report on Public Accounts,' ibid. 1864, app., 189; Seventh Annual Report of the Board of Inspectors of Asylums, Prisons, 1867, *Sessional Papers* 1868, 6

80 Third Annual Report of the Inspector of Penitentiaries 1877, *Sessional Papers* 1878, 10

81 *Statutes of Canada* 1875, c. 44, s. 68; Provincial Penitentiary, Papers and Correspondence between the Dominion Government and the Government of this Province, Supplemental Appendix, *Journals*, 1881, 132; *Statutes of Canada* 1877, c. 38, s. 20

82 C.N. Skinner to Attorney General, and to Lieutenant-Governor of New Brunswick, 22 Feb. 1881, *Journals* 1881, app., 147

83 Sixth Annual Report of the Directors of Penitentiaries, 1873, *Sessional Papers* 1874, 90

84 Second Annual Report of the Directors of Penitentiaries, 1869, ibid. 1870, 45

85 Rules for the Penitentiary, 17 Sept. 1842, MG9, A1, vol. 95, PANB; *Statutes of New Brunswick* 1842, c. 2

86 Provincial Secretary to Commissioners of the Provincial Penitentiary, 26 Nov. 1847, MG9, A1, vol. 95, PANB

87 R. Bartlett to Thomas Dale, 6 May 1861, Tilley Papers, MG27, D15, National Archives of Canada

88 Ibid.

89 John Dale to Samuel Tilley, 28 May 1861, MG27, D15, NAC

90 This is based on a search of entries: St John Penitentiary, Warden's Journal F-700, PANB.

91 Third Annual Report of the Inspector of Penitentiaries, 1877, *Sessional Papers* 1878, 12

92 Second Annual Report of the Inspector of Penitentiaries, 1876, ibid. 1877, 10

93 Ibid. n.p.

94 Sixth Annual Report of the Directors of Penitentiaries, 1873, ibid. 1874, 3

95 W.A. Calder 'Convict Life in Canadian Federal Penitentiaries, 1867–1900' in L.A. Knafla, ed. *Crime and Criminal Justice in Europe and Canada* (Waterloo: Wilfrid Laurier University Press 1979) and 'The Federal Penitentiary System in Canada, 1867–1899: A Social and Institutional History' (PhD thesis, University of Toronto 1979). A contemporary comparison is available in E.C. Wines and Theodore W. Dwight *Report on the Prisons and Reformatories of the United States and Canada Made to the Legislature of New York, January, 1867* (Albany 1867).

96 Report of the Commissioners, 1858, 16

97 Third Annual Report of the Inspector of Penitentiaries, 1877, *Sessional Papers* 1878, 9

98 J. O'Neill to John Quinton, 15 May 1871, Quinton Packet 34, no. 151, NBM

99 A.H. Gordon to Tilley, 29 Mar. 1865, Tilley Papers, NAC

100 Macdonald to Howe, 21 Sept. 1868, Webster Packet, 86, no. 51, NBM

101 J. O'Neill to John Quinton, 15 May 1871, Quinton Packet 34, no. 15, NBM

102 J.W. King to John Quinton, 3 Sept. 1872, Quinton Papers, 34-20, NBM

103 R. Bartlett to Thomas Dale, 6 and 15 May 1861, Tilley Papers, MG27, 1D15, NAC

104 Sixth Annual Report of the Directors of Penitentiaries, 1873, *Sessional Papers* 1874, 90

105 Quinton Diary, MG29 C11, n.p., NBM

106 Sixth Annual Report of the Inspector of Penitentiaries, 1881, *Sessional Papers* 1882, n.p.

107 Warden's Diary, 2 June 1869, NBM

108 Ibid. 7 March 1872

109 First Annual Report of the Directors of Penitentiaries, 1868, *Sessional Papers* 1869, n.p.

110 Warden's Diary, 10 Nov. 1871, NBM

111 Ibid. 9 Jan. 1870

112 Quinton Diary, MG29 C11, NBM; Report of the Warden, Third Annual Report of the Inspector of Penitentiaries, 1877, *Sessional Papers* 1878, 102

113 Third Annual Report of the Inspector of Penitentiaries, 1877, ibid. 1878, 9
114 Ibid. 7
115 Fifth Annual Report of the Inspector of Penitentiaries, 1880, ibid. 1881, 14
116 See especially Gildemeister *Prison Labor and Convict Competition* 196–248.
117 Eric H. Monkkonen 'The Organized Response to Crime in Nineteenth-
    and Twentieth-Century America' *Journal of Interdisciplinary History* 14 (1983)
    113
118 Discussions of the efficacy of prison labour preoccupied federal penal offi-
    cials well into the twentieth century, without further resolution: *Report of
    the Royal Commission to Investigate the Penal System of Canada* (Ottawa: King's
    Printer 1938) 135–8.
119 Comparisons can readily be made between American prisons, such as the
    Norfolk Penal Colony, and the Saint John Penitentiary. See David J. Roth-
    man *Conscience and Convenience: The Asylum and Its Alternatives in Progressive
    America* (Boston: Little, Brown 1980) 379–424.

14

Prisoners for Profit: Convict Labour in the Ontario Central Prison, 1874–1915

JOSEPH GONDOR BERKOVITS

The Ontario Central Prison was shut down in ignominy in 1915, its once modern buildings dank and archaic and its revolutionary philosophies dated and discredited. After temporary use during World War I as a military prison, it was sold for its land value alone and, soon after, demolished. Today, a rather utilitarian-looking industrial plant occupies the site adjacent to the railway tracks in the city of Toronto, just north of the present-day Canadian National Exhibition grounds.[1]

As unlamented and largely forgotten as it is, when it opened in 1874, the Central Prison was the linchpin of the Ontario government's new approach to crime and incarceration. Conceived as an industrial prison for men, and designed and largely financed by a private consortium, the Central Prison was going to be the first in a new wave of similar provincial reformatories. Members of the 'criminal class,' unenlightened as they were by the salutary habits of industry and sobriety, would be put to work in the prison, their labour under contract to a private manufacturer. Convicts would be taught the moral value of labour as well as the new skills required outside by an industrializing economy. Best of all, they would be earning their keep, and even a profit for the government. It was surely capitalism's most brilliant meeting with confinement. Productive convict labour would be the new answer to the already vexing problem of incarceration. Ontario's lawbreakers would no longer languish in a state of idleness and depravity in the province's local jails. Over its forty-year history, politicians, bureaucrats, prison officials, and close to 30,000 inmates struggled in vain to make the bold proposition work. But like most panaceas, it never did.

Many paid the price for the failure of the Central Prison. For the prison's first contractor, the cost was financial: within ten months, the Canada Car Company went bankrupt after investing over a quarter of a million dollars. Other financial misadventures were to follow. The government, in the wake of political fallout over an increasingly scandal-ridden institution, was forced to look to even more desperate methods to try to make the prison work. Private industry had to cope with a new and unwelcome competitor. The labour union movement faced the demoralizing spectre of fellow members of the working class transformed into a virtual slave labour force. While the incarcerated toiled for the provincial treasury, their families lost their livelihood. Devoted penologists, too, saw their cherished adage of labouring 'in the sweat of thy face' reveal itself to be the biblical curse that it truly was, for the sheer horror of forced labour hardened more than it elevated, and it punished more than even the most reactionary had ever anticipated. And so finally, and most significantly, while they were not alone in their adversity, the real victims of the Central Prison were the inmates themselves. In the end, though, as an industrial institution, the Central Prison was no better or worse than any other. It simply manufactured the one product that all prisons seem to produce best: punishment.[2]

Indeed, what makes the study of convict labour so valuable is how intertwined it is with the evolution of the concept of the penitentiary itself. As the years have passed, both have changed, but neither one has existed without the other. The story of the Central Prison is instructive because it chronicles both the beginning of one cycle and the end of another in the continuing development of incarceration. Convict labour at the Central Prison may have developed beyond the mindless tasks of the past, such as turning the crank and running the treadmill, but prison labour as true vocational training was still, and perhaps ever will be, a distant development. The goals and practices of prison labour defined the kind of place that the Central Prison became just as markedly as the limitations of incarceration embodied the experience of labour in the prison. Equally, reformatories like the Central Prison were as much a product of the history of convict labour before them as they were a precursor of the kinds of prisons that followed their closure.

By the time the Central Prison opened in 1874, the penitentiary was still a relatively new development in the history of criminal justice, having arrived only about forty years earlier, but its philosophies quickly became predominant. Before the nineteenth century, society had little faith in the reformatory qualities of incarceration. It was only mandated in the cases of persons awaiting trial or punishment and in the instance of convicted debtors. Prisons were then seen as unruly temporary clearing-houses for criminals on their way to experience the true majesty of the law in the form of some other judicial sanction; they hardly qualified as punishments in their own right. The establishment of the penitentiary, then, was a massive change in the view of the role of incarceration. In sentencing a man convicted of petty theft to the Kingston Reformatory in 1841, an Upper Canadian judge exuded the new vocabulary of rehabilitative labour:

It may teach some of the convicts that repugnance to bodily exertion may be conquered by habit ... There will be a portion of the convicts, no doubt, and I fear the largest portion, who being naturally lazy, and having destroyed their strength and energy by vicious habits, are not likely to overcome their aversion to labour, and with such persons the dread of being condemned to a round of wearisome toil in every sense unprofitable to them, may have the effect at least of deterring them from a repetition of their crime.

As severe as the judge's remarks may seem, they exemplified two important beliefs – that criminals were capable of rehabilitation and that labour was the vehicle to this reformation. But why was work thought to be the answer? This is a subject of considerable debate among historians. The judge saw the labour as corrective but also clearly valued it for its sheer punitiveness. Indeed, Calder argues that constant hard labour was part and parcel of the purposely 'punitive' and 'disagreeable' character of the new penitentiary.[3]

This had become a troublesome dichotomy. Labour could be punishing, but so too could an absence of labour. Atlantic prisoners, for example, were frequently locked in their cells for months at a time for lack of work, and as for American prisons, Rothman relates how, by the turn of the century, 'idleness was rampant and every observer knew it.' Mainstream historians of the prison have come to realize that exposing the contradictions of the past only underlines the quandaries of the present. '[T]he dilemma posed by the attempt to punish and reform criminals,' Beattie remarks, 'has yet to be solved.' Writing about the Central Prison, Oliver wonders why Ontario prison officials never saw any measure of incompatibility between their objectives for hard labour, namely that it could serve as a punishment, provide industrial training, and inculcate an appreciation of the value of work. Failing in these reformative goals, the Central Prison, Oliver argues, ultimately ended up simply serving society's need to terrify the criminal element. Without labour, however, in whatever form, the penitentiary lost its reason for existence. Overt punishment was no longer enough. Labour was the paradoxical nexus of both punishment and rehabilitation, one seemingly inconceivable without the other. The penitentiary movement, with all its seductive promises, cloaked as it was in the language of tough practicality, was more of a faith than a science, and like most movements of faith, it did not matter if it sometimes transcended logic. Indeed, why else would it have had such extraordinary staying power? The penitentiary, with all its problems, has yet to be replaced.[4]

The Central Prison, then, was the outgrowth of a prison system that itself was in a constant state of crisis. Unless they were sentenced to terms of over two years, lawbreakers were a provincial government responsibility. That meant that these lesser offenders would go to locally run jails. These were generally ramshackle affairs, with little discipline, lax security, and crude facilities. There was usually nothing for the inmates to do while incarcerated, except fester in these conditions. Worse still, many jails also served the additional functions of unofficial shelters for the indigent elderly, disabled, and poor, further diluting their carceral identities. The jails were becoming a disappointing and embarrassing reminder of more primitive times. They did nothing to reflect the new ideas of the prison reform movement that were sweeping North America, and they seemed to do little to either reform or deter. Indeed, it is probable that the Central Prison would never have been built had it not been for the crisis in the provincial jails. By 1859, prison inspectors were complaining about their lack of any uniform standards: '[I]n one prison the discipline is severe, in another it is nought; in one prison the accommodation is tolerably good, in another it is abominable; here the diet is hardly enough to sustain life, there it is superabundant; here the prisoners work, there the prisoners (those even whom the Courts specially condemn to hard labour) do absolutely nothing; in some prisons breaches of prison discipline are punished, in others there is neither discipline nor punishment.' One report goes on sarcastically to call the jails nothing better than 'government boarding houses' where their 'residents' 'meet freely old or new friends,' and 'plot against society, organize their next campaigns, and enroll fresh recruits into their ranks.' 'The present system of our Gaols (which is in fact an utter absence of all system) ... fails entirely in effecting the objects of penal institutions. We do not punish, or we punish improperly. We do not deter from crime, and we do not reform the criminal.' Eventually the problem with the jails seemed to be narrowed down into one central issue: lack of convict labour. 'Enter the corridors of any of our gaols,' reads an 1869 report, 'and the first thing that strikes an observer is the utter idleness that prevails throughout the Prison, not the weary, wearing, silent idleness consequent to solitary confinement, but vitiating, associated idleness that is so much coveted and sought after by certain criminals and pests of society.'5

'Idleness' became almost a code word; one needed only to mention it and everything that was wrong with the jail system and prisons in general could be explained. Eliminate that inactivity and one would eliminate crime, the high expenses of prisons, discipline problems, and recidivism. 'It is contrary to reason and common sense that idleness and sloth should form the chief characteristics of a Prison,' the prison inspector wrote in 1869, 'better for a return to the degrading but exploded device of the crank and the tread wheel than continue a system that affords every opportunity for the nurture and spread of vice and crime.' Turning to finances, the inspector wondered why inmates could not pay for their own keep. Prison officials looked to the examples of the big American industrial prisons like Detroit and Albany, and optimistically concluded that 'where the system has been properly managed, large amounts [of revenue] are received from convict labour.' It did not seem to be significant at the time, however, that these institutions, unlike the proposed Central Prison, housed thousands, not hundreds, of inmates, serving years, not months, in which to be moulded into vast squadrons of skilled industrial workers. But idleness was not only supposedly losing the province money, it was also robbing the institution of a central role: '[I]t should never be lost sight of,' reads an 1867 report, 'that the primary object of their incarceration is punishment for crime ... no branch of which would have a more wholesome or deterrent effect than the establishment of a proper system of hard or penal labour.' '[I]t is a perfect farce,' argues another report, 'to suppose that cutting a few sticks of wood can by any possibility be construed into hard labour.' Proposing an industrial prison, then, which by its very definition was designed to get rid of idleness, would answer all these concerns, and would produce an environment which would facilitate the 'punishment, restraint and reformation of criminals.' Indeed, there seemed to be no limit to what the elimination of idleness could accomplish.6

Ontario's prison officials travelled to the United States to see the famous American penitentiaries, and they were impressed. The example of the federally run Kingston Penitentiary must have been on their minds as well. Indeed, in many ways, the Ontario Central Prison was a monument to provincial pride. Even though it was needed only for several hundred inmates, generally serving no more than a few months at a time, and none of them serious offenders, the Central Prison had all the trappings of a big penitentiary, and consequently, all the inherent logistical and disciplinary problems.

But when the Central Prison opened in 1874, the government criminologists could not have been more pleased. The Canada Car Company, a blue-chip consortium of railway car builders with some of the province's most successful businessmen on its board, was firmly entrenched in the prison with a seven-year contract, with an option for a further seven years' renewal. The company had spent a quarter of a million dollars of its own money outfitting the prison to its specific needs, and was furthermore committed to paying the government a starting wage of fifty cents a day per prisoner, which would eventually increase to sixty cents a day over the course of the contract. Not even the long-term convicts at the Kingston Penitentiary earned more for their jailers than forty cents a day. (No wages, of course, were paid to either the federal or provincial inmates themselves.) Building railway cars entailed complex mechanics, fine carpentry, and metalworking. These were the ideal kinds of labour the prison designers had envisioned: productive, skilled, elevating, and educative for the prisoners, and highly profitable for the government.

When the company went bankrupt within ten months of the Central Prison's opening without having paid a cent in wages, the institution's troubles began and never ended. To add insult to injury, the government was forced to pay the company over $15,000 in compensation in an out-of-court settlement.[7] The company reorganized, and was promptly given one of its several successive contracts for the manufacture of various woodenware products. Contracts were successive because the new company, pleading financial woes which unfortunately were real, became adept at renegotiating the contract whenever pressed for payment. It was not a happy partnership for either side. But what was the province to do? Here was a brand-new, half-million-dollar facility, filled with over three hundred convicts suddenly having nothing to do. Things got even worse with the release of the report of an 1876 royal commission appointed to 'Inquire into the Value of The Central Prison Labour.'

It recommended that the government re-evaluate its hopes for convict labour, concluding that the Canada Car Company was being charged considerably more for convict labour than it was worth. Suddenly and very early on, an essential argument for prison labour, profit, was seriously deflated.

The prison's first warden, Captain William Stratton Prince, a military man and a former Toronto chief of police, was not much later relieved of his duties at the Central Prison. In the interim, the irony of the captain's notorious alcohol problem was not lost on members of opposition in the Legislative Assembly. Whether it was caused by the mounting difficulties of the Central Prison, or merely exacerbated by them, a warden's lack of sobriety in a reformatory was ultimately not a character trait to be held in his favour, especially in light of the prohibitionist sentiment sweeping the province at the time as well as the Central Prison's stated goal of eradicating drunkenness. The prison's second warden, James Massie, a retired politician, helped solidify the prison's scandalous status by inspiring yet another royal commission in 1885, this time looking into allegations of the cruelty of the prison management. Depictions of corporal punishment, starvation, squalid conditions, and staff confrontations, luridly covered by the press, disgusted and titillated the public for months. Massie was blamed for some problems, exonerated for most, and continued in office for another fourteen years. In the meantime, the prison attempted the manufacture of over fifty different products, with poor to fair results.[8]

In fact, at least on a private level, Massie did try his best, and developed some lasting relationships with many of the prisoners. This is indicated by the vast body of letters between him and thousands of discharged inmates, full of affectionate greetings and fatherly warnings, all left behind in the prison case files. Dr John Gilmour, an MD and also a former member of the legislature, took over in 1899 as the prison's third and final warden. Like Massie, he knew how to talk tough, but he too had a humanitarian streak. He quickly became preoccupied with securing early releases for his prisoners, which was probably an indication of his opinion of the good of being incarcerated at the Central Prison. '[L]et me say,' the minister of justice wrote to Gilmour in reference to one of his parole recommendations, 'that I think the language you use in your letter is rather vigorous. No doubt you have written exactly as you feel about the case ... when you cry out so emphatically for "Justice! Justice!"' The minister finally asked the warden whether he thought it was 'my duty [to] substitute your judgement for my own.'[9]

By 1908, a change in government and a renewed faith in the possibilities of rehabilitation generated a subsequent wave of reforms, evidenced by another royal commission. The groundwork began to be laid for a new type of prison labour: decidedly non-industrial and anti-technological, a return to more ideal agrarian times, when simple uncomplicated work could be done outside in the fresh air. A scandal over the acceptance of campaign funds by the Ontario provincial secretary from a Central Prison contractor, allegedly in return for more favourable terms, dominated the 1913 session of the Legislative Assembly and was probably the final nail in the coffin of the old contract labour system. Prison architects began planning a new reformatory, the Guelph Prison Farm, later the Ontario Reformatory, an institution whose chief attraction when it opened in 1910 seemed to be its conscious distancing of itself from the ambitions of the Central Prison.

The Central Prison was a failure for many reasons. Apart from their fear of punishment, prisoners were never given any real incentive to work. Brutal punishments, too, often did more to strengthen rather than to weaken inmate resistance. Many arrived too ill to do any work in the first place, and because of the unsanitary conditions and poor diet at the prison, even the healthy did not long stay that way. The multitude of serious industrial accidents in the workshops underlined the fact that prison officials were unequipped to properly train the inmates in the complicated trades in which they were expected to work. With the mostly unskilled inmates serving no more than an average of six months at a time, this was hardly surprising. Successive contractors soon found out that even the low wages they paid the government for convict labour were no bargain. As both the government and the business struggled to make their respective investments in the prison pay, contracts constantly hovered between non-payment and forfeiture. Recessionary times, poor prison management, and labour union protests exacerbated the problems. Survival, much less than profit, became the best viability for prison contractors. Ultimately, though, contractors could bail out. The government, however, had to keep the prison running whether its inmates were employed or not.

Its proponents had envisioned the Central Prison as a profit-making institution for the province and one of hard work and new hopes for the inmates. In reality, the prison had failed to succeed in more than just financial terms; it was a place of idleness, sickness, and human misery. Inmates learned few useful skills in the prison, and when released, a criminal record made jobs even harder for them to find. They were lucky to leave the prison alive and uninjured, with a view to some-how putting the terrible experience of incarceration into the past.

THE CANADA CAR COMPANY DEBACLE

It was exhilarating at first. All the province had to do was sit back and watch the Canada Car Company foremen turn criminals into skilled labourers, and collect the financial and reformatory rewards. All the while, prison bureaucrats, the Ontario government, Warden Prince, and Canada Car Company officials seemed very nearly to bask in their own collective glory. The remarkable testimonials, like so many paeans to the virtues of prison labour, never seemed to stop. The foreman of the moulding shop, who like all foremen was an employee of the Canada Car Company, said, 'The prisoners are doing better than any lot of free men I ever saw in my life, taking the time at which they have been at work into account.' The foreman of the lumber yard seemed to concur: 'The men are as good as free men in all respects.' Warden Prince joined in with the happy chorus, reporting that the convicts had very few complaints, adding that he was 'happy to note the interest displayed by the prisoners, and the diligence and willingness with which they labour, and the remarkable celerity with which many prisoners attain proficiency.' But what truly made those ten months of fantasy the cause for celebration was that this was the one and only time the government could claim that the idea of prison labour, the idea that was responsible for the building of the Central Prison, had been proved right – financially right, yes, but perhaps most importantly, morally right: 'The large proportion of the prisoners who are so highly spoken of were committed for crimes of which idleness and intemperance were the first cause. Enforced sobriety, and seclusion from bad influences have induced the first great principle of reformation – Industry.' All this elation must have been tinged with a measure of desperation. The signs of the impending bankruptcy were there to see for all concerned: the constant supply shortages, machine breakdowns, and most dam-aging, the continued idleness of the prisoners.[10]

Indeed, there were problems early on. The largest number of prisoners ever actually employed was 183 out of a prison population of over 300. This figure included convicts assigned to gardening work and prison construction. By January, out of a population of 304 inmates, there were only 31 who were actually working. Company officials, while extolling the virtues of convict labour, were employing free labour in ever-increasing numbers in the prison shops, with tacit government approval. The warden warned that the practice 'was notably demoralizing to the prisoners, and subversive of discipline [and] dangerous to the safety of the prison.' The company even went so far as to request that prisoners be allowed to work outside of the institution, a request that the government was obviously not willing to meet. The company had every right to be nervous. Under the terms of the contract, the company was required to pay for the labour of the convicts whether they were employed or not. But by March 1876, the Canada Car Company was bankrupt and Ontario Attorney General and Premier Oliver Mowat had the duty of informing the lieutenant-governor that it would be 'advisable that for a time offenders should not be sentenced to the Central Prison.'[11]

The failure of the Canada Car Company was a watershed in the history of the prison. The ensuing royal commission of inquiry's revelations of the company's questionable financial dealings with the government further discredited the contract system, and prison capitalism permanently lost some of its sheen. The Canada Car Company got its contract without any competition and without prior knowledge of the Legislative Assembly. It was required to pay neither rent nor taxes. The deal began to look even more suspicious when it was revealed that the company had been leasing with an option to purchase some acreage in the proposed Central Prison site, land with coveted railway line frontage. This lease appeared to be all too conveniently relinquished to the government in return for a favourable contract. In many ways, the contract exemplified the government's approach to convict labour in general. It was an agreement made in haste, and without sufficient forethought. The deal's terms looked favourable, but their execution was harder than anyone, publicly, and perhaps privately, had anticipated.[12]

No amount of political circumspection, however, could have prevented the inquiry from making its chief conclusion – that prison labour was worth only one-third of the value of free labour. This was a simply devastating development. The government had calculated the value of the Central Prison inmates to be as much as sixty cents a day; the commission in turn pegged the real value at thirty-seven cents. And this did not apply to work such as improving the grounds or kitchen and general maintenance work, which the government routinely liked to term labour. The commission also acknowledged that, as employers of convicts, contractors would never have full control of their employees. This was 'to be anticipated from the necessarily divided control of the prisoners' operations.' The province had also failed to take into account the possibility of economic downturns. 'Contractors employing prisoners must continue the business and pay for their labour, whether the market for the commodities is favourable or not.' Companies could shut down production, but industrial prisons did not have the option of closing when the economy declined, as it did so promptly at the time of the prison's completion. But perhaps most damaging to the proponents of prison labour in general was the commissioners' prediction that, no matter what the province did, prison labour would never be as good as free labour, for various reasons: '[T]he prisoners cannot be relied on for experienced work except after considerable time consumed in instructing them, and then only for the period of their imprisonment, which is short, as compared with the period of time citizens who usually work at a given occupation ... [T]he labour of prisoners is measurably a forced labour, the prisoners not being actuated actively by the ordinary incitements and ambition belonging to citizens and freemen at their work.'[13]

A more complex picture emerges, however, from the inquiry's transcript, comprising some three hundred pages of testimony of foremen, free workers, company officials, guards, prison experts, bureaucrats, and captains of industry. Canada Car Company lawyers and representatives seem to have very shrewdly taken firm control of the agenda, dominating the questioning and with their own witnesses offering the majority of the answers. This was a good business decision. The more devastating the evidence, the more financial leverage the company could hope to exert, both in terms of financial compensation from the government, as well as in future contracts. Accordingly, it was driven home how prisoners wilfully broke machinery and stole tools and might even have been setting fires. The company bullied guards, foremen, and even the warden himself into admitting to these acts of vandalism. In a word, prisoners were terrible workers. They refused to learn. They could not learn the trades anyway, since most apprentices served seven years before mastering a vocation. These were all legitimate concerns, but it was also precisely the kind of evidence Canada Car Company officials wanted to hear. Company Vice-President John McBean's testimony was typical:

Q. Has much loss been incurred in consequence of machines or tools being broken by the prisoners?
A. Frequently some parts of the machines have been broken and sometimes

this would not have taken place had free men been engaged at work, and sometimes it would be otherwise; I know that the loss has been considerable. Even a short time ago, damage was caused which cost us fifty dollars; it was all done because a prisoner became a little angry with the foreman; to repair the damage cost us fifty dollars.

Q. Was this done through ignorance?

A. No, no. It was done on purpose; and only a month ago another case occurred; a tap was turned, and a whole barrel of varnish allowed to be lost. It flowed over a great part of the place.

Worse, officials complained, goods that were produced for the company were defective. Prison-made pails were one example. '[I]f any very considerable weight is put in the pail, the handle comes off, and the pail goes to pieces. This is, I think, all due to the fact that the men have no interest in doing their work as it should be performed.' All these dilemmas were, incidentally, virtually the same arguments that the Canada Car Company had offered the government for its inability to pay for the contracted labour.

Nevertheless, E.B. Eddy, a major manufacturer of wooden goods, along with other representatives of industry, testified that they were losing money because of the competition of the Canada Car Company. 'We do not object to prison labour,' he maintained, but to 'prison labour if obtained for nothing.' In view of the company's record of payment, Eddy was probably closer to the truth than he realized. Indeed, if the goods were so defective, why would private industry protest over the competition? The royal commission exposed the flaws of prison labour, but in a calculated way it was also a whitewash for the system. It portrayed convict labour as virtually useless, and therefore nonthreatening. As a matter of fact, though, private industry was suffering, and for all of the reincarnated Canada Car Company's woes, they were doing serious damage to their competitors. But the commission's findings virtually validated the company's excuses for non-payment, and perhaps laid the groundwork for future manipulations by subsequent contractors willing to try their luck with a demoralized prison labour programme. The province may well have been out of its depth when in came to understanding the intricacies of capitalism.[14]

For all its brinkmanship, however, the Canada Car Company was still bankrupt. The lenient terms of the contract could not outweigh the fact that prisoners were indifferent workers at best and that the economy had declined to the point that there was little demand for new railway cars. The reorganized company's subsequent forays were probably less an expression of faith in convict labour than rather desperate attempts to recoup its substantial investments in the prison. Despite the low wages, future contractors knew that they ventured into the prison purely at their own risk.

CONVICT LABOUR IN PRACTICE

After the Canada Car Company disaster, officials tried to carry on as best they could. They worked with other contractors, and attempted the profitable manufacture of almost every imaginable product, from toy sleds to sausages, from bricks to bouquets of flowers. The prison, for all its creative efforts, never once broke even. Prison productivity figures, for example, were not high. The highest number of convicts engaged in labour never exceeded 73 per cent in the years between 1890 and 1912. These numbers become even less impressive when one realizes that up to 20 per cent and never under 10 per cent of those days of work were spent in domestic duties. Therefore, an already bad year like 1907, when only 63 per cent of inmates were working on any given day, becomes worse when it is considered that 16 per cent of all inmates, calculated into the total deemed working, were engaged in domestic duties. In reality, then, only 47 per cent of the inmates were truly employed in industrial work. Granted, an average of 10 per cent of the total prison population might have been unfit to work, under punishment, or under some kind of medical attention on any given day, but that does not make the figures look much more favourable.

And just because inmates were listed as working did not necessarily mean that their labour was of remunerative value. In the beginning, convicts were used to rebuild portions of the prison complex. The original towers for the armed guards, for example, were so poorly designed and badly built that they were useless.[15] A high proportion of inmates were engaged in domestic duties, such as cooking, cleaning, routine maintenance and gardening. Another group, on average just under 9 per cent of the prison population, was employed in the tailoring shop, useful at least, but not exactly the kind of heavy industry the province had envisioned. The average 30 per cent of inmates who were not given work to do were either left in their cells or marched about in military drill seven hours a day.

Even those employed in the industrial shops did not always do the province much credit. Like the Canada Car Company deal, the second large contract, given to Messrs McMurray and Fuller, a woodenware manufacturing company, was also awarded without advertisement. The company was affiliated with the liquidators of the Canada Car Company and soon found itself being liquidated. The province received no compensation for the labour of its prisoners from this contractor and was forced to admit that a factor in the company's bankruptcy was that 'there was very considerable waste of raw materials by unskilled workers.'[16]

By 1878, the province was clearly losing faith in the prisoners' ability to perform complex industrial labour and began a search for 'some kind of employment for prisoners requiring hard labour only and little or no mechanical skill.' Ultimately, however, the government decided to stay with an industrial focus for the prison, although the wardens had different ideas. Warden Prince seriously considered introducing oakum picking and fibre-mat making; only the poor availability of supplies prevented him from pursuing the plan. Warden Massie, too, flirted with the idea of reintroducing perpetual solitary confinement, under which refractory prisoners would pick wool in their cells.[17]

The fact was that prisoners could not be relied on to produce when they had to. When the binder twine factory had to be rebuilt, the warden brought in expensive free labour, instead of convict labour, because a large contract was in the making and the province could not afford to wait while convict labour took its usual slow course. As for the quality of the binder twine, opposition members in the legislature detailed complaints that 'the convicts were careless in their work, and did not take the trouble to unite ends which became disconnected.' Indeed, one client, the Massey-Harris Company, refused to pay for $1592 worth of the rope because of its poor quality. Any complex mechanical jobs, as well as routine machinery maintenance, had to be contracted out to more skilled, more reliable, and more expensive free workers.[18]

Shoddy or not, goods manufactured at the Central Prison still raised the ire of labour and private industry alike. Convict-made brooms were typically singled out. According to evidence tabled at the legislature, cheap brooms made at the prison were responsible for the fact that free broom-makers made the lowest wages of any skilled mechanics. Testifying at the 1889 royal commission into the relationship between labour and capital, a Hamilton broom-maker identified the Central Prison as a direct cause for the lay-offs in his industry. The commissioners considered stamping 'prison made' on convict-manufactured goods, making them virtually unsaleable. Meanwhile, the prison contractor complained about completed brooms whose handles habitually came loose and whose heads routinely flew off. It seemed that the province just could not please anyone. Citing shoddy workmanship, contractors refused to pay for the same goods that were apparently putting their competitors out of business.[19]

Soon it became apparent that the province was willing to try anything. Brick-making was recommended 'owing to its simplicity.' Evidently, officials had overestimated the convicts. In 1892, the Central Prison was left with an inventory of over two million misshapen bricks left over from the previous year alone, with no prospect of selling them. The government ended up buying many of these bricks itself, and they lined the interior walls of the new provincial parliament buildings, which were being erected in the same year. Eventually, nothing became too far-fetched to try. Convicts tried growing flowers for provincial institutions. Rope-making, selected because of its 'simplicity,' was in fact so simple that this industry typically hired young children, not grown men. In 1896, the prison attempted pig-breeding, but a cholera epidemic among the animals necessitated the slaughtering of them and the burning down of the barn.[20]

This was unusual only inasmuch that prison officials were more frequently fighting fires than setting them – seven major blazes in all. The fires cost the province thousands of dollars – in the case of the paint shop fire of 1888, for example, the building was completely filled with manufactured goods which were just about to be shipped to the contractors. Negligence undoubtedly led to many fires. Inmate resistance may well have been a factor as well. There were certainly enough convicted arsonists residing in the prison with the incentive and the professionalism to indulge themselves, if they so wished. These disasters left even more prisoners in a state of idleness and caused serious lapses of discipline. Carelessness at the Central Prison had become such a big problem that Warden Gilmour devoted his entire report of 1898 to possible methods of fire prevention.[21]

Perhaps the best indication of how desperately prison officials wanted the convicts to begin working more productively was their experiment with a prison bonus system, in which convicts would get small cash gratuities in return for better productivity. The idea of paying inmates for labour probably flew in the face of contemporary theories; it was supposed to rehabilitate, not renumerate the prisoners, and to be a way of paying for the costs of the institution, not creating further overhead. Nevertheless, a trial programme was reluctantly authorized by Warden

Massie in 1881, mainly out of urgency. The broom contractor was very anxious for an increase in output and was willing to pay prisoners a bonus of ten cents per dozen for all brooms made over the prescribed limit. Half of the money was to be kept in trust for the convicts upon their release. It was obvious that Prison Inspector Langmuir had high hopes for the experiment. 'In the broom shop,' he wrote, 'there is a disposition, shewn by some prisoners to shirk work, but it is expected that, when the bonus system is commenced, it will not only give greater stimulation to industry, but will reduce the punishments and deprivations awarded to prisoners in the shop.' Warden Massie had the unpleasant duty of yet again bringing the prison inspector down to earth, informing him that not only had the prisoners failed to produce the extra brooms, they had also not even met the contractor's original requirements. The program was suspended after two months.[22]

In fact, prisoners did try to earn the bonuses. As a consequence of their incarceration, many of their families were in dire financial straits. The case files are filled with prison-issued cheques, sometimes for less than a dollar, urgently sent home to their wives and mothers. The problem was that prisoners, for a variety of reasons, had enough trouble meeting their quotas, let alone exceeding them. The prison, in turn, had little incentive to lower its already desperately unmarketable daily work tasks. Probably for lack of any other alternative, the system was nevertheless tried again in successive years, and in the 1890s, an average of $2000 in bonuses was given out each year, or just under $4.00 for each prisoner upon discharge, not a great sum. The very few mechanically skilled inmates sometimes earned from two to five dollars a month. The money paid out declined sharply after the turn of the century, indicating a phasing out of the system. In any case, the fact that the government was willing to pay convicts anything at all was a major concession on their part.[23]

The Central Prison was not an inexpensive place to maintain, either. The government tried to present the figures in as good a light as possible in the annual reports. The charts indicating revenues always seemed to be as far away as possible from the charts indicating the losses, and more often than not, there appeared to be some very creative accounting. Revenues, for example, included maintenance jobs done by the convicts, calculated at the inflated figure of fifty cents a day. One member of the legislature went so far as to charge that the prison's system of accounting was 'bogus.' It is not difficult to concede the member's point. In 1883, for example, revenues for the Central Prison totalled $26,764, but with expenses of $51,001, it became clear that the Central Prison was really quite costly. That year, the men at the Central Prison were not producing much more in the way of wages for the province on a per capita basis than the women in the Mercer institution were, nor did the costs of Central Prison inmates compare favourably with those of the provincial jails.[24]

Unsellable goods were calculated into revenues as well, creating a rosier picture than actually was the case. In 1892, for example, the government calculated the value of stock remaining on hand at over $46,000, but the actual value of it must have been close to nothing. Oftentimes, too, the industries with the highest revenues also had the highest expenses. In 1893, for instance, the cordage shop netted a commendable $42,859.87. A few pages later, a different chart reveals that it also incurred expenses of $59,958.49. By 1895, the cordage shop was posting losses of close to $60,000. As annual losses of close to a $100,000 a year became the norm, wardens understandably tried to focus on cutting costs. In 1896, Warden Gilmour proudly announced that the per capita cost per diem for the maintenance of the inmates had decreased by 0.008 cents. This was a minuscule victory, but the warden had to show the province something. And if the money could not be earned from the convicts through labour, it would be taken away from them through budget reductions.[25]

No amount of frugality, however, could obscure the fact that prison officials made poor entrepreneurs. When a new Conservative administration was installed in 1905, government investigators were appalled by the financial chaos they found at the prison. New Provincial Secretary William Hanna released statistics that revealed that, from 1903 to 1905, the government-operated North Shop earned the minuscule sum of three-fifths of a cent per man each ten-hour day, and in some cases, even less. Under the terms of the Brandon Management Company agreement of 1881, convicts were supposed to earn the government fifty cents a day. In fact, the contract had cut that amount down to twenty-five cents, and ultimately not even that had been collected. There was also the labour vote to be considered. While the government ostensibly discontinued the brush and broom industry because of free labour protest, net proceeds were so low, about nineteen cents per man per ten-hour day, that there was hardly any point in making an issue out of it.[26]

The prison management was also not in touch with external business practices. Manufactured goods were sold well below market value, and raw materials were bought well above it. Hanna pointed to the instance of one manufacturing company which happily left its own machinery idle while it purchased the underpriced prison goods instead. When the manager of the North Shop was asked to give the cost of the goods he was turning out, he was unable to give a straight answer, and the books were of no use either. When government inspectors came in to make an inventory of lumber purchased for the woodenware industry, where one-quarter of the inmates worked, they discovered that of the 51,000 feet of basswood bought from a supplier, 22,000 were substandard. In his own defence, the contractor replied 'that it had been verbally understood in his former dealings with the Government that the written specifications would not be exacted.' Varnish bought for two dollars a gallon was not worth more than seventy-five cents on the open market. No matter what the government could do to remedy the situation, Hanna conceded to the legislature that there would be no escaping the fact that there would be a daily average of sixty men with nothing to do at the Central Prison.[27]

YEARS OF IDLENESS AND FRUSTRATION

The profound setbacks at the Central Prison caused shock, and then bitterness. The forward-looking and intellectual discussions about the promise of prison labour that had characterized earlier reports of the prison inspector seemed to disappear. Until the possibility of a Guelph prison farm started to be discussed around the turn of the century, prison officials in Ontario seemed to operate in almost an intellectual vacuum, turning their attentions inward. It was not prison labour as an ideal that concerned them now, but the more pressing problem of how to cope with the prisoner himself and keep the prison industries running at the minimum level of efficiency. This attitude was exemplified by the conditions that produced the need for the 1885 royal commission into allegations of cruelty at the Central Prison and the report's callous dismissal of almost all of the charges. Prison reform no longer seemed important. Officials had enough trouble keeping the prison as it was functioning.

The defeatist atmosphere was exacerbated by the sheer monotony of life in the Central Prison. The institution was set up to instil working habits into its inmates, but it consistently failed to provide employment for them. With decreased respect came smaller government allocations, and, not being able to afford enough guards, authorities were forced in 1894 to put the unemployed prisoners into the workshops along with those prisoners who were selected to work. This tactic of mixing working prisoners with non-working prisoners was not conducive to good behaviour. Unemployed prisoners were also often subjected to the military drill, an activity, noted the surgeon, that was only just marginally more hated than the 'purgatory' of the broom shop. 'Many pretenses are devised,' he wrote, and as the surgeon he would have known, 'to escape these objectionable employments in lieu of less disagreeable and lighter labour.' Other industries were seasonal. Brick-making, for example, could only be pursued in the summer months. For the rest of the year, convicts assigned to it frequently had nothing to do. Prison Inspector Christie noted in 1882 that 'it is most desirable to add ... such suitable labour as can be prosecuted at all seasons and in all weathers.' Warden Gilmour complained in 1906, for example, that, out of a population of three hundred inmates, he had to cope with up to sixty unemployed men. 'Enforced idleness for a period of several consecutive months is more injurious to the average convict,' he wrote, 'than our words can express. This places the prisoner out of touch with the social and industrial conditions of the day, and when he leaves the prison he is more helpless than when he entered.'[28]

To make matters even worse, a consistently high proportion of inmates sent to the Central Prison were unfit to work. As early as 1875, the province's Attorney General pointed out that 'in some instances aged, maimed, and otherwise physically incapable persons, as well as lunatics and paralytics, have inadvertently been sentenced to the Central Prison.' He urged that proper medical examinations of the convicted be conducted at their trials to determine their fitness for hard labour. Warden Massie, however, saw this trend as no accident. '[T]he Central Prison,' he argued, 'is neither an almshouse nor an insane asylum, and should not be used as such simply to relieve municipalities of their burdens.' In one typical year, no fewer than twenty-five prisoners were sent, 'comprising lunatics, imbeciles, men deficient of hands or fingers, epileptics, and old men of sixty five and seventy.'[29]

There was no guarantee that even a healthy new inmate would stay that way. In his twenty years in office, Prison Surgeon Aikins waged what seemed to be a one-man crusade against what he felt was one of the two greatest threats to the convicts' good health – poor ventilation. (The other one was 'self abuse.') Aikins was convinced that the rancid air in the prison caused a host of fatal respiratory sicknesses. Uncirculating air, he advised, coupled with poor drainage and an impure water supply, also caused the typhoid deaths that plagued the prison year after year. The doctor was especially concerned that the dark cells, which were virtual pits dug into the ground with an iron hatch on the roof for entry, had no ventilation at all. No wonder the prisoners called the dark cell the 'sewer.' For his part, Warden Prince was un-moved. '[S]ome cases of typhoid fever,' he wrote, 'must invariably exist though quartered in the healthiest situation and under the strictest san-itary regulations.' While undergoing punishment in the dark cell, pris-oner R.H. Wood wrote the Warden, 'if I remain in this cell I will only be a fit subject for the Hospital when my term expires.' When one prisoner complained of having to bathe in water that had been used by twenty prisoners before him, the inspector countered that until more bathtubs were purchased, there was nothing that could be done.[30]

Guards joined the prisoners in complaining of tainted meat and im-properly boiled potatoes. One prisoner alleged that chloride of lime was used to keep down the smell of the rotten meat being served. Prisoners complained, too, of finding worms and bugs in their soup and tarred rope in their bread. Prison investigators were clearly unsympathetic, concluding that 'the State is not bound to treat its vicious members so daintily in prison that they would be better off by reason of their vice ... while many of its virtuous members outside are suffering from hunger.' Dr Aikins also argued that the punishment diet of bread and water 'weakened every power in the body.' 'Every old woman,' he told Warden Massie, 'knew that a variety in diet was necessary.' Apparently, there did not seem to be much of a will to rectify the situation. As late as 1902, Warden Gilmour, who was, after all, a medical doctor him self, was sufficiently worried about the threat of tuberculosis to devote almost his entire annual report to the topic. Unlike the previous ward-ens, Gilmour had more personal reasons for an interest in health con-ditions. At the time, he was just recovering from a lengthy bout of typhoid fever.[31]

LIFE IN AN INDUSTRIAL PRISON

Dangerous work, unsanitary conditions, putrid food, and brutal dis-cipline all took their toll on the inmates. For many, despair greeted them the moment they entered the prison. Prisoner John Currie wrote: 'To the unfortunate transgressor of the law who has received a sentence, his first glimpse of the Old Central Prison as he approaches it tends to discourage and dishearten him. The fancy stone walls, with guards on top, gun on shoulder and the black iron bars bear a cold forbidden aspect to the new arrival to enter within the old grey portals to spend years perhaps.' The diary of prisoner Percy Ebbitt expressed a similar sentiment: 'On entering in the large, spacious grounds in front of the prison you will see very pretty flowers, trees, etc., which you will no doubt notice to take a look at, because it may be a long time before you see them again.'[32]

The inmates reacted in a variety of ways. Many escaped, and some died in the attempt. There were a few suicides. Many simply refused to work; the majority worked indifferently. Discipline became such a problem that the wardens even lobbied to have separate punishment buildings constructed. It almost came to the point where discipline was meant to be an end in itself. Even if the Central Prison was not to make a profit, Warden Massie avowed, all was not lost: 'I do not wish it to be understood that all my efforts are directed towards one object, that of conducting the prison solely on business principles with a view to financial results. The strict rules and discipline the prisoners are required to observe, combined with the moral restraint and substitution of active employment for idleness, has an elevating and reforming tendency.' The warden expressed concern whether the guards, who were hardly an indulgent lot, were tough enough and urged that the discipline at the Central Prison be 'even more stringent than that of a Penitentiary.' The authors of the 1891 Royal Commission on Prisons and Reformatories in Ontario seemed to understand well what kind of atmosphere this attitude would produce:

It seems a matter of regret that no attempt has yet been made to introduce a system of rewards as well as punishment in the Central Prison. Punishment alone has never been found sufficient for the suppression of crime, or the reformation of criminals. 'Hope,' says an eminent penologist, 'is the master spring of human action ... Hope is the great inspiration to exertion in free life. Why should it not be made to fulfill the same benign office in prison life? Can anything else supply its place? Hope is just as truly, just as vitally, just as essentially the root of all right prison discipline as it is of all vigorous and successful effort in free life.[33]

One way to react to this 'hopeless' regime was by escaping. Despite the risk of corporal punishment if caught, or death while being pursued, prisoners planned for escape, they dreamt about escapes, and they followed through with a near epidemic of them. Prisoner Percy Ebbitt included a fanciful plan of escape, written in the form of a story, in his confiscated diary. The protagonist takes advantage of the noise of a passing train to muffle the sound of his filing the bars on his cell window. The guard dog is put out of commission by being fed some crushed glass. His accomplice gives him a secret bird call and he scales the walls.[34] In 1882 there were an unprecedented ten escapes, three of them successful. In 1883, for example, there were six escape attempts, one of them by prisoner Robert Scott, who was shot dead by the guards. Not having heard the news, the young man's brother wrote him, wondering why he was not responding to his letters.[35]

Inmates found work in the Central Prison to be sheer drudgery. Eighteen-year-old Henry Howell wrote the warden a long, plaintive letter:

Sir, Mr. Massie, I cannot understand it. I've been in trouble ever since you sent me in the Brick yard. Mr. Massie it's just like this. After I have been weeling about two hours, my feet get sore & my legs get weak & commences to pain me in the knee joint & then I walk kind of lame, & when night come I am played clean out, & when I come up to my cell, I take a couple of mouths full of Bread & a sip of tea & then I undress my self & get into Bed, & I am sound a-sleep before I know it, but I most allways wake up about one or two o'clock in the morning, & then I feel all Broke up, my legs pain me all over, & my feet feels sore, & the cords or sinuses each side & around my neck feels sore & I feel all stiff ... in my knee, my legs are all stiffened up & I can scarcely turn my head around, because it is so stiff in the mornings. That rope I have around my neck seems to tear my neck all to pieces ... Mr Massie, I hope you will not have any more hard feelings against me. I've only got 32 more days, so I ask you will you be so kind as to give me another job ... [J]ust give me an other job & try me, & see if I cant keep my word. (Just give me one chance & I shall be the best boy in the prison).

Prisoner James Quinn wrote the warden to ask him that after years of being an army nurse and a newspaper compositor, would he 'allow a man that humbly boasts of having some intelligence and abilities to waste eighteen months of his life in the Machine shop where' he is 'absolutely of no use'?[36]

The guard, who did more than anyone else to ensure that production kept moving, played a pivotal role in defining the inmate's experience in prison. Gilbert Hartley was the guard in charge of the broom shop, the prison's largest industry, and he certainly took his job very seriously. No guard came close to filing as many misconduct reports as he did, nor did any other guard write them in such detail. Historians ought to be grateful to him for this. The prisoners reciprocated by treating Hartley with every imaginable discourtesy and disrespect, which he in turn dutifully and comprehensively reported for posterity in his inimitably juvenile pencil scrawl. A typical report was that for 18 August 1885:

I herein desire to report the following incident that occurred this morning at 6:00 o'clock when at that hour I unlocked the cell gate of cell #64 occupied by Pris. Vanetton, to allow him to get his breakfast ration, he said to me, 'no wonder you can eat mouldy bread, you are fit to eat anything.' Not quite understanding him, I asked him what he said. He then repeated what he had said before. I asked him, why? He then went on to say, 'any man who would make such a report as you made, can eat anything.' I asked him what the report was. He said, 'If you didn't want me to go to the closet, why didn't you put a bucket at my machine.' He continued in this strain at some length. I told him he had better be careful how he talked. He would say what he liked or some words to that effect. In explanation of what he said about mouldy bread, I might add on Saturday noon, he showed me his ration of bread which was a little mouldy under the crust and asked me if that was fit to give a man to eat. I asked him if he had never eat bread a little mouldy. He said he had not. I told him he was of the epicures, that I had eaten it before now. G. Hartley Gd.

Christopher Vanetton eventually was to undergo corporal punishment. Vanetton's treatment was one of the cases examined, and approved, by the 1886 inquiry into cruelty at the Central Prison.[37]

Prisoner Edward Dorsey had the following comments to make about Hartley when visited by medical staff while undergoing punishment in the dark cell: 'He put me in the Dark Cell. He would not tell me what he put me in for. God Damn him the "Grey Son of a bitch." ... I will kill the God Damned bugger and go to hell. By God I will. I am not able to do the task [of making brooms]. If I do it one day I get pains in my shoulders the next – The prisoner was still talking when I closed the cell door. S. Hunt, Hospital Guard.' Prisoner George Smith, age twenty-three, put it to Guard Hartley succinctly: 'If you make any more reports about me, I'll [knock] the hell out of you.' Guard Hartley's dedication, however, was unassailable in the case of his exposing prisoner John McCullogh's false claim to diarrhoea. Had Hartley not examined the prisoner's night bucket for evidence, McCullogh would have successfully shirked his duties. Hartley did have his sentimental side, though, and no doubt the prisoners were aware of this fact as well. The guard recounts the following incident involving prisoner Charles Russell, age eighteen, serving a fourteen-month term for burglary:

January 9th, 1889. Russell sent for me last evening and begged me in piteous words and tears to try and save him from being whipped, promising sincerely to give no cause for trouble again while here ... Outside of his bad temper which is at times apparently uncontrollable and which leads to conduct I don't pretend to defend, he has been a very good prisoner and a good worker. I would ask as a favor, if you can possibly do it at this state of affairs, to give him another chance as he certainly did last night seem thoroughly penitent and conquered.

Russell was spared. However, a Hartley misconduct report on 11 June 1888 earned Russell fifteen lashes. A similar intercession was made on behalf of Benjamin Graham to restore the prisoner to his cell.[38]

William Cooper, an eighteen-year-old serving a twenty-three-month sentence for stealing one dollar, was another of Hartley's charges. He wrote the warden in 1891:

Dear Sir, I write these lines to you in hope you will not be angry ... I do try to do all I can up in the shop and every place ... Do not think me a crank for writing but I cant help it. You have been given report after report [about me] ... That day I was reported for getting behind in my work, it was not all my fault. Mr Hartley put me doing some crooked corn that kept me busy all the morning. About half past two Mr. Hartley came and spoke to me rather stern and said there was not a bundle of strait corn for the next day and he went and reported me. I told him I did all I could but he would not listen to me so I was in your hands and I thank you for letting me off. I do try my best to do what is right and keep from them reports but I dont know what to do at all, all the blame was put on me that time so I dont see what he meant when he reported me for I do as much and more as much work as some men making 15 cents and 25 cents a day overtime ... [I]f I speak to [Mr. Hartley] about the corn he dont give me a strait answer. He is always stern to me yet he can laugh and talk with others. I have often been so bad before that he has taken a strong dislike for me. I would do any work than be in the broom shop. Don't be vexed with me for writing with ink. I asked [Guard] Logan about it. He said I could use it in my cell. I am learning to write with it, that is all. I am trying to do right and I am trying to put the other half of my time in without a report. If I was out of the broom shop I would be happy. This is all. I mean what I say and it is true. Yours sincerely, William Cooper.

Hartley's punishment records, as well as the punishment reports of the other guards, show how immense their power was to make life at prison a misery, all in the name of maintaining order and keeping up production. The records also show how, in the face of such absolute authority, prisoners were still willing to endure severe punishment for the simple and life-affirming pleasure of showing them their defiance.[39]

But the guards did not have the easiest of times either. In 1888, for example, one was stabbed to death by a prisoner and another was thrown from a gallery and died from the injuries. Writing to his fiancée, Guard Hartley complained that surely his dangerous work was worthy of a little more respect. Missionaries, he protested, 'of both sexes,' will 'pet some of the vilest creatures who only laugh at what they say, will make them presents of books, bouquets, handkerchiefs, and other trifles but scarcely recognize any of us.' Given that, surely he 'deserve[d] some sympathy from men and women who profess to be Christians?'[40]

Convicts may have failed to see the educative and elevating value of labour, but they did see its punitive effect. They had to battle the effects of fatigue, favouritism, their fear of misconduct reports, and quotas that seemed impossible to achieve. The fact that they were not paid for their work, except in very rare cases of skilled work, did not help morale either. Indeed, one of the most frequent discipline infractions was a refusal to work, punished by the dark cell, confinement in irons, and the lash. But probably the safest way that prisoners found to express their displeasure was by slowing the production line. The wardens were well aware of this tactic, and Warden Massie would often complain that 'every increase of the daily task has been strongly opposed by the prisoners.'[41]

THE PERIL OF INDUSTRIAL ACCIDENTS

Obstructing the railroad tracks: it sounds like the quintessential boyish prank. The judge probably thought that when he was sentencing sixteen-year-old Thomas Slater to the Central Prison he would smarten him up to the value of safety. He sent him to the wrong place. Three months into his term, Slater became another victim of an industrial accident. About twenty-five workers from the cordage shop where Slater was working were sent out to unload a tanker car. Conveniently, a railway line ran through the prison yard and so these expeditions were routine. There was only one guard, and when his back was turned, Slater snuck out of his place, climbed over the railway car, and struck up an illicit conversation with a friend named Nelson, whom he had met in the lock-up while awaiting trial. While talking, he realized his boot had become caught in the track. The car started moving. Too afraid of being caught breaking the rules, he did not yell out for help. '[A]s he did not give any intimation of being caught till thrown down by the wheel passing up on his leg,' Warden Massie wrote to the boy's family lawyer, 'those in the rear end at the sides of the car were ignorant of his position, till attracted by his cries, when as quickly as possible the car was backed off him.' Slater died of shock in the prison hospital. As he had acted 'in direct violation of prison rules,' the warden concluded, 'no blame is chargeable to anyone but himself.' In fact, the prison was to blame. The coroner recommended that rail yard safety procedures be put in place.[42]

But time and time again, basic precautions were not taken. And the result was that prisoners ran the risk of being maimed into unemployability or killed by the very machinery that was supposed to rehabilitate them. Charles Furler lost an eye while breaking stones. His lawyer asked the warden why Furler was not supplied with a mask to protect his face. The warden wrote back simply, 'If you consult the statutes governing such cases, you will find we are in no way liable.' When called into account by the inspector of prisons, the warden explained, 'Furler was breaking stone. He volunteered for the work. He had no mask. Masks have never been used here in the past ... [H]e was given the benefit of the best treatment procurable. We furnished Furler with an artificial eye.' Joseph Bellao, a man with cataracts, was put to work on the circular saw, the most dangerous machine in the prison. He injured his thumb, and the prison inspector angrily ordered the prison to give him ten dollars as compensation. Joshua Bennett, a skilled machinist, was partially blinded by a piece of steel flying into his right eye. But even with Warden Massie on side, he was given no compensation. Prisoner Edward Carroll succeeded in getting a pardon. He lost a finger on the circular saw while cutting ladder steps. For a professional typist, an early release was hardly adequate compensation. A stonecutter,

George McDonald, lost the use of his right hand in an accident in the North Shop. Because of his occupation, he was granted $50 in compensation by the government, which, in light of his 'irresponsible character,' was 'to be meted out to McDonald as his necessities may require.'[43]

As far as the prison and the government were concerned, they were ultimately not responsible for any of the industrial deaths or injuries at the prison. The official line was that any accident that occurred was caused by either prisoner carelessness or disobedience of orders. The fact that these workers were men and boys with in many cases no knowledge of the trades to which they were assigned never seemed to be considered. Unskilled, underfed, and overtired, and in constant terror of punishment as they were, it was hardly surprising that they were not always cautious. There is no mention, either, of any precautions the prison took to prevent future acts of 'carelessness' on the part of the prisoners, by either modifying the tasks they performed or by adapting the machinery on which they worked. In any case, prisoners were not eligible for compensation. '[A]s you are well aware,' Warden Gilmour wrote to a lawyer representing one prisoner, 'prisoners come under the same heading as soldiers and sailors while on duty.' Because he was a prisoner, this man who had lost fingers and the use of a hand while working on a binder twine machine, Gilmour concluded, had 'no legal status.' It was as if the hazards of convict labour were part of its punitive value.[44]

In fact, anything more than token compensation would only encourage more accidents. 'I find,' wrote the inspector of prisons, 'that there is a danger to be apprehended in giving any large grants, in as much as prisoners have been known to willfully mutilate themselves in the hope of obtaining them.' With a dismal safety record, made worse by a draconian disciplinary regime, and a callous attitude towards compensation, one is left to wonder just how serious the Central Prison was in its rehabilitative aspirations. Just how likely were these injured men to become self-supporting?[45]

THE REHABILITATIVE VALUE OF PRISON LABOUR

All the dangers of the Central Prison might almost have been justifiable if the prison had succeeded in teaching the inmates jobs that would have been helpful to them in starting a new life on the outside. For the families of the younger prisoners, this was one of the few consolations available to them as they worried about their sons. The parents of prisoner Robert 'Curly' Fields, for example, wrote Warden Massie, requesting him to have their son 'learn some employment that will be of use to him when he gets out.' There always was a certain amount of belief in the community that the prison could teach trades. One prisoner, a sixty-five-year-old army veteran, even claimed that he committed his crime on purpose, so that he would have the chance of learning the tailoring profession.[46]

But such faith was not justified. The prison register lists the occupations of the prisoners as well as their prison work assignments. Teaching skills was a nice ambition, but with most trades requiring long apprenticeships to master, providing prisoners even wanted to learn these trades, there just was not enough time. For the most part, therefore, the prison was run on the skilled labour of convicts who had been trained on the outside. Convicted tailors invariably went to the tailor shop, shoemakers went to the shoe shop, barbers went to the barber shop, farmers worked in the garden or the stable, varnishers found work in the paint shop, carpenters were likewise directed to the carpentry shop, and bartenders and cooks were sent to the kitchen. Prison management even went so far as to 'recruit' the labour of skilled criminals from other institutions. Warden Gilmour instructed the bailiff to try to find out how many tailors there were at Toronto's Don Jail, and, if possible, to have them transferred to the Central Prison. On another occasion, Gilmour somehow found out that a skilled tailor was awaiting trial and asked the presiding judge to sentence the man, if convicted, to the Central Prison.[47]

Wardens Massie and Gilmour, however, did want to see the discharged prisoners succeed. While they were willing to accept the human costs of convict labour, this did not mean that they did not believe in its promised benefits. Punishment was one issue, but getting a job was the only way a prisoner could put his criminality behind him. The wardens were well aware of the prison's failings, in some ways more so than anyone else, but they believed that, if a released convict could get a job, the message of productive prison labour, whatever its difficulties, was in great measure vindicated. Warden Massie made a point of getting to know the families of his prisoners, their circumstances, their backgrounds. He did not hesitate to write letters of recommendation to his own friends urging them to hire discharged convicts. For example, he wrote to the wife of a bed frame manufacturer asking her that she persuade her husband to give prisoner William Brooks a job at his factory. 'I will be very pleased if your husband will give him employment, if not continuously, at least till he gets a start, after he will make his way. He is very impressible, and if you speak a word of encouragement to him when opportunity presents, it will go a long way towards overcoming all difficulties.' Massie urged the family not to give up on their son. After all, he wrote, it was the middle of an economic depression. He sent them two dollars of his own money for Christmas and said that he could not give more because he gave so much to local charities that 'I find them a very considerable drain on my limited income.' He promised to visit them when he next visited Rochester, where the family lived. Massie campaigned for a pardon for Alexander Ovens. When he got it, the warden offered him a job as a guard. To help a former convict along with his new fruit-growing business, Massie placed a big order of peaches from Stephen Ferrminger, only to be disheartened by their poor quality when they arrived. Massie even lent prison tools along with ten dollars to discharged prisoner Albert Swain to help him get a start in the pattern-making trade in Peterborough.[48]

Warden Gilmour regularly wrote letters of recommendation for prisoners who were about to be released. 'Louis Pokorney goes out on the 28th inst.,' Gilmour wrote to one prospective employer. 'Had he been working on salary, he could not have been a better man. Can you do anything for him by way of employment on the C.P.R.? I hope you may.' Gilmour was even willing to bend the truth a little bit if it would help. Discharged prisoner Charles Price, for example, wrote to Gilmour assuring him that 'I am sure of the job if you don't have to state in the recommend that I was in the Central.' Gilmour sent the following recommendation to the potential employer on a blank sheet of paper with his home address typed on the top: 'Charles Price has applied to me for a reference, and I beg to say that Price was in our employ for a considerable time, something over a year. He is a competent brush hand, enameling beds. We found him steady, industrious and temperate, and I can cordially recommend him to anyone requiring such help. I might say that he left on his own account ... J.T. Gilmour, Manager.' Gilmour, in addition to having a dry sense of humour, knew that without work experience it is difficult to get a job, and that having a prison record made things even worse. The vigorous effort extended by both wardens in trying to secure jobs for discharged inmates brings credit to their often maligned roles, and to the Central Prison's often forgotten idealism.[49]

Perhaps the best way, though, to measure the success of the prison's rehabilitative ambitions is to find out what happened to inmates after they left. Some interesting clues are provided by the letters former convicts and their families wrote the prison after their release. For various external reasons, some did well, while others did not. Former prisoner Edward Swain was just scraping by, living off the charity of former prisoner William Gill's father, and was thinking about going off to live in the woods. Discharged prisoner Henry Watkins was spotted 'in the company with some other idle men on one of the wharfs last week, looking very dirty and ragged.' He had just served his third term for vagrancy. John Millar could not find a job and so enlisted in the US Navy. He travelled a great deal, making a point to (voluntarily) inspect the prisons at each stop. He promised to send the warden a picture of himself in full dress uniform. 'I seen a lot of the Boys during my travels,' he offered, 'Some was doing well and some was not.' William McCutcheon became the foreman at a Toronto tailor shop. Richard Sevalie hired out with a farmer and hated the work. 'I would rather have a place in a factory if you can get me one,' he wrote Warden Massie, 'as the farm work is very hard on my wrist especially milking.' Stuart Pocock was attending to a big stock of cattle. John Laroque homesteaded in Holland, Manitoba. He pollinated his flowers with bees sent to him from the prison hive. George Whitfield became a bookkeeper for the New York Pennsylvania Railroad and earned $125 a month. Discharged prisoner H.F. Clarke liked to keep in touch with his friends in prison. He wrote prisoner John Lyons this update:

I am working still at Wagner's Piano factory and am getting good money. Bunker and me has got down a jig together and a hot one too. I seen Charley Rose the other night and was talking to him. He's working here to[o]. There is one thing that caused me to Blush and that was getting full 4 times the first week but I had very good luck and got off safe. But poor Frenchy is doing 30 days over at the don [jail] for a drink. He comes out on the first of September I think for I don't Remember the very night for I was Busy myself. I hope you are in good health now and keeping out of the sewer [the dark cell] and be a good 'BOY.'

At this rate, it looked as if Clarke might soon be joining some of his prison-mates. Lyons was not given this letter, for obvious reasons. James Browning was making preparations to go prospecting for gold in Africa. Warden Massie tried to talk him out of it. As World War I approached, many prisoners took advantage of the paroles being offered conditional on enlistment, and signed up. Inmates did their best to get on with their lives after imprisonment. There does not appear to be, however, much evidence to indicate that their prospects were materially improved by the experience.⁵⁰

The labour union movement's response to prison labour can be characterized as a mixture of economic and emotional arguments. On one level, it viewed forced labour as an insult to the dignity of free working people. On another, training and employing criminals in the skilled trades was an even greater affront. Worse still were the financial implications of a workforce getting paid less than a third of the free labour rate. This could not help but reduce free workers' wages and take away jobs. Better, then, that these convicts be put to work at undesirable jobs, which involved no threat to skilled workers. At a meeting of the Canadian Labour Union, one delegate suggested the following vocation for prisoners: 'Prison labour might be employed in making the banks of the Don a beautiful place. (Laughter) It would improve the city very much, and in the part which needed it most.' 'There was plenty of new land,' suggested another representative, 'that might be improved and made ready for settlement by convicts, instead of bringing them into competition with mechanical tasks.' It was clearly insulting to see lawbreakers being initiated into the secrets of artisanry. '[T]o teach a convict a trade,' the session resolved, 'might be called placing a premium upon crime.' Many in the movement also felt unfairly singled out, as if the concerns of skilled craftspersons were somehow viewed by the government as expendable in the way that those of the other classes were not. '[W]hy should the mechanical element,' an artisan wrote to the editor of the Ontario Workman, 'have to suffer all the degradation and competition from this lawless class.'⁵¹

Yet workers also understood that the majority of these convicts were from their own ranks and that their criminality was in great measure caused by the very injustices the movement was fighting to eradicate. The *Ontario Workman* wrote: 'Poor pay is a great temptation to theft. You have plenty and to spare – the one you employ nothing but poverty. It is hard for him to reason that such a state of affairs is right – that you should ride in a coach, while he cannot spare a sixpence to patronize a car after hours of hard work ... Is it strange then that so many should fail to keep the straightforward path?' The *Labour Union* ran a seven-part series of first-hand accounts of prison life in Ontario, teeming with outrage over the brutal conditions. An article in the *Ontario Workman* highlighted famous works of literature written by prisoners, from Boethius to Sir Walter Raleigh. At the same time as union members railed against convict labour with their wallets and their craft pride, the prisoner's exploited status clearly found some resonance in their hearts.[52]

Yet what influence on the government did the labour movement exert? Early on, the province declared that it would be impervious to labour union protest:

The opinion that prevails to some extent in Canada, that prison labour is antagonistic and destructive to ordinary skilled industry ... is utterly unworthy of the spirit of this Province which at the present moment is putting forth every effort to attract to its shores all classes of artisans ... And when the welfare of the whole Province in this respect is put into the scale against the interests of a few who may be interested in the particular trade or branch of industry adopted for the employment of prisoners, the objections urged against the system are unworthy of notice or comment.

But when faced with a potential strike by the prison's own free workers, the warden was considerably less sanguine, sounding the alarm all the way to the national minister of justice.[53]

Indeed, behind the scenes, a different scenario might have been unfolding. Pentland has suggested that the Ontario government and Canadian Labour Union made a secret deal, whereby protests against the Central Prison would be forgone in return for a Mechanics' Lien Act, passed in 1873, and an amended Master and Servant Act, passed in 1876. Pentland cites as evidence mention in the union minutes of a meeting with the Attorney General to object to the Canada Car contract. As a consequence, convict labour was then relegated to a lesser role at a planned protest rally, which instead emphasized the Mechanics' Lien Act and the Master and Servant Act. Prison labour was also subsequently absent from future union minutes. If Pentland is correct, then the union's willingness to trade away the convict labour issue may well have signified their view that the labour of prisoners was not as big a threat to their livelihood as they liked to admit publicly. But Pentland's claim is difficult to prove. A look at the minutes will prove, as Pentland himself admits, that the whole idea of planning a mass protest against convict labour was born out of the failure of the union to sway the government from its plans for the Central Prison. Furthermore, there is no talk whatsoever in the minutes of any deal being struck. The convict labour issue may have been abandoned by the union for any number of reasons. Perhaps the union leadership realized, as a consequence of the meeting with the minister, that on reflection the cause was hopeless and decided to campaign for more easily won victories. Perhaps, again, the union did not feel prison labour to be as threatening as they first thought it would be. The picture is just not clear. Indeed, Pentland's theories exemplify the difficulties of fathoming the true measure of influence the labour union movement had on forging government decisions on prison labour. Behind the rhetoric of injured labour pride on the one side and heroic reformatory building on the other, it is difficult to ascertain the exact dynamic of labour and government's interaction. In the final analysis, if we ask whether the Central Prison was closed because of labour union protests, we can really only guess. Indeed, when the time came to close the prison, the government was more than ready to take credit for its responsiveness to labour unions. Although the movement was certain to have played some role, in the end the easiest response to the question of labour union influence is that the Central Prison was shut down because it had enough problems in its own right.[54]

THE REBIRTH OF PRISON LABOUR

In its last ten years, the Central Prison had become to the province what the jails had been forty years previously. It was now the institution in need of reform. And so the last ten years of the Central Prison were in many ways like its early days. Instead of casting the individual prisoner as an obstacle to the prison's success, as he was in the middle years of the prison's history, prison officials began again to focus their attention on how the institution could be better tailored to his needs. The provincial secretary's remarks reflected the return to this approach: 'I mention this only as confirming what those who have given it any attention know to be true, that the short-term prisoner with the first offense is not as black as he is sometimes painted. He would gladly be better if given half a chance. Would the solution that we have in mind here give the prisoner a better chance? I believe it would.' Prison Inspector Bruce Smith even suggested in 1905 that prisons might not be the answer after all. Rather, governments must concentrate on the social conditions that produce crime. 'The system of reformation that aims at the study and correction of the [social] conditions at the source,' he argued, 'is the only rational system.' 'The time has come,' he suggested, 'when a careful study of the methods employed in dealing with the criminal class is called for. It would seem that we have yet much to learn in the study of this subject.' 'Prevention of crime,' wrote Inspector Edwin Rogers a year later on the same theme, 'not the punishment of it, should be the watchword of the future.' In the same year, Inspector Bruce Smith wrote in his report: '[w]e hold too much in view the offense, not the offender; what he has done, not what he is; what he has failed to be, not what he may become.' In 1907 Smith was saying essentially the same thing, adding that '[t]he torture idea of punishment has lingered too long ... In short, punishment is what has been aimed at instead of reformation.'[55]

The Guelph prison farm would attempt to correct the social wrongs that had been foisted upon the criminal. Away from the evils of the inner city and out in 'God's out of doors,' the prisoners would in no time become reformed characters. There would be no more need for dark cells, striped suits, and heavy surveillance. Labour would be elevating, not punishing, and performed for the sake of the prisoner's rehabilitation, not the government's profit. In 1910, Warden Gilmour reported an almost idyllic situation at the Guelph institution, which was then being built by inmates sent over from the Central Prison: 'During the long summer evenings in the place of pining in a cell, the men were playing baseball, pitching quoits, or engaged in other healthful and harmless amusement. There is an indefinable something in outdoor treatment that makes men better, imparting them health, courage and energy ... We must have the physical foundation right before we can build the moral structure on it.' 'The work at Guelph,' officials pledged, 'should be healthful, uplifting and educational.' 'Regard' would be had 'for the development of the mechanical taste and manual dexterity of the inmates, rather than the specialization of labour and the rapid production of goods by machinery.'[56]

The changes sought to avoid all the brutal features of the Central Prison, as well as the impossible financial goals, but the core idea of productive prison labour seemed to remain. For as much as the Guelph prison farm seemed to be a fresh start, it seemed to carry over most of the essential principles of the Central Prison. There was still talk of how much idleness was to blame for criminality. The 1908 Special Committee into Prison Labour that formally recommended the establishment of the Guelph institution might well have been arguing for the Central Prison decades earlier when it wrote that 'idleness in a prison is a crime alike against the prisoner and the State.' 'The chief weakness of the average inmate of a prison,' the commissioners observed, 'is that he not only does not know a trade, but that he has not been drilled consistently in any kind of labor. Habits of idleness have been developed within him, until he has preferred to obtain his sustenance from the labor of others by unlawful means.' The experts were apparently not so eager to give up on the idea of prison labour. Instead, they sought new ways to make it viable.[57]

Designed to be Ontario's premier industrial institution, the Central Prison seemed better suited to producing scandals than manufactured goods. Instead of keeping convicts busy in workshops, it allowed up to half of them to languish in idleness in their cells, or even less comfortably in the punishment block. Many were too old, sick, or mentally handicapped to be able to work in the first place. And what the prison did manage to make was often unfit to sell. The Central Prison never made a profit for the province, and spent the better part of its existence drifting from one contingency plan to another. By the time its successor, the Guelph Industrial Farm, opened, its chief attraction was its distinctiveness from the Central Prison. It took forty years for the province to undo the apparently simple solutions offered by convict labour. In this era, then, of quick political fixes and neo-conservative ideology, with its new prison 'boot camps' and 'get-tough' approaches to crime, it is well to remember the legacy of the Ontario Central Prison.

NOTES

The author owes a great debt of gratitude to Professors James Phillips and Peter Oliver for their long-standing guidance. His sincere thanks also go to Professors Ian Radforth and John Beattie. Research was assisted by the financial support of the Social Sciences and Humanities Research Council of Canada and the Department of History at the University of Toronto.

1 See contemporary city map and photo of the prison in Michael Klucker *Toronto: The Way It Was* (Toronto: Whitecap Books 1988) 126. An ancillary building remains, which was part of the Inglis plant.
2 The Genesis 3:19 verse 'In the sweat of thy face shalt thou eat bread' was often quoted by criminologists. See, for example, Warden Massie's testi-

mony in Canada *Royal Commission on the Relations of Capital and Labour in Canada 1889*, Ontario Evidence.

3 W.A. Calder 'Convict Life in Canadian Federal Penitentiaries, 1867–1900' in L.A. Knafla, ed. *Crime and Criminal Justice in Europe and Canada* (Waterloo: Wilfrid Laurier University Press 1985) 298; John Beattie *Attitudes towards Crime and Punishment in Upper Canada, 1830–1850: A Documentary Study* (Toronto: University of Toronto Centre of Criminology 1977) 53

4 Ibid. 302; David Rothman *Incarceration and Its Alternatives in Twentieth Century America* (Washington: Department of Justice 1979) 40; Beattie *Attitudes* 35; Peter Oliver 'A Terror to Evil-Doers: The Central Prison and the "Criminal Class" in Late Nineteenth-Century Ontario' in R. Hall et al., eds. *Patterns of the Past: Interpreting Ontario's History* (Toronto: Dundurn Press 1988) 217–18

5 Canada *Board of Inspectors of Prisons, Asylums and Public Charities 1859*, 9–10; Ontario *Annual Report of the Inspector of Prisons* (hereafter AR) 1868–9, 4–5

6 AR 1868–9, 5; House of Commons *Report of the Board of Inspectors of Asylums, Prisons, &c.* 1858–9, 5; AR 1868–9, 6; AR 1867, 3; AR 1868–9, 5–7

7 Report of Evidence Taken before the Royal Commission Appointed to Inquire into the Value of the Central Prison Labour, in Ontario *Sessional Papers 1877*, 7

8 For an account of Warden Prince's career as Toronto police chief see Nicholas Rogers 'Serving Toronto the Good' in V. Russell, ed. *Forging a Consensus: Historical Essays on Toronto* (Toronto: University of Toronto Press 1984). See also Ontario 'Newspaper' *Hansard* 2 and 3 Feb. 1877, 26 Feb. 1873.

9 Archives of Ontario, Central Prison Case Files 21403 and 17501 (hereafter CF)

10 AR 1874, 46–9, 108

11 AR 1874, 46–9; AR 1875, 58–9

12 See, for example, Ontario 'Newspaper' *Hansard* 3 Feb. 1876; AR 1871–2, 90.

13 AR 1871–2, 90; AR 1877, 75, 84

14 Ontario *Report of Evidence, Royal Commission 1877*, 266, 139, 86

15 AR 1874, 210

16 AR 1878, 84

17 AR 1878, 84; AR 1875, 68; AR 1889, 87–88

18 AR 1896, 13; Ontario, 'Newspaper' *Hansard* 18 Feb. 1902, 20 Apr. 1900; AR 1891, 84

19 Ontario 'Newspaper' *Hansard*, 5 Apr. 1895; Canada *Royal Commission on the Relations of Capital and Labour in Canada 1889*, Ontario Evidence, 907; Ontario *Report of Evidence*, Royal Commission, 1877, 139

20 AR 1878, 84; AR 1892, 82; Ontario, 'Newspaper' *Hansard* 5 Apr. 1893; AR 1892, 81; AR 1906, x; AR 1896, 13

21 AR 1888, 88; AR 1898, 15–16

22 AR 1881, 170–1, 427

23 AR 1877, 84

24 Ontario, 'Newspaper' *Hansard* 7 Mar. 1899. In 1884, it cost the province some fifty-two cents a day to maintain its inmates, but, in the same period, it cost just over twenty cents a day in a jail: see AR 1883.

25 AR 1892, 81; AR 1893, 146; AR 1895, 10–11; AR 1896, 9

26 'History of the Contract System in the Toronto Central Prison. A Record of Continuous Failures. The Outlook for the Future' *Speech of the Hon. W.J. Hanna, Provincial Secretary to the Ontario Legislature* (Toronto 1907) 3–7

27 Ibid. 8–9

28 AR 1894, 11–12; AR 1879, 441; AR 1882, 59; AR 1906, x

29 AR 1875, 59; AR 1896, 1; AR 1885,83; AR 1879, 148; AR 1877, 71; AR 1896, 1: AR 1887, 94

30 AR 1878, 398; A sixteen-year-old prisoner was put in the dark cell for fighting in the paint shop. After one hour 'he cried bitterly, and begged to be forgiven & would not offend again. Released. James Massie, Warden': CF 7847; AR 1878, 390; CF 16787; AR 1878, 91.

31 Toronto *Globe* 31 July 1885; Royal Commission Appointed to Inquire into Certain Charges against the Warden of the Central Prison and into the Management of the Said Prison, Ontario *Sessional Papers* 1886, 11–12; Toronto *Globe* 19 Aug. 1885; AR 1902, 45–6

32 CF 29649. John Currie left behind a thoughtful account of his prison experience: CF 17111. Percy Ebbitt was a twenty-four-year-old bookkeeper from Ottawa serving a one-year sentence in 1900 for the forgery of three cheques totalling $28.50. As an inmate, he wrote a vast memoir detailing daily life in the Central Prison. His writings were impounded by the prison.

33 AR 1882, 66; AR 1878, 390; AR 1880, 159; Ontario *Report of the Commissioners Appointed to Inquire into the Prison and Reformatory System of Ontario* 1891, 152

34 See note 32 above.

35 AR 1882; AR 1883; CF 5920

36 CF 7518, 17124

37 Peter Oliver has immortalized Guard Hartley in his article on the Central Prison. Quoting from the guard's private papers, Oliver cites letters written by Hartley to his fiancée which interspersed long, approving accounts of floggings with touching descriptions of sunsets and profound biblical truisms. Sharing as he did with her such often gruesome details, it is no wonder that Hartley found it necessary to chide his fiancée for her 'distaste for letter writing': City of Toronto Archives, Gilbert Hartley Papers, Gilbert to Mary, 8 June 1879. One is also afforded the opportunity to meet Hartley

through the punishment records and case files: see CF 6730 and *Report of the Royal Commission Appointed to Enquire Into Certain Charges against the Warden of the Central Prison and into the Management of the Said Prison* (Toronto: Warwick & Sons 1886) 46–7.

38 CF 6262, 8792, 6149, 9236
39 CF 11721
40 AR 188, 90; Hartley Papers, Gilbert to Mary, 2 Mar. 1879
41 AR 1881, 427
42 CF 13992
43 CF 16163, 16968, 13162, 21337, 14764
44 CF 19064
45 CF 17124
46 CF 12457, 15172
47 See, for example, Archives of Ontario, Central Prison Register, Prisoner Numbers 10730, 17328, 16457, 17729, 17868, 17274, 17308, 20171, 20733; CF 16357, 19980.
48 CF 11202, 12935, 13379
49 CF 15436, 15115
50 CF 9101, 16391, 11458, 14988, 7691, 7478, 10501. CF 25770 provides an account of the prevalence of enlistment.
51 Toronto *Globe* 10 Aug. 1877; *Ontario Workman* 19 Dec. 1872
52 *Ontario Workman* 25 July 1872, 3 July 1873
53 AR 1870; CF 16794
54 H. Clare Pentland *Labour and Capital in Canada 1650–1860* (Toronto: Lorimer 1981) 21; Robert S. Kenny Collection, Thomas Fisher Rare Book Library, University of Toronto, Minutes of the Toronto Trade Assembly/Canadian Labour Union, Meetings of 4 and 18 Oct., 15 Nov., and 10 Dec. 1892; 17 Jan. and 7 Feb. 1873; and 16 Jan. 1878. Cited with the permission of the Thomas Fisher Rare Book Library, University of Toronto.
55 *Speech of Hon. W.J. Hanna* 15; AR 1905, 7–9; AR 1906, v, 8; AR 1907, 9
56 AR 1910, 51; Ontario *Report of the Special Committee on Prison Labour* (Toronto 1908) 5
57 Ontario *Report on Prison Labour 1908*, 4–5, 43

15

'To Govern by Kindness':
The First Two Decades of the
Mercer Reformatory for Women

PETER OLIVER

In the late nineteenth century, a few jurisdictions in North America opened prisons for women, including notably Indiana, Massachusetts, and New York State. Although the number of women's prisons would proliferate in the twentieth century, in the earlier period they were rare. It is curious, therefore, that a society as conservative in its social values as was Ontario should be one of a handful of jurisdictions to embark on what seemed to be a relatively radical experiment. Why should a society as traditional as Ontario, with a legislature dominated by rural interests and a government as cautious as that of Oliver Mowat, decide to establish a prison run by women and for women, and this in an era when women could not vote and experienced wide-ranging restrictions on many aspects of their involvement in the public life of the community?

Beyond any doubt, the decision to establish a women's prison launched Ontario on a quite fascinating experiment in social engineering. What makes it particularly intriguing is that the Mercer was the joint effort of one of the most despised and downtrodden elements of late-nineteenth-century life, a bunch of prostitutes and pilfering servants, together with another element, not despised, to be sure, but also treated by the province's male establishment with condescension and indifference, a group of middle-class women trying to make their way in a male-dominated society. At issue, then, is not only the reasons for the establishment of the Mercer but the degree to which it may be said to have succeeded in a society as tradition-bound as late-nineteenth-century Ontario.

In these circumstances, it is natural to approach the study of the Mercer as an exercise in understanding in a late-nineteenth-century society aspects of the lives of women, those who ran the Mercer and those who were prisoners in it. To date, most of the work on women's prisons in Europe and North America takes this as its focus: what does the women's prison have to tell us about women, power, and social change in late-nineteenth-century societies? How in the life of the women's prison do issues of gender interact with those of class and occasionally of ethnicity to enlighten us about social change in the lives of both prisoners and officers?

These questions are central to the current agenda of women's and social history, and an analysis of this subject seems ideally suited to provide insights and answers. Those who have pursued this approach in the study of women's prisons have significantly extended our understanding of the complex mix which constituted the patterns of gender, class, and ethnic relationships in their respective societies. In carrying out this research agenda such scholars as Freedman and Rafter writing about the United States and Dobash and Zedner for Britain have reached similar conclusions about the women's prison movement.[1]

Estelle Freedman puts it most forcefully, arguing that the ideology of separate spheres which attempted to achieve rehabilitation through the application of a prison discipline which drew on the special nurturing qualities inherent in the feminine character contained within itself flaws and contradictions which severely limited its success. In Freedman's view this social or maternal feminist strategy, like the separate but equal ideology of racial segregation, 'rested on a contradictory definition of equality. The nineteenth-century prison reformers did seek to expand women's rights ... But at the heart of their program was the principle of innate sexual difference, not sexual equality.'[2] This kind of differential treatment, while not without some benefits, for example the rescuing of female prisoners from the sexual harassment experienced in the old mixed prisons, served to channel women into sexually stereotyped programs of character training and skills development. This, it is argued, reinforced the very disadvantages which had led many women to crime in the first place.

In any case, Freedman and others conclude, it was too much to expect that the special nurturing qualities suggested by the concept of maternal feminism could succeed in effecting change in the inherently hostile environment of a prison. No matter how much female prison officers pretended to be creating a family-like environment designed to befriend and assist the prisoners, it was impossible to overcome the reality that a prison remained a prison and inmates were there against their will as punishment. In this environment, the notion of sisterhood based on gender identity inevitably yielded to new relationships reflecting the unbreachable distance between middle-class and working-class values, between jailers and prisoners. A programme designed by middle-class women to socialize working-class women by imposing an alien value system had no hope of success. Freedman concludes that 'power triumphed over sisterhood not because these were single-sex institutions but because they were prisons.' As a result, the women's reformatories simply 'recapitulated the histories of other nineteenth-century institutions' for deviants and criminals.[3] In a word, they failed.

Because of the quality of her analysis and the pioneering nature of her work, Freedman's study set an interpretive pattern which has endured and became almost a formula for later studies. Certainly all who read Carolyn Strange's valuable study of the Mercer Reformatory will recognize this interpretive framework. 'Established on little more than faith in women's talent for maternal care,' the Mercer Reformatory, Strange argues, 'faltered soon after its founding.' In applying a feminist formula to assess the first twenty years of the Mercer, Strange argues that its 'central problem' lay in the impossibility of maintaining a prison 'as an "ordinary well conducted household." No matter how motherly the superintendent, she could never transform cells, workhouses and dungeons into a home.'[4]

An interpretation emphasizing contradictory impulses, hence failure, is plausible. The Mercer conformed closely to the pattern of the late-nineteenth-century American women's reformatory. In its objectives, its administration, and its discipline, it replicated the vision of a conservative, middle-class institution made familiar by recent feminist scholarship. Given the extent of the similarities and the prevalence to date of this particular interpretive pattern, it is hardly surprising that we should be told that the Mercer, like its sister American institutions, finally embodied constraints of class and culture so powerful that they produced relationships of dominance and subordination which defeated the objectives of its founders.

Such conclusions have the virtue of being clear and plausible for those whose principal analytic interest lies in women's history. For these scholars, America's first generation of feminist women are to be admired for their courage and their efforts as pioneers but they fell sadly short in terms of later feminist objectives. Numerous works of scholarship have concluded that the achievements of these late-nineteenth-century feminists were severely constrained by their own middle-class values and conservative goals. Described by feminist historians as social or maternal feminists, they are criticized because they failed to demand equality for its own sake. Rather, the maternal feminists proclaimed for women a separate sphere of influence in which their presumed maternal qualities, nurturing instincts, and superior moral virtues could be brought more fully to bear on a range of social and public issues. Constricted by the ideological fetters of maternal feminism, they led a movement whose achievements fell far short of what some believe ought to have been accomplished. Thus, Jill Conway in a groundbreaking article said of the maternal feminists that 'intellectually they had to work within the tradition which saw women as civilizing and moralizing forces in society.' And for Lois Banner 'the social feminist rationale for the participation of women in reform and government was ... anti-feminist in implication' because it was 'based on the traditional image of the woman.'

Considering the prestige of this analysis, bolstered by an impressive array of feminist historical writing, it is not surprising that scholars who employ this formula in the study of women's reformatories should reach negative conclusions. Applying this perspective, Nicole Hahn Rafter concluded that the efforts of female reformatory leaders 'had ironic implications for both their own work and that of later female prison officials. Almost by definition, social feminists clung to and amplified gender stereotypes.' Most seriously, this 'encouraged – virtually mandated – them to apply the double standard to their charges.'[5]

There is, however, another approach to the study of women's prisons which must be considered. For the criminal justice historian, the focus must be not on gender but on the entire range of issues which shaped the nineteenth-century prison experience. From that more encompassing point of departure the contribution made by maternal feminists to the prison enterprise seems fundamentally different, and what becomes most interesting in the reformatory programme is not the alleged spectacle of feminism constrained but the relatively enlightened objectives and, even more significant, the substantial achievements of the women's leadership.

It bears emphasis at this point that both perspectives, criminal justice history broadly conceived and the study of women's reformatories which places issues of gender in the foreground to the neglect of the wider context, agree on one point, or at least they seem to agree. And this is the importance to the analysis of the question of success. The feminist scholars of women's prisons, as noted above, have concluded that such institutions failed because finally they failed to demand gender equality and accepted the maternal feminist principle of separate spheres which soon resulted in separate but unequal. Similarly, many of the classic accounts of prison history written by criminal justice historians of widely differing ideological persuasions focus on the issue of success. 'By what criterion,' asked David Rothman, author of two celebrated books on prisons and other total institutions, 'is a penitentiary an improvement' over previous systems of punishment? And he concludes that in the end it failed.[6]

Recent criminology has been equally fascinated by efforts to measure success. Most notably, a famous report commissioned by the state of New York in the late 1960s with a team headed by Robert Martinson examined hundreds of studies done in Western societies since World War II which had been designed to assess the success of both institutional and non-institutional treatment programs. Martinson's conclusion to the effect that no study yet undertaken provided reliable data on which to judge the success of any existing rehabilitative program set off an enduring international debate among criminologists and correctional workers.[7]

For present purposes the significance of the Martinson debate is that it served to point to innumerable pitfalls and complexities in all efforts to measure 'success,' even while it underlined once again the importance to those in the field of developing appropriate criteria by which to evaluate treatment programmes aimed at convicted offenders. After Martinson, it became increasingly apparent how flawed most studies actually were. Raw recidivism rates, for example, could be interpreted variously and in any case had little to say about numerous aspects of the rehabilitative process. Success, in short, is both a vital and elusive concept and any effort to evaluate the prison experience which begins with an interest in any single-issue approach, whether class, ethnicity, or, in this case, gender, is seriously at risk. To what extent, this essay will ask, does the early history of the Mercer Reformatory contribute, not to our understanding of issues of gender and power in the prison environment, but, equally significant, to the successes and failures of the women's prison in Ontario between 1880 and 1900?

ANTECEDENTS AND ORIGINS

Why was the Mercer established in 1880 and what were its principal objectives? To answer these questions it is useful to look briefly at the imprisonment of women in Ontario earlier in the century. Even after the opening of Kingston Penitentiary in 1835, most female offenders continued to be sent to local jails, and it is evident that disproportionate numbers in comparison to men were sent to jail for offences against morality.[8] It is also apparent that by the late 1850s and the 1860s the numbers of women being sent to jail were increasing substantially, a result of growing urbanization and the numerous by-laws being passed by incorporated communities. Women who were repeat offenders or who committed serious crimes might be sent to Kingston Penitentiary. Between 1835 and 1847, the number committed fluctuated between two and fourteen per year, although the number in the institution at any one time was larger – sixty-eight, for example, in 1859. For penitentiary officials, their presence was regarded as a nuisance, and they were shifted around into whatever part of the institution suited the convenience of the moment. The fact that they were 'too few to count' largely shaped their treatment, and usually they were denied reasonable access to workshops or recreational facilities. In Kingston as elsewhere, female prisoners were regarded as almost impossible to manage, far worse than men in their behaviour, and all but impossible to reform. In 1851, for example, the Catholic chaplain called them 'the most refractory and unmanageable' prisoners in the penitentiary and in 1853 the Protestant chaplain described them as most susceptible on release to returning to a career of crime. The explanation he offered for this was that for women a sentence to Kingston was usually 'the termination of a long course of intemperance and vice.' The female prisoners were under the care of a series of matrons who were paid at a lower rate than male officers in similar positions and who exercised no real authority.[9]

Then, in the mid fifties, this entirely negative image of the female convict changed very rapidly with the appointment as matron of Martha Walker, 'an English widow lady' of genteel station. Mrs Walker, who was better paid and better treated than her predecessors, seemed to exercise authority with considerable assurance and to win the respect both of male officers and of her charges. By 1859 Dr Wolfred Nelson, one of the inspectors, was persuaded that the female portion of the penitentiary was, 'without exception, the most easily governed and the least expensive' part of the penitentiary. By this time, too, both the Catholic chaplain, Angus MacDonell, and the inspector, Wolfred Nelson, were articulating a Catholic perspective on the treatment of women prisoners. Catholic female prisoners, they argued, should be removed from the penitentiary environment and sent to the care of female religious orders where 'they would be treated with motherly kindness, watched with strict surveillance, and ... have constant examples of charity and religion before them.' At an early date they would be 'permitted to leave this benign and hospitable retreat' and be received 'in the bosom of some respectable family as assistants or domestics.' If women must be incarcerated in a prison, Nelson argued, it should be in an entirely separate facility and never within the walls of another prison, and they should receive a discipline entirely different than that used for male convicts.¹⁰ There is no evidence that this Catholic social philosophy had any influence on Canadian penal policy. It would be a quarter of a century before the foundation of the Mercer, at which point other influences had emerged. Nonetheless, the Catholic voice of the 1850s which argued that women would be best rehabilitated by other women in an environment of kindness and sisterhood would find striking resonances in Ontario reformatory policy in the 1880s.

The immediate influences on Ontario policy makers were American. J.W. Langmuir, in the period following his appointment in 1868 as Ontario's prison inspector, made several tours south of the border to study American correctional and welfare facilities. In particular, he visited the Detroit House of Correction, which then was headed by the most innovative American prison warden of the second half of the century, Zebulon Brockway. It was from Brockway's Detroit that he acquired many of the ideas influential in Ontario's decision to establish an intermediate prison at Toronto for men serving sentences between six months and two years. Langmuir deplored the influence on prisoners of the lack of classification and the state of idleness which prevailed in the local jails and he persuaded the Sandfield Macdonald government to establish industrial prisons where habitual offenders and those sentenced to more than six months could be put to hard labour. Langmuir visited Detroit in 1869 and 1871 during Brockway's tenure and while there would have observed the efforts of Emma Hall as teacher and matron of the House of Shelter, an adjunct to the House of Correction which opened in 1868. According to Brockway, whose ideas about a women's reformatory had been influenced by a Massachusetts school for delinquent girls, 'we are profoundly convinced that little can be done to reclaim fallen women except through the sisterly care, counsel and sympathy of their own sex.'[11] Under Hall, the facility was described as a family; it emphasized religious and educational training and moral and domestic influences. Langmuir made it clear in his annual reports that he was greatly impressed by Brockway's Detroit and also that he was well aware of the great prison reform movement which in the late 1860s and early 1870s had become an influential force in American prison circles.[12] Certainly he was familiar with the monumental 1867 *Report on the Prisons and Reformatories of the United States and Canada* commissioned by the New York State Prison Commission and authored by E.C. Wines and Theodore Dwight. Wines and Dwight made the case for entirely separate prisons for women largely on moral grounds, arguing that the presence in the same institution of both sexes had led to numerous abuses and problems. But most of all it was the famous Cincinnati Declaration of 1870 with its unswerving support for separate prisons for women rather than the perspective of any single individual, even Brockway, which probably served to make the Ontario inspector an unswerving and lifelong advocate of the separate prison doctrine.

The Cincinnati Declaration was the product of the first National Prison Congress ever held in the United States and it propounded a series of principles which laid out all the significant prison reform proposals of the next half century, including earned remission, staged progress, and the indeterminate sentence. The inclusion in this all-important statement of the ideals of the women's reformatory movement gave that cause unprecedented prestige in American reform circles. J W Langmuir does not seem to have fully grasped the reformist implications of the Cincinnati program but he did become imbued with the ideal of the industrial reformatory as applied to both men and women and it was his determined advocacy which brought both these institutions to Ontario.

Impressed as always by the views of 'experts' and armed with the prestige of American reformist opinion, John Langmuir returned to Ontario and worked to persuade the Sandfield Macdonald government to establish intermediate prisons for both men and women. The inspector's advice to the premier was unambiguous: 'Respecting the advisability of confining both sexes in the same prison, the very highest authorities in the specialty of prison administration have declared themselves in favour of separate establishments for women, and the National Congress on Penitentiary and Reformatory Discipline, which met at Cincinnati,

Ohio, in their "Declaration of Principles" adopted and promulgated this principle, and already several States have passed laws creating separate prisons for women.' Langmuir at that time was totally convinced of the rightness of the American position. It was 'not to be doubted,' he had told Sandfield, that the separate principle was the correct one and the time was not far distant when 'Ontario will found an industrial reformatory for women, with the official staff attendants, keepers and instructors of the same sex. Then, and only then, will women be fully able to exercise and wield their great power and influence, in practical ways towards reclaiming the criminal and fallen of their sex.'[13]

It would be the better part of a decade before the Ontario government accepted this advice and built a women's prison but Langmuir's advocacy never flagged and when the decision was taken it was clear to everyone that the father of the women's prison in Ontario was John Langmuir. And herein lay not only an irony but, as some have perceived it, a problem. Carolyn Strange in her account of the Mercer's early years has argued that it was gravely weakened at the moment of birth by the fact that its origins were 'not rooted in a popular protest or reform movement.' Because there was 'not yet a solid base of support for the reform ethos,' she concludes, 'this hollow base proved to be a source of weakness in Mercer's management.'[14] There is little indication of any public movement in Ontario to establish a women's prison, yet it is not entirely clear why the province took no early action to establish such a facility, or even to build a women's section attached to the Central Prison. When Langmuir was attempting in this period to win the government's support for a women's prison, he did claim that 'Judges, Grand Jurors, Prison Officials and philanthropists generally' had all urged the establishment of such an institution.[15] Little evidence has come to light to support this claim, and it seems likely that such officials were probably merely urging that, with recidivist males now being sent to an intermediate prison, women should receive similar treatment. It seems unlikely that criminal justice officials in Ontario, whether judges, police, or jailers, knew enough about the American reformatory movement to become advocates for such a women's prison in the full sense of the term.

Later, when the Mowat government did accept Langmuir's recommendation to establish a women's prison, and introduced a resolution to give effect to the new policy, the members of the House seemed quite indifferent to this measure. They also seemed bored the following year when the government presented the statute establishing the new prison. The newspapers were equally indifferent, the Hamilton *Spectator*, for example, using the occasion neither to attack nor applaud the principle of separate but equal but to complain that the city of Toronto already had too many public buildings.[16] In fact, prisons are not established as a result of a ground swell of popular demand; and the absence of some kind of reform movement at the Mercer's foundation was irrelevant to its future success or failure. The process operates the other way around, and the public becomes involved in prison reform only in reaction to some perceived threat, scandal, or disorder. What is deserving of comment is less that there was little evidence of popular support but rather the sheer indifference of the public to what was, after all, in the context of the day a somewhat radical or at least unorthodox initiative.

There was a moment of danger, perhaps, when the Public Accounts Committee in 1879 was examining proposed expenditures on a women's prison. W.R. Meredith, the Tory leader, although holding advanced views on many social problems, was in every sense a traditionalist on women's questions. The committee was examining Langmuir when Meredith asked whether it would have been possible to combine the facility for women with the Central Prison. Langmuir said not, because the occupations of women were entirely different than for men. But Meredith persisted, noting that women and men were in the same institution at Kingston. Langmuir rebutted that there were few women at Kingston, and he believed it would have been 'a very great mistake' to join the women's prison with the men's. Liberal Cabinet minister Arthur Hardy came to his assistance, suggesting there was no precedent in North America for the kind of arrangement Meredith was suggesting. Langmuir quickly concurred, 'Not in prisons of that kind – In reformatories they are quite separate.' When the inspector emphasized that 'those acquainted with the subject' believed it 'extremely improper' to put men and women in the same facility, Meredith was not prepared to challenge this argument from authority. Meredith also seemed uneasy with Langmuir's position that the head of the prison should be a woman, but Hardy intervened again, noting that the reformatory at Massachusetts had a female head. Meredith, clearly outmanoeuvred, was in no position to challenge Langmuir's well-informed and expert opinions.[17]

Was it just, then, the neat bureaucratic mind of John Langmuir desiring parallel intermediate facilities, male and female, which led to the establishment of the Mercer? Or was the decision thrust upon the province by the growing number of female prisoners, perhaps even by a perceived crisis of female criminality? In 1868 in his first report Langmuir pointed out that women were a 'large and increasing proportion' of jail inmates. Of 8015 commitments over the previous fifteen months, 2530 were females. He estimated that three-quarters of the women were prostitutes and expressed alarm that 140 were under sixteen years of age. Jail imprisonment, he pointed out, offered neither employment nor education and 'very often, through contamination, the evil sought to be remedied is aggravated and increased.' Most of all, he suggested, the women regarded jail terms as no punishment at all, as 'a large portion of females of this class are committed to Gaol from twenty to twenty-five times before they attain the age of twenty-five.' Langmuir's first priority was the juveniles, and he urged the province to establish a reformatory 'somewhat of the character of a Magdalene Asylum' for those under sixteen if there was to be any hope at all of saving them from a life of crime.[18] In the 1870s middle-class Ontarians were thinking actively of establishing industrial schools and of moving on several fronts to address more aggressively what many saw as an approaching crisis of juvenile criminality.

It was at this point that the more general problem of adult female crime presented itself most forcefully. When Langmuir inspected the Toronto jail in 1868 he encountered 60 women and 61 men; the following year there were 86 women and only 61 men. Yet over the next several years the proportions of male to female in the jails fluctuated so considerably that numbers alone can scarcely account for the decision to establish a women's prison. In his 1874 report the inspector noted that there had been no appreciable increase in the numbers of females committed to jail since 1869. Five years later, in 1879, he pointed to a small but significant increase. The number of males sent to prison dropped from 11,595 in 1878 to 10,017 while the number of females increased from 1886 to 2013. Yet the 1880 report, which provided eleven-year averages, demonstrated that commitments for women between 1869 and 1880, the very years that a prison for women was under active consideration, 'did not increase in anything like the same proportion as those of the men.' The increase for women was 11 per cent and for men 145 per cent, and female commitments went from 1680 to 1863. The decline continued into the 1880s, the inspector's 1886 report showing substantial decreases in the percentages of female prisoners to the total of jail commitments from 1869, when the women represented 29.7 per cent, to 18.41 per cent in 1874, 15.65 per cent in 1879, 14.22 per cent in 1884, 13.19 per cent in 1885, and 13.28 per cent in

1886. Yet if Ontario was experiencing no dramatic expansion in female criminality, the increasing numbers of women confined in city jails, such as that of Toronto, at least made the problem highly visible. As Langmuir put it in his 1878 report, 'the fact that the annual commitments have reached 2,000 is sufficiently alarming to warrant the adoption of the most progressive measures known in prison reform, in regard to that class of our prison population.'[19]

Clearly, then, there was no sudden or rapidly escalating crisis of female criminality to account for the government's belated decision to follow Langmuir's almost-decade-old advice. Given the extent of the inspector's influence in the provincial government, it seems likely that for most of the 1870s, he himself, although a supporter of a women's prison, had had other and more pressing priorities, including the reformation of Penetanguishene Reformatory and the opening of several new asylums for the mentally ill. Then, in 1878, when the province came into a windfall of $100,000 from the estate of Andrew Mercer and Premier Mowat asked his inspector how the funds might best be spent, the time for a women's reformatory had at last arrived. In his considered response Langmuir's justification was not the increasing extent of female criminality but rather the great merit of differential treatment as enunciated by American experts. Langmuir filled the premier in on the background in an 1878 letter, telling him that his own experience in the decade since he had recommended a women's prison to Sandfield had confirmed his earlier views. His report to his political masters was a complete brief statement of the women's prison ideology: for a reformatory for women to fulfil its promise, he all but lectured the premier, 'it should be completely isolated' from any men's prison. 'The buildings, their interior arrangements, the disciplinary management, industrial pursuits and general surroundings of a Reformatory for females, are altogether different from those for males.' And, in an afterthought dear to the hearts of Ontario's late-nineteenth-century politicians, he assured the premier that women's prisons, both in construction and in administration, were 'of a far less costly character' than men's prisons.[20] Mowat was persuaded; Ontario at long last would have its women's prison.

DIFFERENTIAL TREATMENT

What did Langmuir understand by the concept of a totally different 'disciplinary management'? Seeking to deepen his knowledge he made another trek south to visit several American facilities, and he was singularly unimpressed by how Americans were putting into practice the separate but equal ideology enunciated at Cincinnati.

He reported that the Ingleside Home for Women at Buffalo, whose inmates were primarily prostitutes, had failed because it possessed no 'structural means' of enforcing discipline. He was critical even of the famous reformatory at Framingham, Massachusetts, because the buildings were too scattered to permit adequate supervision, which he said was essential because in a female facility 'influence and example are the most powerful factors in the reclamation of the inmates.'[21] This emphasis on role models was an important insight of the reformatory movement which differentiated its approach from that used in traditional male custodial institutions, where guards had no role at all in any rehabilitative process.

Langmuir also was an ardent supporter of what American reformers had postulated about the architectural distinctiveness of the female reformatory. It was 'of the utmost importance,' he argued, 'that the structure should externally, be as free as possible from prison appearance' in order to add to the home-like atmosphere most apt to assist the rehabilitative process.[22] With its attractive design and ornamental towers, the Mercer was a large and rather handsome building which could easily have been mistaken for a hospital or an educational facility. As Langmuir had wished, this was a compact structure, three storeys high, with a raised basement. Wisely, it was built not by convict labour but under contract. It contained 147 cells and rooms and 49 isolation cells in the basement, enabling it to hold 196 women. The Industrial Refuge for Juveniles was located in an entirely separate wing with space for 50 girls.

But the part of the Mercer design most reflective of its reformatory function was its interior arrangements. The Mercer was designed, as Langmuir proudly reported, so as to obtain 'as perfect a system of classification as it is possible to have ... There are twelve distinct corridors or wards in the building, to each of which is attached a separate workroom, and in addition the general workshop is divided into two flats and five distinct apartments ... and there are also four distinct yards for airing and exercise.' The objective was to provide distinct and separate accommodation for four grades of prisoners. On arrival each inmate was to be placed in a small cell, which Langmuir described as 'prison-like,' from whence she might be 'promoted' to better and larger cells and improved surroundings. Continued good conduct could be further rewarded by transfer to a single room in another wing. After another period of good conduct which demonstrated 'marked evidence of reformation,' the prisoner could be moved for a final time to an area 'in which few or no prisoner surroundings' were evident and where every inmate would 'be furnished with a good sized single room and a window opening in each.'[23] With its system of two levels of cells and two of rooms, the Mercer was equipped with the most advanced system of reformatory prison discipline available in any nineteenth-century Canadian prison.

For reasons which are not readily apparent, the commitment to classification and grading which had been incorporated into the Mercer's original design never assumed a large role in actual practice. The original intention that all the inmates would be required actually to earn their progress through two types of cells and two types of rooms seems to have been entirely lost to view. About all that was done was to try to separate older, hardened offenders from the younger women. There is a suggestion in the 1882 report that madames were taking advantage of their stay in the reformatory to actively recruit young girls. The report that year announced that women under twenty-one would be separated 'from the wretched women in whose houses they have led lives of sin.'

At this time Mercer superintendent Mary Jane O'Reilly instituted the practice used in some American and British reformatories by which new arrivals were placed in isolation for a month, partly in order to allow officers to gain 'a knowledge of the character and capabilities of the new prisoner.'[24] Two years later, however, the inspector reported that this system was being discontinued; henceforth new arrivals would be admitted at once to the general ward and the space previously reserved for them would be used for the refractory class. This significant change was put into effect at once. The objective, as expressed by the inspector, was to encourage new prisoners 'to maintain their position by good behaviour' and to place them in the refractory ward only if they faltered.[25] Although the annual reports provide scanty information about subsequent classification procedures, this apparently meant that the inmates began their stay with most available privileges, and that they could lose them as a form of punishment. In the twentieth century when this approach to good behaviour classification became increasingly common it was often criticized for leading prisoners to regard privileges as inalienable rights, contributing thereby to the problems of institutional management.

From this point on, about all that was done in the area of classification was to appoint an attendant to keep girls under eighteen separate from older women. In 1887 there was so little evidence of any classificatory system that a grand jury called it a disgrace that women who were penitentiary graduates or insane were being allowed to mix with young girls. Mercer officials indignantly denied this charge, yet it is noteworthy that their rebuttal said not a word about what arrangements for classification actually did exist.[26] Certainly the elaborate scheme envisaged when the Mercer was established had disappeared. Most likely this was because the Mercer's physical arrangements had proved inadequate; or perhaps the staff was not up to the demands such a system entailed. More positively, O'Reilly may have objected on humanitarian grounds to a system which forced many inmates into a solitary and penal phase. It is not unlikely that she quietly dropped so structured an approach on her own authority in favour of the more informal and personal system which endeavoured to treat all inmates equally.

STAFFING

There was little in the thirty-one brief clauses of the 1879 Andrew Mercer statute to convey to the public any sense that an interesting social experiment was being launched. The statute simply proclaimed the establishment of the new prison, described officially as the Andrew Mercer Reformatory for Women, and asserted that the lieutenant-governor 'may' appoint a female superintendent and schoolmistress, with no reference being made to the sex of other officers and guards. Potentially the role of women managers was challenged by the authority given to Langmuir as inspector to 'make rules and regulations for the management, discipline and police of the said Reformatory, and for fixing and prescribing the duties and conduct of the Superintendent and every other officer or servant' as well as for every other aspect of the prison's life.[27]

Yet if ultimate statutory authority rested with the inspector, there is no doubt that the Mercer's first superintendent had full control over the daily life of the prison, and she maintained it virtually unchallenged for the next two decades. The statute gave her the same authority as a male prison warden. She was to live in the institution and as chief executive officer, under the direction of the inspector, to have 'the entire execution, control, and management of all its affairs.' Possibly the strong-willed Langmuir would have been tempted to interfere but he retired in 1882 and none of his successors seems to have been inclined to question O'Reilly's management. The prison, of course, functioned as part of a wider welfare bureaucracy in which financial control was particularly tight. Mrs O'Reilly, for example, had to make a case for even the smallest expenditures, a few dollars for books or money to paint the chapel. Within those constraints, however, she was in charge, and one suspects that she revelled in the challenge and responsibility. Mary Jane O'Reilly shaped the Mercer in the image of a model women's reformatory.

She herself was a perfect example of a female superintendent. Genteel and upper middle class, the widow of James O'Reilly, a prominent Kingston lawyer (he prosecuted the murderer of D'Arcy McGee) and Tory member of Parliament, she possessed all the qualities of breeding, judgment, and firmness which the position was deemed to demand.[28] Perhaps, too, as a Roman Catholic of Irish descent she had some special sympathy for many of those under her care and protection. Not even the dull formality of two decades of official reports to Queen's Park can disguise the warmth and caring which Mary Jane O'Reilly offered her charges and wards. If the Mercer Reformatory ultimately fell short of the aspirations of its founders, it was not because of any lack of dedication or mismanagement at the top.

Nor was it because the institution's staff fell short of the ideal of being entirely female. The bursar Robert Laird, who also performed the duties of storekeeper, as the husband of the assistant superintendent lived in an apartment in the building. There was also a male engineer and a night guard, and by the late 1880s this position was held by James Kenny, a former sergeant-major in the Royal Artillery. Another constant male presence was Dr John King, the institution's physician. Yet the assistant superintendent was always a woman, as was the schoolteacher and most of the guards. Most important, there was never any doubt that it was Mary Jane O'Reilly who established priorities and shaped the discipline which distinguished the Mercer so sharply from the Central Prison.

Perhaps Mrs O'Reilly faced more of a struggle to retain control than is apparent in the official reports. One sign of a lingering reluctance to place confidence in a female administration appeared in 1880 over the appointment of a Sunday school superintendent. The position was a significant one because of the important place volunteer activities were to occupy in the prison's rehabilitative machinery and S.H. Blake, the long-time president of the Prisoners' Aid Association, had serious reservations about giving it to a woman. He spoke to Langmuir and gave him, as Langmuir explained to the provincial treasurer, 'some strong reasons why the proposition for the Sunday School at the Reformatory to be controlled by a lady should be modified so as to allow of the appointment of a male superintendent.' It was Blake's judgment that 'if a man were appointed, his business habits and knowledge of discipline and general management, would enable him to take a practical and common sense view of matters, which a woman would not perhaps always do.' The name of William Howland, a future Toronto mayor well known for his philanthropic efforts, was suggested, and Langmuir recommended 'that Mr. Blake's request be acceded to.' As a result, Howland became superintendent of the Mercer Sunday school programme.[29] There was, undeniably, a strong and influential male presence in Ontario's model women's prison.

COMMITTAL AND RELEASE

Feminist historians agree that 'the heart of the women's reformatory model lay in its assumptions about commitment.'[30] These procedures, it is argued, differed fundamentally from past practices. While men convicted of most public order and morals offences were sent to a local jail or not incarcerated at all, women now began to be sent to reformatories. As well, those American states which opened women's prisons instituted sentencing schemes which made it possible to imprison female misdemeanants for relatively long periods of time. Women's reformatories, Nicole Rafter asserts, created a category of female prisoner that had no male counterpart: they were 'based on acceptance – indeed, willing embrace – of differential standards for the imprisonment of women and men.' Those American states which instituted reformatories, it is argued, 'gave legal force to a double standard that punished women more severely than men who had committed the same offences.'[31]

These practices, it is suggested, originated in the intent to create a reformatory environment geared to rehabilitation. The first committal law in the Massachusetts Reformatory permitted it to receive only women who had committed minor offences; and the overwhelming majority of committals during the late nineteenth century were for petty moral offences. New York's practices were even more exclusive. That state's two late-nineteenth-century women's reformatories accepted only women convicted of petty larceny, habitual drunkenness, and prostitution and the state also legislated an age limit which rejected older women deemed unlikely to be receptive to reformative influences. Notably, too, almost no black women were admitted.

As for sentence length, the reformatories of the northeastern United States pioneered in the use of indeterminate sentences. This practice reflected the belief that even in the case of minor offenders, reformatory discipline needed an adequate time in which to achieve behavioural changes. The law establishing the Massachusetts Reformatory set a two-year maximum for many offences which previously had carried a six-month maximum, but it set no minimum, and many prisoners continued to be released in less than a year. When reformers objected, an 1880 law set one year as a minimum sentence. New York State established the astounding maximum for minor offenders of five years but some judges refused to commit women on this basis. Reformatory officials countered that the courts did not understand that the objective was to help women achieve rehabilitation. Still, in 1899 the maximum was lowered to three years.[32]

The interpretive consensus about these committal and release practices is that, however well-meaning they were in intention, they resulted in forms of differential treatment that effected a double standard which discriminated against women. Rafter's conclusion is typical. Even after New York's reduction of the maximum for female minor offenders from five to three years, she writes, it remained true that 'female minor offenders were still liable to far longer imprisonment than before the reformatories were founded, and that no similar extension of state control occurred in the case of men convicted of petty crimes.'[33] Even in the new reformatories, it seemed, women had once again emerged as victims.

Using this analysis for purposes of comparison, did law and practice in the province of Ontario reveal similar inequities? According to Strange, it was Langmuir's intention to complement the motherly discipline provided by the female staff by sending to the institution 'daughterly subjects' who were 'the most suitable persons for Reformatory discipline and treatments.'[34] In fact, there is little evidence to prove that the Mercer in this respect replicated the American reformatory ideal. When the Mercer was discussed by the Public Accounts Committee in 1879, Tory leader W.R. Meredith asked the inspector, 'what class of women do you expect to get in that Reformatory?' The answer was unequivocal: those committed for 'the same kind of offences as warrant the commitment of men to the Central Prison.'[35] In his reports of the previous decade Langmuir had frequently pointed to the presence in the jails of a hardened class of female recidivists and this was the element which soon filled the Mercer. Out of the first group of thirty women sent to the Mercer, the Annual Report noted that 'in nearly every case, the women were habitual offenders ... and the lives of many of them had been largely spent in Common Gaols.' To the Public Accounts Committee Langmuir described them bluntly as 'the criminal class.'[36]

The committal clauses of the Mercer statute did not differ substantially from those of the Central Prison. By Clause 12 all females confined in the jails might be transferred to the prison by the provincial secretary; by Clause 13 every court before which any female was convicted of any offence punishable by a jail sentence might sentence such female directly to the reformatory; and by Clause 17 the superintendent of the Mercer was required to receive every offender sentenced to that facility. The only clause which permitted a degree of selectivity was number 14, which gave the provincial secretary authority to transfer prisoners from the Mercer back to the common jail. In his 1879 report Langmuir emphasized the similarity between these committal clauses and those for the Central Prison. If Langmuir had intended to populate the Mercer with 'daughterly subjects' deemed most suitable for correction, he would have written the statute differently. Instead the Mercer, like the Central Prison, was soon filled by the most notorious repeat offenders from the local jails.

That this indeed was the intention is suggested in Langmuir's 1881 report. There he commented that a year's observation of the actual working of the new institution had led him to conclude that the Mercer was fulfilling its original objectives 'in a very satisfactory way.' This was especially the case, he continued, 'when it is considered that a large number of the prisoners for whom it is intended furnish perhaps the very worst material to work upon with a view to reclamation.' Even prisoners of this class, he boasted, instead of spending their time in idleness in the common jails, 'are now kept fully employed, and for the time being, at least, are restrained in their evil courses.' Hard labour and incapacitation, now being achieved in the Mercer to Langmuir's satisfaction, were precisely the same as the objective previously established for the notoriously penal Central Prison. In Langmuir's judgment, it was the hardened offenders and recidivists who were most in need of the lengthy sentences which could be better enforced in a prison than in a jail.

One of the most persistent themes in the annual reports was the request of the superintendent for longer sentences. These were deemed absolutely essential for the prison programme to be effective.[37] It is important to note, however, that such requests were consistently ignored by the sentencing authorities. Nearly 65 per cent of Mercer in-

TABLE 1
Sentence Length of Central Prison and Mercer Inmates, 1880–1900

	Central Prison		Mercer Reformatory	
	n	%	n	%
1 month and under to 3 months	4436	31.2	182	6.9
3 months, 1 day to 6 months	5976	42.0	1517	57.7
6 months, 1 day to 9 months	629	4.4	69	2.6
9 months, 1 day to 12 months	1592	11.2	406	15.4
12 months, 1 day to 18 months	790	5.6	150	5.7
18 months, 1 day to 24 months	755	5.3	288	11.0
2 years, 1 day to 5 years	43	0.3	17	0.6

TABLE 2
Sentence Length of Central Prison and Mercer Inmates, 1880–1900

	Central Prison		Mercer Reformatory	
	n	%	n	%
1 month and under to 6 months	10412	73.2	1699	64.6
6 months, 1 day to 12 months	2221	15.6	475	18.1
12 months, 1 day to 24 months	1545	10.9	438	16.7
2 years, 1 day to 5 years	43	0.3	17	0.6

mates received sentences of six months or less. The most common sentences were for between three and six months, representing 57.7 per cent of all sentences (see table 1).

Still, a greater proportion of Mercer inmates (35.4 per cent) received sentences longer than six months than did Central Prison inmates (26.8 per cent; see table 2).[38] One can only speculate as to the reasons. It is hard to believe that judges across the province were more willing to listen to the superintendent of the Mercer than to the warden of the Central Prison in this respect. Possibly the differential reflects a lingering sentiment among criminal justice officials that women were harder to reform than men, or it may equally represent a feeling that women were more reformable than men, and therefore worth the investment of a longer sentence.

What is most significant about these figures, however, relates to the argument of American feminist historians about the double standard inherent in the significantly longer sentences given to women convicted

TABLE 3
Offences Committed by Mercer Inmates, 1881–1900*

	1881–1885		1886–1890		1891–1895		1896–1900		1881–1900	
	n	%	n	%	n	%	n	%	n	%
Crimes against the person	12	1.4	17	2.6	16	2.8	19	3.6	64	2.5
Crimes against property	160	18.9	350	20.8	112	19.7	123	23.0	530	20.4
Crimes against public morals	283	33.4	214	33.0	197	34.6	162	30.3	856	32.9
Crimes against public order	268	31.6	245	37.8	197	34.6	165	30.9	875	33.7
Other offences	125	14.7	37	5.7	47	8.3	65	12.2	274	10.5
Drink-related offences only	169	19.2	78	12.0	67	17.8	73	13.7	387	14.9
Prostitution-related only	278	31.7	209	32.3	190	33.4	155	29.0	832	32.0
All other offences	401	49.1	361	55.7	312	54.8	306	57.3	1380	53.1

*Figures for 1880 are not available.

of minor offences. The sentences of most women imprisoned in the Mercer were brief, between three and six months, despite the continual plea of the woman who headed the Mercer that they be made longer. Mercer inmates most emphatically were not sentenced to long periods of incarceration for minor transgressions. And there were no indeterminate sentences available to make it possible for reformatory officials to retain prisoners until they deemed their behaviour satisfactory or their prognosis good.

It is true, nonetheless, that women were sentenced to the reformatory for crimes which were less serious than those which landed men in the Central Prison. As an analysis of offence patterns demonstrates, over two-thirds of the inmates were convicted of public order and morals offences (see table 3). The relatively harmless nature of most female offences is emphasized by the low proportion of Mercer women sentenced for assault or other crimes against the person. For the whole period 1881–1900, only 64 women, or 2.5 per cent of the total population, were committed for such crimes. By comparison, even in a period when women were more actively entering the labour force and frequenting other formerly male preserves, they remained much less prone to violent activities than men.

Similarly there continued to be a great disparity between the numbers of men and women imprisoned for property offences. Between 1881

TABLE 4
Five Most Common Offences Committed by Mercer Inmates, 1881–1900*

	1881–1885		1886–1890		1891–1895		1896–1900		1881–1900	
	n	%	n	%	n	%	n	%	n	%
Vagrancy	206	24.3	180	27.8	164	28.8	140	26.3	690	26.5
Larceny	142	16.7	115	17.7	93	16.3	110	20.6	460	17.7
Keeping/inmate of house of ill-fame	126	14.9	83	12.8	102	17.9	71	13.3	382	14.7
Drunkenness†	123	14.5	36	5.6	41	7.2	62	11.6	262	10.1
Keeping/inmate of disorderly house	90	10.6	49	7.6	39	6.9	42	7.9	220	8.5
Total	687	81.0	463	71.5	439	77.2	425	79.6	2014	77.5
All other Offences	161	19.0	185	28.5	130	22.8	109	20.4	585	22.5

*Figures for 1880 are not available.
†Includes those convicted of simply drunkenness *only*.

and 1890, 530 women, or 20.4 per cent of the population, were in the Mercer for property crimes. This compared to 7595 men in the Central Prison; for the 1874–1900 period, 55.7 per cent of Central Prison inmates were there for property crimes. The difference is striking. Presumably men in need stole while women sold their bodies.

A total of 32.9 per cent of the Mercer women, compared to 4.1 per cent of the Central Prison men, were committed for public morals offences. Since morals offences included prostitution, this is far less striking than the male-female disparity in crimes against public order, which accounted for 33.7 per cent of female committals and only 19 per cent of male. These encompassed vagrancy and drunk and disorderly, but not drunkenness, which was listed under 'other' offences. The disparity is explained by the number of female vagrants who were prostitutes. In the table 4 list of five most common offences, vagrancy is well in the lead at 26.5 per cent. Put another way, the total of public morals and public order offences is 66.6 per cent, compared to 23.1 per cent for men. In late-nineteenth-century Ontario, men, it seems, specialized in property offences and crimes of violence and women in morals-related offences.

It is true, therefore, that the offences for which women were sent to the Mercer could be regarded as 'less serious' than the offences which sent men to the Central Prison. But perhaps they were just different, which is hardly surprising because they reflected what society for centuries, whether 'fairly' or 'unfairly,' had recognized as widely different patterns of male and female criminality. But it is just not accurate to insist that somehow this pattern of committal should be attributed primarily to the women's reformatory movement. It originated centuries earlier and reflected a bewildering variety of enduring gender-based attitudes and social circumstances, including society's different perceptions of improper behaviour in men and women, as well as changes brought about by centuries-long processes of industrialization and urbanization which gradually altered the male and female spheres of social and economic activity. To suggest that this pattern represented a double standard either achieved or exaggerated by the maternal feminism of women's reformatory advocates is to distort a far more complex reality. A double standard did indeed exist but it was one which rewarded and punished both men and women in numerous different ways, and committal practices as they existed at least at the Mercer did little, much to Mary Jane O'Reilly's regret, to fundamentally reshape that reality.

If there is nothing in the Mercer's committal practices to substantiate the argument that this was a facility designed specifically to deal with 'daughterly subjects' who had gone astray by committing relatively minor offences, it was equally true that there was nothing about the Mercer's discharge procedures to distinguish it from male facilities. Under the American system, the deployment of indeterminate sentences was premised on the idea that well-behaved young women could earn early release from detention through good conduct and by offering other evidence of rehabilitation while those who were undeserving would be retained for longer periods.[39] In Ontario Clause 7 of the Mercer statute asserted the desirability of putting an earned remission system in place 'in order to encourage good behaviour and industry,' yet no remission system was implemented in this period. In 1881 Langmuir supported remission in principle, pointing out that many women were 'anxious to know whether good conduct would earn for them a remission of a portion of their sentences.' Yet he noted that nearly every woman in the Mercer was a hardened offender and that sentences were already too brief to achieve rehabilitation. He was therefore at that time not prepared to recommend 'that full effect be given to that portion of the law providing for the shortening of a sentence on account of good conduct.' All he was willing to do was to make special recommendations in the case of deserving individuals. In the same report O'Reilly pointed to the great benefits of remission systems used in other countries and expressed regret that nothing had been done to reward good behaviour in the Mercer. She must have been disappointed by Langmuir's decision because it placed discretionary power entirely in the inspector's hands and was no substitute for a full-scale programme shaped to meet institutional needs and standards.[40]

Over the years O'Reilly returned to the question of remission many times. Many of the best-behaved inmates, she reported, 'frequently ask me if there is any probability that some of their time will be remitted for good conduct' and she found it frustrating to be able to offer no hope. 'Every year since this Reformatory has been in operation,' she asserted in 1886, 'I have hoped that those vested with authority would introduce a law, by which our inmates could merit this remission of sentence.' Such clemency, she argued, would be recommended only for first offenders sentenced to at least one year. 'The hope of having the sentence shortened, ever so little, by their own efforts would I feel sure prove a strong incentive to good conduct.' Fully a decade later O'Reilly had made no progress and repeated the customary plea. 'If the hope of time being remitted for good conduct were held out to them,' she suggested plaintively, 'it would be a strong incentive to good behaviour.'[41] A remission system was at this time in effect in Kingston Penitentiary and the failure to make use of an approach which had proved its utility is difficult to explain. Possibly provincial officials did not want to hold out such a prospect to the type of repeat offenders who were in the Central Prison and believed it inappropriate to employ a system in the Mercer which they were not prepared to use in the male facility. In any case, the persistent failure to heed O'Reilly's advice placed an important limitation on her ability to manage the Mercer in her own fashion.

At the same time, O'Reilly's efforts continued to be constrained by the statutory obligation to accept all prisoners sent to the Mercer by the sentencing authorities. Repeatedly she did her best to educate or persuade the judicial authorities to consider the institutional implications. Short sentences, she argued in 1886, were particularly regrettable for addicts. Habitual drunks, who usually received six months, invariably were released with their appetites sharpened. In Massachusetts, she noted with approval, a term of two years had been established for women with prior convictions for drunkenness.[42] Following a visit in 1890 to reformatories in the United States, she suggested that longer sentences there contributed a great deal to institutional order. The discipline received had time to take root and she did not observe there 'that restlessness and excitability I have seen among the women sent for shorter terms to this Reformatory.'[43] The inspector concurred, arguing in 1898 that little would be achieved in the Mercer 'until commitments are for a longer period, or what would be better still an indeterminate period.' Canada, he urged, should follow the American practice and enact the important reform of the indeterminate sentence.[44] At the very least, O'Reilly believed, it would serve as a deterrent if the sentence length were increased for each successive conviction. Yet, in contrast to the American model, Ontario during O'Reilly's tenure neither effected longer sentences nor legislated earned remission or indeterminate sentences.

Throughout her tenure O'Reilly's belief in the good work done in the Mercer was balanced by her consciousness of the extent of recidivism. The 1882 report, for example, noted that 212 women had been admitted during the year, and 35 of these were recommittals; in 1886 O'Reilly reported that 27 out of a population of 88 were recidivists. Offsetting the high rate of recidivism, however, was a consistent drop in total numbers confined. From 1885, when the number in custody was 262, there was a drop to 167 in 1898. Nonetheless, neither O'Reilly nor James Noxon, the inspector, had become any more willing to make claims of rehabilitative success. Noxon emphasized in 1899 that structural changes were finally being made which would permit a superior system of classification to be put in place, but even when a complete classification was possible, Noxon asserted, the Mercer would remain 'a reformatory only in name, being impotent because of the short term of sentence, to influence the lives' of the inmates for permanent good. At this point Noxon took an extreme view, asserting that if any faith still existed 'in the possibility under favourable conditions' of reforming the lives of at least some of the inmates, then every effort must be made to secure the indeterminate sentence. According to Noxon, this was 'the all important organic change absolutely necessary to successful reformatory efforts.'[45]

INDUSTRIAL PROGRAMMES

In one other respect, the Mercer and the Central Prison shared a common characteristic: each was established as an industrial reformatory and represented the province's concerted attack on the state of idleness which prevailed in the common jails and which was so offensive to middle-class Ontarians. Thus Langmuir habitually referred to the Mercer as an industrial reformatory and O'Reilly also regarded the work programme as central to the prison regimen. She fully accepted the conventional wisdom about the relationship between idleness and crime, asserting that 'of all wretched women the idle are the most wretched.' 'We try to impress upon them the importance of labor, and we look upon this as one great means of their reformation.'[46] To ensure that there should be no misunderstanding about this, Langmuir, with the Mercer about to open, asked the premier to address a circular to all sentencing authorities outlining the objectives of the Mercer. Mowat obliged by telling the judges and the magistrates that normally no woman should be sentenced to the reformatory for less than six months and that 'No one should be sentenced to this Reformatory where hard labour is not intended to be imposed or without the certificate of the Gaol Surgeon that the convict is physically and mentally capable of performing ordinary day labour.' If there was any doubt, the woman should be sent to the local jail for possible future removal to the Mercer. 'Of course,' he concluded, 'no one who is not sentenced to hard labour will be removed to the Reformatory.'[47]

For Langmuir, in the period when the Mercer was being organized, the manner in which the inmates were to be employed was 'perhaps the most important problem in connection with this institution, which has to be solved.' He took it for granted that it would be 'an act of folly' to congregate large numbers of women in prison without furnishing suitable employment. The statute, he emphasized, 'very properly' made provision for the enforcement of sentences of hard labour.[48] For Langmuir this not only encompassed discipline and punishment but also was a means of ensuring that prisoner labour relieved the government of much of the institution's operating expenses. In this respect, the income received was not very significant. In 1882, for example, institutional costs were $29,105.21 and the proceeds of labour came to $3076.46. The figures did not change dramatically over the course of O'Reilly's tenure. In 1899 operating expenses were $23,635.74 and total revenue $4212.06. With daily costs per inmate running at about 50 cents to an annual total of about $182 per inmate, the financial burden assumed by the province was hardly excessive.[49]

There was one fundamental difference between approaches to labour in the Mercer and the Central Prison. In the former there was a strong initial effort to make the work regimen part of a wider programme of good behaviour classification. 'There should be a variety of labour,' Langmuir indicated in his 1879 report, 'commencing with that of a more menial order, such as washing etc., so that the continued good conduct of an inmate might be rewarded by advancement to a higher grade of work, such as machine-sewing etc.' The inspector advised the government to establish facilities for a range of work, including shoemaking, paper-box making, tailoring, and sewing by both machine and hand. He also intended to allow private contractors to make proposals to come into the prison and hire the inmates for different types of labour.

All this came to little. There were problems finding contractors to employ the Mercer women, and before long a single task, laundering, dominated all others. To a lesser extent, sewing, knitting, and prison domestic work were also carried out. It is difficult to know why Langmuir's original plan failed so completely. No doubt it had a good deal to do with the character of the inmate population and the lack of any semblance of the work ethic. O'Reilly and her colleagues seem to have quickly concluded that the vast majority of Mercer prisoners were working-class women fitted only for the most menial tasks; and they rationalized their position by arguing that the provision of training in the basic skills required of a domestic servant was most likely to lead to post-release employment.[50]

In fact, the Mercer population was even more strongly working class than that of the Central Prison. In table 5 an amazing 87.5 per cent of the inmates were reported as holding occupations. Of this group, only 4 per cent held positions which could be described as middle class, although the position listed as 'housekeeper' in the domestic category poses a problem. It is possible that this refers to what today would be called a housewife. But even if it is assumed that such persons were not gainfully employed, there still remain 75.3 per cent reporting occupations. The category 'no occupation,' which accounts for 12.5 per cent of the inmates, is equally problematic in attempting to determine class, but there is no reason to believe that any substantial proportion of this category was other than working class. If this is so, it appears that almost 96 per cent of the population was working class. But what sets the class composition of the Mercer most dramatically apart from that of the Central Prison is the larger proportion of unskilled workers. Unskilled workers, including both domestics and prostitutes, but omitting those with no occupation, made up 82.3 per cent of the inmate population, compared to 47.1 per cent in the Central Prison.

Some explanation is needed for the decline in the number reporting the occupation of prostitute from 29.7 per cent in 1881–5 to just 5.6 per cent in 1896–1900. Although this may reflect the success of police anti-prostitution campaigns, the extent of the change suggests it may be more logically attributable, to a labelling change as the authorities

TABLE 5
Occupation of Mercer Inmates, 1881–1900*

	1881–1885		1886–1890		1891–1895		1896–1900		1881–1900	
	n	%	n	%	n	%	n	%	n	%
Domestic[1]	490	56.6	365	56.3	398	69.9	374	70.0	1627	62.6
Industrial[2]	7	0.8	7	1.1	9	15.8	6	1.1	29	1.1
Prostitute	252	29.7	171	26.4	59	10.4	30	5.6	512	19.7
Other[3]	35	4.1	20	3.1	28	4.9	22	4.1	105	4.0
No occupation	64	4.0	86	13.3	75	13.2	101	18.9	326	12.5

* Figures for 1880 are not available.
[1] Includes charwomen, cooks, housekeepers, laundresses, servants, domestics, washerwomen, and ladies' maids.
[2] Includes lace-makers, box-makers, basket-makers, bookbinders, book-folders, brush-makers, factory girls, labouring women, presser in dye works, rag-pickers, weavers, paper-box makers, spinners, whitewashers, cane-chair makers, and knitters.
[3] Includes clerks, dressmakers, furriers, milliners, pedlars, seamstresses, tailors, dressmakers, teachers, waitresses, nurses, market women, second-hand dealers, store-keepers, hotel-keepers, midwives, and telegraph operators.

became increasingly reluctant to dignify prostitution by calling it an occupation.

Also noteworthy is the increase in the number of domestics from about 57 per cent in 1886–90 to 70 per cent in 1891–1900, further confirming the popular impression that the Mercer was home to a population composed primarily of members of the servant class.

Table 6, the five leading occupations of Mercer inmates, further highlights the very low number of Mercer women reporting skills. The leading four occupations, representing 79.4 per cent of all inmates, were all unskilled. The fifth largest category, dressmaker, seamstress etc., accounted for only 2.9 per cent of the inmates. Clearly, in late-nineteenth-century Ontario unskilled women were far more likely to turn to criminal activity than were unskilled men.

Yet while O'Reilly's judgment of the skill-level and abilities of the inmates may have been a realistic one, undeniably the work training offered in the Mercer confirmed and reinforced their position at the lowest level of Ontario society. Perhaps the decision was the only one possible and was best suited to the social circumstances and post-release needs of Mercer graduates. O'Reilly in 1891 was frank in stating that 'we have tried to keep discharged inmates in view, and provide situations for those who are willing to go into service.'[51]

Certainly there is no doubt that many of the Mercer women were

TABLE 6
Five Leading Occupations of Mercer Inmates, 1881–1900*

	1881–1885		1886–1890		1891–1895		1896–1900		1881–1900	
	n	%	n	%	n	%	n	%	n	%
Servant/domestic	355	41.9	258	39.8	262	46.0	209	39.1	1084	41.7
Prostitute	252	29.7	171	26.4	59	10.4	30	5.6	512	19.7
Housekeeper	70	8.3	59	9.1	72	12.6	115	21.5	316	12.2
Charwoman	41	4.8	33	5.1	42	7.4	36	6.7	152	15.8
Seamstress, tailoress, dressmaker	30	3.5	12	1.9	19	3.3	14	2.6	75	2.9
Total	748	88.2	533	82.3	454	79.8	404	75.7	2139	82.3
All other occupations	100	11.8	115	17.7	115	20.2	130	24.3	460	17.7

*Figures for 1880 are not available.

TABLE 7
Literacy of Central Prison and Mercer Inmates, 1880–1900

	Central Prison		Mercer Reformatory	
	n	%	n	%
Read and Write	11300	79.5	1401	53.3
Read only	802	5.6	545	20.7
Illiterate	2119	14.9	683	26.0

entirely uneducated and, as the 1882 report put it, 'almost wholly ignorant of the plainer duties of domestic work.' Differences in status and opportunities explain the enormous disparity between male and female prisoners in the level of literacy (see table 7). Almost four-fifths of the men were recorded as literate and barely more than half the women. The literacy level given for men, however, seems surprisingly high. In this regard it is significant that evidence from the Mercer prison register suggests that Mrs O'Reilly exercised considerable care in examining incoming inmates. Her conclusion that only about half the inmates could read and write may well be a more accurate measurement of the literacy abilities of late-nineteenth-century Canadian prisoners generally than that provided by Central Prison records. There was, then, much practical justification for putting the prisoners to work at domestic drudgery.

But considerations of class, status, and ability were not alone in determining that the Mercer never took up the challenge of training its inmates in a broader range of work activities. The 1882 inspection minutes made a claim which, if true, is a tragic commentary on the social circumstances as well as the medical condition of many distressed and lower-class women in late-nineteenth-century Ontario. 'Owing to their mental and physical debasement,' they indicated, 'not more than one-fourth of the women when committed to the Reformatory are capable of doing any kind of work properly.' In these circumstances, it was an achievement of sorts to be able to assert, as the inspector did in 1882, that 'quite a number' of women left the Mercer well-trained and able to earn a good living.[52]

Altogether the state of work in the Mercer contrasts favourably with the disciplinary and practical problems which arose in the Central Prison. In 1887, a typical year, revenue earned was $2090.63 from laundering, $740.22 from making clothes for inmates, $521.58 from sewing, and $243.50 from knitting. Although efforts were made, with some success, to obtain orders for prison products from private business, these were often hard to come by. The 1889 report pointed out that laundry had become the principal employment because it had become difficult to obtain needlework of any description and there was 'no immediate prospect of securing large orders for clothing, etc.' At this point the prison's meticulously kept statistics showed that the laundry that year had completed 87,064 pieces for the Central Prison, 61,856 for various groups in the city, and 22,809 for the CPR. By this time, too, the garden, not a part of the Mercer's original design, was producing great quantities of vegetables for internal consumption. Despite the difficulties, especially the failure to relate work programmes to good conduct classification, 'women's work' seemed easier to provide and simpler to carry out than the occupations found at the Central Prison. The Mercer women, as the peaceful state of the facility and the lightness of punishments suggests, showed little of the resistance to work routines which was so prominent a part of the cycle of violence in the Central Prison.[53]

COMPLETING THE INMATE PROFILE

Other aspects of the inmate profile highlight both similarities and distinctions between male and female prison populations in the 1880–1900 period.

Thus tables 8 and 9, the analysis of national origin of inmates, confirm earlier work on the Central Prison demonstrating that immigrant status

TABLE 8
Nativity of Mercer Inmates, 1880–1900

	1881–1885		1886–1890		1891–1895		1896–1900		1881–1900	
	n	%	n	%	n	%	n	%	n	%
Canadian	407	46.4	358	55.2	350	61.5	354	66.3	1469	55.9
English & Welsh	132	15.0	98	15.1	75	13.2	53	9.9	358	13.6
Irish	211	24.0	105	16.2	79	13.9	60	11.2	455	17.3
Scottish	23	2.6	22	3.4	14	2.5	16	3.0	75	2.9
American	85	9.7	52	8.0	47	8.3	44	8.2	228	8.7
Other	20	2.3	13	2.0	4	0.7	7	1.3	44	1.7

TABLE 9
Nativity of Mercer Inmates, 1880–1900

	1881–1885		1886–1890		1891–1895		1896–1900		1881–1900	
	n	%	n	%	n	%	n	%	n	%
Canadian	407	46.4	358	55.2	350	61.5	354	66.3	1469	55.9
Foreign-born	471	53.6	290	44.8	219	38.5	180	33.7	1160	44.1

was a far more powerful indicator of criminal propensity than was ethnicity. As the Ontario population became gradually more Canadian in origin between the 1881 and 1891 census years, so too did the female criminal population. Unfortunately, the census did not consider the nativity of men and women separately, but overall between 1881 and 1891 the Canadian-born increased from 77.8 per cent of the population to 80.9 per cent. In the same period, the proportion of Canadian-born in the province's two intermediate prisons went from 48 per cent to 56.1 per cent. The group of women demonstrating the greatest decline in level of imprisonment over the twenty-year period 1880–1900 is the Irish, reflecting the decreasing numbers of Irish emigrating to Canada in the late nineteenth century. Nonetheless Irish women were imprisoned at a much higher rate than were Irish men. For the 1874–1900 period, 12.9 per cent of the inmates of the Central Prison were Irish compared to 17.3 per cent of Mercer inmates for the 1880–1900 period. Throughout most of the century, both literary and quantitative evidence continually confirmed that Irish women were imprisoned in the entire range of correctional facilities at rates higher than were men.

Table 10, an index of over-underrepresentation by country of origin for all Ontario jails, the Mercer, and the Central Prison, uses census

TABLE 10

Index of Over-underrepresentation in all Ontario Jails, the Ontario Central Prison, and the Mercer Reformatory, 1880-1900

Country of origin	All jails	Central Prison	Mercer Reform.
Canada	0.6	0.7	0.7
England and Wales	2.0	1.9	1.8
Ireland	3.3	2.0	2.9
Scotland	1.3	1.1	0.8
United States	3.1	4.9	4.0
Other	1.6	1.8	1.0

TABLE 11

Religion of Central Prison and Mercer Inmates, 1880-1900

	Central Prison		Mercer Reformatory		Ontario population, 1891	
	n	%	n	%	n	%
Episcopalian	4510	31.7	917	34.9	706,838	17.6
Roman Catholic	4916	34.6	897	34.1	679,139	16.9
Methodist	2183	15.4	449	17.1	1,245,536	31.0
Presbyterian	1764	12.4	217	8.3	871,461	21.7
Baptist	461	3.2	121	4.6	212,718	5.3
Other	387	2.7	28	1.1	299,390	7.5

data to compare the imprisonment rates of ethnic groups with their representation in the entire Ontario population. A score of less than one means that a national group was underrepresented and a score of more than one that it was overrepresented. While Canadians were somewhat underrepresented, English and Irish males had almost exactly the same rate of overrepresentation. Irish women scored significantly higher than English women. Like American men, American women scored highest, again confirming official concern over the number of tramps and drifters crossing the border at will.

In general, however, the comparison between the Mercer and the Central Prison on the basis of country of origin reveals few significant differences between the sexes.

The same is true in table 11 for religious comparisons. One feature of the inmate profile of both prisons is the overrepresentation of Catholics. This might tend to reinforce the popular stereotype of an underprivileged and alienated Catholic proletariat largely segregated from the Protestant population and manifesting its alienation by a far higher

TABLE 12
Age of Central Prison and Mercer Inmates, 1880–1900

	Central Prison		Mercer Reformatory	
	n	%	n	%
Under 18	810	5.7	369	14.0
18–20	1422	10.0	316	12.0
21–30	5929	41.7	938	35.7
31–40	2933	20.6	504	19.2
41–50	1719	12.1	324	12.3
51–60	975	6.9	120	4.6
61+	433	3.0	58	2.2

crime rate. What offsets this image, however, are the figures for Episcopalians, who were overrepresented in both prisons in almost the same proportion as were Catholics. In contrast, Methodists and Presbyterians were particularly law-abiding.

If existing nativity and religious data can reveal few distinctions between Mercer and Central Prison inmates, age, marital status, and drinking habits do highlight more substantial differences. As table 12 demonstrates, the inmates of the Mercer tended to be younger. Fully 14 per cent were under eighteen years of age compared to 5.7 per cent for the Central Prison. Almost two-thirds of the Mercer women were aged thirty or younger, and 81 per cent were forty or younger. The relative youth of Mercer inmates probably helped sustain official belief in the facility's reform potential. However, the youthfulness of Mercer's population is not unrelated to the high proportion of the inmates who were prostitutes, not the most likely group to be rehabilitated.

The fact that 43.4 per cent of Mercer women were married compared to 29.5 per cent of Central Prison men (table 13) also seems suggestive. For men, it would seem that the married state contributed to stability and lessened inclinations to crime. For women, often left destitute by the death of a spouse, ill-treated or abandoned, marriage did not necessarily bring economic security. Many married women may have been forced to resort to crime to support themselves and their families.

One can only speculate as to why a significantly higher proportion of the men were reported as intemperate than of the women (table 14). But once again this fact may suggest significant economic differences between men and women in late-nineteenth-century society.

To summarize, the Mercer inmate population was younger, less lit-

TABLE 13
Marital Status of Central Prison and Mercer Inmates, 1880–1900

	Central Prison		Mercer Reformatory	
	n	%	n	%
Single/widowed	10029	70.5	1489	56.6
Married	4192	29.5	1140	43.4

TABLE 14
Drinking Habits of Central Prison and Mercer Inmates, 1881–1900

	Central Prison		Mercer Reformatory	
	n	%	n	%
Temperate	3021	22.1	1098	42.2
Intemperate	10640	77.9	1051	57.8

erate, more temperate, and more likely to be married than the male population in the Central Prison. Also it was serving sentences which were somewhat longer. Almost no women were imprisoned in the Mercer for crimes against the person; two-thirds of the inmates were there for public morals and public order offences. As was true of the Central Prison inmates, immigrant status was far more important than ethnicity in accounting for criminality. But the most pervasive reality shaping the Mercer inmate profile was class. The Mercer housed a population composed almost entirely of the unskilled and the disadvantaged, women who had little to lose from engaging in criminal activities.

GOVERNING BY KINDNESS

If neither work discipline nor committal and discharge procedures were strikingly different between the Mercer and the Central Prison, it might seem necessary to conclude that herein lies the explanation for the willingness of conservative Ontarians to establish and support a women's prison. The institution, it seems, except for the prominence given to women in its administration and some statistical differences in inmate profile which would have been largely unnoticed by most contemporaries, essentially replicated the familiar procedures of the Central Prison. And even with respect to female governance, men held several important positions in the prison and the male inspectors, Langmuir and his successors, probably were perceived as being finally in control. But any such dismissive conclusion simply misunderstands the extent of Langmuir's commitment to the social feminist vision of prison administration and it misses a great deal about what went on in both of Ontario's late-nineteenth-century prisons. It is at this point that the words and actions of O'Reilly and her colleagues must be taken very seriously, for when looked at closely it soon becomes evident that the Mercer as managed by Mary Jane O'Reilly had almost nothing in common with the punitive male prison.

Contemporaries were clear in their own minds and entirely frank about the differences between the Central Prison and the Mercer. The former was planned and run with the objective of deterrence; it was designed, as some put it, to be 'a terror to evil doers' and anyone familiar with its rather sordid and unhappy history will agree that it easily achieved this objective. Men were sent to the Central Prison for punishment and women to the Mercer, as O'Reilly explained it, for discipline in the context of kindness, friendship, and support. It is impossible to imagine any official associated with Ontario's men's prison setting out objectives similar in any respect to those O'Reilly regularly enunciated for the Mercer. As she put it in 1881, her purpose was to inspire the inmates 'with a feeling of self-respect, and to teach them that they can cherish pure thoughts, perform good actions and live soberly, impressing upon them the fact that true reformation must begin with themselves. Our aim has been to govern with kindness, and we have found this the most effectual way of influencing them, treating them as human beings who have a claim upon our charity as well as upon our justice.'[54] Perhaps it was because both officers and prisoners understood and to a degree accepted these high-minded and strikingly modern objectives that O'Reilly was able to run the facility without resort to frequent punishments or other harsh disciplinary tools. The absence of scandal or riot meant in turn that O'Reilly seldom faced the threat of outside interference. As a result, the praise offered by the inspectors in the annual reports for O'Reilly's administration is as frequent as is O'Reilly's own praise for both the inmates and the members of her staff. In innumerable ways, then, O'Reilly's expressed intent 'to govern by kindness' is difficult to document but was felt and experienced by all members of the prison community. As such it contributed to an exceptional administrative success, which made the Mercer in this period one of the most harmonious prisons anywhere.

During her tenure of office, Mary Jane O'Reilly would prove again and again that her administration in every respect lived up to this carefully articulated goal of governing by kindness, just as fully as the Central Prison did to its own repressive mission. Consider, for example, the evidence offered by two decades of prison reports. Such documents must always be regarded critically for, in general, they reflected only what their authors wanted to be known about the life of the prison. Almost always, however, they reveal rather more than a cursory reading would suggest, and this is true of O'Reilly's Mercer reports. At first these documents seem to offer little to compel attention or to suggest that the prison was the setting for a worthwhile social experiment. Certainly there was little of the sense of drama or danger which even the casual reader gains from most reports of life in male prisons. Year after year, the government inspector could find little to comment upon; there were no life-threatening issues and apparently no great achievements in the work of reforming the inmates. About the most O'Reilly ever claimed was her 1881 comment that perhaps 'good seeds have been sown among the briars and weeds.'[55] Moving beyond metaphor, the place was clean, the food fairly acceptable, the prisoners relatively compliant. In a typical comment, the inspector in 1893 told the government that there was 'nothing of importance to report.'

With the benefit of hindsight, it would be more accurate to conclude that the conventional and complacent male bureaucrats who succeeded Langmuir in the inspector's office simply lacked the insight to understand what was really happening in the Mercer. On one level at least O'Reilly's achievement seems enormous. Under her leadership, there were no scandals, riots, charges of brutality, or other incidents characteristic of punitive prisons everywhere. The contrast between the ambience of the Mercer and the unruly, often violent behaviour which Kingston Penitentiary officials complained had characterized female behaviour in that institution in the 1840s and early 1850s is striking. Although the extent and precise nature of violence in the nineteenth-century female prison remains largely unprobed, and although the gendered nature of such violence doubtless differentiated it from that in male prisons, its existence should be neither doubted nor underestimated. As Philip Priestly notes for England, women 'were by no means immune' from such outbreaks. In the punitive institution, prisoners react to official oppression, contempt, and brutality by returning it in full measure, and they develop a subculture which helps them cope with the pains of imprisonment which is reflective of the anger and hatred which pervade such facilities.[56] The official comments about the Mercer that there was 'nothing to report' strongly suggest that somehow this institution was not a community characterized by a subculture of resistance and hatred.

In the more traditional areas of rehabilitative endeavour the Mercer, in common with women's reformatories elsewhere, made a substantial effort to provide both educational programmes and religious succour, with far more success in the latter area than in the former. When the Central Prison was opened the decision had been made not to appoint a resident chaplain but to use the services of the Toronto Ministerial Association to provide a rotation of ministers of different denominations for Protestant services while putting Catholic needs in the hands of the Bishop of Toronto. Langmuir explained his preference for a voluntary system as opposed to the paid full-time chaplaincy service which existed in Kingston Penitentiary by arguing that such an approach best suited a community where religious pluralism prevailed.[57] In June 1880, with the Mercer about to open, he told the provincial treasurer that about $200 would be required to fund Protestant services and $100 for Catholic. Although the Ministerial Association assumed responsibility for nominating clergymen, the work among Protestant prisoners was formally directed, as Langmuir told the treasurer, by the Prisoners' Aid Association of Toronto.[58] This was a group of prominent philanthropically minded citizens whose efforts dated back to the late 1860s and the establishment of the Toronto Jail Mission. The name Prisoners' Aid Association had been assumed in the early 1870s when Langmuir encouraged their active involvement in the new Central Prison. Success among the Central Prison men, however, was at best mixed, and the opening of the Mercer seems to have led to renewed enthusiasm among association workers.

In the absence of a resident chaplain, it became the responsibility of Mrs O'Reilly or the deputy superintendent to conduct the daily reading of prayers, while more formal services were performed by the clergymen sent by the Ministerial Association on Sundays and on one weekday. O'Reilly reported that the rule obliging inmates to be present at religious services was 'rigidly enforced' and claimed that much that was positive about the Mercer was attributable 'to the good influence these religious services have on the minds of the inmates.'[59]

Similar assertions about the effectiveness of religious ministrations are prominent in innumerable reports on nineteenth-century North American and European correctional institutions and in every case they pose formidable problems of interpretation. Certainly there is no gain-saying the enthusiasm and commitment of middle-class men and women, clergy and volunteers alike, as they pressed their evangelical vision on a lower-class and truly captive audience. It is impossible, how-ever, to more than speculate about how ill-educated prostitutes and servant-women really regarded the weekly word intended, as the Pris-oners' Aid Association report put it in 1881, to bring each inmate 'face to face with the fact of their own sinfulness and the way of Salvation through our Lord Jesus Christ.'[60]

The Prisoners' Aid Association asserted its influence on the Mercer primarily through the Sabbath school under William Howland. As well, as the association report put it, 'the government decided, for various reasons, that the staff of teachers should consist entirely of ladies' and 'a Lady Superintendent was also appointed' in the person of Liz Har-vie.[61] The school opened in 1881; each week an average of thirteen teachers, some of them experienced veterans from the Central Prison, instructed the inmates in Christian homilies, distributed religious tracts, and encouraged recitations. Not surprisingly, the choir, which enabled the women to have some contact with children from the Industrial Ref-uge, was a popular feature. School attendance was voluntary, and in 1881 it averaged fifty-nine from the reformatory and eleven from the refuge. In their first annual report, Howland and Harvie proudly re-sorted to the rhetoric of maternal feminism to describe their efforts: 'We frequently hear sweeping assertions about the hardness and severity manifested by the virtuous Christian woman towards her fallen sister, but we gladly state that in this city there are women of culture and refinement, who are giving not only the tear of sympathy, but the kindly word and the helping hand to fallen sisters.'[62]

Year after year, the reports of Howland and Harvie proclaimed their own marvellous success. The women, it seemed, paid rapt attention, never causing the slightest disturbance. Their behaviour was always 'orderly and correct in every respect,' and they had frequently shown 'by the quivering lip and starting tear, that not only has the attention been arrested but the heart impressed.' The 1882 report, which claimed that 'not even one case of bad conduct or even inattention' had occurred, was repeated year after year.[63] Perhaps this was all true. The women of the Mercer, young, poor, uneducated, and in trouble, may have been overawed by the formidable ladies of the Sabbath School Association and have eagerly accepted the message that through belief and coop-eration they would achieve salvation and even temporal success. Or perhaps they were responding primarily to the evident interest and kindness being offered and a kind of feminine bonding was being achieved through friendship and solicitude. Or possibly the prisoners regarded it all as entertainment, a welcome diversion from the drudgery of the laundry, while ignoring or rejecting the message itself. Scattered evidence does suggest that this approach did reach a more receptive audience in the Mercer than in the Central Prison, where religious ministrations occasionally led to unpleasant incidents.[64]

There was a practical side, however, to the proffered hand of friendship which doubtless accounts in some measure for the receptiveness of the Mercer women to the efforts of the Sabbath ladies. The teachers provided clothing and other necessaries on release, they made gifts of crochet hooks and other supplies which could be used for recreational purposes, and they met the women 'at the prison gate' and helped them find lodging and work. As time passed, these after-care services expanded considerably. By the mid-1880s such work in Ontario may finally have achieved the level reached much earlier in such American states as New York and Massachusetts.

From the beginning, the Prisoners' Aid Association had used the services of a full-time employee, Henry Softley, who under the title 'missionary agent' visited ex-prisoners and helped them find food, lodging, and employment. In 1882 a considerable advance was made in after-care work when the association acquired a house at 148 Bay Street as an office for its agent and a meeting place for volunteers and former prisoners. One evening a week a Bible class was held in the Bay Street house, and the 1882 report claimed that 'quite a number' of discharged inmates attended. A woman representing the association was available for an hour each evening 'for the purpose of assisting and advising' prisoners discharged from both the Mercer and the jail. Occasionally clothing, brought by the teachers, was distributed. Liz Harvie also held regular Saturday meetings for former inmates desiring religious instruction, the average attendance in 1882 being twenty-five.[65]

On the whole Howland and the association leadership did not make excessive claims about rehabilitation but neither did they underestimate the results of their work. In 1886 Howland and Harvie asserted that the teachers were 'cheered from time to time' by evidence of moral improvement and of 'a work of grace in the heart.' In 1891, when the numbers in the Mercer were declining, Howland was bolder, attributing the reduction at least in part to the Sabbath school. At this point the association was paying a 'Bible woman' to visit women after discharge; in 1893 she visited sixteen women regularly every two weeks and reported that she had paid 130 visits to women in their own homes. The association and its supporters had no doubt about the benefits of their evangelical activities. For Howland in 1891 'the word of God is the best means for the reformation of the fallen' and he insisted that 'the steady persistent teaching of this word bears more fruit than any other method.' Mrs O'Reilly, delighted with the assistance offered by the association, frequently reiterated her conviction that religious training was at the heart of rehabilitation. And Maude Keith, the Bible woman, when asked about the success of her work, would point out that 'many of these dear women have said, "I praise the Lord that I ever was sent to the Mercer Reformatory."'[66]

Each year the association published extracts from letters sent by former prisoners expressing their gratitude in language which could only have been acquired during imprisonment. As one eighteen-year-old, who had been placed as a servant in a Christian home, put it, 'You must not feel anxious about me for I am going to try to be a good girl for the rest of my life, for I do think that I have worked for Satan long enough.' No precise assessment can ever be made of the actual results of the association's efforts. But assuredly the words of Maude Keith, who spoke with such feeling of 'these dear women,' were part of a different world indeed than that inhabited by Gilbert Hartley, the Central Prison guard who found in that institution 'nothing that is elevating and refining all is base and vile.'[67]

Nonetheless the volunteers of the Prisoners' Aid Association worked diligently on behalf of men as well as women, and a sharper contrast between the milieus of male and female prisons is found in the attitudes and approaches of the paid employees of the respective facilities. In the old-fashioned custodial prison, especially the men's prison, it was axiomatic that the guards, poorly trained and ill educated, would be allowed to have almost no contact with the inmates. In theory at least, guard and inmate were not even to converse other than on a limited range of absolutely essential matters. The staff's role in the Mercer, as laid down in the 1882 report by the inspector, reversed the normal practice in every possible respect. To effect inmate reform, the inspector announced, it would be necessary to select only such attendants 'as are likely to be thoroughly interested in their work ... The fact that the inmates are daily and hourly in contact with these attendants, and have the opportunity of consulting with them for their benefit, is sufficient evidence that in the hands of the staff rests, one, if not the chief, agency' for inmate reformation.

It was, of course, one thing to assert this ideal, the ideal of guard as role model, and another to put it into practice. In addition to the natural constraint between jailer and prisoners there were formidable barriers of class between the Mercer inmates and middle-class women like O'Reilly and Deputy Superintendent Lucy Coad. Whether real bonding ever took place or could occur between a woman like O'Reilly and a frightened and ignorant young prostitute is almost impossible to determine. But to an extent unequalled by any other nineteenth-century Canadian prison, O'Reilly and her staff made the effort. And it helped a good deal that there was a practical side to much of the assistance rendered. This applied especially to some extraordinary initiatives in the neglected field of after-care. In her 1881 report O'Reilly pointed out that of 108 discharged inmates, jobs had been obtained for fifteen by officers of the reformatory and seventeen were 'taken in charge' by the Sunday school staff, while others had been directed to such institutions as the Toronto Magdalene Asylum and a local convent. O'Reilly suggested that twenty women seemed to have returned to their former activities. 'As in former years,' she noted in 1884, 'we have continued to keep up a correspondence with discharged inmates, visiting from time to time with those within our reach.'

Through visitations and correspondence, O'Reilly was able to provide estimates of how many girls managed to keep out of trouble and hold down jobs. In 1886 she reported that 23 of 137 discharged inmates seemed to have fallen back into their old ways, but the others were doing well. O'Reilly's comment that 'we strive to keep the discharged inmates in view as far as we can' was no idle boast. 'Every member of the staff,' she asserted proudly, 'does her utmost to help and encourage discharged inmates.' Between this staff work and the help provided by the Prisoners' Aid Association, itself in receipt of a provincial subsidy, the women who left the Mercer could receive assistance, both practical and moral, if they wished to have it. The inspector was right to be pleased in 1889 that 'this very important question of the future welfare of the inmates has in the past and continues to be so well looked after.' It is hard to believe that either staff or inmates would encourage such a post-release relationship unless bonds of trust and friendship had somehow been nurtured in the environment created at the Mercer by O'Reilly and her colleagues.[68]

Of course, not all institutional programmes met with the same degree of success. At first O'Reilly had believed that a considerable dint could be made in the institution's high illiteracy rate by a programme of compulsory secular education. As the 1881 report expressed it, the plan was to try to ensure that all women confined for longer sentences emerged able 'to read and write a little.' In contrast to the Central Prison, where no provision was made for a teacher, the Mercer was able to use the teacher employed at the Industrial Refuge to offer regular night classes. The resulting programme was not a success. In 1884 O'Reilly concluded that 'it is utterly useless to compel women over thirty years of age to attend school. With few exceptions they are unwilling to be taught.' The night school continued on a voluntary basis and a new programme began during the morning for younger women and for one hour in the afternoon for older women anxious to learn to read and write. In 1889 O'Reilly confirmed that the number of illiterates was 'the same as usual, about three-fifths,' but she had not changed her opinion that compulsion was useless. If O'Reilly was disappointed by the results, at least she was providing educational opportunities for those who wished them, and the availability of different classes for varying age groups and levels of ability suggests a degree of flexibility seldom found in the nineteenth-century prison.

In the prison environment, small kindnesses often assume considerable significance. It was important, for example, that O'Reilly understood that those inmates who could read would be unlikely to have any interest in the 500 volumes donated to the Mercer library by the Department of Education, which she described as 'far beyond the comprehension of the majority.'[69] In 1886 she complained that the library contained only bibles, catechisms, and school books, but as 'almost all young girls have a craving for fiction' she urged that a judicious selection be made in this area. In 1887 she reported that a special appropriation for the library was 'much appreciated.' Beyond a willingness to acquire novels for the library, O'Reilly essayed several other unusual steps to relax the oppressive prison environment. In 1893 she urged that a boardwalk be constructed in the yard for use during bad weather. This was 'the only opportunity these poor women have of breathing the fresh air and getting some out-door exercise.' In 1898 she asked for the addition of 'a recreation room for the inmates ... where they could meet' for the two-hour daily period of freedom from labour. For inmates unable to read, 'some harmless amusement could be provided.' O'Reilly in her reports was always anxious to say good things about the inmates, noting, for example, the excellent care they kept of the books in the library. On several occasions she expressed surprise that women who almost without exception were so cooperative while in prison should fall back into their old lives on release. O'Reilly's positive approach extended to her staff. She worked to persuade the government to supply improved facilities for them as well, including a sitting-room, and she commented frequently on their cooperation and dedication. A prison, of course, can never be a normal community but in a real way O'Reilly created in the Mercer a sense that officers and inmates were working together in a positive environment, one whose purpose was not to punish but to assist.

The essential kindness and humaneness of O'Reilly's approach was even more apparent in her attitude to punishment. She clearly grasped that the enforcement of frequent punishments would undermine any prospect of winning the cooperation of the inmates. 'We seldom use the dark cells,' she wrote astutely in 1882, 'for our experience has taught us, that to degrade a woman for some trivial offence, when an admonition would suffice, is injudicious.' O'Reilly may have found it politic to say little in her reports about the relaxation of the rule of silence, but it is fairly clear that she obviated much of the need to inflict harmful punishments by permitting the inmates to engage in a wide range of social discourse. At times the resulting clamour alarmed some of the more traditional members of her staff, and in 1887 she clamped down somewhat. 'I have striven,' she wrote, 'to enforce stricter discipline requiring perfect silence in the workshops.' The implication is that even at this point the women were allowed to converse freely among themselves on most other occasions. The statistics confirm the infrequency of punishments. Over the whole of 1884 only 43 inmates were punished and a total of 131 punishments administered. According to O'Reilly, these statistics proved 'that the number of refractory women is small, and that a very large number are never guilty of any breach of the Reformatory rules.'[70] Even under the tighter discipline administered in 1887, the number of offences totalled only 171. O'Reilly was vague as to what these punishments entailed, but they seem to have amounted to little more than reprimands, the withdrawal of privileges, and occasionally being placed in a solitary cell. The dark cell was used only fourteen times in 1885, three times in 1886, and six in 1887. In 1890 she reported proudly that there had been no dark cell punishments at all. Such an achievement offers a startling contrast to the painful reality which pervaded almost all male prisons of the era.

Further evidence of a kindly and nurturing approach to the inmates was evident in the work of the institution's long-time surgeon, Dr John S. King. Often the doctor becomes one of the most hated authority figures in the prison because he regards it as his special task to search out malingerers, to send them back to work at the first possible moment. By contrast, so far as one can tell from official reports, John King was genuinely concerned about the state of health of the inmates, which he often found to be deplorable, and over the years he worked conscientiously to do all in his power to be of assistance. On admission, each woman received a physical examination, and during the period of incarceration Dr King often referred with some pride to weight gains and other evidence of physical improvement. King regarded it as his responsibility to ensure that the prisoners received a nutritious diet and that the facility was well heated and ventilated, and the regular inspections he carried out helped make the Mercer a healthy place in which to live. The prison avoided such medical emergencies as epidemics, its death rate was low, and it seems likely that the doctor was entirely accurate in his judgment that most of the women were altogether healthier inside the prison than they had been in the world of poverty and alcohol which they knew outside.[71]

Dr King's reports provide a sad commentary on the life of disadvantaged women in late-nineteenth-century Ontario. Many women on admission he described as 'wholly unfitted' for any work but knitting, either from general debility or disease. Some were so weakened 'from debauch, disease or want of nourishment' as to be totally incapacitated. The most serious problem was syphilis. It affected thirty-two inmates in the prison's first year and was prevalent throughout its early history. Rigid segregation was imposed, and those infected confined in a separate ward. In King's judgment, Mercer's inmates came almost entirely from two classes: prostitutes and chronic drunks.[72]

One of King's responsibilities highlighted the distinctiveness of the women's prison. In the early years, King delivered two or three babies annually. Occasionally the numbers increased, and in 1893 he reported eleven births and the arrival of a number of new inmates with child in arms. Mercer officials had mixed feelings about this situation. The presence of mothers with children had a humanizing effect on institutional life, but it also disrupted routines and at one point thought was given to closing the nursery. The presence in a separate wing of the Industrial Refuge for Girls also distinguished the Mercer from the Central Prison. On occasions, such as during choir practices, there was contact between the Mercer women and the girls in the refuge, surely another softening feature of reformatory life.

By the mid-1880s Dr King was pointing in his reports to the presence of increasing numbers of persons he regarded more as unfortunates than as criminals. In 1884 he regretted that every year 'several insane cases are sent to the Reformatory.' The institution, he commented, was 'forced into becoming a sort of refuge for old and debilitated cases.' Soon both King and O'Reilly were commenting regularly on the increasing numbers who were severely retarded or of such low intelligence as to be unable to perform the most menial tasks. Although O'Reilly found such women far more difficult to deal with than ordinary criminals, she believed that 'these poor unfortunates are not as responsible as others more gifted by nature' and she expressed grave fears that 'when they regain their liberty they will fall back into their old ways.' By the early 1890s O'Reilly was conscious of the fact that the Mercer was becoming, like the jails, a congregate facility housing a disparate population of the criminal, the destitute, and the ill. 'A number of incapables are sent to us every year,' she pointed out in 1893, 'old women charged with vagrancy guilty of no crime, subjects for a home rather than a reformatory. We have also in the house at the present time two insane women, besides some half-dozen who are weak-minded. The infant population also is largely on the increase.'

THE SUCCESS OF THE MERCER?

There are two critical questions pertaining to the early history of the Mercer: the nature of the differential treatment and the issue of success. The first of these is more easily dealt with. The Mercer, as we have seen, in several important respects did not follow the pattern of the American women's reformatory. That, of course, is hardly surprising as there was no common trajectory; each jurisdiction had its own distinct traditions and priorities and reformatory institutions evolved somewhat differently everywhere. The Mercer naturally reflected the political priorities and social values of the Ontario elite and, equally inevitably, the administrative style of the powerful inspector, Langmuir. As such, it was a prison administered by a woman; its committal policies required it to accept women who were frequent offenders; and it had only very modest expectations as to rehabilitation. Nonetheless, it applied disciplinary methods which were gender specific and distinctly feminine and it created an environment which distinguished it in many respects from its male counterpart, the Central Prison.

Any discussion of differential discipline, however, leads inexorably to the larger question: just what did this discipline achieve? The question of success, of 'what works,' has been the central concern of correctional workers throughout the modern history of the prison and in the twentieth century, in particular, has preoccupied discussion and debate. For these reasons, the conclusion of feminist scholars that the women's reformatory was a failure is of great interest both historically and in its implications for present prison policy. Leaving aside the debate about current policy towards single-sex facilities and their management as beyond the confines of this analysis, the negative conclusions of recent scholarship about the relationship between social and maternal feminism and prison reform remain important and intriguing.[73] In the late nineteenth and early twentieth centuries women's prisons were at the height of their influence. For many jurisdictions they offered a real alternative to previous approaches to the confinement and punishment of what some describe as 'fallen sisters.' For the reasons cited above, there is reason to conclude that in many respects the experience of the Mercer was substantially superior to what happened in the more traditional institution Ontario provided for male offenders, the Central Prison. Yet the entire history of efforts to assess prison success confirms the problematic nature of all such endeavours. For the early years of the Mercer the problem is compounded by the absence of any substantial body of case files, of private correspondence, or of public investigations of the type which take us behind the scenes at the Central Prison. Most of what we know must be based on inference derived from official reports and from occasional snippets in manuscript sources.

There is, however, evidence from one contemporary effort to help us judge the success of the Mercer, the work of the 1891 commission chaired by Langmuir to 'Enquire into the Prison and Reformatory System of Ontario.' Although this commission dealt with the Mercer only briefly (evidence perhaps of continued confidence in O'Reilly's management), some of the testimony which was given has been used to substantiate the argument that the Mercer was a failure. And two of O'Reilly's senior colleagues used the 1891 investigation as an opportunity to vent their frustration with important aspects of O'Reilly's management.

Their testimony and the comments of the commissioners have led one student of the Mercer to conclude that the reformatory was, in fact, a failure. The views expressed by O'Reilly's colleagues, it is argued, were 'particularly damning,' demonstrating that the reformatory had 'faltered soon after its founding' largely because the agenda of maternal feminism had proved inadequate to create within the walls of a prison a home-like environment where real reform might be achieved.[74]

The hostile testimony came first from Lucy Coad, the long-time deputy superintendent. Asked whether there was any difficulty in maintaining discipline, Coad seemed positively eager to respond: 'oh, yes,' she asserted at once, the women were allowed 'too much liberty.' And this made it 'very hard to keep them in order.' In some cases, she continued, 'they are very wild when they come in; they dance around and do all sorts of things.' 'I hardly slept last night through worrying about two women who broke everything in their rooms.' Eventually Coad locked these two up in a corridor but she expressed great regret that 'the dark cells are hardly ever used.'[75]

Coad was not without remedies for this sad state of affairs. Better discipline could be achieved if the punishment cells were placed in an area removed from all communication with other parts of the building. And even more could be achieved by enforcing the rule of silence. Not only were the women allowed to sit together at meals, she complained, but, 'while at work they are always talking. Their tongues are always going. With us, there are no gates, there is nothing to keep the women in the corridors apart during recreation time. They are continually going from one place to another if they wish to speak to each other.' Coad found this state of affairs deplorable. Recently, she told the commissioners, she had visited the women's reformatory in Massachusetts and 'there was no comparison at all' between discipline there and in the Mercer. At the Massachusetts facility 'no woman lifted her eyes ... There was no laughing or talking, nothing but the utmost decorum.' As had long been the ideal in the great custodial prisons, all the prisoners had their faces 'turned one way,' constantly observed by a guard on an elevated platform. 'Not a sound came from them,' the envious Coad related. 'Our women sit together and laugh and talk and sing sometimes.' Altogether, Coad argued, the Mercer inmates had 'too much liberty' and 'they abuse it.' The remedy? Coad would impose the rule of silence. Such a system, she pointed out, 'has never been enforced with us' and any attempt to institute it might cause a little trouble at first, but she was confident 'it could be done.'[76]

Obviously concerned about the lack of discipline in an institution in which prisoners could not only talk but sometimes even sing, the male members of this naturally all-male commission questioned Lucy Coad closely. Charles Drury, a prominent Liberal politician, elicited the fact that no formal set of rules was in place. Drury was shocked by this revelation. The superintendent and deputy superintendent were in charge of the discipline alternate weeks, and Coad claimed that in these circumstances the absence of written rules had led to confusion between her and Mrs O'Reilly. Coad had shown O'Reilly a copy of the rules in force in Massachusetts but had failed to persuade her to make any changes; when she made the same case to the inspector, he too, she reported, 'thought it would be wiser not to interfere with the existing system at the Mercer.' Evidently the inspector either was not concerned about the absence of written rules or preferred not to disturb a system which seemed to be working. Drury, however, was not persuaded. Bluntly, he asked, had the Mercer 'done the kind of work it was designed for?' The response was equally blunt. 'No, it is just simply a place of detention.' Not surprisingly, Drury's conclusion from all this was entirely negative: 'So then we have a public institution erected and maintained for reformatory purposes, and it is not doing any good at all; but you find another institution on the same line, that is carrying on the work elsewhere that ours ought to do here. You see wherein the weakness of our institution lies, but you are not allowed to do anything to improve it? A. That is true.'[77]

The next witness, Robert Laird, the bursar and storekeeper, spoke from a wealth of experience. He had been in the Mercer since it opened. Laird confirmed almost everything Coad had to say. He told the commissioners there was 'little reformation among the prisoners' and that 'it would be advisable if a little more strict discipline were enforced.' The staff, he suggested, was not as dedicated as it should be, and he hinted that this was the result of appointments made on the basis of patronage. But Laird's greatest complaint related to the existence of two 'classes' among the staff, by which he meant Catholics and Protestants, and he told the commissioners that many disagreements resulted from this division. Since both Coad and Laird argued that tensions could be lessened if Catholics and Protestants were dealt with in separate facilities, their criticisms may have been inspired in part by personal ambition or by religious prejudice against the Catholic O'Reilly. There was also a suggestion that Laird believed that a stronger male presence was required. '... it would be very advisable,' he asserted, 'if there were a judicious advisory board of gentlemen who would visit the institution and interest themselves in its management.'[78]

O'Reilly's own testimony, which preceded that of Coad and Laird, should have allowed the commissioners to place these negative opinions in some perspective. She began by providing some very revealing clarification of the institution's statistical profile. Although only two women had been committed the previous year for drunk and disorderly, as opposed to thirty-four for vagrancy and twenty-five for larceny, most of those committed in the latter categories were also drunks. Similarly, although the statistics showed only six admitted as prostitutes, Mrs O'Reilly told the commissioners that 'many more than half' those committed the previous year plied that trade.

But what differentiated O'Reilly's testimony from that of her colleagues was her confident assertion that there was no great difficulty in controlling such a population. 'There are not more than half a dozen at all refractory that I cannot manage without punishing' and even those 'eventually succumb to discipline.' Commissioner Timothy Anglin responded that some female convict prisons in England were notorious for 'periodical revolts' in which the women 'destroy property, smash the furniture and break the windows.' Such cases had been very rare in the Mercer, said O'Reilly, and had not involved any number of women acting in concert. Given the absence of such outbreaks, O'Reilly was able to respond with confidence when the commission chairman, John Langmuir, seemed perturbed by the absence of printed rules. 'Cast-iron rules,' she replied firmly, 'do not always work well.' She made sure that all the women understood the general rules when they came in and, in any case, she added, it would be of little use to post printed rules with a majority of the inmates unable to read.

The other critical issue the commissioners raised was rehabilitation. Could much good be done, they wanted to know, in the absence of a better system of classification? Given the prison's design, she responded, it was 'not easy to classify them as we would wish'; but it was always impossible to prevent contamination in a prison environment by any system short of complete solitary confinement, an approach of which she decidedly disapproved. In an ideal structure, she argued, the women would be housed in cottages and classified according to age, character, and nature of their offence.

O'Reilly's intelligence and confidence were apparent in the way she responded to several perplexing yet naive questions. Asked whether she was accomplishing everything she could, given the Mercer's flawed design, she told the commissioners: 'that is a pretty hard question to answer.' Asked next how many of the eighty-five women then imprisoned she could hope to reclaim, she rebutted skilfully, 'you ask me one difficult question, and then you follow it up by asking another.' Still, some response was required and she told the commissioners that 'with the modes of treatment that we adopt now we are doing a great deal of good, and ... a good many never come back to us after they are released.' The staff followed up on what happened after release as far as possible, and although 'there are very many who do well for a few months ... afterwards a good few of them fall away.' She refused to take credit for a recent decrease in the average annual inmate population. 'I do not know how to account for it.'[79]

The commissioners were not sufficiently impressed by the views expressed by O'Reilly's critics to challenge her administration. Perhaps the women's prison, so long as it was efficiently administered, did not interest them very much. Probably John Langmuir at least, as the founder of the Mercer, retained some memory of the feminist ideals present at the beginning and understood the truly reactionary implications of the disciplinary proposals advanced by Lucy Coad and Robert Laird. In their brief recommendations the commissioners proposed improved classification, the use of the indeterminate sentence for recidivists or their committal for longer periods, and the diversification of the work programme, all goals Mrs O'Reilly had herself advocated many times in the past.[80]

Mary Jane O'Reilly carried on as superintendent for another decade. In subsequent annual reports the provincial inspector was once again generous in his praise of her efforts. For O'Reilly this was no mean achievement. As Canada's first female prison superintendent, she had established the Mercer very much in her own image and for two decades had responded to all challenges and administered it without scandal, riot, or even sustained complaint or criticism. Under O'Reilly the Mercer was indeed a reformatory for women run by women and there is little doubt, as she herself so cautiously claimed, that many of those unfortunates who lived for a time under her roof benefited from the experience.

If the Mercer in any sense could be described as a failure, surely it was not because it proved impossible to apply feminist methods in a prison environment. It was, after all, a prison, and the limitations inherent in that reality would survive so long as prisons themselves. But within institutions of that description there existed almost every possible kind of horror and cruelty, and, far less frequently, occasional glimmers of hope and humanity. Prisons, like every other human institution, must be judged and assessed in all their variety and circumstances, not condemned generically by formula or ideology. It is scarcely possible to miss the point more totally than to condemn a prison for being a prison.

When considered as a historical institution and in the context of the social values of its own day, the Mercer's history as outlined above makes it problematic, even ahistorical, to emphasize its failures over its achievements. In many ways it is remarkable that the women's prison went so far as it did to devise and apply gender-specific methods appropriate to the contemporary female condition. To add yet one more example, Matilda Elliot, who was in charge of the Industrial Refuge, in a rather matter-of-fact way provided the 1891 commissioners with an interesting piece of information. After pointing out that the refuge, like the Mercer itself, had no hard and fast rules and that her objective was 'to bring the girls up as if they were at home,' she added: 'I never lock up my rooms. The front door is always open and Mrs. O'Reilly's quarters are the same, and have been the same for all these years.'[81] For anyone knowledgeable about prison history, it is impossible to conceive of a more significant or of a more symbolic contrast between the Mercer and the male prison than Mary Jane O'Reilly's door, which was kept open 'for all these years.' By itself, this was, quite simply, an astounding, indeed a symbolic, commentary on the truly profound differences between the world of the Mercer and that of Kingston Penitentiary and the Central Prison. And as such it represents a glowing tribute to Mary Jane O'Reilly, to her colleagues, and, perhaps most of all, to her charges, the petty thieves and prostitutes of late-nineteenth-century Ontario.

In all these ways, then, the Mercer did not fail either as a women's prison or in its efforts to apply feminist principles in a prison environment. The failure of the Mercer rather related to the failure of Langmuir, Noxon, and all those other male bureaucrats who were so utterly unable to even consider, much less comprehend, that there might be a larger social significance to the Mercer's accomplishments, one which had relevance for penal strategies generally. The Ontario community had much to learn from the efforts of Mary Jane O'Reilly and her colleagues in the Mercer, if only it had tried to understand. Its failure to make the effort contributed not a little to the enduring tragedy of Canadian prison life poised to enter the twentieth century with its harsh, rigid, and unspeakably cruel structures still firmly in place. The failure of recent scholarship equally to appreciate the nature and extent of this late-nineteenth-century achievement of a few middle-class

women and a lot of prostitutes and pilferers is perhaps less understandable and even more regrettable.

NOTES

1 The pioneering and still most perceptive study is Estelle B. Freedman *Their
  Sisters' Keepers: Women's Prison Reform in America, 1830–1930* (Ann Arbor: University of Michigan Press 1981). A more recent and also perceptive study of
  the American experience is Nicole Hahn Rafter *Partial Justice, Women Prisons
  and Social Control* 2nd ed. (New Brunswick, NJ: Transaction Publishers 1990)
  and also Rafter 'Prisons for Women, 1790–1980' *Crime and Justice: An Annual
  Review of Research* vol. 5 (1983). Good accounts of the British experience are
  R.P. Dobash, R.E. Dobash, and S. Gutteridge *The Imprisonment of Women* (Oxford: Basil Blackwell 1986) and Lucia Zedner *Women, Crime and Custody in Vic-
  torian England* (Oxford: Clarendon Press 1991). See too Lucia Zedner
  'Women, Crime and Penal Responses: A Historial Account,' *Crime and Justice:
  A Review of Research* 14 (1991). For Canadian accounts see Carolyn Strange
  '"The Criminal and Fallen of Their Sex": The Establishment of Canada's
  First Women's Prison, 1874–1901' *Canadian Journal of Women and the Law* 1/1
  (1985) and 'The Velvet Glove: Maternalistic Reform at the Andrew Mercer
  Ontario Reformatory for Females 1874–1927' (MA thesis, University of Ottawa 1983); see too Jennifer Brown, 'Influences Affecting the Treatment of
  Women Prisoners in Toronto, 1880–1890' (MA thesis, Wilfrid Laurier University 1975) and Ellen Adelberg and Claudia Currie *Too Few to Count: Canadian Women in Conflict with the Law* (Vancouver: Press Gang Publishers 1987).
2 Freedman *Their Sisters' Keepers* 47
3 Ibid. 105–6
4 Strange 'Canada's First Women's Prison' 92
5 Rafter *Partial Justice* 46. For the Conway and Banner articles, see ibid.
6 David Rothman *The Discovery of the Asylum* (Boston: Little, Brown 1971) xv
7 Robert Martinson 'What Works? Questions and Answers about Prison Reform' *Public Interest* Spring 1974. The Martinson study is discussed in almost
  every work in criminology published since it appeared. See, for example,
  Todd R. Clear and George F. Cole *American Corrections* (Pacific Grove, Calif.:
  Brooks, Cole 1990).
8 For a useful study, see the unpublished paper read at the Canadian Historical Association 1983 meeting, R. Sundstrom '"Snakes and Snails and
  Puppy-Dog Tails": The Neglected Question of Female Juvenile Offenders in
  Toronto in the 1840's.'

9 See Canada, *Sessional Papers*, Annual Report, Penitentiary Inspectors, 1851, 1853.

10 Annual Report, 1856, 1858, and 1860. And see Andrew Curtis et al. *Kingston Penitentiary, the First Hundred and Fifty Years 1835–1985* (Ministry of Supply and Services Canada 1985) chap. 7.

11 For Emma Hall and the Detroit House of Shelter, see Rafter *Partial Justice* 24–8. For references to Langmuir's visits to Detroit see Ontario, *Sessional Papers*, Annual Report of the Inspector of Asylums, Prisons, etc., 1869, 1870, and 1871. For a fuller analysis of American influences on the establishment of intermediate prisons in Ontario see Peter Oliver '"A Terror to Evil-Doers": The Central Prison and the "Criminal Class" in Late Nineteenth-Century Ontario' in Roger Hall et al., eds. *Patterns of the Past* (Toronto: Dundurn Press 1988). Throughout, my comparisons of female and male prisons are between the Mercer and the Central Prison and much of my understanding of the Mercer derives from my earlier work on the male facility.

12 Ontario, Prison Inspector, Annual Reports, 1869–71. Subsequently, references to the Ontario Inspectoral Reports are referred to as AR. These are brief documents, readily available in the *Sessional Papers*, and when the report date is cited in the text, I do not usually provide a footnote reference.

13 AR 1878

14 Strange 'Canada's First Women's Prison' 83

15 AR 1878

16 Stephen B. Connors 'John Woodburn Langmuir and the Development of Prisons and Reformatories in Ontario, 1868–1882' (MA thesis, Queen's University 1982) 112.

17 Ontario *Journals of the Legislative Assembly* 1879 Session, vol. 12, Appendix (no. 1), 30–3.

18 AR 1868

19 AR 1878

20 Ibid. The 1878 order-in-council on the Mercer did offer one suggestive hint as to contemporary Ontario thinking when it asserted that the Mercer would be 'maintained and managed in the same way as the Reformatory at Penetanguishene, and be for the reception of females, irrespective of age' (1878 AR) It was characteristic of much late-nineteenth-century social legislation that women and children were equated as being legally and physically disadvantaged and in need of special legislative protection.

21 AR 1878

22 Ibid.

23 Ibid.

24 AR 1882
25 AR 1884
26 AR 1887
27 *Statutes of Ontario* chap. 38, An Act Respecting the Andrew Mercer Reformatory for Females, Assented to 11 Mar. 1879
28 I thank Mrs Margaret Angus of Kingston, Ontario, for biographical information. Mrs O'Reilly received about the same amount of training for her work as had Colonel Prince when appointed warden at the Central Prison. The 1880 AR notes that she was sent to visit the Women's Reformatory at Framingham and the assistant superintendent was sent to Indianapolis. As the ever-confident Langmuir put it, they were 'thereby enabled to enter upon their duties with the confidence which can only be gained from practical knowledge.'
29 Provincial Archives of Ontario (PAO), RG8, Provincial Secretaries Papers, Special Series, box 6, Langmuir to the Provincial Treasurer, 12 Oct. 1880
30 Rafter *Partial Justice* 35
31 Ibid. 36
32 Generally see Rafter *Partial Justice* chap. 2.
33 Ibid. 38
34 Strange 'Canada's First Women's Prison' 86
35 Ontario, *Journals of the Legislative Assembly*, 1879 Session, vol. 12 (no. 1) 30-3
36 Ibid.
37 For example, see AR 1890.
38 I thank my research assistants, Michelle Corbett and John Choules, for their invaluable efforts in preparing the statistical analysis of the first twenty years of the Mercer, and the comparisons with the Central Prison. The analysis used both published statistics and materials taken from the prison registers. Of course, prison statistics must be used with caution but from their very nature such data as sentence length and nature of offence are far more reliable than, for example, statistics dealing with such difficult subjects as the amount of crime in society.
39 Rafter *Partial Justice* 37-8
40 AR 1881
41 AR 1896
42 AR 1890
43 Ibid.
44 AR 1898
45 AR 1899
46 AR 1881

47 PAO, RG8, Provincial Secretaries Papers, Langmuir to A.S. Hardy, Provincial Secretary, 26 Aug. 1880, and Circular, Oliver Mowat, Attorney General, 21 Sept. 1880

48 AR 1879

49 Ibid. 1899

50 AR 1891

51 Ibid.

52 AR 1882

53 See the Central Prison case files in the Ontario Archives for repeated evidence of determined resistance to work programmes in the male prison.

54 AR 1881

55 Ibid.

56 Studies of prison subcultures are tremendously influential and have evolved from the early efforts of sociologists writing in the 1930s–1950s period, who offered a functional analysis, to the 'importation' theory posited by most studies done since the 1960s. See especially Donald Clemmer *The Prison Community* (Boston: Christopher 1940), Gresham Sykes *Society of Captives* (Princeton: Princeton University Press 1958), and, as the most influential example of importation theory, John Irwin *Prisons in Turmoil* (Boston: Little, Brown 1980). There is as yet no satisfactory study of an Ontario facility; W.E. Mann *Society behind Bars: A Sociological Scrutiny of Guelph Reformatory* (Toronto: Second Science Publishers 1967) is flawed but useful. James B. Jacobs *Stateville* (Chicago: University of Chicago Press 1977) is the best study of an American prison, drawing on both functional and importation theory, while Rose Giallombardo's *Society of Women: A Study of a Woman's Prison* (New York: John Wiley and Sons 1966) is the classic attack on functionalism in the environment of the women's prison. Modern studies of course rely on participant-observer methodology while nineteenth-century studies present a far greater challenge. For an introduction to aspects of the subculture of a nineteenth-century prison, see my article on the Central Prison. And see Philip Priestley *Victorian Prison Lives, English Prison Biography 1830–1914* (London: Methuen 1985) 21.

57 PAO, RG8, box 6, Provincial Secretaries Papers, Langmuir to the Provincial Treasurer, 9 June 1880

58 Ibid.

59 AR 1884, 1889. Mrs O'Reilly argued that religion made it easier to enforce the discipline and, above all, that it was critical to rehabilitation. In the 1889 *Report* she insisted that 'we realize more and more that religion alone will produce a true reformation of character.' Many men in the Central Prison

were disruptive and contemptuous during religous services. See Oliver *Central Prison.*

60 PAO, *Seventh Annual Report of the Prisoners' Aid Association,* 1881

61 Ibid.

62 The *First Report* of the Mercer Sunday school was part of the 1881 Prisoners' Aid Association *Annual Report.*

63 AR, PAA, 1882

64 See especially, 1886, 1891, and 1893 Mercer, ARs.

65 AR 1882, PAA

66 Ibid. 1893, PAA

67 For Gilbert Hartley's version of life in the Central Prison, see Oliver *Central Prison.*

68 By contrast, the rules and regulations of male prisons in the nineteenth century forbade all but the most formal contact within the institution, and prison officers who had contact with prisoners after release were subject to harsh discipline.

69 AR 1881

70 AR 1884

71 In 1882, for example, Dr King noted that 143 of 177 inmates discharged during the year had gained weight.

72 AR 1882

73 For aspects of the current debate in a Canadian context, see Adelburg and Currie *Too Few to Count.*

74 Strange 'Canada's First Women's Prison' 88–9 and 92

75 Ontario *Report of the Commissioners Appointed to Enquire into the Prison and Reformatory System of Ontario* (Toronto 1891). The pages of testimony dealing with the Mercer are 730–8 and 744–52.

76 Ibid. 747

77 Ibid.

78 Ibid. 752

79 Ibid. 734

80 Ibid. 217–18

81 Ibid. 738

Index

PUBLICATIONS OF THE OSGOODE SOCIETY